Intermediate GCSE Mathematics:

Revision and Practice

Intermediate GCSE Mathematics:

Revision and Practice

D. Rayner

Oxford University Press 1994

Oxford University Press, Walton Street,, Oxford OX2 6DP

Oxford New York
Athens Auckland Bangkok Bombay
Calcutta Cape Town Dar es Salaam Delhi
Florence Hong Kong Istanbul Karachi
Kuala Lumpur Madras Madrid Melbourne
Mexico City Nairobi Paris Singapore
Taipei Tokyo Toronto

and associated companies in
Berlin Ibadan

First published 1994

ISBN 0 19 914575 X

Artwork by Nick Hawken, Oxford Illustrators and Julian Page

Typeset and illustrated by Tech-Set, Gateshead, Tyne and Wear
Printed and bound in Great Britain by
Butler & Tanner Ltd, Frome and London

Preface

This book is for candidates working through Key Stage 4 towards a GCSE in Mathematics: it covers the National Curriculum for Levels 5 to 8. The book can be used both in the classroom and by students working on their own. There are explanations, worked examples and numerous exercises which, it is hoped, will help students to build up confidence. The author believes that people learn mathematics by *doing* mathematics. The questions are graded in difficulty throughout the exercises.

The book can be used either as a course book over the last two or three years before the Key Stage 4 examinations or as a revision text in the final year. The contents list shows where all the topics appear in the National Curriculum and an index at the back of the book provides further reference.

The work is collected into sections on Number, Algebra, Shape and Space, Handling Data, Probability, and Using and Applying Mathematics. This is done for ease of reference but the material can be taught in any convenient order. Most teachers will prefer to alternate freely between topics from each of the sections with the basic proviso that work at Level 5 is done before that at Level 6, and so on.

At the end of the book, there are several revision exercises which provide mixed questions across the curriculum. There are also multiple choice questions for variety.

The section on Using and Applying Mathematics contains a selection of starters for coursework projects which have been tried and tested. They can be used to provide practice in the strategies involved in attempting 'open-ended' problems.

The author is indebted to the many students and colleagues who have assisted him in this work. He is particularly grateful to Julie Anderson, Philip Cutts and Micheline Rayner for their invaluable work.

D. Rayner 1994

CONTENTS

1 Shape and space 1

1.1 Accurate drawing

4/5a

Some questions involving bearings or irregular shapes are easy to solve by drawing an accurate diagram.

Navigators on ships use scale drawings to work out their position or their course.

To improve the accuracy of your work, follow these guidelines.

- Use a *sharp* HB pencil.
- Don't press too hard.
- If drawing an *acute* angle make sure your angle is less than 90°.
- If you use a pair of compasses make sure they are fairly stiff so the radius does not change accidently.

Exercise 1

Use a protractor and ruler to draw full size diagrams and measure the sides marked with letters.

1.
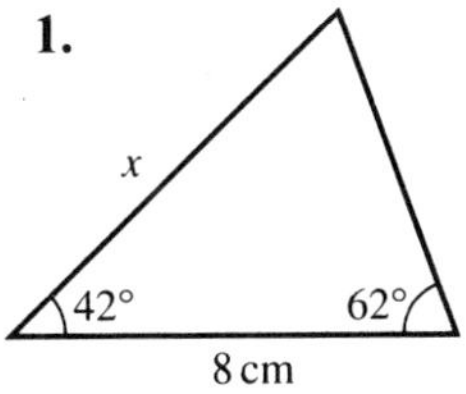

2.
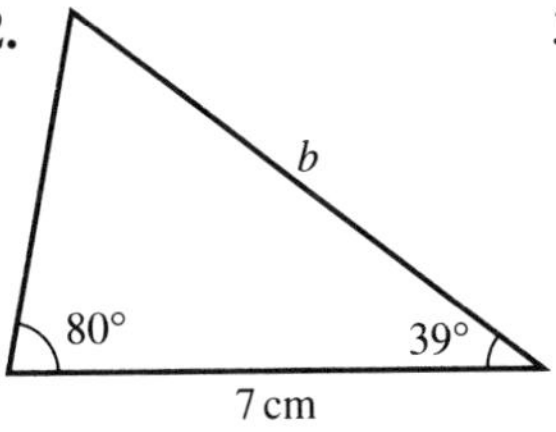

3.
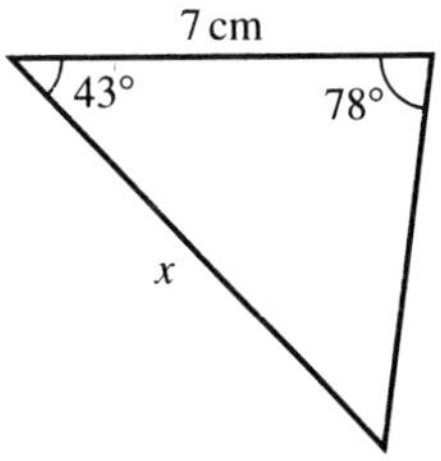

4.
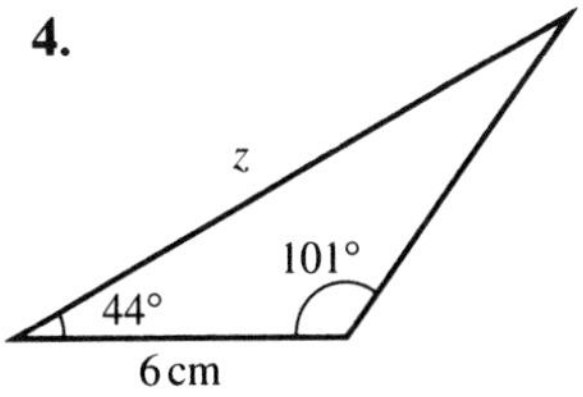

5.

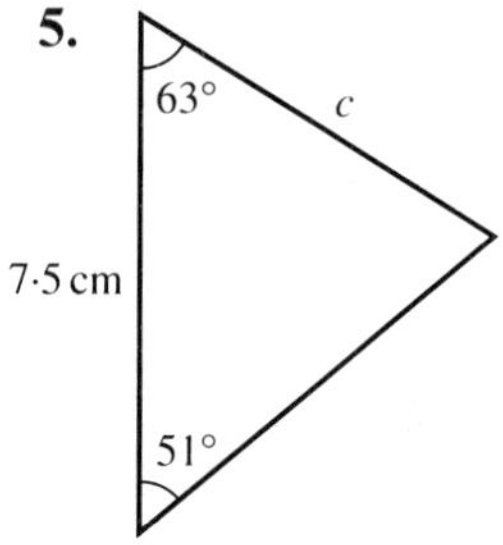

6.

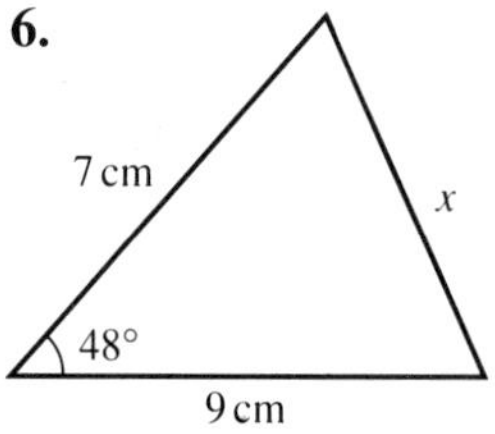

7.

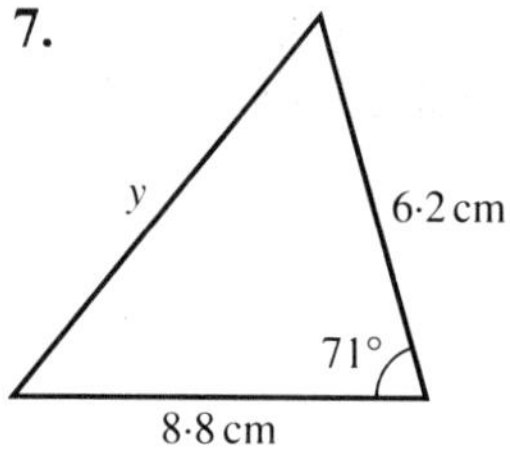

8.

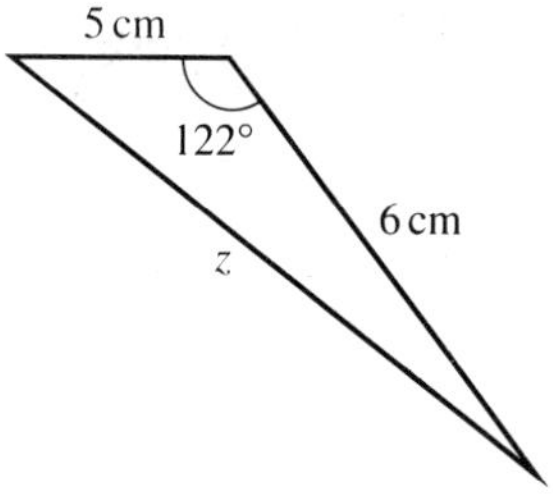

9.

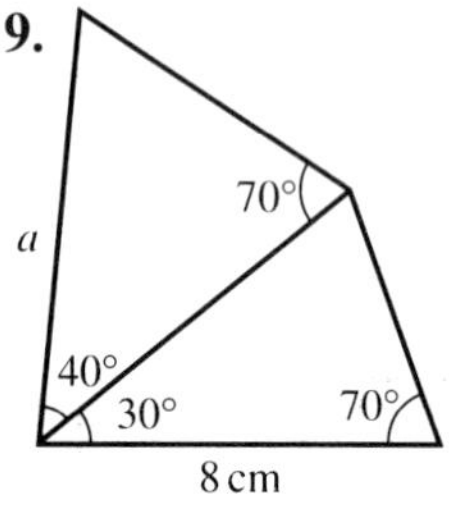

10.

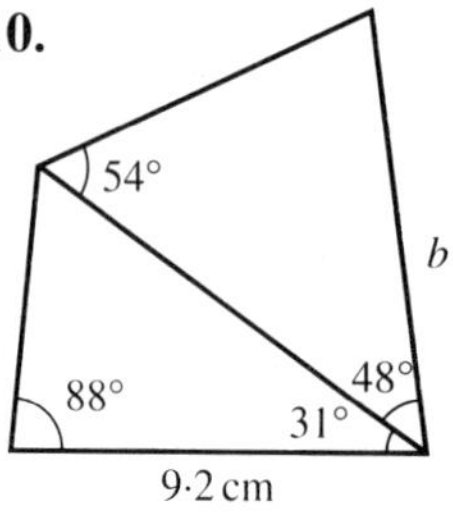

11.

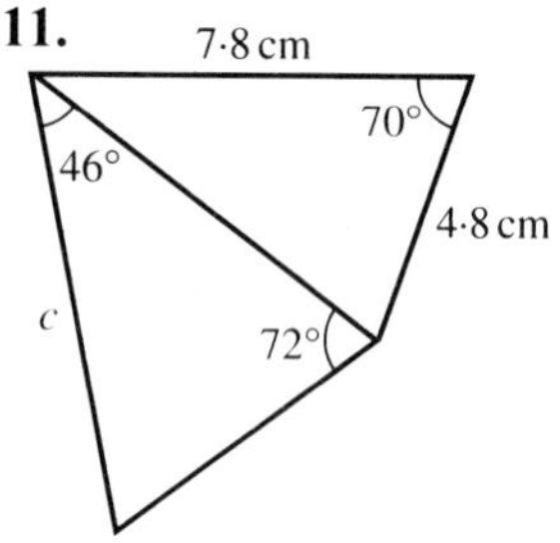

12.

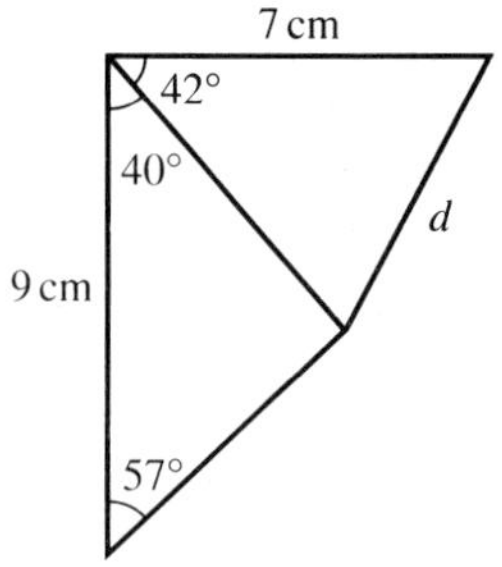

In Questions **13** to **16** construct the triangles using a pair of compasses. Measure the angles marked with letters.

13.

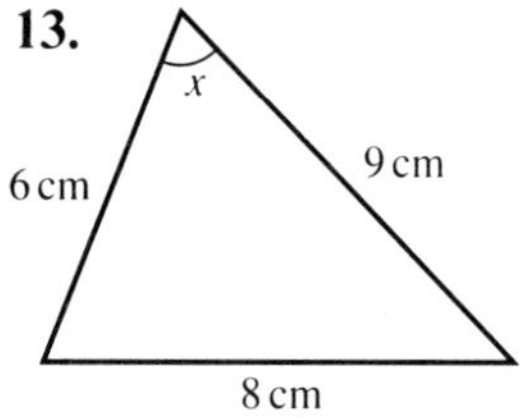

14.

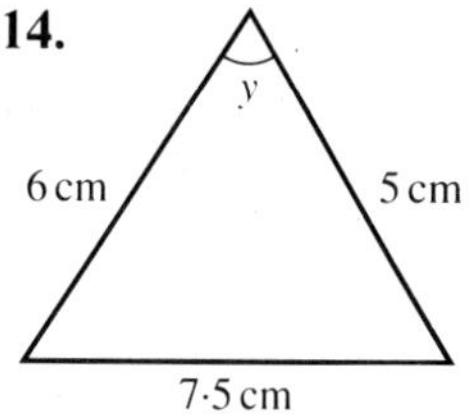

15.

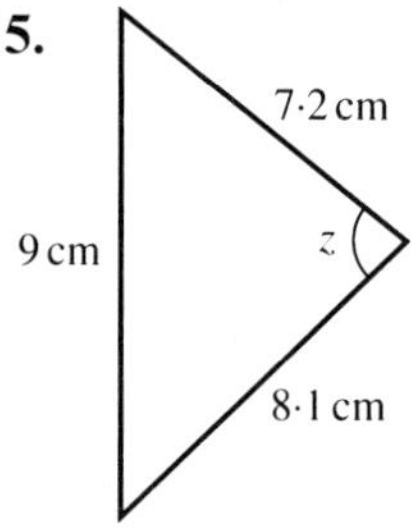

16.

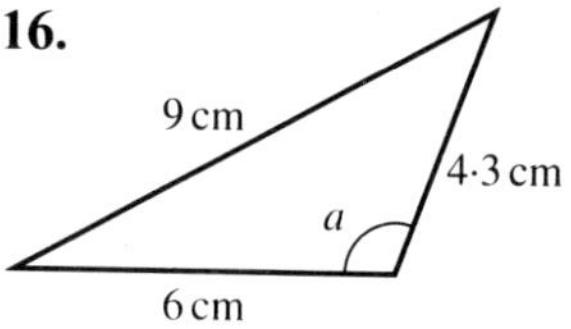

17. Farmer Gibson has to work out the area of his field to calculate his EC subsidy. The field is not a rectangle or parallelogram or any standard shape. He has measured the four sides of the field and one of the diagonals.

(a) Make a scale drawing of the field, using a scale of 1 cm to 10 m.

(b) Measure the lengths of the dotted lines and hence work out the total area of the field to the nearest 100 m^2.

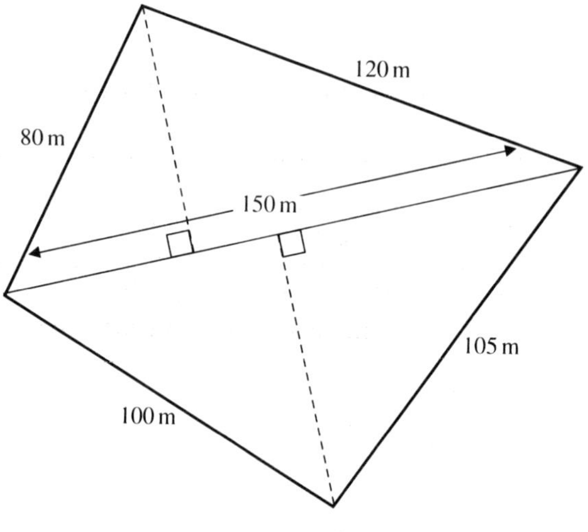

18. Make a scale drawing to calculate the area of this field, correct to the nearest 100 m^2.

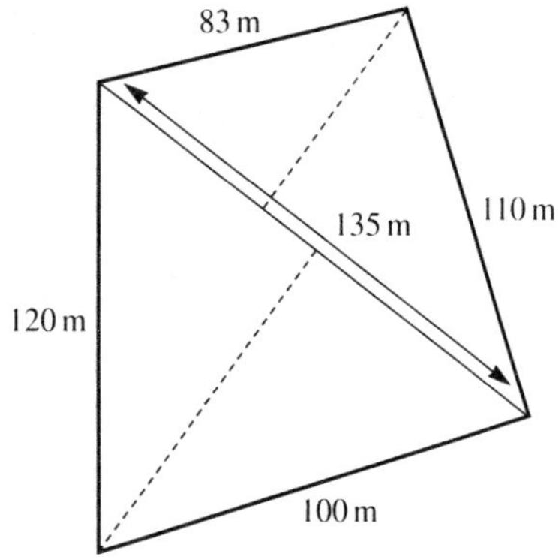

Nets

If the cube here was made of cardboard, and you cut along some of the edges and laid it out flat, you would have the *net* of the cube.

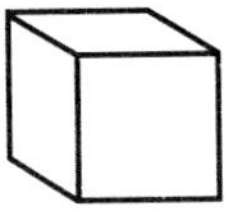

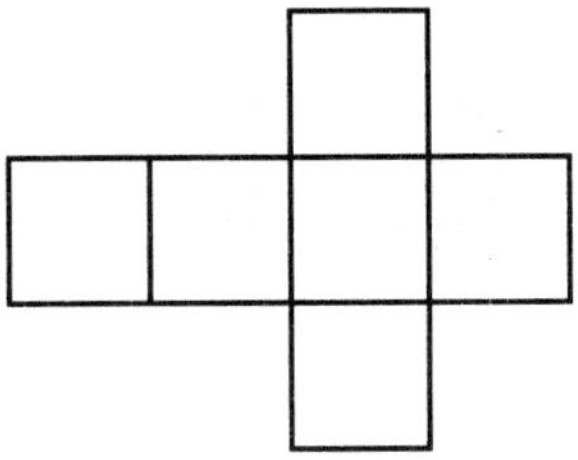

Here is the net for a square-based pyramid.

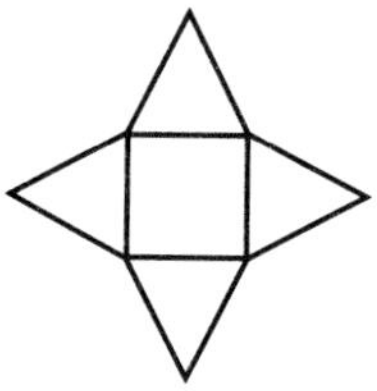

Exercise 2

1. Which of the nets below can be used to make a cube?

(a)

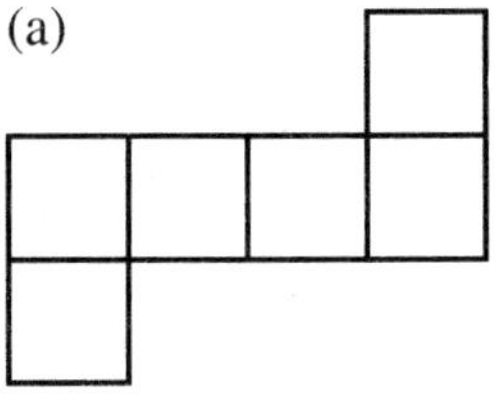

(b)

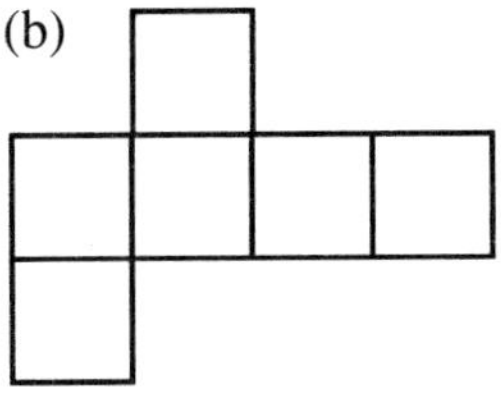

(c)

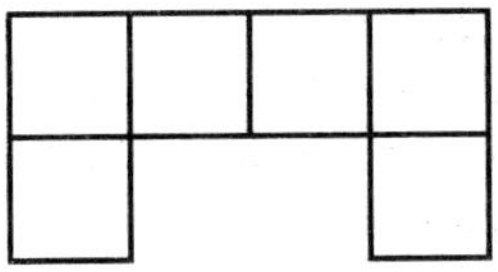

(d)

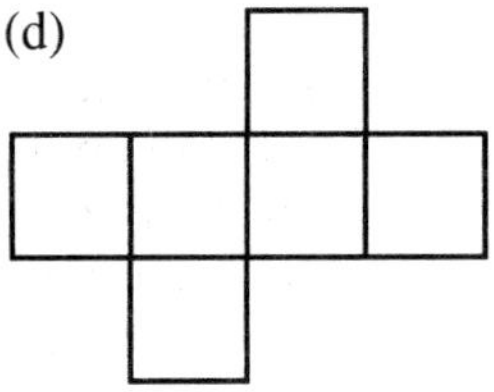

2. The numbers on opposite faces of a dice add up to 7. Take one of the possible nets for a cube from Question 1 and show the number of dots on each face.

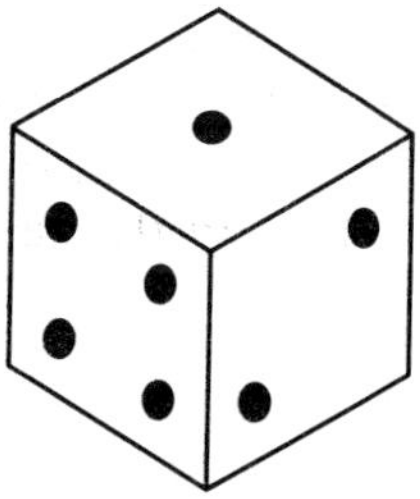

3. Here we have started to draw the net of a cuboid (a closed rectangular box) measuring 4 cm × 3 cm × 1 cm. Copy and then complete the net.

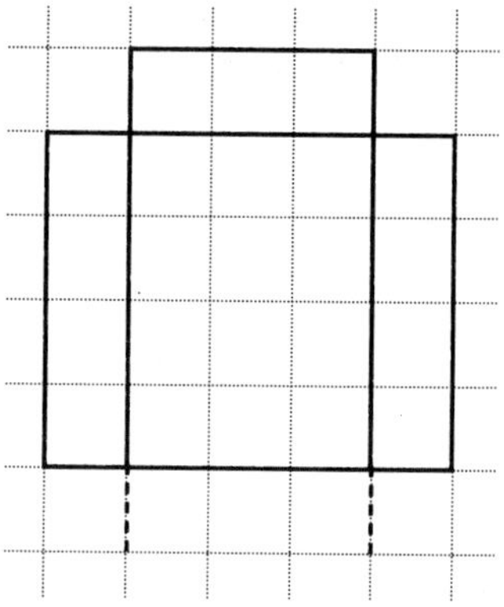

4. A cube can be dissected into three equal pyramids.
Make three solids from the net shown and fit them together to make a cube. All lengths are in cm.

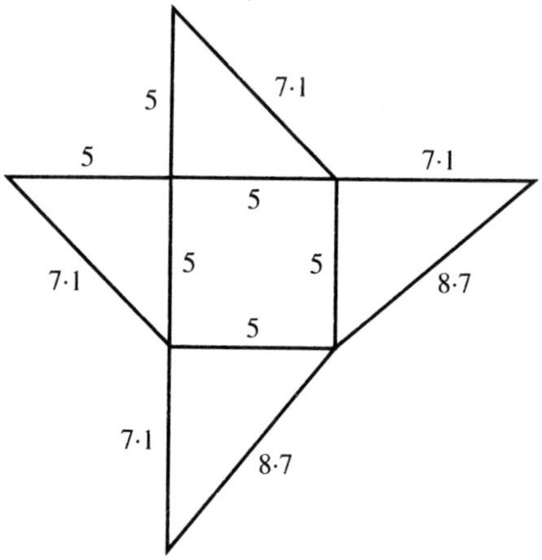

5. Describe the solid formed from each of these nets.

(a)

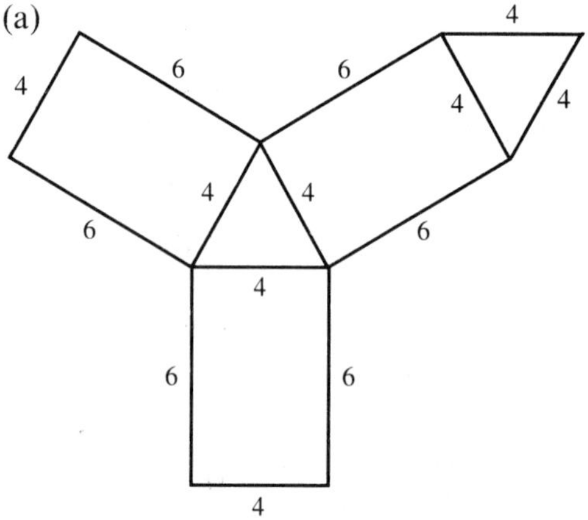

(b)

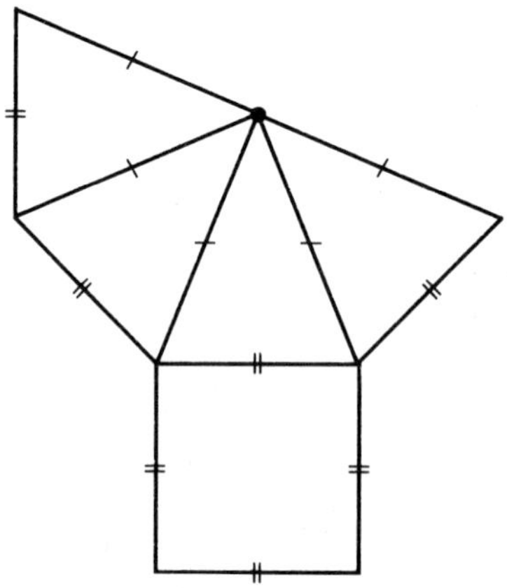

6. Sketch a possible net for each of the following:
(a) a cuboid measuring 5 cm by 2 cm by 8 cm
(b) a prism 10 cm long whose cross-section is a right-angled triangle with sides 3 cm, 4 cm and 5 cm.

7. The diagram shows the net of a pyramid. The base is shaded. The lengths are in cm.

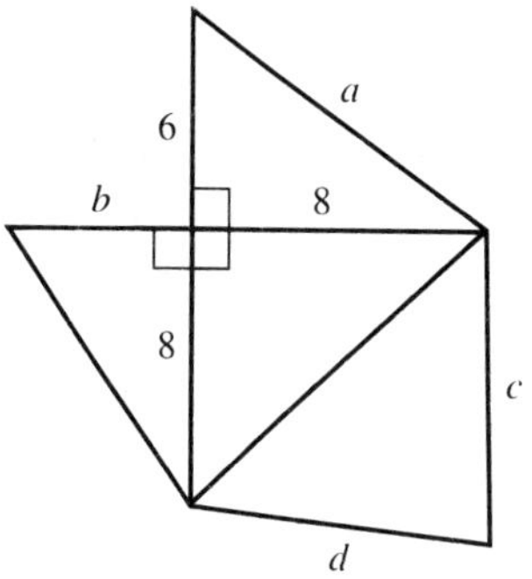

(a) How many edges will the pyramid have?
(b) How many vertices will it have?
(c) Find the lengths a, b, c, d.
(d) Use the formula $V = \frac{1}{3}$ base area$\times$height to calculate the volume of the pyramid.

1.2 Angle facts

4/5b

The angles at a point add up to 360°.
The angles on a straight line add up to 180°.

(a)

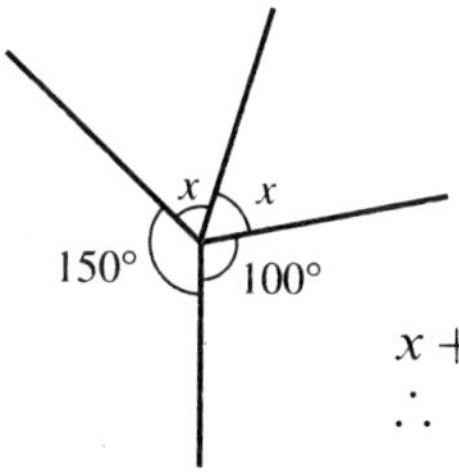

$$x + x + 150 + 100 = 360$$
$$\therefore\ 2x = 360 - 250$$
$$x = 55°$$

(b)

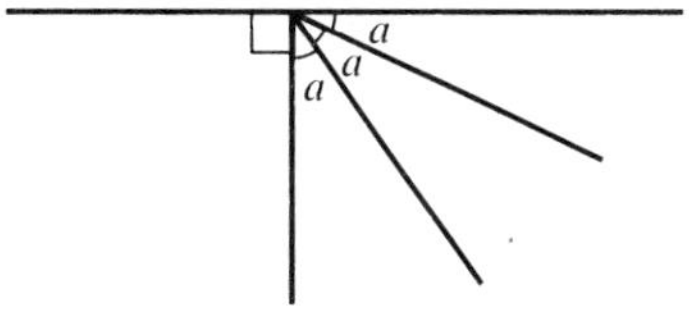

$$3a + 90 = 180$$
$$3a = 90$$
$$a = 30°$$

Exercise 3

Find the angles marked with letters. The lines AB and CD are straight.

1.
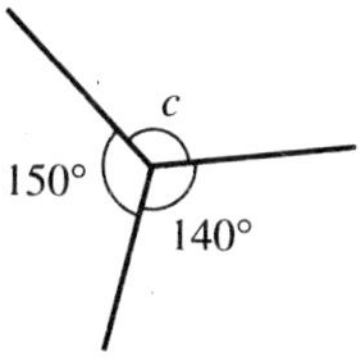

2.
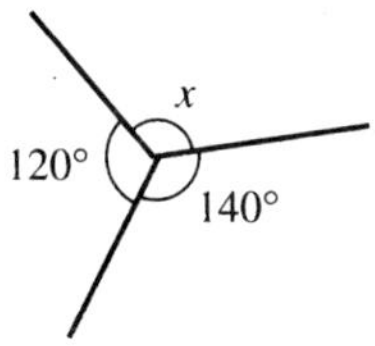

3.
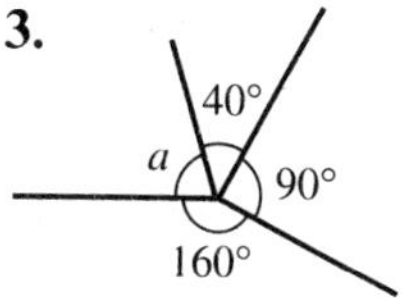

4.
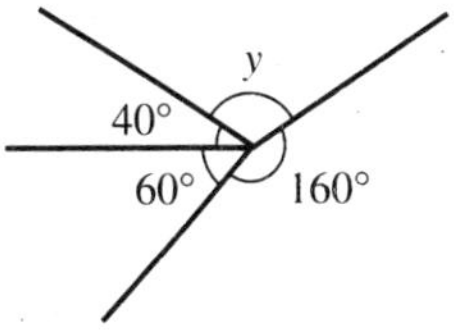

5.
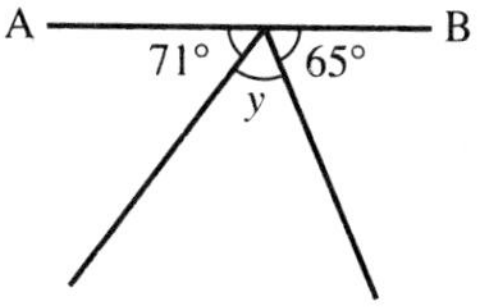

6.
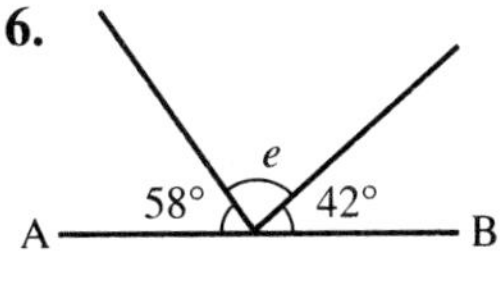

7.
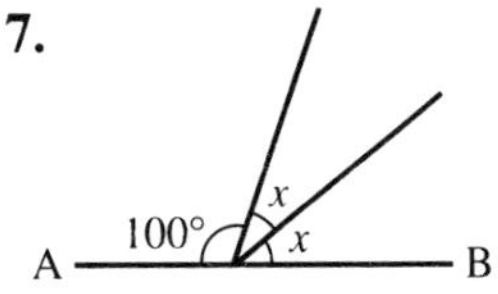

8.
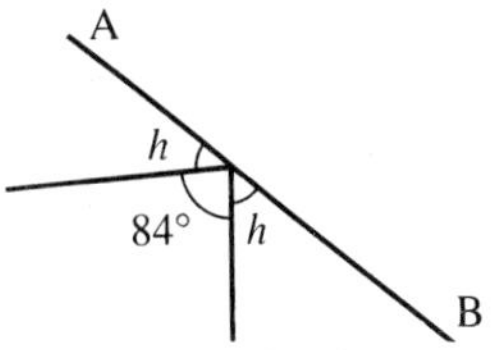

9.
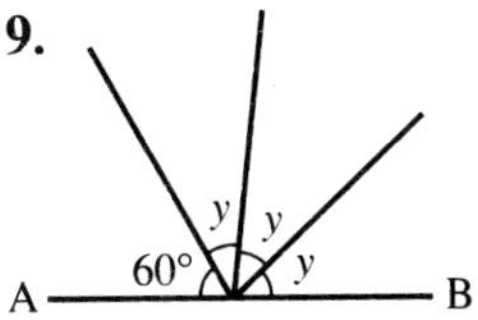

10.
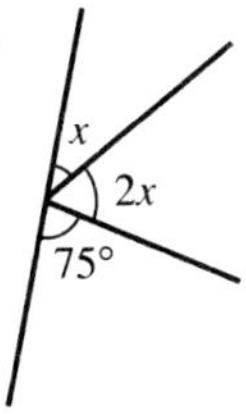

11.
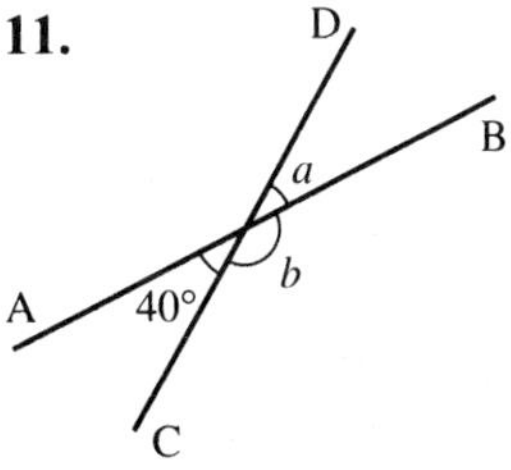

12.
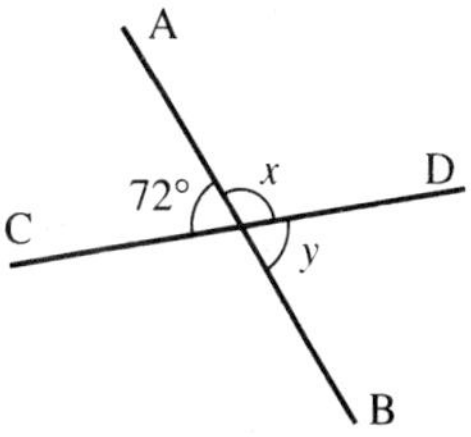

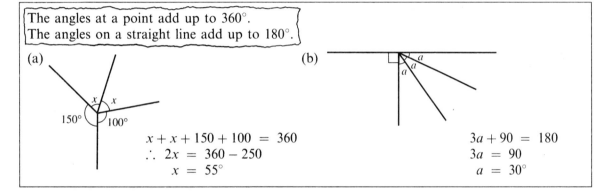

Triangles

The angles in a triangle add up to 180°.

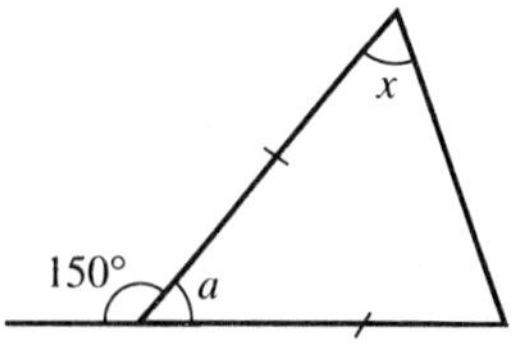

$a = 180 - 150° = 30°$

The triangle is isosceles $\therefore$ $2x + 30 = 180$

$2x = 150$

$x = 75°$

Exercise 4

Find the angles marked with letters. For the more difficult questions it is helpful to draw a diagram.

1.

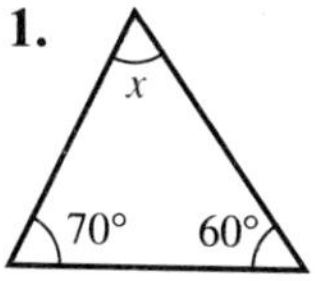

2.

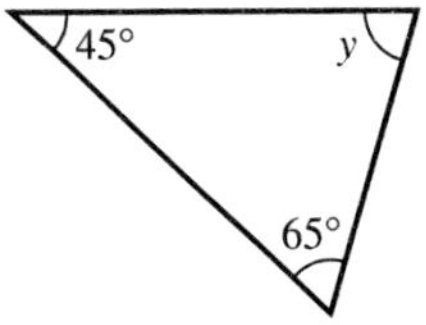

3.

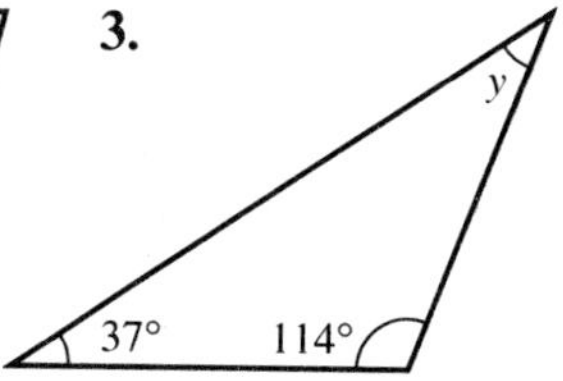

4.

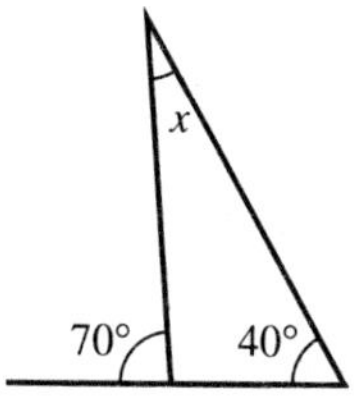

5.

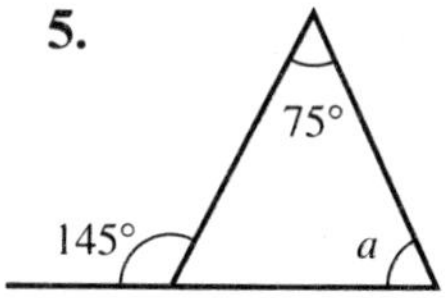

6.

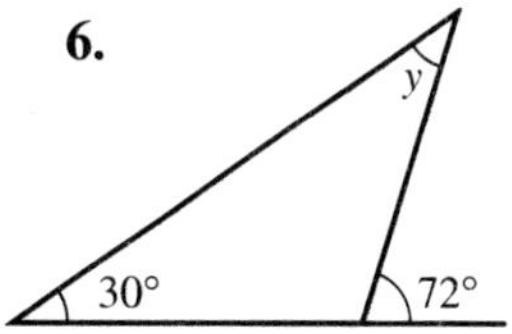

7.

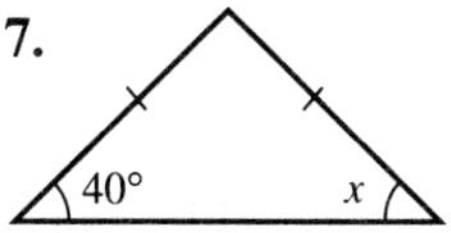

8.

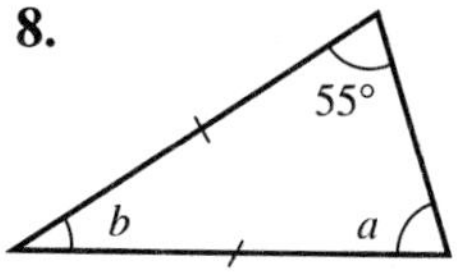

9.

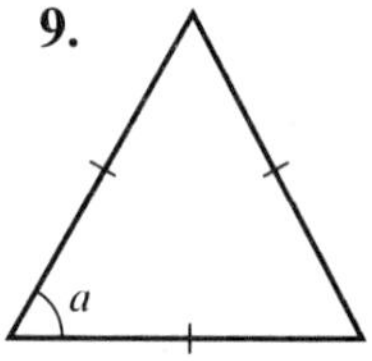

10.

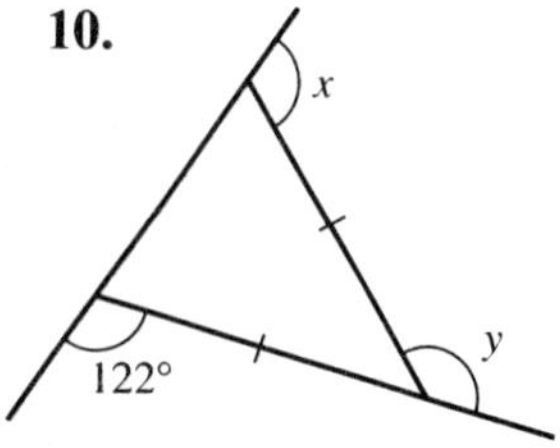

11.

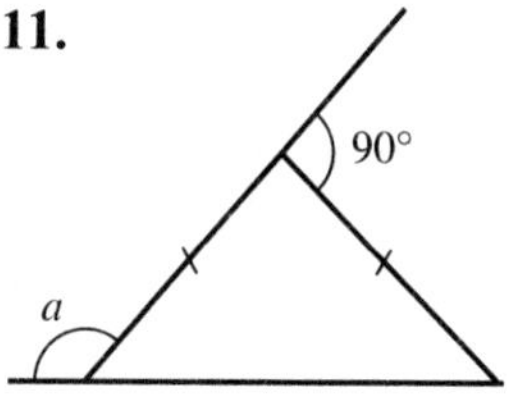

12.

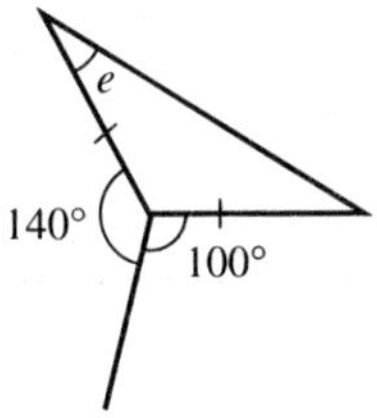

13.

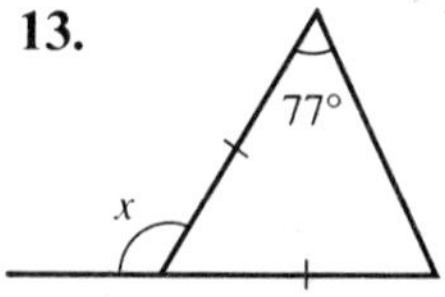

14.

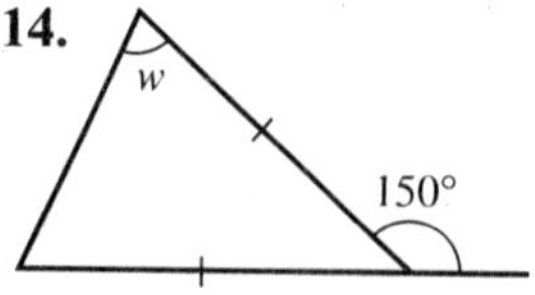

15.

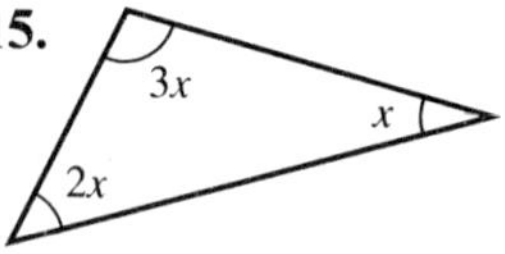

16.

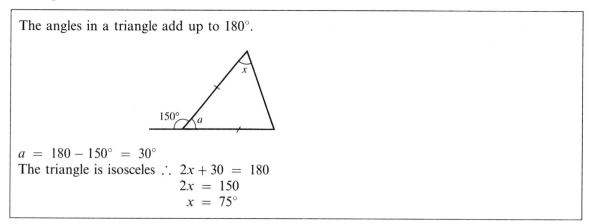

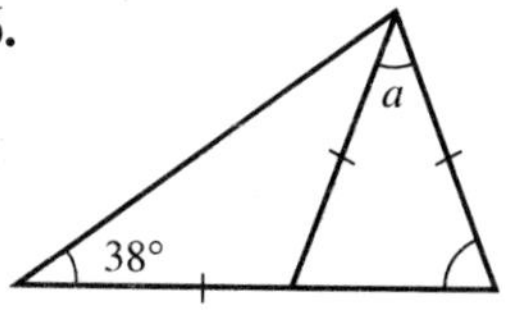

Parallel lines

When a line cuts a pair of parallel lines all the acute angles are equal and all the obtuse angles are equal.

(a)

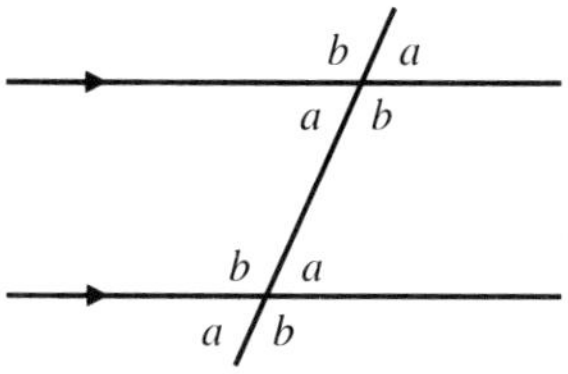

Some people remember:
'F angles'

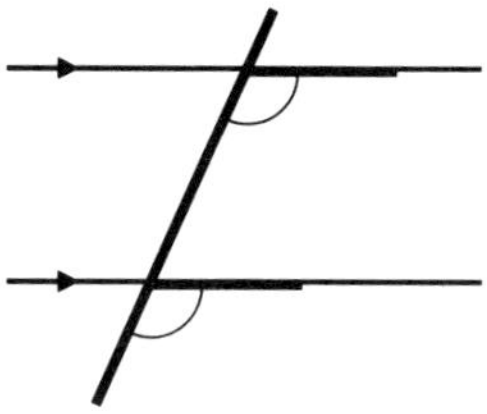

and 'Z angles'

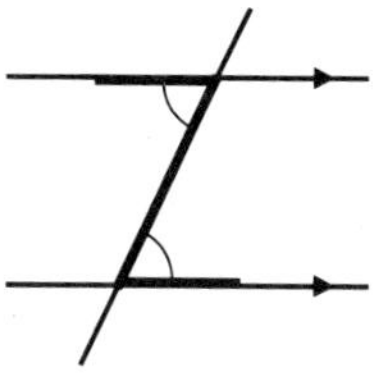

Exercise 5

Find the angles marked with letters.

1.

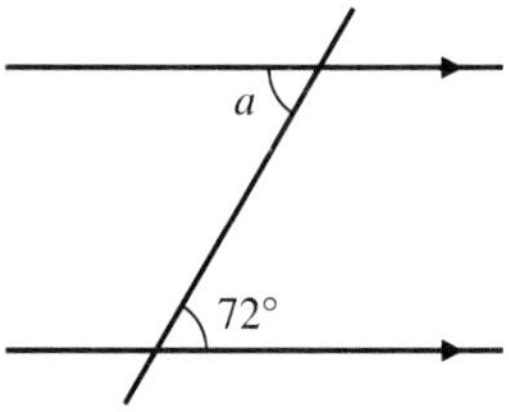

2.

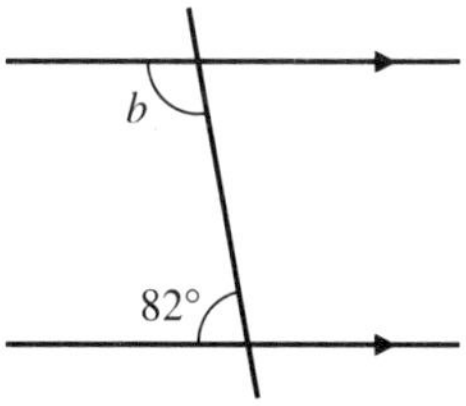

3.

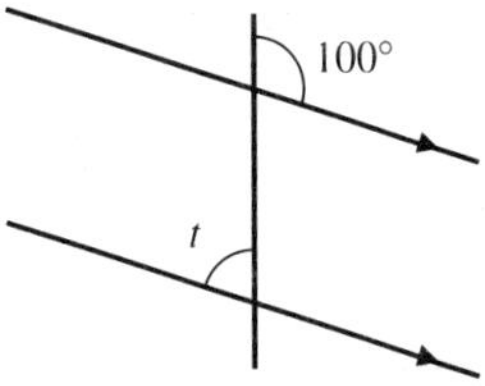

4.

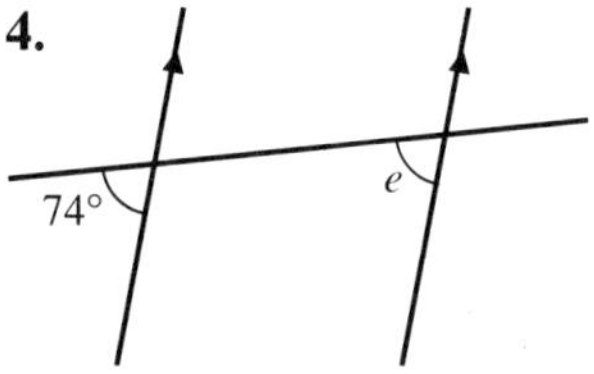

5.

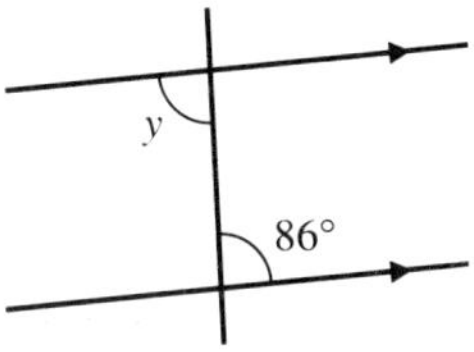

6.

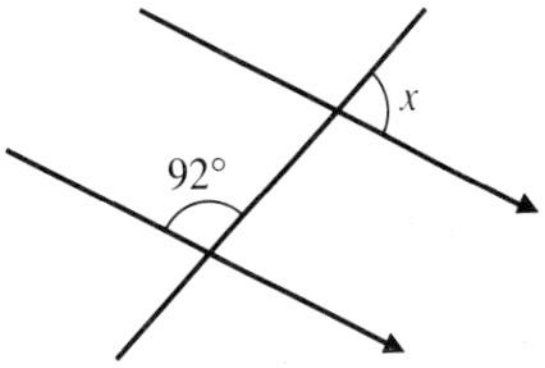

7.

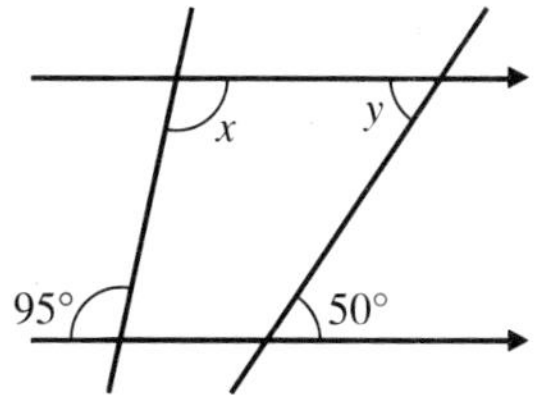

8.

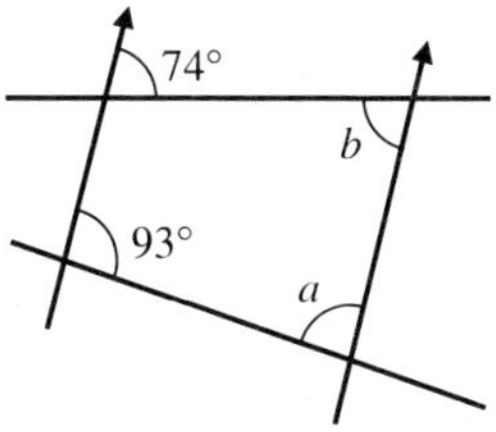

9.

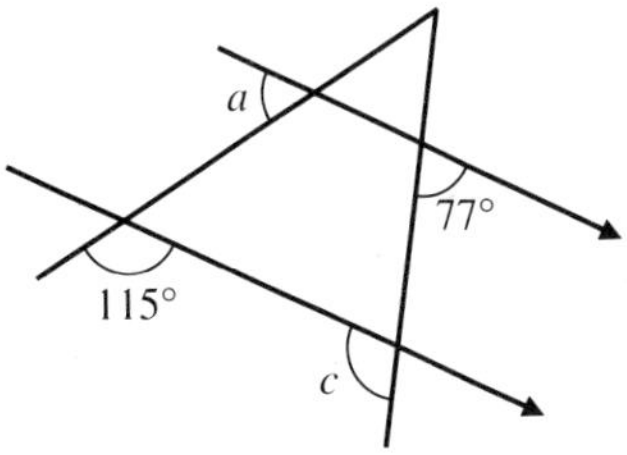

10.

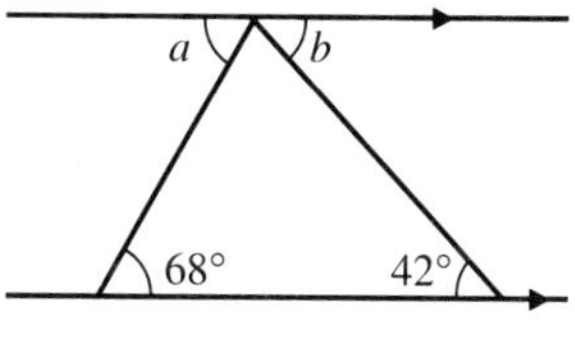

11.

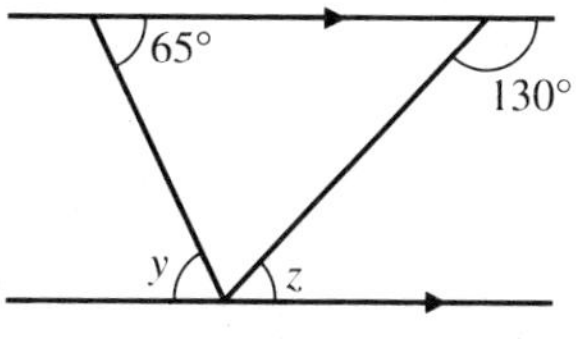

12.

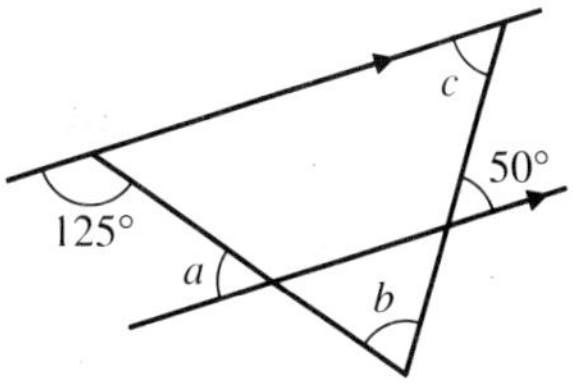

Quadrilaterals and regular polygons

(a) The quadrilateral PQRS has been split into two triangles.
We know that $a+e+f = 180°$
and that $b+c+d = 180°$
$\therefore\ a+b+c+d+e+f = 360°$.
But the angles of the quadrilateral are $(a+b)$, c, $(d+e)$ and f.

$\therefore$ The sum of the angles in a quadrilateral is 360°.

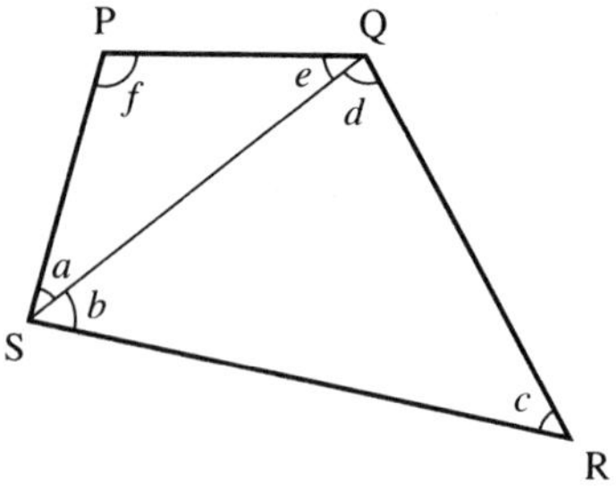

(b) The angles at the centre of a regular polygon are equal.

For example:

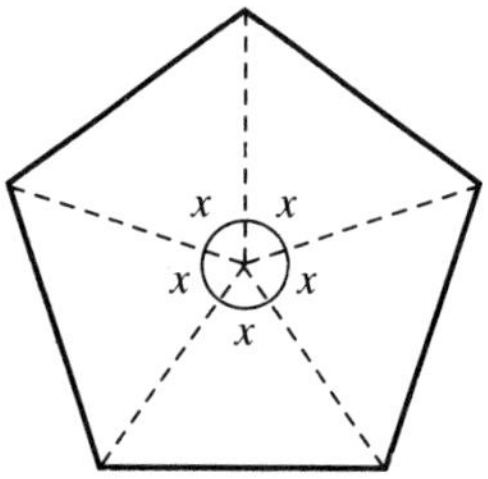

Regular pentagon:
$x+x+x+x+x = 360°$
$\therefore\ x = 72°$

Exercise 6

Find the angles marked with letters.

1.

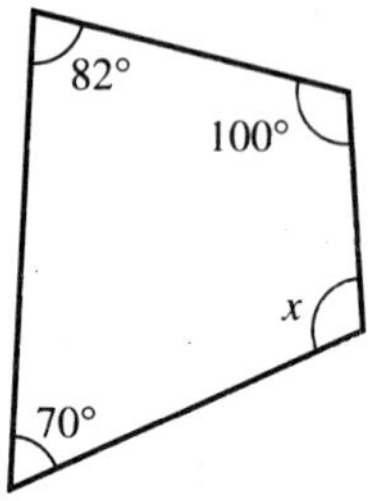

2.

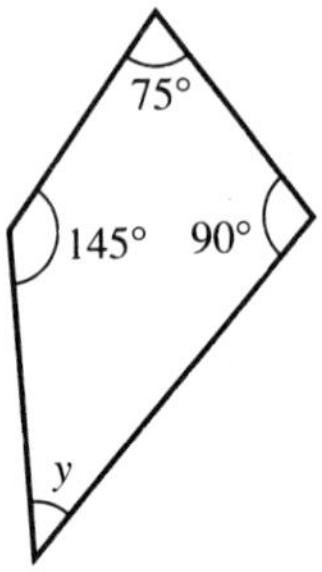

3.

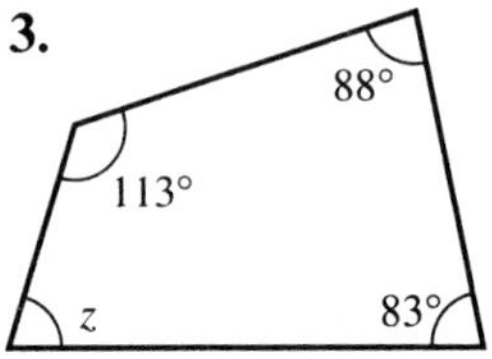

4.

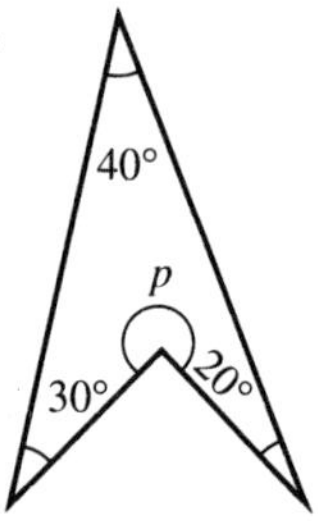

5.

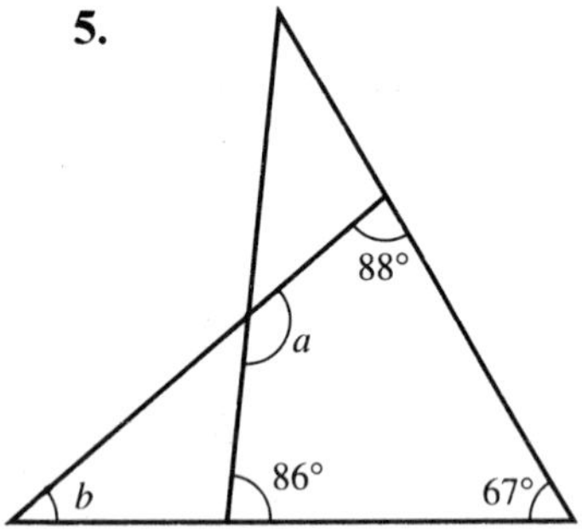

6.

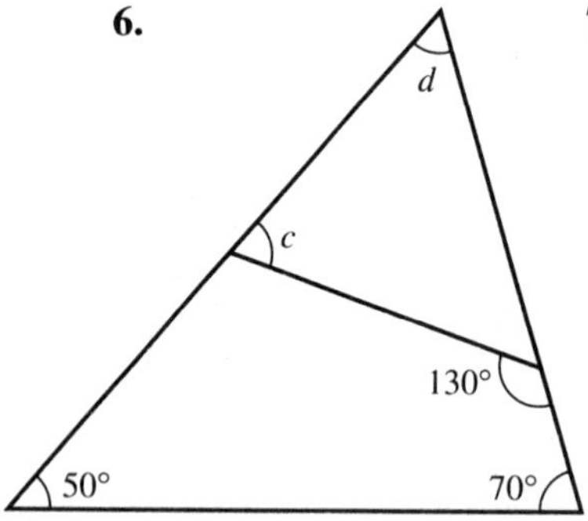

7.

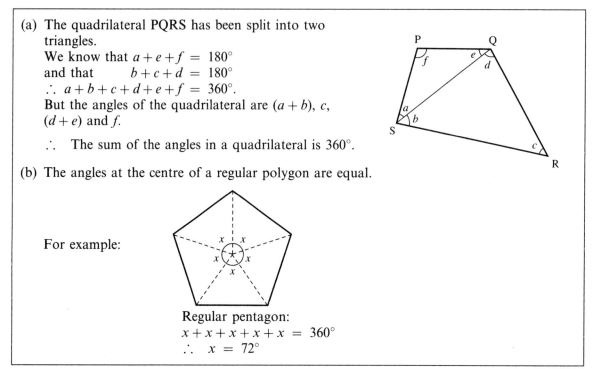

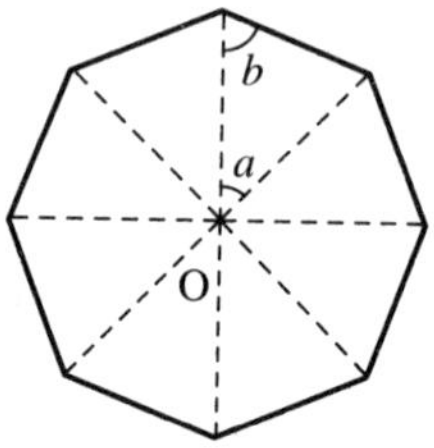

regular octagon
O is the centre.

Mixed questions

The next exercise contains questions which summarise the work of the last four exercises.

Exercise 7

Find the angles marked with letters.

1.
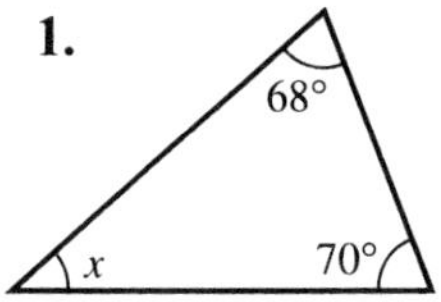

2.
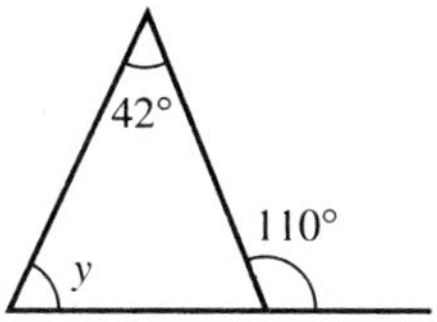

3.
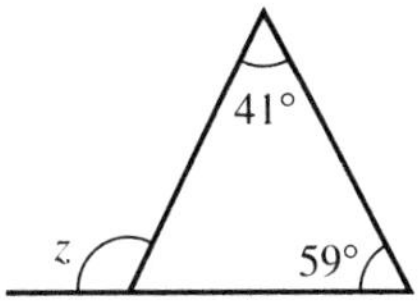

4.
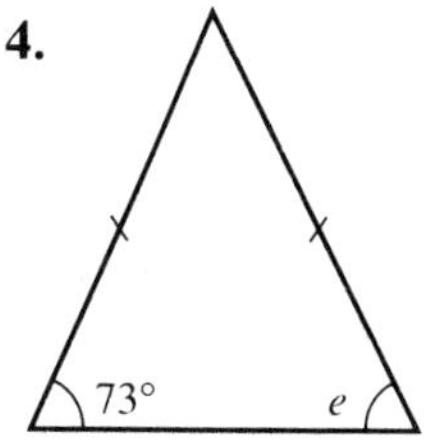

5.
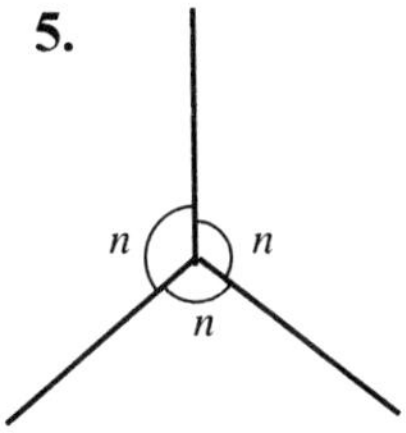

6.
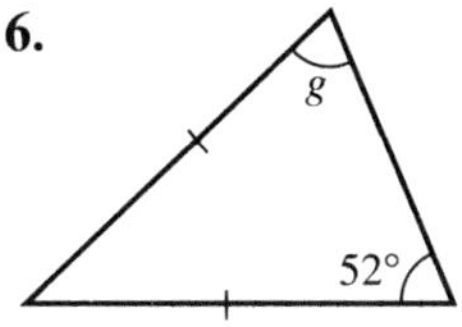

7.
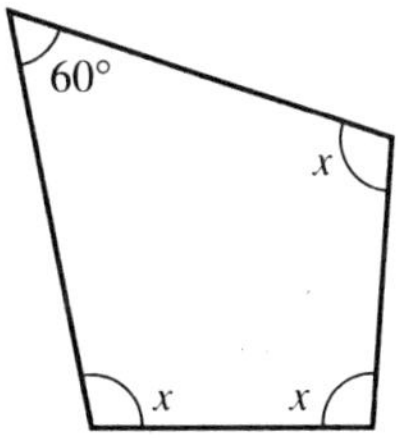

8.
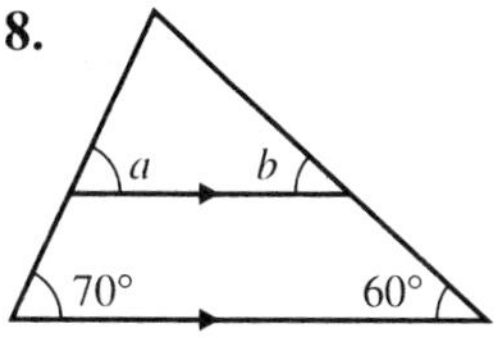

9.
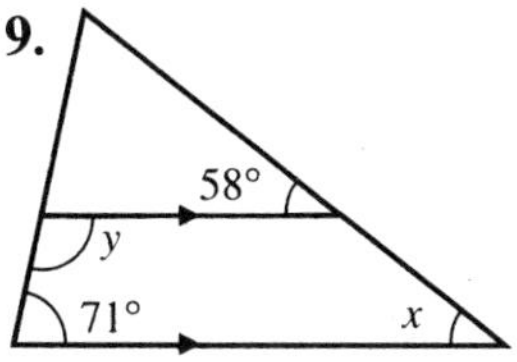

10.
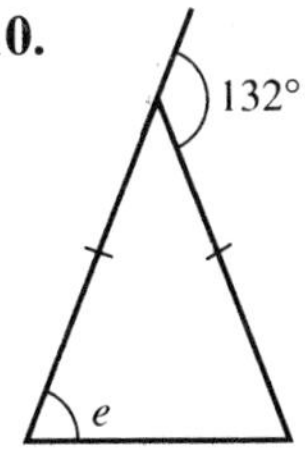

11.
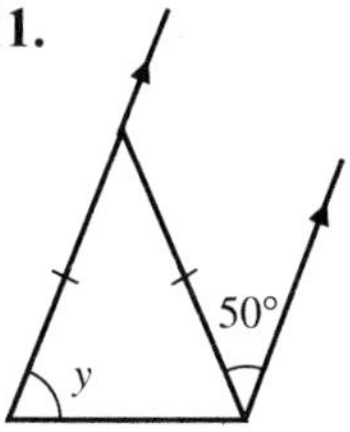

12.
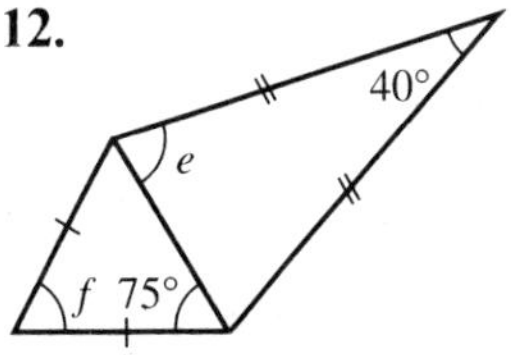

13.
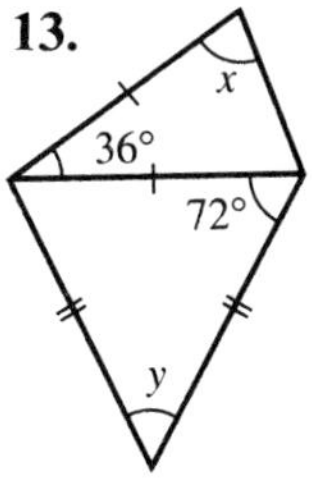

14.
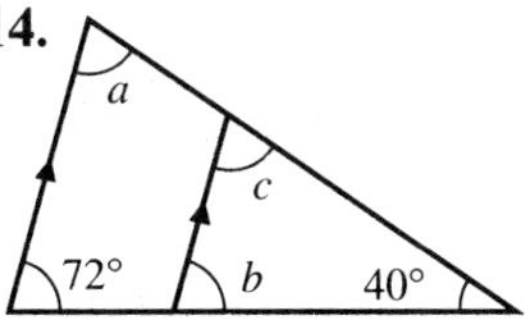

15.
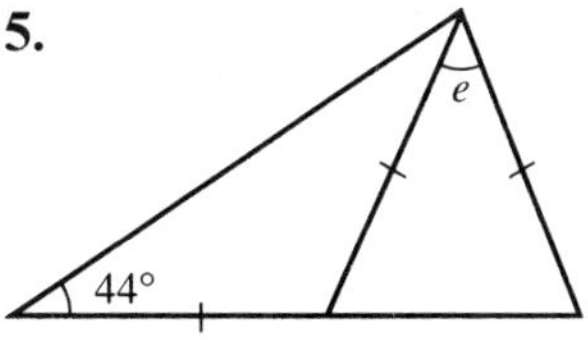

16.
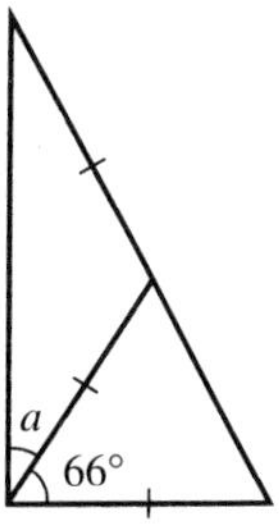

17.
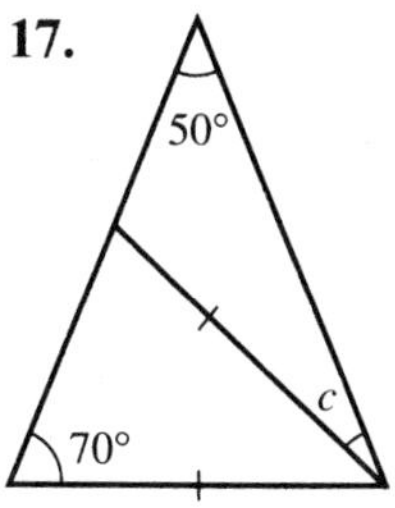

18.
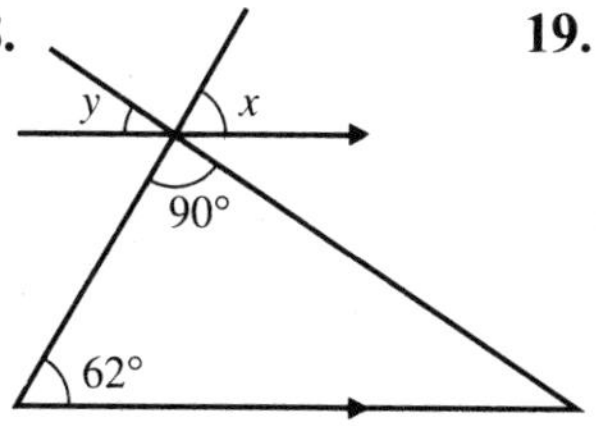

19.
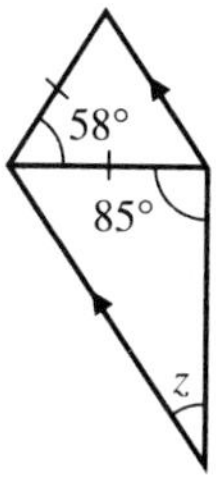

20.
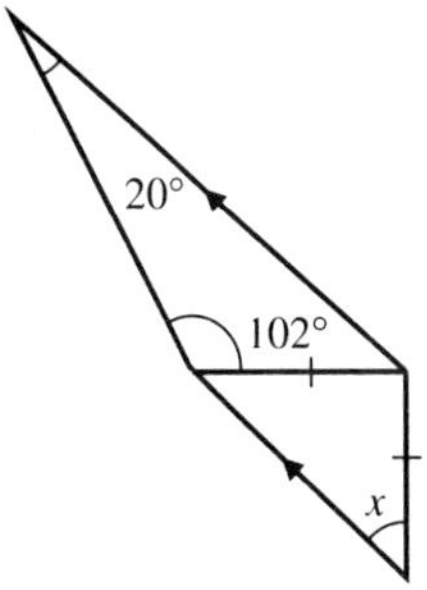

21.

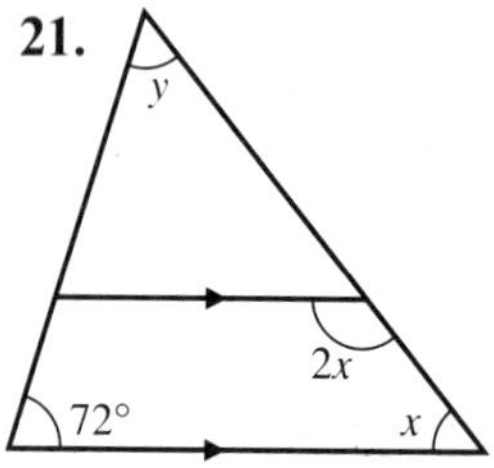

22.

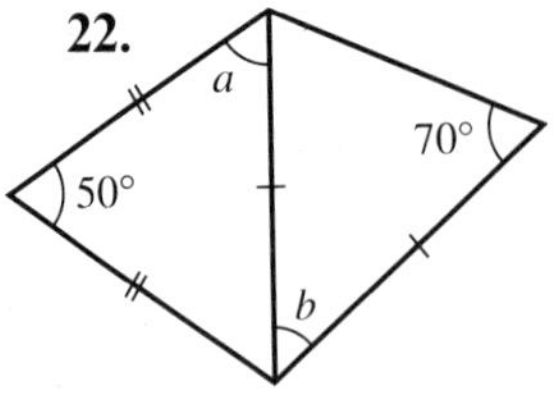

23.

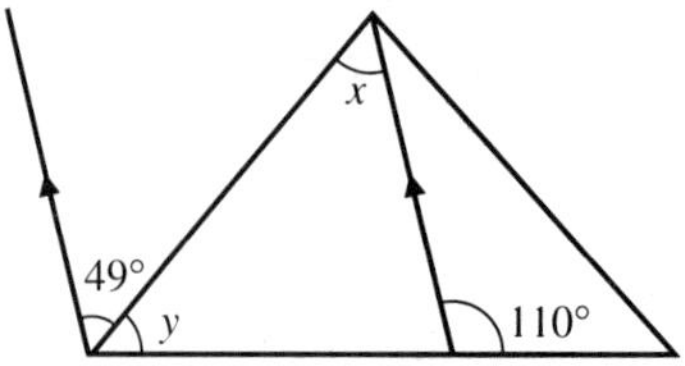

24.

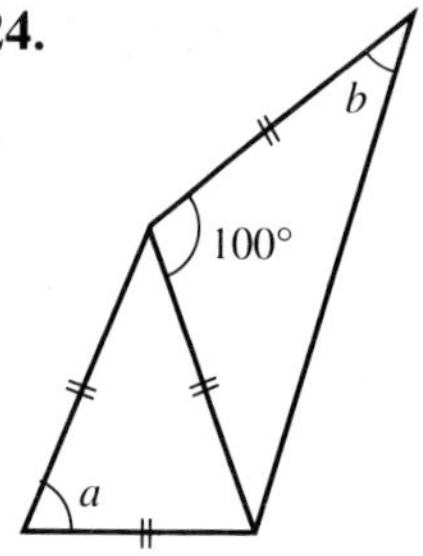

25. The diagram shows two equal squares joined to a triangle. Find the angle x.

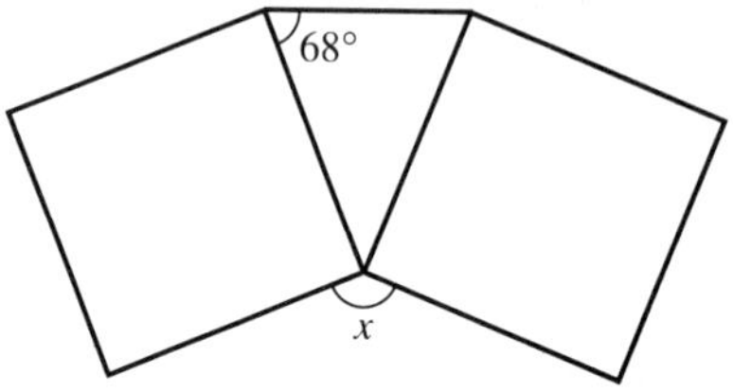

26. Find the angle a between the diagonals of the parallelogram.

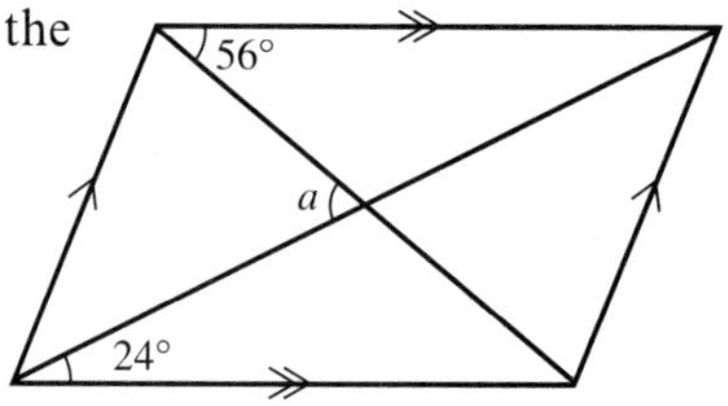

27. The diagram shows the cross section of a roof of a chalet. PQ and RS are horizontal and ST is vertical. Work out angles x, y and z.

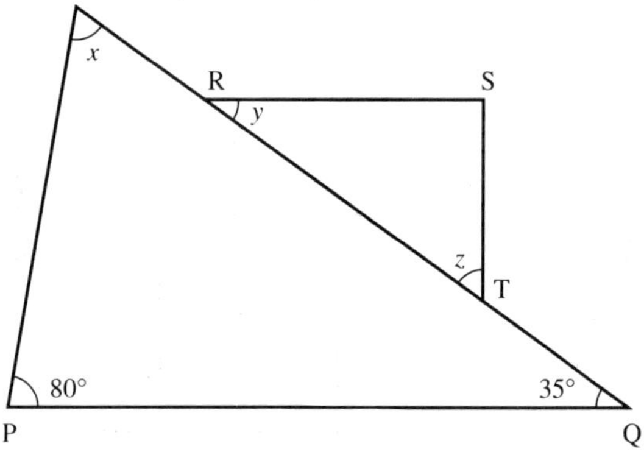

28. Given AB = AC and DA is parallel to EC, find x.

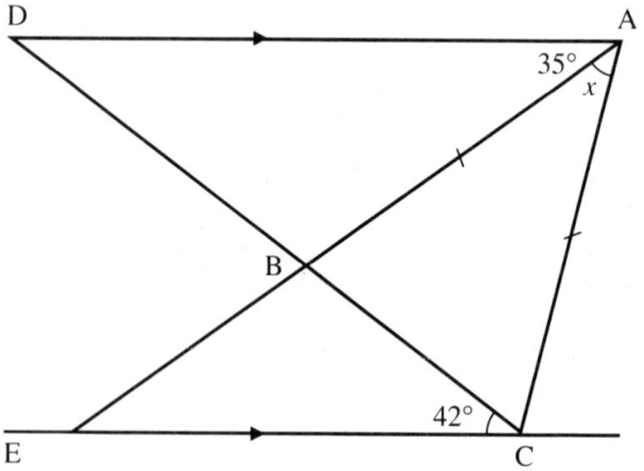

1.3 Symmetry

4/5b

(a) Line symmetry

The letter M has one line of symmetry, shown dotted.

(b) Rotational symmetry

The shape may be turned about O into three identical positions. It has rotational symmetry of order three.

Exercise 8

For each shape state:
(a) the number of lines of symmetry
(b) the order of rotational symmetry.

1. 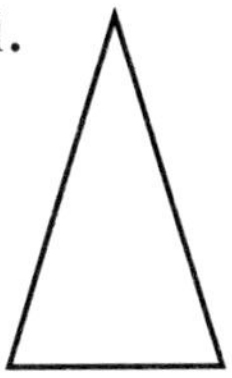

2. 

3. 

4. 

5. 

6. 

7. 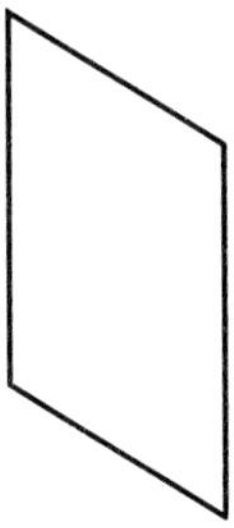

8. 

9. 

10. 

11. 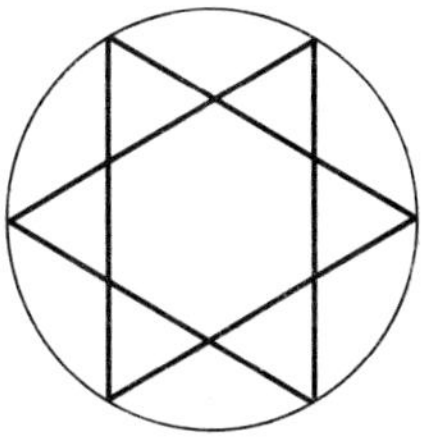

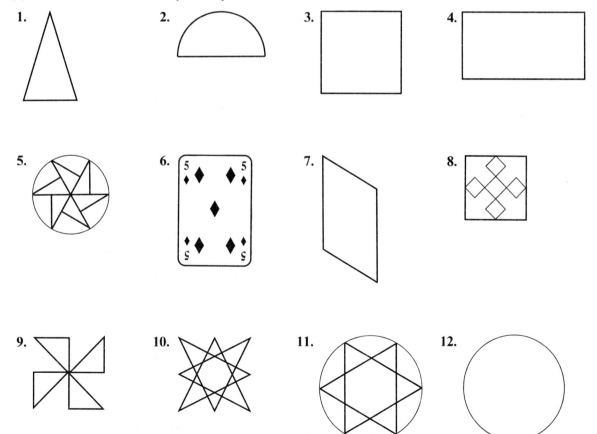

12. 

Exercise 9

In Questions **1** to **8**, the broken lines are axes of symmetry. In each question only *part of the shape* is given. Copy what is given onto squared paper and then carefully complete the shape.

1.

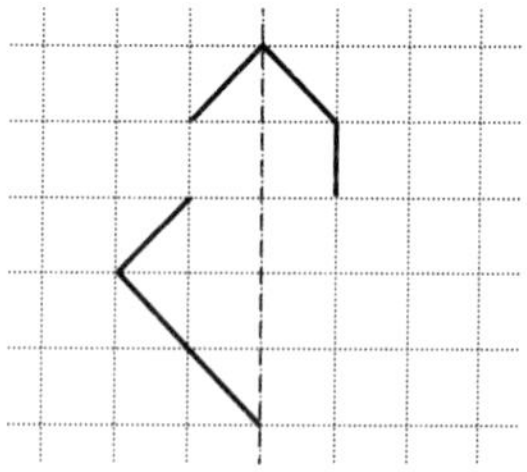

2.

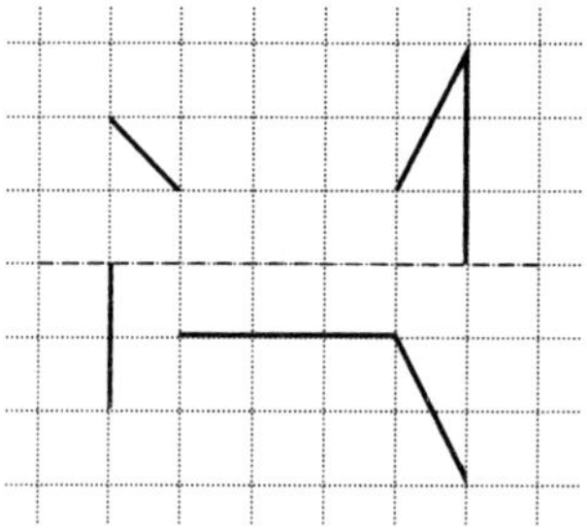

3.

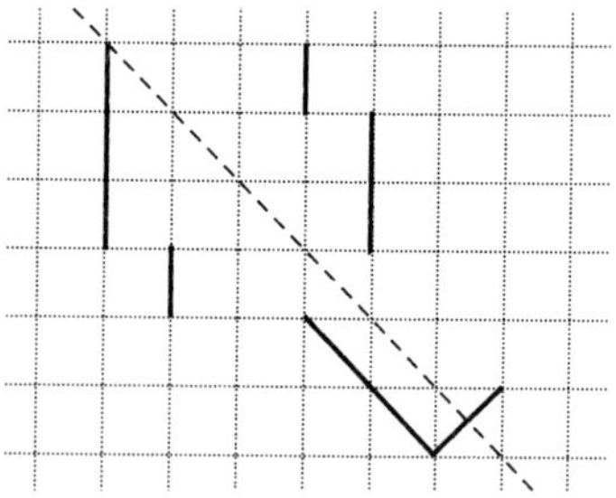

4.

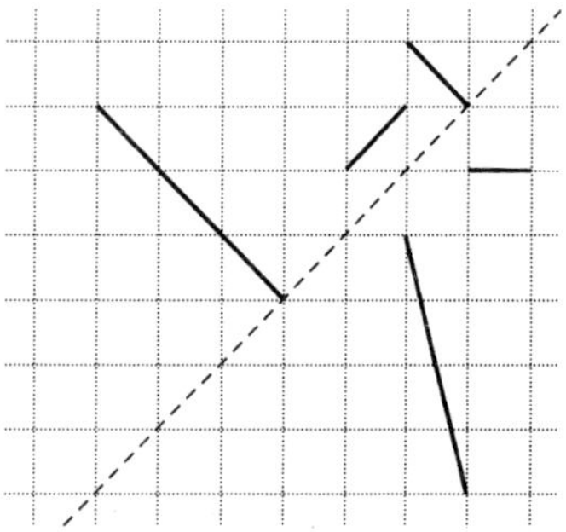

5.

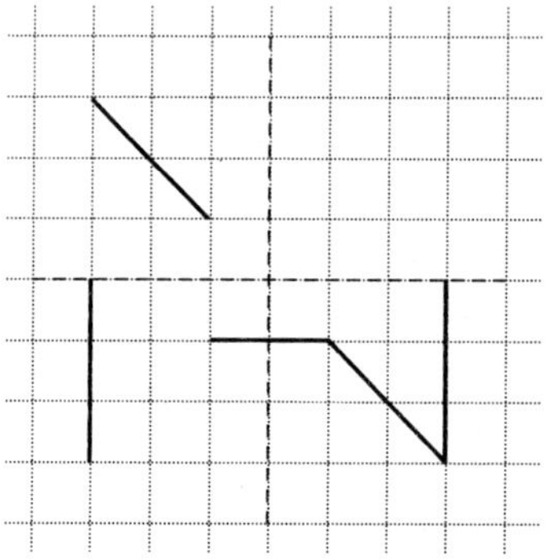

6.

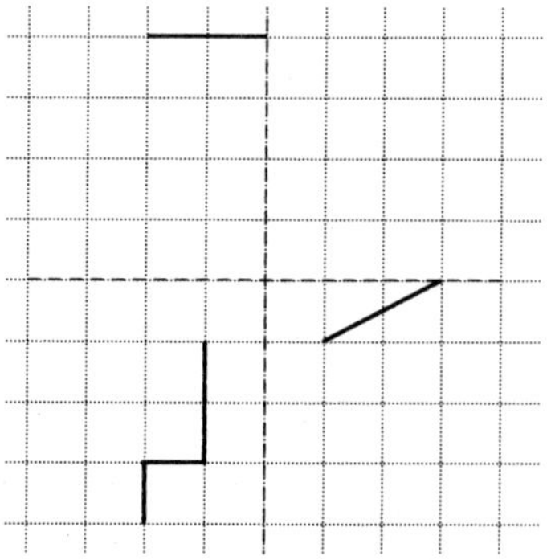

7.

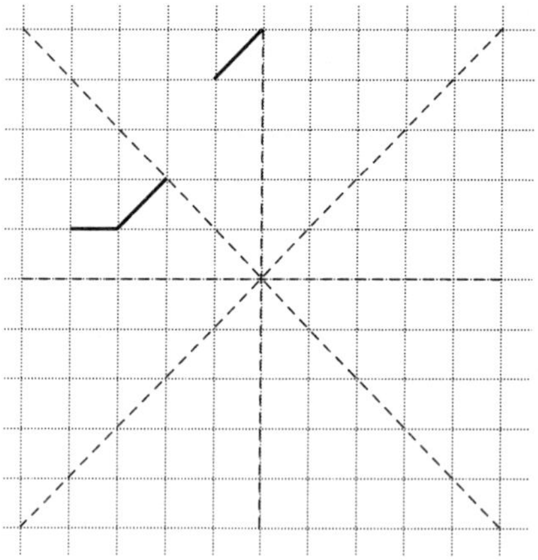

8.

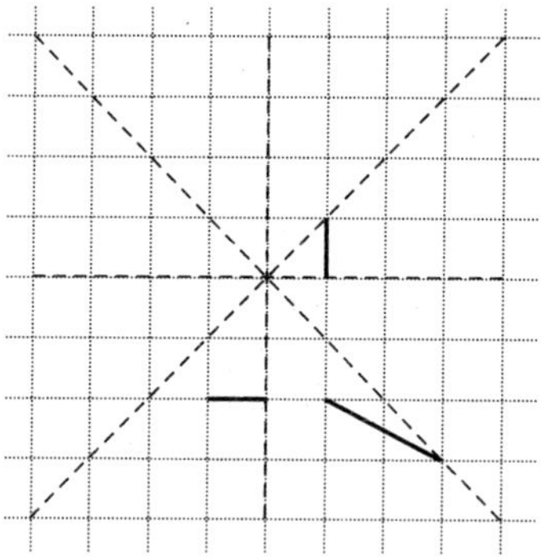

9. Fold a piece of paper twice and cut out any shape from the corner. Stick the cut-out into your book stating the number of lines of symmetry and the order of rotational symmetry.

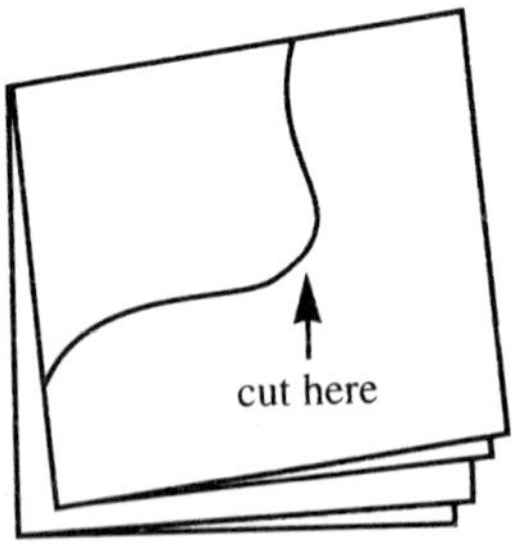

Planes of symmetry

A plane of symmetry divides a 3-D shape into two congruent shapes. One shape must be a mirror image of the other shape.

The shaded plane is a plane of symmetry of the cube.

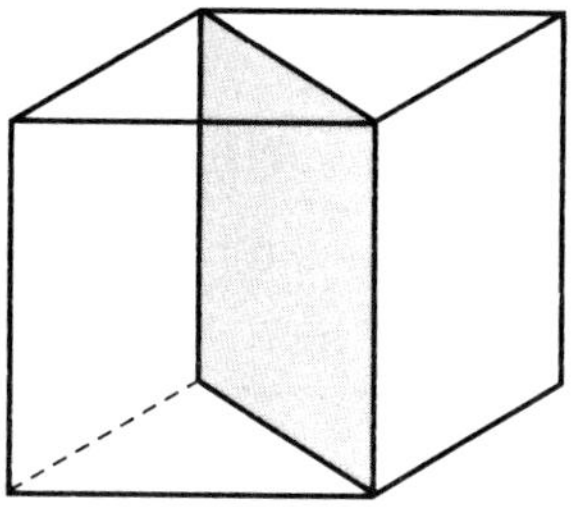

Exercise 10

1. How many planes of symmetry does this cuboid have?

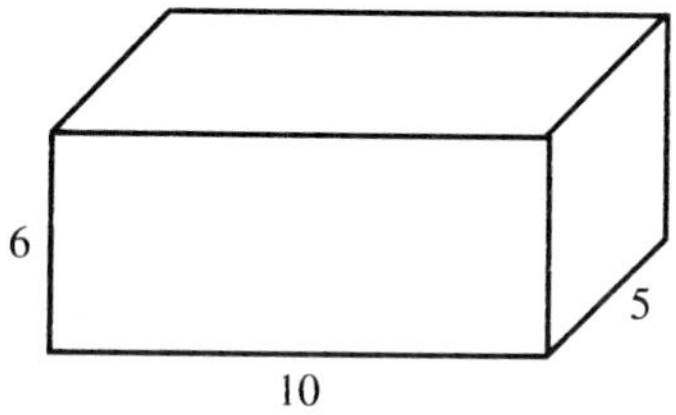

2. How many planes of symmetry do these shapes have?

(a)
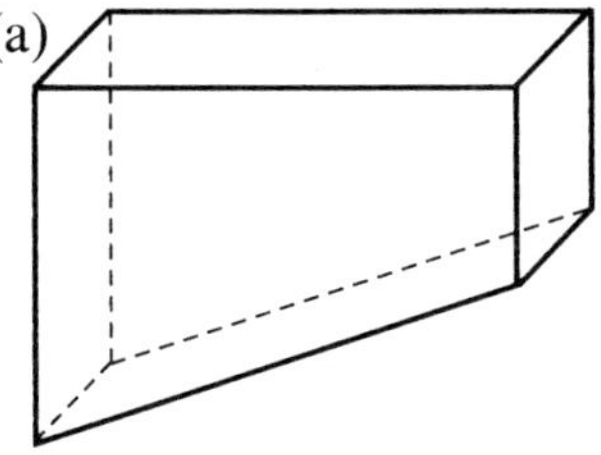
(b)
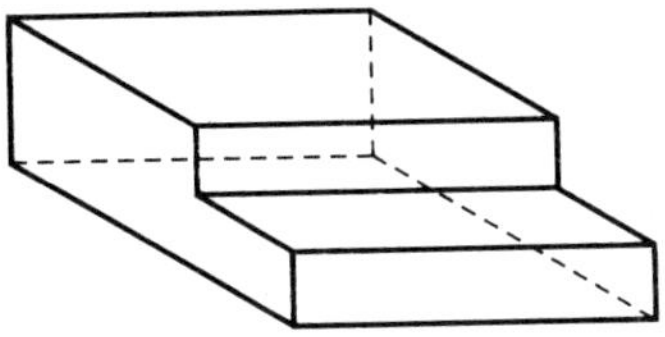
(c)
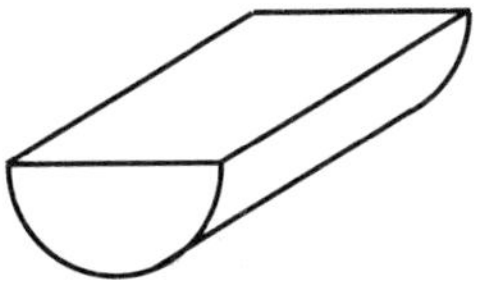

3. How many planes of symmetry does a cube have?

4. Draw a pyramid with a square base so that the vertex of the pyramid is vertically above the centre of the square base. Show any planes of symmetry by shading.

5. The diagrams show the plan view and the side view of an object.

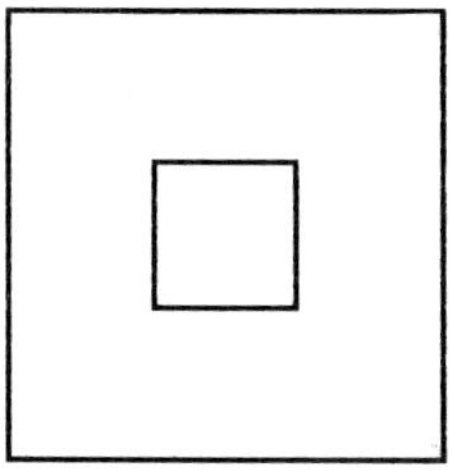
plan view

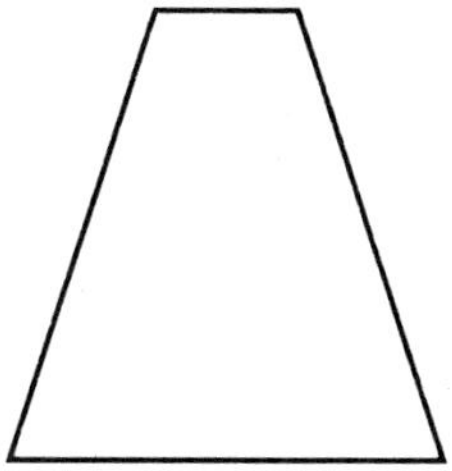
side view

How many planes of symmetry has this object?

1.4 Networks

4/5c

A map shows rivers, woods, churches, roads, railway lines and so on as they appear on an aerial photograph.

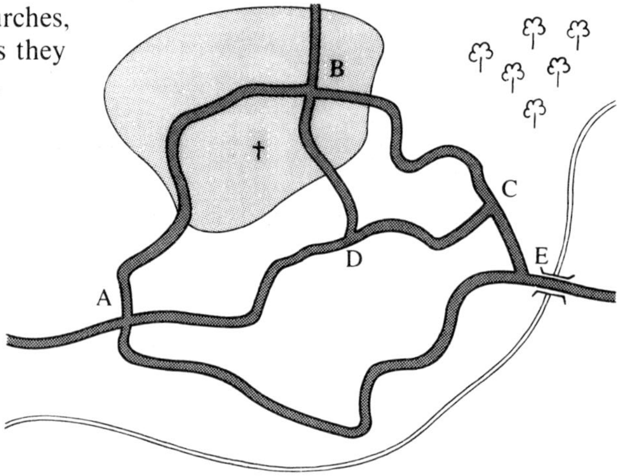

If we are only interested in the lengths of the roads a network diagram without all the curves is simpler.
The shortest route from A to E, which passes through B, C and D, is
A → B → D → C → E which is 13 miles.
Another route is A → D → B → C → E and this is 15 miles.

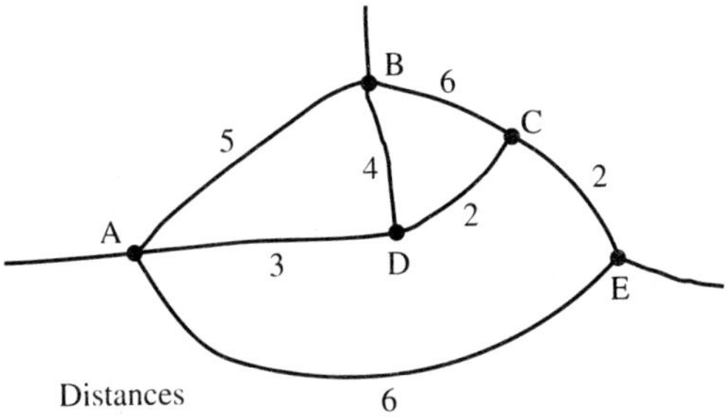

The plan of the London Underground is a network diagram. The lines and stations are shown clearly but the distances between stations all look to be the same, which is not in fact the case.

Networks are used in finding shortest routes for journeys and in planning problems such as deciding where a new bridge is to be built.

Exercise 11

1. A network is *traversable* if it can be drawn without lifting your pen from the paper and without going over any line twice. State which of the following networks are traversable.

(a)

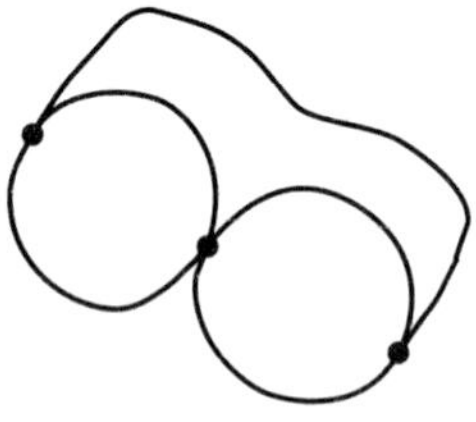

(b)

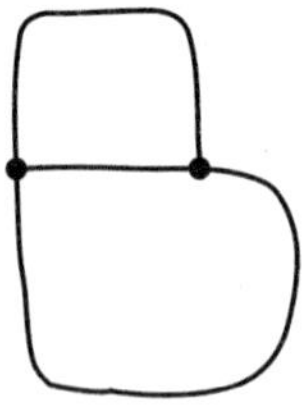

(c)

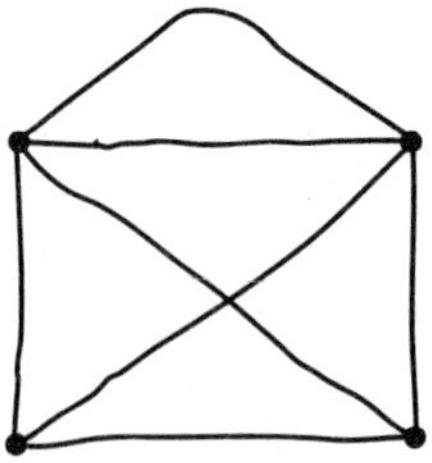

(d)

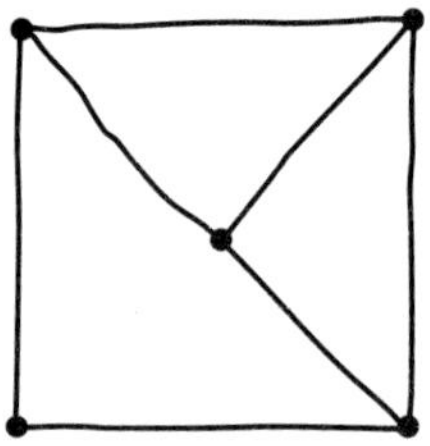

(e) 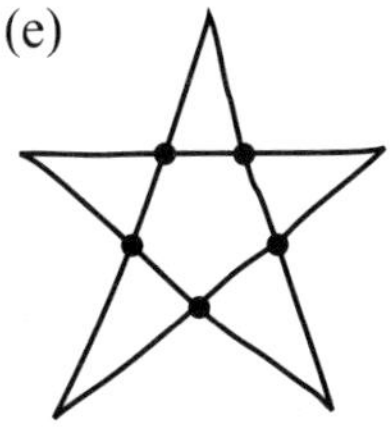

(f) 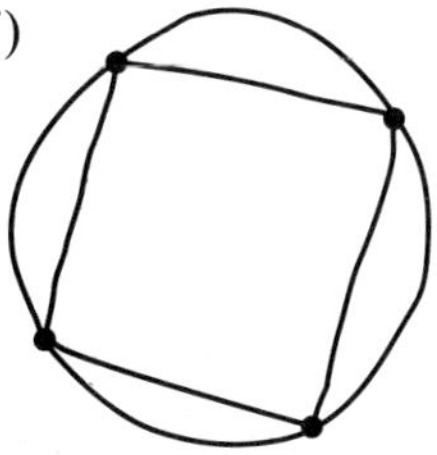

(g) 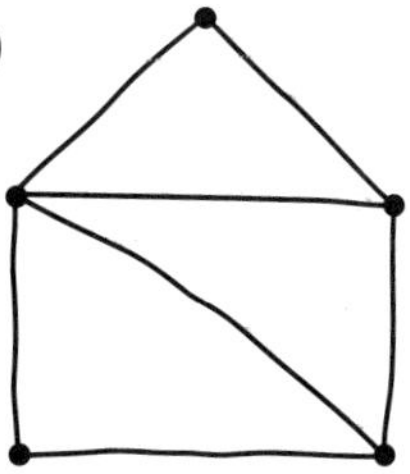

(h) 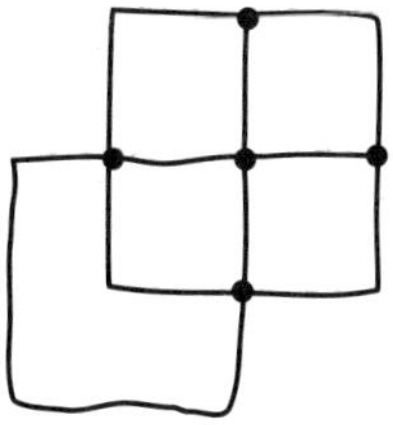

2. The diagram shows the lengths in miles of the roads between points A, B, C, ... G.

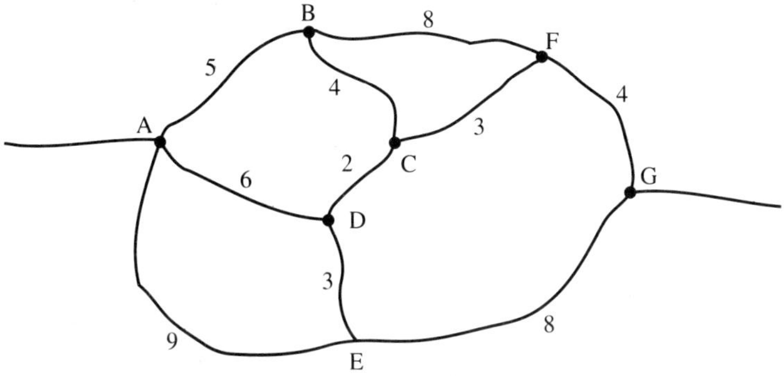

(a) Find the shortest route from A to G.
(b) Find the shortest route from A to G which involves passing through all the towns B, C, D, E, F on the way. You can if you wish travel along any road more than once.
(c) A rather dishonest taxi driver wants to increase the size of his fare. Find the longest route from A to G which involves passing through each of the towns B, C, D, E, F.

3. For the network below, find
(a) the shortest route from A to I
(b) the shortest route from A to I which passes through all the towns B, C, D, E, F, G, H on the way.

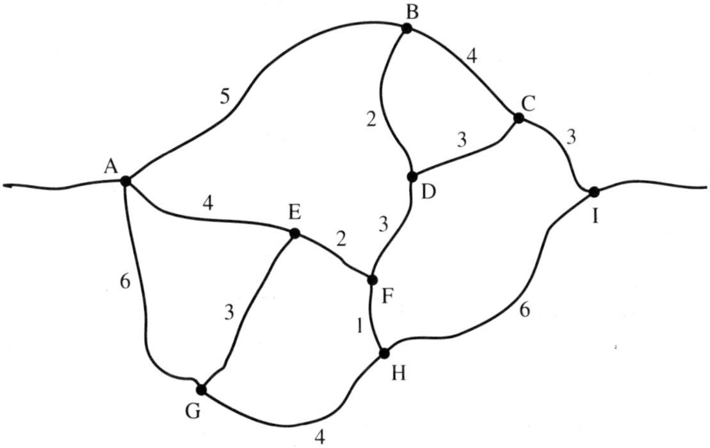

4. A postman starts and finishes at A and has to walk along each road at least once. For (a), (b), (c) and (d) below find the route which involves walking the minimum possible distance. Describe the route in the form A → B → E etc and write down the length of the route.

(a)

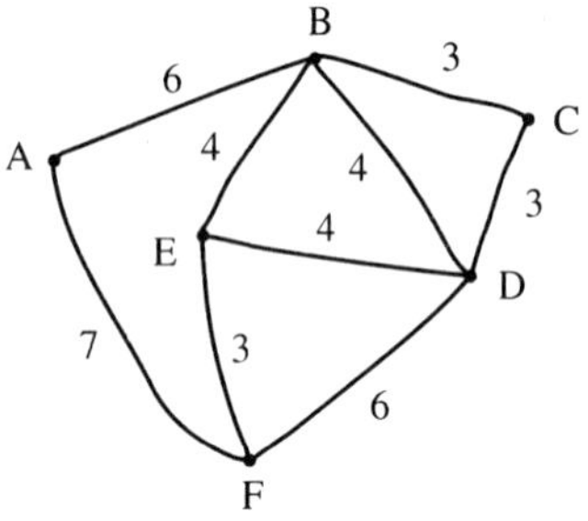

(b)

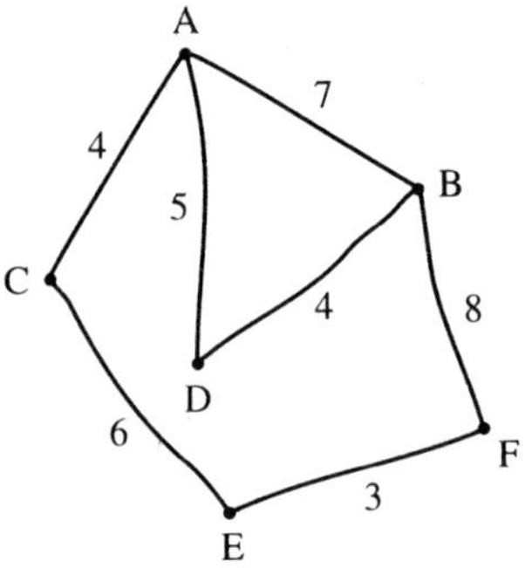

(c)

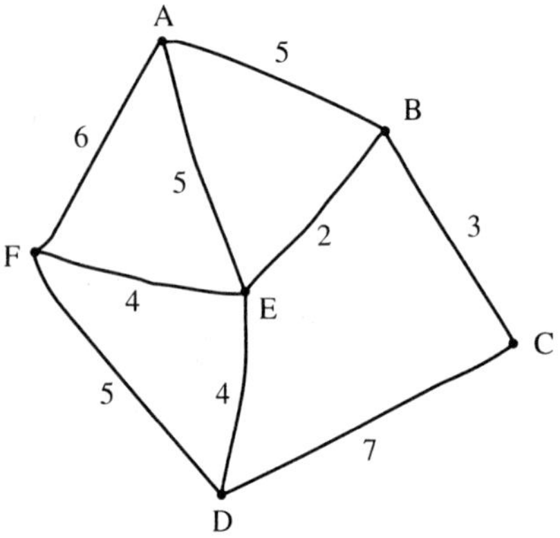

(d)

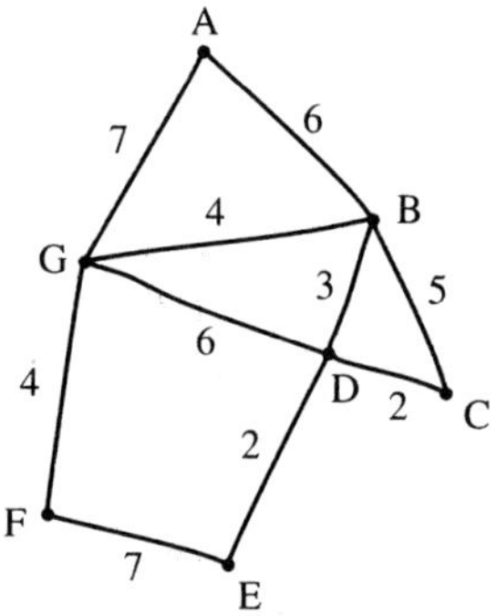

5. A groundsman is painting the white lines for the pitches below and wants to walk the shortest possible distance.
The diagrams are drawn to scale.
Sketch the diagrams and show with a jagged line [⋀⋀⋀] the places where he has to walk along the same line twice.

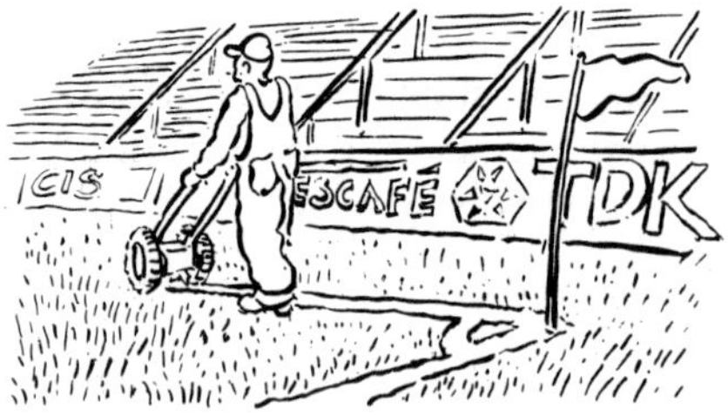

(a)

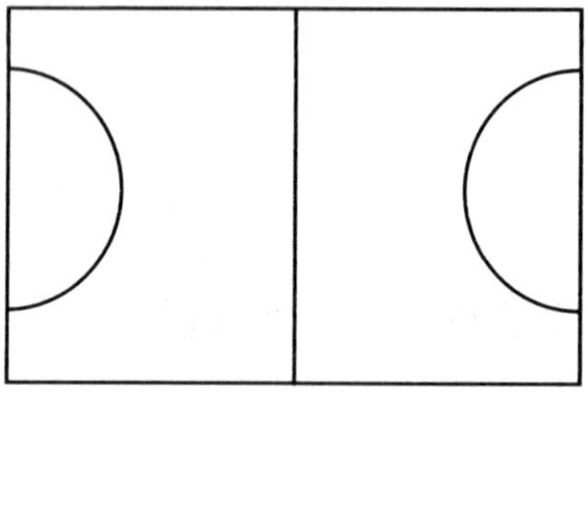

(b)

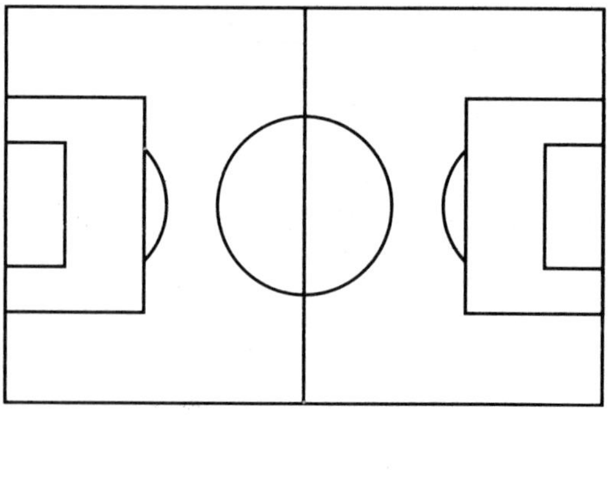

1.5 Circle calculations

4/5d, 4/6d

Circumference of a circle

The circumference of the circle below is given by $C = \pi d$

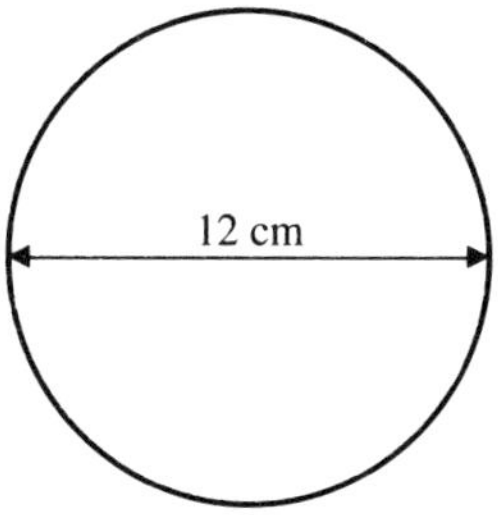

$C = \pi \times 12$ cm
$C = 37{\cdot}7$ cm (to 3 s.f.)
We have used the 'π' button on a calculator. The value of π (pi) is 3·142 approximately.

Exercise 12

Find the circumference. Use the 'π' button on a calculator or take $\pi = 3{\cdot}142$. Give the answers correct to 3 significant figures.

1.
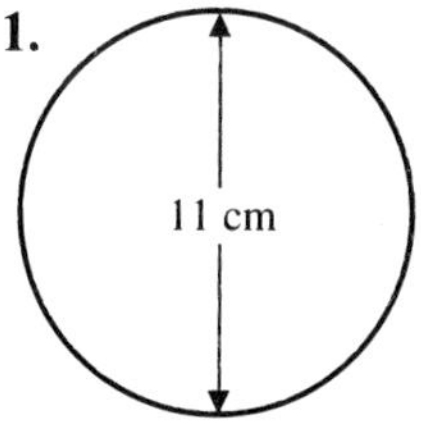

2.
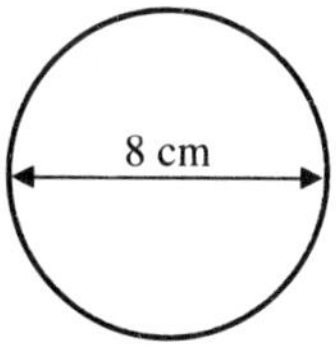

3.
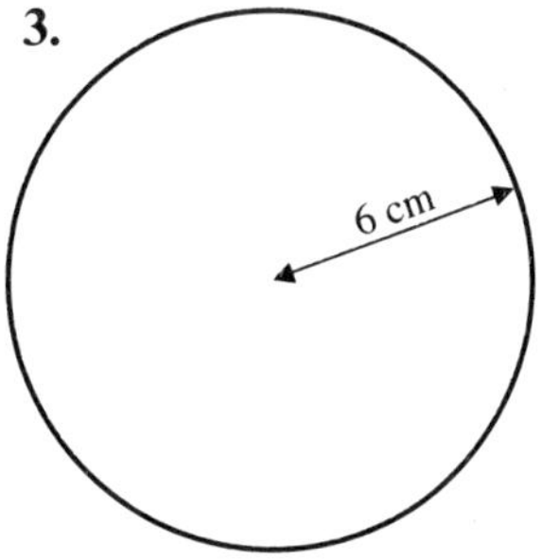

4.
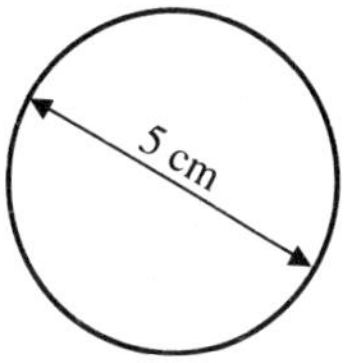

5.
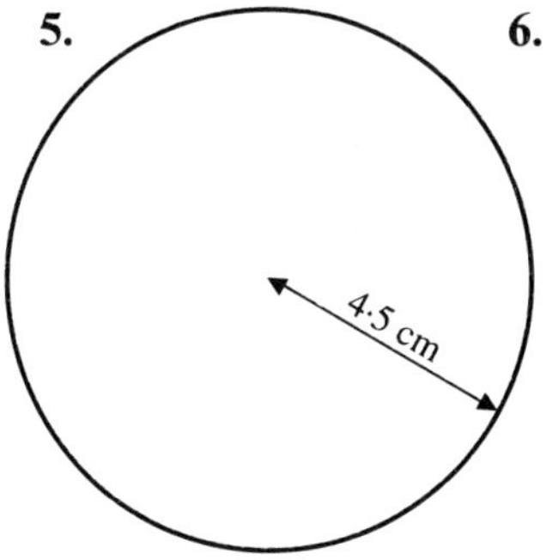

6.
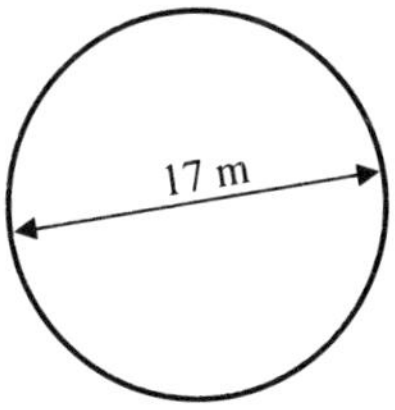

7.
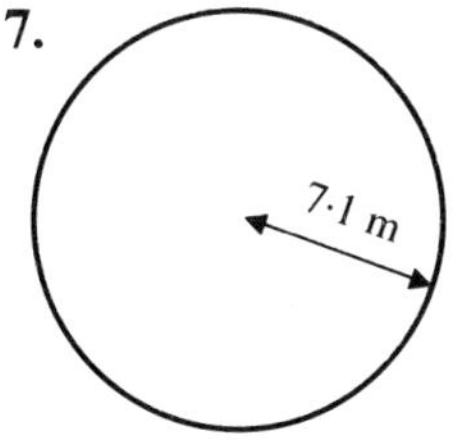

8.
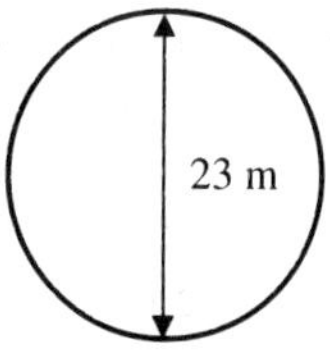

9. A 'new' 10p coin has a diameter of 2·4 cm and the 'old' 10p coin has a diameter of 2·8 cm.

How much longer, to the nearest mm, is the circumference of the old coin?

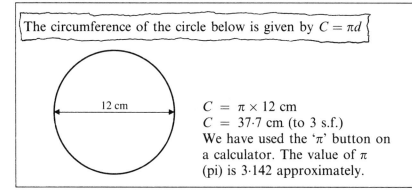

10. A circular pond has a diameter of 2·7 m. Calculate the length of the perimeter of the pond.

11. How many complete revolutions does a cycle wheel of diameter 60 cm make in travelling 400 m?

12. A running track has two semicircular ends of radius 34 m and two straights of 93·2 m as shown.

Calculate the total distance around the track to the nearest metre.

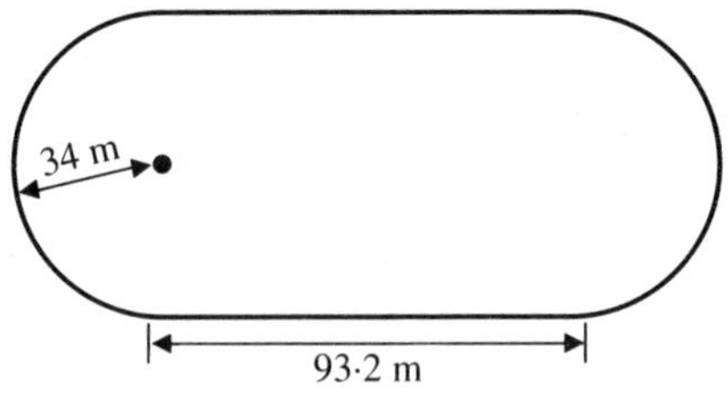

13. A fly, perched on the tip of the minute hand of a grandfather clock, is 14·4 cm from the centre of the clock face.
How far does the fly move between 12:00 and 12:15?

14. A penny-farthing bicycle is shown.
In a journey the front wheel rotates completely 156 times.
(a) How far does the bicycle travel?
(b) How many complete turns does the rear wheel make?

15. The diagram shows a framework for a target, consisting of 2 circles of wire and 6 straight pieces of wire. The radius of the outer circle is 30 cm and the radius of the inner circle is 15 cm.
Calculate the total length of wire needed for the whole framework.

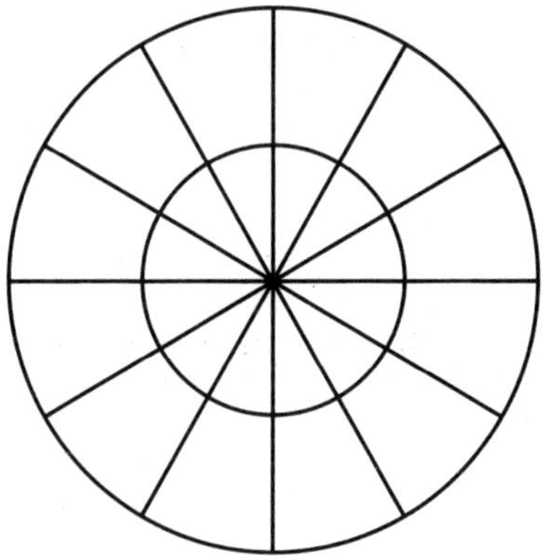

16. For a meeting, chairs are arranged in a large circle. The width of each chair is 40 cm.
How many chairs are needed to form a circle of diameter 3 m?

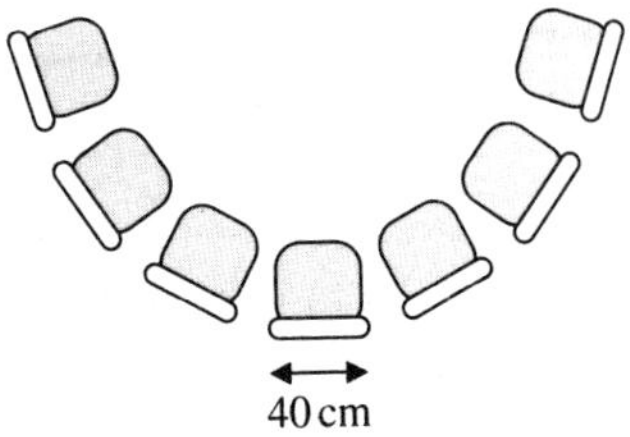

17. Lord Gibson decides to build a circular wall of radius 200 m around his stately home.

The diagram shows a section of the wall. Estimate, to the nearest thousand, the number of bricks required for the complete wall.

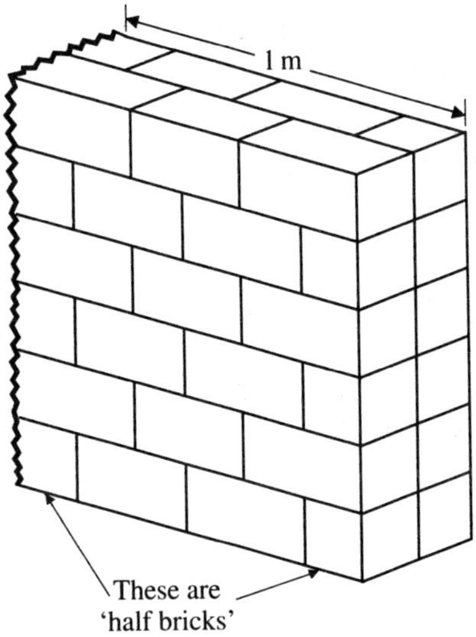

Area of a circle

Find the area of the circle shown.

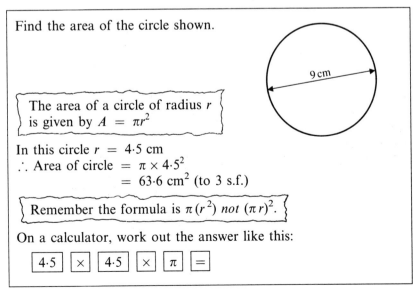

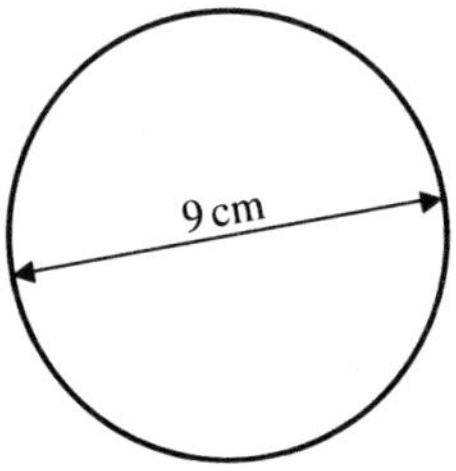

The area of a circle of radius r is given by $A = \pi r^2$

In this circle $r = 4{\cdot}5$ cm

$\therefore$ Area of circle $= \pi \times 4{\cdot}5^2$

$= 63{\cdot}6\ \text{cm}^2$ (to 3 s.f.)

Remember the formula is $\pi(r^2)$ *not* $(\pi r)^2$.

On a calculator, work out the answer like this:

[4·5] [×] [4·5] [×] [π] [=]

Exercise 13

In Questions **1** to **8** find the area of the circle. Use the 'π' button on a calculator or use $\pi = 3{\cdot}14$. Give the answers correct to three significant figures.

1.

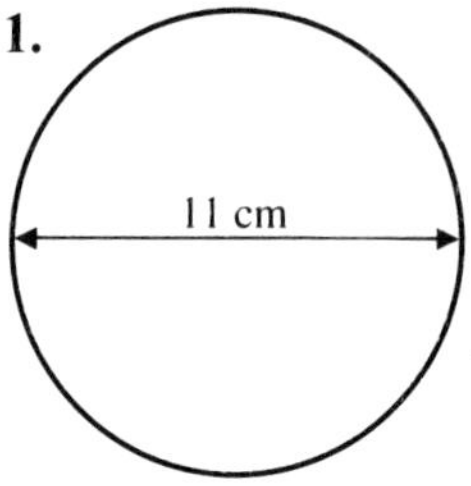

2.

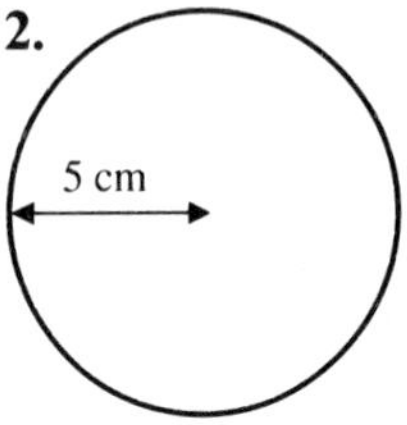

3.

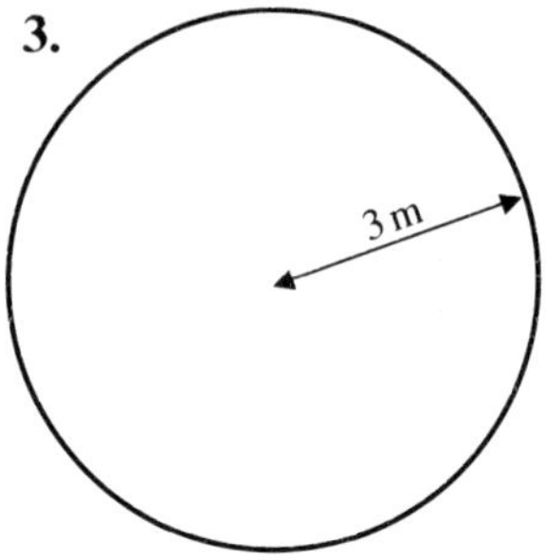

4.

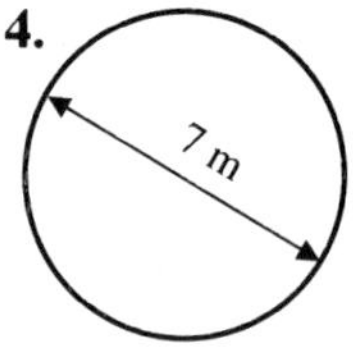

5.

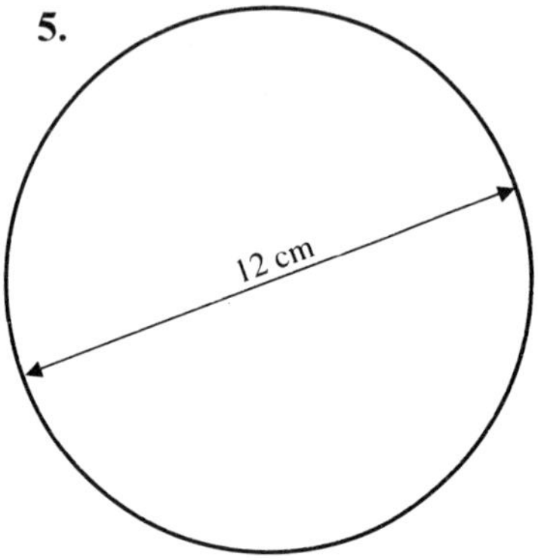

6.

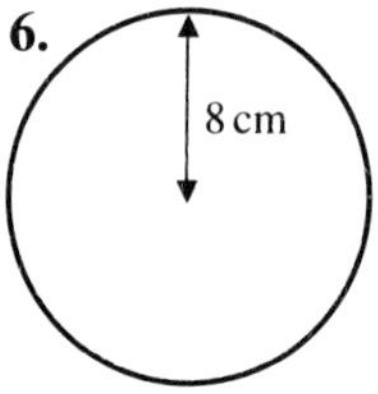

7.

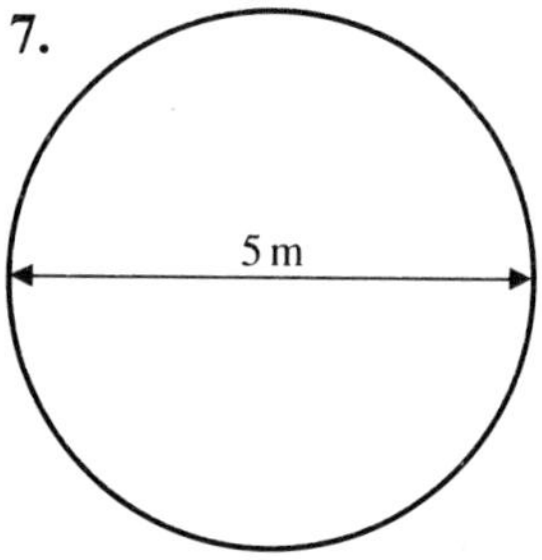

8.

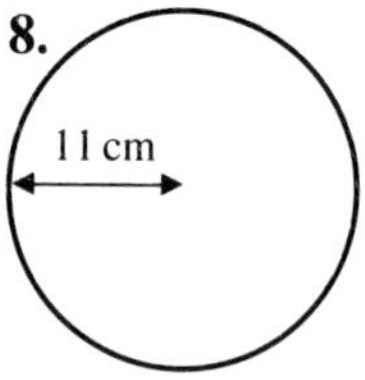

9. A spinner of radius 7·5 cm is divided into six equal sectors.
Calculate the area of each sector.

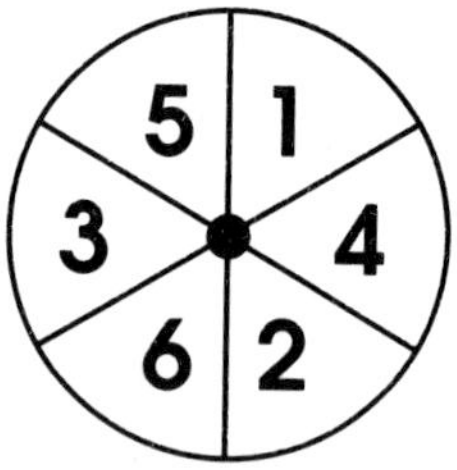

10. A circular swimming pool of diameter 12·6 m is to be covered by a plastic sheet to keep out leaves and insects.
Work out the area of the pool.

11. A circle of radius 5 cm is inscribed inside a square as shown.
Find the area shaded.

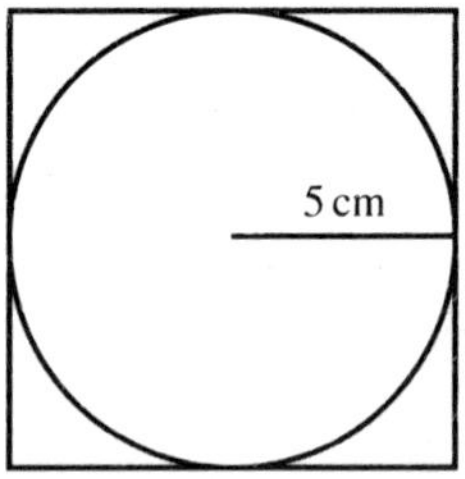

12. A large circular lawn is sprayed with weedkiller. Each square metre of grass requires 2 g of weedkiller. How much weedkiller is needed for a lawn of radius 27 m?

13. Discs of radius 4 cm are cut from a rectangular plastic sheet of length 84 cm and width 24 cm.

How many complete discs can be cut out? Find
(a) the total area of the discs cut
(b) the area of the sheet wasted.

14. A circular pond of radius 6 m is surrounded by a path of width 1 m.
(a) Find the area of the path.
(b) The path is resurfaced with astroturf which is bought in packs each containing enough to cover an area of 7 m^2. How many containers are required?

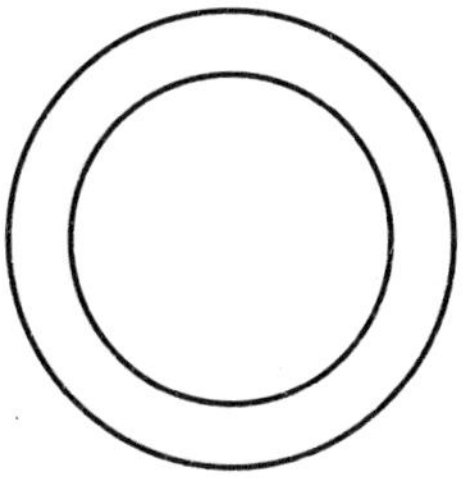

15. The diagram below shows a lawn (unshaded) surrounded by a path of uniform width (shaded). The curved end of the lawn is a semicircle of diameter 10 m.

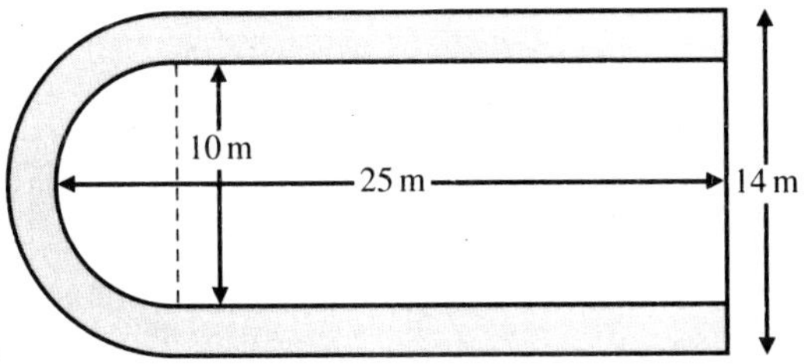

Calculate the total area of the path.

More complicated shapes

For the shape below find:

(a) the perimeter,
(b) the area.

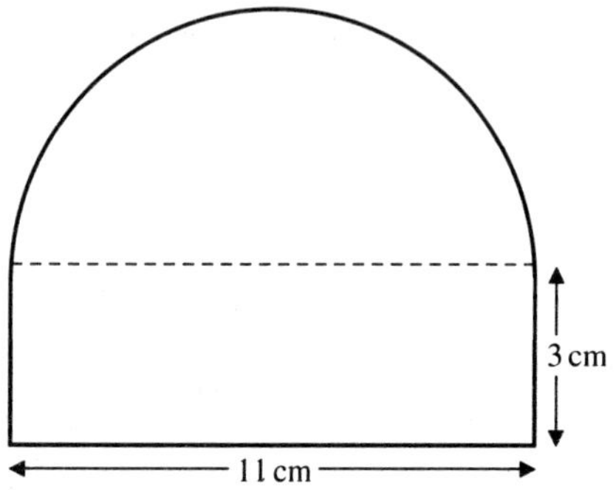

(a) Perimeter $= \left(\frac{\pi \times 11}{2}\right) + 11 + 3 + 3$

$= 34{\cdot}3$ cm (3 s.f.)

(b) Area $= \left(\frac{\pi \times 5{\cdot}5^2}{2}\right) + (11 \times 3)$

$= 80{\cdot}5\ \text{cm}^2$ (3 s.f.)

Exercise 14

Use the 'π' button on a calculator or take $\pi = 3{\cdot}14$. Give the answers correct to 3 s.f. For each shape find the perimeter.

1.
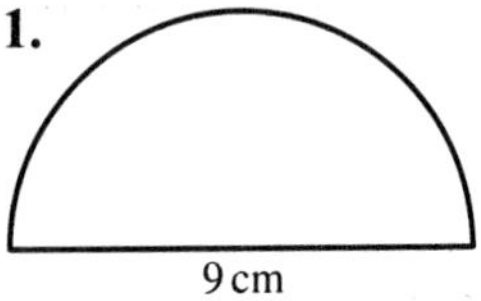

2.
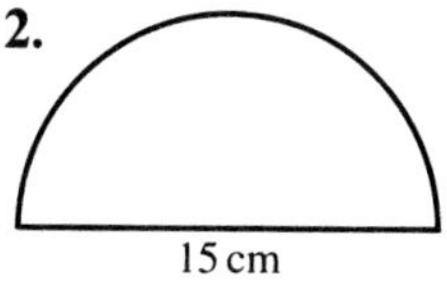

3.
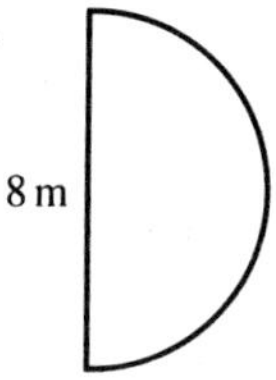

4.
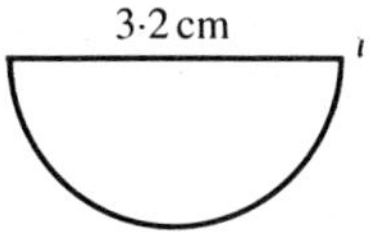

5.
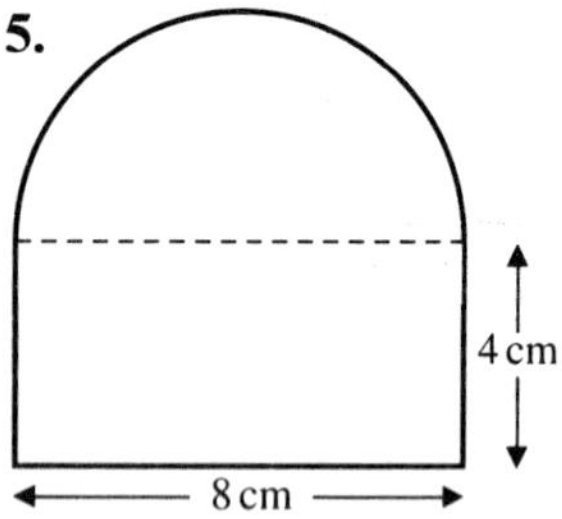

6.
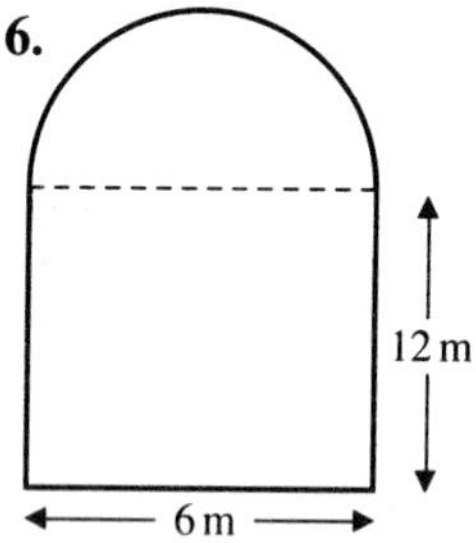

7.
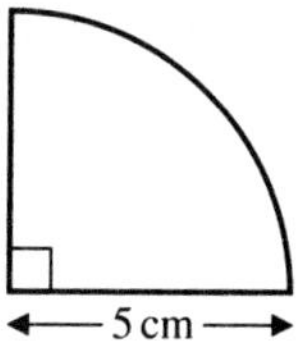

8.
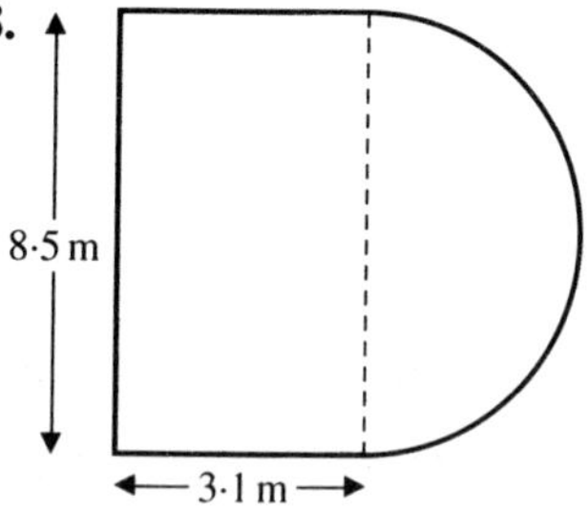

9.
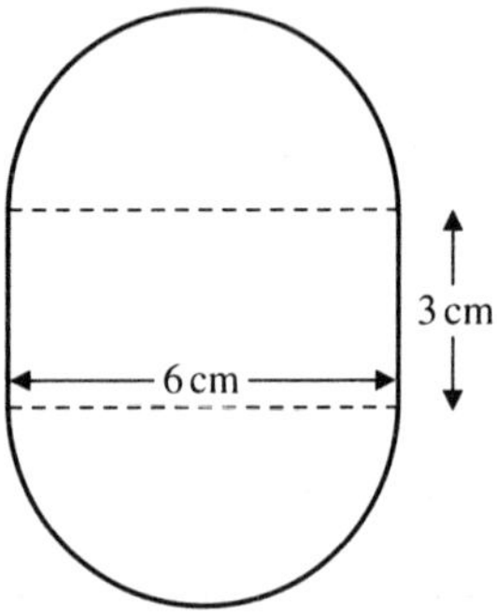

10.
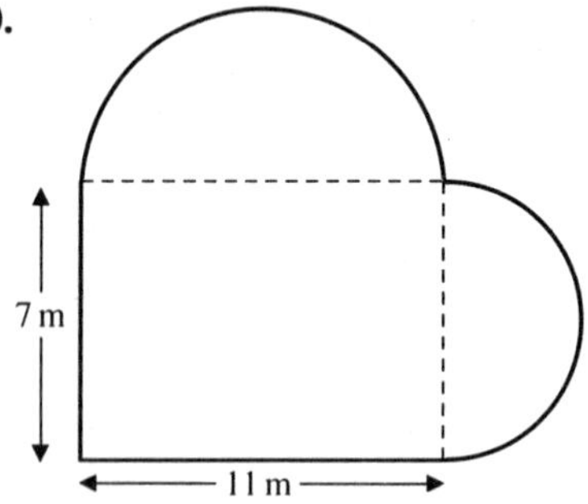

11.
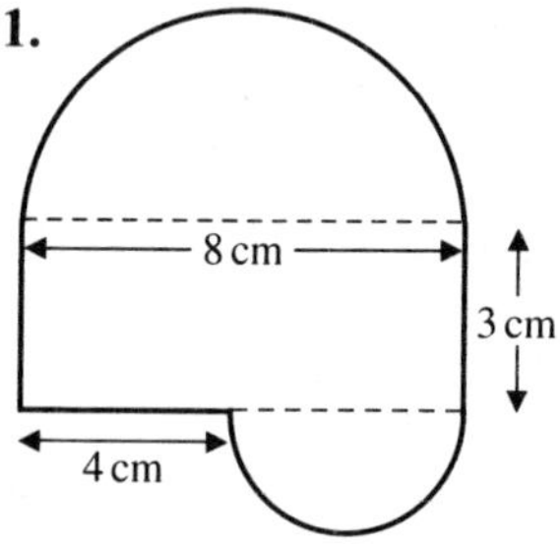

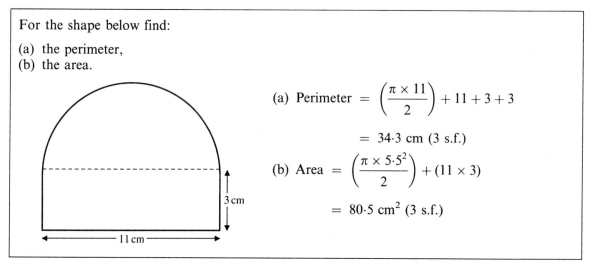

Exercise 15

Find the area of each shape. All lengths are in cm.
In Questions **4, 5, 6** find the shaded area.

1.

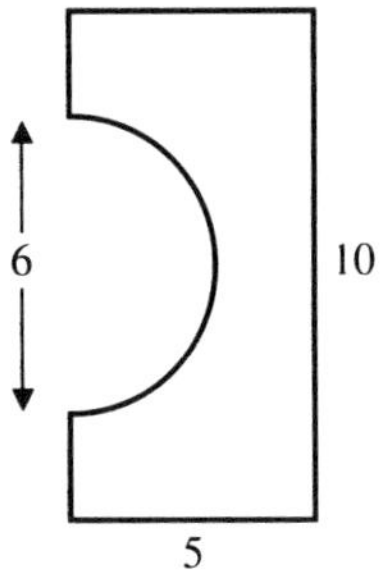

2.

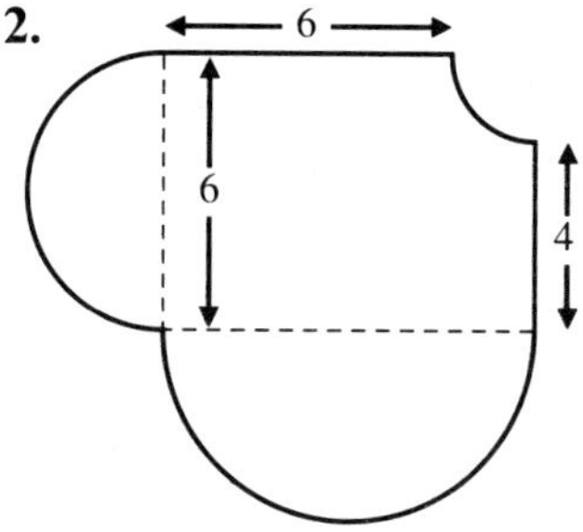

3.

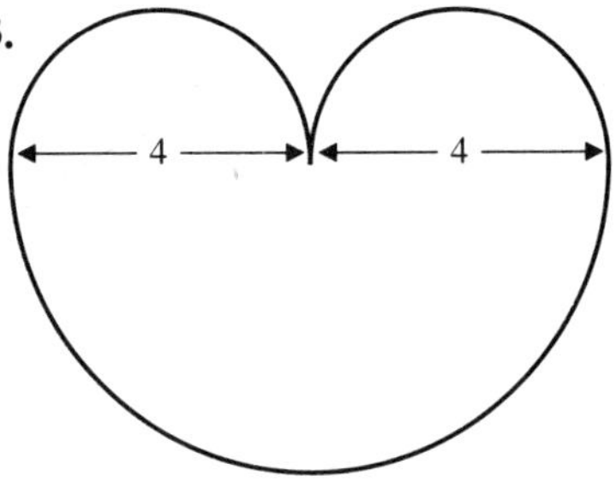

4.

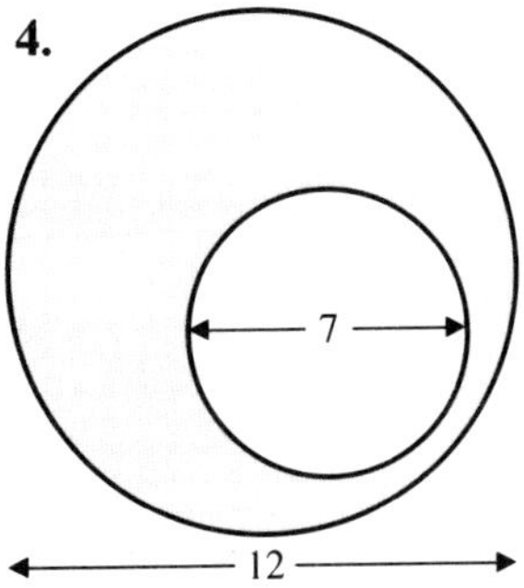

5.

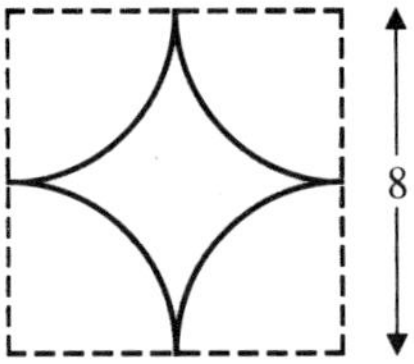

6.

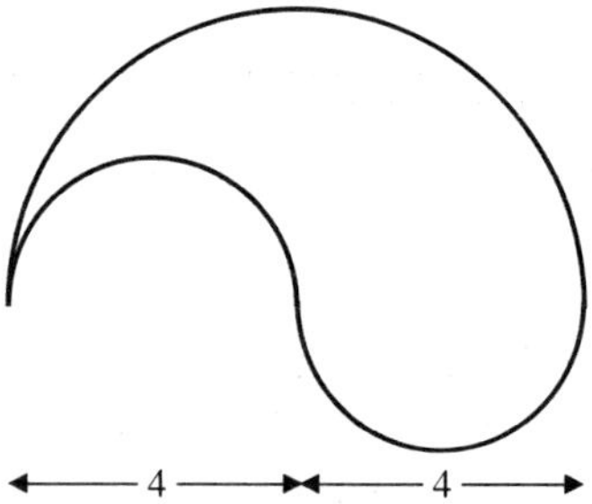

7. (a) Find the area of triangle OAD.
(b) Hence find the area of the square ABCD.
(c) Find the area of the circle.
(d) Hence find the shaded area.

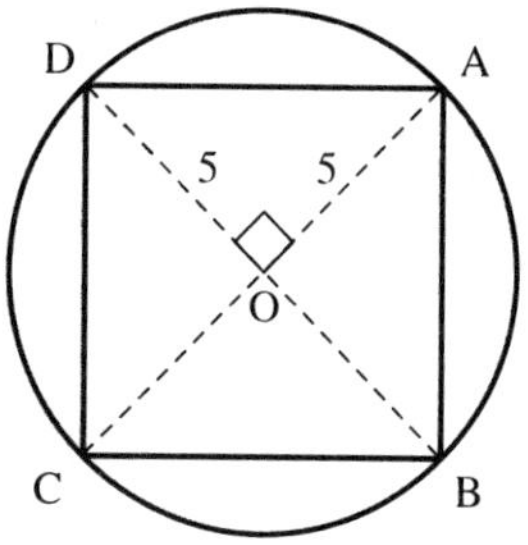

Finding the radius of a circle

Sometimes it is difficult to measure the diameter of a circle but it is fairly easy to measure the circumference.

(a) The circumference of a circle is 60 cm. Find the radius of the circle.

$$C = \pi d$$
$$\therefore\ 60 = \pi d$$
$$\therefore\ \frac{60}{\pi} = d$$
$$\therefore\ r = \frac{(60/\pi)}{2} = 9{\cdot}55 \text{ cm (to 3 s.f.)}$$

(b) The area of a circle is 18 m^2. Find the radius of the circle.

$$\pi r^2 = 18$$
$$r^2 = \frac{18}{\pi}$$
$$r = \sqrt{\left(\frac{18}{\pi}\right)} = 2{\cdot}39 \text{ m (to 3 s.f.)}$$

Exercise 16

In Questions **1** to **10** use the information given to calculate the radius of the circle. Use the 'π' button on a calculator or take $\pi = 3{\cdot}14$.

1. The circumference is 15 cm

2. The circumference is 28 m

3. The circumference is 7 m

4. The area is 54 cm^2

5. The area is 38 cm^2

6. The area is 49 m^2

7. The circumference is 16 m

8. The area is 60 cm^2

9. The circumference is 29 cm

10. The area is 104 cm^2

11. An odometer is a wheel used for measuring long distances. The circumference of the wheel is exactly one metre.
Find the radius of the wheel.

12. A sheet of paper is 32 cm by 20 cm. It is made into a hollow cylinder of height 20 cm with no overlap.

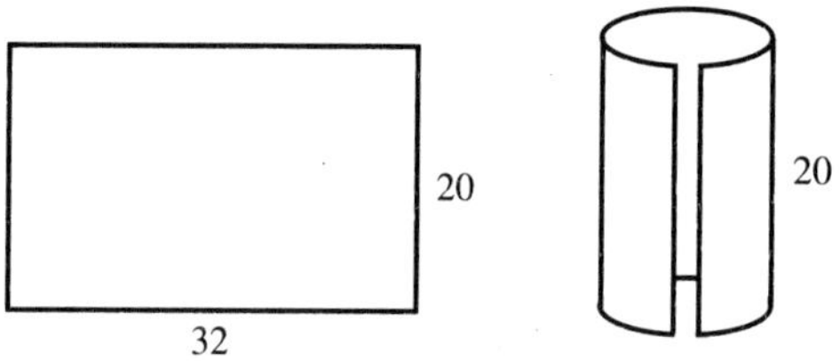

Find the radius of the cylinder.

13. The area of the centre circle on a football pitch is 265 m^2.
Calculate the radius of the circle to the nearest 0·1 m.

14. Eight sections of curved railway track can be joined to make a circular track of circumference 184 cm.
Each section is 23 cm long.
Calculate the diameter of the circle.

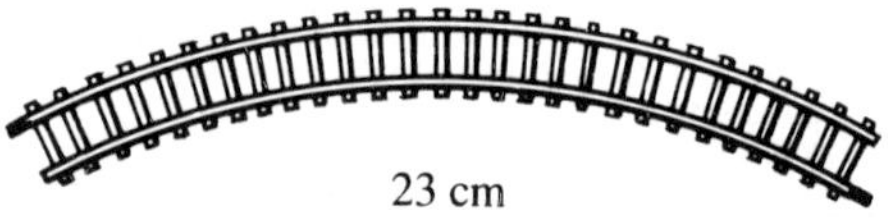

15. Calculate the radius of a circle whose area is equal to the sum of the areas of three circles of radii 2 cm, 3 cm and 4 cm.

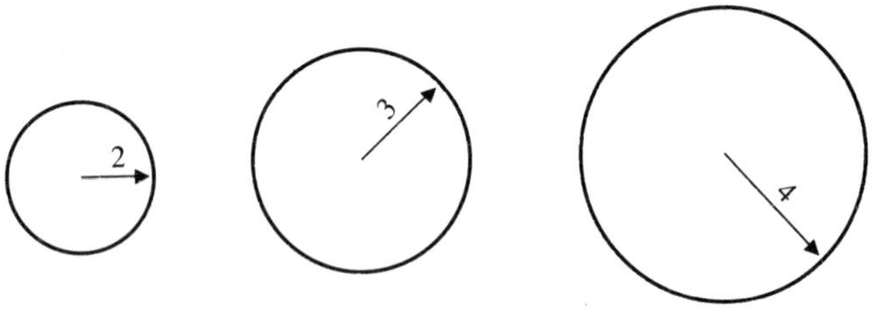

16. The handle of a paint tin is a semicircle of wire which is 28 cm long.
Calculate the diameter of the tin.

17. A television transmitter is designed so that people living inside a circle of area 120 000 km^2 can receive pictures.
What is the radius of this reception circle? Give your answer to the nearest km.

18. The circle and the square have the same area.
Find the radius of the circle.

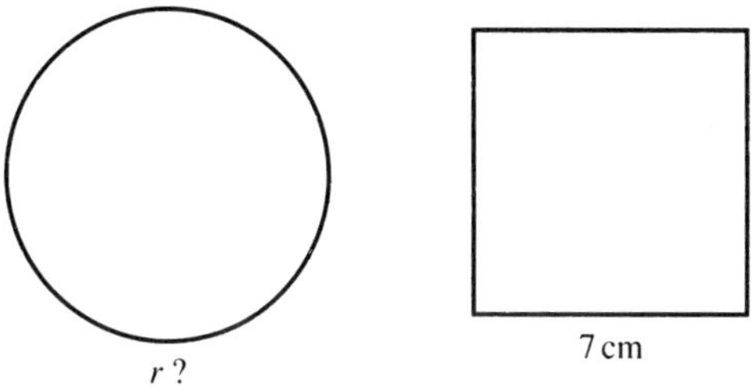

19. The circumference of this circle is 52 m.
Find its area.

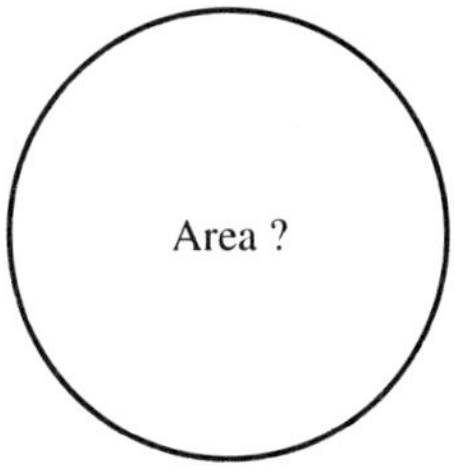

20. The area of a circular target is 1·2 m^2. Find the circumference of the target.

21. The perimeter of a circular pond is 85 m long. Work out the area of the pond.

22. The sector shown is one quarter of a circle and has an area of 23 cm^2.
Find the radius of the circle.

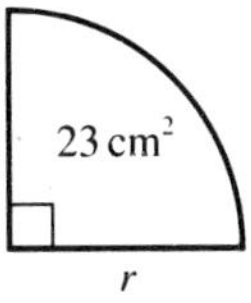

23. 'Muirfield' grass seed is sown at a rate of 40 grams per square metre and one box contains 2·5 kg. The seed is just enough to sow a circular lawn. Calculate the radius of this lawn to the nearest 0·1 metre.

1.6 Area

4/5d, 4/6d

Rectangle and triangle

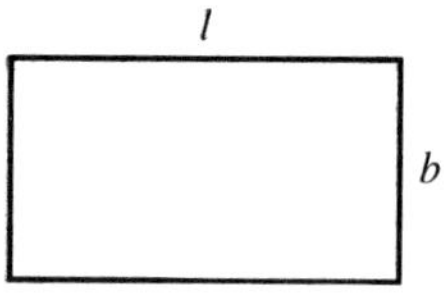

Rectangle:
area $= l \times b$

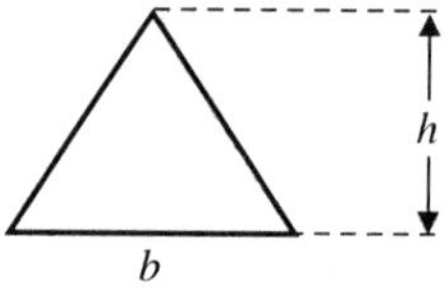

Triangle:
area $= \dfrac{b \times h}{2}$

Exercise 17

Work out the area. All lengths are in cm.

1.
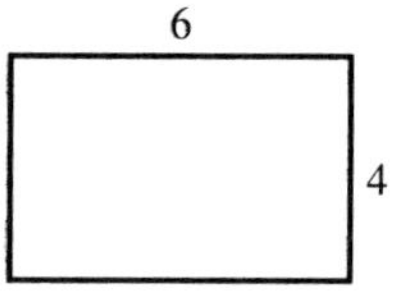

2.
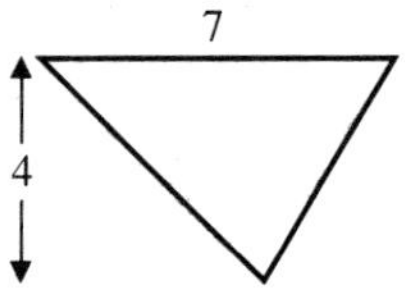

3.
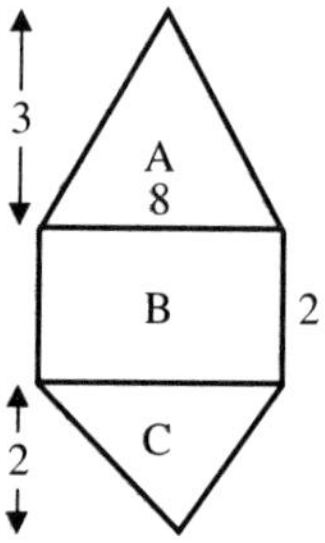

4.
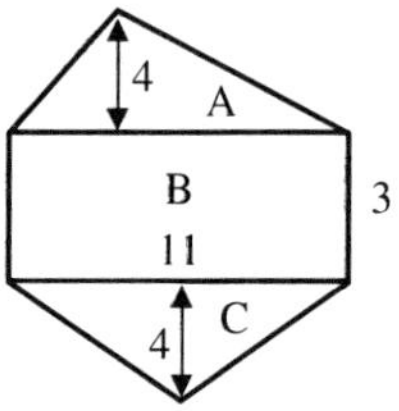

5.
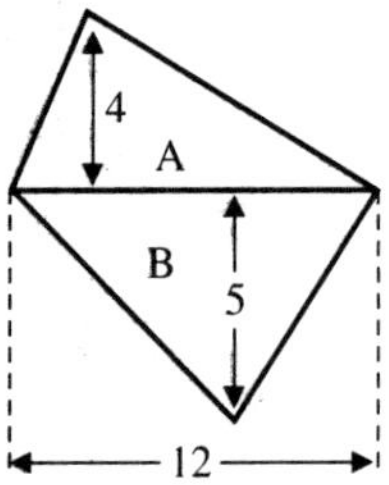

6.
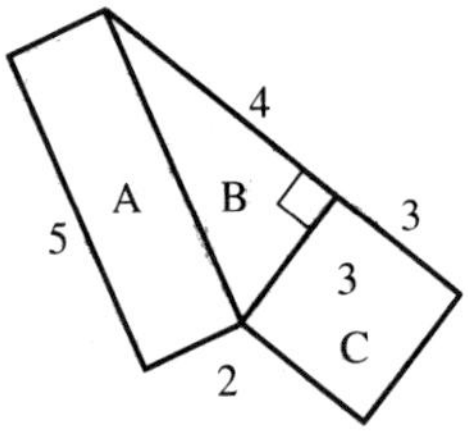

7.
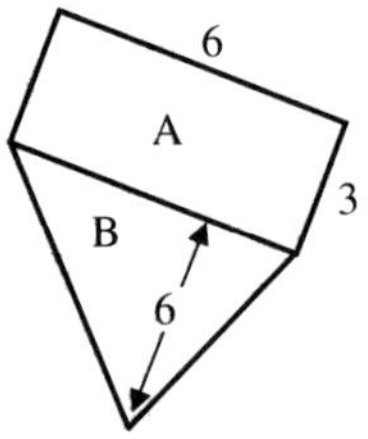

8.
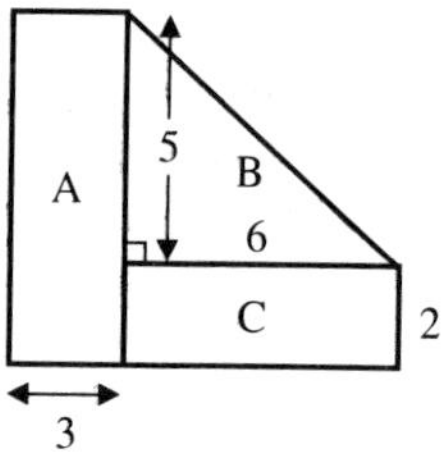

9.
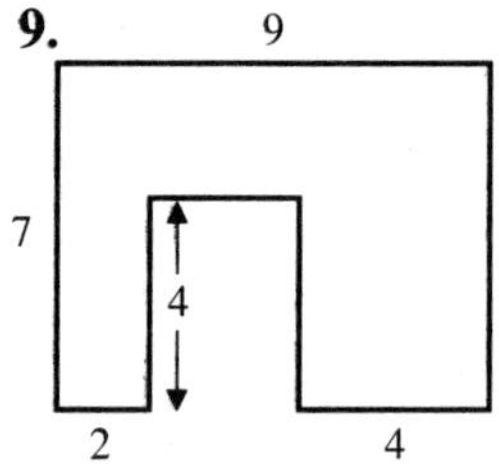

10.
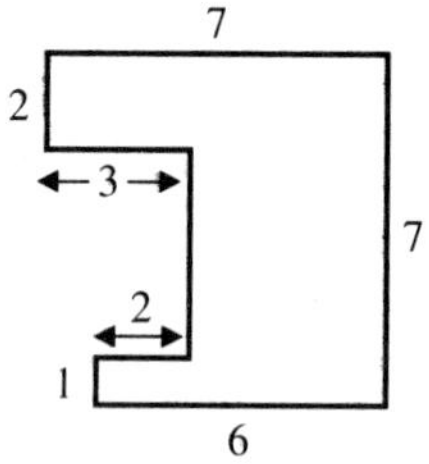

11.
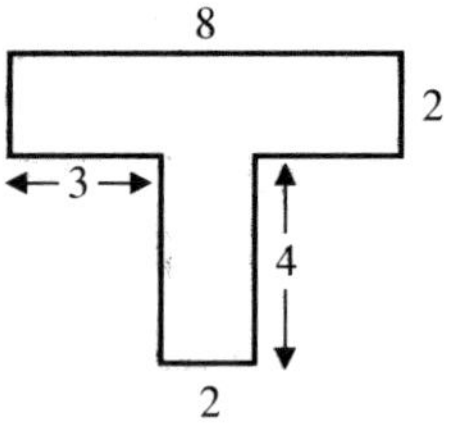

12.
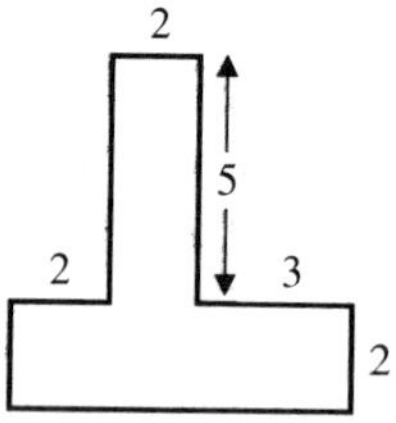

13.
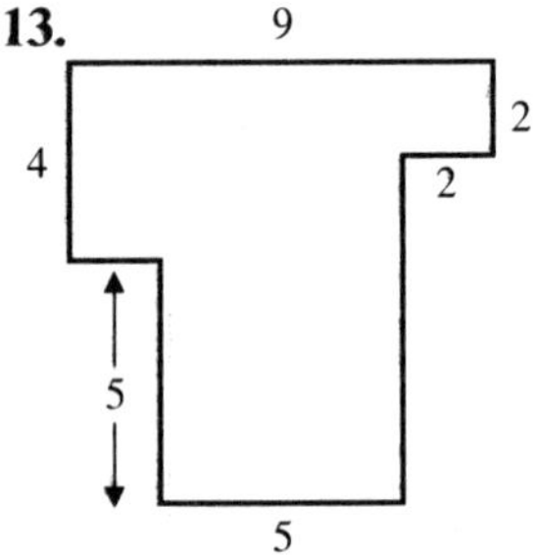

14.
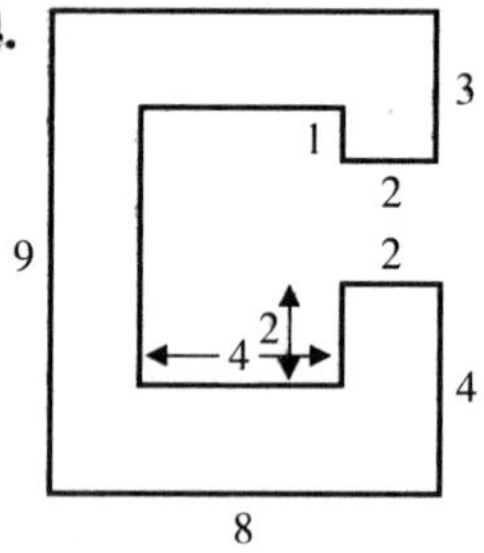

15.
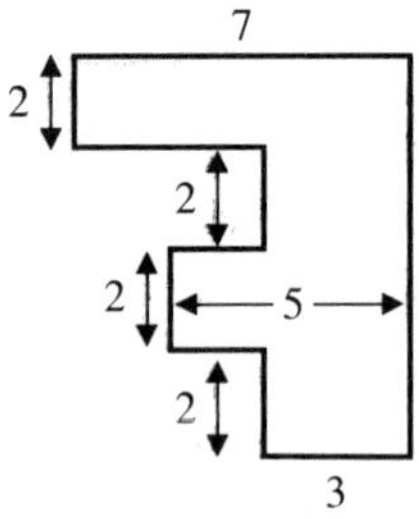

16.
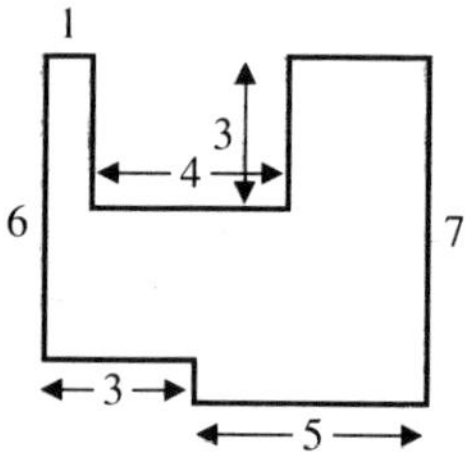

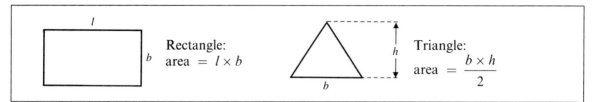

Exercise 18

A decorator works out how many rolls of wallpaper he needs for a room from the table below.

Height from skirting	Measurement round walls (including doors and windows) in metres									
	8·6	9·8	11·0	12·2	13·4	14·6	15·8	17·0	18·2	19·4
2·20 m	4	4	5	5	6	6	7	7	8	8
2·35 m	4	4	5	5	6	6	7	8	8	9
2·50 m	4	5	5	6	6	7	7	8	8	9
2·65 m	4	5	5	6	6	7	8	8	9	9
2·80 m	4	5	6	6	7	7	8	9	9	10
2·95 m	5	5	6	7	7	8	9	9	10	10
3·10 m	5	5	6	7	8	8	9	10	10	11

1. A plan of one room is shown.
Work out
(a) the total length round the walls (the perimeter).
(b) the number of rolls of wallpaper he needs.
(c) the total cost of the wallpaper if one roll costs £3·20.
(d) the area of the ceiling of the room.

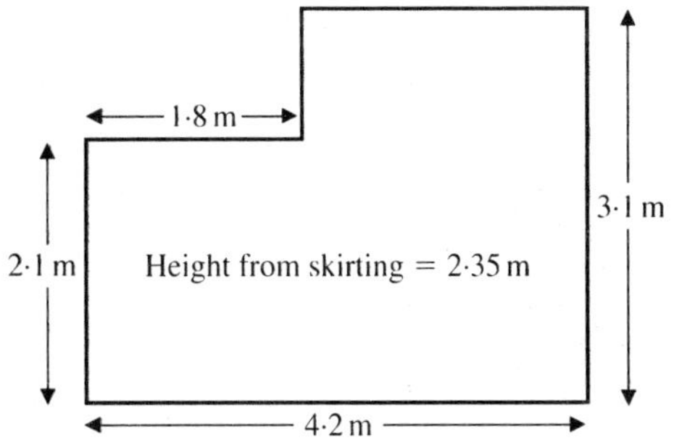

2. Work out the answers to parts (a), (b), (c) and (d) for each of the rooms shown below.

A.

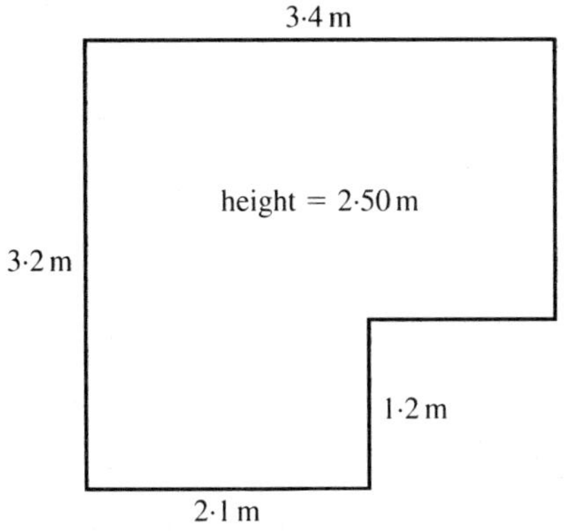

B.

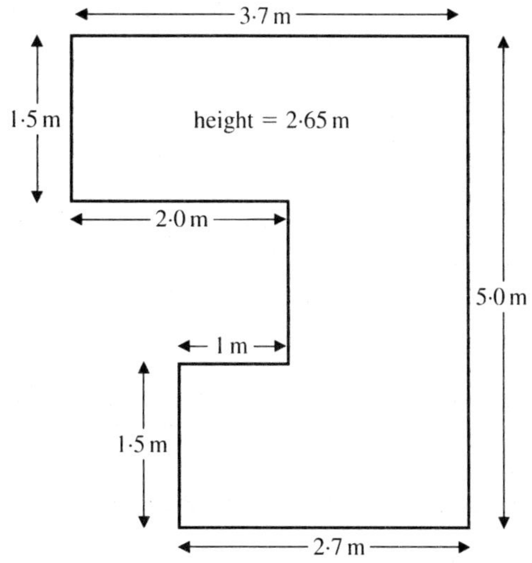

Exercise 19

1. (a) Copy the diagram.
(b) Work out the areas of triangles A, B and C.
(c) Work out the area of the square enclosed by the broken lines.
(d) Hence work out the area of the shaded triangle. Give the answer in square units.

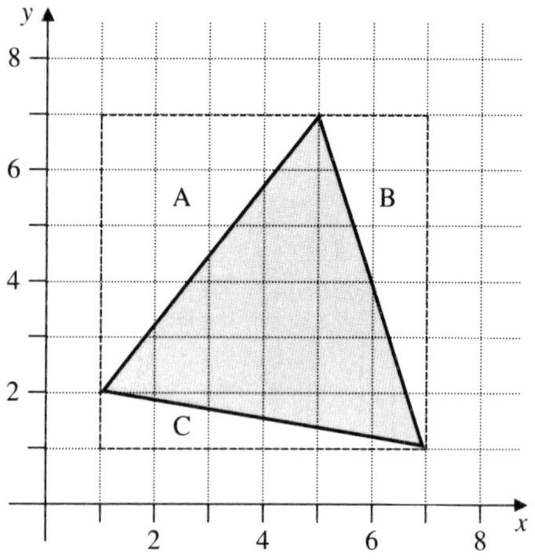

2. (a) Copy the diagram.
(b) Work out the areas of triangles A, B and C.
(c) Work out the area of the rectangle enclosed by the broken lines.
(d) Hence work out the area of the shaded triangle. Give the answer in square units.

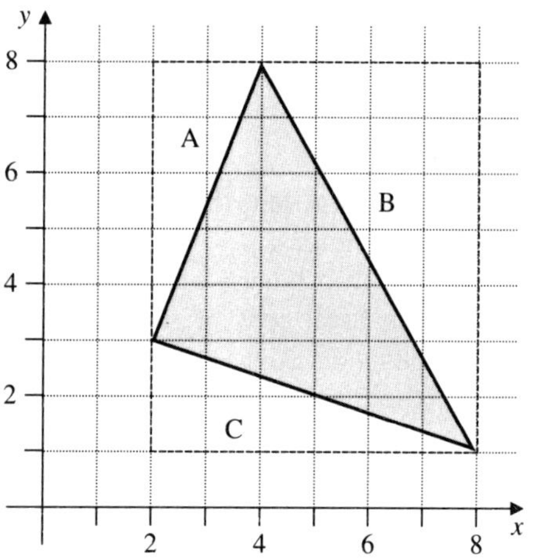

For Questions **3** to **7**, draw a pair of axes similar to those in Questions **1** and **2**. Plot the points in the order given and find the area of the shape enclosed.

3. (1,4), (6,8), (4,1)

4. (1,7), (8,5), (4,2)

5. (2,4), (6,1), (8,7), (4,8), (2,4)

6. (1,4), (5,1), (7,6), (4,8), (1,4)

7. (1,6), (2,2), (8,6), (6,8), (1,6)

8. A wooden cuboid has the dimensions shown.
(a) Calculate the total surface area.
(b) The cuboid is painted using paint from a tin sufficient to cover 3 m^2. How many cuboids can be painted using the paint in one tin?

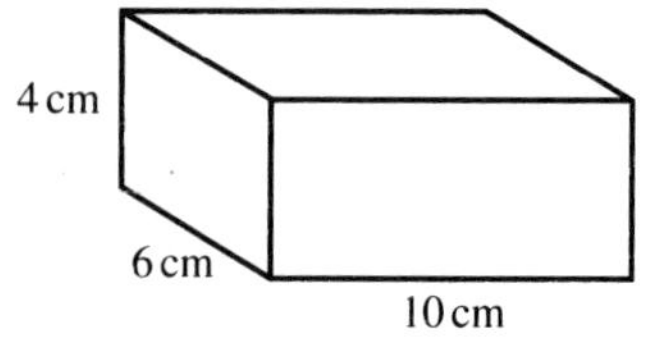

Trapezium and parallelogram

Trapezium (two parallel sides)

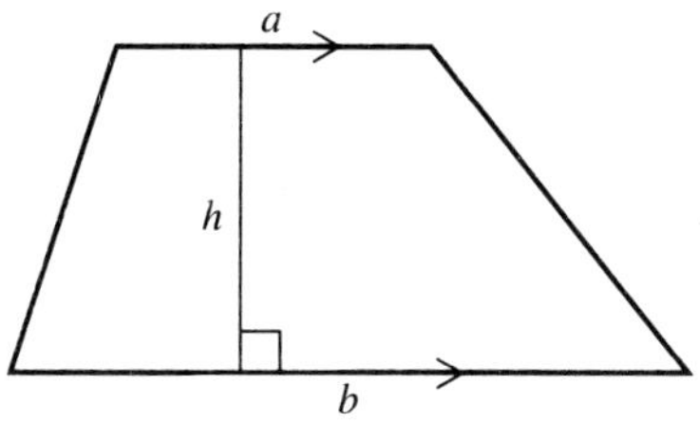

$$\text{area} = \frac{1}{2}(a+b) \times h$$

Parallelogram

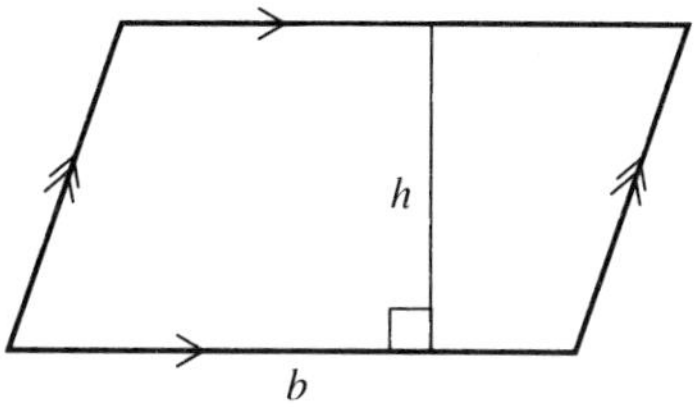

$$\text{area} = b \times h$$

Exercise 20

Find the area of each shape. All lengths are in cm.

1.

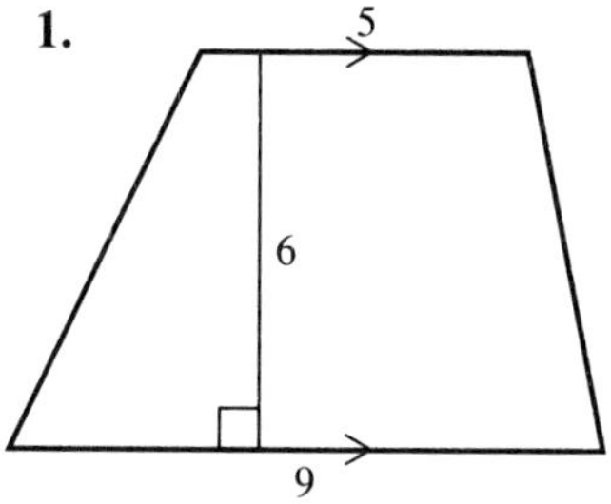

2.

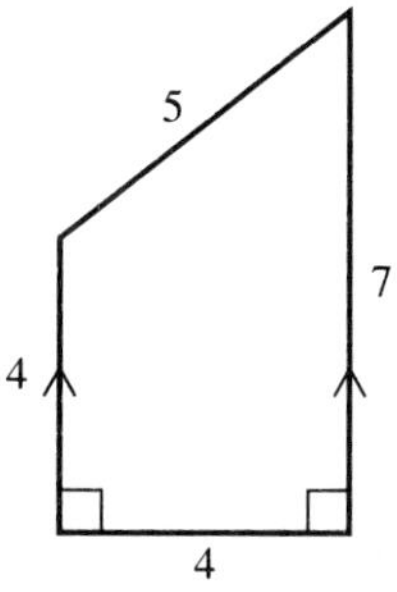

3.

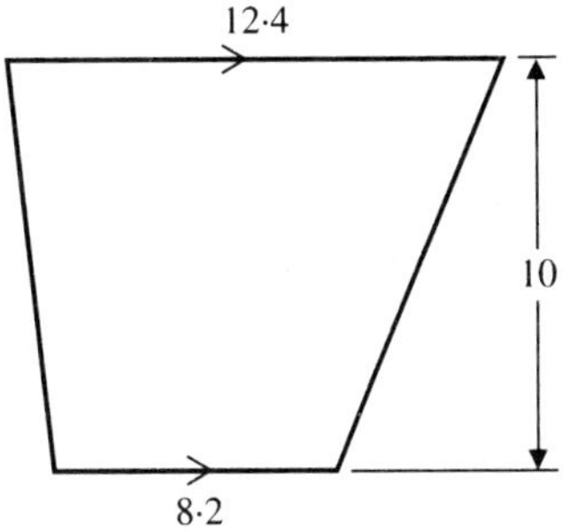

4.

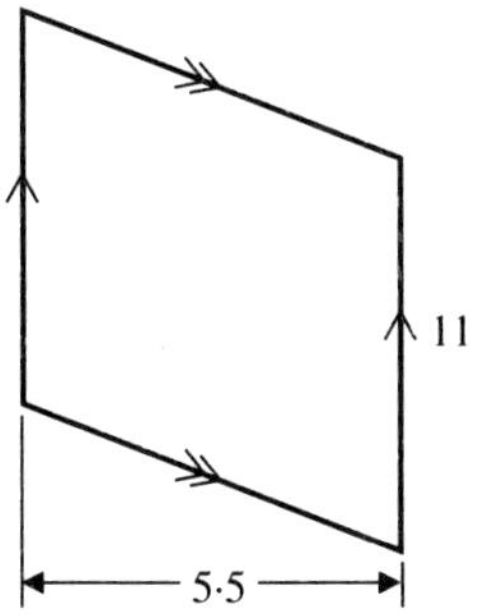

5.

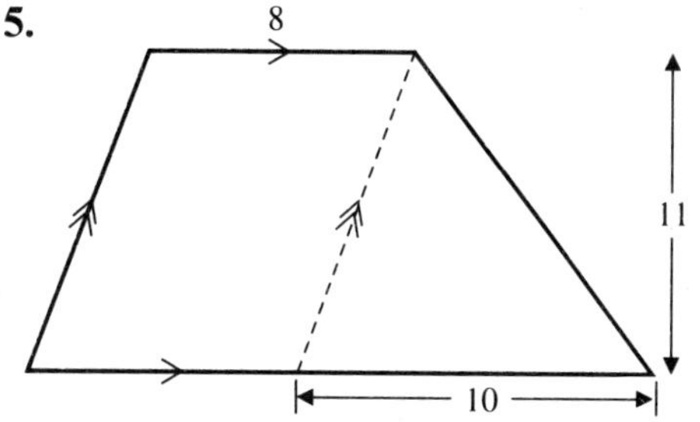

6.

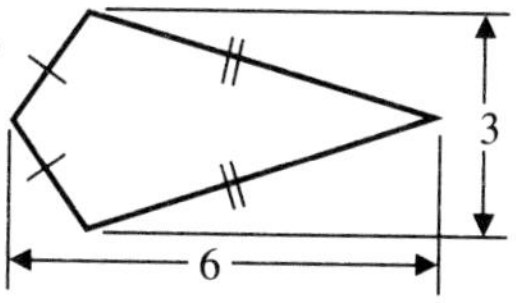

7.

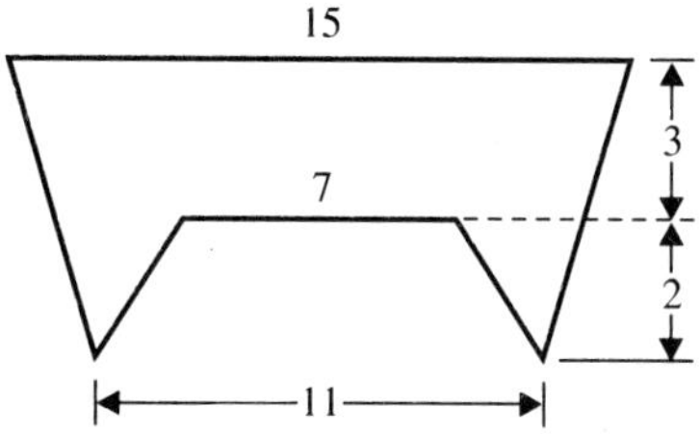

8.

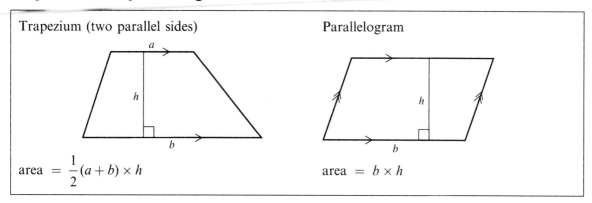

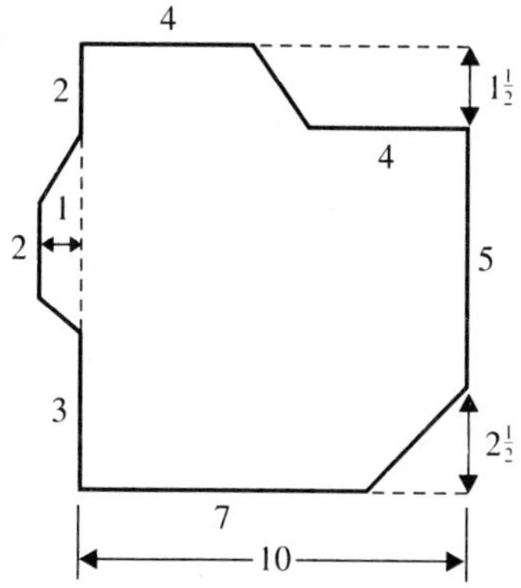

9. Large areas of land are measured in hectares. One hectare = 10 000 m^2. The Imperial unit, used in the past, is the acre. One hectare is approximately 2.5 acres.
Copy and complete the statements below:

(a)

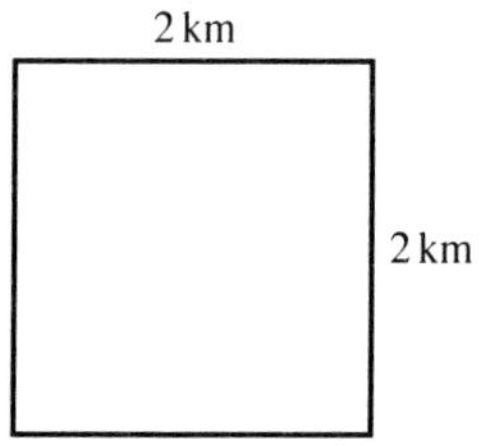

area of square = ________ m^2
area of square = ________ hectares.

(b)

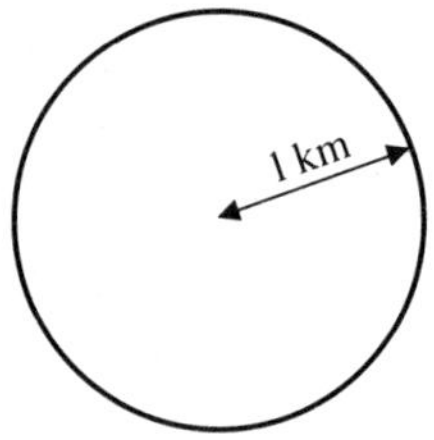

area of circle = ________ hectares.
area of circle is approximately ________ acres.

10. The field shown is sprayed at the rate of 2 litres per hectare. The cost of the spray is £25 for 100 litres.
How much will it cost to spray this field, to the nearest pound?

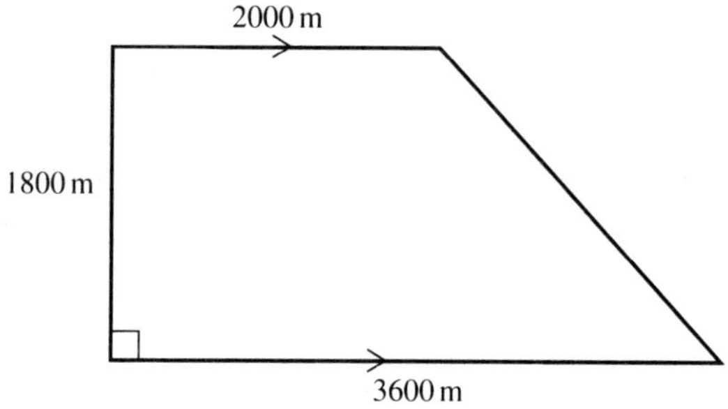

Designing square patterns

The object is to design square patterns of different sizes. The patterns are all to be made from smaller tiles all of which are themselves square.
Designs for a 4 × 4 square:

(a)

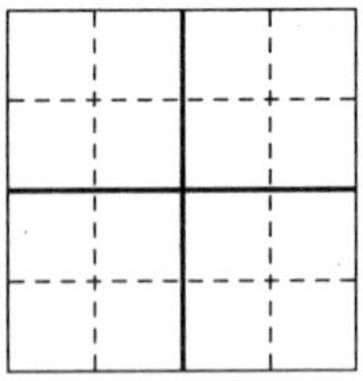

This design consists of four tiles each 2 × 2. The pattern is rather dull.

(b) Suppose we say that the design must contain at least one 1 × 1 square.

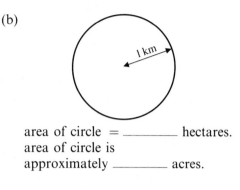

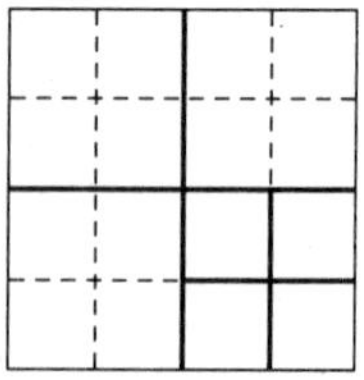

This design is more interesting and consists of seven tiles.

Exercise 21

1. Try the 5 × 5 square. Design a pattern which divides the 5 × 5 square into eight smaller squares.
2. Try the 6 × 6 square. Here you must include at least one 1 × 1 square. Design a pattern which divides the 6 × 6 square into nine smaller squares. Colour in the final design to make it look interesting.
3. The 7 × 7 square is more difficult. With no restrictions, design a pattern which divides the 7 × 7 square into nine smaller squares.
4. Design a pattern which divides an 8 × 8 square into ten smaller squares. You must not use a 4 × 4 square.
5. Design a pattern which divides a 9 × 9 square into ten smaller squares. You can use only one 3 × 3 square.
6. Design a pattern which divides a 10 × 10 square into eleven smaller squares. You must include a 3 × 3 square.
7. Design a pattern which divides an 11 × 11 square into eleven smaller squares. You must include a 6 × 6 square.

1.7 Volume

4/5d, 4/6a

Prisms and cuboids

(a) A prism is an object with a uniform cross section.

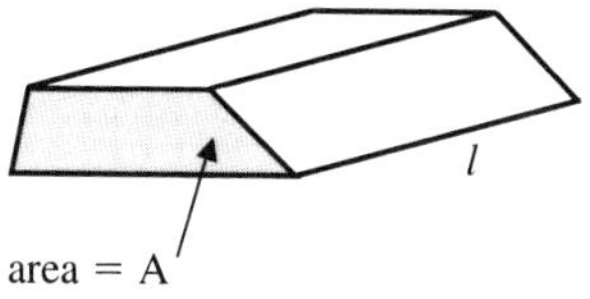

Volume $= A \times l$.

(b) A cuboid is a prism whose cross section is a rectangle.

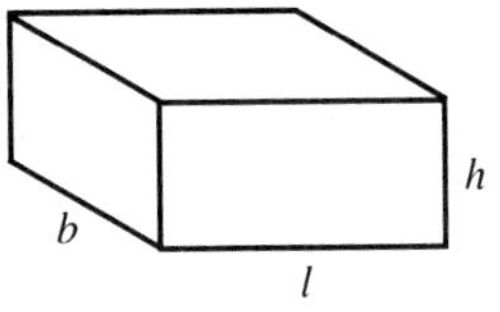

Volume $= l \times b \times h$

Exercise 22

Find the volume of each prism.

1. 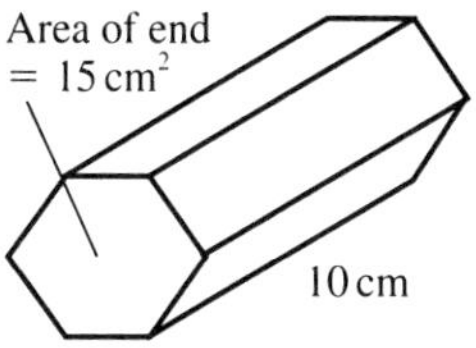

2. 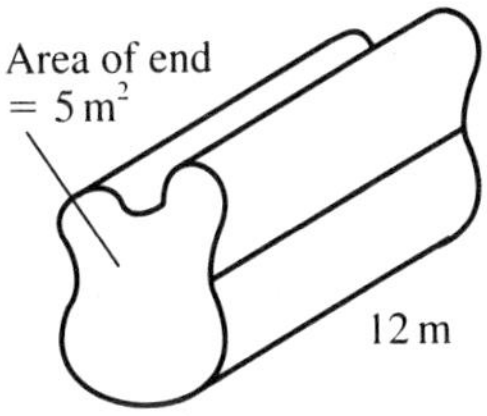

3. 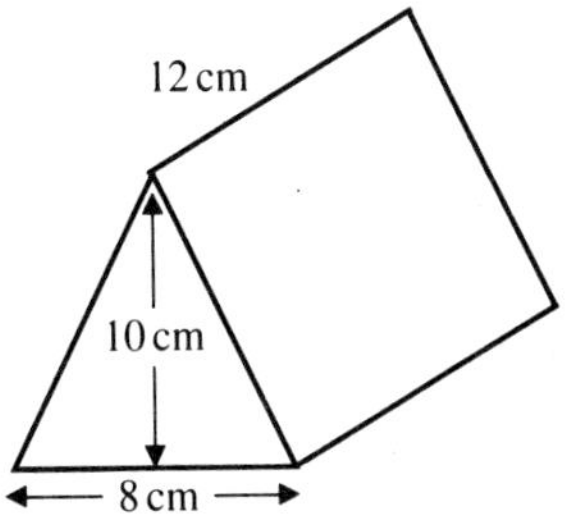

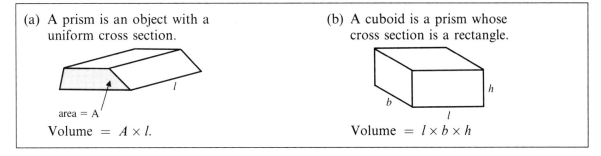

3. A rectangular block has dimensions 20 cm $\times$ 7 cm $\times$ 7 cm. Find the volume of the largest solid cylinder which can be cut from this block.

4. Brass washers are to be made 2 mm thick with a circular cross section as shown below.

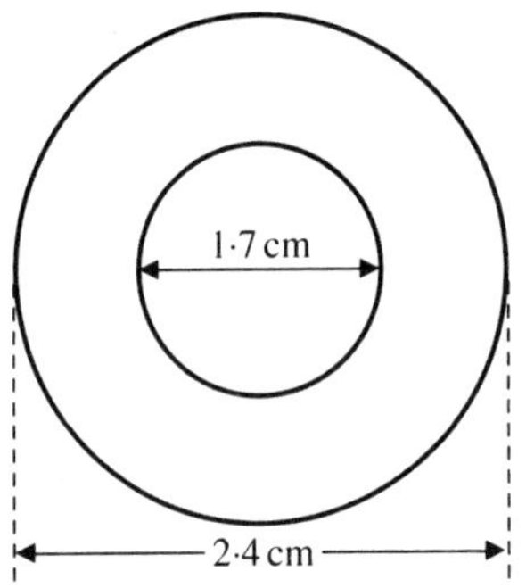

(a) Find the area of the flat surface of the washer.
(b) Calculate the volume of the washer.
(c) Find in cm^3 the volume of brass needed to make 10 000 of these washers.

5. A cylindrical water tank has internal diameter 40 cm and height 50 cm and a cylindrical mug has internal diameter 8 cm and height 10 cm. If the tank is initially full, how many mugs can be filled from the tank?

6. The diagram shows the cross section of a steel girder which is 4 m long.

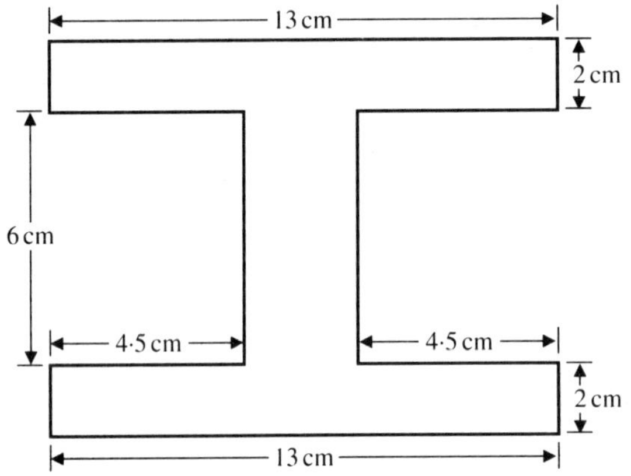

(a) Calculate the cross-sectional area in cm^2.
(b) Calculate the volume of the girder in cm^3.
(c) If 1 cm^3 of steel weighs 7·8 g find the weight of the girder in kg.
(d) How many girders can be carried on a lorry if its total load must not be more than 8 tonnes? (1 tonne = 1000 kg).

7. In the diagram all the angles are right angles and the lengths are in cm.
Find the volume.

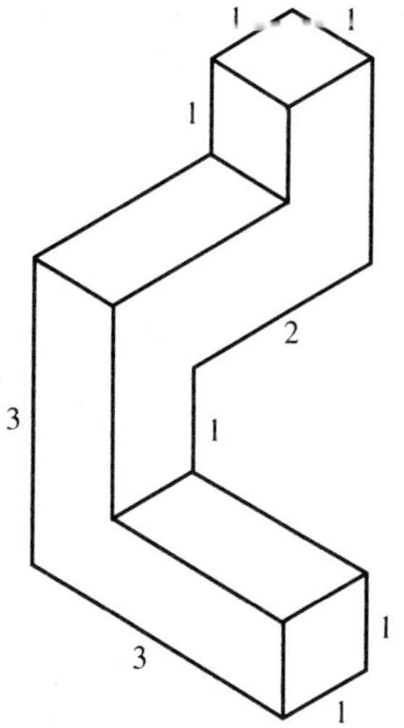

8. Mr Morton builds a fence at the end of his garden. The planks for the fence measure 1 m by 12 cm by 1 cm. The posts to which the planks are nailed are 10 cm square in cross section and 1·40 m long.

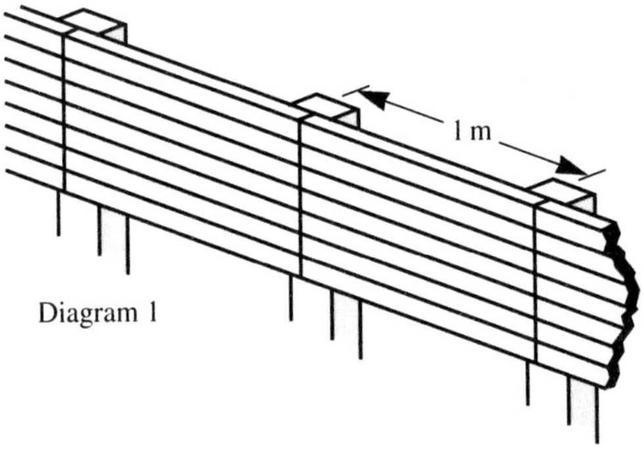

Diagram 1

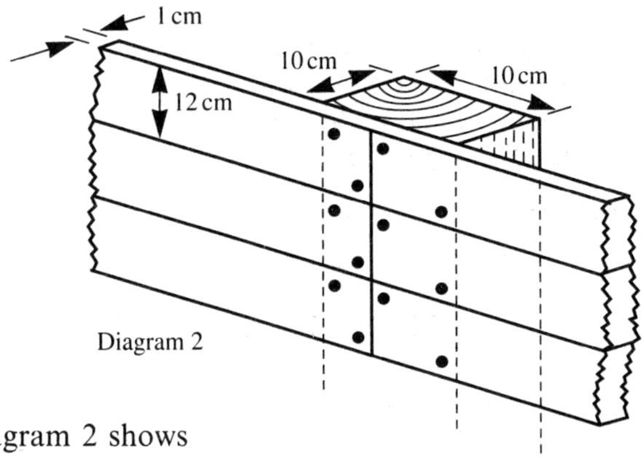

Diagram 2

Diagram 1 shows a part of the fence and Diagram 2 shows details of its construction.

(a) How many planks are there between each pair of posts?

(b) If the fence is 5 m long,
  (i) how many planks are needed?
  (ii) how many posts are needed? (There is a post at each end of the fence).

(c) Calculate the volume in cm^3 of
  (i) each plank
  (ii) each post

(d) Wood of the required quality costs 4p per 100 cm^3, irrespective of the thickness. Calculate the cost of
  (i) each plank
  (ii) each post
  (iii) all the wood for the whole fence.

(e) Each end of a plank is nailed to a post with two nails. How many nails are needed for the whole fence?

9. Mr Gibson decided to build a garage and began by calculating the number of bricks required. The garage was to be 6 m by 4 m and 2·5 m in height. Each brick measures 22 cm by 10 cm by 7 cm. Mr Gibson estimated that he would need about 40 000 bricks. Is this a reasonable estimate?

10. A cylindrical metal pipe has external diameter of 6 cm and internal diameter of 4 cm. Calculate the volume of metal in a pipe of length 1 m. If 1 cm^3 of the metal weighs 8 g, find the weight of the pipe.

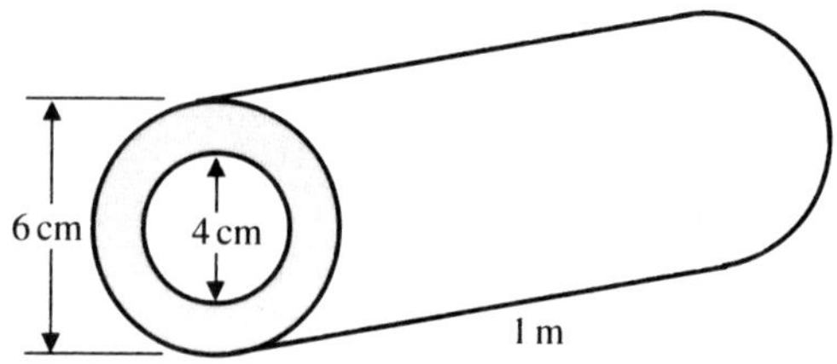

11. A cylindrical tin of height 15 cm and radius 4 cm is filled with sand from a rectangular box. How many times can the tin be filled if the dimensions of the box are 50 cm by 40 cm by 20 cm?

12. Rain which falls onto a flat rectangular surface of length 6 m and width 4 m is collected in a cylinder of internal radius 20 cm. What is the depth of water in the cylinder after a storm in which 1 cm of rain fell?

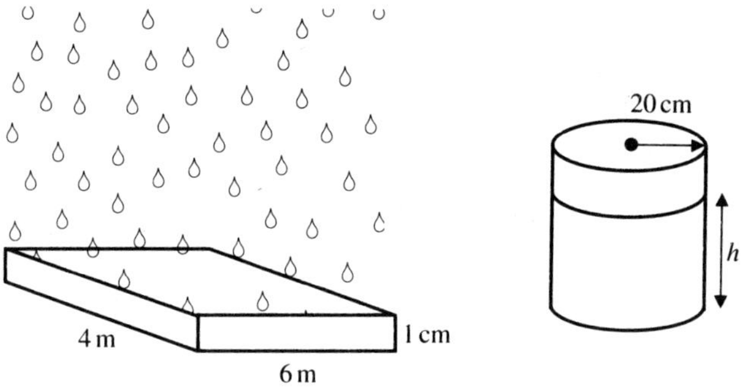

13. Water pours into the trough shown at a rate of 2 litres/min. How long, to the nearest minute, will it take to fill the trough?

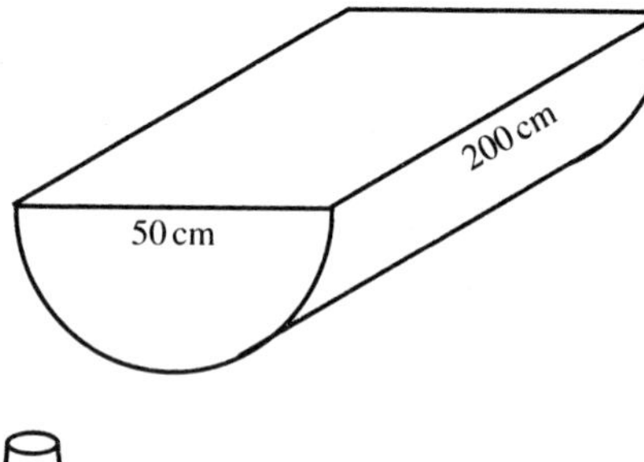

14. Water is poured from the cylindrical bottle shown into ice-cube moulds which are then put in a freezer. How many complete ice cubes of side 2·5 cm can be made?

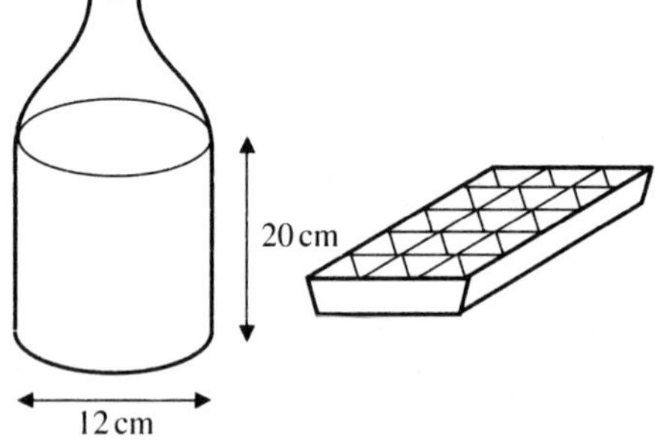

Drawing solids

When we draw a solid on paper we are making a 2-D representation of a 3-D object.
Here are two pictures of the same cuboid, measuring $4 \times 3 \times 2$ units.

(a) On ordinary squared paper

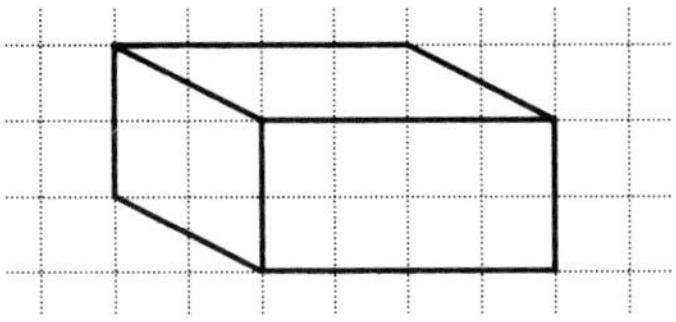

(b) On isometric paper [a grid of equilateral triangles]

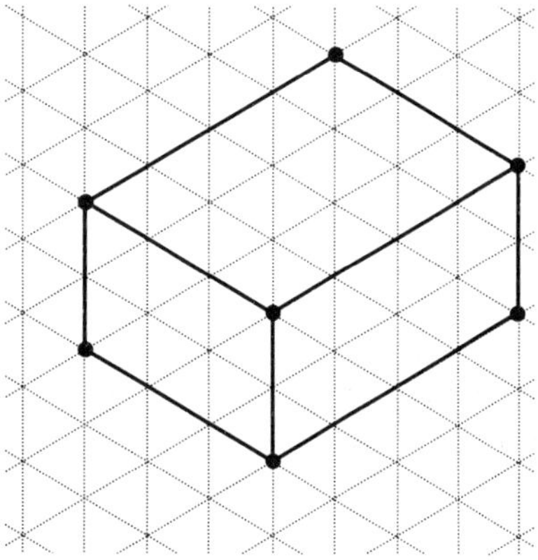

The dimensions of the cuboid cannot be taken from the first picture but they can be taken from the picture drawn on isometric paper.
Instead of isometric paper you can also use 'triangular dotty' paper like this:
Be careful to use it the right way round (as shown here).

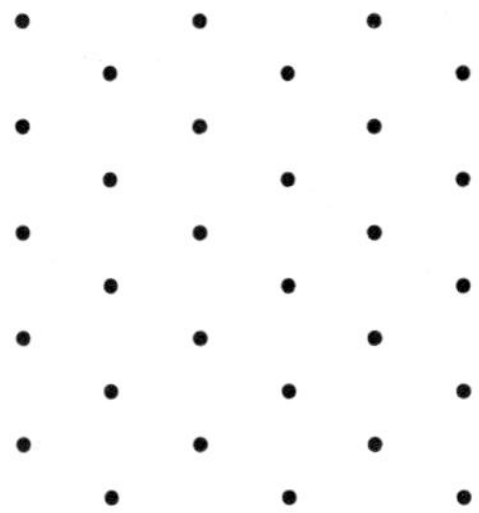

Exercise 25

In Questions **1** to **5** the objects consist of 1 cm cubes joined together. Draw each object on isometric paper (or 'triangular dotty' paper) and write down its volume.
Questions **1** and **2** are already drawn on isometric paper.

1.

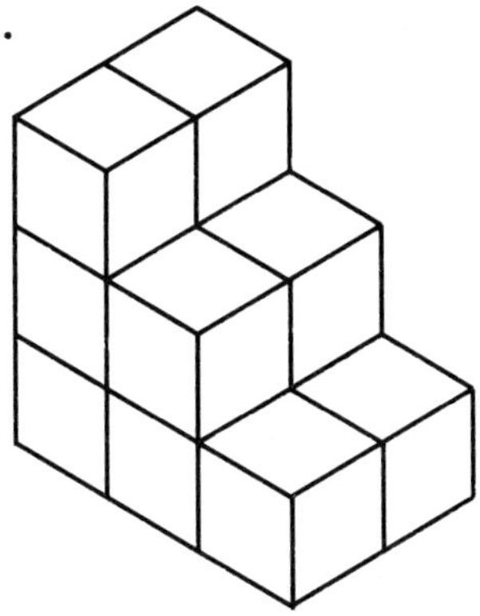

2.

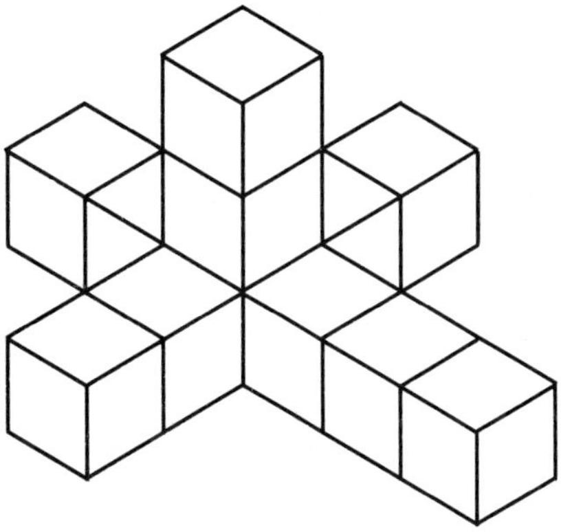

3.
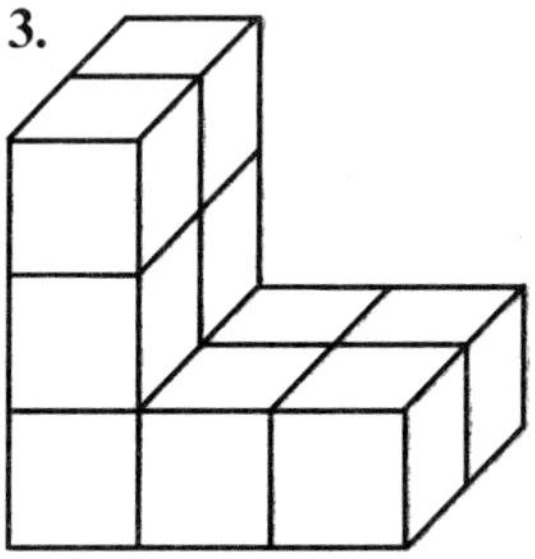

4.
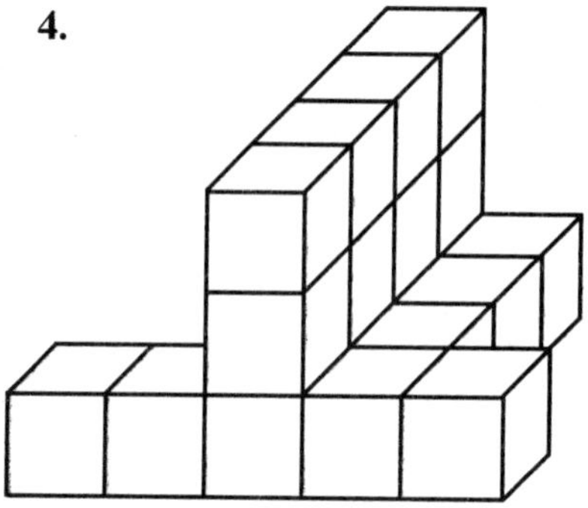

5.
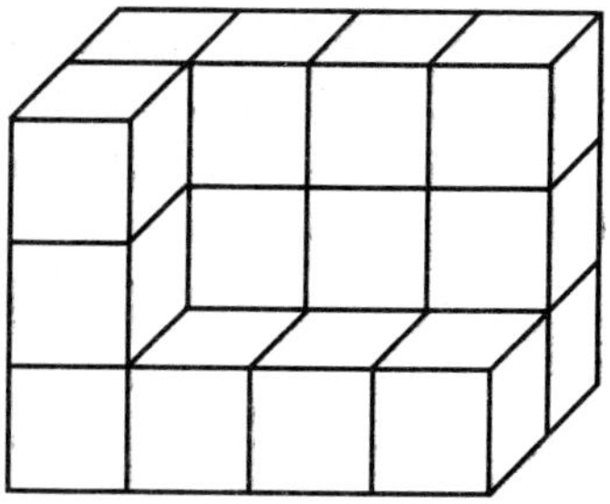

6. On isometric paper draw a cuboid with dimensions $6 \times 4 \times 2$ units.

7. (a) The side view and plan view (from above) of object A are shown.

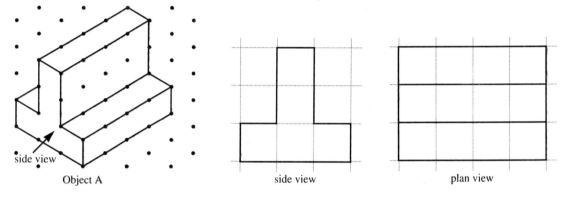

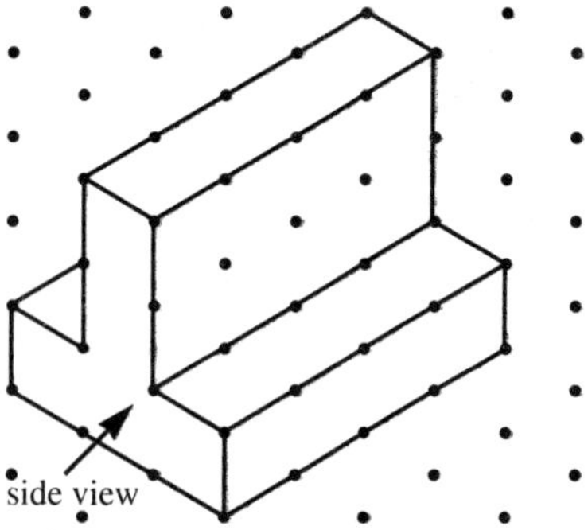

Object A

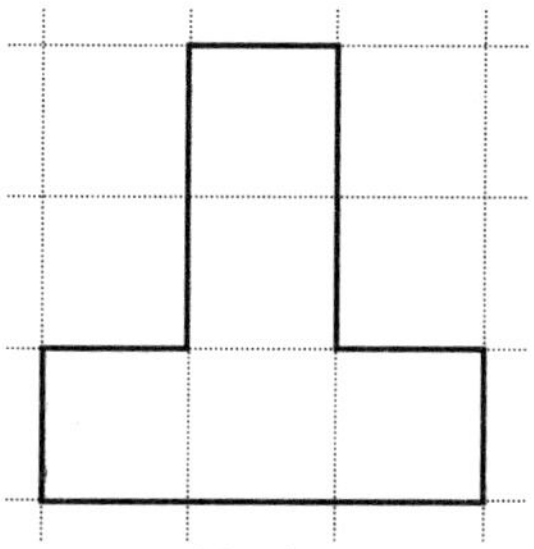
side view

plan view

(b) Draw the side view and plan view of objects B and C.

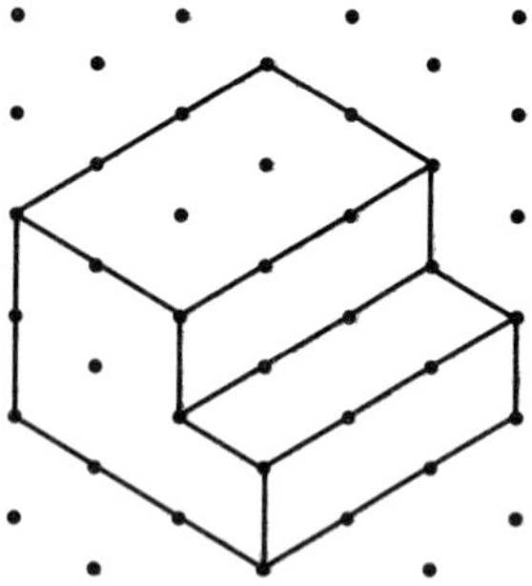
Object B

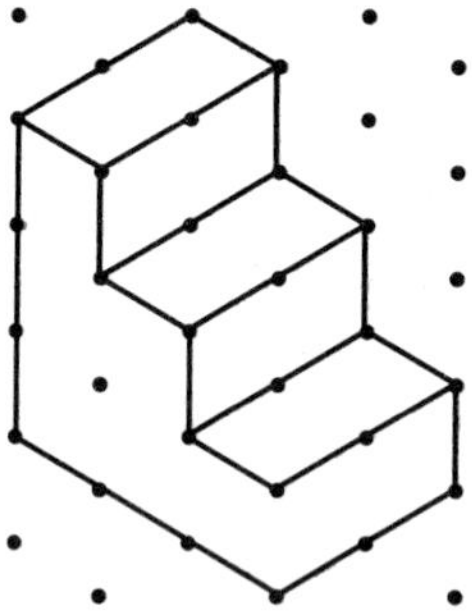
Object C

8. Using four unifix cubes, make as many different shaped objects as possible. Draw each object on isometric paper.

2 Algebra 1

2.1 Sequences

3/5a, 3/5b, 3/6a

Exercise 1

1. Here is the start of a sequence: 1, 3, 4, ...
Each new term is found by adding the last two terms.
For example $4 = 1 + 3$.
The next term will be 7.
(a) Write down the next six terms.
(b) Use the same rule to write down the next four terms of the sequence which starts 2, 5, 7, ...

2. (a) Write down the next two lines of the sequence:
$3 \times 4 = 3 + 3^2$
$4 \times 5 = 4 + 4^2$
$5 \times 6 = 5 + 5^2$
$=$
$=$
(b) Complete the lines below
$10 \times 11 =$
$30 \times 31 =$

3. The fractions $\frac{1}{2}, \frac{2}{4}, \frac{3}{6}$ are all the same since $\frac{2}{4}$ and $\frac{3}{6}$ cancel down to $\frac{1}{2}$. We say that $\frac{1}{2}, \frac{2}{4}, \frac{3}{6}$ are equivalent fractions.
Find the missing numbers in these sequences of equivalent fractions.
(a) $\frac{1}{3}, \frac{2}{6}, \frac{3}{*}, \frac{4}{12}, \frac{5}{*}, \frac{6}{18}, \frac{*}{21}, \frac{*}{*}$.
(b) $\frac{2}{5}, \frac{4}{10}, \frac{*}{15}, \frac{*}{20}, \frac{10}{*}, \frac{12}{*}, \frac{*}{35}$.
(c) $\frac{1}{4}, \frac{2}{8}, \frac{3}{*}, \frac{*}{16}, \frac{5}{*}, \frac{*}{24}$.
(d) $\frac{3}{7}, \frac{6}{*}, \frac{*}{21}, \frac{12}{*}$.

4. For the sequence 2, 3, 8, ... each new term is found by squaring the last term and then subtracting one.
Write down the next three terms.

5. The sequence 3, 3, 5, 4, 4 is obtained by counting the letters in 'one, two, three, four, five, ...'.
Write down the next three terms.

6. Find the next number in each sequence.

(a) 3, 6, 12, 24, (b) 14, 19, 25, 32,
(c) 200, 100, 50, 25, (d) 88, 99, 110,
(e) 2, 6, 18, 54, (f) 560, 56, 5·6,
(g) 1, 2, 6, 24, 120, (h) 1, 1, 2, 3, 5, 8, 13,

7. The odd numbers 1, 3, 5, 7, 9,... can be added to give an interesting sequence.

1	1	$1 \times 1 \times 1$
$3 + 5$	8	$2 \times 2 \times 2$
$7 + 9 + 11$	27	$3 \times 3 \times 3$
$13 + 15 + 17 + 19$	64	$4 \times 4 \times 4$

1, 8, 27, 64 are *cube* numbers.

We write $2^3 = 8$ ['two cubed equals eight']
$4^3 = 64$

Or the other way round:
$\sqrt[3]{8} = 2$ ['the cube root of eight equals two']
$\sqrt[3]{27} = 3$

(a) Continue adding the odd numbers in the same way as before.
Do we *always* get a cube number?

(b) Write down
(i) $\sqrt[3]{125}$ (ii) $\sqrt[3]{1000}$ (iii) 11^3.

8. (a) Write down the next three lines of this pattern.

$$1^3 = 1^2 = 1$$
$$1^3 + 2^3 = (1 + 2)^2 = 9$$
$$1^3 + 2^3 + 3^3 = (1 + 2 + 3)^2 = 36$$

(b) Work out as simply as possible
$1^3 + 2^3 + 3^3 + 4^3 + 5^3 + 6^3 + 7^3 + 8^3 + 9^3 + 10^3$.

9. This question is about 'happy numbers'.
Start by writing a list of square numbers.
[1, 4, 9, 16, ... 100].

(a)
32
↙ ↘
3^2 2^2
↓ ↓
9 + 4 = 13
↙ ↘
1^2 3^2
↓ ↓
1 + 9 = 10
↙ ↘
1^2 0^2
↓ ↓
1 + 0 = 1

32 is a so-called 'happy' number because it ends with 1.

(b) Try a different number: 70. This time we will simplify the working by doing the squaring without writing it down.

70
↙ ↘
49 + 0 = 49
↙ ↘
16 + 81 = 97
↙ ↘
81 + 49 = 130
↙ ↓ ↘
1 + 9 + 0 = 10
↙ ↘
1 + 0 = 1

So 70 is also a 'happy' number.

(c) Find out whether the following numbers are 'happy' or 'unhappy':
23, 85, 49, 40, 44, 14, 15, 94
Hint: Write single digit numbers with a nought in front:
$4 \to 04$
$6 \to 06$
This helps to maintain the pattern.
Look out for patterns of numbers which repeat themselves. This will save a lot of working.

(d) If 23 is happy, is 32 happy?
If 24 is unhappy, is 42 happy?
If 25 is unhappy, is 52 happy?

(e) Draw a number square from 1 to 100.
Draw a red ring around all the happy numbers.
As a check there are 20 numbers.

1	2	3	4	5	6	7	8	9	10
11	12	13	14	15	16	17	18	19	20
21	22	23	24	25	26	27	28	29	30
31	32	33	34	35	36	37	38	39	40
41	42	43	44	45	46	47	48	49	50
51	52	53	54	55	56	57	58	59	60
61	62	63	64	65	66	67	68	69	70
71	72	73	74	75	76	77	78	79	80
81	82	83	84	85	86	87	88	89	90
91	92	93	94	95	96	97	98	99	100

10. Copy the pattern and write down the next three lines.

$1 + 9 \times 0 = 1$
$2 + 9 \times 1 = 11$
$3 + 9 \times 12 = 111$
$4 + 9 \times 123 = 1111$
$5 + 9 \times 1234 =$

Exercise 2

1. Here is the sequence of the first six odd and even numbers.

	1st	2nd	3rd	4th	5th	6th
odd	1	3	5	7	9	11
even	2	4	6	8	10	12

Find (a) the 8th even number (b) the 8th odd number
(c) the 13th even number (d) the 13th odd number.

2. You can use a rule to work out the answers.
(a) If the 57th even number is 114, what is the 57th odd number?
(b) Write down
(i) the 45th even number (ii) the 53rd odd number
(iii) the 100th odd number (iv) the 219th odd number.

3. Here we have written the numbers in three columns.

			Line
1	2	3	1
4	5	6	2
7	8	9	3
10	11	12	4
13	14	15	5
16	17	18	6
19	20	21	7

left ↗ ↑ ↖ right
middle

(a) What number will you get on the right of
(i) line 8 (ii) line 12 (iii) line 25?

(b) Write down the number in the middle of
(i) line 8 (ii) line 12 (iii) line 20.

(c) What number will you get in
(i) line 10 on the left
(ii) line 13 on the right
(iii) line 17 in the middle
(iv) line 30 on the left?

(d) Find the missing number:
(i) 120 is on the right of line ____.
(ii) 61 is on the left of line ____.
(iii) 92 is in the middle of line ____.
(iv) 148 is on the left of line ____.

4. (a) In this sequence we get row B from row A by multiplying by 2 and then adding 5.

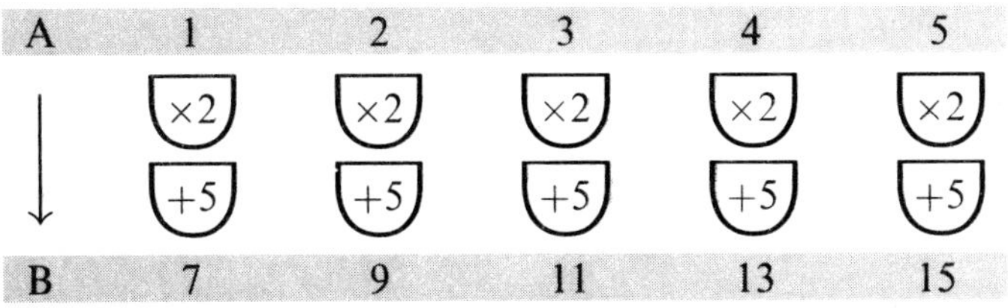

(b) Find the numbers in sequence B using the operations shown.

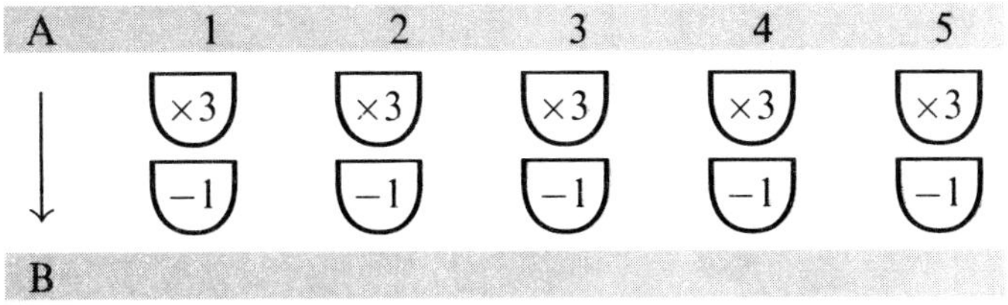

5. Find the operations which go in the boxes.

(a)

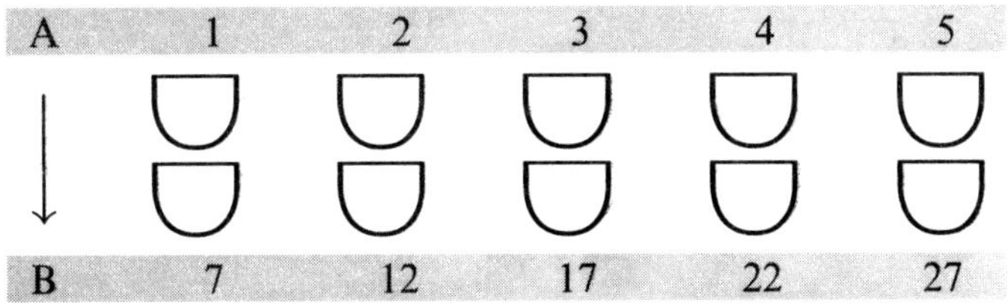

(b)

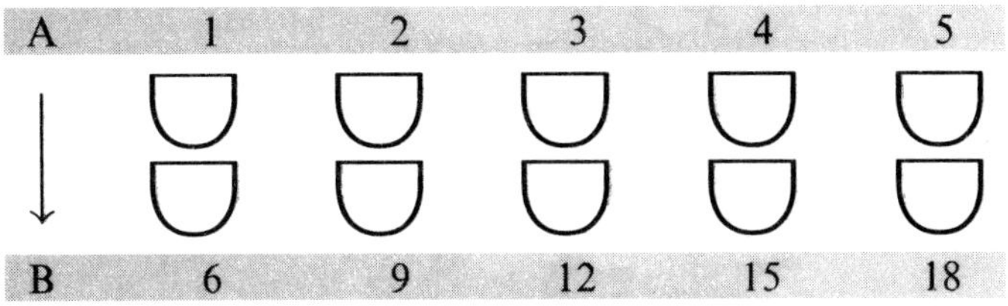

6.

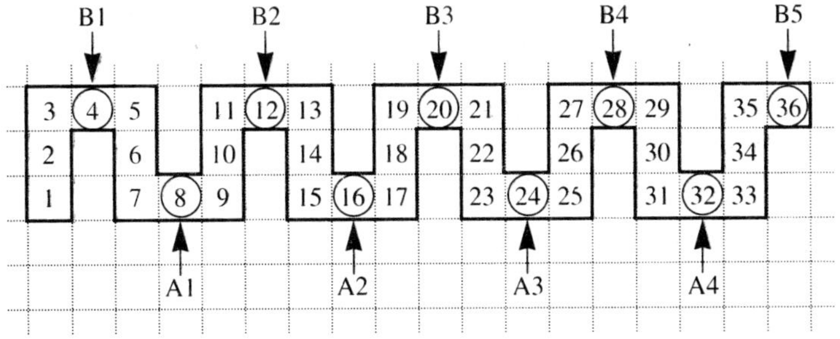

Look at the sequences A1, A2, A3, A4... and B1, B2, B3, B4...

Write down

(a) A6 (b) A10 (c) B7

(d) B11 (e) A15 (f) B20

What rule can you use to write down any number in the 'A' sequence?

7.

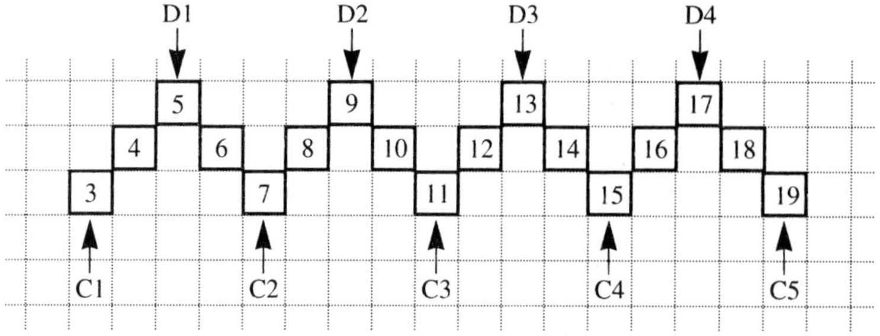

Write down

(a) D7 (b) D10 (c) D70

(d) C15 (e) C20 (f) C100

8.

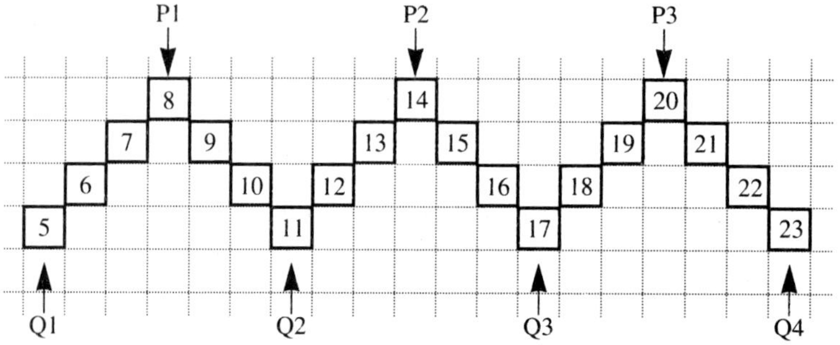

Write down

(a) P7 (b) Q7 (c) Q100

What rule can you use to find any number in the 'Q' sequence?

Differences in sequences

In the sequence of diagrams below, we will count the points p on the circle and the number of lines l that have been drawn. Each point is joined to every other point on the circle.

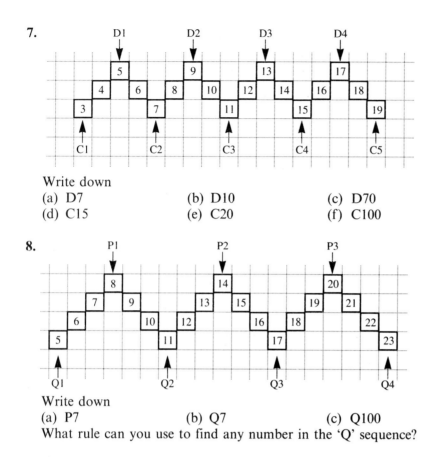

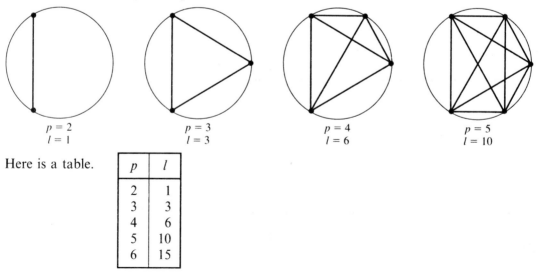

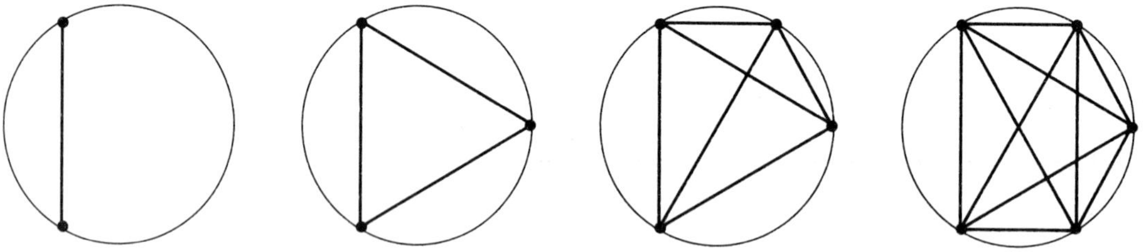

$p = 2$, $l = 1$ $p = 3$, $l = 3$ $p = 4$, $l = 6$ $p = 5$, $l = 10$

Here is a table.

p	l
2	1
3	3
4	6
5	10
6	15

(a) The *differences* in the l column form a pattern

p	l	difference
2	1	
		2
3	3	
		3
4	6	
		4
5	10	
		5
6	15	

(b) We can use the differences to predict the next values for l.

p	l	difference
2	1	
		2
3	3	
		3
4	6	
		4
5	10	
		5
6	15	
		6
7	(21)	
		7
8	(28)	

↑ These two are predictions.

This technique is useful for making predictions in many investigations. We can easily confirm that the predictions work by drawing a circle with 7 points and then 8 points.

Exercise 3

1. Here is a sequence of matchstick squares.

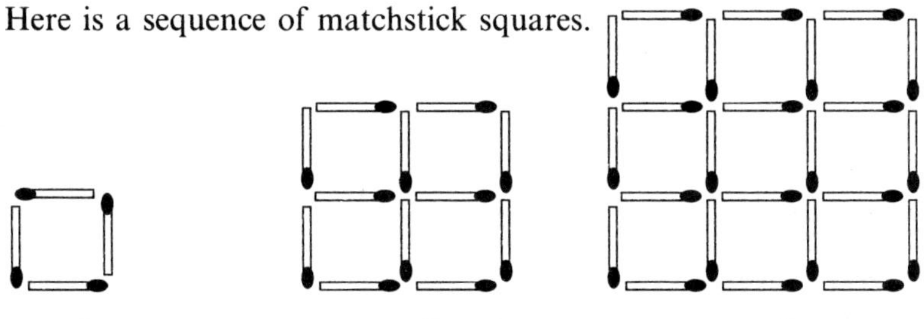

$n = 1$ $n = 2$ $n = 3$

Diagram number n	No. of matches m	difference
1	4	
		8
2	12	
		12
3	24	
		16
4	40	
5	?	

Use the differences to predict the number of matches in diagram number 5.

2. Here we have matchstick triangles.

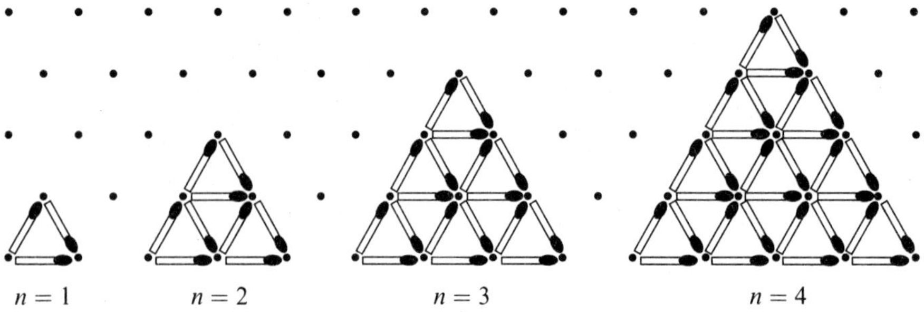

Count the number of matches m in each diagram and make a table.

n	m	difference
1	3	
2	9	
3		
4		

(a) Use differences to predict the number of matches in Diagram Number 5 ($n = 5$).
(b) Now draw Diagram 5 to see if you prediction is correct.

3. Look at the coordinates of the points on this curve.
The x-coordinates form an obvious pattern but what about the y-coordinates?
Write the y-coordinates in a column.

3
8
15
24
35

Use differences to work out the next number in this sequence.

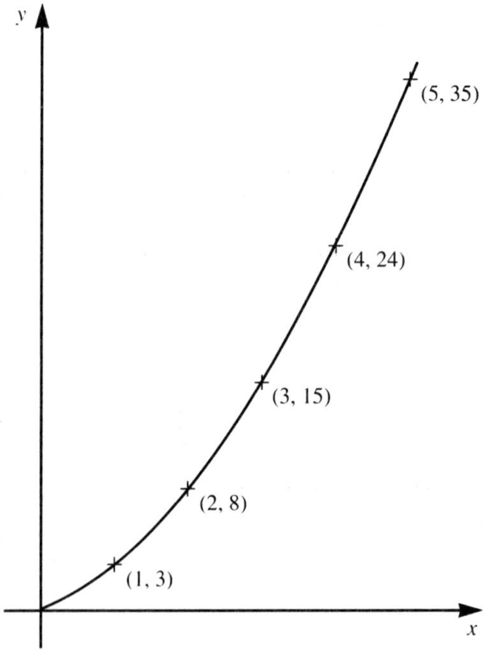

4. Here is a quadrilateral, a pentagon and a hexagon.

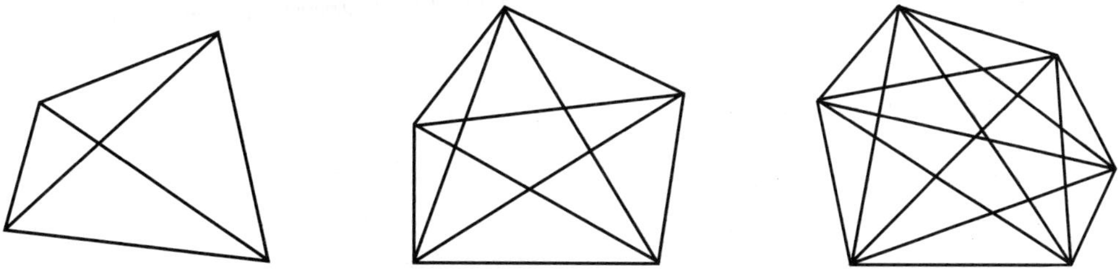

2 diagonals   5 diagonals   9 diagonals

(a) How many diagonals are there in a polygon with seven sides?
(b) Use the sequence to predict the number of diagonals in a polygon with 10 sides.

5. Look at the tables and use differences to find the missing number.

(a)

n	r
2	10
3	18
4	28
5	40
6	?

(b)

n	t
2	3
3	6
4	10
5	15
6	?

(c)

n	r
1	4
2	9
3	16
4	25
5	?

6. Find the next two numbers in each sequence.
(a) 4, 9, 17, 28
(b) 7, 15, 25, 37
(c) 2, 5, 10, 17, 26

7. (a) This sequence is more difficult.

number	difference
2	
	3
5	
	6
11	
	10
21	
	15
36	

(b) The first differences make no obvious pattern. Try the next set of differences.

number	difference	second difference
2		
	3	
5		3
	6	
11		4
	10	
21		5
	15	
36		?
	?	
?		

Find the missing numbers.

8. The number square opposite is formed by writing numbers in a spiral.

(a) Look at the sequence of numbers along diagonal A.

1
3
13
31
57

Use differences to work out the next *two* numbers in the sequence.

(b) The numbers in diagonal B form the sequence 1 5 17 37 65. Find the next two numbers in this sequence.

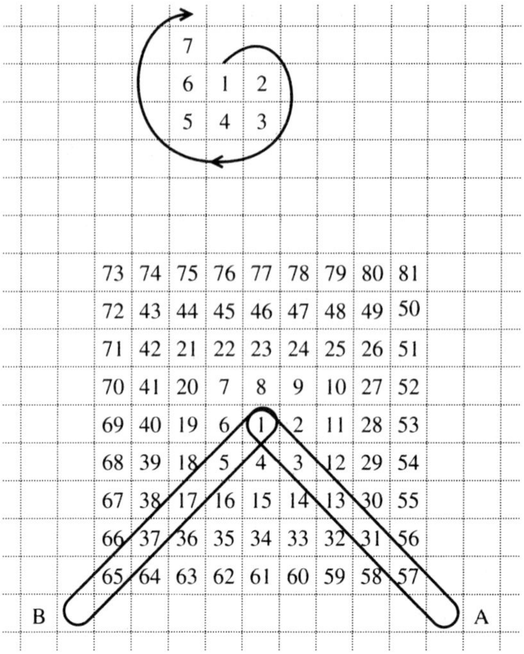

9. Use the method of Question **7** to find the missing numbers.

(a)	(b)	(c)
2	2	2
8	9	9
20	28	20
40	65	36
70	126	58
?	?	?

10. This is a harder sequence. Find the first differences, second differences, third differences and so on until you find a pattern.
Use the differences to find the next number in the sequence.

15
39
119
315
711
1415

Sequences on a computer

Exercise 4

1. Here is a short computer program written in BASIC.

```
10    FOR A = 1 TO 15
20    M = A * A
30    PRINT M
40    NEXT A
50    END
RUN
```

Line 10, together with line 40, tells the computer to start by making a variable A equal to 1. The computer will then follow the commands in line 20 and line 30 and will then 'loop back' to line 10.
It will automatically increase the value of A by 1.
This process will continue until A equals 15.
Line 20 tells the computer to make a variable M equal to A × A (computers use * for 'multiply' to avoid confusion with the letter X).
Line 30 tells the computer to print the current value of M.
Line 50 is the end of the program.

RUN Type this, press RETURN, and the program will work.

What do we expect to see on the screen?

Here is a table of values of A and M.

A	M
1	1
2	4
3	9
4	16
.	.
.	.
.	.
.	.

The computer should print the values of M in a column (very quickly!)
Type the program on a computer and see what happens.

2. Now let's make two small changes.
   (a) New line: '10 FOR A = 1 TO 9' tells the computer to go around the loop just 9 times.
   In fact you can write any other number instead of 9.
   (b) New line: '20 M = A * A * A'
   Keep the same lines 30, 40, 50.
   What do you expect to see on the screen?
   Run the program to see if you are right.

3. New line: '20 M = A + A + 2'
Again write down what you expect to get and then see if you were right.

4. Here are some more suggestions for line 20.
For each one write down the sequence you expect and then run the program on the computer.
   (a) 20 M = A * 3 + 5
   (b) 20 M = A/10 + 10
   (c) 20 M = A * (A + 1)
   (d) 20 M = (A + 1)/A

5. Now choose your own ideas for line 20. See if you get what you predict.

2.2 Solving equations

3/6b

We can think of equations as weighing scales which are balanced.
The scales stay balanced so long as you add or take away the same weight from both sides.
The same is true of equations.

Exercise 5

The scales are balanced. Work out the weight of the object x in each case. Each small weight □ is 1 kg.

1.
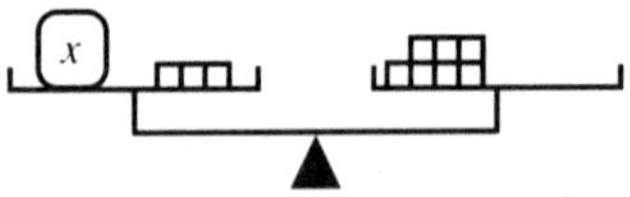

2.
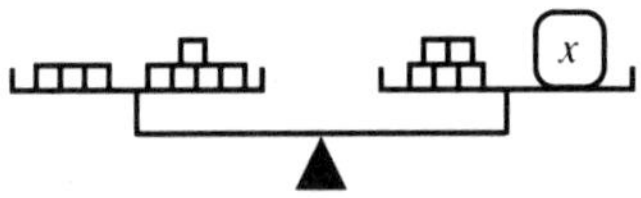

3.

4.
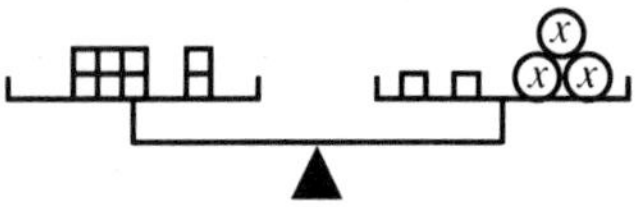

5.
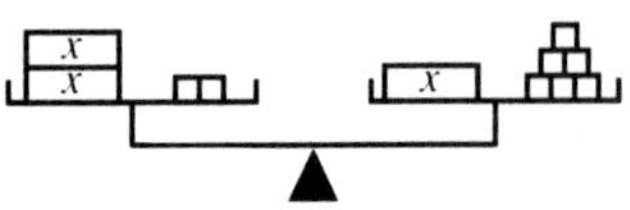

6.
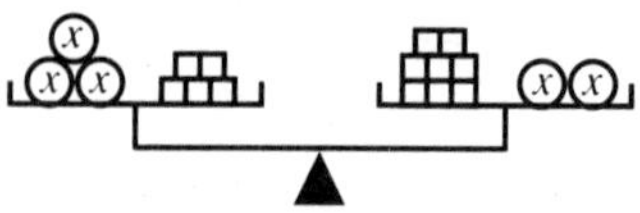

> We solve equations by doing the same thing to both sides.
>
> (a) $x + 6 = 11$
> $x = 11 - 6$ [take away 6]
> $x = 5$
>
> (b) $3x + 14 = 16$
> $3x = 16 - 14$ [take away 14]
> $3x = 2$
> $x = \frac{2}{3}$ [divide by 3]
>
> (c) $4x - 5 = -2$
> $4x = -2 + 5$ [add 5]
> $4x = 3$
> $x = \frac{3}{4}$ [divide by 4]
>
> (d) $7 = 2x + 15$
> $-15 + 7 = 2x$ [take away 15]
> $-8 = 2x$
> $-4 = x$ [divide by 2]

Exercise 6

Solve the equations.

1. $x - 7 = 5$
2. $x + 11 = 20$
3. $x + 12 = 30$
4. $x - 6 = -2$
5. $x - 8 = 9$
6. $x + 5 = 0$
7. $x - 13 = -7$
8. $x + 10 = 3$
9. $5 + x = 9$
10. $9 + x = 17$
11. $y - 6 = 11$
12. $y + 8 = 3$
13. $3x + 1 = 16$
14. $4x + 3 = 27$
15. $2x - 3 = 1$
16. $5x - 3 = 1$
17. $3x - 7 = 0$
18. $2x + 5 = 20$
19. $6x - 9 = 2$
20. $7x + 6 = 6$
21. $9x - 4 = 1$
22. $11x - 10 = 1$
23. $15y + 2 = 5$
24. $7y + 8 = 10$
25. $4y - 11 = -8$
26. $3z - 8 = -6$
27. $4p + 25 = 30$
28. $5t - 6 = 0$
29. $9m - 13 = 1$
30. $4 + 3x = 5$
31. $7 + 2x = 8$
32. $5 + 20x = 7$
33. $3 + 8x = 0$
34. $50y - 7 = 2$
35. $200y - 51 = 49$
36. $5u - 13 = -10$
37. $9x - 7 = -11$
38. $11t + 1 = 1$
39. $3 + 8y = 40$
40. $12 + 7x = 2$
41. $6 = 3x - 1$
42. $8 = 4x + 5$
43. $9 = 2x + 7$
44. $11 = 5x - 7$
45. $0 = 3x - 1$
46. $40 = 11 + 14x$
47. $-4 = 5x + 1$
48. $-8 = 6x - 3$
49. $13 = 4x - 20$
50. $-103 = 2x + 7$

Equations with x on both sides

> Solve the equations
>
> (a) $8x - 3 = 3x + 1$
> $8x - 3x = 1 + 3$
> $5x = 4$
> $x = \frac{4}{5}$
>
> (b) $3x + 9 = 18 - 7x$
> $3x + 7x = 18 - 9$
> $10x = 9$
> $x = \frac{9}{10}$

Exercise 7

1. $7x - 3 = 3x + 8$
2. $5x + 4 = 2x + 9$
3. $6x - 2 = x + 8$
4. $8x + 1 = 3x + 2$
5. $7x - 10 = 3x - 8$
6. $5x - 12 = 2x - 6$
7. $4x - 23 = x - 7$
8. $8x - 8 = 3x - 2$
9. $11x + 7 = 6x + 7$
10. $9x + 8 = 10$
11. $5 + 3x = x + 8$
12. $4 + 7x = x + 5$
13. $6x - 8 = 4 - 3x$
14. $5x + 1 = 7 - 2x$
15. $6x - 3 = 1 - x$

16. $3x - 10 = 2x - 3$
17. $5x + 1 = 6 - 3x$
18. $11x - 20 = 10x - 15$
19. $6 + 2x = 8 - 3x$
20. $7 + x = 9 - 5x$
21. $3y - 7 = y + 1$
22. $8y + 9 = 7y + 8$
23. $7y - 5 = 2y$
24. $3z - 1 = 5 - 4z$
25. $8 = 13 - 4x$
26. $10 = 12 - 2x$
27. $13 = 20 - 9x$
28. $8 = 5 - 2x$
29. $5 + x = 7 - 8x$
30. $3x + 11 = 2 - 3x$

(a)
$$\begin{aligned} 3(x-1) &= 2(x+7) \\ 3x - 3 &= 2x + 14 \\ 3x - 2x &= 14 + 3 \\ x &= 17 \end{aligned}$$

(b)
$$\begin{aligned} 5(2x+1) &= 3(x-2) + 20 \\ 10x + 5 &= 3x - 6 + 20 \\ 10x - 3x &= -6 + 20 - 5 \\ 7x &= 9 \\ x &= 1\tfrac{2}{7} \end{aligned}$$

Exercise 8

Solve the equations

1. $2(x + 1) = x + 5$
2. $4(x - 2) = 2(x + 1)$
3. $5(x - 3) = 3(x + 2)$
4. $3(x + 2) = 2(x - 1)$
5. $5(x - 3) = 2(x - 7)$
6. $6(x + 2) = 2(x - 3)$
7. $10(x - 3) = x$
8. $3(2x - 1) = 4(x + 1)$
9. $4(2x + 1) = 5(x + 3)$
10. $3(x - 1) + 7 = 2(x + 1)$
11. $5(x + 1) + 3 = 3(x - 1)$
12. $7(x - 2) - 3 = 2(x + 2)$
13. $5(2x + 1) - 5 = 3(x + 1)$
14. $3(4x - 1) - 3 = x + 1$
15. $2(x - 10) = 4 - 3x$
16. $3x + 2(x + 1) = 3x + 12$
17. $4x - 2(x + 4) = x + 1$
18. $2x - 3(x + 2) = 2x + 1$
19. $5x - 2(x - 2) = 6 - 2x$
20. $3(x + 1) + 2(x + 2) = 10$
21. $4(x + 3) + 2(x - 1) = 4$
22. $3(x - 2) - 2(x + 1) = 5$
23. $5(x - 3) + 3(x + 2) = 7x$
24. $3(2x + 1) - 2(2x + 1) = 10$
25. $4(3x - 1) - 3(3x + 2) = 0$

Equations with fractions

Solve the equations

(a)
$$\begin{aligned} \frac{7}{x} &= 8 \\ 7 &= 8x \\ \frac{7}{8} &= x \end{aligned}$$

(b)
$$\begin{aligned} \frac{3x}{4} &= 2 \\ 3x &= 8 \\ x &= \frac{8}{3} \\ x &= 2\tfrac{2}{3} \end{aligned}$$

Exercise 9

Solve the equations

1. $\dfrac{3}{x} = 5$
2. $\dfrac{4}{x} = 7$
3. $\dfrac{11}{x} = 12$
4. $\dfrac{6}{x} = 11$
5. $\dfrac{2}{x} = 3$
6. $\dfrac{5}{y} = 9$
7. $\dfrac{7}{y} = 9$
8. $\dfrac{4}{t} = 3$
9. $\dfrac{3}{a} = 6$
10. $\dfrac{8}{x} = 12$
11. $\dfrac{3}{p} = 1$
12. $\dfrac{15}{q} = 10$
13. $\dfrac{x}{4} = 6$
14. $\dfrac{x}{5} = 3$
15. $\dfrac{y}{5} = -2$

16. $\frac{a}{7} = 3$

17. $\frac{t}{3} = 7$

18. $\frac{m}{4} = \frac{2}{3}$

19. $\frac{x}{7} = \frac{5}{8}$

20. $\frac{2x}{3} = 1$

21. $\frac{4x}{5} = 3$

22. $\frac{3y}{2} = 2$

23. $\frac{5t}{6} = 3$

24. $\frac{m}{8} = \frac{1}{4}$

25. $8 = \frac{5}{x}$

26. $19 = \frac{7}{y}$

27. $-5 = \frac{3}{a}$

28. $-6 = \frac{k}{4}$

29. $\frac{n}{7} = -10$

30. $4 = \frac{33}{q}$

31. $\frac{x}{2} = 110$

32. $\frac{500}{y} = -1$

33. $-99 = \frac{98}{f}$

34. $\frac{x}{3} + 5 = 7$

35. $\frac{x}{5} - 2 = 4$

36. $\frac{2x}{3} + 4 = 5$

37. $\frac{x}{6} - 10 = 4$

38. $\frac{6}{x} + 1 = 2$

39. $\frac{5}{x} - 7 = 0$

40. $5 + \frac{3}{x} = 10$

Exercise 10

In this exercise □, △, ○ and ∗ represent weights which are always balanced.

1. (a)

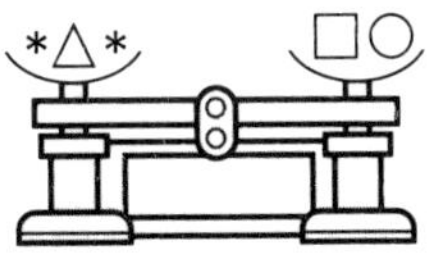

(b)

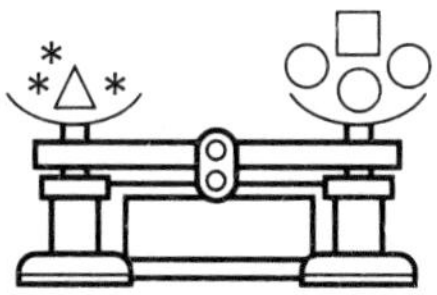

(c)

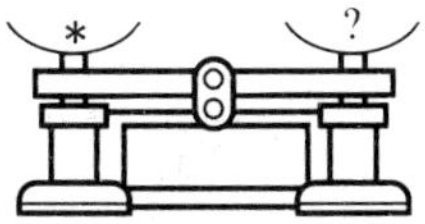

How many ○'s?

2. (a)

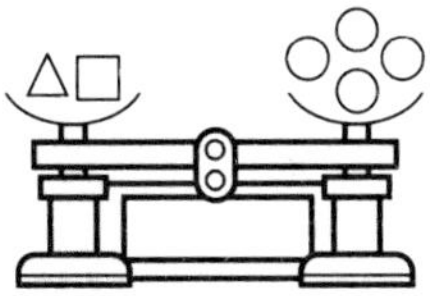

(b)

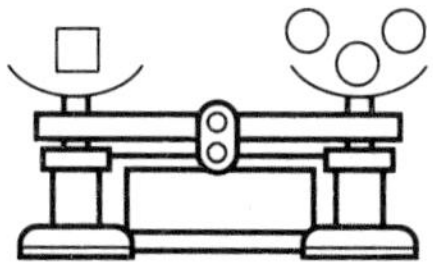

(c)

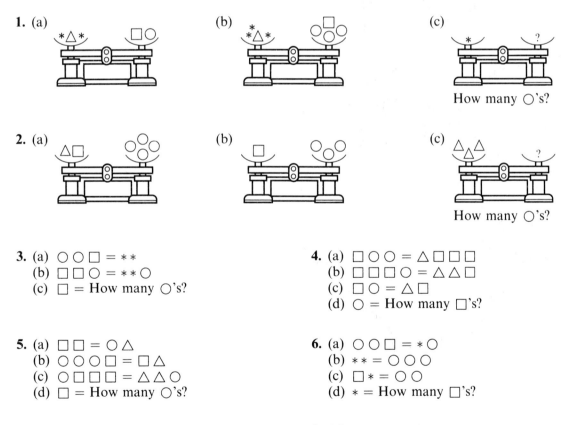

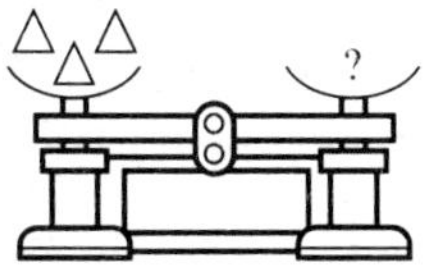

How many ○'s?

3. (a) ○ ○ □ = ∗ ∗
(b) □ □ ○ = ∗ ∗ ○
(c) □ = How many ○'s?

4. (a) □ ○ ○ = △ □ □ □
(b) □ □ □ ○ = △ △ □
(c) □ ○ = △ □
(d) ○ = How many □'s?

5. (a) □ □ = ○ △
(b) ○ ○ ○ □ = □ △
(c) ○ □ □ □ = △ △ ○
(d) □ = How many ○'s?

6. (a) ○ ○ □ = ∗ ○
(b) ∗ ∗ = ○ ○ ○
(c) □ ∗ = ○ ○
(d) ∗ = How many □'s?

7. (a) ○ □ □ = △ ∗
(b) ∗ ∗ ∗ = △ △
(c) ○ □ = △
(d) △ △ △ △ = How many □'s ?

8. (a) ○ □ = △
(b) ○ = □ ∗
(c) ○ ○ □ = △ ∗ ∗
(d) □ = How many ∗'s?

Solving problems with equations

If I multiply a 'mystery' number by 2 and then add 3 the answer is 14. Find the 'mystery' number.

Let the mystery number be x.

$$\begin{aligned} \text{Then } 2x + 3 &= 14 \\ 2x &= 11 \\ x &= 5\tfrac{1}{2} \end{aligned}$$

The 'mystery' number is $5\frac{1}{2}$

Exercise 11

Find the 'mystery' number in each question by forming an equation and then solving it.

1. If I multiply the number by 3 and then add 4, the answer is 13.

2. If I multiply the number by 4 and then add 5, the answer is 8.

3. If I multiply the number by 2 and then subtract 5, the answer is 4.

4. If I multiply the number by 10 and then add 19, the answer is 16.

5. If I add 3 to the number and then multiply the result by 4, the answer is 10.

6. If we subtract 11 from the number and then treble the result, the answer is 20.

7. If we double the number, add 4 and then multiply the result by 3, the answer is 13.

8. If we treble the number, take away 6 and then multiply the result by 2, the answer is 18.

9. If we double the number and subtract 7 we get the same answer as when we add 5 to the number.

10. If we multiply the number by 5 and subtract 4, we get the same answer as when we add 3 to the number and then double the result.

11. If we multiply the number by 6 and add 1, we get the same answer as when we add 5 to the number and then treble the result.

12. If I add 5 to the number and then multiply the result by 4, I get the same answer as when I add 1 to the number and then multiply the result by 2.

The length of a rectangle is twice the width. If the perimeter is 36 cm, find the width.

(a) Let the width of the rectangle be x cm. Then the length of the rectangle is $2x$ cm.

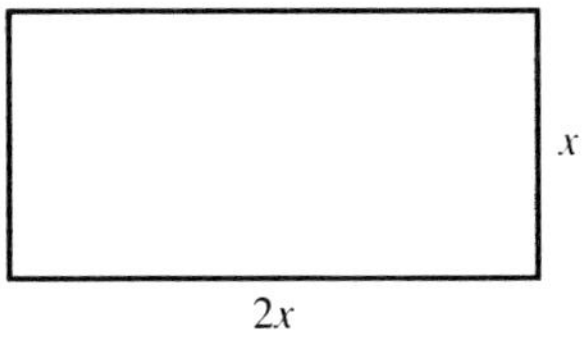

(b) Form an equation.

$$x + 2x + x + 2x = 36$$

(c) Solve

$$6x = 36$$
$$x = 6$$

The width of the rectangle is 6 cm.

Exercise 12

Answer these questions by forming an equation and then solving it.

1. Find x if the perimeter is 7 cm.

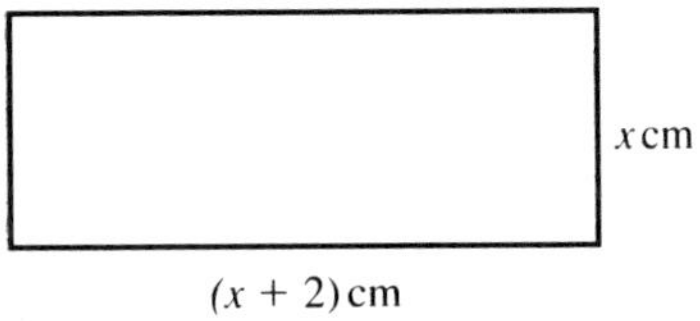

2. Find x if the perimeter is 5 cm.

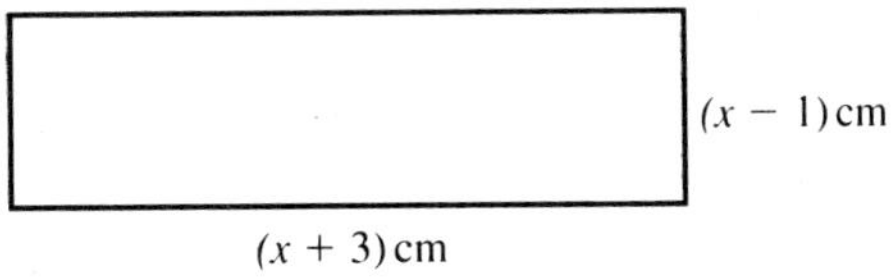

3. The length of a rectangle is 3 times its width. If the perimeter of the rectangle is 11 cm, find its width.
Hint: Let the width be x cm.

4. The length of a rectangle is 4 cm more than its width. If its perimeter is 13 cm, find its width.

5. The width of a rectangle is 5 cm less than its length. If the perimeter of the rectangle is 18 cm, find its length.

6. Find x in the following rectangles:

(a)

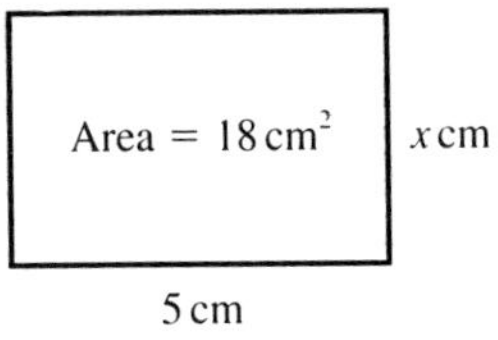

(b)

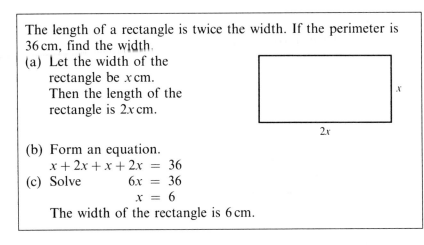

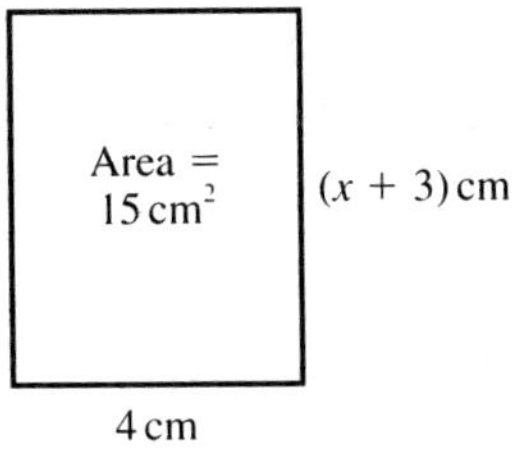

7. Find x in the following triangles:

(a)

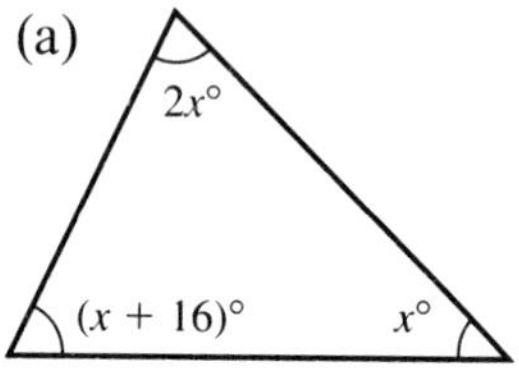

(b)

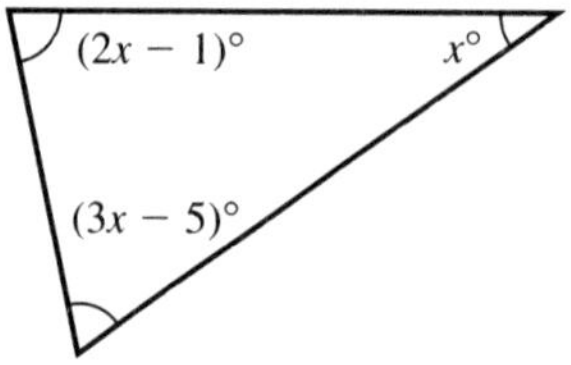

8. The angles of a triangle are 32°, $x°$ and $(4x + 3)°$. Find the value of x.

9. Find a in the diagrams below

(a)

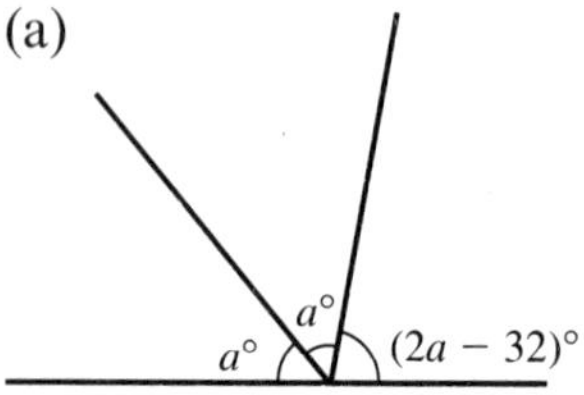

(b)

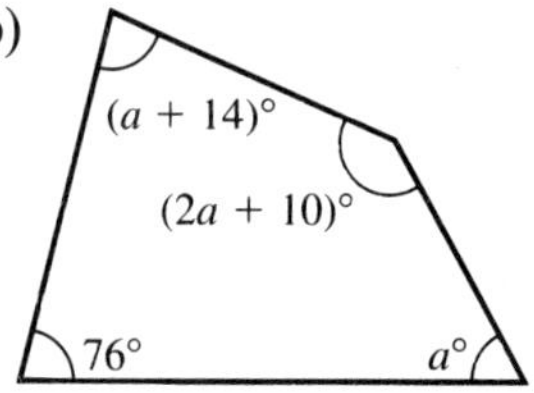

10. The sum of three consecutive whole numbers is 168. Let the first number be x. Form an equation and hence find the three numbers.

11. The sum of four consecutive whole numbers is 170. Find the numbers.

12. In this triangle AB = x cm.
BC is 3 cm shorter than AB.
AC is twice as long as BC.
(a) Write down, in terms of x, the lengths of
 (i) BC
 (ii) AC
 The perimeter of the triangle is 41 cm.
(b) Write down an equation in x and solve it to find x.

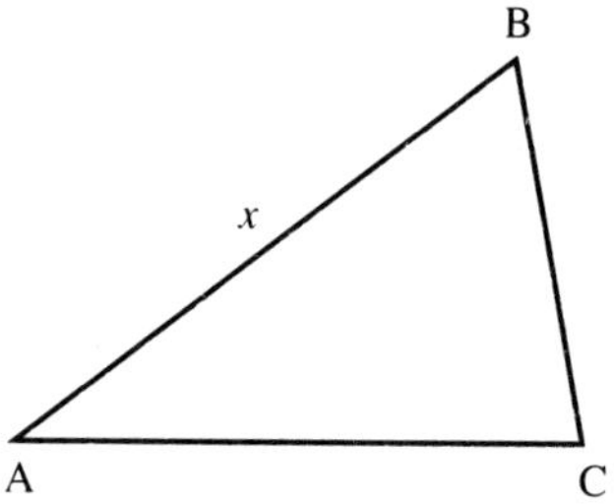

13. This is a rectangle. Work out x and hence find the perimeter of the rectangle.

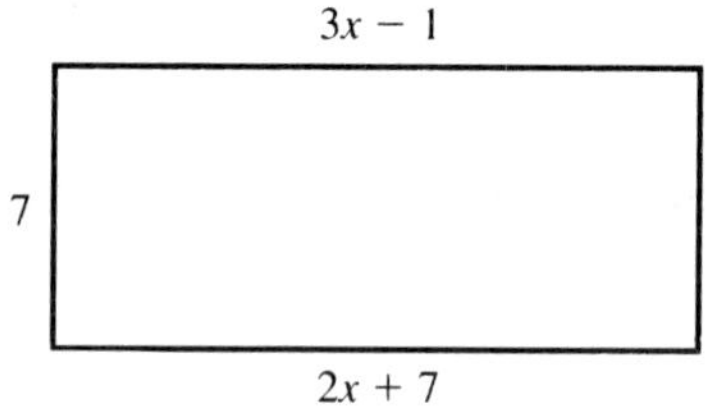

14. Find the length of the sides of this equilateral triangle.

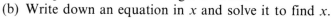

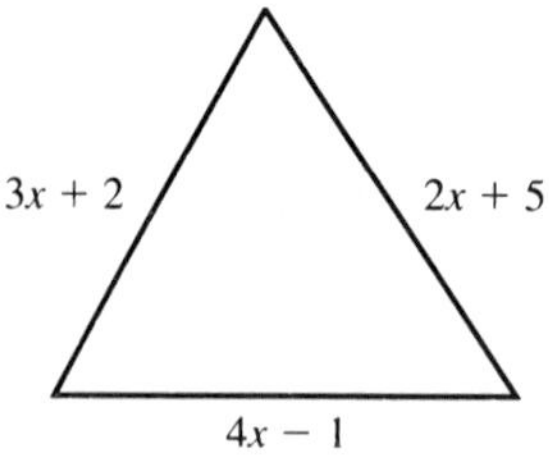

15. Petra has £12 and Suki has nothing. They both receive the same money for doing a delivery job.
Now Petra has three times as much as Suki.
How much did they get for the job?

16. The area of rectangle A is twice the area of rectangle B. Find x.

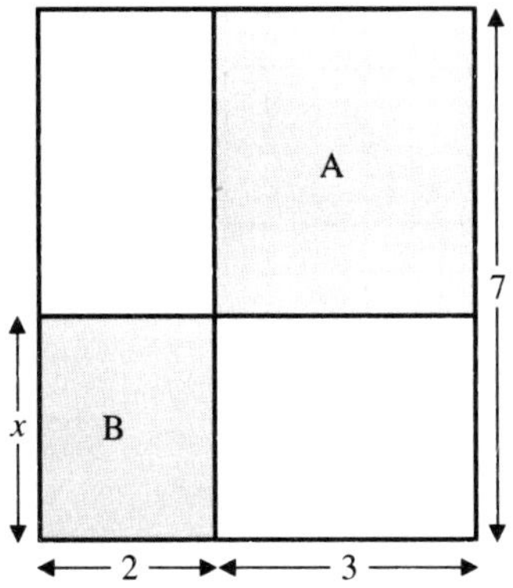

17. Pupils and teachers from Gibson College went on an outing to London in 4 full coaches. Two teachers had to go by train.

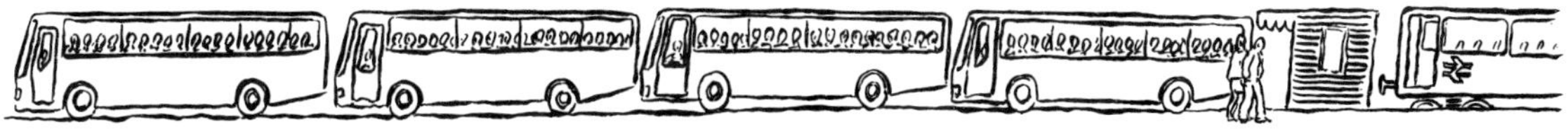

Unfortunately 3 of the coaches were parked illegally in London and their wheels were clamped. For the return journey there was one full coach and the other 143 pupils and teachers had to go back by train.

Use x to stand for the number of people in one full coach. Make an equation involving x and solve it to find the number of people on a coach.

18. Cory has nine teddy bears and she decides they each need a new ribbon.

She buys two long pieces of material to cut into nine equal ribbons.
From the first piece of material she cuts 7 ribbons and has 11 cm left over.
From the second piece of material she cuts 2 ribbons and has 146 cm left over.
How long is each ribbon?

2.3 Drawing graphs

3/6c

Draw the graph of $y = 4 - 2x$ for values of x from -2 to $+3$

(a)

x	-2	-1	0	1	2	3
4	4	4	4	4	4	4
$-2x$	4	2	0	-2	-4	-6
y	8	6	4	2	0	-2

(b) Plot the values of x and y from the table

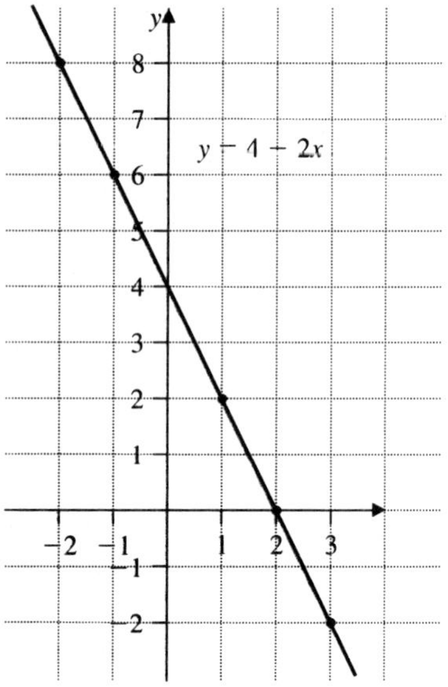

Exercise 13

For each question make a table of values and then draw the graph. Suggested scales: 1 cm to 1 unit on both axes, unless otherwise stated.

1. $y = 2x + 1$; x from -3 to $+3$.

x	-3	-2	-1	0	1	2	3
$2x$	-6	-4					
$+1$	1	1	1				
y	-5	-3					

2. $y = 3x - 5$; x from -2 to $+3$.

3. $y = x + 2$; x from -4 to $+4$.

4. $y = 2x - 7$; x from -2 to $+5$.

5. $y = 4x + 1$; x from -3 to $+3$.
(Use scales of 1 cm to 1 unit on the x-axis and 1 cm to 2 units on the y-axis.)

6. $y = x - 3$; x from -2 to $+5$.

7. $y = 2x + 4$; x from -4 to $+2$.

8. $y = 3x + 2$; x from -3 to $+3$.

9. $y = x + 7$; x from -5 to $+3$.

10. $y = 4x - 3$; x from -3 to $+3$.
(Use scales of 1 cm to 1 unit on the x axis and 1 cm to 2 units on the y-axis.)

11. $y = 4 - 2x$; x from -3 to $+3$.

x	-3	-2	-1	0	1	2	3
4	4	4	4	4			4
$-2x$	6	4					-6
y	10	8					-2

12. $y = 8 - 2x$; x from -2 to $+4$.

Curved graphs

Draw the graph of $y = x^2 + x - 2$ for values of x from -3 to $+3$.

(a)

x	-3	-2	-1	0	1	2	3
x^2	9	4	1	0	1	4	9
$+x$	-3	-2	-1	0	1	2	3
-2	-2	-2	-2	-2	-2	-2	-2
y	4	0	-2	-2	0	4	10

(b) Plot the x and y values from the table.

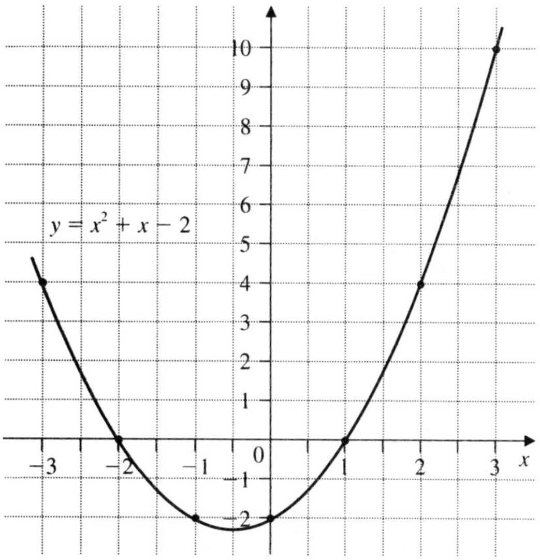

Exercise 14

For each question make a table of values and then draw the graph. Suggested scales: 2 cm to 1 unit on the x-axis and 1 cm to 1 unit on the y-axis.

1. $y = x^2 + 2$; x from -3 to $+3$.

x	-3	-2	-1	0	1	2	3
x^2	9	4	1	0	1		
$+2$	2	2	2				
y	11	6	3				

2. $y = x^2 + 5$; x from -3 to $+3$.

3. $y = x^2 - 4$; x from -3 to $+3$.

4. $y = x^2 - 8$; x from -3 to $+3$.

5. $y = x^2 + 2x$; x from -4 to $+2$.

x	-4	-3	-2	-1	0	1	2
x^2	16	9					4
$+2x$	-8	-6					4
y	8	3					8

6. $y = x^2 + 4x$; x from -5 to $+1$.

7. $y = x^2 + 4x - 1$; x from -2 to $+4$.

8. $y = x^2 + 2x - 5$; x from -4 to $+2$.

9. $y = x^2 + 3x + 1$; x from -4 to $+2$.

These graphs are more difficult.

10. $y = x^3 + 1$; x from -3 to $+3$.
Scales: 2 cm to 1 unit for x;
1 cm to 5 units for y.

11. $y = \frac{12}{x}$; x from 1 to 12.

12. $y = 2x^2 + 3x - 1$; x from -4 to $+2$.
Scales: 2 cm to 1 unit for x;
1 cm to 1 unit for y.
(Remember $2x^2 = 2(x^2)$. Work out x^2 and then multiply by 2).

13. $y = \frac{16}{x}$; x from 1 to 10.
Scales: 1 cm to 1 unit for x;
1 cm to 1 unit for y.

14. A rectangle has a perimeter of 14 cm and length x cm. Show that the width of the rectangle is $(7 - x)$ cm and hence that the area A of the rectangle is given by the formula $A = x(7 - x)$. Draw the graph, plotting x on the horizontal axis with a scale of 2 cm to 1 unit, and A on the vertical axis with a scale of 1 cm to 1 unit. Take x from 0 to 7. From the graph find,

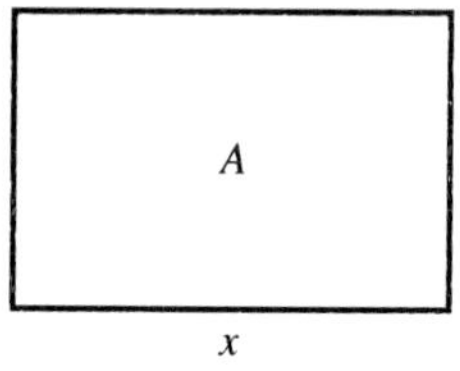

(a) the area of the rectangle when $x = 2{\cdot}25$ cm,
(b) the dimensions of the rectangle when its area is 9 cm^2,
(c) the maximum area of the rectangle,
(d) the length and width of the rectangle corresponding to the maximum area.

15. The diagram shows the net of an open box, with the base shaded.

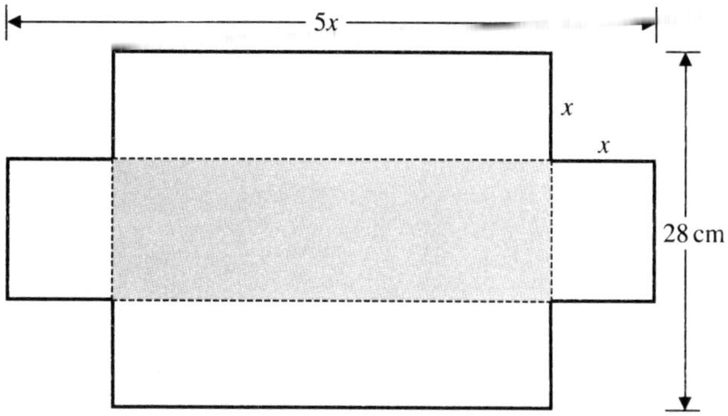

(a) Explain why the area, $A\,\text{cm}^2$, of the base of the box is given by the formula

$$A = 3x(28 - 2x)$$

(b) Plot the graph of A against x for values of x from 4 to 10. Use a scale of 2 cm to 1 unit for x and a scale of 2 cm to 10 units for A. Draw the A-axis with values from 240 to 300.

(c) From your graph, find the value of x which gives the maximum value of A.

(d) For this value of x, calculate the volume of the box.

16. A ball is thrown upwards at 35 m/s. After t seconds its height in metres is given by the equation

$$h = 35t - 5t^2.$$

(a) Copy and complete this table

Time t	0	1	2	3	4	5	6	7
Height h								

(b) Draw a graph, using a scale of 2 cm to 1 second across the page and 2 cm to 10 m up the page.

(c) A second ball is thrown and its height is given by

$$h = 20t - 5t^2.$$

On the same page draw a graph for this ball, taking t from 0 to 4.

(d) When is the first ball at its highest point?

(e) For how long is the first ball above 50 m?

(f) What is the greatest height reached by the second ball?

3 Number 1

3.1 Long multiplication and division

2/5a

To work out 327 × 53 we will use the fact that 327 × 53 = (327 × 50) + (327 × 3)
Set out the working like this.

```
  327
   53 ×
16350 → This is 327 × 50
  981 → This is 327 × 3
17331 → This is 327 × 53
```

Here is another example.

```
  541
   84 ×
43280 → This is 541 × 80
 2164 → This is 541 × 4
45444 → This is 541 × 84
```

Exercise 1

Work out, without a calculator.

1. 35 × 23	**2.** 27 × 17	**3.** 26 × 25
4. 31 × 43	**5.** 45 × 61	**6.** 52 × 24
7. 323 × 14	**8.** 416 × 73	**9.** 504 × 56
10. 306 × 28	**11.** 624 × 75	**12.** 839 × 79
13. 694 × 83	**14.** 973 × 92	**15.** 415 × 235

With ordinary 'short' division, we divide and find remainders. The method for 'long' division is really the same but we set it out so that the remainders are easier to find.

Work out 736 ÷ 32

```
     23
 32)736
    64↓
     96
     96
      0
```

(a) 32 into 73 goes 2 times
(b) 2 × 32 = 64
(c) 73 − 64 = 9
(d) 'bring down' 6
(e) 32 into 96 goes 3 times

Exercise 2

Work out, without a calculator.

1. 672 ÷ 21
2. 425 ÷ 17
3. 576 ÷ 32
4. 247 ÷ 19
5. 875 ÷ 25
6. 574 ÷ 26
7. 806 ÷ 34
8. 748 ÷ 41
9. 666 ÷ 24
10. 707 ÷ 52
11. 951 ÷ 27
12. 806 ÷ 34
13. 2917 ÷ 45
14. 2735 ÷ 18
15. 56274 ÷ 19

Exercise 3

Solve each problem without a calculator.

1. A shop owner buys 56 tins of paint at 84p each. How much does he spend altogether?

2. Eggs are packed eighteen to a box.

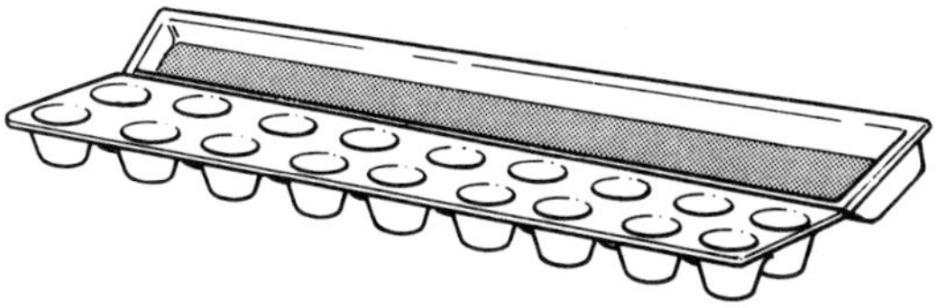

How many boxes are needed for 828 eggs?

3. On average a man smokes 146 cigarettes a week. How many does he smoke in a year?

4. Sally wants to buy as many 23p stamps as possible. She has £5 to buy them. How many can she buy and how much change is left?

5. How many 49-seater coaches will be needed for a school trip for a party of 366?

6. An office building has 24 windows on each of 8 floors. A window cleaner charges 42p for each window. How much is he paid for the whole building?

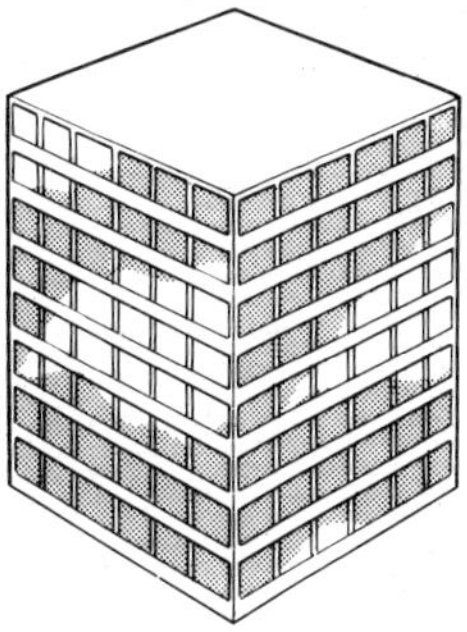

7. A lottery prize of £238 million was won by a syndicate of 17 people who shared the prize equally between them. How much did each person receive?

8. It costs £7905 to hire a plane for a day. A trip is organised for 93 people. How much does each person pay?

9. The headmaster of a school discovers an oil well in the school playground. As is the custom in such cases, he receives all the money from the oil. The oil comes out of the well at a rate of £15 for every minute of the day and night. How much does the headmaster receive in a 24-hour day?

Exercise 4

Each empty square contains either a number or a mathematical symbol (+, −, ×, ÷). Copy each square and fill in the details.

1.

5			→	60
×		÷		
		24	→	44
↓		↓		
	×	$\frac{1}{2}$	→	50

2.

	×	6	→	42
÷		÷		
14	−		→	
↓		↓		
		2	→	1

3.

	×	2	→	38
−		÷		
			→	48
↓		↓		
7	−		→	$6\frac{1}{2}$

4.

17	×		→	170
−		÷		
	÷		→	
↓		↓		
8	−	0·1	→	

5.

0·3	×	20	→	
		−		
11	÷		→	
↓		↓		
11·3	−		→	2·3

6.

	×	50	→	25
−		÷		
		$\frac{1}{2}$	→	0·6
↓		↓		
0·4	×		→	

7.

7	×		→	0·7
÷		×		
	÷		→	
↓		↓		
1·75	+	0·02	→	

8.

	+	8	→	9·4
−				
	×	0·1	→	
↓		↓		
1·3		0·8	→	2·1

9.

	×		→	30
−				
	÷	10	→	0·25
↓		↓		
97·5	+	3	→	

10.

3	÷	2	→	
÷		÷		
8	÷		→	
↓		↓		
	+	$\frac{1}{8}$	→	

11.

		$\frac{1}{16}$	→	$\frac{3}{16}$
×				
	÷	4	→	
↓		↓		
$\frac{1}{8}$		$\frac{1}{4}$	→	$\frac{3}{8}$

12.

0·5	−	0·01	→	
		×		
	×		→	35
↓		↓		
4	÷	0·1	→	

13.

	−	1·8	→	3·4
−		÷		
	×		→	
↓		↓		
	+	0·36	→	1

14.

	×	30	→	21
×		−		
	−		→	35
↓		↓		
	−	49	→	

15.

	×	−6	→	72
÷		+		
4	+		→	
↓		↓		
	+	1	→	−2

3.2 Percentages

2/5b

(a) Work out 22% of £40.

$$\frac{22}{100} \times \frac{40}{1} = \frac{880}{100}$$

Answer: £8·80

(b) Work out 16% of £85 [Alternative method].

Since $16\% = \frac{16}{100}$ we can replace 16% by 0·16

So 16% of £85 = 0·16 × 85
= £13·60

Exercise 5

Work out

1. 20% of £60
2. 10% of £80
3. 5% of £200
4. 6% of £50
5. 4% of £60
6. 30% of £80
7. 9% of £500
8. 18% of £400
9. 61% of £400
10. 12% of £80
11. 6% of $700
12. 11% of $800
13. 5% of 160 kg
14. 20% of 60 kg
15. 68% of 400 g
16. 15% of 300 m
17. 2% of 2000 km
18. 71% of $1000
19. 26% of 19 kg
20. 1% of 6000 g
21. 8·5% of £2400

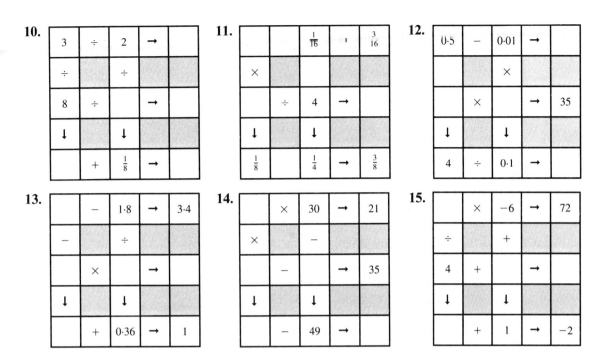

Work out 6·5% of £17·50 correct to the nearest penny.

$$\frac{6 \cdot 5}{100} \times \frac{17 \cdot 5}{1} = \frac{113 \cdot 75}{100}$$

$$= £1 \cdot 1375$$

Answer: £1·14 to the nearest penny.

Exercise 6

Give the answers to the nearest penny where necessary

1. 4·5% of £6·22
2. 17% of £6·84
3. 15% of £8·11
4. 17% of £17·07
5. 37% of £9·64
6. 3·5% of £12·90
7. 8% of £11·64
8. 68% of £54·45
9. 73% of £23·24
10. 2·5% of £15·20
11. 6·3% of £12·50
12. 8·2% of £19·50
13. 87% of £15·40
14. 80% of £62·50
15. 12% of £24·50
16. $12\frac{1}{2}$% of £88·50
17. $7\frac{1}{2}$% of £16·40
18. $5\frac{1}{2}$% of £80
19. $12\frac{1}{2}$% of £90
20. 19% of £119·50
21. 8·35% of £110

A coat originally cost £24. Calculate the new price after a 5% reduction.

$$\text{Price reduction} = 5\% \text{ of } £24$$

$$= \frac{5}{100} \times \frac{24}{1} = £1 \cdot 20$$

$$\text{New price of coat} = £24 - £1 \cdot 20$$

$$= £22 \cdot 80$$

A CD originally cost £11·60. Calculate the new price after a 7% increase.
We could work out 7% of £11·60 as in the example above.
There is, however, a *quicker* way which many people prefer.
If we increase the price by 7% the final price is 107% of the old price.

$$\therefore \text{ new price} = 107\% \text{ of } £11 \cdot 60$$

$$= 1 \cdot 07 \times 11 \cdot 6$$

$$= £12 \cdot 41 \text{ to the nearest penny.}$$

For a 5% *reduction* as in the above example we would multiply by 0·95.

Exercise 7

1. Increase a price of £60 by 5%
2. Reduce a price of £800 by 8%
3. Reduce a price of £82·50 by 6%
4. Increase a price of £65 by 60%
5. Reduce a price of £2000 by 2%
6. Increase a price of £440 by 80%
7. Increase a price of £66 by 100%
8. Reduce a price of £91·50 by 50%
9. Increase a price of £88·24 by 25%
10. Reduce a price of £63 by $33\frac{1}{3}$%

In the remaining questions give the answers to the nearest penny.

11. Increase a price of £8·24 by 46%
12. Increase a price of £7·65 by 24%
13. Increase a price of £5·61 by 31%
14. Reduce a price of £8·99 by 22%
15. Increase a price of £11·12 by 11%
16. Reduce a price of £17·62 by 4%
17. Increase a price of £28·20 by 13%
18. Increase a price of £8·55 by $5\frac{1}{2}$%
19. Reduce a price of £9·60 by $7\frac{1}{2}$%
20. Increase a price of £12·80 by $10\frac{1}{2}$%

Exercise 8

1. In a closing-down sale a shop reduces all its prices by 20%. Find the sale price of a coat which previously cost £44.
2. The price of a car was £5400 but it is increased by 6%. What is the new price?
3. The price of a sideboard was £245 but, because the sideboard is scratched, the price is reduced by 30%. What is the new price?
4. A hi-fi shop offers a 7% discount for cash. How much does a cash-paying customer pay for an amplifier advertised at £95?
5. A rabbit weighs 2·8 kg. After being shot, its weight is increased by 1%. How much does it weigh now?

6. The insurance premium for a car is normally £90. With a 'no-claim bonus' the premium is reduced by 35%. What is the reduced premium?
7. Myxomatosis kills 92% of a colony of 300 rabbits. How many rabbits survive?
8. The population of a town increased by 32% between 1945 and 1985. If there were 45 000 people in 1945, what was the 1985 population?
9. A restaurant adds a 12% 'service charge' onto the basic price of meals. How much do I pay for a meal with a basic price of £8·50?

10. A new-born baby weighs 3·1 kg. Her weight increases by 8% over the next fortnight. What does she weigh then?

11. A large snake normally weighs 12·2 kg. After swallowing a rat, the weight of the snake is increased by 7%. How much does it weigh after dinner?

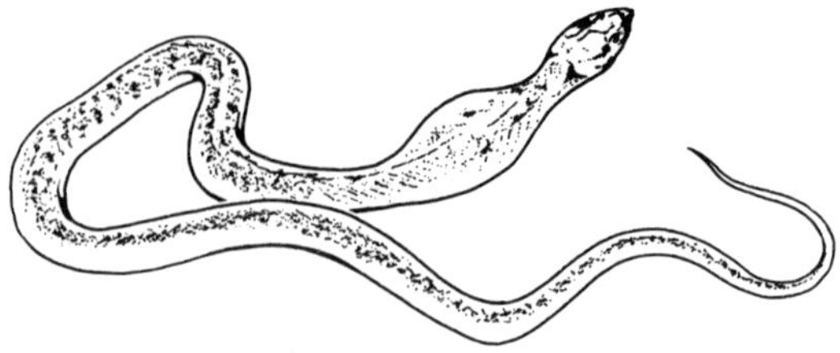

12. At the beginning of the year a car is valued at £3250. During the year its value falls by 15%. How much is it worth at the end of the year?

Exercise 9

In Questions **1** to **4** find the total bill.

1. 2 hammers at £5·30 each
50 screws at 25p for 10
5 bulbs at 38p each
1 tape measure at £1·15
VAT at 17·5% is added to the total cost.

2. 5 litres of oil at 85p per litre
3 spanners at £1·25 each
2 manuals at £4·30 each
200 bolts at 90p for 10
VAT at 17·5% is added to the total cost.

3. 12 rolls of wallpaper at £3·70 per roll
3 packets of paste at £0·55 per packet
2 brushes at £2·40 each
1 step ladder at £15·50
VAT at 17·5% is added to the total cost.

4. 5 golf clubs at £12·45 each
48 golf balls at £15 per dozen
100 tees at 1p each
1 bag at £21·50
1 umbrella at £12·99
VAT at 17·5% is added to the total cost.

5. In a sale a dress priced at £35 is reduced by 20%. At the end of the week the *sale price* is reduced by a further 25%.
Calculate
(a) the price in the original sale
(b) the final price.

6. (a) In 1985 a club has 40 members who each pay £12 annual subscription. What is the total income from subscriptions?
(b) In 1986 the subscription is increased by 35% and the membership increases to 65.
(i) What is the 1986 subscription?
(ii) What is the total income from subscriptions in 1986?

Pay rises

Exercise 10

1. John works for company A and during 1995 he earns £160 per week. From January 1st 1996 company A offer John an extra 5% on his wages and John accepts this offer and is paid this new wage for 52 weeks in 1996.
   (a) How much is John paid each week in 1996?
   (b) How much does John earn in the whole of 1996?

2. Steve works for company B and during 1995 he also earns £160 per week. From January 1st 1996 company B offer Steve an extra 5% but Steve does not accept this and he goes on strike for six weeks, during which time he receives no pay. After six weeks of the strike, company B offer Steve 10% and he immediately accepts this and receives his increased pay for the rest of 1996.
   (a) How much is Steve paid after the strike?
   (b) How much does Steve earn in the whole of 1996?

3. Ann also earns £160 per week during 1995 and she also goes on strike for the first six weeks of 1996. At the end of her strike she accepts a pay offer of 15% and she receives her increased pay for the rest of 1996.
   (a) How much is Ann paid after the strike?
   (b) How much does Ann earn in the whole of 1996?

4. At the beginning of the year the wages of three people working for the same firm are as follows:
   Cleaner £80 per week;
   Secretary £115 per week;
   Personnel manager £25 080 per year.
   (a) The firm awards all of its employees a pay rise of 5%.
      (i) What is the pay increase for a cleaner?
      (ii) What is the pay increase for a secretary?
      (iii) How much does the personnel manager earn in one week before the pay rise?
      (iv) What is the weekly pay increase for the personnel manager?
   (b) The firm's computer makes a mistake with pay increases and awards an increase of 12% for everyone instead of 5%.
      (i) What is the pay increase for a cleaner?
      (ii) What is the pay increase for a secretary?
      (iii) What is the weekly pay increase for the personnel manager?

3.3 Map scales and ratio

2/5b, 2/6b

The map below is drawn to a scale of 1 : 50 000. In other words 1 cm on the map represents 50 000 cm on the land.

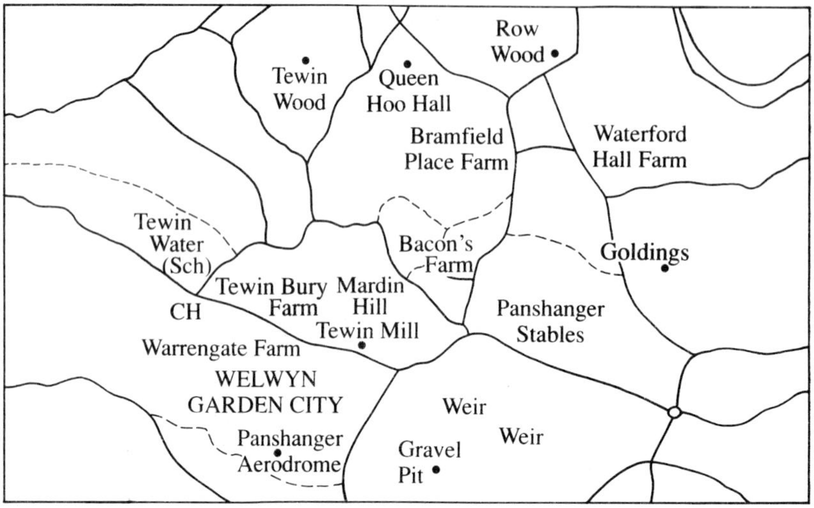

On a map of scale 1 : 25 000 two towns appear 10 cm apart. What is the actual distance between the towns in km?

1 cm on map = 25 000 cm on land
10 cm on map = 250 000 cm on land
250 000 cm = 2500 m
= 2·5 km

The towns are 2·5 km apart.

Exercise 11

1. The scale of a map is 1 : 1000. Find the actual length in metres represented on the map by 20 cm.
2. The scale of a map is 1 : 10 000. Find the actual length in metres represented on the map by 5 cm.
3. Copy and complete the table.

Map scale	Length on map	Actual length on land
(a) 1 : 10 000	10 cm	1 km
(b) 1 : 2000	10 cm	m
(c) 1 : 25 000	4 cm	km
(d) 1 : 10 000	6 cm	km

4. Find the actual distance in metres between two points which are 6·3 cm apart on a map whose scale is 1 : 1000.

5. On a map of scale 1 : 300 000 the distance between York and Harrogate is 8 cm. What is the actual distance in km?

6. A builder's plan is drawn to a scale of 1 cm to 10 m. How long is a road which is 12 cm on the plan?

7. The map on page 70 is drawn to a scale of 1 : 50 000. Make your own measurements to find the actual distance in km between:
(a) Goldings and Tewin Wood (marked •).
(b) Panshanger Aerodrome and Row Wood.
(c) Gravel Pit and Queen Hoo Hall.

The distance between two towns is 18 km.
How far apart will they be on a map of scale 1 : 50 000?

18 km = 1 800 000 cm
1 800 000 cm on land = $\frac{1}{50\,000} \times 1\,800\,000$ cm on map

Distance between towns on map = 36 cm

Exercise 12

1. The distance between two towns is 15 km. How far apart will they be on a map of scale 1 : 10 000?

2. The distance between two points is 25 km. How far apart will they be on a map of scale 1 : 20 000?

3. The length of a road is 2·8 km. How long will the road be on a map of scale 1 : 10 000?

4. The length of a reservoir is 5·9 km. How long will it be on a map of scale 1 : 100 000?

5. Copy and complete the table.

Map scale	Actual length on land	Length on map
(a) 1 : 20 000	12 km	cm
(b) 1 : 10 000	8·4 km	cm
(c) 1 : 50 000	28 km	cm
(d) 1 : 40 000	56 km	cm
(e) 1 : 5000	5 km	cm

6. The scale of a drawing is 1 cm to 10 m. The length of a wall is 25 m. What length will the wall be on the drawing?

Ratio

Share £60 in the ratio 2 : 3.

Total number of shares = 2 + 3 = 5
∴ One share = £60 ÷ 5 = £12
∴ The two amounts are £24 and £36

Exercise 13

1. Share £30 in the ratio 1 : 2.
2. Share £60 in the ratio 3 : 1.
3. Divide 880 g of food between the cat and the dog in the ratio 3 : 5.
4. Divide $1080 between Sam and Chris in the ratio 4 : 5.
5. Share 126 gallons of petrol between Steven and Dave in the ratio 2 : 5.
6. Share £60 in the ratio 1 : 2 : 3.
7. Alan, Brian and Dawn divided £560 between them in the ratio 2 : 1 : 5. How much did Brian receive?
8. A sum of £120 is divided in the ratio 3 : 4 : 5. What is the largest share?
9. At an election 7800 people voted Labour, Conservative or Alliance in the ratio 4 : 3 : 5. How many people voted Alliance?

In a class, the ratio of boys to girls is 3 : 4.
If there are 9 boys, how many girls are there?

Boys : Girls = 3 : 4
Multiply both parts by 3.
Boys : Girls = 9 : 12
So there are 9 boys and 12 girls.

Exercise 14

1. In a room, the ratio of boys to girls is 3 : 2. If there are 12 boys, how many girls are there?
2. In a room, the ratio of men to women is 4 : 1. If there are 20 men, how many women are there?

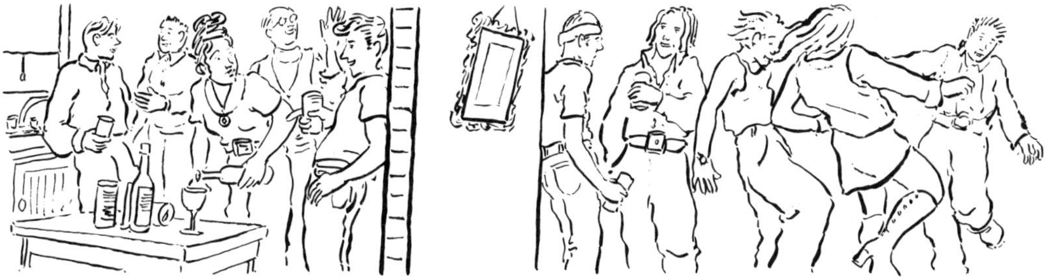

3. In a box, the ratio of nails to screws is 5 : 3. If there are 15 nails, how many screws are there?
4. An alloy consists of copper, zinc and tin in the ratios 1 : 3 : 4. If there is 10 g of copper in the alloy, find the weights of zinc and tin.
5. In a shop the ratio of oranges to apples is 2 : 5. If there are 60 apples, how many oranges are there?
6. A recipe for 5 people calls for 1·5 kg of meat. How much meat is required if the recipe is adapted to feed 8 people?
7. A cake for 6 people requires 4 eggs. How many eggs are needed to make a cake big enough for 9 people?
8. A photocopier enlarges the original in the ratio 2 : 3. The height of a tree is 12 cm on the original. How tall is the tree on the enlarged copy?

original

enlarged copy

9. A photocopier enlarges copies in the ratio 4 : 5. The length of the headline 'BRIDGE COLLAPSES' is 18 cm on the original. How long is the headline on the enlarged copy?
10. A photocopier *reduces* in the ratio 5 : 3. The height of a church spire is 12 cm on the original. How tall is the church spire on the reduced copy?

11. A cake weighing 550 g has three ingredients: flour, sugar and raisins. There is twice as much flour as sugar and one and a half times as much sugar as raisins. How much flour is there?

12. If $\frac{5}{8}$ of the children in a school are boys, what is the ratio of boys to girls?

13. A man and a woman share a bingo prize of £1000 between them in the ratio 1 : 4. The woman shares her part between herself, her mother and her daughter in the ratio 2 : 1 : 1. How much does her daughter receive?

14. The number of pages in a newspaper is increased from 36 to 54. The price is increased in the same ratio. If the old price was 28p, what will the new price be?

15. Two friends bought a house for £220 000. Sam paid £140 000 and Joe paid the rest. Three years later they sold the house for £275 000. How much should Sam receive from the sale?

16. Concrete is made from 1 part cement, 2 parts sand and 5 parts aggregate (by volume). How much cement is needed to make 2 m^3 of concrete?

3.4 Approximations

2/5c

A car travels a distance of 158 miles in $3\frac{1}{2}$ hours. What is the average speed?

$$\text{Speed} = \frac{\text{Distance}}{\text{Time}} = \frac{158}{3{\cdot}5}$$

On a calculator the answer is 45·142 857 14 mph.
It is not sensible to give all these figures in the answer. We have used a distance and a time which may not be all that accurate. It would be reasonable to give the answer as '45 mph'.
We can approximate in two ways:

(a) we can give *significant figures* (s.f.)
(b) we can give *decimal places* (d.p.)

Each type of approximation is described below.

Significant figures

Write the following numbers correct to three significant figures (3 s.f.).

(a) 2·6582 = 2·66 (to 3 s.f.)
↑

(b) 0·5142 = 0·514 (to 3 s.f.)
↑

(c) 84 660 = 84 700 (to 3 s.f.)
↑

(d) 0·04031 = 0·0403 (to 3 s.f.)
↑

In each case we look at the number marked with an arrow to see if it is 'five or more'.

Exercise 15

In Questions **1** to **8** write the numbers correct to three significant figures.

1. 2·3462 **2.** 0·81438 **3.** 26·241 **4.** 35·55
5. 112·74 **6.** 210·82 **7.** 0·8254 **8.** 0·031162

In Questions **9** to **16** write the numbers correct to two significant figures.

9. 5·894 **10.** 1·232 **11.** 0·5456 **12.** 0·7163
13. 0·1443 **14.** 1·831 **15.** 24·83 **16.** 31·37

In Questions **17** to **24** write the numbers correct to four significant figures.

17. 486·72 **18.** 500·36 **19.** 2·8888 **20.** 3·1125
21. 0·071542 **22.** 3·0405 **23.** 2463·5 **24.** 488 852

In Questions **25** to **36** write the numbers to the degree of accuracy indicated.

25. 0·5126 (3 s.f.) **26.** 5·821 (2 s.f.) **27.** 65·89 (2 s.f.) **28.** 587·55 (4 s.f.)
29. 0·581 (1 s.f.) **30.** 0·0713 (1 s.f.) **31.** 5·8354 (3 s.f.) **32.** 87·84 (2 s.f.)
33. 2482 (2 s.f.) **34.** 52 666 (3 s.f.) **35.** 0·0058 (1 s.f.) **36.** 6568 (1 s.f.)

Decimal places

Write the following numbers correct to two decimal places (2 d.p.)

(a) 8·358 = 8·36 (to 2 d.p.)
↑

(b) 0·0328 = 0·03 (to 2 d.p.)
↑

(c) 74·355 = 74·36 (to 2 d.p.)
↑

In each case we look at the number marked with an arrow to see if its is 'five or more'.
Here we count figures after the decimal point.

Exercise 16

In Questions **1** to **8** write the numbers correct to two decimal places (2 d.p.).

1. 5·381 **2.** 11·0482 **3.** 0·414 **4.** 0·3666
5. 8·015 **6.** 87·044 **7.** 9·0062 **8.** 0·0724

In Questions **9** to **16** write the numbers correct to one decimal place.

9. 8·424 **10.** 0·7413 **11.** 0·382 **12.** 0·095
13. 6·083 **14.** 19·53 **15.** 8·111 **16.** 7·071

In Questions **17** to **28** write the numbers to the degree of accuracy indicated.

17. 8·155 (2 d.p.) **18.** 3·042 (1 d.p.) **19.** 0·5454 (3 d.p.) **20.** 0·005 55 (4 d.p.)
21. 0·7071 (2 d.p.) **22.** 6·8271 (2 d.p.) **23.** 0·8413 (1 d.p.) **24.** 19·646 (2 d.p.)
25. 0·071 35 (4 d.p.) **26.** 60·051 (1 d.p.) **27.** −7·30 (1 d.p.) **28.** −5·424 (2 d.p.)

29. Use a ruler to measure the dimensions of the rectangles below.
(a) Write down the length and width in cm correct to one d.p.
(b) Work out the area of each rectangle and give the answer in cm^2 correct to one d.p.

(i)
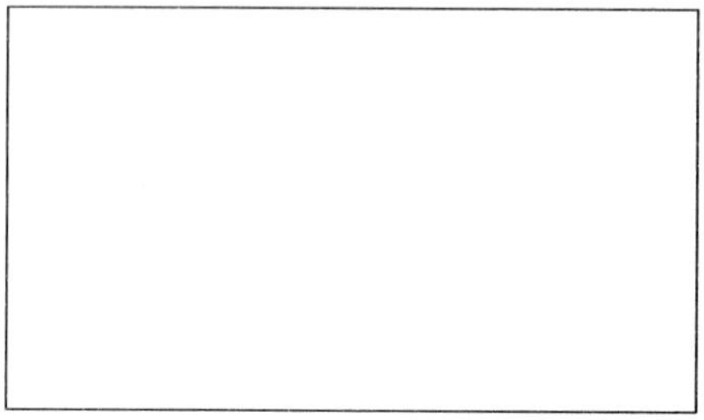

(ii)
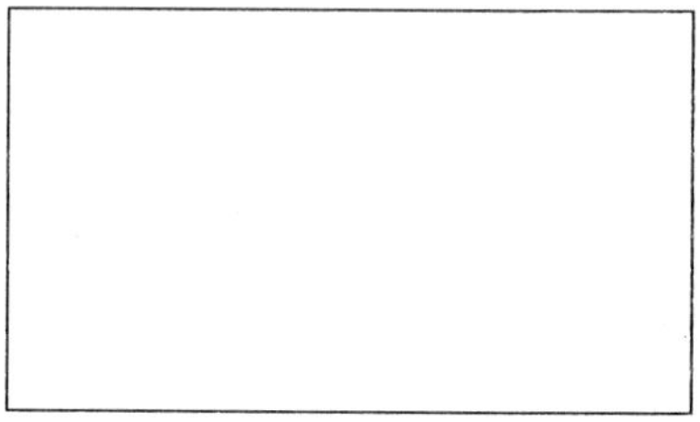

Exercise 17

Write the answers to the degree of accuracy indicated.

1. 0·153 × 3·74 (2 d.p.)
2. 18·09 ÷ 5·24 (3 s.f.)
3. 184 × 2·342 (3 s.f.)
4. 17·2 ÷ 0·89 (1 d.p.)
5. 58 ÷ 261 (2 s.f.)
6. 88·8 × 44·4 (1 d.p.)
7. (8·4 − 1·32) × 7·5 (2 s.f.)
8. (121 + 3758) ÷ 211 (3 s.f.)
9. (1·24 − 1·144) × 0·61 (3 d.p.)
10. 1 ÷ 0·935 (1 d.p.)
11. $78{\cdot}3524^2$ (3 s.f.)
12. $(18{\cdot}25 - 6{\cdot}941)^2$ (2 d.p.)
13. $9{\cdot}245^2 - 65{\cdot}2$ (1 d.p.)
14. (2 − 0·666) ÷ 0·028 (3 s.f.)
15. $8{\cdot}43^3$ (1 d.p.)
16. $0{\cdot}924^2 - 0{\cdot}835^2$ (2 d.p.)

3.5 Metric and Imperial units

2/5d

Metric units

Length: 10 mm = 1 cm	Mass: 1000 g = 1 kg	Volume: 1000 ml = 1 litre
100 cm = 1 m	1000 kg = 1 t	1000 *l* = 1 m^3
1000 m = 1 km	(t for tonne)	Also 1 ml = 1 cm^3

Exercise 18

Copy and complete.

1. 85 cm = m
2. 2·4 km = m
3. 0·63 m = cm
4. 25 cm = m
5. 7 mm = cm
6. 2 cm = mm
7. 1·2 km = m
8. 7 m = cm
9. 0·58 km = m
10. 815 mm = m
11. 650 m = km
12. 25 mm = cm
13. 5 kg = g
14. 4·2 kg = g
15. 6·4 kg = g
16. 3 kg = g
17. 0·8 kg = g
18. 400 g = kg
19. 2 t = kg
20. 250 g = kg
21. 0·5 t = kg
22. 0·62 t = kg
23. 7 kg = t
24. 1500 g = kg
25. 800 ml = l
26. 2 l = ml
27. 1000 ml = l
28. 4·5 l = ml
29. 6 l = ml
30. 3 l = cm^3
31. 2 m^3 = l
32. 5·5 m^3 = l
33. 0·9 l = cm^3
34. 600 cm^3 = l
35. 15 m^3 = l
36. 240 ml = l
37. 28 cm = m
38. 5·5 m = cm
39. 305 g = kg
40. 0·046 km = m
41. 16 ml = l
42. 208 mm = m
43. 28 mm = cm
44. 27 cm = m
45. 788 m = km
46. 14 t = kg
47. 1·3 kg = g
48. 90 l = m^3
49. 2·9 t = kg
50. 19 ml = l

51. Write down the most appropriate metric unit for measuring:
(a) the distance between Glasgow and Leeds
(b) the capacity of a wine bottle
(c) the mass of raisins needed for a cake
(d) the diameter of small drill
(e) the mass of a car
(f) the area of a football pitch.

Imperial units

(a)	12 inches = 1 foot	(b)	16 ounces = 1 pound	(c)	8 pints = 1 gallon
	3 feet = 1 yard		14 pounds = 1 stone		
	1760 yards = 1 mile		2240 pounds = 1 ton		

Exercise 19

1. How many inches are there in two feet?
2. How many ounces are there in three pounds?
3. How many feet are there in ten yards?
4. How many pounds are there in two tons?
5. How many pints are there in six gallons?
6. How many yards are there in ten miles?
7. How many inches are there in one yard?
8. How many pounds are there in five stones?
9. How many pints are there in half a gallon?
10. How many yards are there in half a mile?

In Questions **11** to **30** copy each statement and fill in the missing numbers.

11. 9 feet = yards
12. 16 pints = gallons
13. 2 miles = yards
14. 5 pounds = ounces
15. 10 stones = pounds
16. 4 yards = feet
17. 4 feet = inches
18. 10 tons = pounds
19. 1 mile = feet
20. 6 feet = yards
21. 2 feet 6 inches = inches
22. 5 feet 2 inches = inches
23. 5 stones 6 pounds = pounds
24. 7 stones 3 pounds = pounds
25. $1\frac{1}{2}$ feet = inches
26. $\frac{1}{2}$ pound = ounces
27. 4 feet 10 inches = inches
28. 6 stones 8 pounds = pounds
29. $\frac{1}{4}$ pound = ounces
30. 10 stones 12 pounds = pounds

Changing units

Although the metric system is generally replacing the Imperial system we still need to be able to convert from one set of units to the other.

We will use the following approximate conversions.

1 inch = 2·54 cm	1 gallon = 4·55 litres
1 mile = 1·61 km	1 km = 0·621 mile
1 pound = 0·454 kg	1 litre = 0·22 gallon
1 pint = 0·568 litre	1 kg = 2·2 pounds

(a) Change 3 pints into litres.

1 pint = 0·568 litres
∴ 3 pints = 0·568 × 3 litres
= 1·70 litres (3 s.f.)

(b) Change 2 feet into cm.

2 feet = 24 inches
1 inch = 2·54 cm
∴ 2 feet = 2.54 × 24 cm
= 61·0 cm (3 s.f.)

Exercise 20

Copy each statement and fill in the missing numbers.

1. 10 inches = cm	**2.** 10 gallons = litres	**3.** 100 pounds = kg
4. 100 pints = litres	**5.** 2 miles = km	**6.** 2 pounds = kg
7. 10 miles = km	**8.** 4 inches = cm	**9.** 5 pounds = kg
10. $\frac{1}{2}$ pint = litre	**11.** 10 km = miles	**12.** 100 litres = gallons
13. 3 kg = pounds	**14.** 100 km = miles	**15.** 400 litres = gallons
16. 2 kg = pounds	**17.** 2 km = miles	**18.** 5 litres = gallons
19. 20 kg = pounds	**20.** 20 km = miles	**21.** 1 foot = cm
22. 5 pints = litres	**23.** 3 litres = gallons	**24.** 3 inches = cm

25. A car handbook calls for the oil to be changed every 5000 km. How many miles is that?

26. In a holiday brochure an apartment is described as being '1000 m from a sandy beach'.
(a) Roughly how far is this in miles?
(b) Roughly how long would it take to walk this distance at 'normal' walking speed?

27. (a) On a British road the speed limit is 30 mph. Convert this into a speed in km/h.
(b) On an Italian road the speed limit is 80 km/h. Convert this into a speed in mph.

28. Dutch tomatoes are sold in Britain at 85 pence per pound and the same quality tomatoes are sold in France at 25 francs per kilo. Assume £1 = 10 francs.
(a) Which country has the lower price?
(b) What is the price difference in pence per pound of tomatoes?

29. A car is travelling at a speed of 110 km/h when an accident occurs further along the road. It takes the driver 0·8 seconds to react to the accident. How many *yards* will the car travel in this time interval?

30. A fitter is doing a job which requires a 3 mm drill. He has no metric drills but he does have the following Imperial sizes: $\frac{1}{16}$, $\frac{1}{8}$, $\frac{3}{16}$. Which of these drills is the nearest in size to 3 mm?

31. Convert 1 ounce into grams to the nearest whole number.

Exercise 21

The school's technology department have a wonderful new computer-controlled machine. It is fed with waste plastic and can be programmed to produce any fairly small object. As a demonstration, Mr Evans shows his class how to make dice. He programs the machine to produce centimetre cubes.

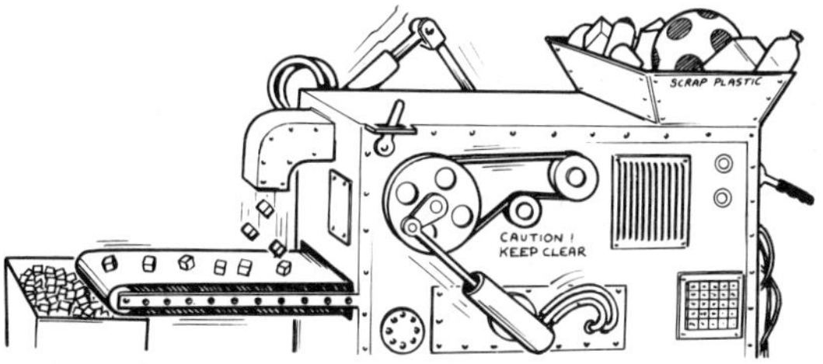

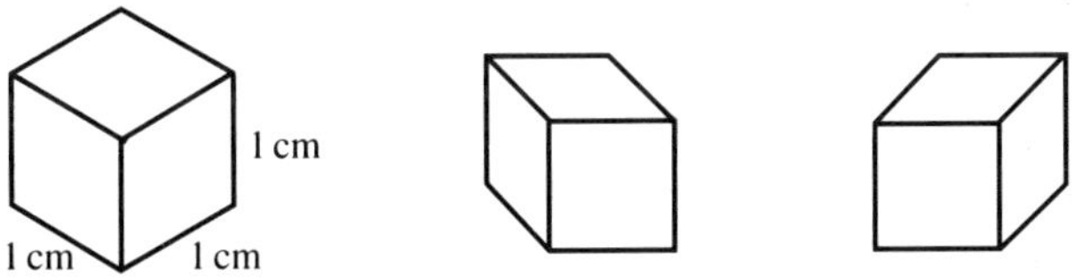

At the end of the afternoon Mr Evans is distracted and he forgets to turn off the machine. As it is a Friday afternoon, the machine works on right through the weekend and by the following Monday morning Mr Evans is the proud owner of one million centimetre cubes, yes one million!
Now Mr Evans is a resourceful man and he decides to sell the cubes for various applications.

1. The million cubes could be stuck together with super glue to make a tower.
Would the tower be as tall as:
(a) Nelson's Column?
(b) The Empire State Building?
(c) Mount Everest?

2. The million cubes could be stuck side by side along the ground.
Would the line be long enough to go:
(a) right around the M25 (115 miles)?
(b) through the Channel Tunnel?

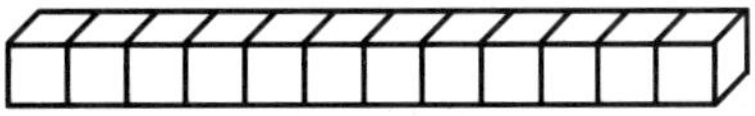

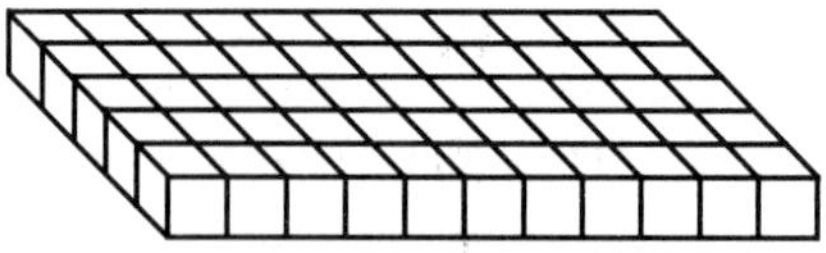

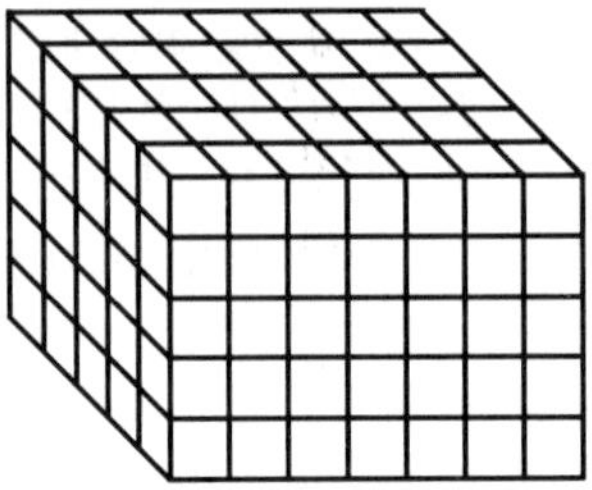

3. If the cubes were placed in a single layer, would there be enough to cover:
(a) the floor of your classroom?
(b) a football pitch?

4. If the cubes were in a solid mass, would there be enough:
(a) to fill your classroom?
(b) to fill a large fridge-freezer?

5. Mrs Evans soon realises the potential of the cubes, which by this time are rather famous, and she sets out to make not a million but a *billion* of the cubes [1,000,000,000].
(a) Would that be enough to fill your classroom?
(b) Placed side by side, roughly how many times would they go around the M25?

3.6 Problems 1

2/6a, 2/6c

Making a profit

A shopkeeper buys potatoes at a wholesale price of £180 per tonne and sells them at a retail price of 22p per kg.
How much profit does he make on one kilogram of potatoes?

He pays £180 for 1000 kg of potatoes. ∴ he pays £[180 ÷ 1000] for 1 kg of potatoes.
i.e. he pays 18p for 1 kg

He sells at 22p per kg.
∴ profit = 4p per kg.

Exercise 22

Find the profit in each case.

Commodity	Retail price	Wholesale price	Profit
1. cans of drink	15p each	£11 per 100	profit per can?
2. rulers	24p each	£130 per 1000	profit per ruler?
3. birthdays cards	22p each	£13 per 100	profit per card?
4. soup	27p per can	£8·50 for 50 cans	profit per can?
5. newspapers	22p each	£36 for 200	profit per paper?
6. box of matches	37p each	£15·20 for 80	profit per box?
7. potatoes	22p per kg	£160 per tonne	profit per kg?
8. carrots	38p per kg	£250 per tonne	profit per kg?
9. T-shirts	£4·95 each	£38·40 per dozen	profit per T-shirt?
10. eggs	96p per dozen	£50 per 1000	profit per dozen?

Commodity	Retail price	Wholesale price	Profit
11. oranges	5 for 30p	£14 for 400	profit per orange?
12. car tyres	£19·50 each	£2450 for 200	profit per tyre?
13. wine	55p for 100 ml	£40 for 10 litres	profit per 100 ml?
14. sand	16p per kg	£110 per tonne	profit per kg?
15. wire	23p per m	£700 for 10 km	profit per m?
16. cheese	£2·64 per kg	£87·50 for 50 kg	profit per kg?
17. copper tube	46p per m	£160 for 500 m	profit per m?
18. apples	9p each	£10·08 per gross	profit per apple?
19. carpet	£6·80 per m^2	£1600 for 500 m^2	profit per m^2?
20. tin of soup	33p per tin	£72 for 400 tins	profit per tin?

Scale readings

Exercise 23

Work out the value indicated by the arrow.

1.
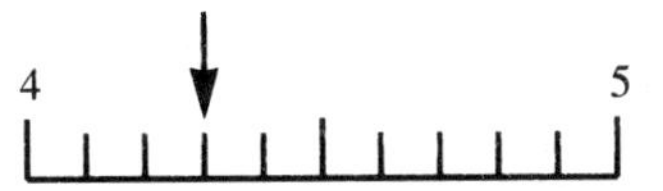

2.
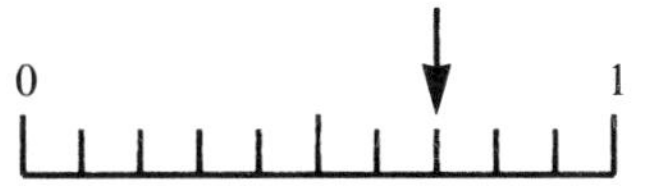

3.
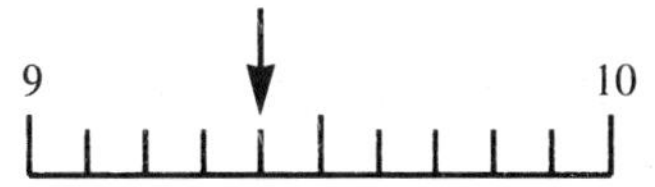

4.
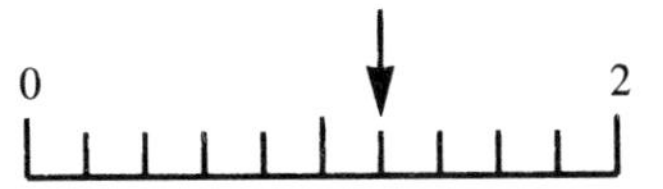

5.
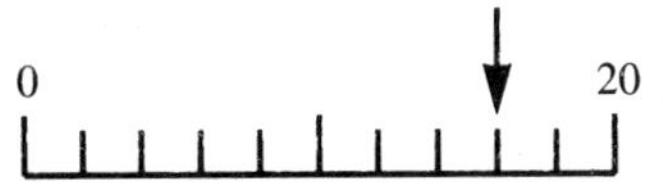

6.
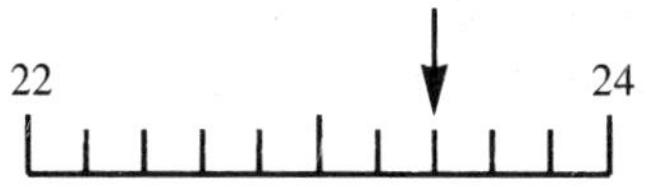

7.
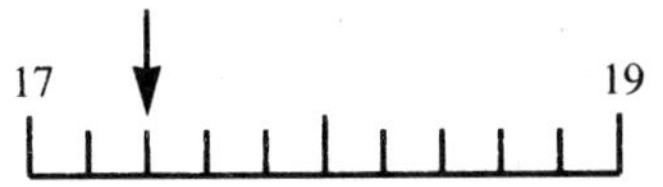

8.
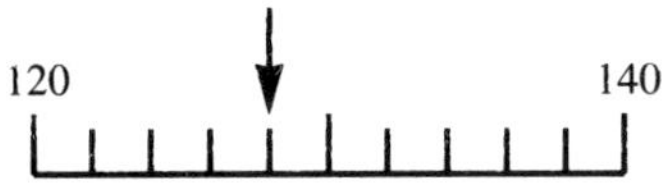

9.
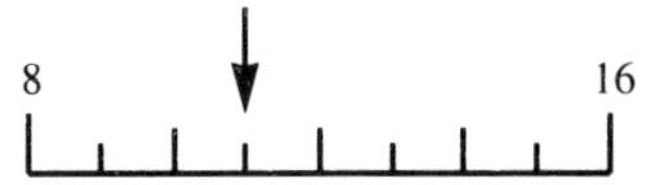

10.
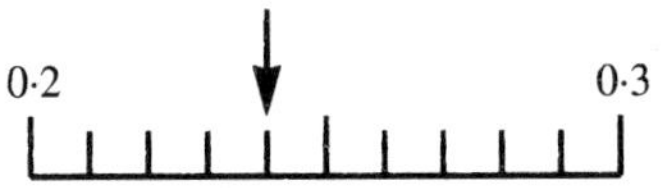

11.
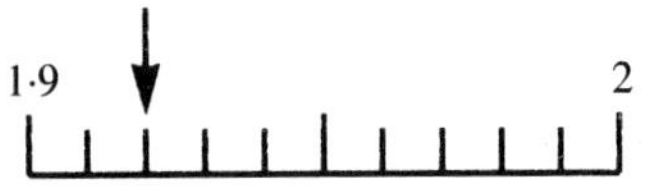

12.

13.
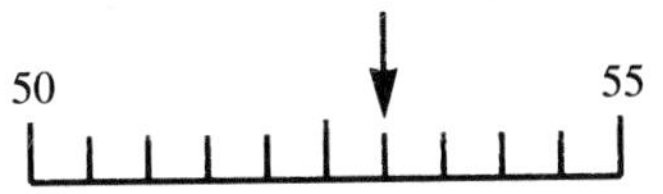

14.
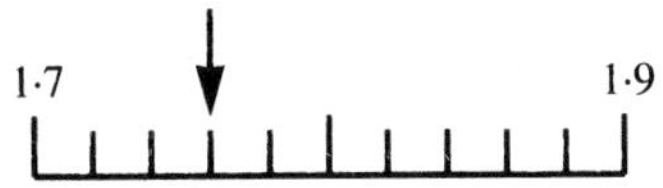

15.
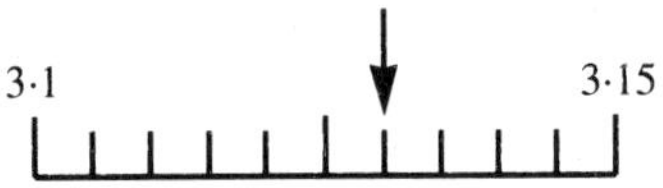

16.
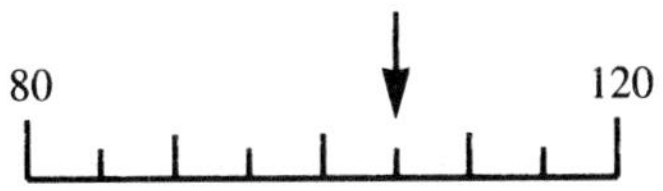

17.
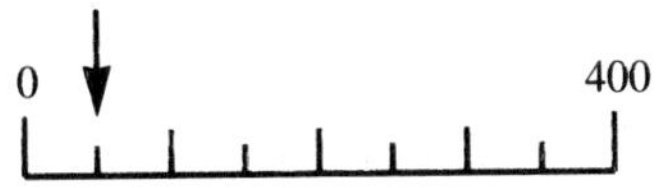

18.
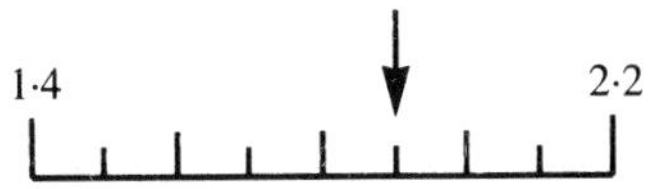

Timetables

Exercise 24

1. For how many minutes do each of the following programmes last:
   (a) 'The money programme',
   (b) 'Fawlty Towers',
   (c) 'Face the press',
   (d) '100 great sporting moments'?
2. How much of a video tape would be used if 'The Jewel in the Crown' and 'The writing on the wall' were recorded?
3. At what time does 'Comrades' start on the 24-hour clock?
4. There were four films on the two channels. What was the title of the shortest film?
5. A video tape is 3 hours long. How much of the tape is not used after taping the two films in the afternoon on Channel 4?
6. How much time is devoted to sport on BBC 2? [Include 'Under sail'].
7. For how many hours and minutes does Channel 4 broadcast programmes?
8. What is the starting time on the 24-hour clock of the programme in which 'Basil' appears?
9. How many programmes were repeats?
10. For how long are 'Pages from Ceefax' broadcast?
11. What is the starting time on the 24-hour clock of the programme in which the 'Redskins' appear?
12. How much of a two hour video tape is not used after taping 'Windmill' and 'The Natural World'?
13. For how many hours and minutes does BBC 2 broadcast programmes?

BBC 2

9.0	**PAGES FROM CEEFAX.**
10.20	**OPEN UNIVERSITY.**
11.25	**PAGES FROM CEEFAX.**
11.50	**CHAMPION THE WONDER HORSE*:** Lost River (rpt). A drought brings danger.
12.15	**WINDMILL:** Archive film on animals.
1.10	**STATES OF MIND:** Jonathan Miller talks to Professor Richard Gregory (rpt.).
2.0	**RUGBY SPECIAL:** Highlights of a County Championship match and a Welsh Cup match.
2.30	**TENNIS:** Benson and Hedges Final.
4.15	**UNDER SAIL:** New series.
4.35	**RACHMANINOV MASTERCLASS.**
5.20	**THINKING ALOUD:** Denis Healey joins a discussion on espionage.
6.0	**NEWS REVIEW,** with Moira Stewart.
6.30	**THE MONEY PROGRAMME:** Guns for Sale. A look at Britain's defence industry.
7.15	**THE NATURAL WORLD:** City of Coral. A voyage beneath the Caribbean.
8.5	**COMRADES:** Educating Rita. The first of 12 films about life in the Soviet Union profiles a young trainee teacher.
8.50	**100 GREAT SPORTING MOMENTS:** Daley Thompson's Gold in the Moscow Olympics.
9.10	**FAWLTY TOWERS:** Basil and Sybil fall out over alterations to the hotel (rpt.).
9.40	**FILM:** A Dangerous Summer (see Film Guide).
11.5	**TENNIS:** Benson and Hedges Final.
11.55	**MUSIC AT NIGHT. 12.10 CLOSE.**

CHANNEL 4

1.5	**IRISH ANGLE — HANDS:** Basket Maker.
1.30	**FACE THE PRESS:** Graham Kelly, Secretary of the Football League, questioned by Ian Wooldridge of the Daily Mail and Brian Glanville of the Sunday Times.
2.0	**POB'S PROGRAMME,** with Patricia Hodge.
2.30	**FILM*:** Journey Together (see Film Guide).
4.15	**FILM*:** The London Blackout Murders, with John Abbot (see Film Guide).
5.15	**NEWS; WEATHER,** followed by **THE BUSINESS PROGRAMME.**
6.0	**AMERICAN FOOTBALL:** Dallas Cowboys at Washington Redskins.
7.15	**THE HEART OF THE DRAGON:** Understanding (rpt.).
8.15	**THE JEWEL IN THE CROWN (T):** The Towers of Silence (rpt.).
9.15	**THE WRITING ON THE WALL:** Who Governs? The political events of 1974 recalled by Robert Kee.
10.25	**FILM*:** Seven Days to Noon (see Film Guide). **12.10 CLOSE.**

Exercise 25

1. There are 1128 pupils in a school and there are 36 more girls than boys. How many girls attend the school?
2. A generous, but not very bright, teacher decides to award 1p to the person coming 10th in a test, 2p to the person coming 9th, 4p to the person coming 8th and so on, doubling the amount each time. How much does the teacher award to the person who came top?
3. A tree was planted when James Wilkinson was born. He died in 1920, aged 75. How old was the tree in 1975?
4. Washing-up liquid is sold in 200 ml containers. Each container costs 57p. How much will it cost to buy 10 litres of the liquid?
5. A train is supposed to leave London at 11 24 and arrive in Brighton at 12 40. The train was delayed and arrived $2\frac{1}{4}$ hours late. At what time did the train arrive?
6. Big Ben stopped for repairs at 17 15 on Tuesday and restarted at 08 20 on Wednesday. For how long had it been stopped?

7. How much would I pay for nine litres of paint if two litres cost £2·30?
8. A television set was advertised at £282·50 for cash, or by 12 equal instalments of £25·30. How much would be saved by paying cash?
9. Eggs are packed twelve to a box. A farmer has enough eggs to fill 316 boxes with unbroken eggs and he has 62 cracked eggs left over. How many eggs had he to start with?
10. A car travels 30 miles on a gallon of petrol and petrol costs £2·20 per gallon. Over a period of one year the car travels a distance of 9600 miles. How much does the petrol cost for the whole year?

Exercise 26

1. Copy and complete the following bill.

$6\frac{1}{2}$ lb of potatoes at 12p per lb = £
4 lb of beef at   per lb = £7·20
   jars of coffee at 95p per jar = £6·65
Total = £

2. A hotel manager was able to buy loaves of bread at £4·44 per dozen, whereas the shop price was 43p per loaf. How much did he save on each loaf?

3. John Lowe made darts history in 1984 with the first ever perfect game played in a tournament, 501 scored in just nine darts. He won a special prize of £100 000 from the sponsors of the tournament. His first eight darts were six treble 20s, treble 17 and treble 18.
(a) What did he score with the ninth dart?
(b) How much did he win per dart thrown, to the nearest pound?

4. How many 50 ml bottles can be filled from a jar containing 7 litres of liquid?

5. (a) Which four coins make a total of 77p?
(b) Which five coins make a total of 86p?
(c) Which five coins make a total of £1·57?

6. Two numbers m and z are such that z is greater than 10 and m is less than 8. Arrange the numbers 9, z and m in order of size, starting with the smallest.

7. One day a third of the class is absent and 16 children are present. How many children are in the class when no one is away?

8. A train leaves Manchester at 09 00 and travels towards London at 100 mph. Another train leaves London for Manchester, also at 09 00, and travels at 80 mph. Which train is nearer to London when they meet?

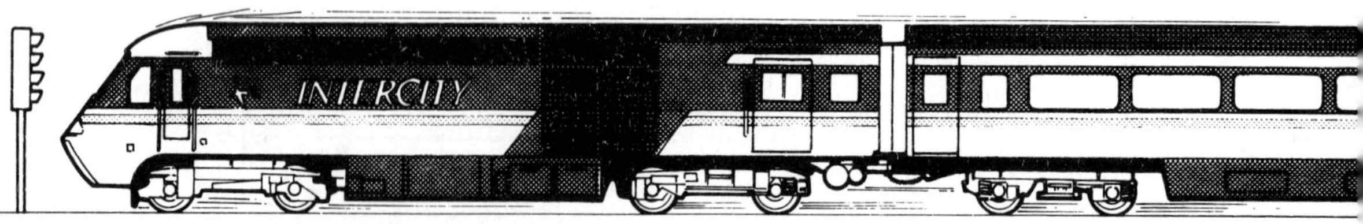

9. A man is 35 cm taller than his daughter, who is 5 cm shorter than her mother. The man was born in 1949 and is 1·80 m tall. How tall is the wife?

10. In a simple code A – 1, B – 2, C – 3, ... Z – 26.
Decode the following messages.
(a) 23, 8, 1, 20
20, 9, 13, 5
4, 15
23, 5
6, 9, 14, 9, 19, 8.
(b) 19, 4^2, (3×7), 18, $(90 - 71)$
1^3, (9×2), $(2^2 + 1^2)$
18, $(\frac{1}{5}$ of $105)$, 2, $(1 \div \frac{1}{2})$, 3^2, 19, 2^3.
(c) 23, $(100 \div 20)$
1, $(2 \times 3 \times 3)$, $(2^2 + 1^2)$
21, $(100 - 86)$, $(100 \div 25)$, 5, $(2^4 + 2)$
1, (5×4), $(10 \div \frac{1}{2})$, 1, $(27 \div 9)$, $(99 \div 9)$.

Exercise 27

1. Twelve calculators cost £102. How many calculators could be bought for £76·50?

2. A car travels 35 m in 0·7 seconds. How far does it travel in
(a) 0·1 s? (b) 1 s? (c) 2 minutes?

3. The outline of a 50p coin is shown below.

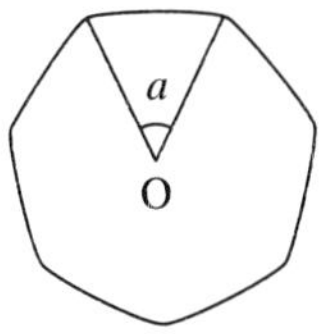

O is the centre of the coin

Calculate the size of the angle, a, to the nearest $\frac{1}{10}$ of a degree.

4. The diagram below shows the map of a farm which grows four different crops in the regions shown.

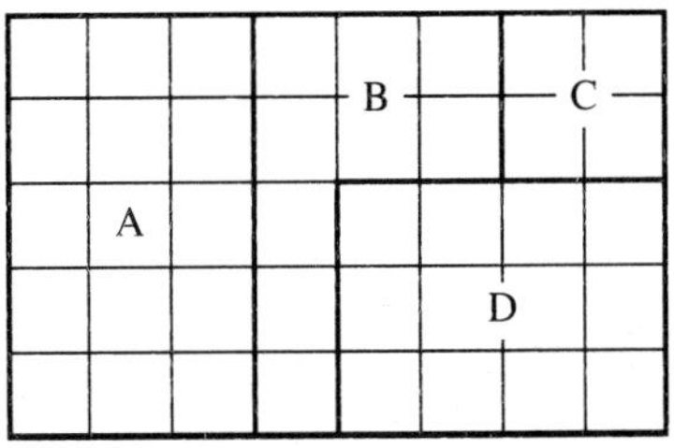

Each square represents one acre.
(a) What is the total area of the farm?
(b) What area is used for crop A?
(c) What percentage of the farm is used for
(i) crop C (ii) crop D
(iii) crop A (iv) crop B?

5. An examination is marked out of a total of 120 marks. How many marks did Alan get if he scored 65% of the marks?

6. A man worked 7 hours per day from Monday to Friday and 4 hours overtime on Saturday. The rate of pay from Monday to Friday is £4·50 per hour and the overtime rate is time and a half. How much did he earn during the week?

7. A man smokes 40 cigarettes a day and each packet of 20 cigarettes costs £1·15. How much does he spend on cigarettes in a whole year of 365 days?

8. A shopkeeper buys coffee at £3·65 per kg and sells it at 95p per 100 g. How much profit does he make per kg?

9. Five 2's can make 25: $25 = 22 + 2 + \frac{2}{2}$

(a) Use four 9's to make 100
(b) Use three 6's to make 7
(c) Use three 5's to make 60
(d) Use five 5's to make 61
(e) Use four 7's to make 1
(f) Use three 8's to make 11

10. Find the missing digits.

(a)

	2	
+	5	4
		7

(b)

	1	7
+		6
	6	

(c)

	5		2
+	1	3	
		1	8

(d)

	4		4
+		5	
	8	2	4

(e)

	8	
−		4
	5	2

(f)

	8		2
−		5	
	2	3	2

Exercise 28

1. A special new cheese is on offer at £3·48 per kilogram. Mrs Mann buys half a kilogram. How much change does she receive if she pays with a £5 note?

2. A cup and a saucer together cost £2·80. The cup costs 60p more than the saucer. How much does the cup cost?

3. A garden 9 m by 12 m is to be treated with fertilizer. One cup of fertilizer covers an area of 2 m^2 and one bag of fertilizer is sufficient for 18 cups.
(a) Find the area of the garden.
(b) Find the number of bags of fertilizer needed.

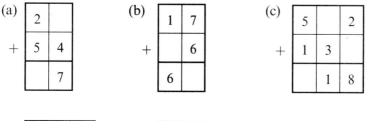

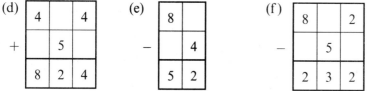

4. Copy and complete the pattern below.

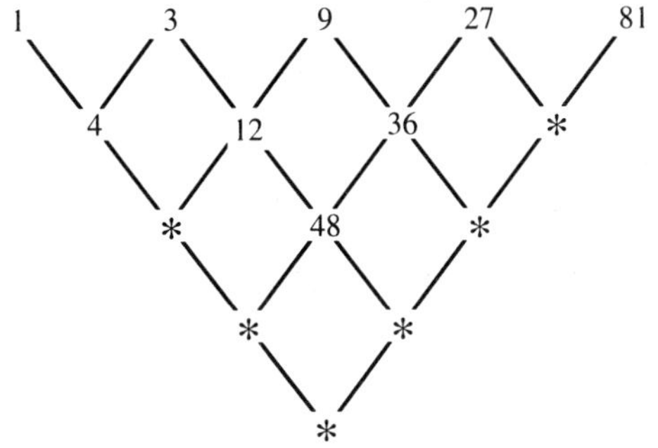

5. Six lamp posts lie at equal distances from each other along a straight road. If the distance between each pair of lamp posts is 20 m, how far is it from the first lamp post to the sixth?

6. An engineering firm offers all of its workers a choice of two pay rises. Workers can choose either an 8% increase on their salaries or they can accept a rise of £800.
(a) A fitter earns £5200 a year. Which pay rise should he choose?
(b) The personnel manager earns £11 500 a year. Which pay rise should he choose?

7. A ship's voyage started at 20 30 on Tuesday and finished at 07 00 on the next day.
How long was the journey in hours and minutes?

8. Work out, without using a calculator.

(a) $0{\cdot}6 - 0{\cdot}06$	(b) $0{\cdot}04 \times 1000$
(c) $0{\cdot}4 \div 100$	(d) $7{\cdot}2 - 5$
(e) 10% of £90	(f) 25% of £160.

9. In 1984 the population of the United States was 232 million. The population was expected to grow by 12% by the end of the century. Find the expected population at the end of the century, correct to the nearest million.

10. Find two numbers which:
(a) multiply to give 12 and add up to 7.
(b) multiply to give 42 and add up to 13.
(c) multiply to give 32 and add up to 12.
(d) multiply to give 48 and add up to 26.

Exercise 29

1. In a simple code A = 1, B = 2, C = 3 and so on. When the word 'BAT' is written in code its total score is $(2 + 1 + 20) = 23$.
(a) Find the score for the word 'ZOOM'
(b) Find the score for the word 'ALPHABET'
(c) Find a word with a score of 40.

2. How many cubes, each of edge 1 cm, are required to fill a box with internal dimensions 5 cm by 8 cm by 3 cm?

3. A swimming pool 20 m by 12 m contains water to a uniform depth of $1\frac{1}{2}$ m. 1 m^3 of water weighs 1000 kg. What is the weight of the water in the pool?

4. Place the following numbers in order of size, smallest first: 0·12, 0·012, 0·21, 0·021, 0·03.

5. The houses in a street are numbered from 1 to 60. How many times does the number '2' appear?

6. Draw a large copy of the square below.

1	2	3	4

Your task is to fill up all 16 squares using four 1's, four 2's, four 3's and four 4's. Each number may appear only once in any row (↔) or column (↕). The first row has been drawn already.

7. Between the times 11 57 and 12 27 the mileometer of a car changes from 23793 miles to 23825 miles. At what average speed is the car travelling?

8. Which of the shapes below can be drawn without going over any line twice and without taking the pencil from the paper? Write 'yes' or 'no' for each shape.

(a)
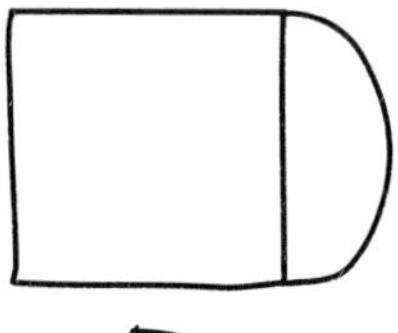

(b)
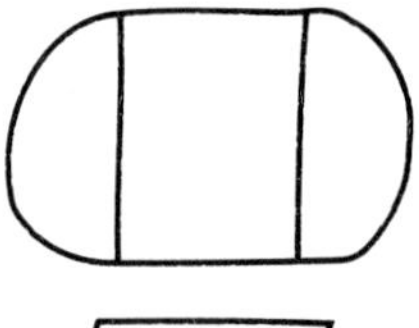

(c)
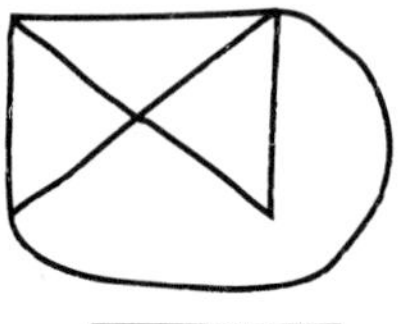

(d)
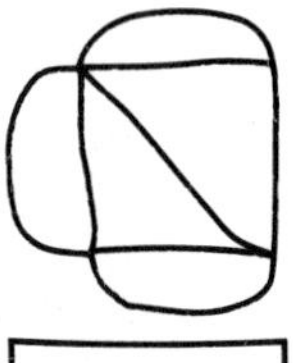

(e)

(f)
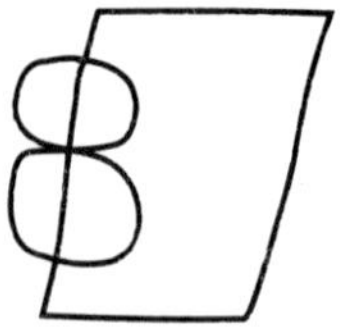

(g)
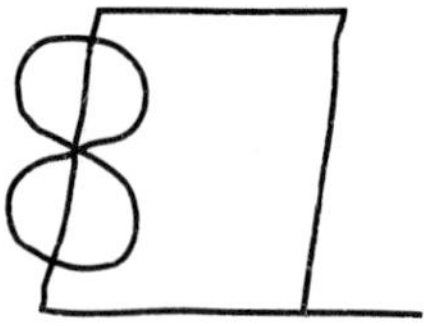

(h)

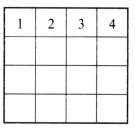

4 Handling data 1

4.1 Displaying data

5/5c

Raw data in the form of numbers is collected when surveys or experiments are conducted. This sort of information is often much easier to understand when either a pie chart or a frequency diagram is drawn.

Pie charts

The pie chart shows the holiday intentions of 600 people.

(a) Number of people camping $= \frac{60}{360} \times 600$
$= 100.$

(b) Number of people touring $= \frac{72}{360} \times 600$
$= 100.$

(c) Number of people at seaside $= \frac{102}{360} \times 600$
$= 170.$

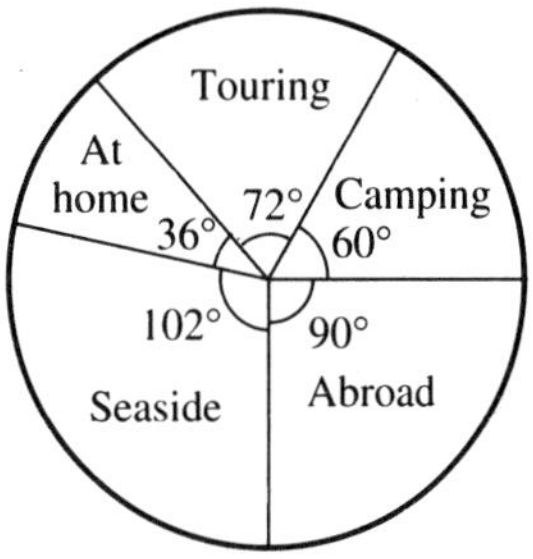

Exercise 1

1. The total cost of a holiday was £900. The pie chart shows how this cost was made up.

(a) How much was spent on food?
(b) How much was spent on travel?
(c) How much was spent on the hotel?
(d) How much was spent on other items?

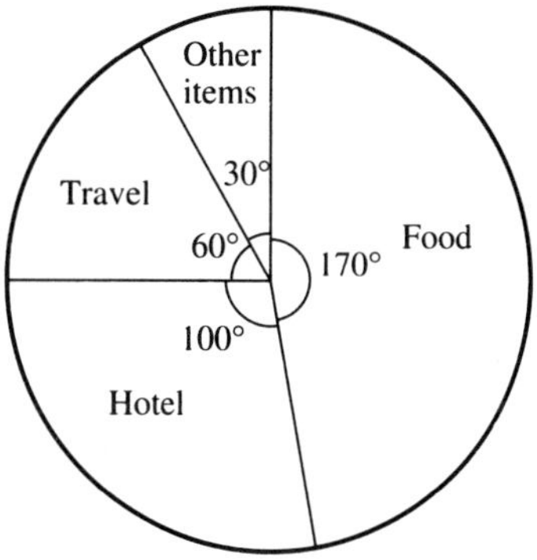

2. Mr Billingsgate had an income of £6000. The pie chart shows how he used the money.

How much did he spend on
(a) Food,
(b) Rent,
(c) Savings,
(d) Entertainment,
(e) Travel?

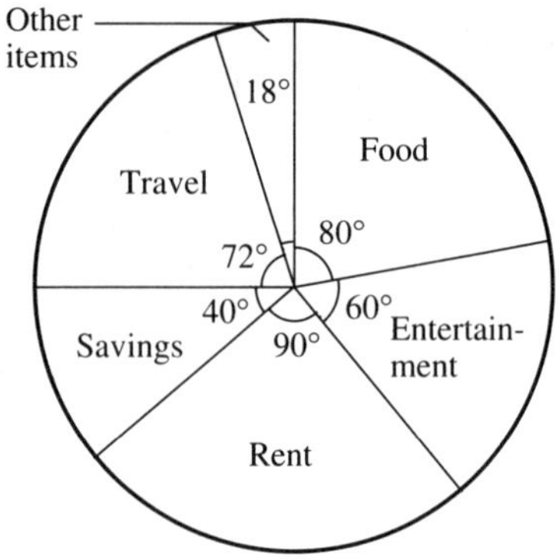

3. The total expenditure of a County Council is £36 000 000. The pie chart shows how the money was spent.

(a) How much was spent on
(i) Education (ii) Social services?
(b) What is the angle representing expenditure on highways?
(c) How much was spent on highways?

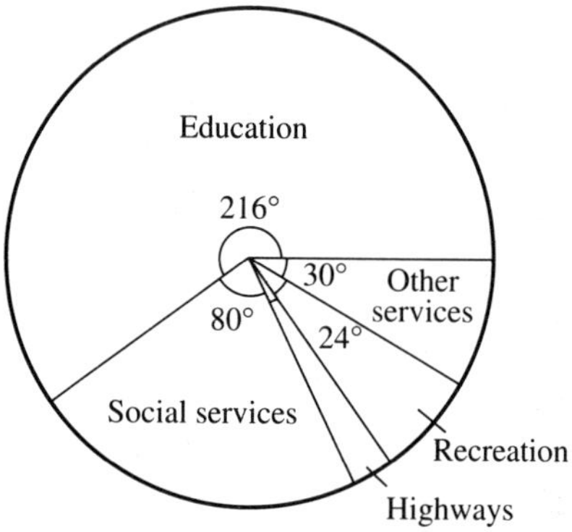

4. The pie chart shows how a pupil spends her time in a maths lesson which lasts 60 minutes.

(a) How much time does she spend:
(i) Getting ready to work,
(ii) Talking,
(iii) Sharpening a pencil?
(b) She spends 3 minutes working. What is the angle on the pie chart for the time spent working?

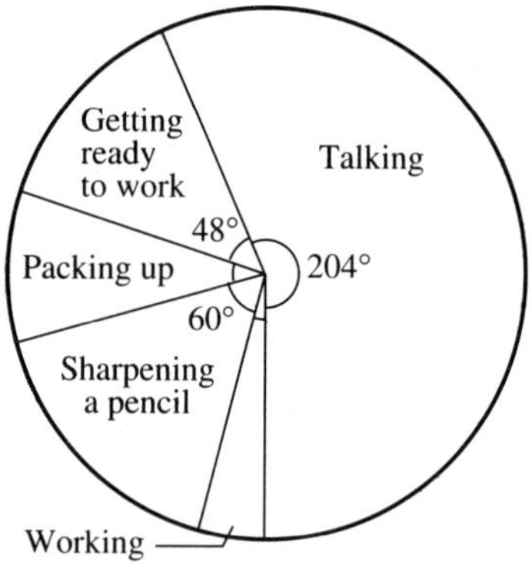

Exercise 2

1. At the semi-final stage of the F.A. Cup, 72 neutral referees were asked to predict who they thought would win. Their answers were:

Spurs	9	Everton	22
Manchester United	40	York City	1

(a) Work out
(i) $\frac{9}{72}$ of 360° (ii) $\frac{40}{72}$ of 360° (iii) $\frac{22}{72}$ of 360° (iv) $\frac{1}{72}$ of 360°
(b) Draw an accurate pie chart to display the predictions of the 72 referees.

2. A survey was carried out to find what 400 pupils did at the end of the fifth year:

120 went into the sixth form
160 went into employment
80 went to F.E. colleges
40 were unemployed.

(a) Simplify the following fractions: $\frac{120}{400}$; $\frac{160}{400}$; $\frac{80}{400}$; $\frac{40}{400}$.

(b) Draw an accurate pie chart to show the information above.

3. In a survey on washing powder 180 people were asked to state which brand they preferred. 45 chose Brand A.

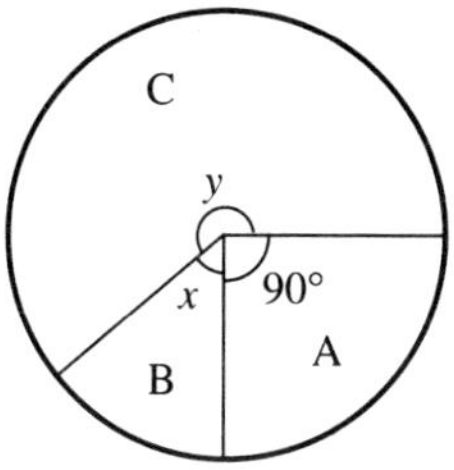

If 30 people chose brand B and 105 chose Brand C, calculate the angles x and y.

4. A packet of breakfast cereal weighing 600 g contains four ingredients as follows:

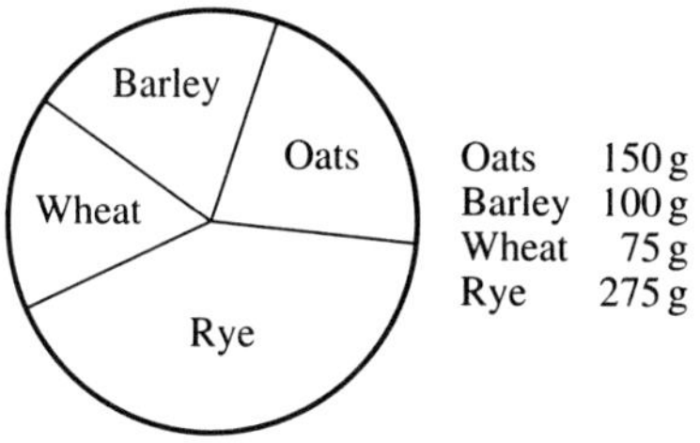

Calculate the angles on the pie chart shown and draw an accurate diagram.

5. The table below shows the share of British car sales achieved by four companies in one year.

Company	A	B	C	D
Share of sales	50%	10%	25%	15%

In a pie chart to show this information, find the angle of the sectors representing:

(a) Company A (b) Company B
(c) Company C (d) Company D.

Frequency diagrams and bar charts

The marks obtained by 36 pupils in a test were as follows.

1	3	2	3	4	2	1	3	0
5	3	0	1	4	0	4	4	3
3	4	3	1	3	4	3	1	2
1	3	4	0	4	3	2	5	3

Here is the tally chart for this data.

Mark	Tally	Frequency
0	||||	4
1	𝍸 |	6
2	||||	4
3	𝍸 𝍸 ||	12
4	𝍸 |||	8
5	||	2

The same information is shown on a frequency diagram.

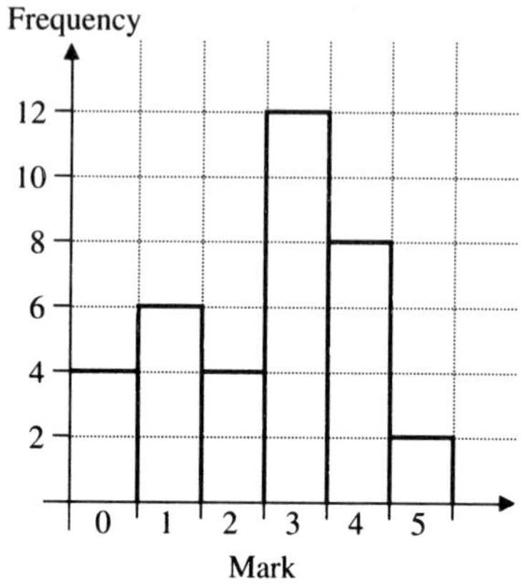

Exercise 3

1. In a survey, the number of occupants in the cars passing a school was recorded.

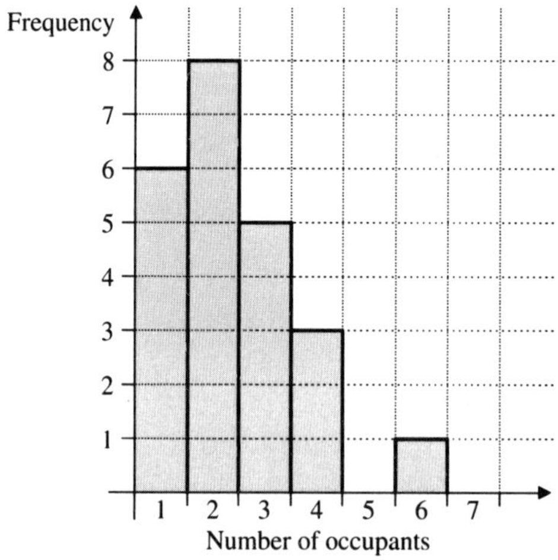

(a) How many cars had 3 occupants?
(b) How many cars had less than 4 occupants?
(c) How many cars were in the survey?
(d) What was the total number of occupants in all the cars in the survey?
(e) What fraction of the cars had only one occupant?

2. In an experiment, two dice were thrown sixty times and the total score showing was recorded.

2	3	5	4	8	6	4	7	5	10
7	8	7	6	12	11	8	11	7	6
6	5	7	7	8	6	7	3	6	7
12	3	10	4	3	7	2	11	8	5
7	10	7	5	7	5	10	11	7	10
4	8	6	4	6	11	6	12	11	5

(a) Draw a tally chart to show the results of the experiment. The tally chart is started below.

Score	Tally marks	Frequency
2	॥	2
3	||||	4
4		
.		
.		

(b) Draw a frequency graph to illustrate the results. Plot the frequency on the vertical axis.

3. The bar chart shows the profit/loss made by a toy shop from September 1994 to April 1995.

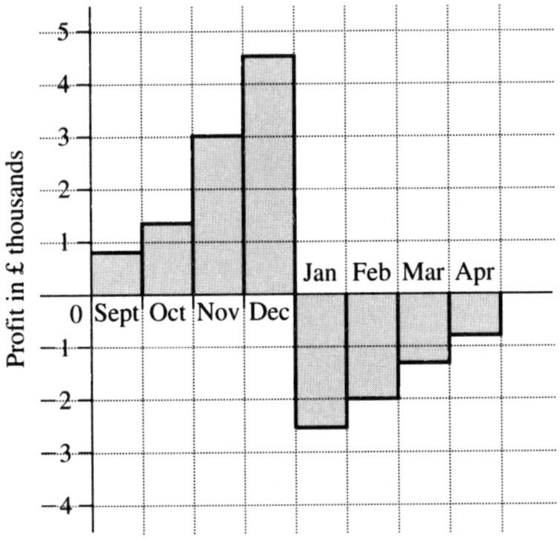

(a) Estimate the total profit in this period.
(b) Describe what is happening to the shop's profits in this period. Try to think of an explanation for the shape of the bar chart.

Grouped data

Sometimes the data to be displayed can take a wide range of values. In such cases, it is convenient to put the data into groups before drawing a tally chart and frequency diagram.

The hand spans  of children were measured as follows:

14·8	20·0	16·9	20·7	18·1	17·5	18·7
19·0	19·8	17·8	14·3	19·2	21·7	17·4
16·0	15·9	18·5	19·3	16·6	21·2	18·4

The smallest value is 14·3 cm and the largest is 21·7 cm.
The data can be grouped as follows and the frequency diagram drawn.

<table>
<tr><th>Class intervals</th><th>Tally</th></tr>
<tr><td>$14 \leqslant s < 16$</td><td>|||</td></tr>
<tr><td>$16 \leqslant s < 18$</td><td>卌 |</td></tr>
<tr><td>$18 \leqslant s < 20$</td><td>卌 |||</td></tr>
<tr><td>$20 \leqslant s < 22$</td><td>||||</td></tr>
</table>

Notice that '20·0' goes into the last group $20 \leqslant s < 22$.

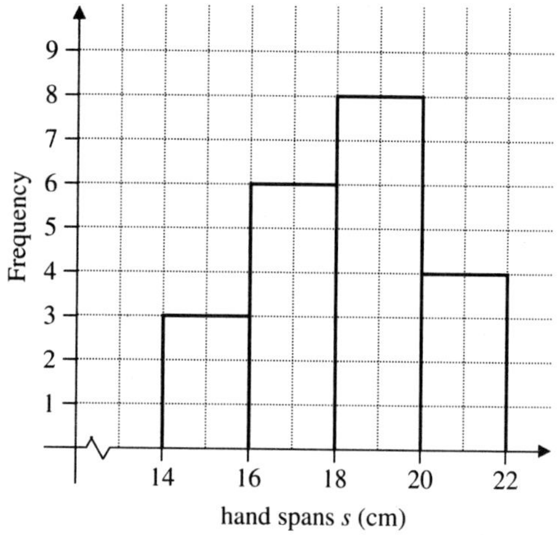

Exercise 4

1. The graph shows the heights of pupils in a class.
   (a) How many pupils were over 150 cm tall?
   (b) How many pupils had a height between 135 cm and 155 cm?
   (c) How many pupils were in the class?
   (d) Would you expect the graph to be this shape or a different shape? Explain why.

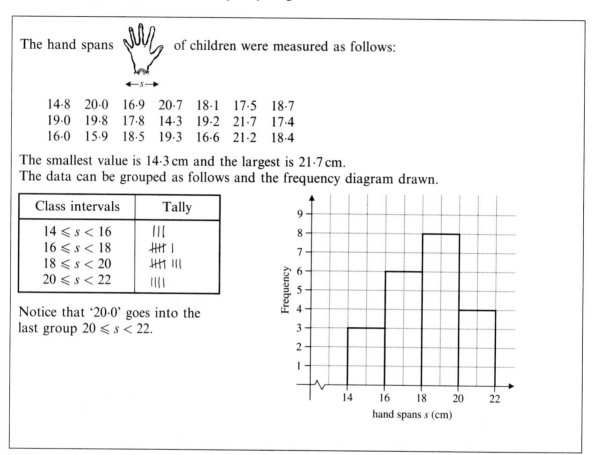

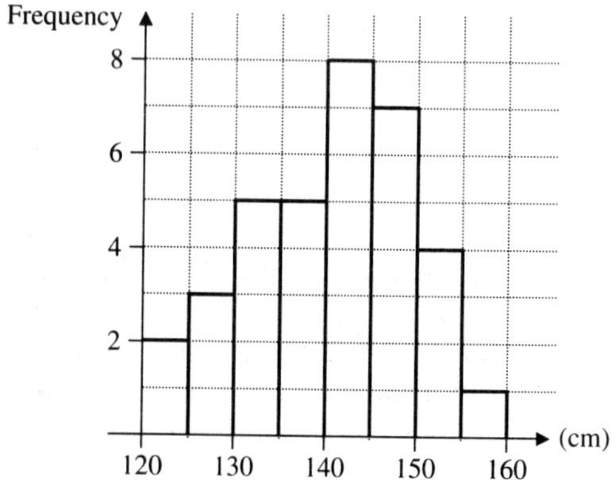

2. In a survey, the heights of children aged 15 were measured in four countries around the world. A random sample of children was chosen by computer, not necessarily the same number from each country.

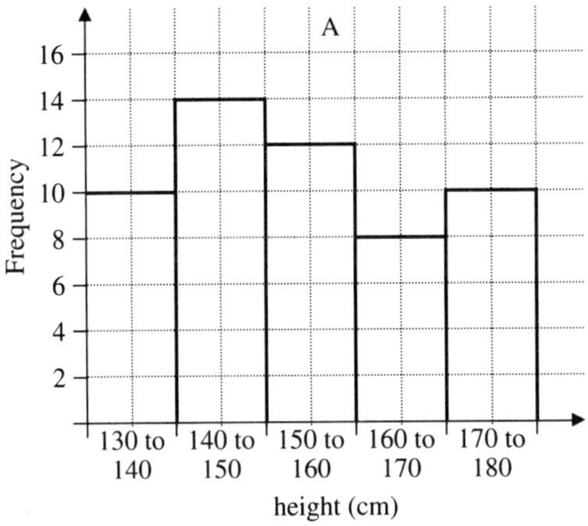

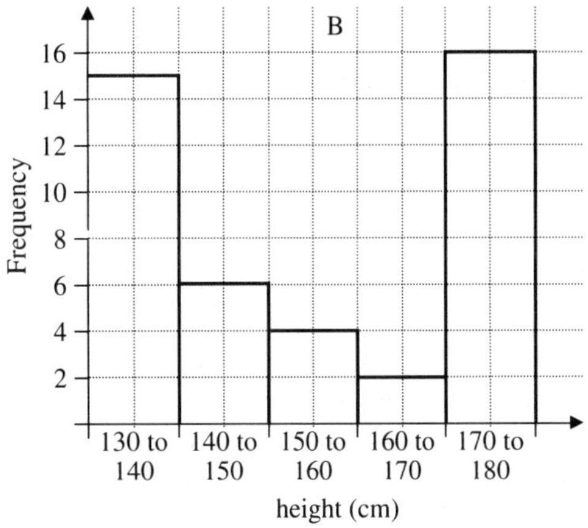

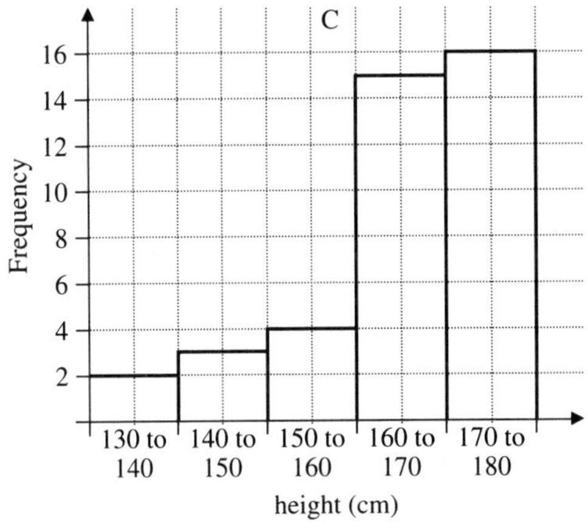

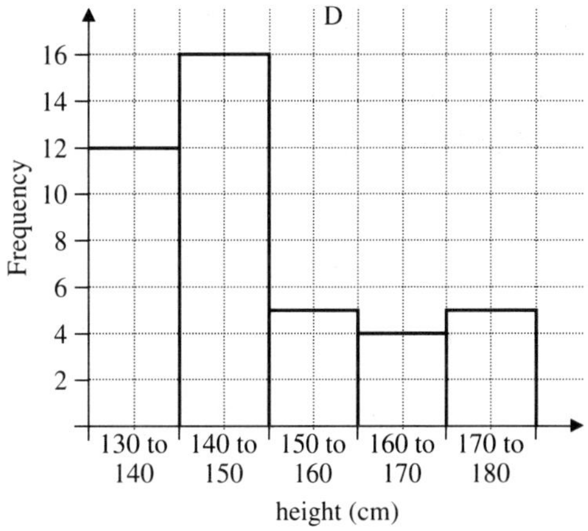

Use the graphs to identify the country in each of the statements below.

(a) Country ____ is poor and the diet of children is not good. Two thirds of the children were less than 150 cm tall.

(b) There were 54 children in the sample from Country ____.

(c) In Country ____ the heights were spread fairly evenly across the range 130 to 180 cm.

(d) Country ____ is famous for producing lots of good high jumpers and basketball players.

(e) The smallest sample of children came from Country ____.

(f) In Country ____ three quarters of the children were either tall or short.

3. Scientists have developed a new fertilizer which is supposed to increase the size of carrots. A farmer grew carrots in two adjacent fields A and B and treated one of the fields with the new fertilizer. A random sample of 50 carrots was taken from each field and weighed. Here are the results for Field A (all in grams).

118	91	82	105	72	92	103	95	73	109
63	111	102	116	101	104	107	119	111	108
112	97	100	75	85	94	76	67	93	112
70	116	118	103	65	107	87	98	105	117
114	106	82	90	77	88	66	99	95	103

Make a tally chart using the groups given.

weight	tally	frequency
$60 \leqslant w < 70$		
$70 \leqslant w < 80$		
$80 \leqslant w < 90$		
$90 \leqslant w < 100$		
$100 \leqslant w < 110$		
$110 \leqslant w < 120$		

The frequency graph for Field B is shown below.

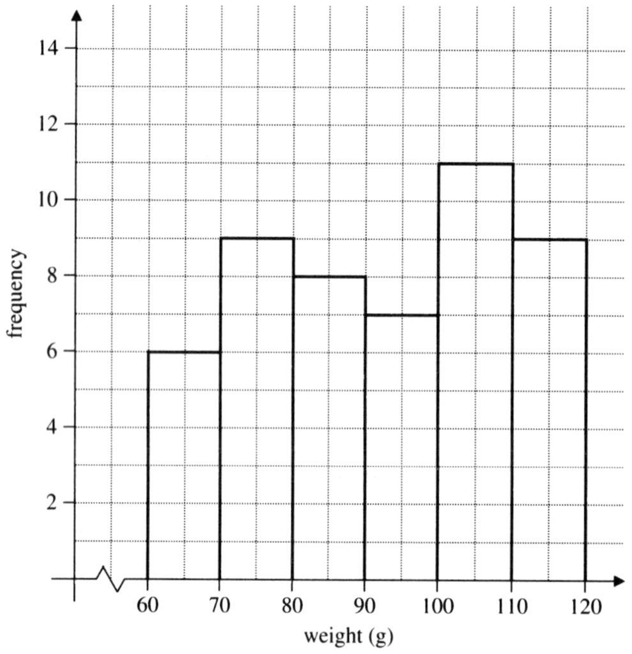

Copy the graph above and, in a different colour, draw the graph for Field A.
Which field do you think was treated with the new fertilizer?

4.

Vitamin
Vitamins take Johnny to the top of the class!
IT'S ALL
It's all in the pills!

Some people think that childrens' IQ's can be increased when they eat extra vitamins.
In an experiment, 52 children took an IQ test before and then after a course of vitamin pills. Here are the results.

Before:

81	107	93	104	103	96	101	102	93	105	82	106	97
108	94	111	92	86	109	95	116	92	94	101	117	102
95	108	112	107	106	124	125	103	127	118	113	91	113
113	114	109	128	115	86	106	91	85	119	129	99	98

After:

93	110	92	125	99	127	114	98	107	128	103	91	104
103	83	125	91	104	99	102	116	98	115	92	117	97
126	100	112	113	85	108	97	101	125	93	102	107	116
94	117	95	108	117	96	102	87	107	94	103	95	96

(a) Put the scores into convenient groups between 80 and 130.
(b) Draw two frequency graphs to display the results.
(c) Write a conclusion. Did the vitamin pills make a significant difference?

Conversion graphs

Exercise 5

Draw the graph and then answer the questions.

1. (a) Convert into dollars
   (i) £2 (ii) £1.60 (iii) £2.40
   (b) Convert into pounds
   (i) \$1 (ii) \$3.50 (iii) \$2.50

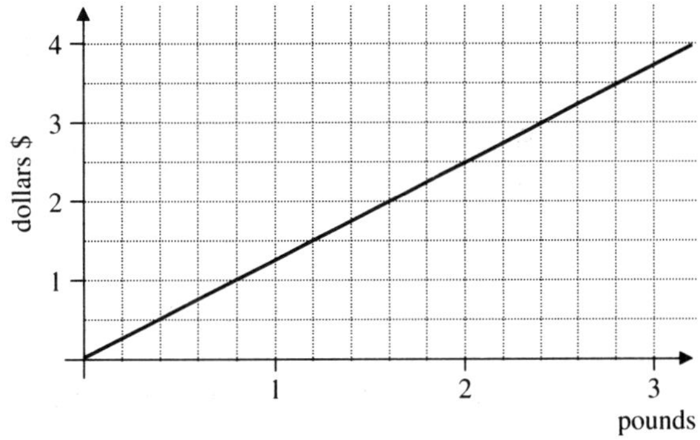

2. Give your answers as accurately as you can.
[e.g. 3 lb = 1·4 kg approximately]
(a) Convert into kilograms
(i) 5·5 lb (ii) 8 lb (iii) 2 lb
(b) Convert into pounds
(i) 2 kg (ii) 3 kg (iii) 1·5 kg
(c) A bag of sugar weighs 1 kg. What is its weight in pounds?
(d) A washing machine has a weight limit of 7 lb. What is the weight limit in kilograms?

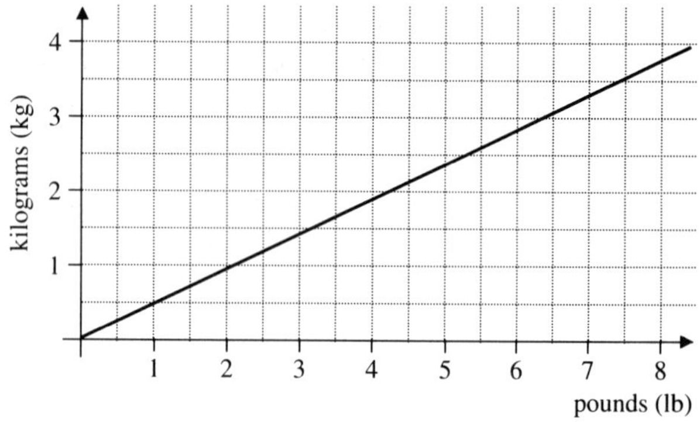

3. Between 1984 and 1994 the value of the pound against the German mark changed.
(a) How much less in DM did you receive for £1 in 1994 compared with 1984?
(b) Express this change as a percentage of the number of marks received in 1984.

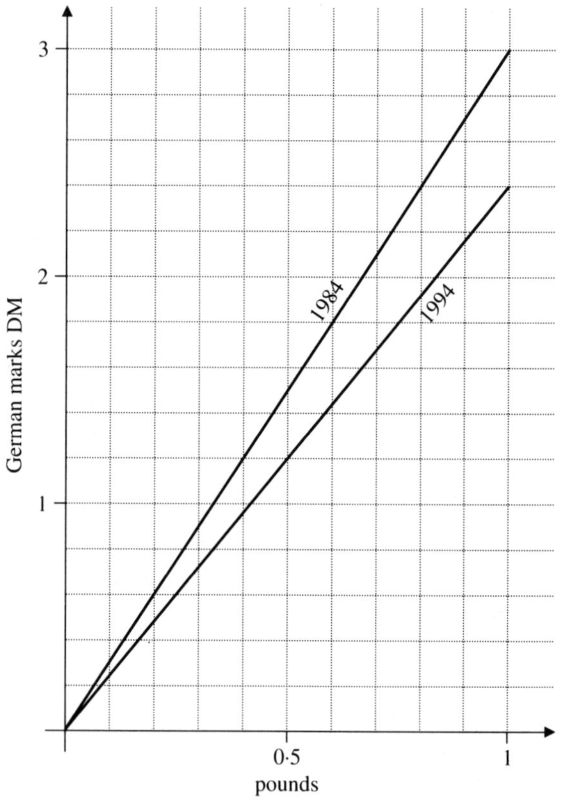

4. Temperature can be measured in °C or in °F. A conversion graph can be constructed using two points as follows:
Draw axes with a scale of 1 cm to 5° as shown.

32° F = 0° C and 95° F = 35° C.

Draw a line through these two points.
Use your graph to convert:
(a) 50° F into °C
(b) 20° C into °F
(c) 0° F into °C

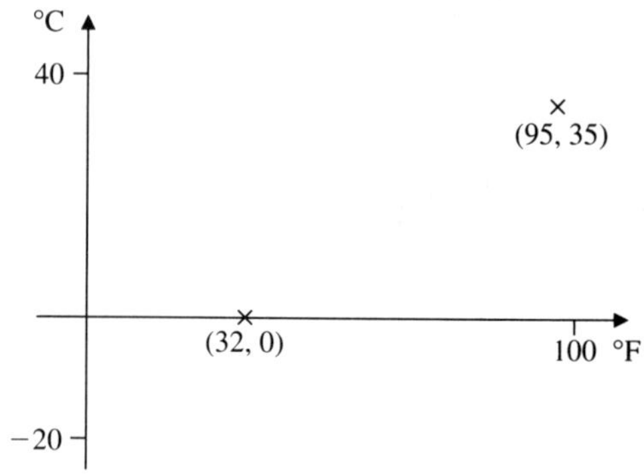

4.2 Questionnaires

3/3b, 3/8a, 3/8a

Surveys are conducted by organisations for a variety of reasons.

- Newspapers publish opinion polls about the voting intentions of people or the popularity of the Prime Minister. They provide interesting stories for the newspaper.

- Car makers conduct surveys to find what features most people want to have in their cars such as radios, electric windows, sun roofs and so on. They then use the survey results to help with the design of future models.

- Supermarkets like Tescos or Sainsburys conduct surveys to discover what things are most important to their customers. They might want to find out how people felt about ease of car parking, price of food, quality of food, length of time queueing to pay, etc.

- Surveys are made to find the popularity of various TV programmes. Advertisers are prepared to pay a large sum for a 30 second advertisement in a programme with an audience of 10 million people.

Most surveys are conducted using questionnaires. It is very important to design the questionnaire well so that:

(a) people will cooperate and will answer the questions honestly
(b) the questions are not biased
(c) the answers to the questions can be analysed and presented for ease of understanding.

Here is a checklist of five things to improve your questionnaire design:

1. Provide an introduction to the sheet so that your subject knows the purpose of the questionnaire.

> 'Proposed new traffic lights'

2. Make the questions easy to understand and specific to answer.
Do *not* ask vague questions like this →

> ~~Did you see much of the Olympics on TV?~~

The answers could be:

'Yes, a lot'
'Not much'
'Only the best bits'
'Once or twice a day'

You will find it hard to analyse this sort of data.

A *better* question is:

> 'How much of the Olympic coverage did you watch?' Tick one box
>
> Not at all ☐
> Up to 1 hour per day ☐
> 1 to 2 hours per day ☐
> More than 2 hours per day ☐

3. Make sure that the questions are not *leading* questions. It is human nature not to contradict the questioner. Remember that the survey is to find out opinions of other people, not to support your own.
Do *not* ask

'Do you agree that BBC has the best sports coverage?'

A better question is

> 'Which of the following has the best sports coverage?'
>
> | BBC | ITV | Channel 4 | Satellite TV |
> |---|---|---|---|
> | ☐ | ☐ | ☐ | ☐ |

You might ask for one tick or possibly numbers 1, 2, 3, 4 to show an order of preference.

4. If you are going to ask sensitive questions (about age or income, for example), design the question with care so as not to offend or embarrass.
   Do *not* ask:
   'How old are you?'
   or 'Give your date of birth'
   A better question is:

'Tick one box for your age group.'			
15–17	18–20	21–30	31–50
☐	☐	☐	☐

5. Do not ask more questions than necessary and put the easy questions first.

Exercise 6

Criticise the following questions and suggest a better question which overcomes the problem involved.
Write some questions with 'yes/no' answers and some questions which involve multiple responses.
Remember to word your questions simply.

1. Do you think it is ridiculous to spend money on food 'mountains' in Europe while people in Africa are starving?
2. What do you think of the new head teacher?
3. How dangerous do you think it is to fly in a single-engined aeroplane?

4. What is your weekly pay?
5. Do you agree that English and Maths are the most important subjects at school?
6. Do you or your parents often hire videos from a shop?
7. Do you think that we get too much homework?
8. Do you think you would still eat meat if you had been to see the animals killed?

Analysis

Having conducted the survey, you need to display your results clearly.
Diagrams like pie charts, frequency diagrams and scatter graphs are a good idea. Do not be afraid to use colours.

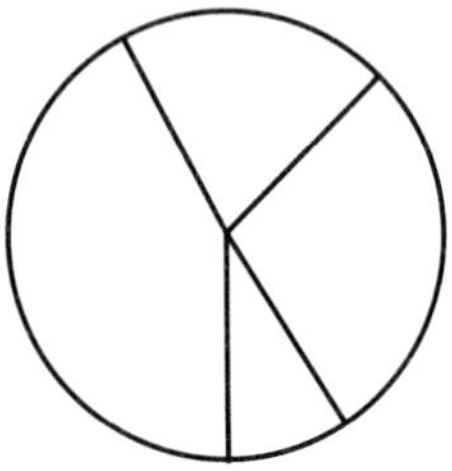
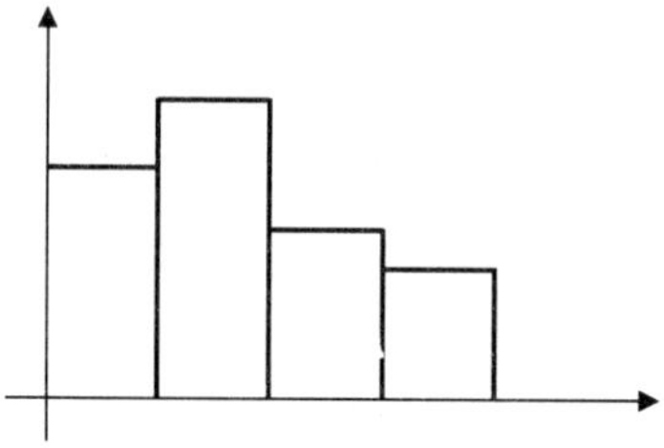
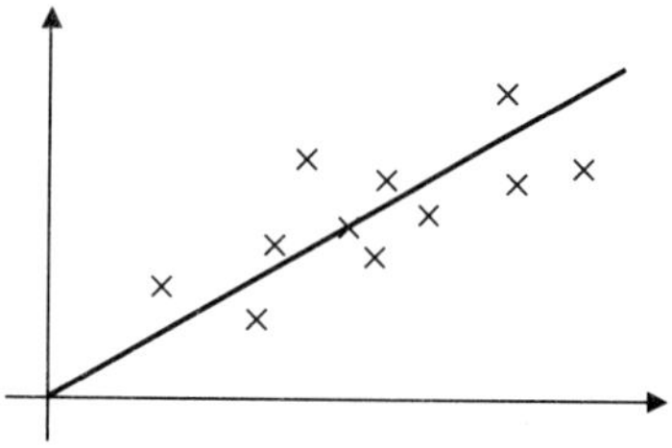

You might want to use a database or spreadsheet program on a computer if you think this would help your work.

Draw *conclusions* from your results but make sure they are justified by the evidence.

The best way to learn about questionnaires is to conduct your own survey on a topic which *you* find interesting.

Hypothesis testing

An hypothesis is defined as 'a statement which may be true, but for which a proof has not been found'. Statisticians are employed to collect and analyse information about a question with the aim of proving or disproving it. Questionnaires are often used for this purpose.
Here are some questions:

A 'Is there too much sport on television?'

B 'Are people who are good at spelling also good at arithmetic?'

castle ✓	$51 \times 17 = 867$ ✓
elefant ×	$0{\cdot}4 \times 0{\cdot}2 = 0{\cdot}08$ ✓
necessary ✓	$5{\cdot}6 - 4 = 5{\cdot}2$ ×
tomorrow ✓	$\frac{1}{6} + \frac{1}{2} = \frac{2}{8}$ ×

C 'Does smoking damage your health?'

D 'Do pupils in Year 7 watch more TV than pupils in Year 11?'

Once you have the question, your first task is to make an hypothesis (make a statement) so that you have something concrete to test. Hypotheses for the above four questions could be:

A Most people would like TV schedules to contain less coverage of sport.

B People who are good at spelling are also good at arithmetic.

C Smokers have a shorter life span than non-smokers.

D Pupils in Year 7 watch more television than pupils in Year 11.

There are several factors which you must consider when making your hypothesis.

1. Can you test it?
In the smokers problem there are many factors which will affect life span – diet, fitness, stress, heredity etc. How can you eliminate these so that it is *only* the smoking which counts?

2. Can you collect enough data to give a reasonable result? Where will you collect your data?
For the spelling/arithmetic problem, you could write your own tests and then ask about 30 pupils, preferably of different ages, to do them. You should try to get people with a range of abilities in spelling and arithmetic.

3. How will you know if you have proved or disproved the hypothesis?
You need to have some idea of the criteria for proof (or disproof) before you start collecting data.
In the question about sport on television, what do you mean by 'most'? Do you mean over half of those questioned? What about 'don't knows'?

4. Can you collect the type of data which you can analyse?
Consider the techniques at your disposal:
mean, median, mode, scatter diagrams, pie charts, frequency graphs. The spelling/arithmetic data, for example could be clearly displayed on a scatter diagram.

5. Do you find it interesting?
If you don't, the whole piece of work will be dull and tedious, both to you and to your teacher.

Your own work

Almost certainly the best idea for an hypothesis will be an idea which *you* think of because *you* want to know the answer.
As a guide, here is a list of questions which some students have looked at. You can use one of these if you find it interesting or if you can't think of a better one yourself.

(a) Young people are more superstitious than older people.
(b) Given a free choice most girls would hardly ever wear a dress in preference to something else.

(c) More babies are born in the Winter than the Summer.
(d) The age for part time jobs should be reduced from 16 to 14.
(e) The school day should start at 0800 and end at 1400.
(f) Most cars these days use unleaded petrol.

4.3 Scatter diagrams

5/6b, 5/7a

Sometimes it is interesting to discover if there is a relationship (or *correlation*) between two sets of data.
Examples

- Do tall people weigh more than short people?
- If you spend longer revising for a test, will you get a higher mark?
- Do tall parents have tall children?
- If there is more rain, will there be less sunshine?
- Does the number of Olympic gold medals won by British athletes affect the rate of inflation?

If there is a relationship, it will be easy to spot if your data is plotted on a scatter diagram – that is a graph in which one set of data is plotted on the horizontal axis and the other on the vertical axis.

Each month the average outdoors temperature was recorded together with the number of therms of gas used to heat the house. The results are plotted on the scatter diagram as shown.
Clearly there is a high degree of *correlation* between these two figures. British Gas do in fact use weather forecasts as their main short-term predictor of future gas consumption over the whole country.

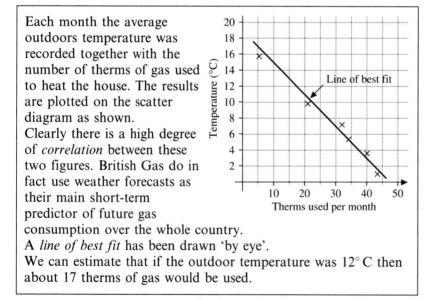

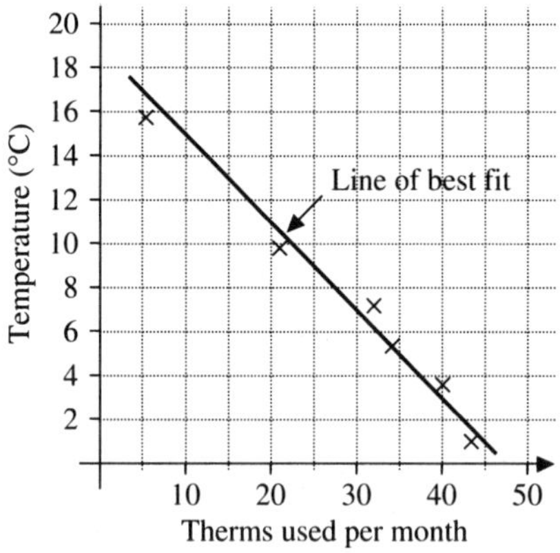

A *line of best fit* has been drawn 'by eye'.
We can estimate that if the outdoor temperature was 12° C then about 17 therms of gas would be used.

Note. You can only predict within the range of values given.
If we extended the line for temperatures below zero the line of best fit predicts that about 60 therms would be used when the temperature is −4° C. But −4° C is well outside the range of the values plotted so the prediction is not valid. [Perhaps at −4° C a lot

of people might stay in bed and the gas consumption would not increase by much. The point is you don't know!]

(a) The line in our example has a negative gradient and we say there is *negative correlation*.

(b) If the line of best fit has a positive gradient we say there is *positive correlation*.

(c) Some data when plotted on a scatter diagram does not appear to fit any line at all. In this case there is no correlation.

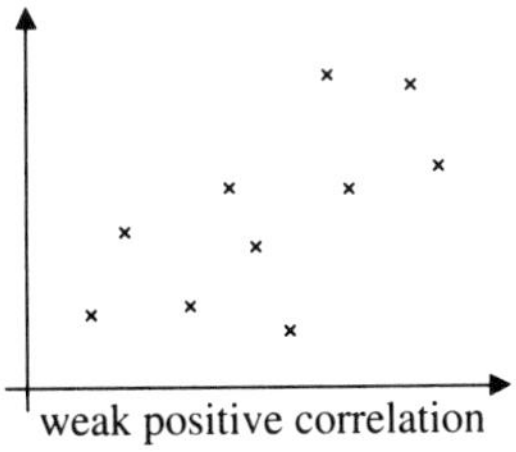

weak positive correlation

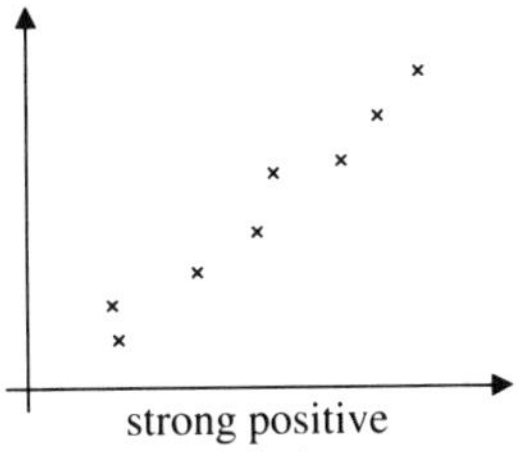

strong positive correlation

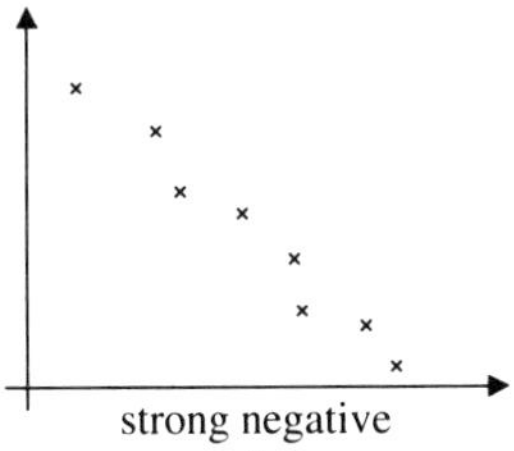

strong negative correlation

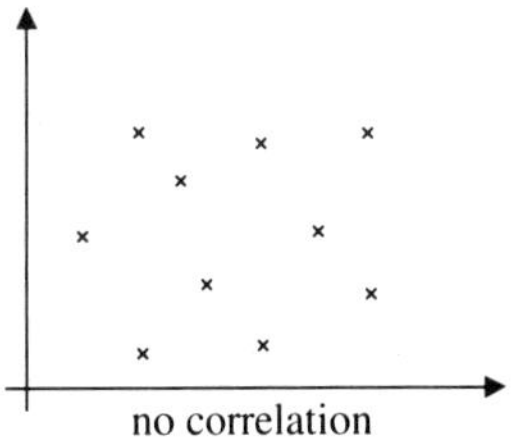

no correlation

Exercise 7

1. For this question you need to make some measurements of people in your class.

(a) Measure everyone's height and 'armspan' to the nearest cm.

Plot the measurements on a scatter graph. Is there any correlation?

(b) Now measure everyone's 'head circumference' just above the eyes.
Plot head circumference and height on a scatter graph. Is there any correlation?

(c) Decide as a class which other measurements [e.g. pulse rate] you can (fairly easily) take and plot these to see if any correlation exists.

(d) Which pair of measurements gave the best correlation?

2. The marks of 7 students in the two papers of a physics examination were as follows.

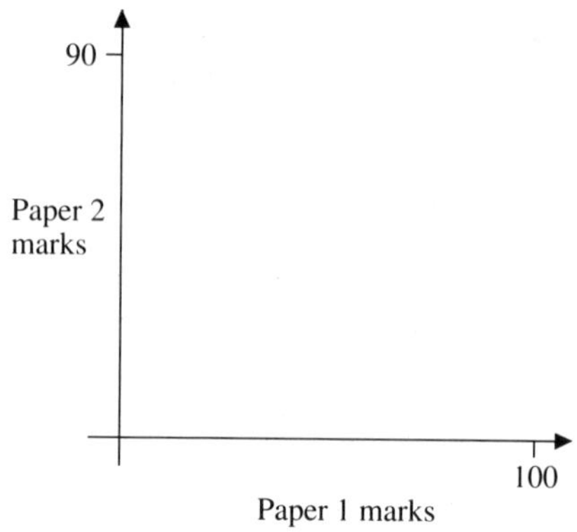

Paper 1	20	32	40	60	71	80	91
Paper 2	15	25	40	50	64	75	84

(a) Plot the marks on a scatter diagram, using a scale of 1 cm to 10 marks, and draw a line of best fit.
(b) A student scored a mark of 50 on Paper 1. What would you expect her to get on Paper 2?

3. The table shows (i) the engine size in litres of various cars and (ii) the distance travelled in km on one litre of petrol.

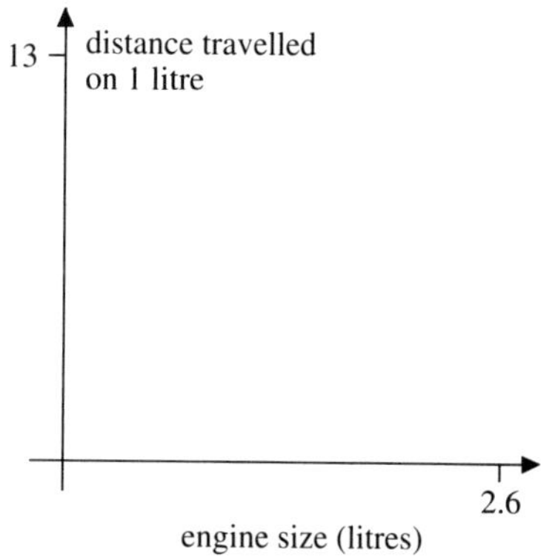

Engine	0·8	1·6	2·6	1·0	2·1	1·3	1·8
Distance	13	10·2	5·4	12	7·8	11·2	8·5

(a) Plot the figures on a scatter graph using a scale of 5 cm to 1 litre across the page and 1 cm to 1 km up the page. Draw a line of best fit.
(b) A car has a 2·3 litre engine. How far would you expect it to go on one litre of petrol?

4. The data shows the latitude of 10 cities in the northern hemisphere and the average high temperatures.

City	Latitude (degrees)	Mean high temperature (°F)
Bogota	5	66
Bombay	19	87
Casablanca	34	72
Dublin	53	56
Hong Kong	22	77
Istanbul	41	64
St Petersburg	60	46
Manila	15	89
Oslo	60	50
Paris	49	59

(a) Draw a scatter diagram and draw a line of best fit. Plot latitude across the page with a scale of 2 cm to 10°. Plot temperature up the page from 40° F to 90° F with a scale of 2 cm to 10° F.

(b) Which city lies well off the line?
Do you know what factor might cause this apparent discrepancy?
(c) The latitude of Shanghai is 31° N. What do you think its mean high temperature is?

5. What sort of pattern would you expect if you took readings of the following and drew a scatter diagram?
(a) cars on roads; accident rate.
(b) sales of perfume; advertising costs.
(c) birth rate; rate of inflation.
(d) petrol consumption of car; price of petrol.

4.4 Two-way tables

5/6b

Here is a two-way table for students at a college. The table shows the number of students in each of four sub-groups.

	Male	Female	
Science	758	249	
Arts	456	642	

It is useful to find the total for each column, the total for each row and the total number of people in the whole table.
We can then extract information from the table.

	Male	Female	Total
Science	758	249	1007
Arts	456	642	1098
Total	1214	891	2105

(a) The percentage of science students who are

$$\text{female} = \frac{249}{1007} \times 100\%$$

$$= 24{\cdot}7\% \text{ (1 d.p.)}$$

(b) The percentage of male students who are studying the arts

$$\text{the arts} = \frac{456}{1214} \times 100\%$$

$$= 37{\cdot}6\% \text{ (1 d.p.)}$$

You have to be careful that you are finding the percentage of the correct figure. In (b) above, there are 1214 male students and of these 456 are studying the arts.

Exercise 8

1. A group of six year olds was asked whether or not they could swim. The results are shown in the two-way table.

	Boy	Girl	Total
can swim	175	114	
cannot swim	389	216	
Total			

(a) Copy the table and find the totals for each row and each column and also the total number of children in the table.
(b) What percentage of the boys can swim?
(c) What percentage of the girls can swim?

2. In a survey, people were asked to state which was their favourite TV channel from BBC1, ITV and BBC2.

	BBC1	ITV	BBC2	Total
under 16	275	452	57	
over 16	195	216	374	
Total				

(a) Copy the table and work out the totals.
(b) What percentage of under 16's chose ITV?
(c) What percentage of those who chose BBC2 were over 16?
(d) What is the main difference between the results for the under 16's and for the over 16's?

3. A survey was made of the ages of cars which took the MOT safety test at a garage.

	Failed test	Passed test	Total
less than 4 years old	15	96	
4 to 7 years old	43	67	
over 7 years old	97	88	
Total			

(a) What percentage of the cars over 7 years old passed the test?
(b) How many cars failed the test?
(c) What percentage of the cars which failed were less than 4 years old?
(d) Are the results of this survey what you expected or do you find them surprising in any way?

4. When listening to the weather forecast, you may have heard the expression 'wind chill'. Wind chill is a measure of how cold it will feel for a given air temperature and wind speed.

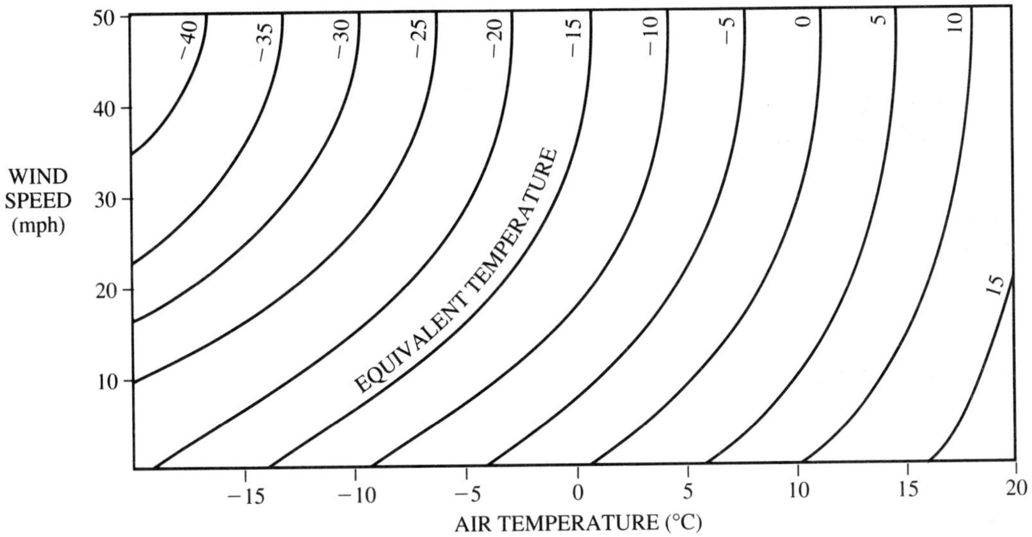

From the table, if the wind speed is 20 mph and the air temperature is 15° C it will 'feel' like 10° C. We call 10° C the equivalent temperature or wind chill. The wind chill lines are drawn every 5° so you will have to estimate some answers.

(a) Find the wind chill if the wind speed is 40 mph and the air temperature is 15° C.

(b) Find the wind chill if the wind speed is 22 mph and the air temperature is 0° C.

(c) One day the wind chill was −15° C and the wind speed was 40 mph. What was the air temperature?

(d) Does it feel colder when the air temperature is 0° C and the wind speed is 30 mph, or when it is 5° below zero and the wind speed is 20 mph?

(e) Forecasters use the following terms as a guide to describe wind chills:

0° → 5° C	Very Cool
−10° → 0° C	Cold
−15° → −10° C	Very Cold
−25° → −15° C	Bitterly Cold
below −25° C	Freezing cold (exposed flesh freezes).

(i) How would the forecaster describe the weather when the temperature is −10° C and the wind speed is 20 mph?

(ii) Would you go skiing if the temperature was −8° C and the wind speed was 35 mph?

5. The carona plant is grown both for its bark and for its fruit. Unfortunately only a fraction of the plants actually produce any fruit each year. The fruit is supposed to have strong medicinal powers and scientists have worked hard to develop a new fertilizer which it is hoped will increase the number of plants producing fruit.
Here are the results for one farmer's crop where some plants were given the fertilizer and others were not.

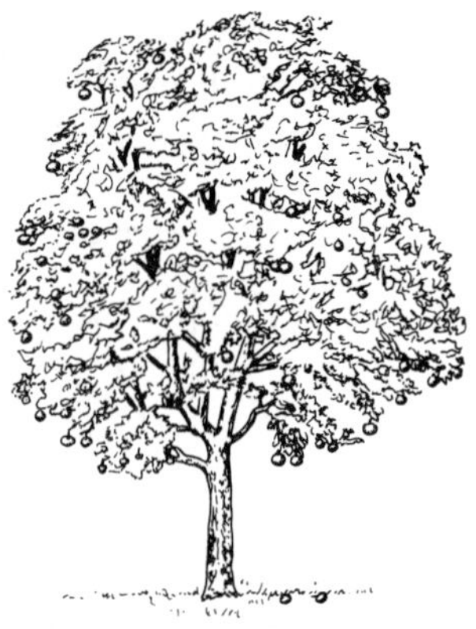

	produced fruit	did not produce fruit	
given fertilizer	314	142	
not given fertilizer	153	98	

We have to decide how effective the fertilizer has been.

(a) What percentage of the plants which were given the fertilizer produced fruit?

(b) What percentage of the plants which were *not* given the fertilizer produced fruit?

(c) What conclusion do you make about this fertilizer?

(d) The Mark II version of the fertilizer produced this set of results.

	produced fruit	did not produce fruit	
given Mk II fertilizer	476	279	
not given Mk II fertilizer	283	159	

What conclusion do you make about the Mark II fertilizer?

5 Shape and space 2

5.1 Transforming shapes

4/6b, 4/7d

Reflection

A′B′C′D′ is the image of ABCD after reflection in the broken line (the mirror line).

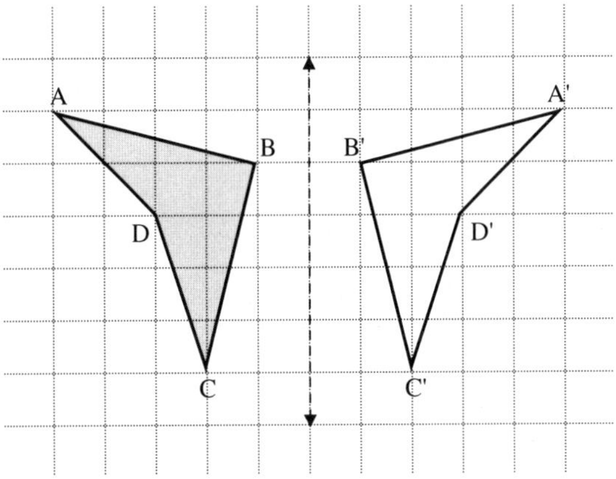

Exercise 1

On squared paper draw the object and its image after reflection in the broken line.

1.

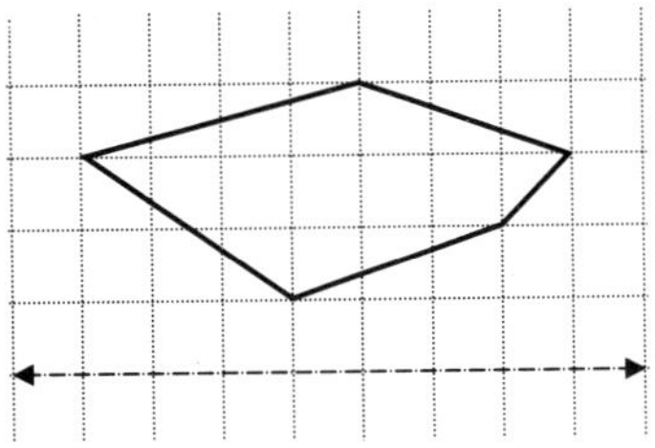

2.

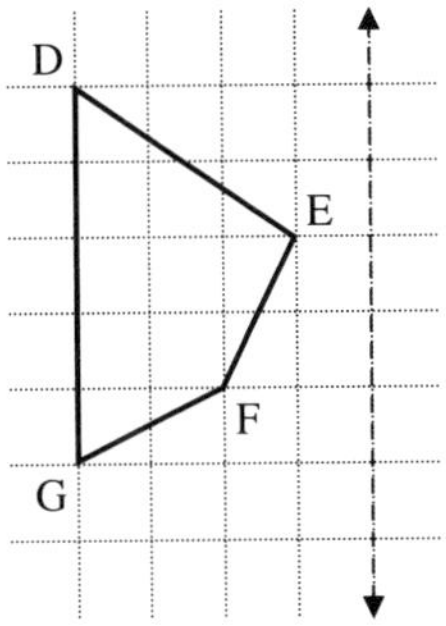

3.

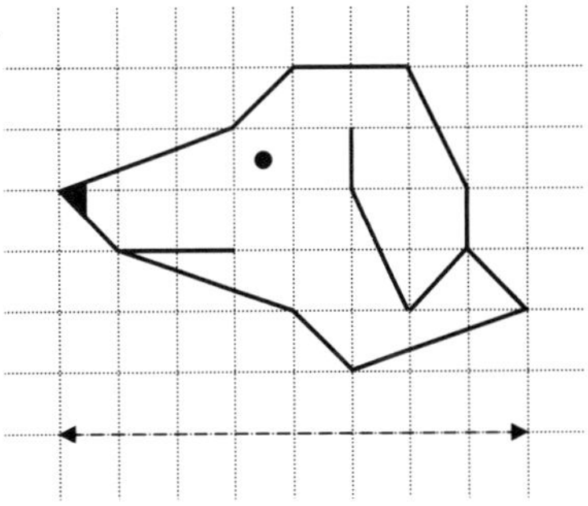

4.

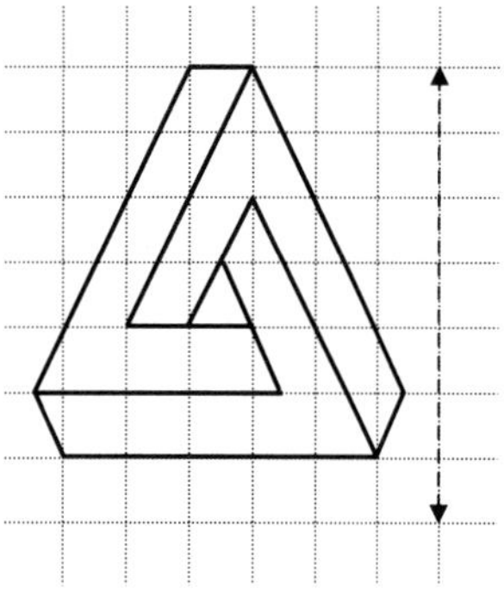

5.

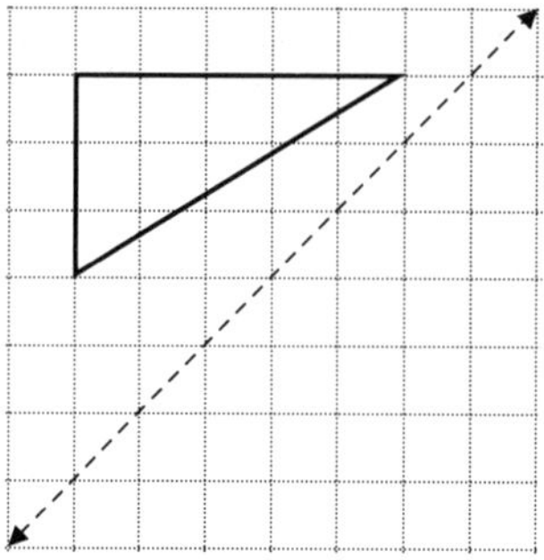

6.

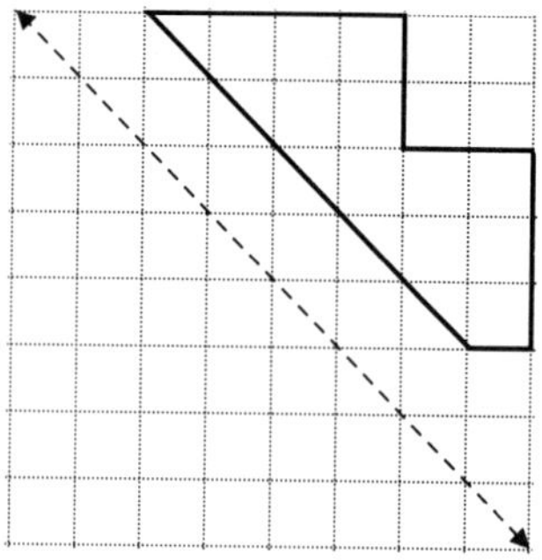

7.

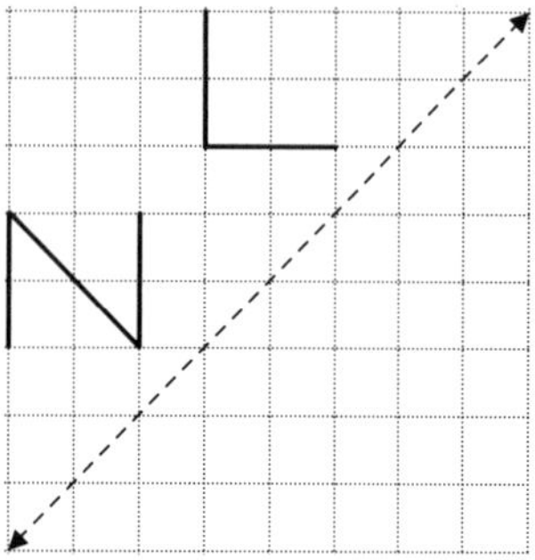

8.

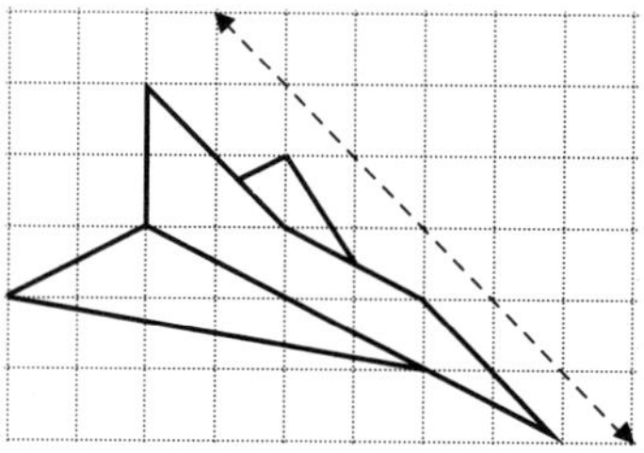

9.

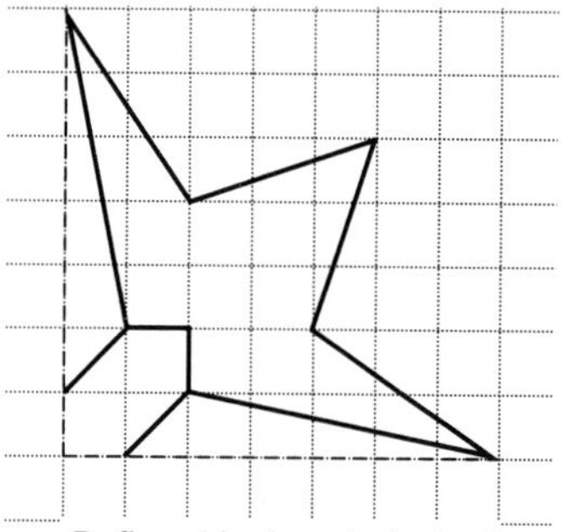

Reflect this shape in *both* of the broken lines.

Exercise 2

1. Copy the diagram below.

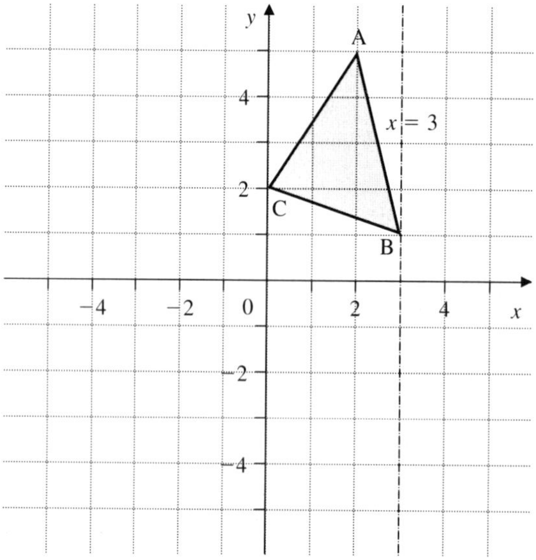

Draw the image of △ ABC after reflection in the lines indicated.

(a) the x-axis. Label it △1.

(b) the y-axis. Label it △2.

(c) the line $x = 3$. Label it △3.

For Questions 2 to 5 draw a pair of axes so that both x and y can take values from -7 to $+7$.

2. (a) Plot and label P(7,5), Q(7,2), R(5,2).
(b) Draw the lines $y = -1$, $x = 1$ and $y = x$. Use dotted lines.
(c) Draw the image of △PQR after reflection in:
(i) the line $y = -1$. Label it △1.
(ii) the line $x = 1$. Label it △2.
(iii) the line $y = x$. Label it △3.
(d) Write down the coordinates of the image of point P in each case.

3. (a) Plot and label L(7,–5), M(7,–1), N(5,–1).
(b) Draw the lines $y = x$ and $y = -x$. Use dotted lines.
(c) Draw the image of △LMN after reflection in:
(i) the x-axis. Label it △1.
(ii) the line $y = x$. Label it △2.
(iii) the line $y = -x$. Label it △3.
(d) Write down the coordinates of the image of point L in each case.

4. (a) Draw the line $x + y = 7$. [It passes through (0,7) and (7,0).]
(b) Draw △1 at (–3,–1), (–1,–1), (–1,–4).
(c) Reflect △1 in the y-axis onto △2.
(d) Reflect △2 in the x-axis onto △3.
(e) Reflect △3 in the line $x + y = 7$ onto △4.
(f) Reflect △4 in the y-axis onto △5.
(g) Write down the coordinates of △5.

5. (a) Draw the lines $y = 2$, $x = -1$ and $y = x$.
(b) Draw △1 at (1,–3), (–3,–3), (–3,–5).
(c) Reflect △1 in the line $y = x$ onto △2.
(d) Reflect △2 in the line $y = 2$ onto △3.
(e) Reflect △3 in the line $x = -1$ onto △4.
(f) Reflect △4 in the line $y = x$ onto △5.
(g) Write down the coordinates of △5.

6. Find the equation of the mirror line for the reflection:
(a) △1 onto △2
(b) △1 onto △3
(c) △1 onto △4
(d) △1 onto △5.

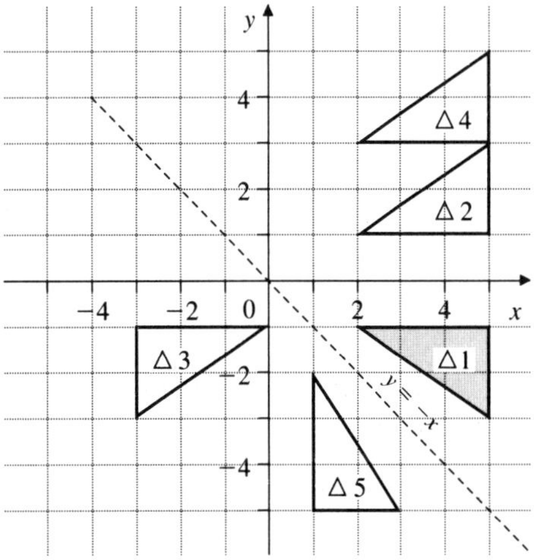

Rotation

$\triangle A'B'C'$ is the image of $\triangle ABC$ after a 90° clockwise rotation about centre O.

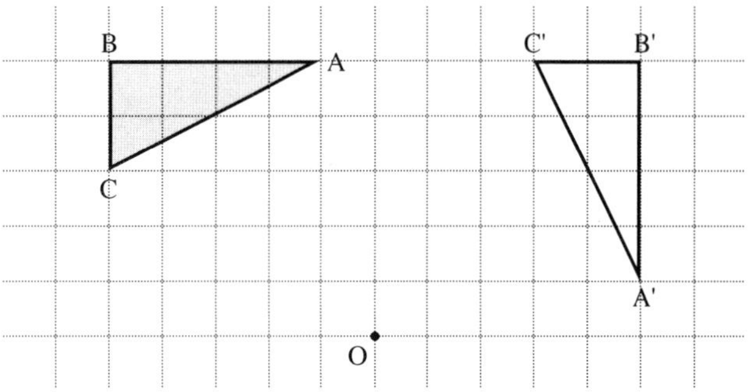

Draw $\triangle ABC$ on tracing paper and then put the tip of your pencil on O. Turn the tracing paper 90° clockwise about O. The tracing paper now shows the position of $\triangle A'B'C'$.
Notice that you need three things to describe a rotation:
(a) the centre
(b) the angle
(c) the direction (e.g. clockwise)

Exercise 3

Draw the object and its image under the rotation given. Take O as the centre of rotation in each case.

1.

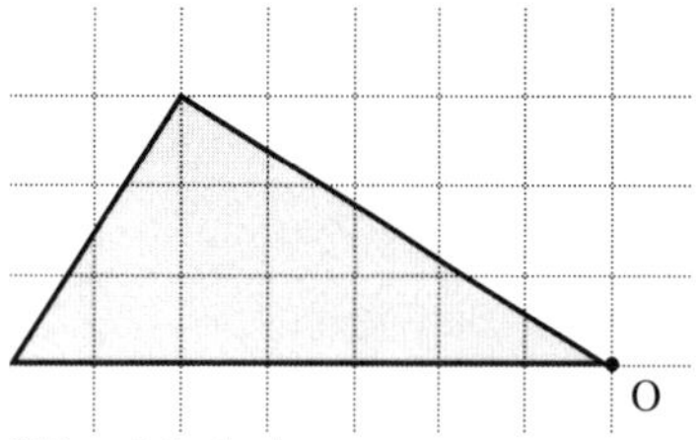

90° anticlockwise

2.

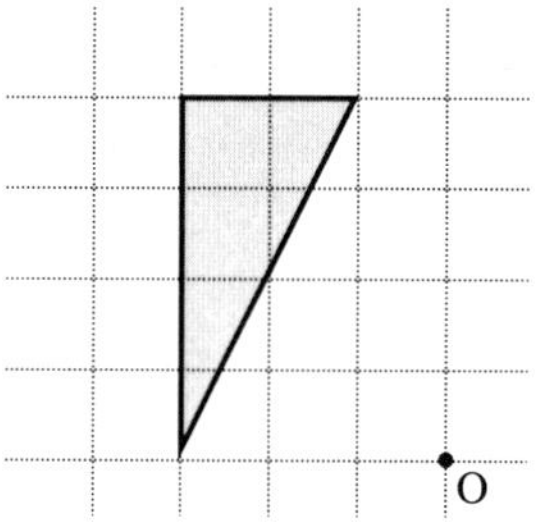

90° clockwise

3.

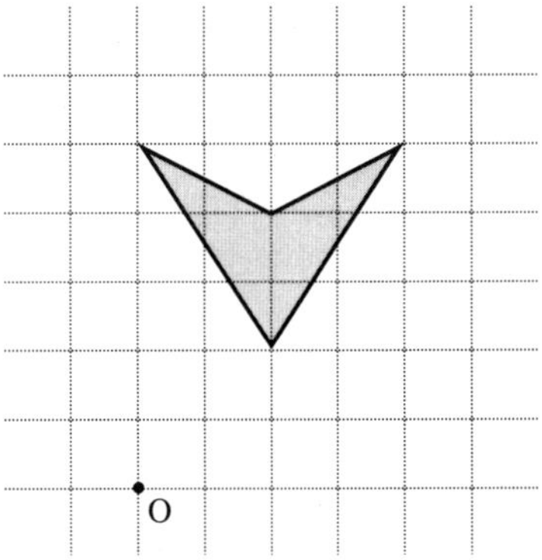

90° clockwise

4.

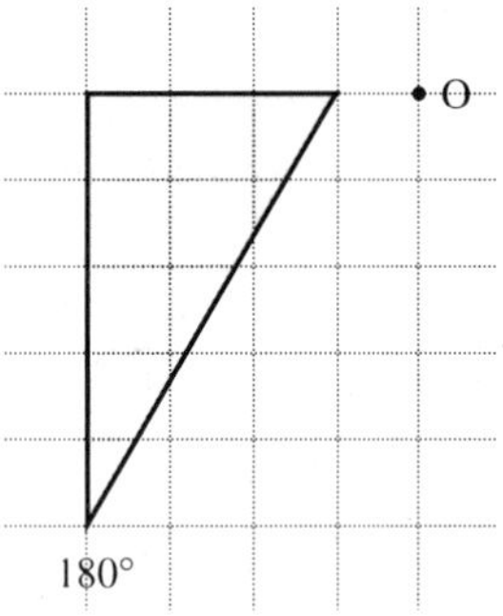

180°

5.

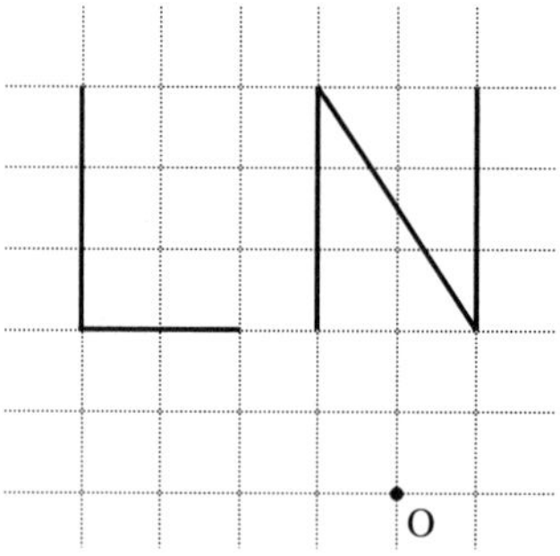

90° clockwise

6.

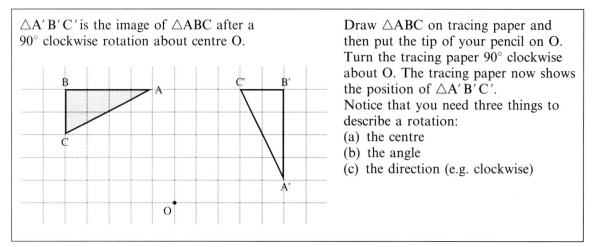

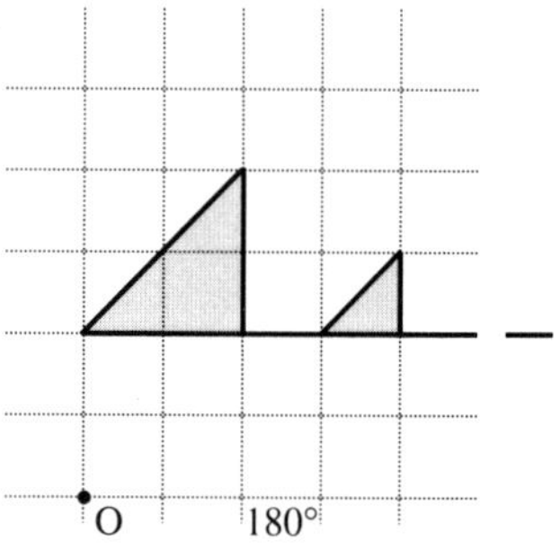

180°

7. The shape on the right has been rotated about several different centres to form the pattern below.

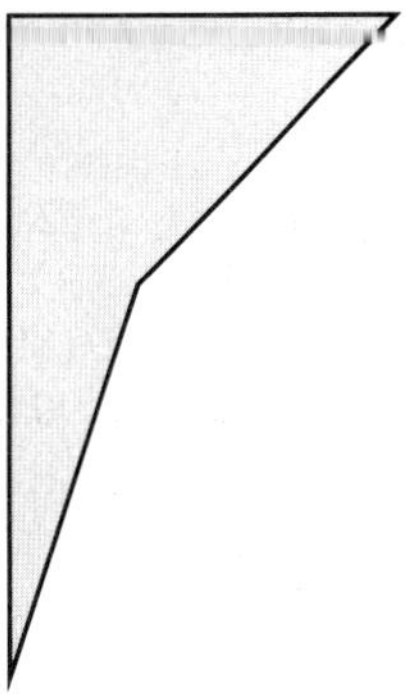

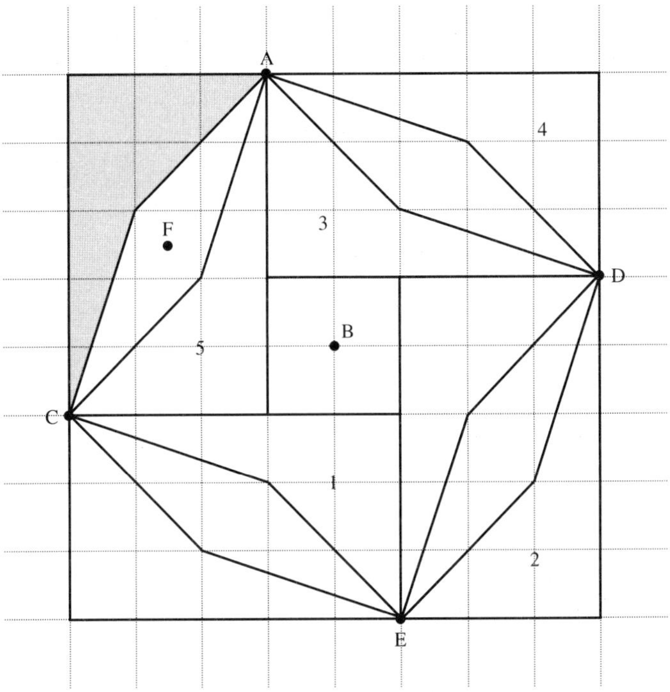

Describe the rotation which takes the shaded shape onto shape 1, shape 2, shape 3, shape 4 and shape 5.
For each one, give the centre (A, B, C, D, E or F), the angle and the direction of the rotation.
[e.g. 'centre C, 90°, clockwise'].

Exercise 4

1. Copy the diagram on the right.

   (a) Rotate △ABC 90° clockwise about (0,0). Label it △1.
   (b) Rotate △DEF 180° clockwise about (0,0). Label it △2.
   (c) Rotate △GHI 90° clockwise about (0,0). Label it △3.

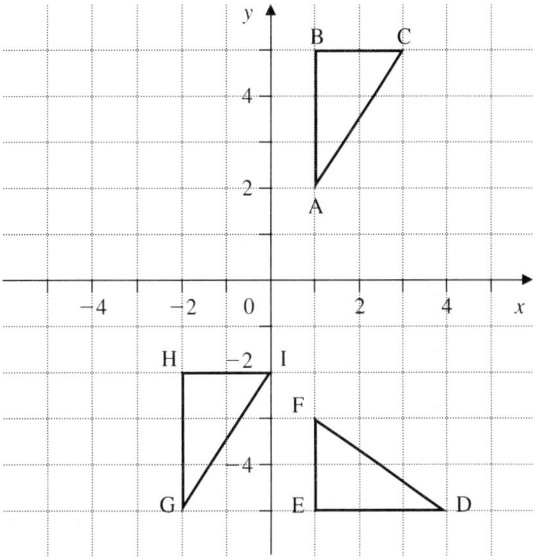

For Questions **2** and **3** draw a pair of axes with values of x and y from -7 to $+7$.

2. (a) Plot $\triangle 1$ at (2,3), (6,3), (3,6).
(b) Rotate $\triangle 1$ 90° clockwise about (2,1) onto $\triangle 2$.
(c) Rotate $\triangle 2$ 180° about (0,0) onto $\triangle 3$.
(d) Rotate $\triangle 3$ 90° anticlockwise about (1,1) onto $\triangle 4$.
(e) Write down the coordinates of $\triangle 4$.

3. (a) Plot $\triangle 1$ at (4,4), (6,6), (2,6).
(b) Rotate $\triangle 1$ 90° anticlockwise about (6,0) onto $\triangle 2$.
(c) Rotate $\triangle 2$ 90° anticlockwise about $(-3,-4)$ onto $\triangle 3$.
(d) Rotate $\triangle 3$ 90° clockwise about $(-3,2)$ onto $\triangle 4$.
(e) Write down the coordinates of $\triangle 4$.

Finding the centre of a rotation

Exercise 5

In Questions **1** to **3** copy the diagram exactly and then use tracing paper to find the centre of the rotation which takes the shaded shape onto the unshaded shape. Mark the centre of rotation with a cross.

1.

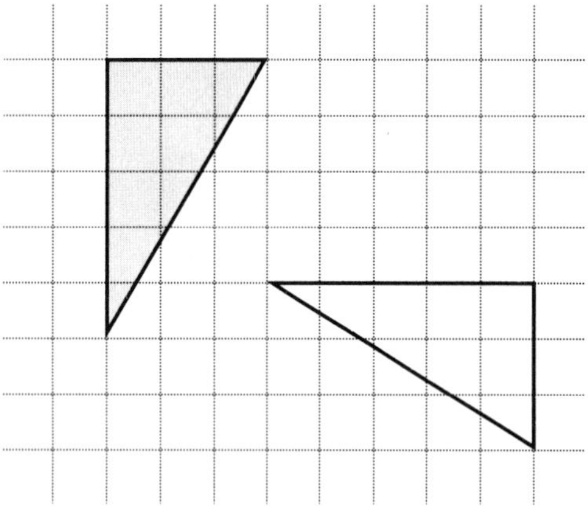

2.

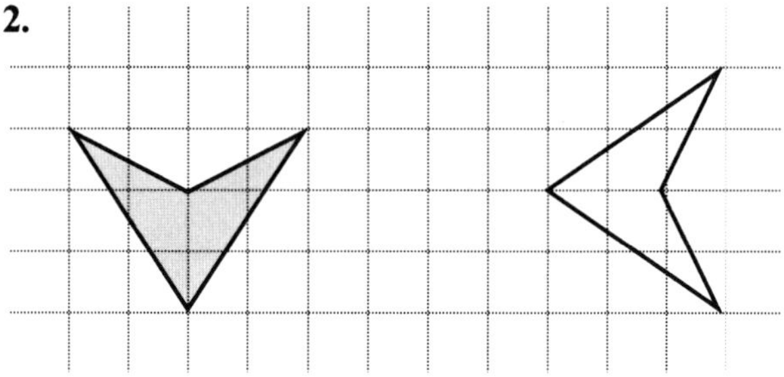

3.

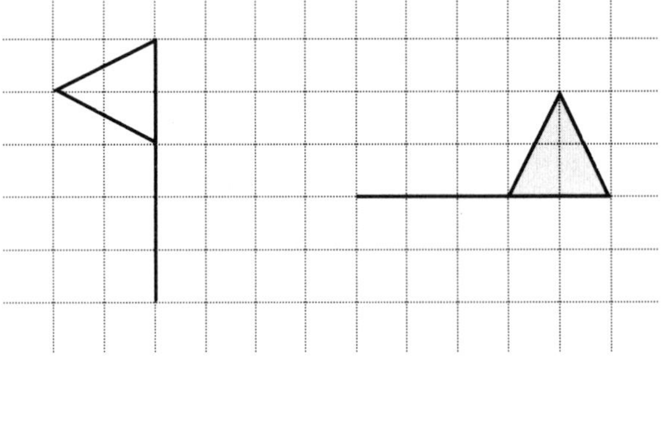

4. Copy the diagram below.

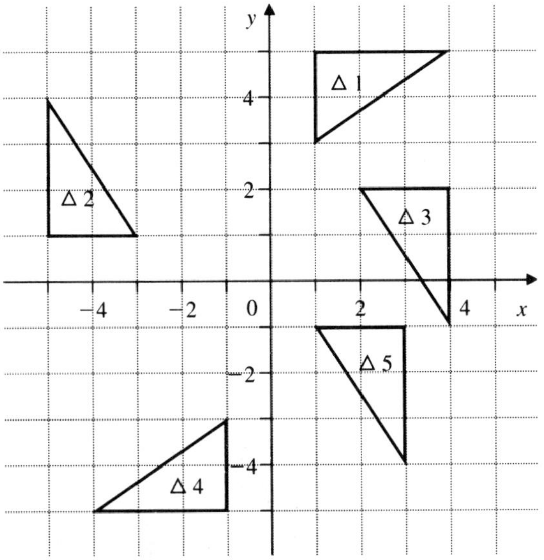

Find the coordinates of the centre of the following rotations:

(a) $\triangle 1 \rightarrow \triangle 2$ (b) $\triangle 1 \rightarrow \triangle 3$
(c) $\triangle 1 \rightarrow \triangle 4$ (d) $\triangle 1 \rightarrow \triangle 5$

For Questions **5**, **6** draw a pair of axes with values of x and y from -7 to $+7$.

5. (a) Plot and label the following triangles:
$\triangle 1$: (3,4), (7,4), (3,7)
$\triangle 2$: (3,2), (6,2), (3,−2)
$\triangle 3$: (−7,−4), (−3,−4), (−3,−7)
$\triangle 4$: (−2,1), (−5,1), (−2,5)
$\triangle 5$: (2,−3), (5,−3), (2,−7)

(b) Find the coordinates of the centre of the following rotations:
(i) $\triangle 1 \rightarrow \triangle 2$ (ii) $\triangle 1 \rightarrow \triangle 3$
(iii) $\triangle 1 \rightarrow \triangle 4$ (iv) $\triangle 1 \rightarrow \triangle 5$.

6. (a) Plot and label the following triangles:
$\triangle 1$: (−4,−3), (−4,−7), (−6,−7)
$\triangle 2$: (−3,4), (−7,4), (−7,6)
$\triangle 3$: (−2,1), (2,1), (2,−1)
$\triangle 4$: (0,7), (4,7), (4,5)
$\triangle 5$: (2,−3), (4,−3), (2,−7)

(b) Find the coordinates of the centre of the following rotations:
(i) $\triangle 1 \rightarrow \triangle 2$ (ii) $\triangle 1 \rightarrow \triangle 3$
(iii) $\triangle 1 \rightarrow \triangle 4$ (iv) $\triangle 1 \rightarrow \triangle 5$.

Enlargement

A

B

C

Photo A has been enlarged to give photos B and C. Notice that the shape of the face is exactly the same in all the pictures.

Photo A measures 22 mm by 27 mm
Photo B measures 44 mm by 54 mm
Photo C measures 66 mm by 81 mm

From A to B both the width and the height have been multiplied by 2. We say B is an enlargement of A with a *scale factor* of 2. Similarly C is an enlargement of A with a scale factor of 3.

Also C is an enlargement of B with a scale factor of $1\frac{1}{2}$.

The scale factor of an enlargement can be found by dividing corresponding lengths on two pictures.

In this enlargement the scale factor is $\frac{21}{14}$ (= 1·5)

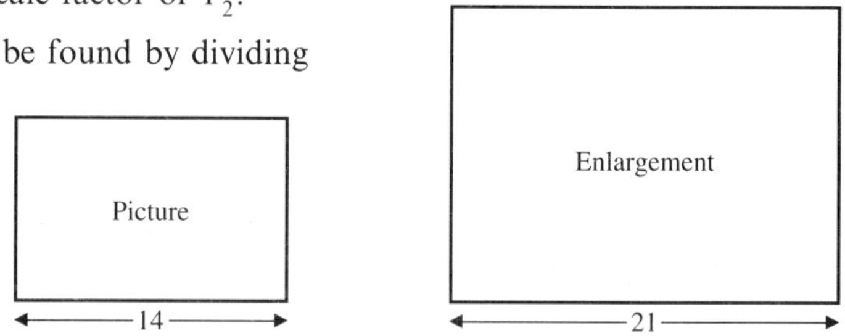

Exercise 6

1. This picture is to be enlarged and we want the enlargement to fit exactly in a frame.
Which of the following frames will the picture fit?
Write 'yes' or 'no'.
(a) 76 mm by 100 mm
(b) 76 mm by 110 mm
(c) 114 mm by 150 mm
(d) 57 mm by 75 mm.

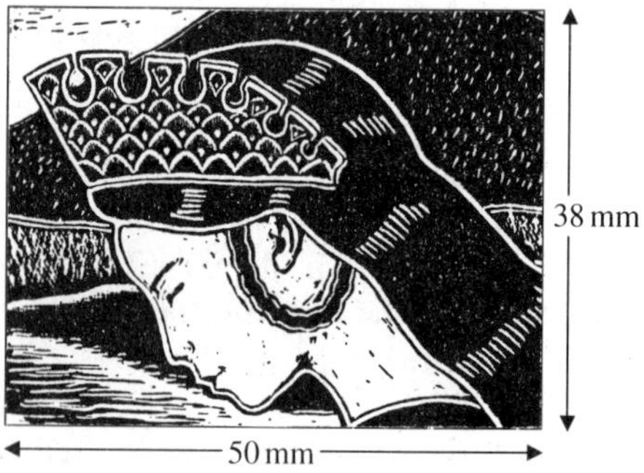

2. This picture is to be enlarged so that it fits exactly into the frame. Find the length x.

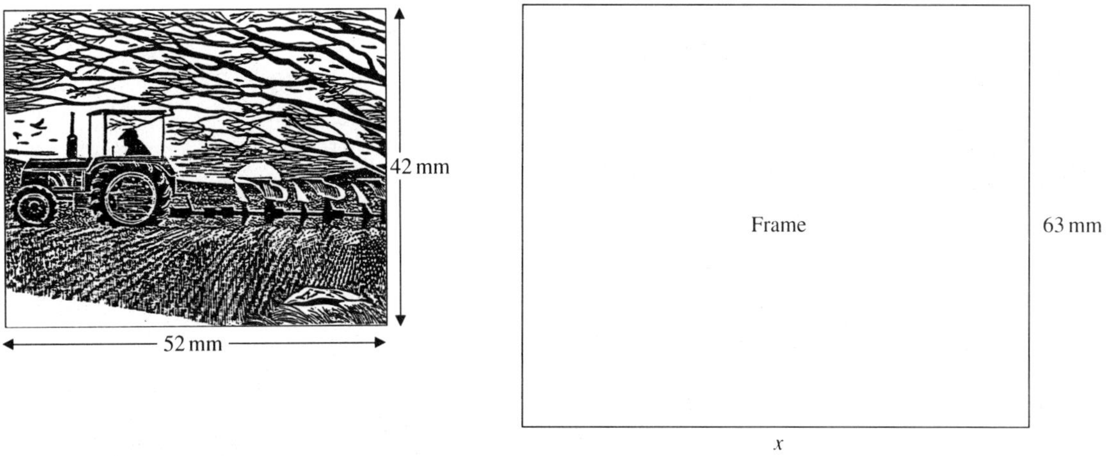

3. This picture is enlarged or reduced to fit into each of the frames shown. Calculate y and z.

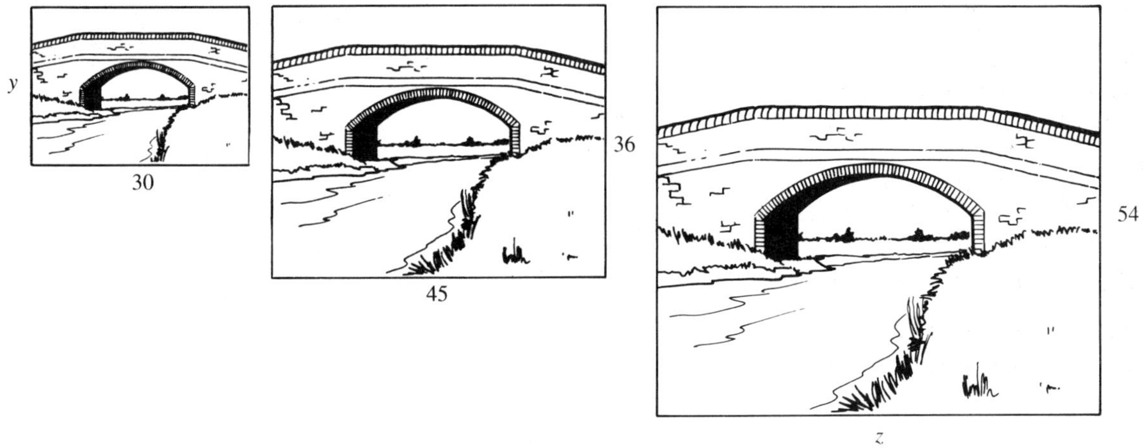

4. Here we have started to draw a two times enlargement of a house using the squares.

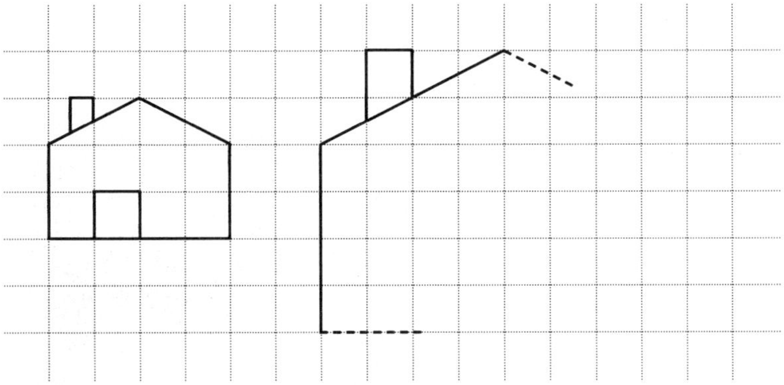

Draw the complete enlargement in your book (use squared paper).

5. Draw a three times enlargement of this figure.

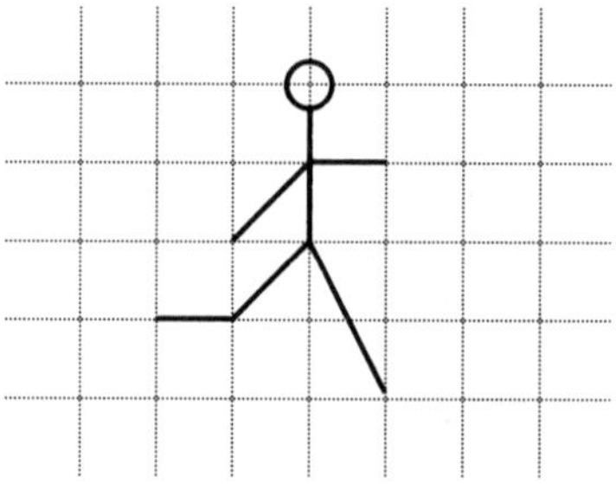

6. Draw a two times and a three times enlargement of this shape. Measure the angles a and b on each enlargement. Write the correct version of this sentence: 'In an enlargement, the angles in a shape are changed/unchanged'.

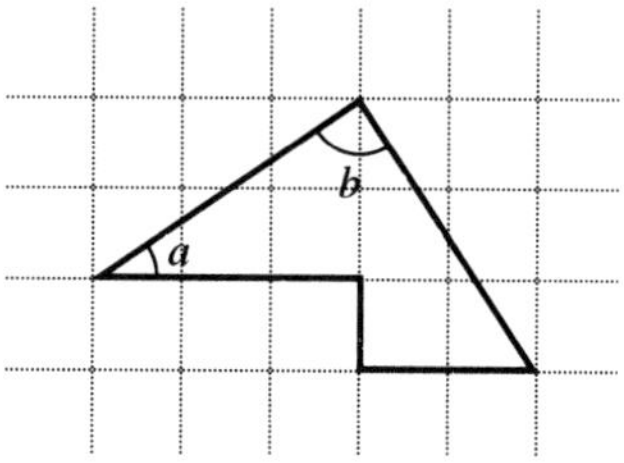

7. This diagram shows an arrowhead and its enlargement. Notice that lines drawn through corresponding points (A, A′ or B, B′) all go through one point O. This point is called the centre of enlargement. Copy and complete:

OA′ = ______ × OA
OB′ = ______ × OB.

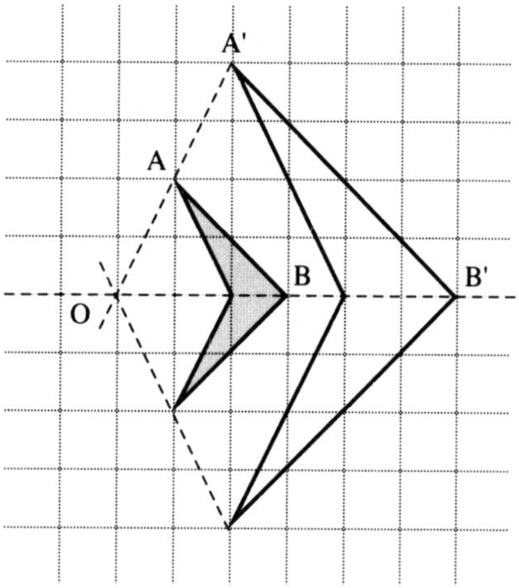

8. Copy this shape and its enlargement. Draw construction lines to find the centre of enlargement.

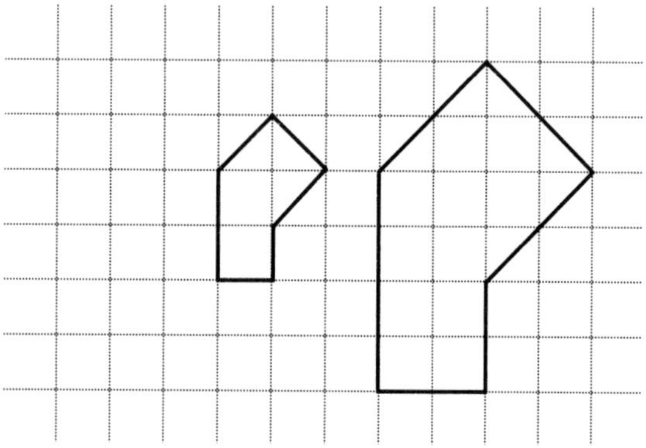

9. In this diagram, $\triangle 1$ is a two times enlargement of the shaded triangle with O_1 as centre of enlargement. Also $\triangle 2$ is a three times enlargement of the shaded triangle with O_2 as centre of enlargement.

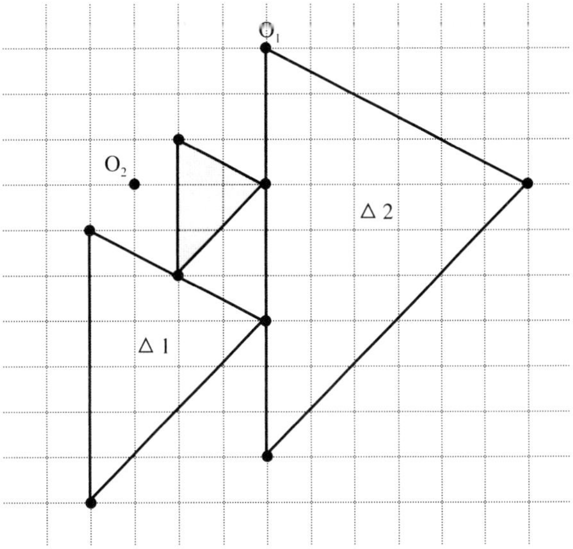

(a) Copy the diagram and draw construction lines to find the centre of enlargement from $\triangle 1$ onto $\triangle 2$.
[Hint: leave space on the left side of the diagram].
(b) What is the scale factor for the enlargement $\triangle 1$ onto $\triangle 2$?

For a mathematical description of an enlargement we need two things.

(a) the scale factor (b) the centre of enlargement.

The triangle ABC is enlarged onto triangle A′B′C′ with a scale factor of 3 and centre O.

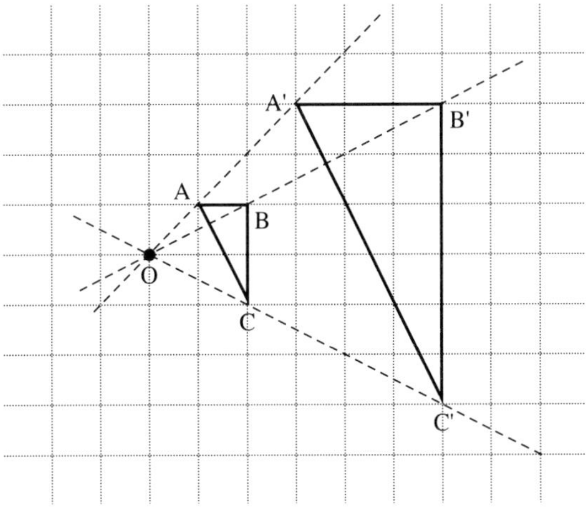

Note: $OA' = 3 \times OA$; $OB' = 3 \times OB$; $OC' = 3 \times OC$.

All lengths are measured from the *centre of enlargement*.

Exercise 7

Copy each diagram and draw an enlargement using the centre O and the scale factor given.

1.

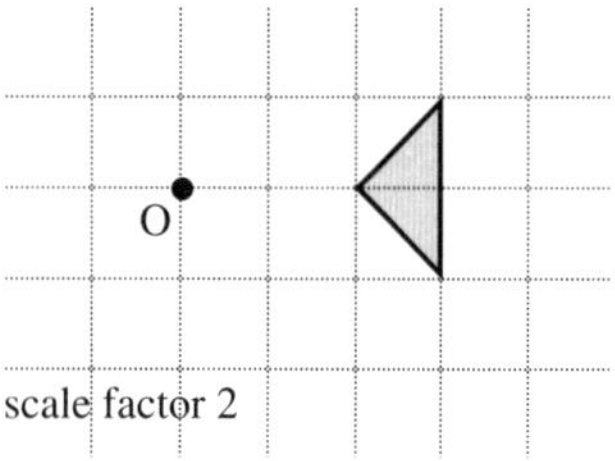

2.

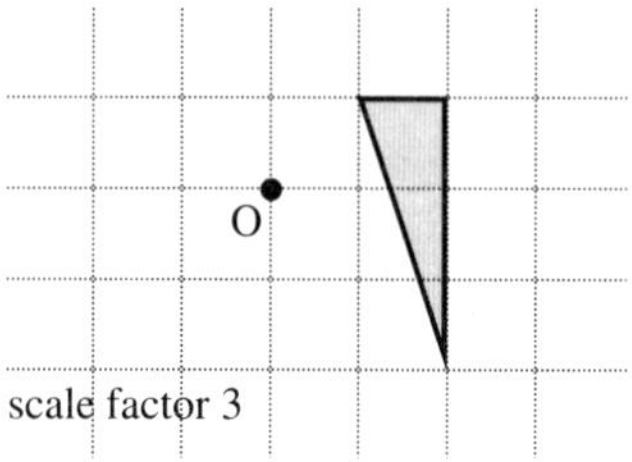

3.

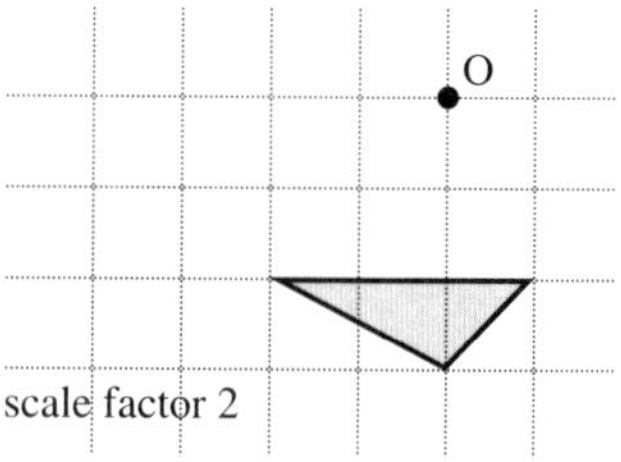

4.

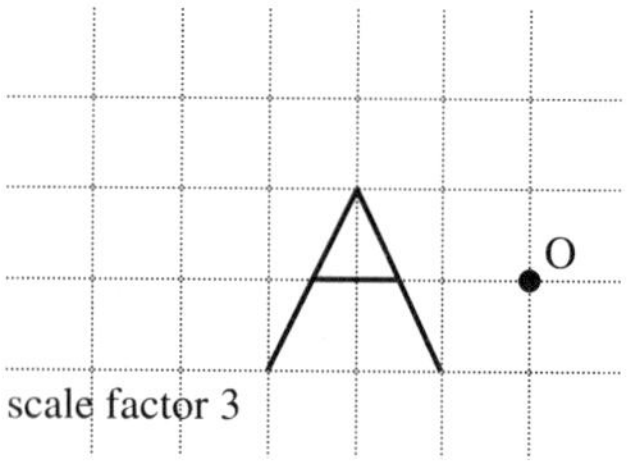

5.

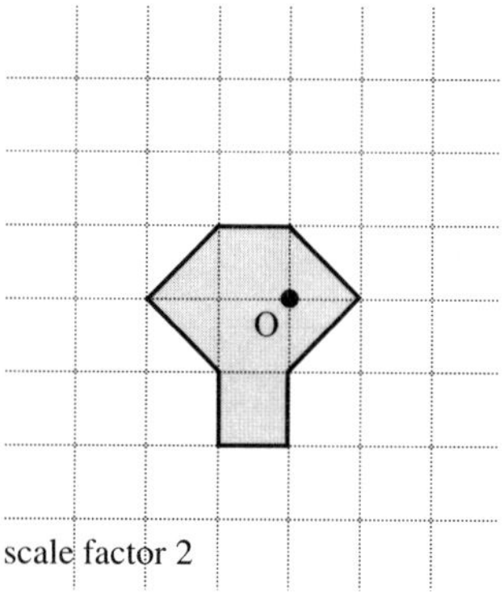

6.

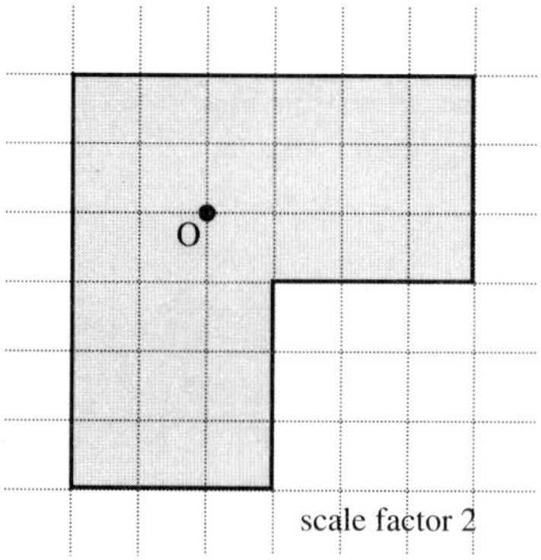

7. (a) Copy the diagram on the right.
(b) Draw the image of △1 after enlargement with scale factor 3, centre (0,0). Label the image △4.
(c) Draw the image of △2 after enlargement with scale factor 2, centre (−1,3). Label the image △5.
(d) Draw the image of △3 after enlargement with scale factor 2, centre (−1,−5). Label the image △6.
(e) Write down the coordinates of the ‘pointed ends’ of △4, △5 and △6. [The ‘pointed end’ is the vertex of the triangle with the smallest angle.]

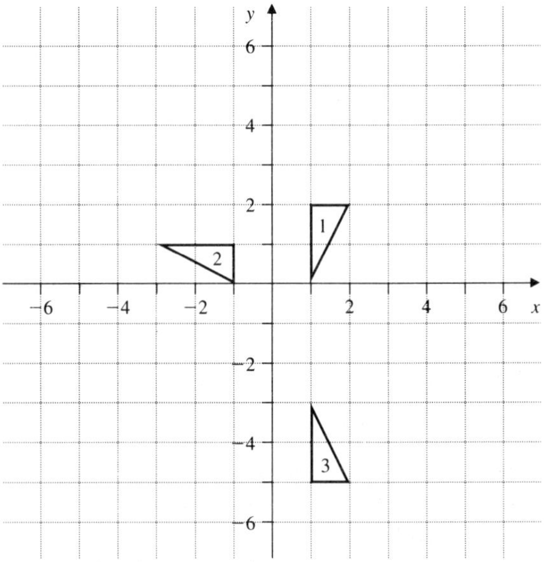

For Questions **8**, **9** draw a pair of axes with values from −7 to +7.

8. (a) Plot and label the triangles
△1: (5,5), (5,7), (4,7)
△2: (−6,−5), (−3,−5), (−3,−4)
△3: (1,−4), (1,−6), (2,−6).
(b) Draw the image of △1 after enlargement with scale factor 2, centre (7,7). Label the image △4.
(c) Draw the image of △2 after enlargement with scale factor 3, centre (−6,−7). Label the image △5.
(d) Draw the image of △3 after enlargement with scale factor 2, centre (−1,−5). Label the image △6.
(e) Write down the coordinates of the 'pointed ends' of △4, △5 and △6.

9. (a) Plot and label the triangles
△1: (5,3), (5,6), (4,6)
△2: (4,−3), (1,−3), (1,−2)
△3: (−4,−7), (−7,−7), (−7,−6).
(b) Draw the image of △1 after enlargement with scale factor 2, centre (7,7). Label the image △4.
(c) Draw the image of △2 after enlargement with scale factor 3, centre (5,−4). Label the image △5.
(d) Draw the image of △3 after enlargement with scale factor 4, centre (−7,−7). Label the image △6.
(e) Write down the coordinates of the 'pointed ends' of △4, △5 and △6.

Enlargements with fractional scale factors (reductions)

The unshaded shape is the image of the shaded shape after an enlargement with scale factor $\frac{1}{2}$, centre O.

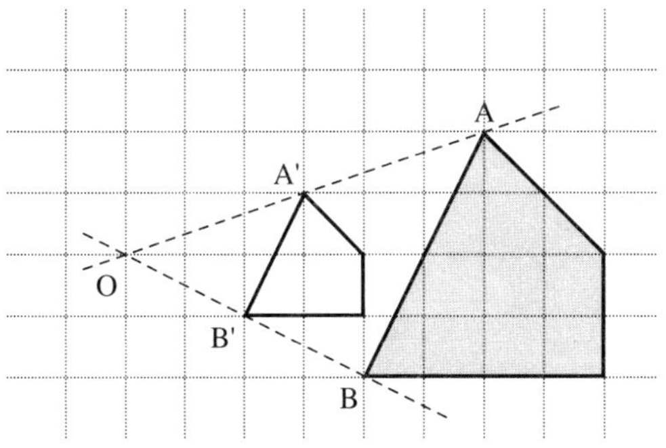

Note that $OA' = \frac{1}{2} \times OA$

$OB' = \frac{1}{2} \times OB$

Even though the shape has undergone a reduction, mathematicians prefer to call it an enlargement with a fractional scale factor.

Exercise 8

Copy each diagram and draw an enlargement using the centre O and the scale factor given.

1.

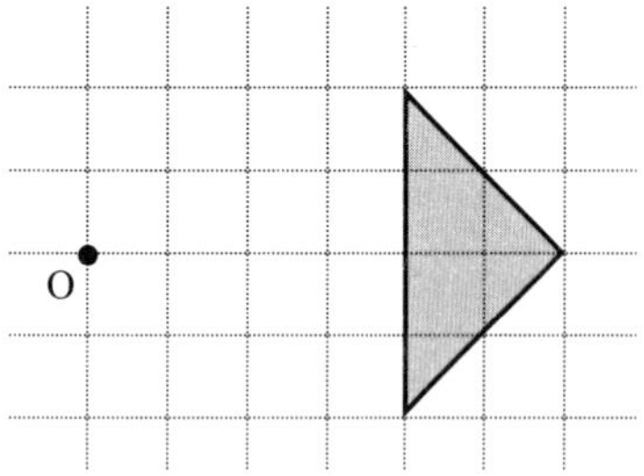

scale factor $\frac{1}{2}$

2.

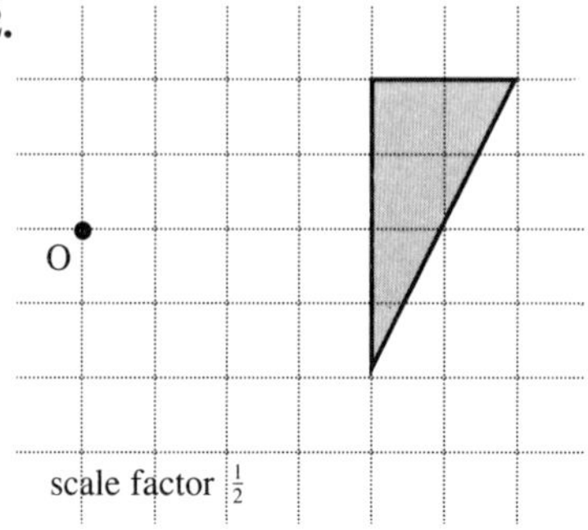

scale factor $\frac{1}{2}$

3.

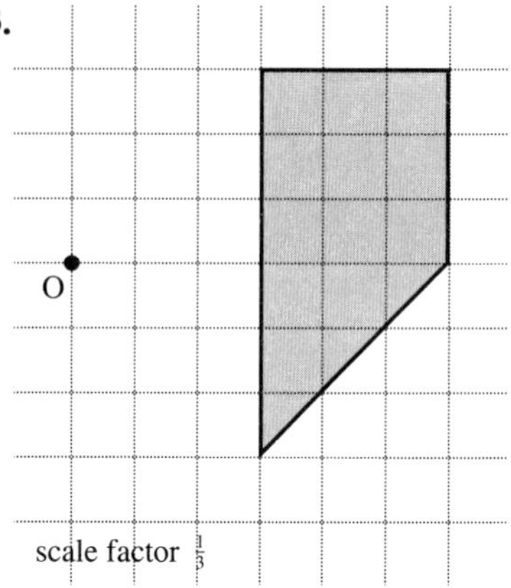

scale factor $\frac{1}{3}$

4. (a) Plot and label the triangles
$\triangle 1$: (7,6), (1,6), (1,3)
$\triangle 2$: (7,−1), (7,−7), (3,−7)
$\triangle 3$: (−5,7), (−5,1), (−7,1).
(b) Draw $\triangle 4$, the image of $\triangle 1$ after an enlargement with scale factor $\frac{1}{3}$, centre (−2,0).
(c) Draw $\triangle 5$, the image of $\triangle 2$ after an enlargement with scale factor $\frac{1}{2}$, centre (−5,−7).
(d) Draw $\triangle 6$, the image of $\triangle 3$ after an enlargement with scale factor $\frac{1}{2}$, centre (−7,−5).

Translation

A translation is simply a 'shift'. There is no turning or reflection and the object stays the same size. In the diagram shown:

(a) $\triangle 1$ is mapped onto $\triangle 2$ by the translation with vector $\begin{pmatrix} 4 \\ 2 \end{pmatrix}$

(b) $\triangle 2$ is mapped onto $\triangle 3$ by the translation with vector $\begin{pmatrix} 2 \\ -3 \end{pmatrix}$

(c) $\triangle 3$ is mapped onto $\triangle 2$ by the translation with vector $\begin{pmatrix} -2 \\ 3 \end{pmatrix}$

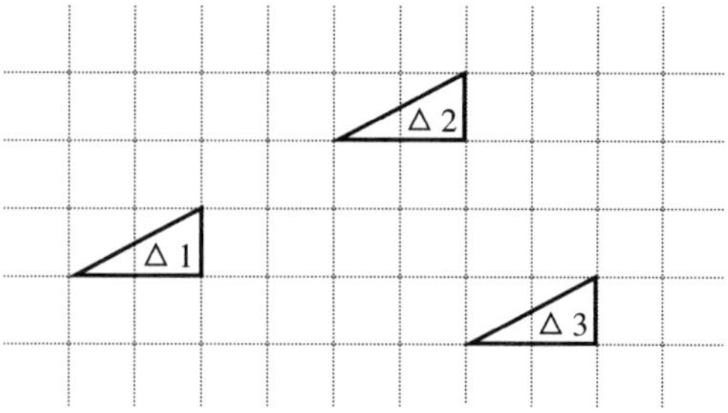

In a vector the top number gives the number of units across (positive to the right) and the bottom number gives the number of units up/down (positive upwards).

So $\begin{pmatrix} 4 \\ 2 \end{pmatrix}$ is 4 across → 2 up ↑ $\begin{pmatrix} -2 \\ 3 \end{pmatrix}$ is 2 across ← 3 up ↑

Exercise 9

1. Look at the diagram shown.

Decide which of these are translations; answer 'yes' or 'no' for each part.

(a) △1 → △2 (b) △1 → △3
(c) △1 → △4 (d) △1 → △5
(e) △1 → △6 (f) △1 → △7
(g) △1 → △8 (h) △2 → △3
(i) △2 → △4 (j) △2 → △5
(k) △2 → △6 (l) △2 → △7
(m) △2 → △8 (n) △3 → △6

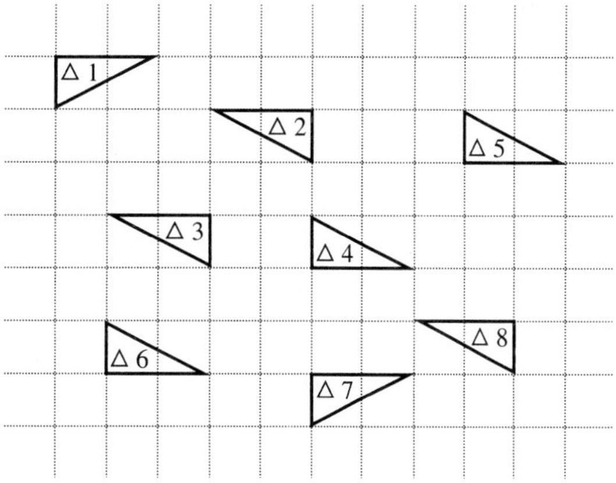

2. Look at the diagram shown.

Write down the vector for each of the following translations:

(a) △1 → △2 (b) △1 → △3
(c) △1 → △4 (d) △1 → △5
(e) △1 → △6 (f) △1 → △7
(g) △1 → △8 (h) △2 → △3
(i) △2 → △4 (j) △2 → △5
(k) △2 → △6 (l) △2 → △8
(m) △3 → △5 (n) △8 → △2

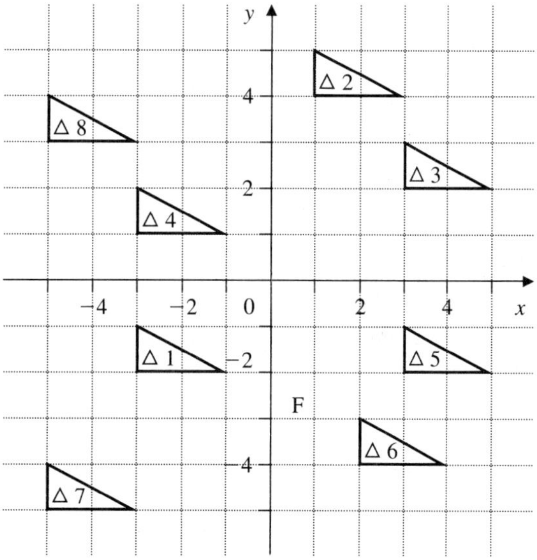

Tessellations

A tessellation is formed when a shape (or shapes) fit together without gaps to cover a surface. Here are some examples.

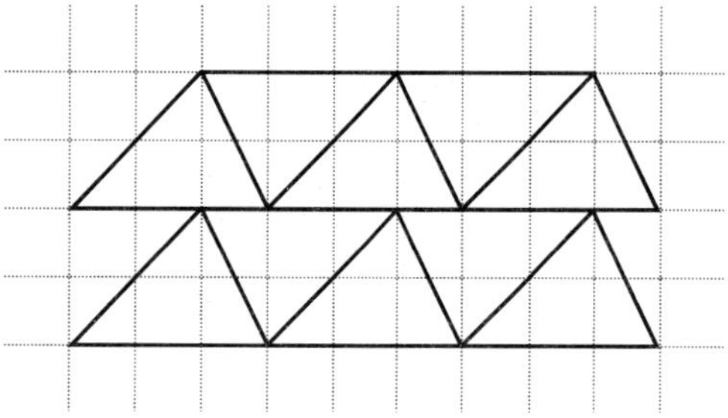

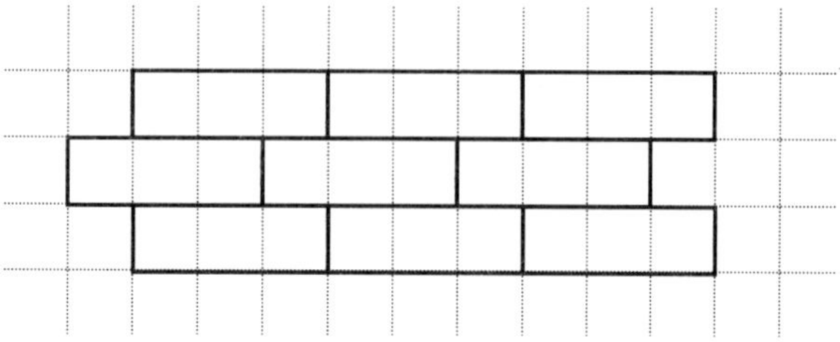

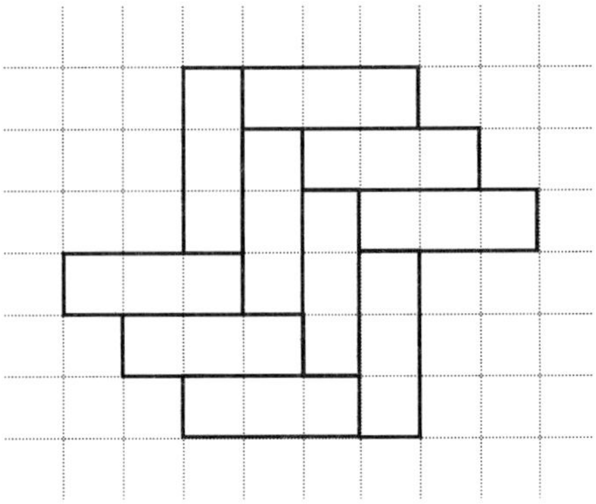

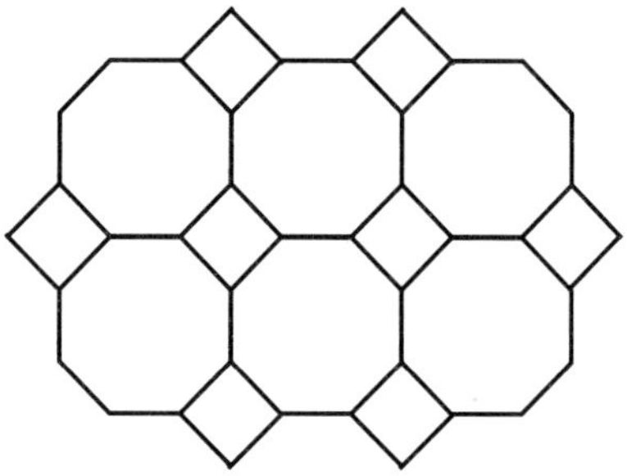

Exercise 10

1. Use squared paper to show that each of the shapes below tessellates.

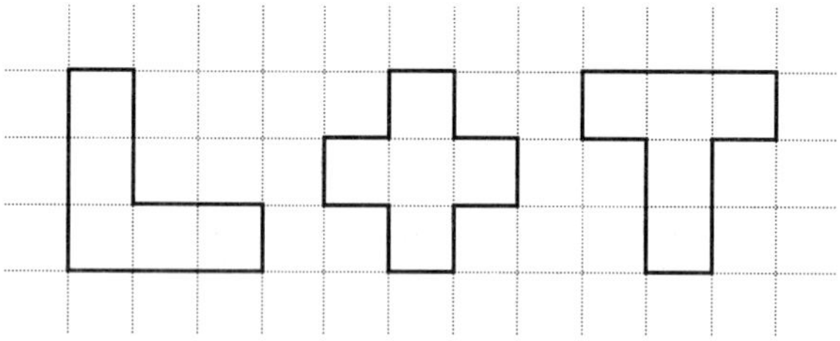

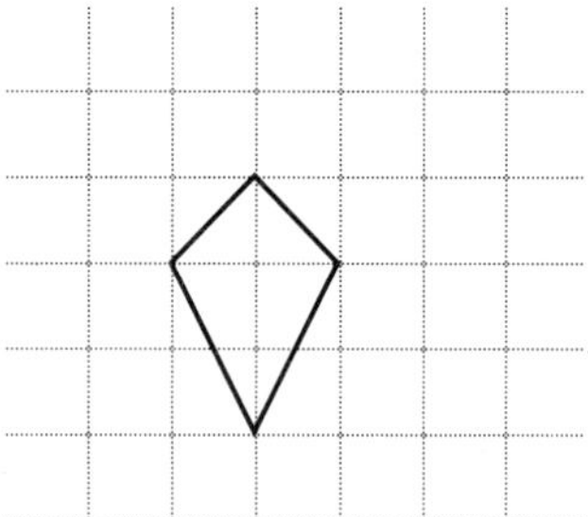

2. (a) Draw any irregular triangle or quadrilateral and cut twenty or so copies from cardboard. Fit them together, like a jigsaw puzzle, to cover a plane.

(b) Say whether the statements below are true or false:

(i) 'all triangles tessellate'

(ii) 'all quadrilaterals tessellate'.

3. Is it true that 'all pentagons tessellate'?

4. Copy each pattern and add a further six tiles of your own.

(a)

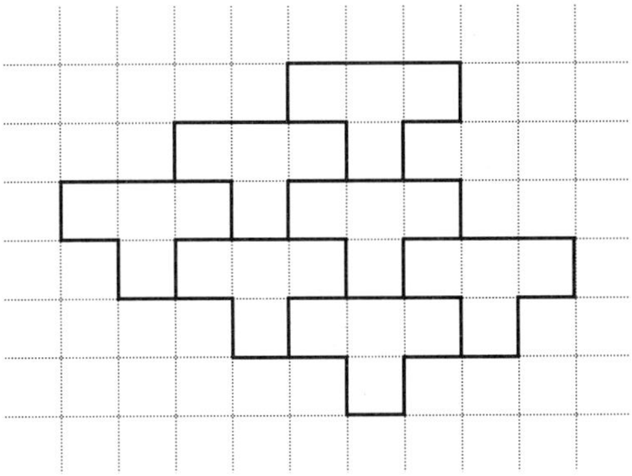

(b)

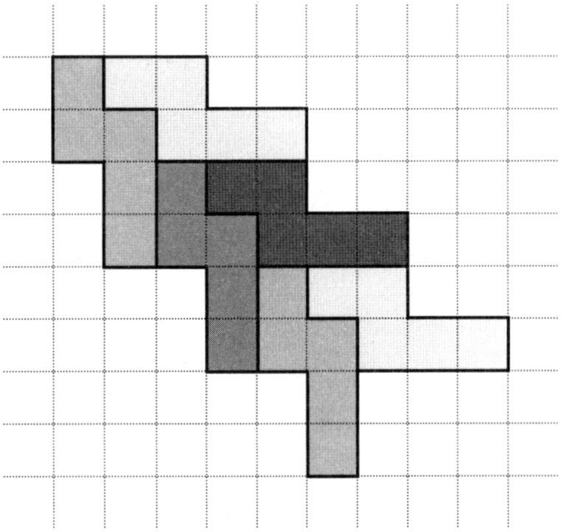

(c) This one is more difficult. Good luck!

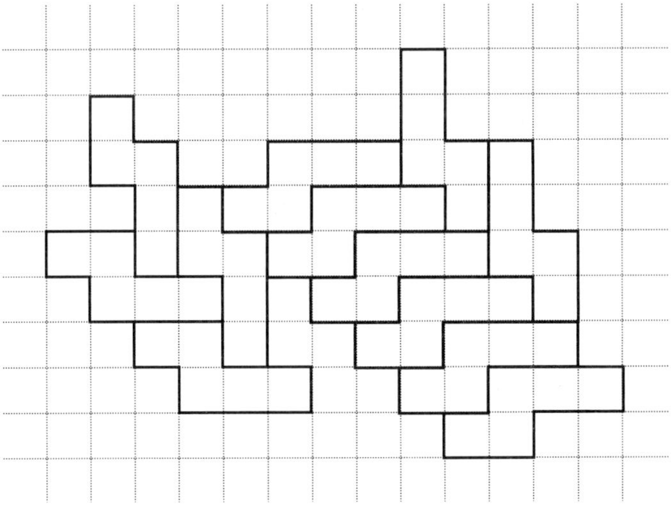

5. Here are two tessellations, each using two shapes.

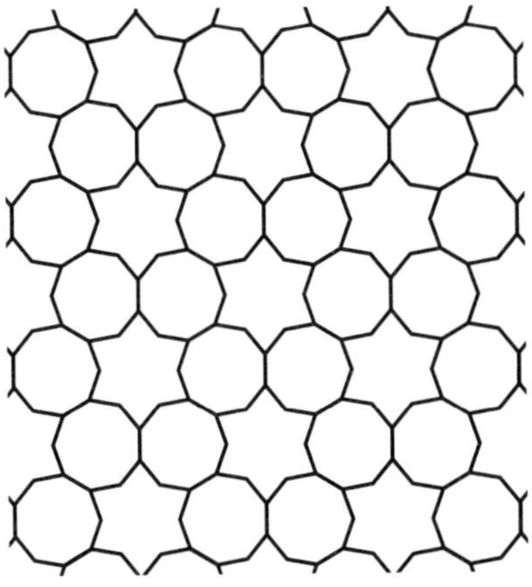

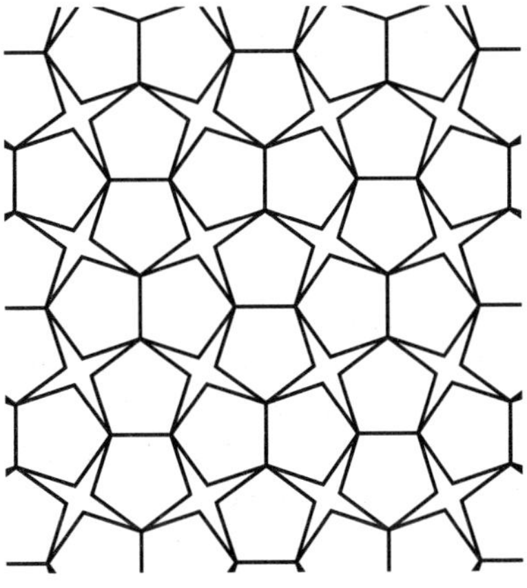

Try to design a tessellation like these.

5.2 Quadrilaterals and other polygons

4/6b

Properties of quadrilaterals

Square: Four equal sides;
All angles 90°;
Four lines of symmetry.

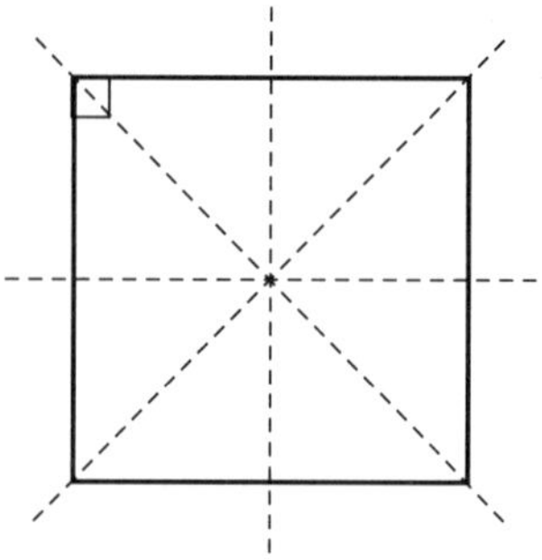

Rectangle (not square): Two pairs of equal and parallel sides;
All angles 90°;
Two lines of symmetry.

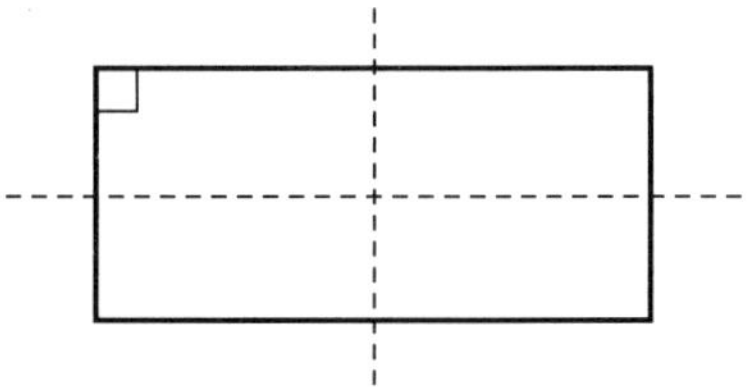

Rhombus: Four equal sides;
Opposite sides parallel;
Diagonals bisect at right angles;
Diagonals bisect angles of rhombus;
Two lines of symmetry.

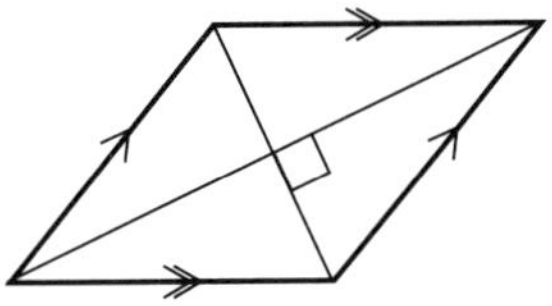

Parallelogram: Two pairs of equal and parallel sides;
Opposite angles equal;
No lines of symmetry (in general).

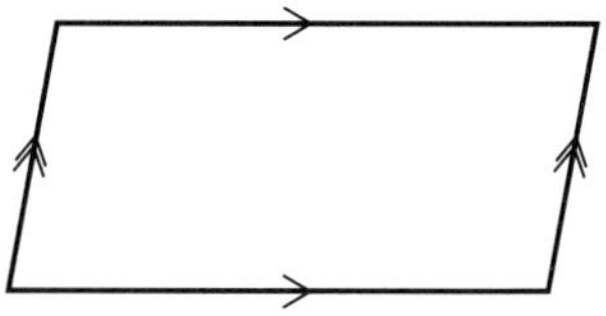

Trapezium: One pair of parallel sides.

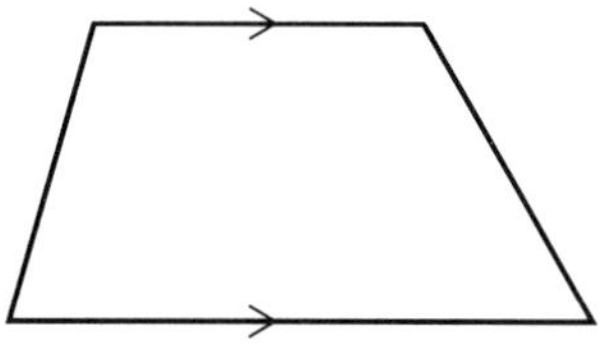

Kite: AB = AD, CB = CD;
Diagonals meet at 90°;
One line of symmetry.

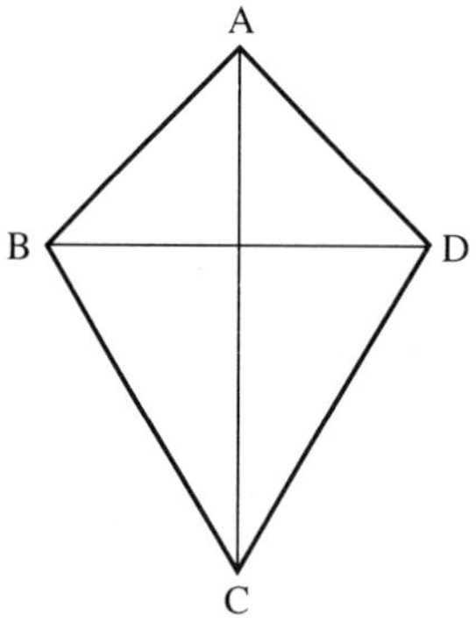

For all quadrilaterals the sum of the interior angles is 360°.

Exercise 11

1. Find the angle x.

(a)

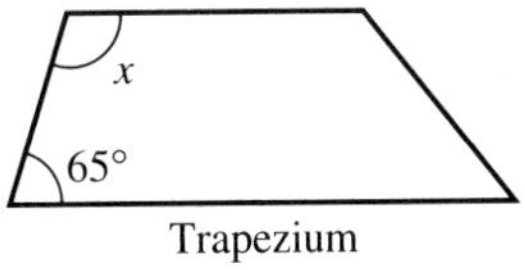

(b)

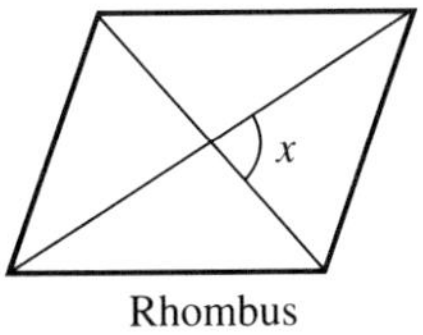

(c)

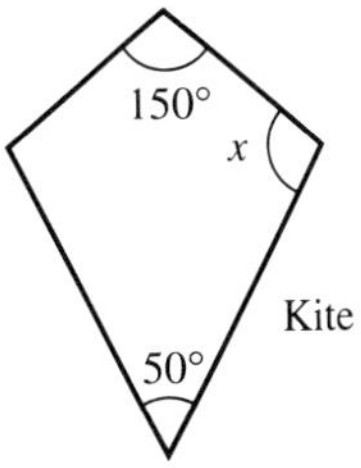

2. Copy the table and fill all the boxes with either ticks or crosses.

	Diagonals always equal	Diagonals always perpendicular	Diagonals always bisect the angles	Diagonals always bisect each other
Square				
Rectangle				
Parallelogram				
Rhombus				
Kite				

3. ABCD is a rhombus whose diagonals intersect at M. Find the coordinates of C and D.

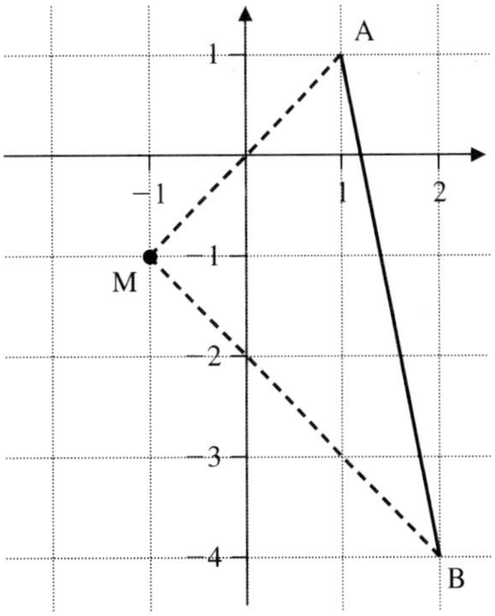

In Questions **4** to **14**, begin by drawing a diagram and remember to put the letters around the shape in alphabetical order.

4. In a rectangle KLMN, $L\hat{N}M = 34°$. Calculate:
(a) $K\hat{L}N$ (b) $K\hat{M}L$

5. In a trapezium ABCD, $A\hat{B}D = 35°$, $B\hat{A}D = 110°$ and AB is parallel to DC. Calculate:
(a) $A\hat{D}B$ (b) $B\hat{D}C$

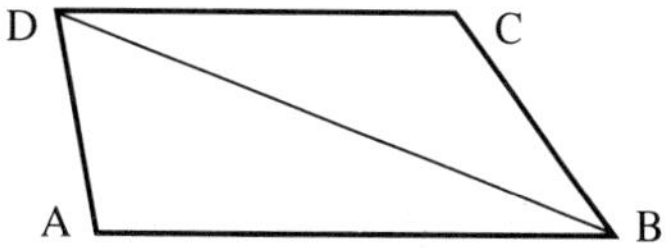

6. In a parallelogram WXYZ, $W\hat{X}Y = 72°$, $Z\hat{W}Y = 80°$.
Calculate:
(a) $W\hat{Z}Y$ (b) $X\hat{W}Z$ (c) $W\hat{Y}X$

7. In a kite ABCD, AB = AD, BC = CD, $C\hat{A}D = 40°$ and $C\hat{B}D = 60°$. Calculate:
(a) $B\hat{A}C$ (b) $B\hat{C}A$ (c) $A\hat{D}C$

8. In a rhombus ABCD, $A\hat{B}C = 64°$. Calculate:
(a) $B\hat{C}D$ (b) $A\hat{D}B$ (c) $B\hat{A}C$

9. In a rectangle WXYZ, M is the mid-point of WX and $Z\hat{M}Y = 70°$. Calculate:
(a) $M\hat{Z}Y$ (b) $Y\hat{M}X$

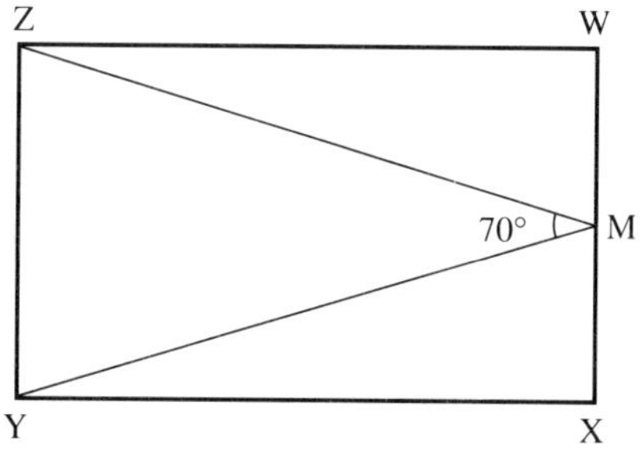

10. In a trapezium ABCD, AB is parallel to DC, AB = AD, BD = DC and $B\hat{A}D = 128°$. Find:
(a) $A\hat{B}D$ (b) $B\hat{D}C$ (c) $B\hat{C}D$

11. In a parallelogram KLMN, KL = KM and $K\hat{M}L = 64°$.
Find:
(a) $M\hat{K}L$
(b) $K\hat{N}M$
(c) $L\hat{M}N$

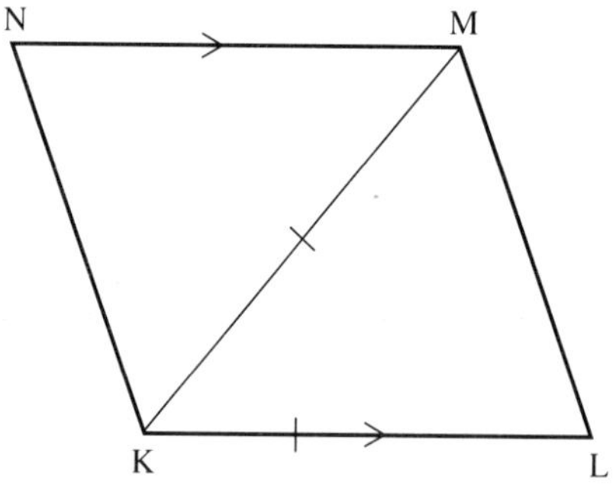

12. In a kite PQRS with PQ = PS and RQ = RS, $Q\hat{R}S = 40°$ and $Q\hat{P}S = 100°$. Find $P\hat{Q}R$.

13. In a rhombus PQRS, $R\hat{P}Q = 54°$. Find:
(a) $P\hat{R}Q$ (b) $P\hat{S}R$ (c) $R\hat{Q}S$

14. In a kite PQRS, $R\hat{P}S = 2P\hat{R}S$, PQ = QS = PS and QR = RS.
Find:
(a) $Q\hat{P}S$ (b) $P\hat{R}S$ (c) $Q\hat{S}R$

5.3 Bearings

4/6c

Bearings are used where there are no roads to guide the way. Ships, aircraft and mountaineers use bearings to work out where they are.

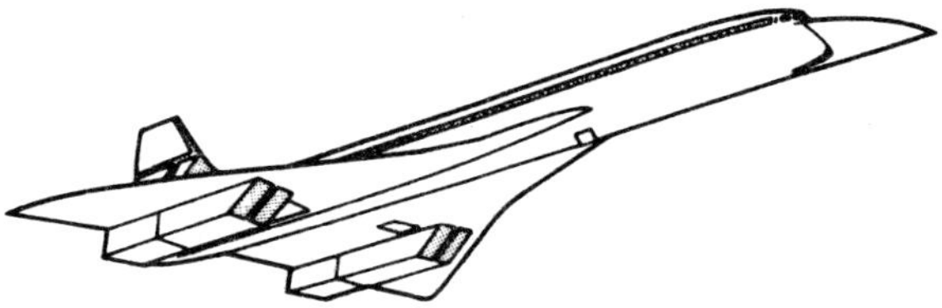

Bearings are measured *clockwise from North.*

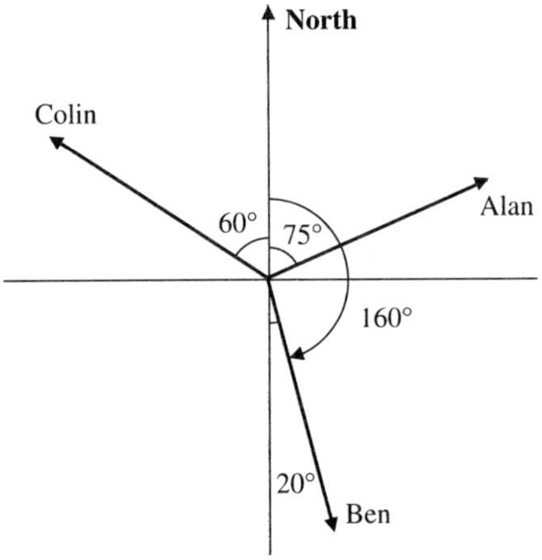

Alan is walking on a bearing of 075°.
Ben is walking on a bearing of 160°.
Colin is walking on a bearing of 300°.

Exercise 12

The diagrams show the directions in which several people are travelling. Work out the bearing for each person.

1.

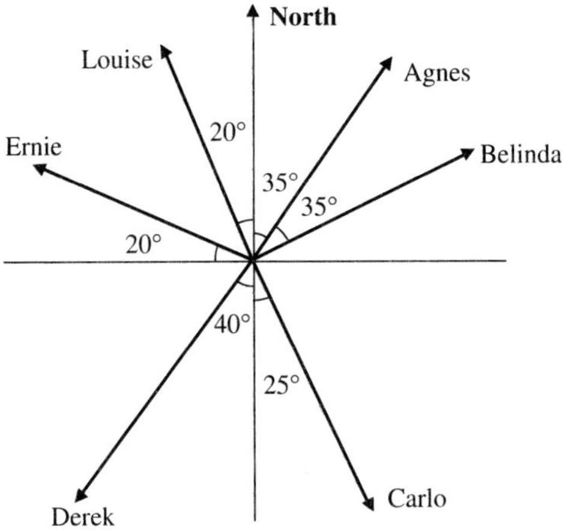

2.

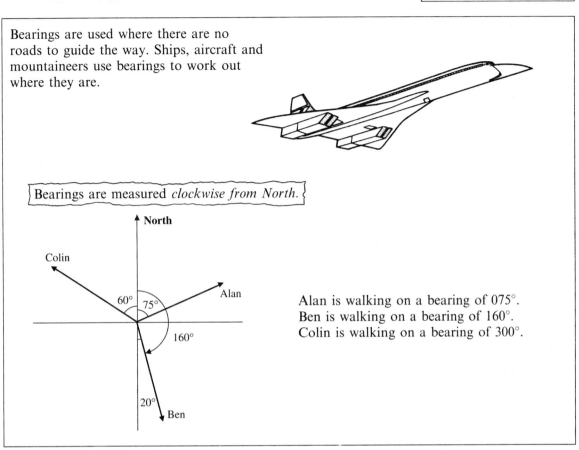

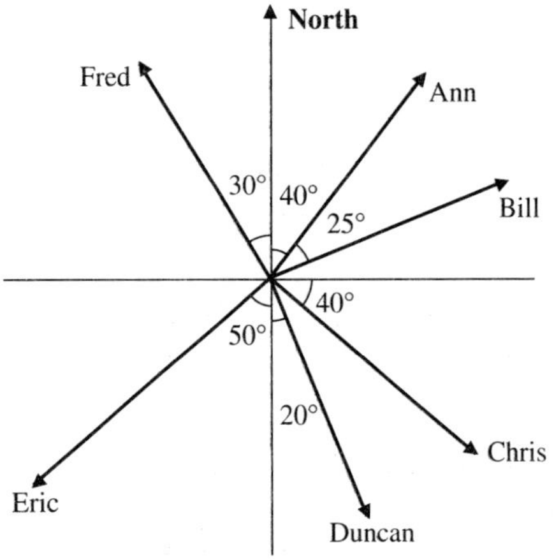

Relative bearings

The bearing of A from B is the direction in which you travel to get to A from B.

It helps to show the journey with an arrow, as below.

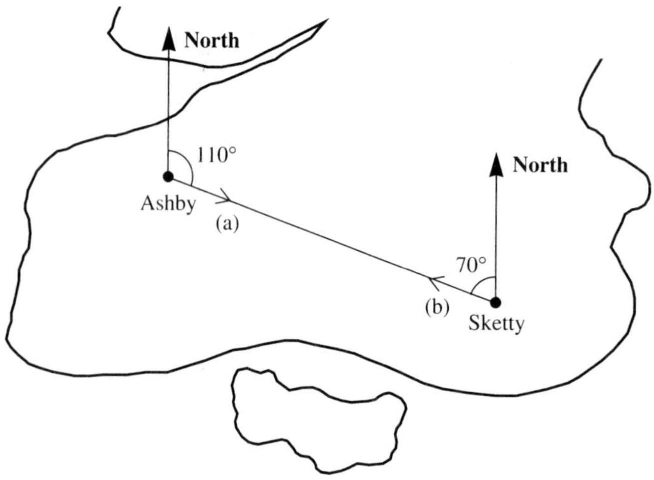

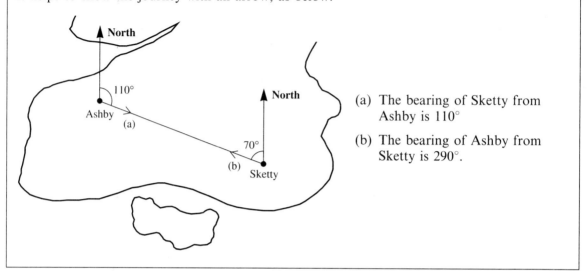

(a) The bearing of Sketty from Ashby is 110°

(b) The bearing of Ashby from Skety is 290°.

Exercise 13

The map of North America shows six radar tracking stations, A, B, C, D, E, F.

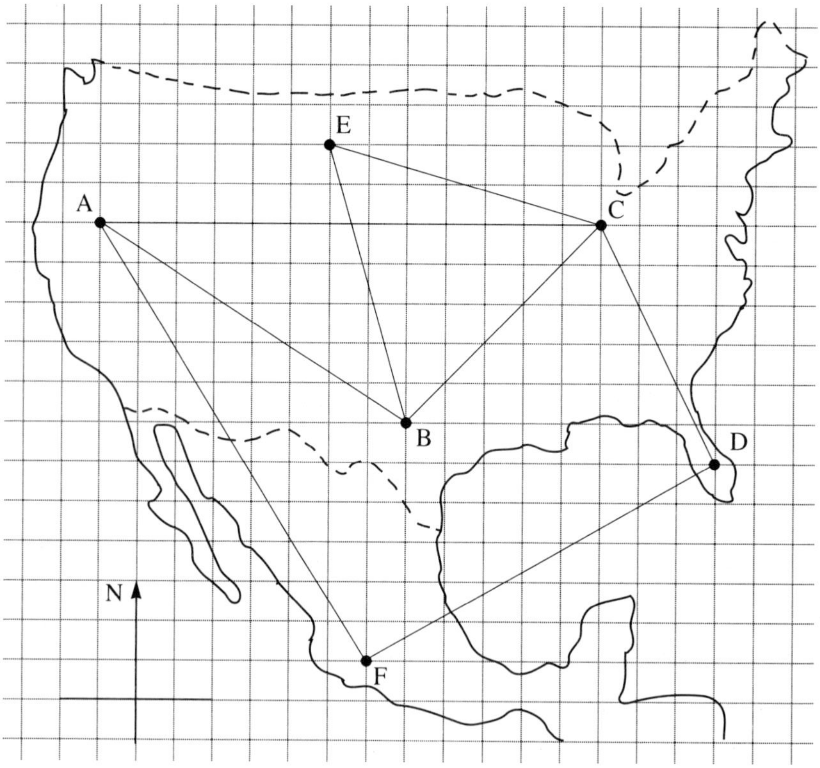

1. From A, measure the bearing of (a) F (b) B (c) C.
2. From C, measure the bearing of (a) E (b) B (c) D.
3. From F, measure the bearing of (a) D (b) A.
4. From B, measure the bearing of (a) A (b) E (c) C.

Ships or aircraft can be located when their bearings from two places are known.

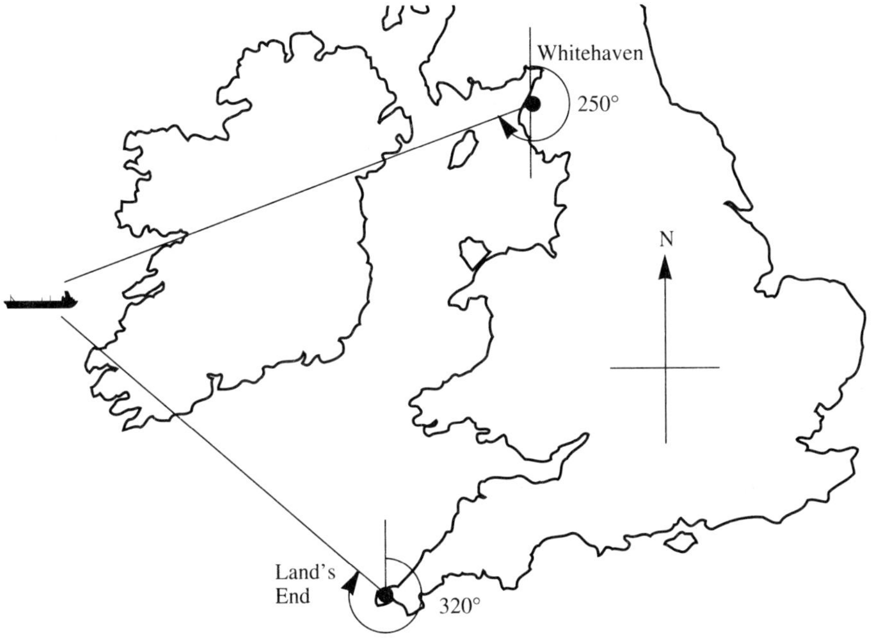

On the map the tanker 'Braer' is on a bearing 320° from Land's End. From Whitehaven, the Braer is on a bearing of 250°.
There is only one place where it can be.

Exercise 14

Draw the points P and Q below in the middle of a clean page of squared paper. Mark the points A, B, C, D and E accurately, using the information given.

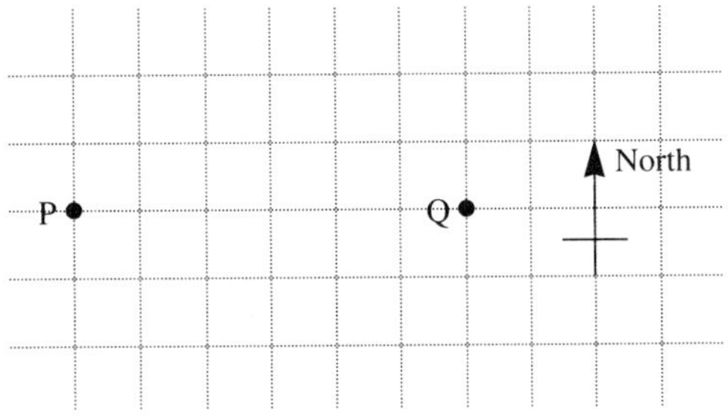

1. A is on a bearing of 040° from P and 015° from Q.
2. B is on a bearing of 076° from P and 067° from Q.
3. C is on a bearing of 114° from P and 127° from Q.
4. D is on a bearing of 325° from P and 308° from Q.
5. E is on a bearing of 180° from P and 208° from Q.

Exercise 15

Draw the points X and Y below in the middle of a clean page of squared paper. Mark the points K, L, M, N and O accurately, using the information given.

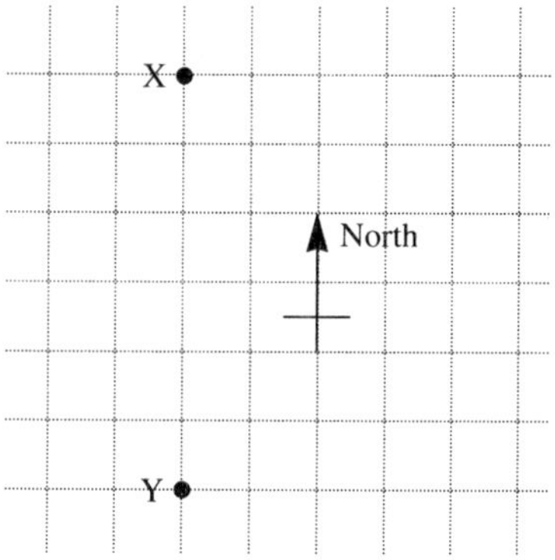

1. K is on a bearing of 041° from X and 025° from Y.
2. L is on a bearing of 090° from X and 058° from Y.
3. M is on a bearing of 123° from X and 090° from Y.
4. N is on a bearing of 203° from X and 215° from Y.
5. O is on a bearing of 288° from X and 319° from Y.

Exercise 16

Make accurate scale drawings with a scale of 1 cm to 1 km, unless told otherwise. Use squared paper and begin each question by drawing a small sketch of the journey.

1. A ship sails 8 km due North and then a further 7 km on a bearing 080°, as in the diagram (which is not drawn to scale).
   How far is the ship now from its starting point?

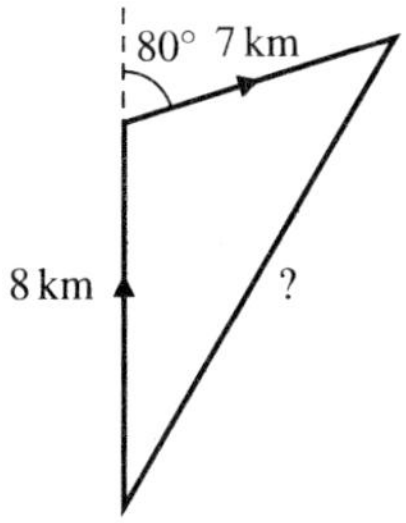

2. A ship sails 9 km on a bearing 090° and then a further 6 km on a bearing 050°, as shown in the diagram.
   How far is the ship now from its starting point?

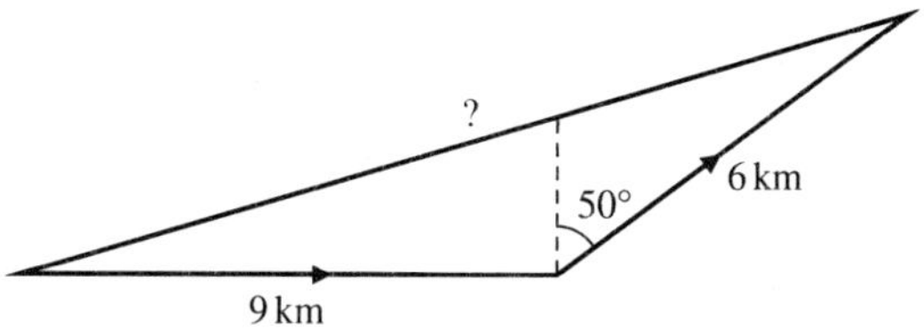

3. A ship sails 6 km on a bearing 160° and then a further 10 km on a bearing 240°, as shown.
   (a) How far is the ship from its starting point?
   b) On what bearing must the ship sail so that it returns to its starting point?

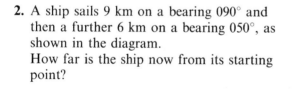

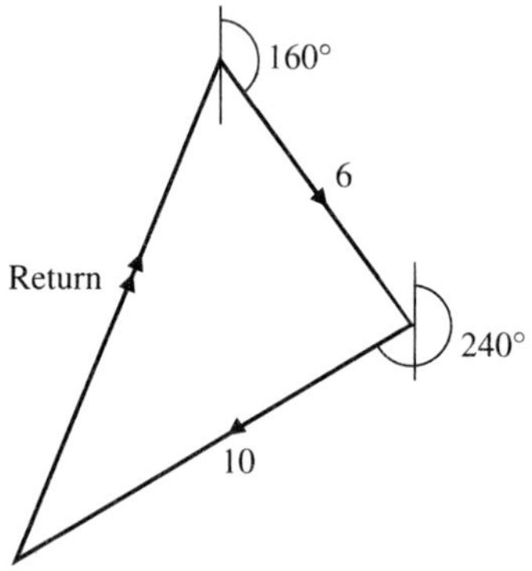

4. A ship sails 5 km on a bearing 030°, then 3 km on a bearing 090° and finally 4 km on a bearing 160°. How far is the ship now from its starting point?

5. Point B is 8 km from A on a bearing 140° from A. Point C is 9 km from A on a bearing 200° from A.
   (a) How far is B from C?
   (b) What is the bearing of B from C?

6. Point Q is 10 km from P on a bearing 052° from P. Point R is 4 km from P on a bearing 107° from P.
   (a) How far is Q from R?
   (b) What is the bearing of Q from R?

7. A laser beam gun L is 120 km from P on a bearing 068°. The laser beam destroys anything on a bearing 270° from L.

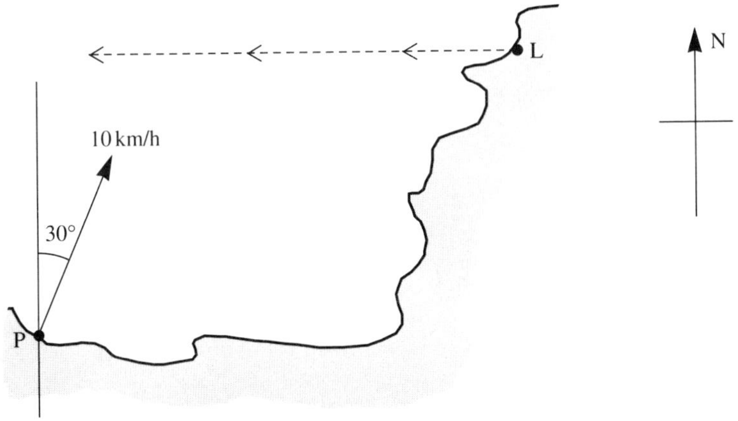

   (a) Draw a diagram, with a scale of 1 cm to 10 km, to show the positions of P and L.
   (b) A ship sails from P at a speed of 10 km/h on a bearing 030°. For how long does the ship sail before being destroyed?

8. Robinson Crusoe is on a tiny island R, dying of starvation. There is an airport at A which is 150 km from R on a bearing 295° from R.

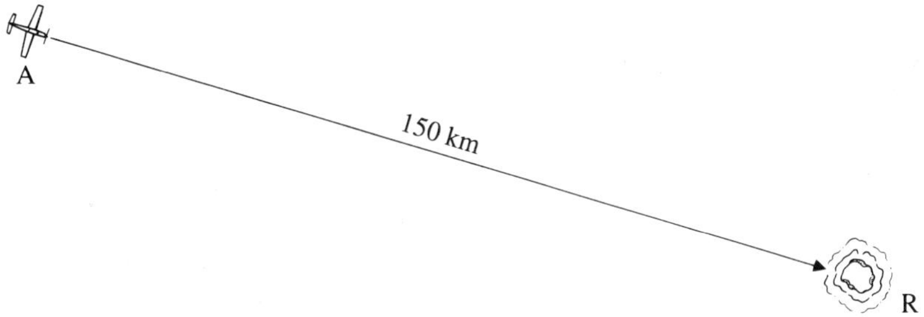

An aircraft flies from A. If the aircraft gets within 40 km of R, the pilot will see Robinson's bonfire and Mr Crusoe will be saved. Will Robinson survive if the plane flies on a bearing of 098°?

5.4 Three-dimensional coordinates

4/7a

In three dimensional space we need three coordinates to describe the position of a point. The coordinates are x, y and z.
In this diagram the coordinates of A are (5, 4, 2)

$$\begin{matrix} \nearrow & \uparrow & \nwarrow \\ x & y & z \end{matrix}$$

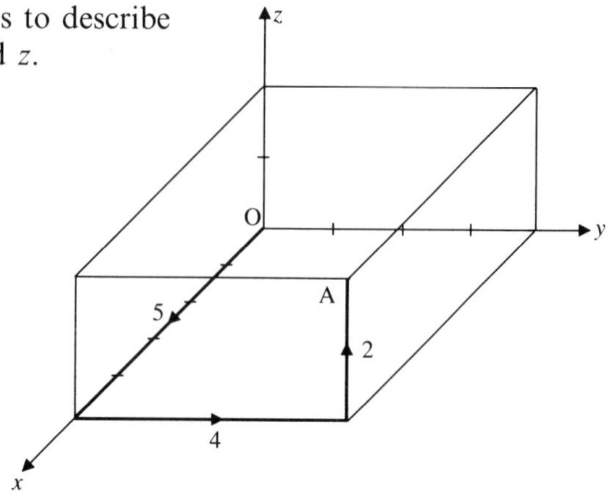

Exercise 17

1. Write down the coordinates of the points A, B, C, D.

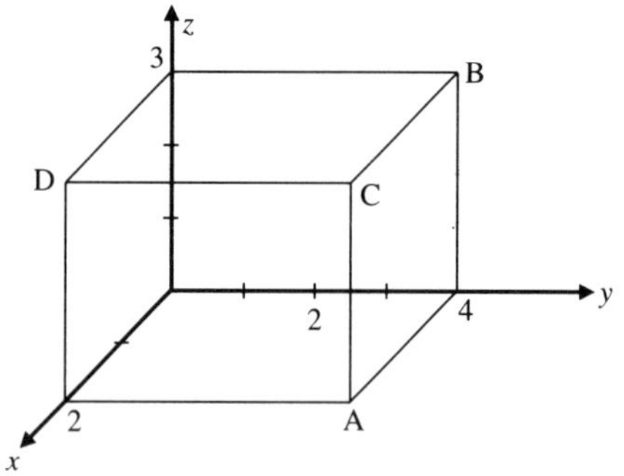

2. (a) Write down the coordinates of B, C, Q, R.

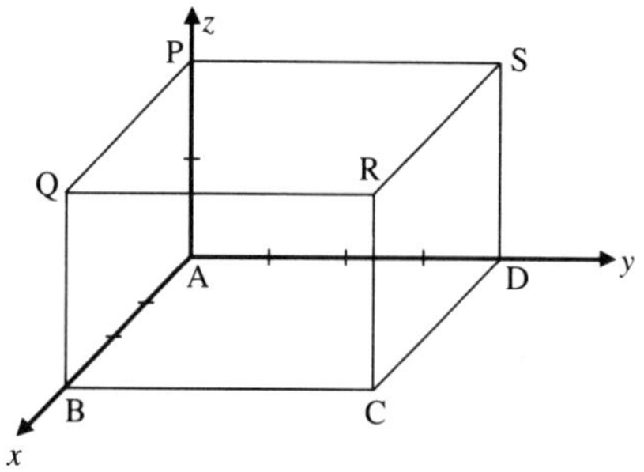

(b) Write down the coordinates of the mid-points of
(i) AD (ii) DS (iii) DC

(c) Write down the coordinates of the centre of the face
(i) ABCD (ii) PQRS (iii) RSDC

(d) Write down the coordinates of the centre of the box.

3. (a) Write down the coordinates of C, R, B, P, Q.

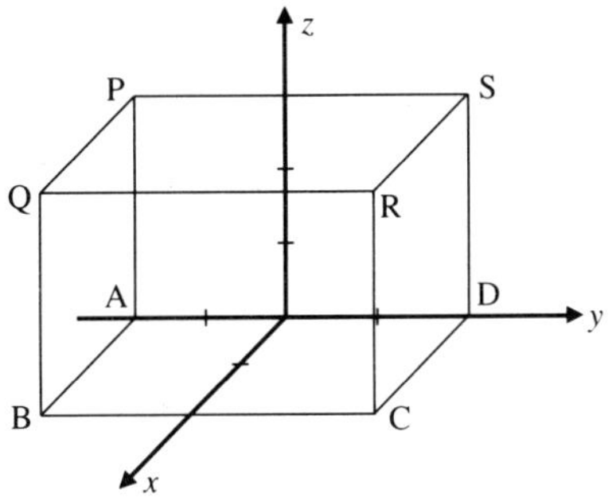

(b) Write down the coordinates of the mid-points of
(i) QB (ii) PQ

4. Use Pythagoras' theorem to calculate the lengths of
(i) LM (ii) LN (iii) NM

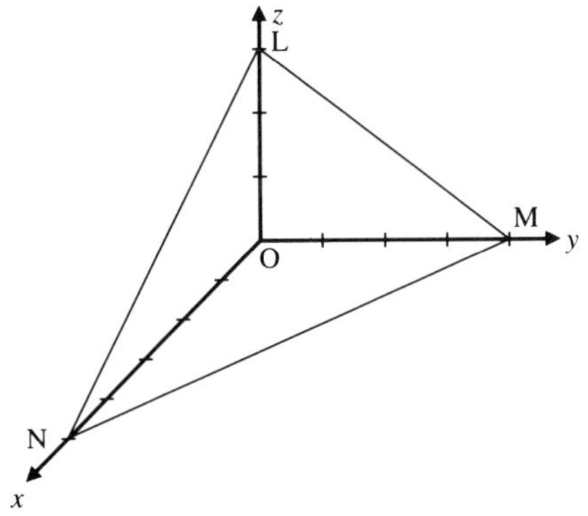

5. In the cuboid below, OP = 4, OQ = 7, OR = 5. Write down the coordinates of the centre of the face
(a) ABCR (ii) BCQD (iii) OPDQ

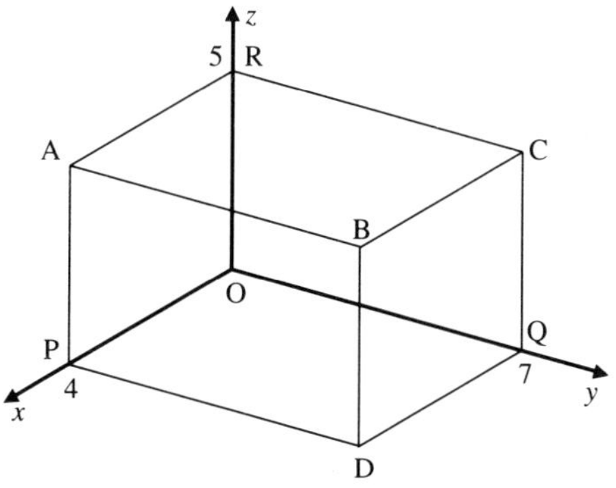

6. Measured from a control tower O, an aircraft is 20 km North, 30 km East and 5 km high. So with origin at O, its coordinates are (20, 30, 5). It is flying east at 3 km per minute.
What are the coordinates of the aircraft after 5 minutes?

7. Draw your own axes and plot the points O (0,0,0), A(3,0,0), B(3,4,0), C(0,0,5).
Work out the length of the following lines.
(a) AB (b) OB (c) CB

8. A solid object has vertices at (0,0,0), (6,0,0), (6,6,0), (0,6,0) and (3,3,4).
Plot the points on a diagram and name the object.

9. Plot the points O(0,0,0), A(6,8,0), B(6,8,10).
Work out (a) OA
(b) angle BOA

10. A prisoner starts his escape tunnel at (0,0,0). He digs in a straight line to a sewer at (5, 3, −2). He then crawls along the sewer to (5, 20, −2). Finally he digs in a straight line to escape at (0,24,0). Work out the total length of the three sections of his escape route. The units are given in metres.

5.5 Locus

4/7b

In mathematics, the word *locus* describes the position of points which obey a certain rule. The locus can be the path traced out by a moving point.

Three important loci

(a) Circle

The locus of points which are equidistant from a fixed point O is shown. It is a **circle** with centre O.

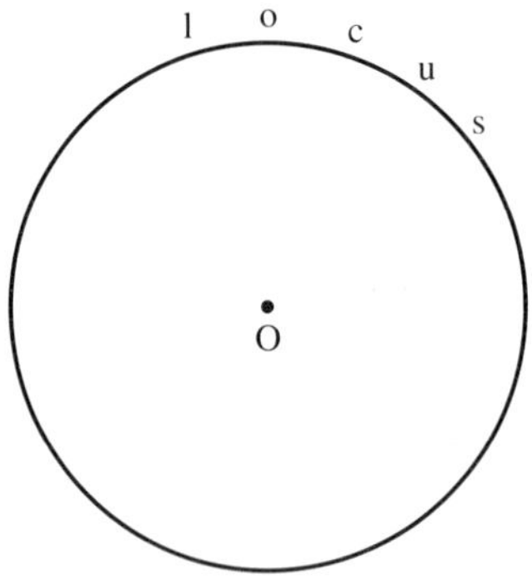

(b) Perpendicular bisector

The locus of points which are equidistant from two fixed points A and B is shown.

The locus is the **perpendicular bisector** of the line AB. Use compasses to draw arcs, as shown, or use a ruler and a protractor.

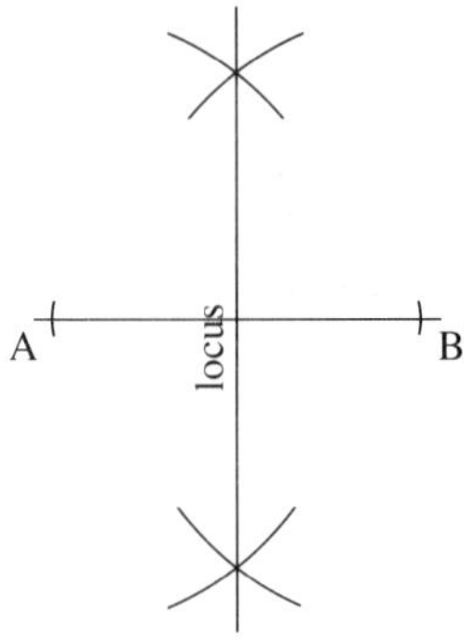

(c) Angle bisector

The locus of points which are equidistant from two fixed lines AB and AC is shown.

The locus is the line which bisects the angle BAC. Use compasses to draw arcs or use a protractor to construct the locus.

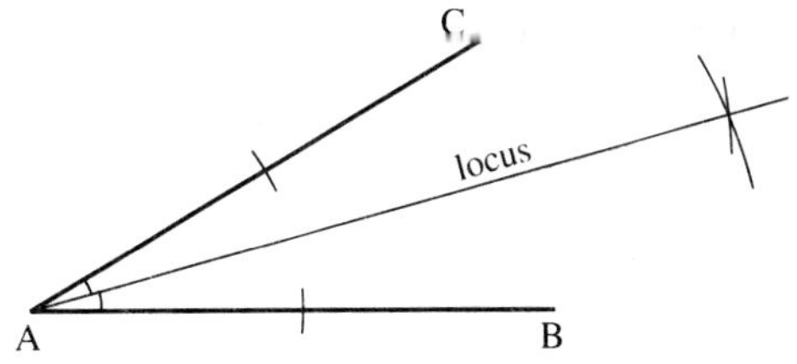

Exercise 18

1. Mark two points P and Q which are 10 cm apart. Draw the locus of points which are equidistant from P and Q.

2. Draw two lines AB and AC of length 8 cm, where $B\hat{A}C = 40°$. Draw the locus of points which are equidistant from AB and AC.

3. (a) Draw the triangle LMN full size.
   (b) Draw the locus of the points which are:
      (i) equidistant from L and N
      (ii) equidistant from LN and LM
      (iii) 4 cm from M
   [Draw the three loci in different colours].

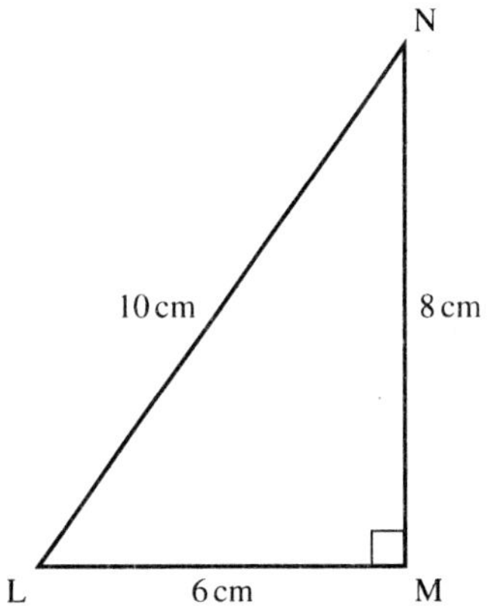

4. Draw a line AB of length 6 cm. Draw the locus of a point P so that angle ABP = 90°.

5. The diagram shows the walls of a rectangular shed measuring 8 m by 5 m. A goat is tied outside the shed to the corner C by a rope 7 m long. Make a scale drawing to show the boundary of the area which the goat can reach.

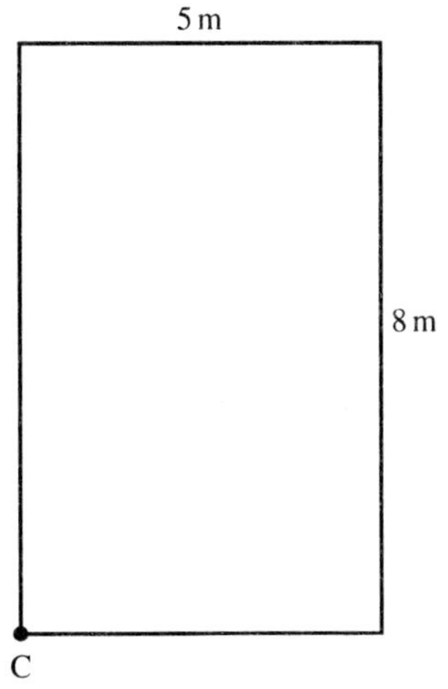

6. Channel 9 in Australia is planning the position of a new TV satellite to send pictures all over the country. The new satellite is to be placed:
(a) an equal distance from Darwin and Adelaide.
(b) not more than 2000 km from Perth.
(c) not more than 1600 km from Brisbane.

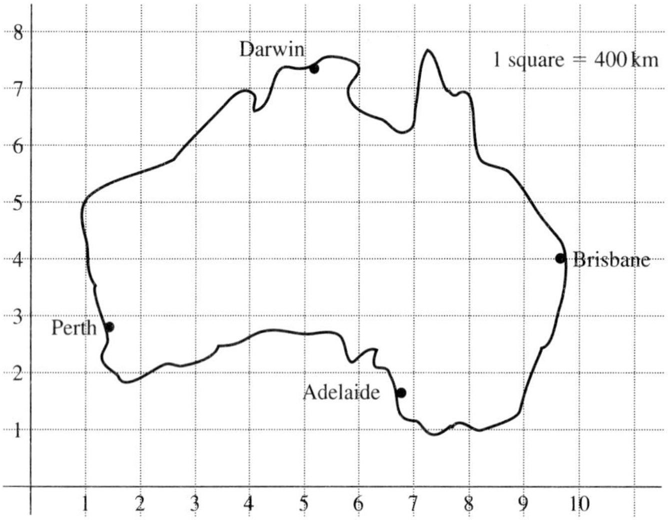

Make a copy of the map on squared paper using the grid lines as reference.
Show clearly where the satellite could be placed so that it satisfies the conditions (a), (b), (c) above.

7. A and B are fixed pegs 10 cm apart. A piece of string of length 15 cm is tied to A and B and passes through a small ring R which can slide along the string.

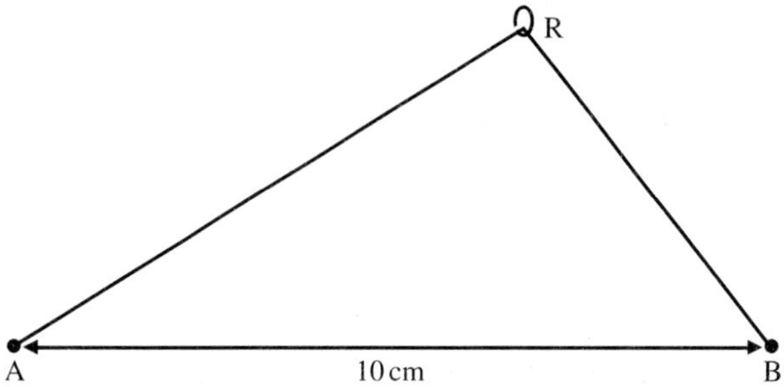

Draw, as accurately as you can, the locus of R if the string is always kept taut.
The locus of the point R where AR + BR = 15 cm is a curve called an ellipse.

8. Rod AB rotates about the fixed point A. B is joined to C which slides along a fixed rod. AB = 15 cm and BC = 25 cm.

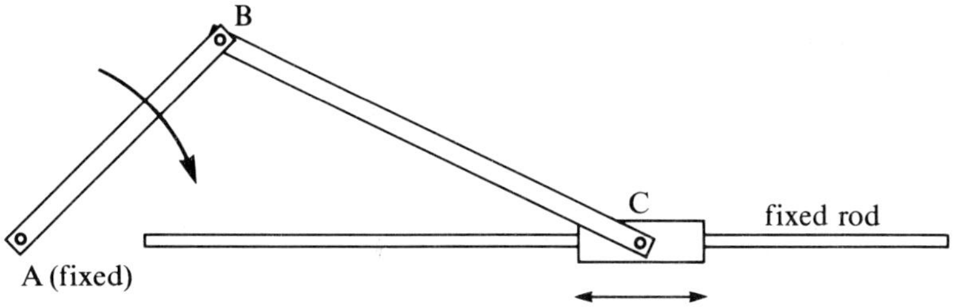

Describe the locus of C as AB rotates clockwise about A.
Find the smallest and the largest distance between C and A.

9. Cog A has 36 teeth and cog B has 24 teeth.

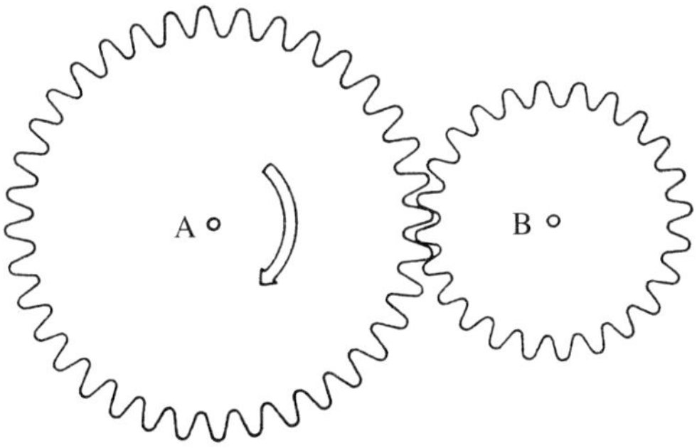

(a) When cog A turns clockwise in what direction does cog B turn?
(b) When cog A makes 10 complete revolutions how many times does cog B rotate?
(c) If cog B is rotating at a speed of 300 revolutions per minute at what speed is cog A rotating?

10. Draw two points M and N 16 cm apart. Draw the locus of a point P which moves so that the area of triangle MNP is $80\,cm^2$.

11. Describe the locus of a point which moves in three dimensional space and is equidistant from two fixed points.

12. A circle of radius 2 cm rolls around the perimeter of a square of side 8 cm.
Sketch the locus of the centre of the circle.

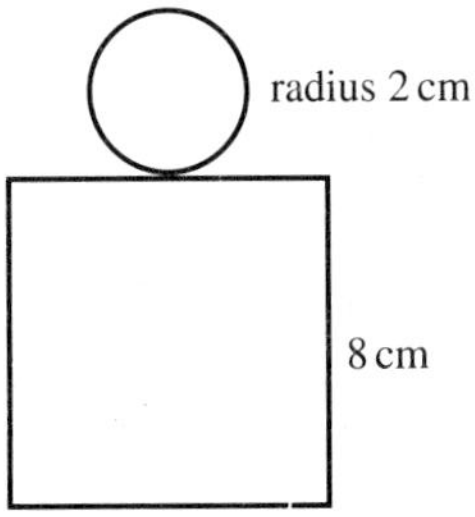

5.6 Pythagoras' theorem

4/7c

In a right-angled triangle the square on the hypotenuse is equal to the sum of the squares on the other two sides.

$a^2 + b^2 = c^2$

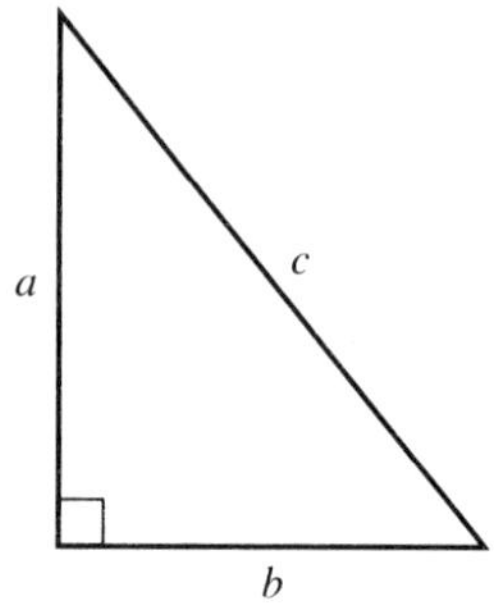

Find the side marked d.

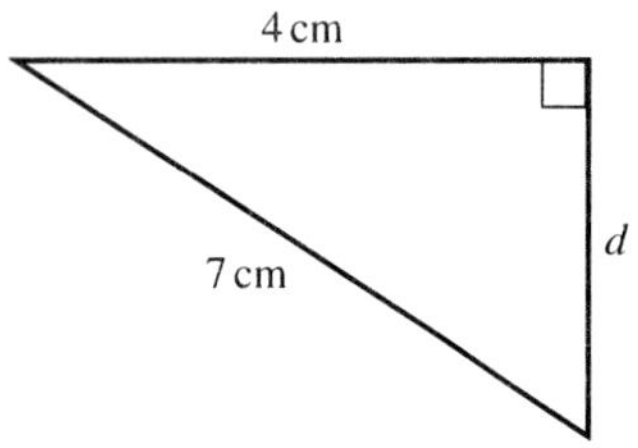

$$d^2 + 4^2 = 7^2$$
$$d^2 = 49 - 16$$
$$d = \sqrt{33} = 5{\cdot}74 \text{ cm (3 S.F.)}$$

The *converse* is also true:
'If the square on one side of a triangle is equal to the sum of the squares on the other two sides, then the triangle is right-angled.'

Exercise 19

In Questions **1** to **4**, find x. All the lengths are in cm.

1.

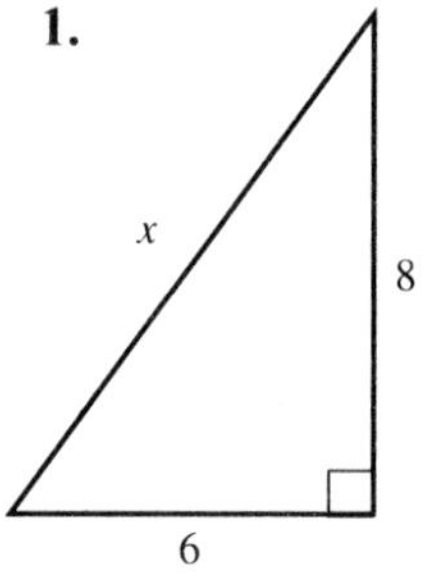

2.

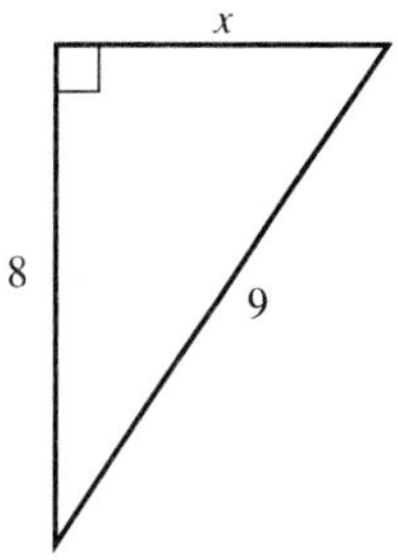

3.

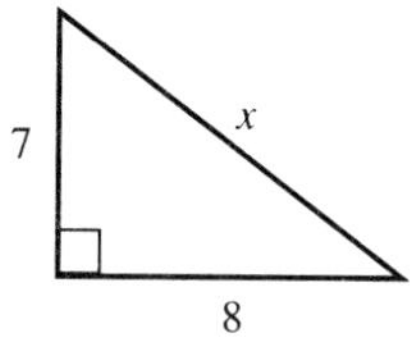

4.

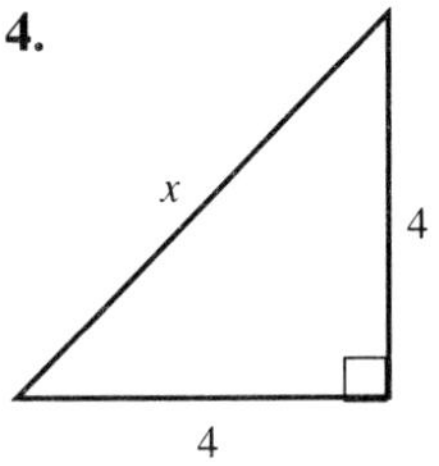

5.

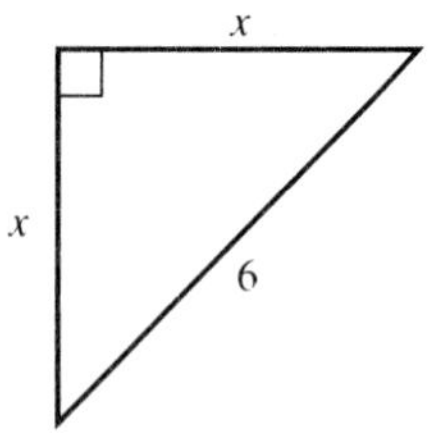

6.

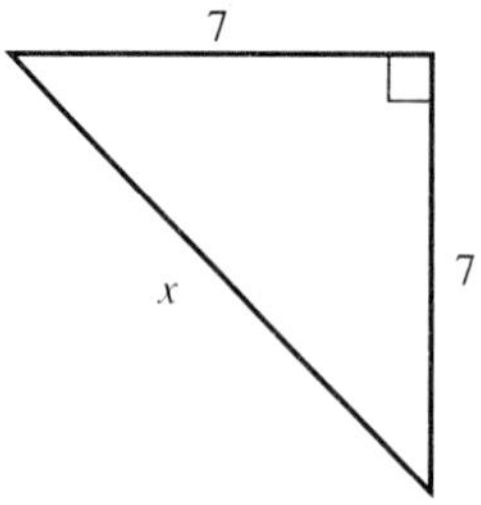

7.

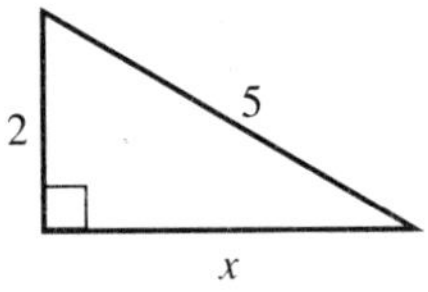

8.

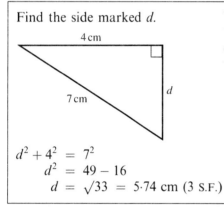

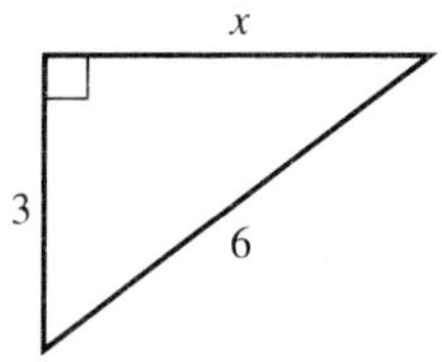

9. Find the length of a diagonal of a rectangle of length 9 cm and width 4 cm.

10. A square has diagonals of length 10 cm. Find the sides of the square.

11. A 4 m ladder rests against a vertical wall with its foot 2 m from the wall. How far up the wall does the ladder reach?

12. A ship sails 20 km due North and then 35 km due East. How far is it from its starting point?

13. A thin wire of length 18 cm is bent in the shape shown.

Calculate the length from A to B.

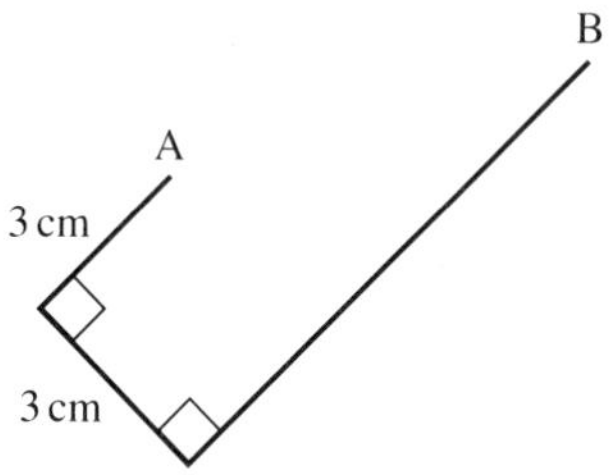

14. A paint tin is a cylinder of radius 12 cm and height 22 cm. Leonardo, the painter, drops his stirring stick into the tin and it disappears. Work out the maximum length of the stick.

15. In the diagram A is (1, 2) and B is (6, 4)

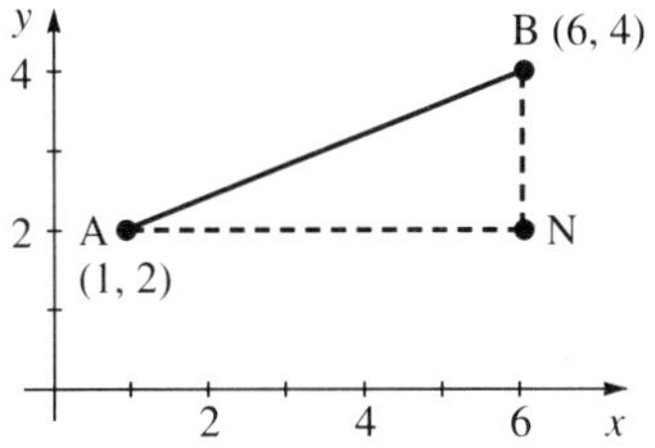

Work out the length AB. (First find the length of AN and BN).

16. On squared paper plot P(1, 3), Q(6, 0), R(6, 6). Find the lengths of the sides of triangle PQR. Is the triangle isosceles?

In Questions **17** to **22** find x.

17.

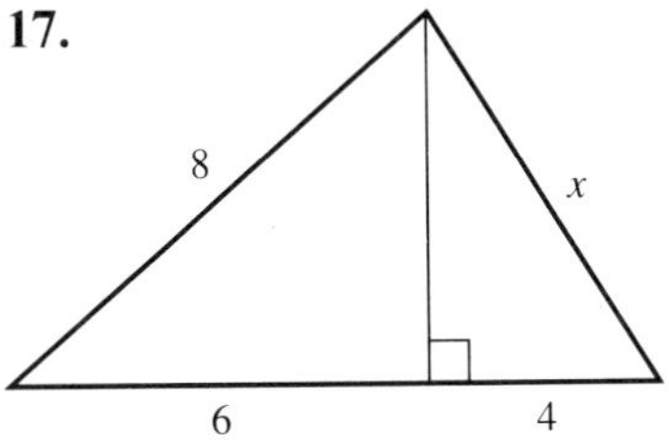

18.

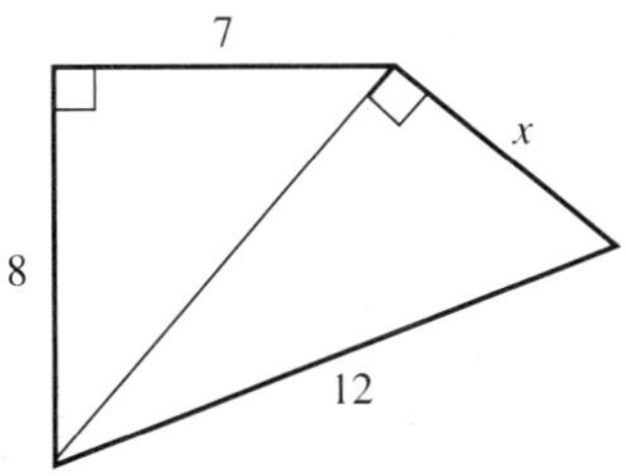

19.

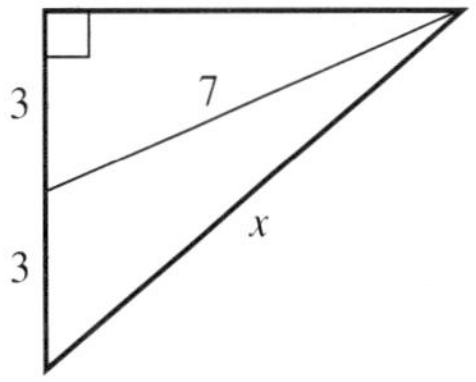

20.

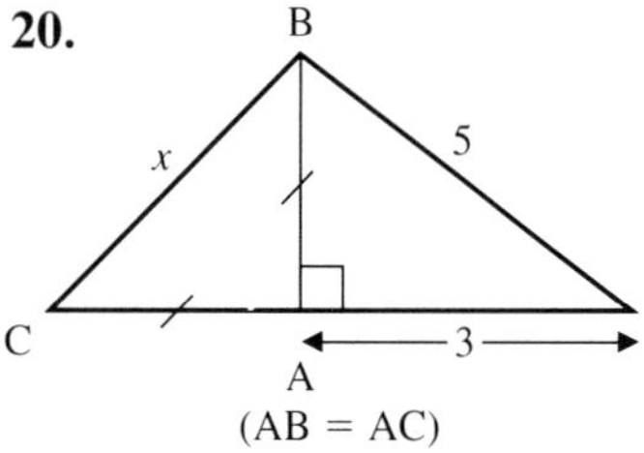

21.

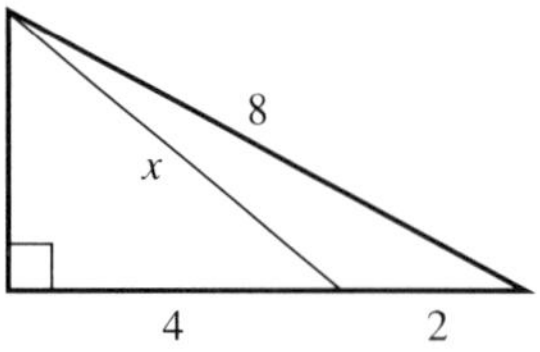

22.

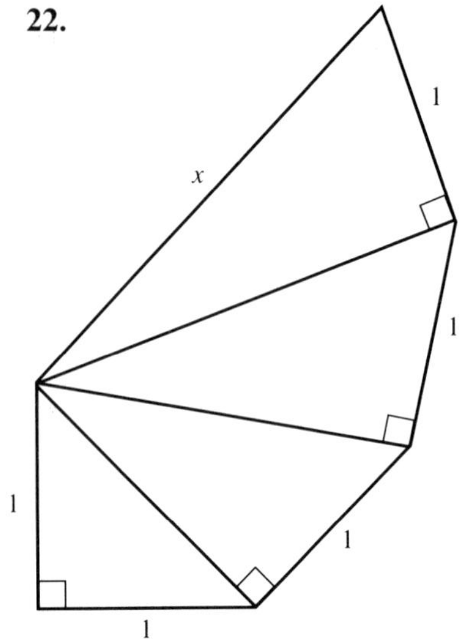

23. The most well known right-angled triangle is the 3, 4, 5 triangle $[3^2 + 4^2 = 5^2]$.
It is interesting to look at other right-angled triangles where all the sides are whole numbers.

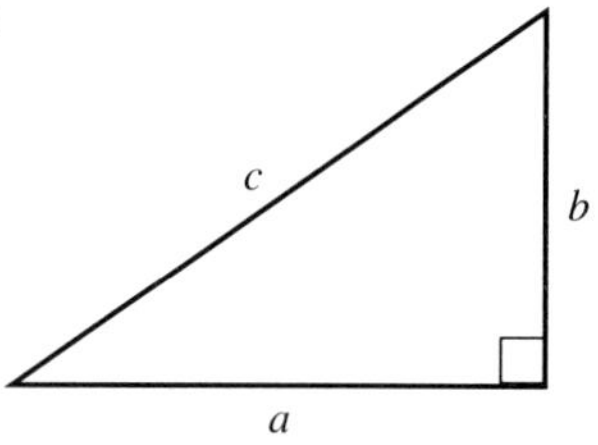

(a) (i) Find c if $a = 5$, $b = 12$
(ii) Find c if $a = 7$, $b = 24$
(iii) Find a if $c = 41$, $b = 40$

(b) Write the results in a table.

a	b	c
3	4	5
5	12	?
7	24	?
?	40	41

(c) Look at the sequences in the 'a' column and in the 'b' column. Also write down the connection between b and c for each triangle.
(d) Predict the next three sets of values of a, b, c. Check to see if they really do form right-angled triangles.

24. The diagram shows a rectangular block.

Calculate (a) AC (b) AY

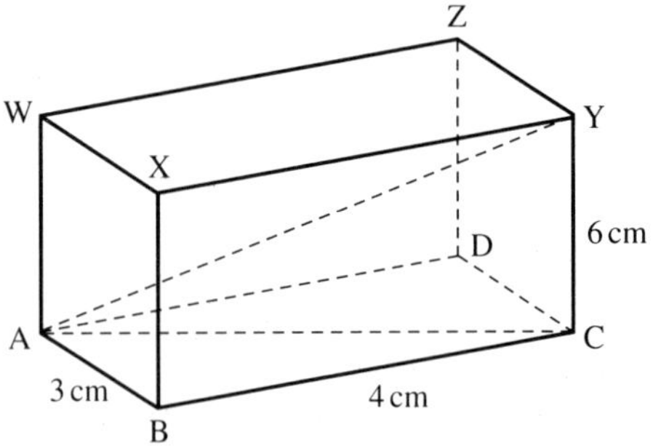

25. The diagram shows a rectangular block.

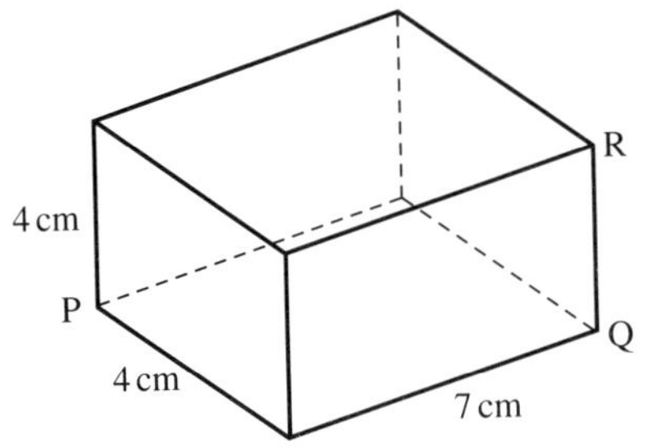

Calculate (a) PQ (b) PR

26. Alexis and Philip were arguing about a triangle that had sides 10 cm, 11 cm and 15 cm. Alexis said the triangle had a right angle, and Philip said that it did not. Who was correct?

5.7 Problems in area and volume

4/7d

Exercise 20

1. Find the capacity in litres of the oil drum shown below. (1000 cm^3 = 1 litre).

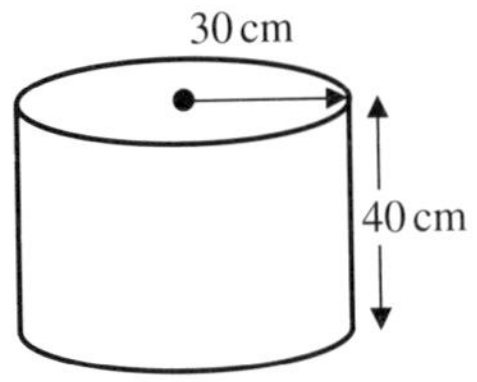

2. Find the volume in litres of a cylinder of height 55 cm and diameter 20 cm.

3. The diagram shows a square ABCD in which DX = XY = YC = AW. The area of the square is 45 cm^2.

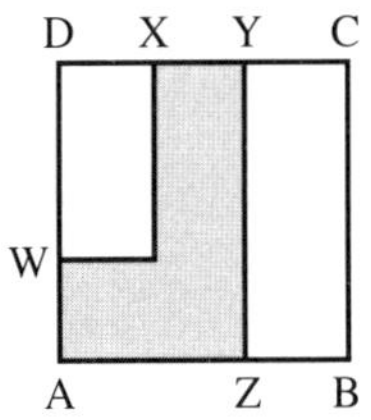

(a) What is the fraction $\frac{DX}{DC}$?

(b) What fraction of the square is shaded?
(c) Find the area of the unshaded part.

4. A floor 5 m by 20 m is covered by square tiles of side 20 cm. How many tiles are needed?

5. A rectangular field, 400 m long, has an area of 6 hectares. Calculate the perimeter of the field. [1 hectare = 10 000 m^2].

6. Find the shaded area. The lengths are in centimetres.

(a)

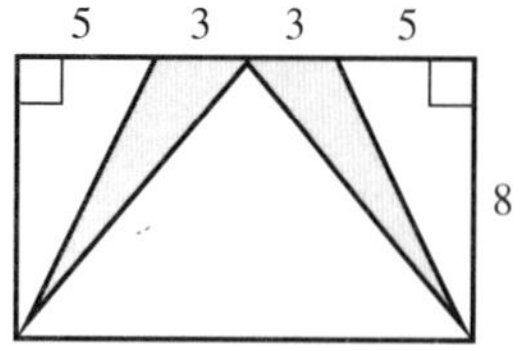

(b)

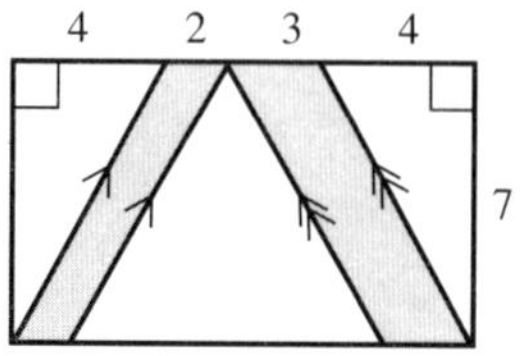

7. Calculate the volume of the object below. The lengths are in centimetres.

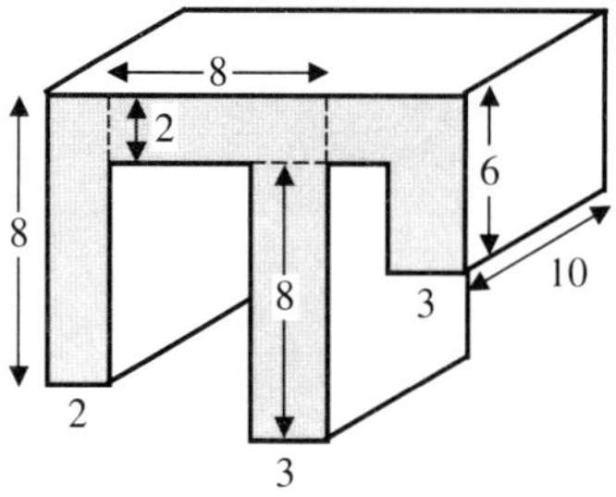

8. The arrowhead has an area of 3·6 cm^2. Find the length x.

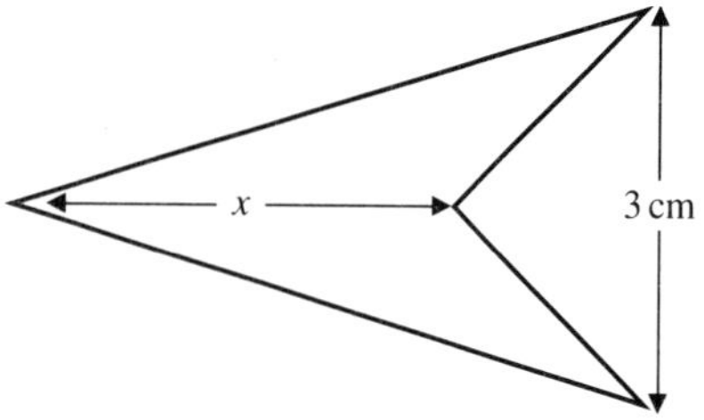

9. Find the length x.

(a)

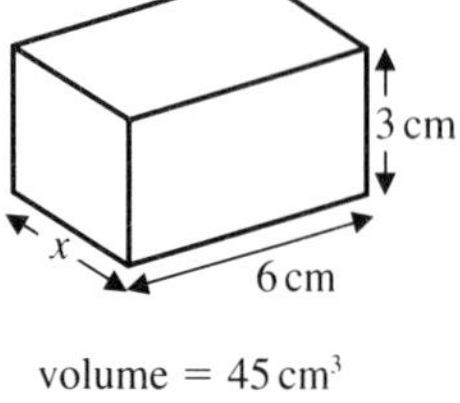

(b)

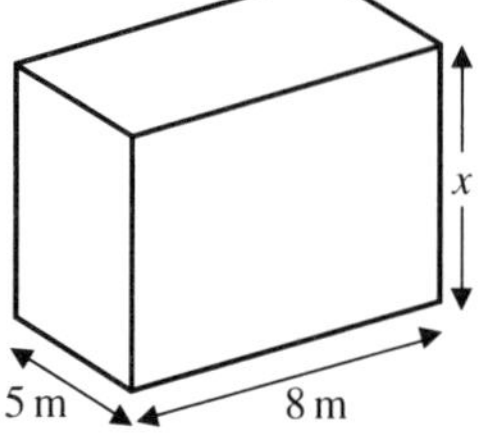

10. A rectangular block of metal has dimensions 20 cm × 16 cm × 8 cm. It is melted down and recast into cubes of edge length 4 cm. How many cubes will be cast?

11. A freezer makes ice cubes which are rectangular blocks $5 \text{ cm} \times 3 \text{ cm} \times 2 \text{ cm}$. How many ice cubes can be made from 3 litres of water?

12. A wall, 12 m long, 150 cm high and 15 cm thick is constructed using bricks which measure $20 \text{ cm} \times 15 \text{ cm} \times 10 \text{ cm}$. How many bricks are needed (ignoring the cement)?

13. The diagonals of a rhombus measure 24 cm and 32 cm.
(a) Work out the area of the rhombus
(b) Work out the perimeter of the rhombus

14. The solid object shown is made from 27 small cubes each 1 cm by 1 cm by 1 cm. The small cubes are glued together and then the outside is painted red. Calculate
(a) the number of cubes with one face painted
(b) the number of cubes with two faces painted
(c) the number of cubes with three faces painted
(d) the number of cubes with no faces painted
(Check that the answers to (a), (b), (c) and (d) add up to the correct number.)

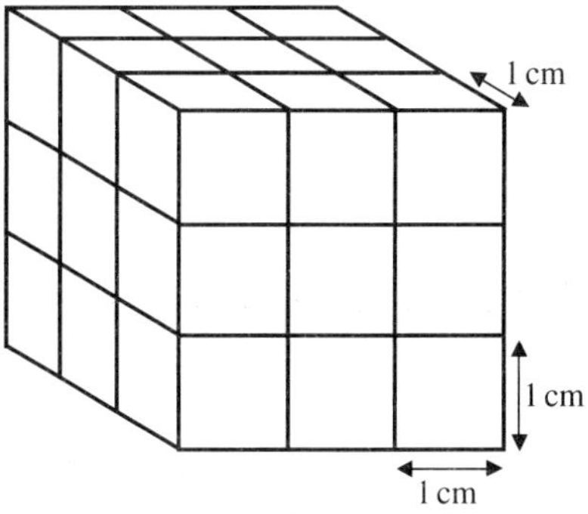

6 Algebra 2

6.1 Finding a rule

3/7a

Here is a sequence of'houses' made from matches.

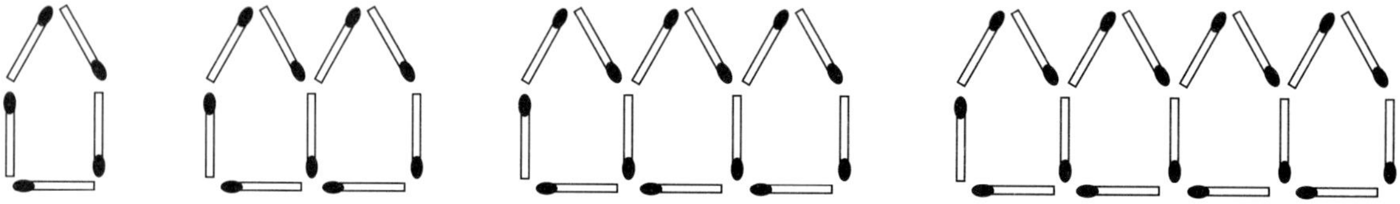

The table on the right records the number of houses h and the number of matches m.

h	m
1	5
2	9
3	13
4	17

If the number in the h column goes up one at a time, look at the number in the m column. If it goes up (or down) by the same number each time, the function connecting m and h is linear. This means that there are no terms in h^2 or anything more complicated.

In this case, the numbers in the m column go up by 4 each time. This suggests that column for $4h$ might help.

h	m	$4h$
1	5	4
2	9	8
3	13	12
4	17	16

Now it is fairly clear that m is one more than $4h$.

So the formula linking m and h is $m = 4h + 1$

The table shows how r changes with n. What is the formula linking r with n?

n	r
2	3
3	8
4	13
5	18

Because r goes up by 5 each time, try writing another column for $5n$.
The table shows that r is always 7 less than $5n$, so the formula linking r with n is
$r = 5n - 7$

n	r	$5n$
2	3	10
3	8	15
4	13	20
5	18	25

Unfortunately if the numbers on the left do not go up by one each time, this method does not work. In that case you have to think of something clever!

Exercise 1

1. Below is a sequence of diagrams showing black tiles b and white tiles w with the related rable.

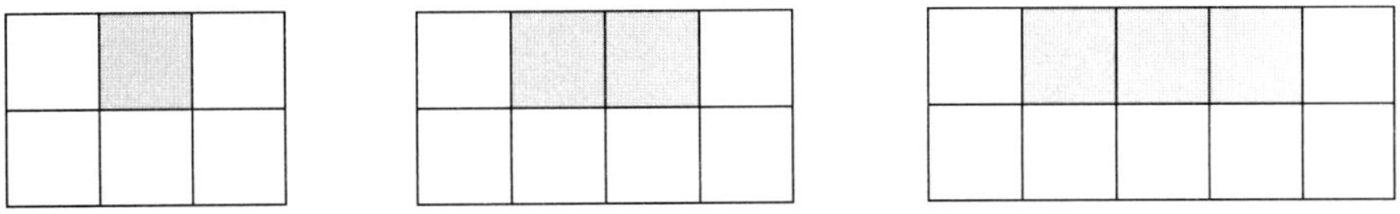

b	w
1	5
2	6
3	7
4	8

What is the formula for w in terms of b? [i.e. write '$w = \dots\dots\dots$']

2. This is a different sequence with black tiles b and white tiles w and the related table.

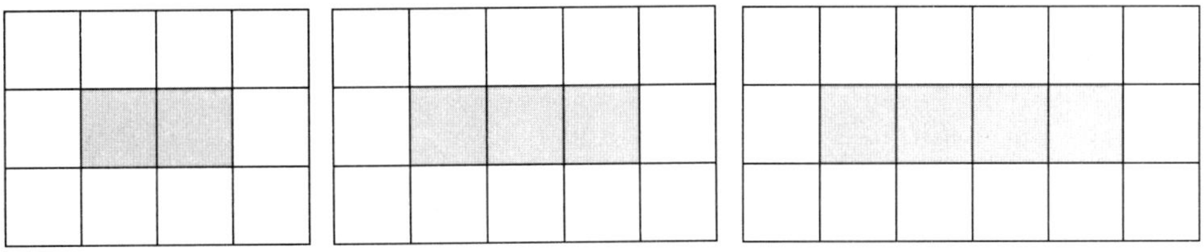

b	w
2	10
3	12
4	14
5	16

What is the formula? Write it as $w = \dots$

3. Here is a sequence of I's.

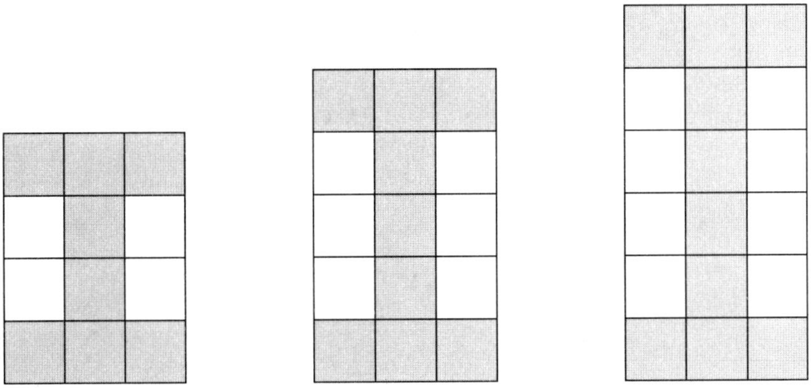

Make your own table for black tiles b and white tiles w. What is the formula for w in terms of b?

4. In this sequence we have matches (m) and triangles (t).

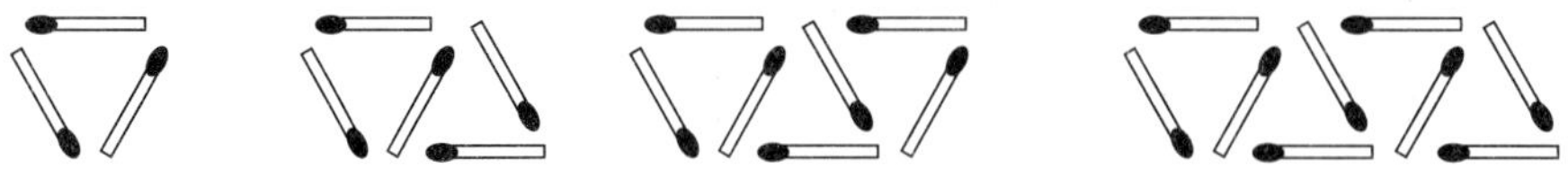

Make a table for t and m. It starts like this:

t	m
1	3
2	5
⋮	⋮

Continue the table and find a formula for m in terms of t.
Write '$m = \ldots\ldots$'.

5. Here is a different sequence of matches and triangles.

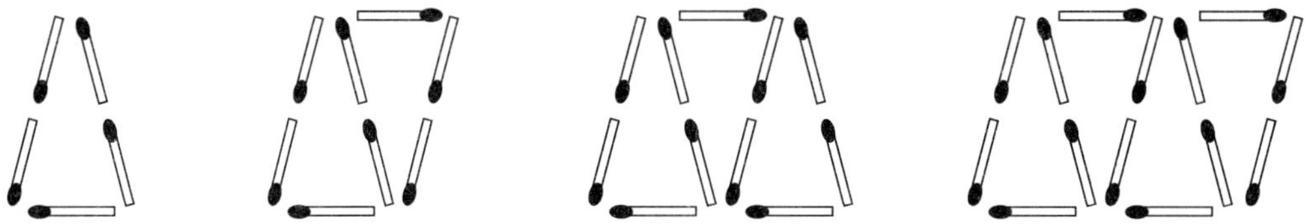

Make a table and find a formula connecting m and t.

6. In this sequence there are triangles (t) and squares (s) around the outside.

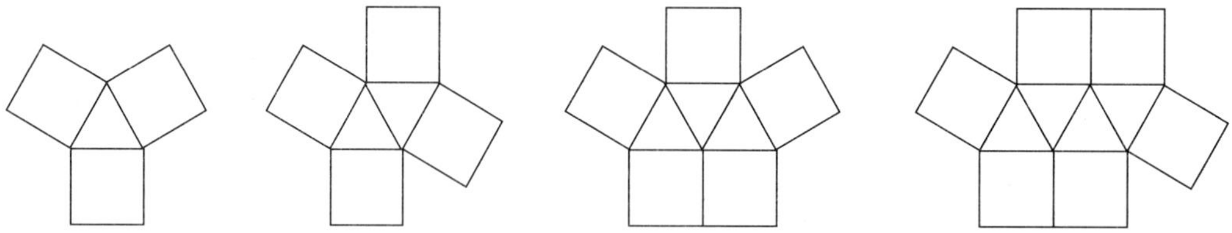

What is the formula connecting t and s?

7. Look at the tables below. In each case, find a formula connecting the two letters.

(a)

n	p
1	3
2	8
3	13
4	18

write '$p = \ldots$'

(b)

n	k
2	17
3	24
4	31
5	38

write '$k = \ldots$'

(c)

n	w
3	17
4	19
5	21
6	23

write '$w = \ldots$'

8. In these tables it is harder because the numbers on the left do not go up by one each time. Try to find a formula in each case.

(a)

n	y
1	4
3	10
7	22
8	25

(b)

n	h
2	5
3	9
6	21
10	37

(c)

n	k
3	14
7	26
9	32
12	41

9. This is one member of a sequence of cubes (c) made from matches (m).

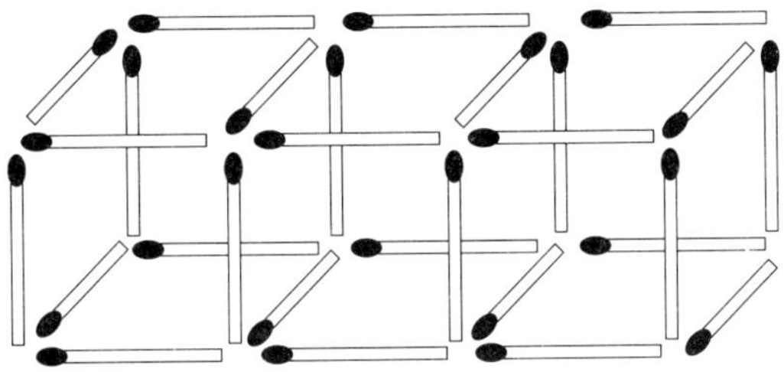

Find a formula connecting m and c.

10. You can make some nice loops by fitting pentagon tiles together.

Diagram $n = 1$

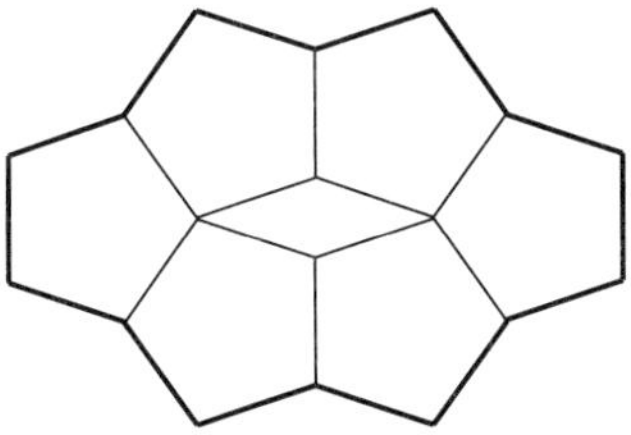

6 tiles (t)
14 external edges (e)

Diagram $n = 2$

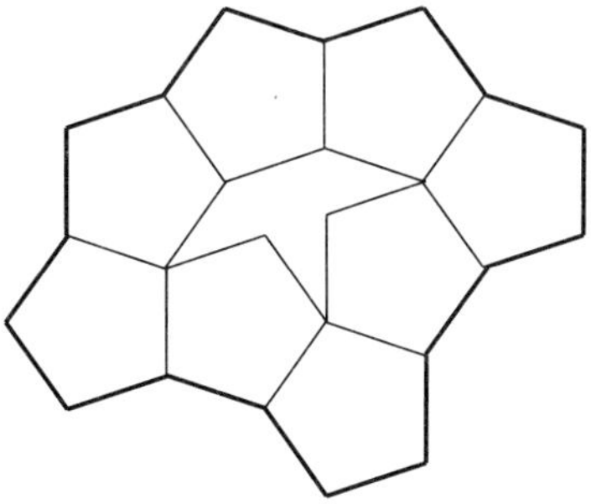

8 tiles (t)
17 external edges (e)

Diagram $n = 3$

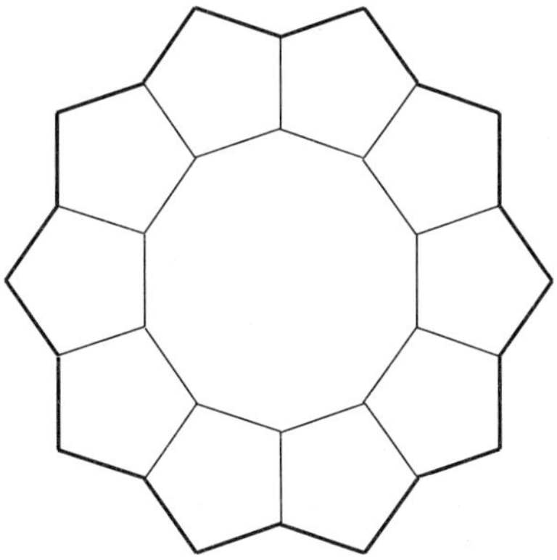

10 tiles (t)
20 external edges (e)

Make your own tables involving n, t and e.

(a) Find a formula connecting n and t.
(b) Find a formula connecting n and e.
(c) Find a formula connecting t and e.

6.2 Trial and improvement

3/6b, 3/7b

Some problems cannot be solved using linear equations. In such cases, the method of 'trial and improvement' is often a help.

Exercise 2

1. Think of a rectangle having an area of $72\,\text{cm}^2$ whose base is twice its height.

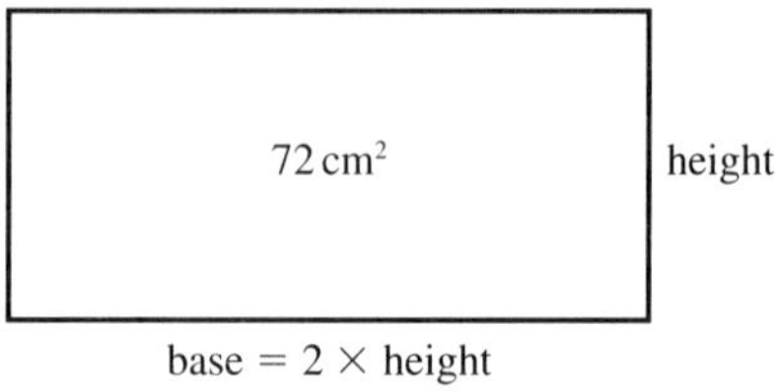

Write down the length of the base.

2. Find a rectangle of area $75\,\text{cm}^2$ so that its base is three times its height.

3. In each of the rectangles below, the base is twice the height. The area is shown inside the rectangle. Find the base and the height.

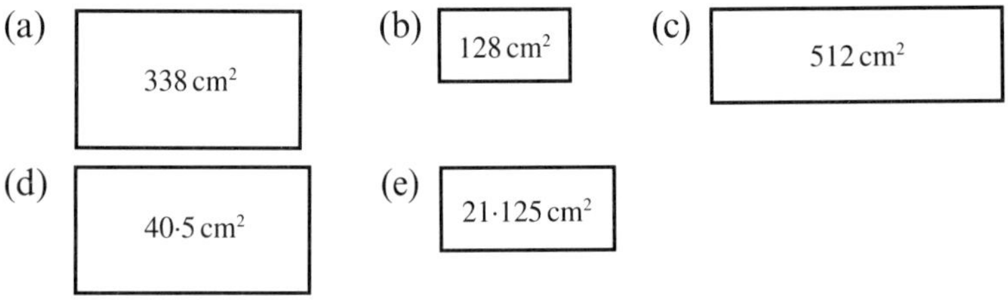

4. In this rectangle, the base is 1 cm more than the height and the area is $90\,\text{cm}^2$.

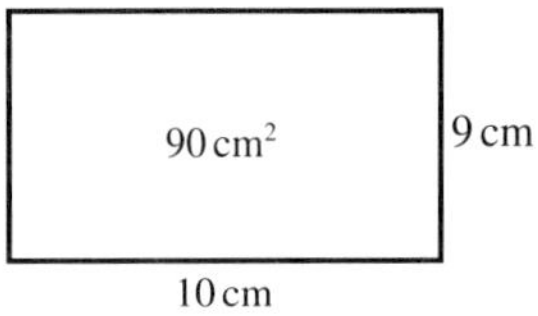

In each of the rectangles below, the base is 1 cm more than the height. Find each base and height.

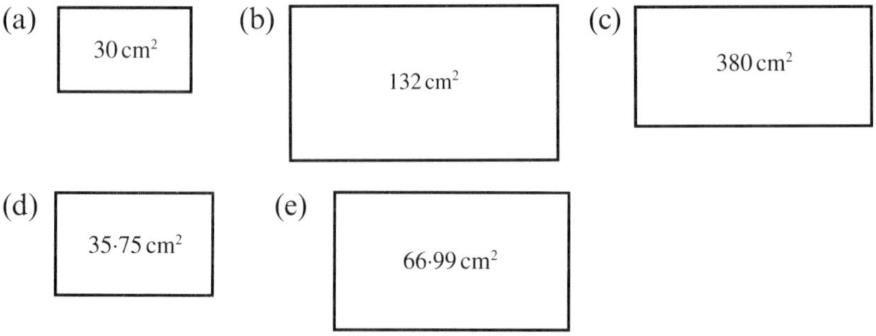

5. A problem! Once again the base of the rectangle is 1 cm more than the height.
Try to find the base and the height of the rectangle.

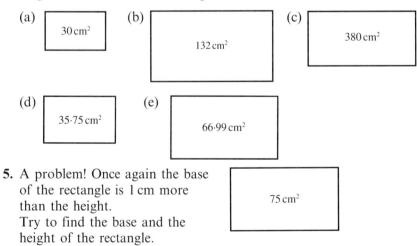

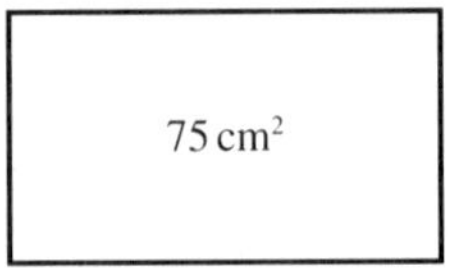

Inexact answers

In some questions it is not possible ever to find an answer which is precisely correct. However, we can find answers which are nearer and nearer to the exact one, perhaps to the nearest 0·1 cm or even to the nearest 0·01 cm.

In this rectangle, the base is 1 cm more than the height h cm. The area is 80 cm^2.
Find the height h.

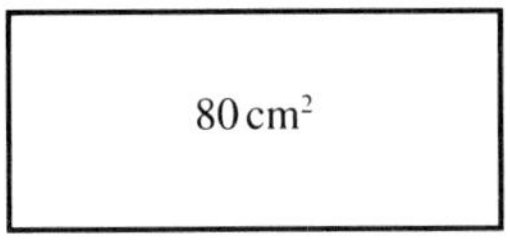

Try a special case and be systematic.

(a) Suppose $h = 8$.

$8(8 + 1) = 72 < 80$

This is too small.
Draw a line. Write 'too small' on the left-hand end and 'too big' on the right-hand end. Put 8 on the 'too small' end.

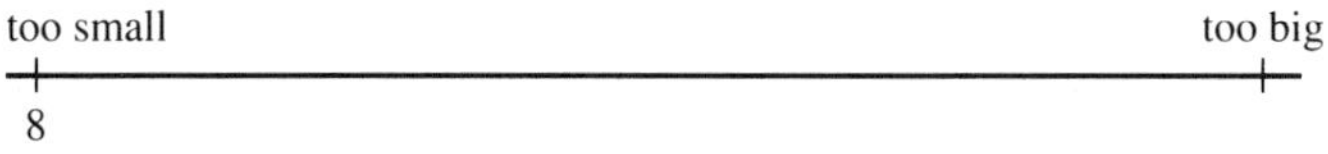

(b) Try $h = 9$.

$9(9 + 1) = 90 > 80$

This is too big, so put the result on the right-hand end.

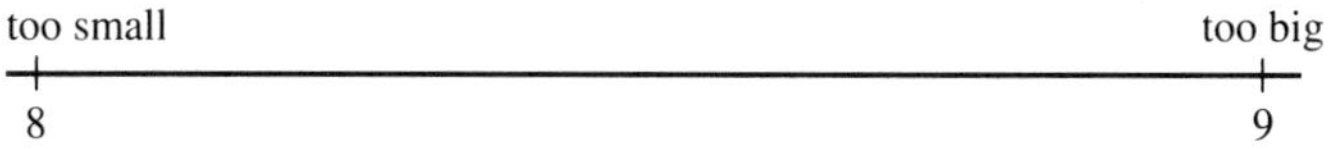

(c) Try an intermediate number, say $h = 8{\cdot}5$.

$8{\cdot}5(8{\cdot}5 + 1) = 80{\cdot}75 > 80$

This is slightly too big. Put the result on the right. Do *not* put it in the middle!

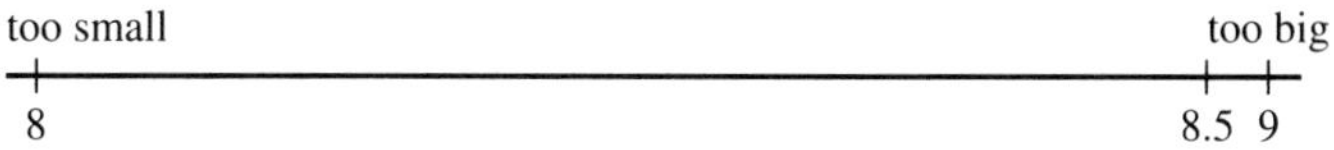

(d) Carry on adjusting the number you try, placing it suitably on the line. The number in brackets is the result of the calculation each time.

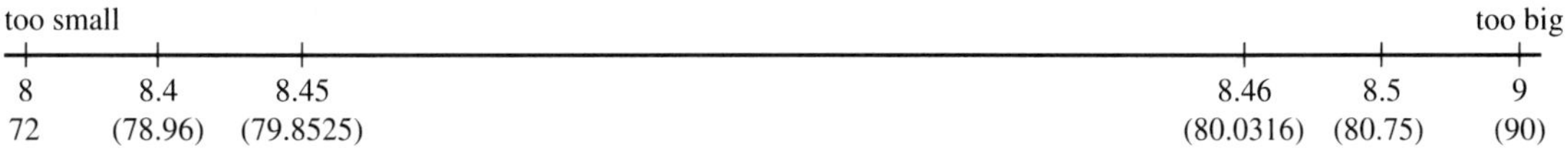

Clearly the value for h is 'between 8·45 cm and 8·46 cm'.
For many problems, this will be accurate enough. Further trials will give further improvement in accuracy, e.g. h is 'between 8·458 cm and 8·459 cm'.

Exercise 3

1. In these two rectangles, the base is 1 cm more than the height.

(a) 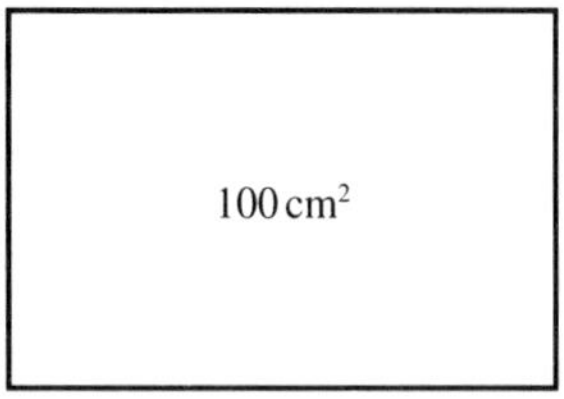

(b) 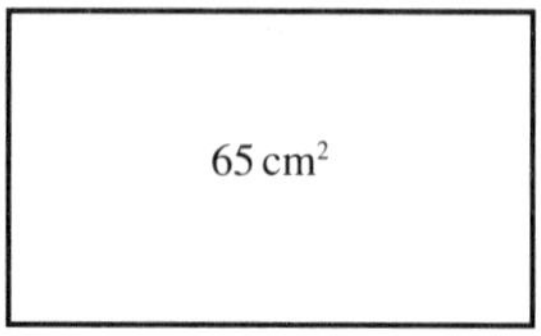

Find the height of each one, writing the answer as 'h is between _ cm and _ cm'. The two numbers should be 0·01 cm apart.

2. Find solutions to the following equations, giving the answer in the form 'x is between _ and _'. The two numbers should be 0·01 apart.

(a) $x(x-3) = 11$ (b) $3x(x-2) = 21$

(c) $x^3 = 300$ (d) $x^2(x+1) = 50$

(e) $x + \frac{1}{x} = 6$ (f) $x^5 = 313$

(g) $x^x = 100$. Here you need a calculator with a $\boxed{x^y}$ button.

3. An engineer wants to make a solid metal cube of volume 526 cm³.
Call the edge of the cube x and write down an equation.
Find x giving your answer in the form given in Question 2.

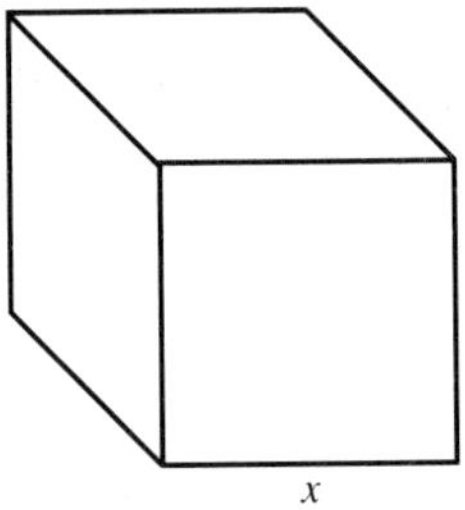

4. In this rectangle, the base is 2 cm more than the height.
Find h if the diagonal is 15 cm.

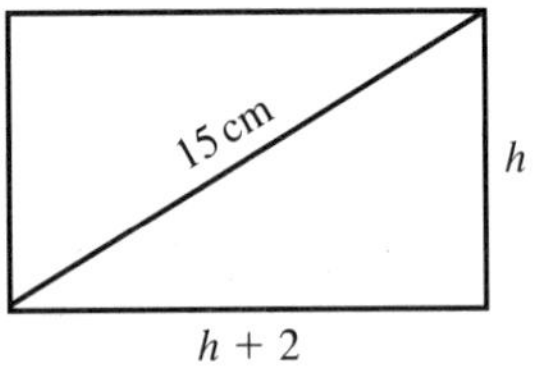

5. A designer for supermarket chain wants to make a cardboard box of depth 6 cm. He has to make the length of the box 10 cm more than the width.

(a) What is the length of the box in terms of x?
The box is designed so that its volume is to be 9000 cm³.

(b) Form an equation involving x.

(c) Solve the equation and hence give the dimensions of the box to the nearest cm.

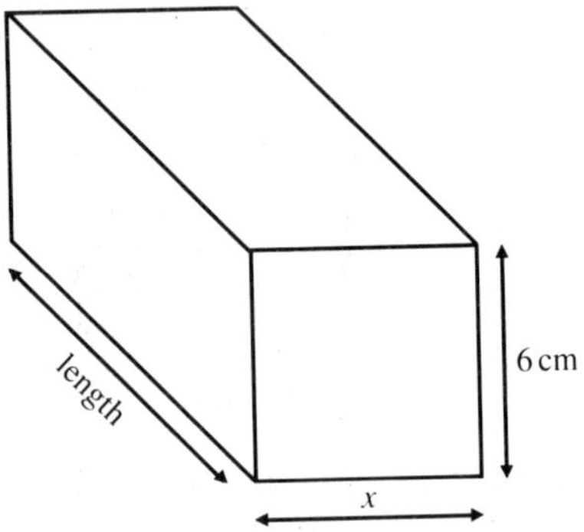

6. The diagram represents a rectangular piece of paper ABCD which has been folded along EF so that C has moved to G.

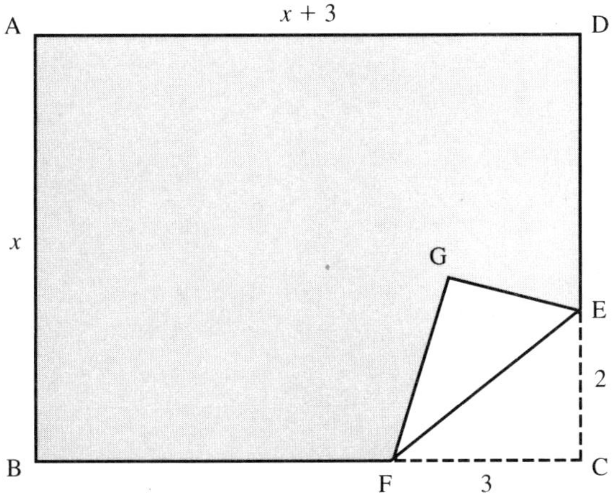

All lengths are in cm.

(a) Calculate the area of △ ECF.

(b) Find an expression for the shaded area ABFGED in terms of x.

Given that the shaded area is $20\,\text{cm}^2$, show that $x(x+3) = 26$

Solve this equation, giving your answer correct to one decimal place.

7. In the rectangle PQRS, PQ $= x$ cm and QR $= 1$ cm. The line LM is drawn so that PLMS is a square.

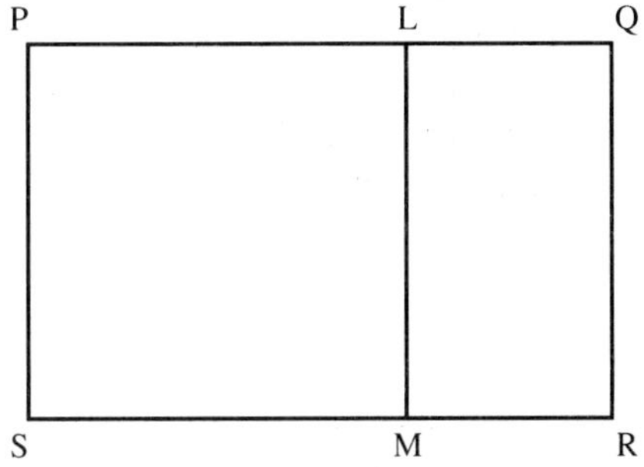

(a) Write down, in terms of x, the length LQ.

(b) If $\dfrac{PQ}{QR} = \dfrac{QR}{LQ}$, obtain an equation in x.

Hence find x correct to two decimal places.

6.3 Simultaneous equations

3/7b

Graphical solution

Louise and Philip are two children and Louise is 5 years older than Philip. The sum of their ages is 12 years. How old is each child?

Let Louise be x years old and Philip be y years old.

We can say $x + y = 12$ [sum = 12]
and $x - y = 5$ [difference = 5]

Suppose we draw on the same page the graphs of $x + y = 12$
and $x - y = 5$

$x + y = 12$ goes through (0,12), (2,10), (6,6), (12,0).
$x - y = 5$ goes through (5,0), (7,2), (10,5).

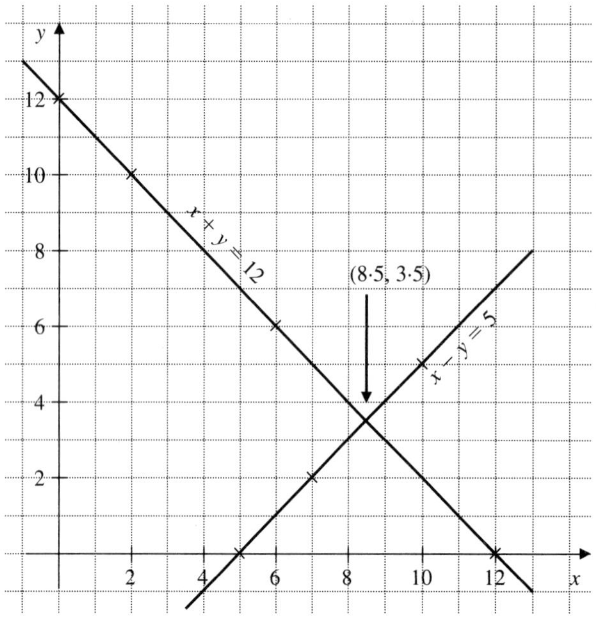

The point (8·5, 3·5) lies on both lines at the same time.

We say that $x = 8{\cdot}5$, $y = 3{\cdot}5$ are the solutions of the **simultaneous** equations $x + y = 12$, $x - y = 5$.

So Louise is $8\frac{1}{2}$ years old and Philip is $3\frac{1}{2}$ years old.

Exercise 4

1. Use the graphs to solve the equations below.

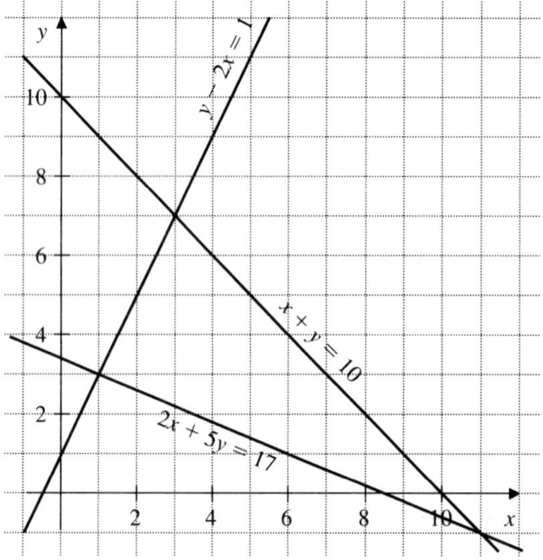

Solve (a) $\begin{aligned} x + y &= 10 \\ y - 2x &= 1 \end{aligned}$ (b) $\begin{aligned} 2x + 5y &= 17 \\ y - 2x &= 1 \end{aligned}$ (c) $\begin{aligned} x + y &= 10 \\ 2x + 5y &= 17 \end{aligned}$

In Questions **2** to **6**, solve the simultaneous equations by drawing graphs. Use a scale of 1 cm to 1 unit on both axes.

2. $x + y = 6$
$2x + y = 8$
Draw axes with x and y from 0 to 8.

3. $x + 2y = 8$
$3x + y = 9$
Draw axes with x and y from 0 to 9.

4. $x + 3y = 6$
$x - y = 2$
Draw axes with x from 0 to 8 and y from -2 to 4.

5. $5x + y = 10$
$x - y = -4$
Draw axes with x from -4 to 4 and y from 0 to 10.

6. $a + 2b = 11$
$2a + b = 13$
In this one the unknowns are a and b. Draw the a-axis across the page from 0 to 13 and the b-axis up the page also from 0 to 13.

7. There are four lines drawn here.

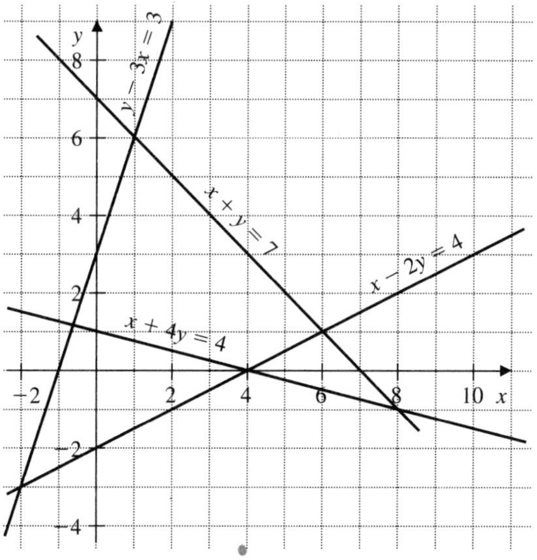

Write down the solutions to the following:

(a) $x - 2y = 4$
$x + 4y = 4$

(b) $x + y = 7$
$y - 3x = 3$

(c) $y - 3x = 3$
$x - 2y = 4$

(d) $x + 4y = 4$
$x + y = 7$

(e) $x + 4y = 4$
$y - 3x = 3$ (For this one give x and y correct to 1 d.p.)

Simultaneous equations: algebraic solution

We can also solve simultaneous equations without drawing graphs.
There are two methods: substitution and elimination.
You can choose for yourself which one to use in any question.

(a) Substitution method

This method is used when one equation contains a single 'x' or 'y', as in equation [2] of the example below.

Solve the simultaneous equations

$$3x - 2y = 0 \quad \ldots [1]$$
$$2x + y = 7 \quad \ldots [2]$$

From [2] $2x + y = 7$

$y = 7 - 2x$

Substituting in [1]

$3x - 2(7 - 2x) = 0$

$3x - 14 + 4x = 0$

$7x = 14$

$x = 2$

Substituting in [2]

$2 \times 2 + y = 7$

$y = 3$

The solutions are $x = 2$, $y = 3$.

These values of x and y are the only pair which simultaneously satisfy *both* equations.

Exercise 5

Use the substitution method to solve the following:

1. $2x + y = 5$, $x + 3y = 5$

2. $x + 2y = 8$, $2x + 3y = 14$

3. $3x + y = 10$, $x - y = 2$

4. $2x + y = -3$, $x - y = -3$

5. $4x + y = 14$, $x + 5y = 13$

6. $x + 2y = 1$, $2x + 3y = 4$

7. $2x + y = 5$, $3x - 2y = 4$

8. $2x + y = 13$, $5x - 4y = 13$

9. $7x + 2y = 19$, $x - y = 4$

10. $b - a = -5$, $a + b = -1$

11. $a + 4b = 6$, $8b - a = -3$

12. $a + b = 4$, $2a + b = 5$

13. $3m = 2n - 6\frac{1}{2}$, $4m + n = 6$

14. $2w + 3x - 13 = 0$, $x + 5w - 13 = 0$

15. $x + 2(y - 6) = 0$, $3x + 4y = 30$

16. $2x = 4 + z$, $6x - 5z = 18$

17. $3m - n = 5$, $2m + 5n = 7$

18. $5c - d - 11 = 0$, $4d + 3c = -5$

It is useful, at this point to revise the operations of addition and subtraction with negative numbers.

Simplify:

(a) $-7 + -4 = -7 - 4 = -11$

(b) $-3x + (-4x) = -3x - 4x = -7x$

(c) $4y - (-3y) = 4y + 3y = 7y$

(d) $3a + (-3a) = 3a - 3a = 0$

(b) Elimination method

Use this method when the first method is unsuitable (some prefer to use it for every question).

	$2x + 3y = 5$	... [1]
	$5x - 2y = -16$	... [2]
[1] × 5	$10x + 15y = 25$	... [3]
[2] × 2	$10x - 4y = -32$	... [4]
[3] − [4]	$15y - (-4y) = 25 - (-32)$	
	$19y = 57$	
	$y = 3$	
Substitute in [1]	$2x + 3 \times 3 = 5$	
	$2x = 5 - 9 = -4$	
	$x = -2$	

The solutions are $x = -2$, $y = 3$.

Exercise 6

Use the elimination method to solve the following:

1. $2x + 5y = 24$, $4x + 3y = 20$

2. $5x + 2y = 13$, $2x + 6y = 26$

3. $3x + y = 11$, $9x + 2y = 28$

4. $x + 2y = 17$, $8x + 3y = 45$

5. $3x + 2y = 19$, $x + 8y = 21$

6. $2a + 3b = 9$, $4a + b = 13$

7. $2x + 3y = 11$, $3x + 4y = 15$

8. $3x + 8y = 27$, $4x + 3y = 13$

9. $2x + 7y = 17$, $5x + 3y = -1$

10. $5x + 3y = 23$, $2x + 4y = 12$

11. $7x + 5y = 32$, $3x + 4y = 23$

12. $3x + 2y = 4$, $4x + 5y = 10$

13. $3x + 2y = 11$, $2x - y = -3$

14. $3x + 2y = 7$, $2x - 3y = -4$

15. $x - 2y = -4$, $3x + y = 9$

16. $5x - 7y = 27$, $3x - 4y = 16$

17. $3x - 2y = 7$, $4x + y = 13$

18. $x - y = -1$, $2x - y = 0$

19. $y - x = -1$, $3x - y = 5$

20. $x - 3y = -5$, $2y + 3x + 4 = 0$

Problems solved by simultaneous equations

Exercise 7

Solve each problem by forming a pair of simultaneous equations.

1. Find two numbers with a sum of 15 and a difference of 4. [Let the numbers be x and y].
2. Twice one number added to three times another gives 21. Find the numbers, if the difference between them is 3.

3. The average of two numbers is 7, and three times the difference between them is 18. Find the numbers.

4. Here is a puzzle from a newspaper. The ? and * stand for numbers which are to be found. The totals for the rows and columns are given.

Write down two equations involving ? and * and solve them to find the values of ? and *

?	*	?	*	36
?	*	*	?	36
*	?	*	*	33
?	*	?	*	36
39	33	36	33	

5. The line, with equation $y + ax = c$, passes through the points (1, 5) and (3, 1). Find a and c.
Hint: For the point (1, 5) put $x = 1$ and $y = 5$ into $y + ax = c$, etc.

6. The line $y = mx + c$ passes through (2, 5) and (4, 13).
Find m and c.

7. A stone is thrown into the air and its height, h metres above the ground, is given by the equation

$$h = at - bt^2.$$

From an experiment we know that $h = 40$ when $t = 2$ and that $h = 45$ when $t = 3$.
Show that $a - 2b = 20$
and $a - 3b = 15$.
Solve these equations to find a and b.

8. A television addict can buy either two televisions and three video-recorders for £1750 or four televisions and one video-recorder for £1250. Find the cost of one of each.

9. A pigeon can lay either white or brown eggs. Three white eggs and two brown eggs weigh 13 ounces, while five white eggs and four brown eggs weigh 24 ounces. Find the weight of a brown egg and of a white egg.

10. A bag contains forty coins, all of them either 2p or 5p coins. Let there be x 2p coins and y 5p coins. If the value of the money in the bag is £1·55, find the number of each kind.

11. A slot machine takes only 10p and 50p coins and contains a total of twenty-one coins altogether. If the value of the coins is £4·90, find the number of coins of each value.

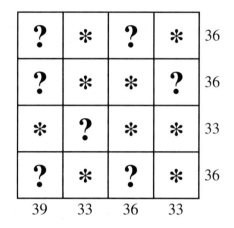

12. A tortoise makes a journey in two parts; it can either walk at 0·4 m/s or crawl at 0·3 m/s.

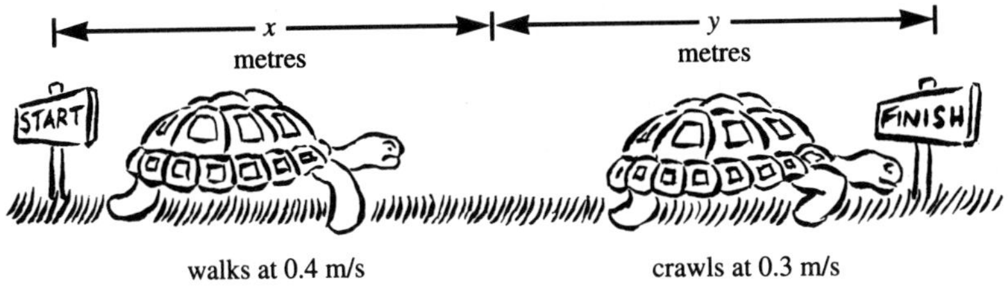

If the tortoise walks the first part and crawls the second, the journey takes 110 seconds.
If it crawls the first part and walks the second, the journey takes 100 seconds.
Let x metres be the length of the first part and y metres be the length of the second part.
Write down two simultaneous equations and solve them to find the lengths of the two parts of the journey.

13. The diagram shows segments of three straight lines.

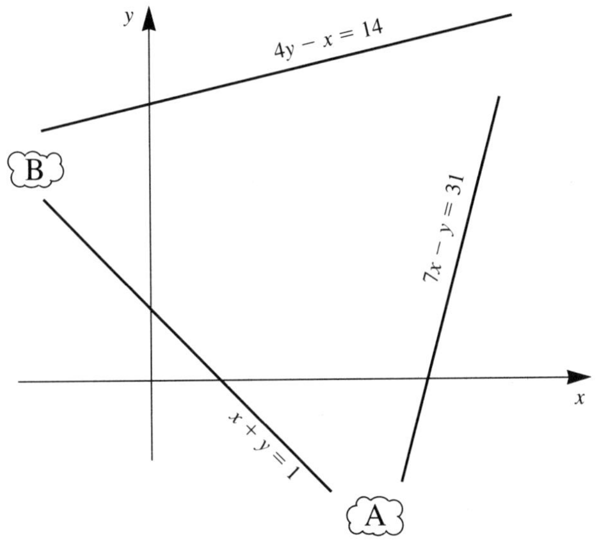

Find the coordinates of the points A and B.

14. The wage bill for five men and six women workers is £670, while the bill for eight men and three women is £610. Find the wage for a man and for a woman.

15. A kipper can swim at 14 m/s with the current and at 6 m/s against it. Find the speed of the current and the speed of the kipper in still water.

6.4 Interpreting graphs

3/7b, 3/8c

Travel graphs

Exercise 8

1. The graph shows a return journey by car from Leeds to Scarborough.
   (a) How far is it from Leeds to York?
   (b) How far is it from York to Scarborough?
   (c) At which two places does the car stop?
   (d) How long does the car stop at Scarborough?
   (e) When does the car
       (i) arrive in York,
       (ii) arrive back in Leeds?
   (f) What is the speed of the car
       (i) from Leeds to York,
       (ii) from York to Scarborough,
       (iii) from Scarborough to Leeds?

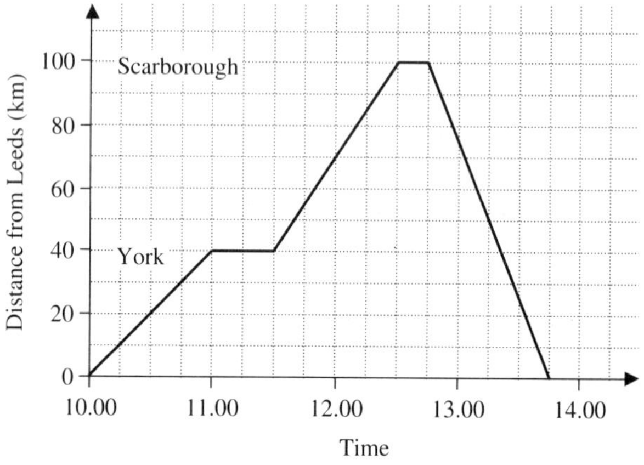

2. Steve cycles to a friend's house but on the way his bike gets a puncture, and he has to walk the remaining distance. At his friend's house, he repairs the puncture, has a game of snooker and then returns home. On the way back, he stops at a shop to buy a book on how to play snooker.
   (a) How far is it to his friend's house?
   (b) How far is it from his friend's house to the shop?
   (c) At what time did his bike get a puncture?
   (d) How long did he stay at his friend's house?
   (e) At what speed did he travel
       (i) from home until he had the puncture,
       (ii) after the puncture to his friend's house,
       (iii) from his friend's house to the shop,
       (iv) from the shop back to his own home?

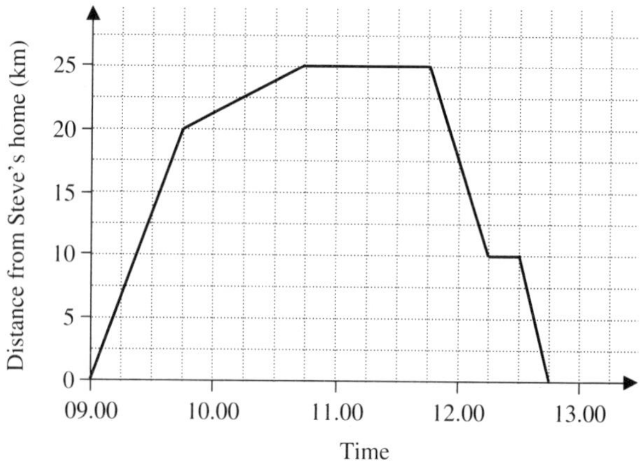

3. Mr Berol and Mr Hale use the same road to travel between Aston and Borton.

(a) At what time did
  (i) Mr Berol arrive in Borton,
  (ii) Mr Hale leave Aston?

(b) (i) When did Mr Berol and Mr Hale pass each other?
  (ii) In which direction was Mr Berol travelling?

(c) Find the following speeds:
  (i) Mr Hale from Aston to Stanley,
  (ii) Mr Berol from Aston to Borton,
  (iii) Mr Hale from Stanley to Borton,
  (iv) Mr Berol from Borton back to Aston.

(d) (More difficult) When did Mr Hale arrive in Borton?

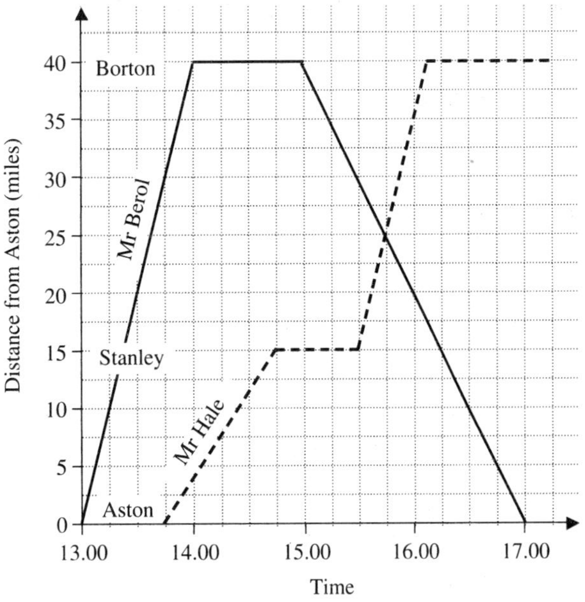

4. The graph shows the journeys made by a van and a car starting at York, travelling to Durham and returning to York.

(a) For how long was the van stationary during the journey?

(b) At what time did the car first overtake the van?

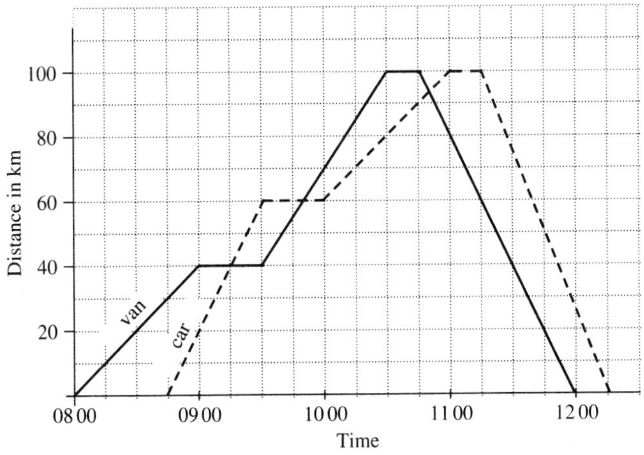

(c) At what speed was the van travelling between 09 30 and 10 00?

(d) What was the greatest speed attained by the car during the entire journey?

(e) What was the average speed of the car over its entire journey?

5. The graph shows the journeys of a bus and a car along the same road. The bus goes from Leeds to Darlington and back to Leeds. The car goes from Darlington to Leeds and back to Darlington.

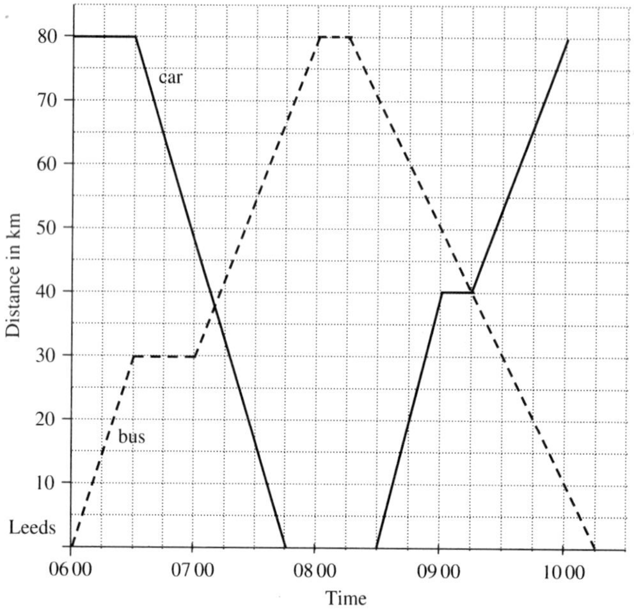

(a) When did the bus and the car meet for the second time?
(b) At what speed did the car travel from Darlington to Leeds?
(c) What was the average speed of the bus over its entire journey?
(d) Approximately how far apart were the bus and the car at 09 45?
(e) What was the greatest speed attained by the car during its entire journey?

In Questions **6, 7, 8,** draw a travel graph to illustrate the journey described. Draw axes with the same scales as in Question **5**.

6. (a) Mrs Chuong leaves home at 08 00 and drives at a speed of 50 km/h. After $\frac{1}{2}$ hour she reduces her speed to 40 km/h and continues at this speed until 09 30. She stops from 09 30 until 10 00 and then returns home at a speed of 60 km/h.
(b) Use a graph to find the approximate time at which she arrives home.

7. (a) Mr Coe leaves home at 09 00 and drives at a speed of 20 km/h. After $\frac{3}{4}$ hour he increases his speed to 45 km/h and continues at this speed until 10 45. He stops from 10 45 until 11 30 and then returns home at a speed of 50 km/h.
(b) Use the graph to find the approximate time at which he arrives home.

8. (a) At 10 00 Akram leaves home and cycles to his grandparents' house which is 70 km away. He cycles at a speed of 20 km/h until 11 15, at which time he stops for $\frac{1}{2}$ hour. He then completes the journey at a speed of 30 km/h. At 11 45 Akram's sister, Hameeda, leaves home and drives her car at 60 km/h. Hameeda also goes to her grandparents' house and uses the same road as Akram.

(b) At approximately what time does Hameeda overtake Akram?

Real life graphs

Exercise 9

1. The graph shows how the share price of the chemical firm ICI varied over a period of weeks. The share price is the price in pence paid for one share in the company.

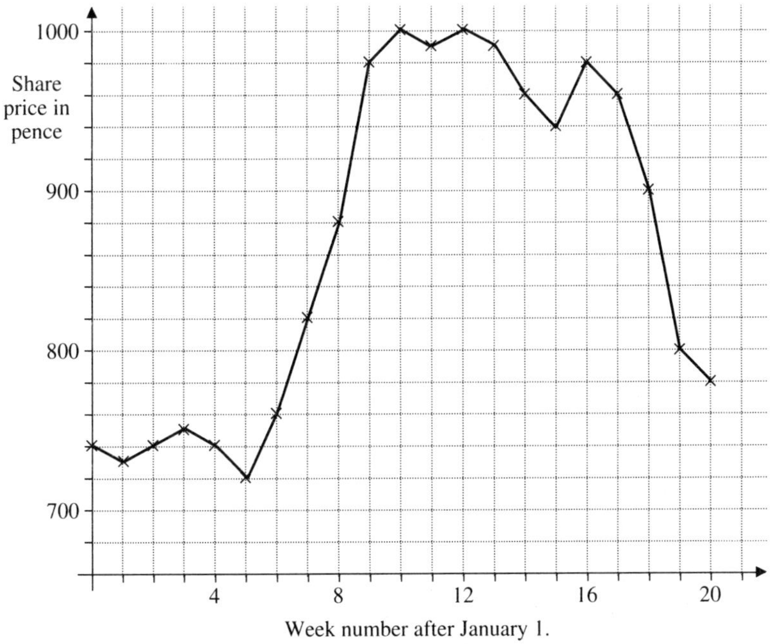

(a) What was the share price in Week 4?

(b) Naomi bought 200 shares in Week 6 and sold them all in week 18. How much profit did she make?

(c) Mr Gibson can buy (and then sell) 5000 shares. He consults a very accurate fortune teller who can predict the share price over coming weeks. What is the maximum profit he could make?

(d) When there is a full moon the fortune teller's predictions can be fairly disastrous. What is the maximum *loss* Mr Gibson could make?

2. The graph shows the number of pupils on the premises of a school one day.

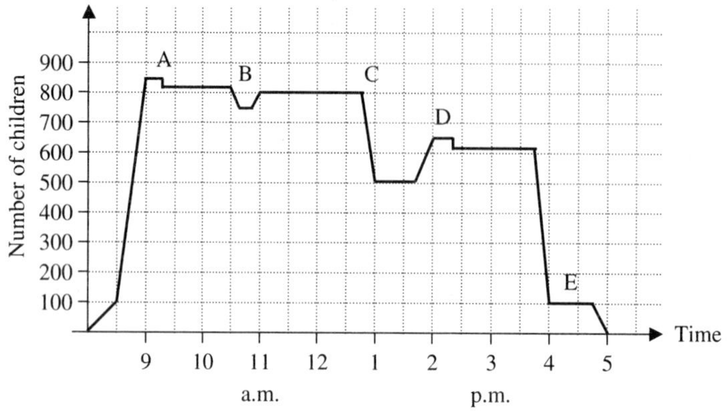

The graph tells you some interesting things. Referring to the points A, B, C, D, E, describe briefly what happened during the day. Give an explanation of what you think might have happened.

3. The graph below shows average television and radio audiences throughout a typical day in 1989.

United Kingdom

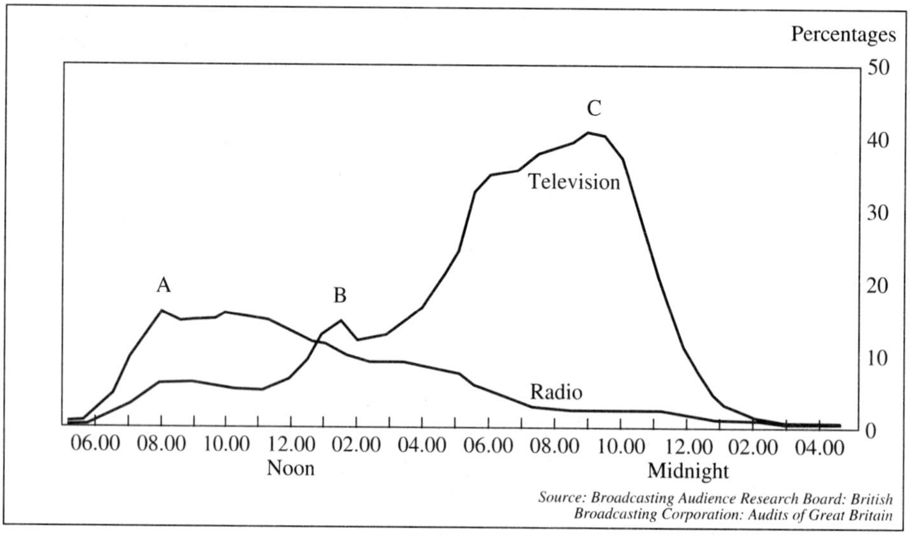

From: Social Trends, 1990, chart 10.5

Source: Key Data 1990/91

(a) When are the 'peak times' for
 (i) radio audiences (ii) television audiences?
(b) Give reasons which explain the shapes of the graphs at times A, B and C.

4. A car travels along a motorway and the amount of petrol in its tank is monitored as shown on the graph.
   (a) How much petrol was bought at the first stop?
   (b) What was the petrol consumption in miles per gallon:
      (i) before the first stop,
      (ii) between the two stops?
   (c) What was the average petrol consumption over the 200 miles?

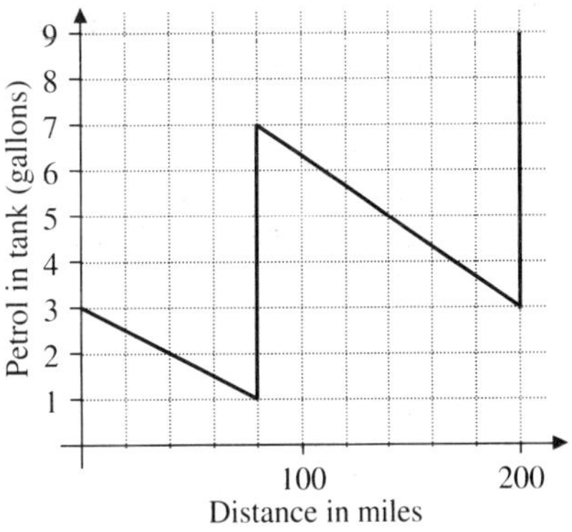

After it leaves the second service station the car encounters road works and slow traffic for the next 20 miles. Its petrol consumption is reduced to 20 m.p.g. After that, the road clears and the car travels a further 75 miles during which time the consumption is 30 m.p.g. Draw the graph above and extend it to show the next 95 miles. How much petrol is in the tank at the end of the journey?

5. Kendal Motors hires out vans.

Copy and complete the table where x is the number of miles travelled and C is the total cost in pounds.

x	0	50	100	150	200	250	300
C	35			65			95

Draw a graph of C against x, using scales of 2 cm for 50 miles on the x-axis and 1 cm for £10 on the C-axis.
Use the graph to find the number of miles travelled when the total cost was £71.

6. Jeff sets up his own business as a plumber.

Copy and complete the table where C stands for his total charge and h stands for the number of hours he works.

h	0	1	2	3
C		33		

Draw a graph with h across the page and C up the page. Use scales of 2 cm to 1 hour for h and 2 cm to £10 for C. Use your graph to find how long he worked if his charge was £55·50

Sketch graphs

Exercise 10

1. Which of the graphs A to D below best fits the following statement: 'Unemployment is still rising but by less each month.'

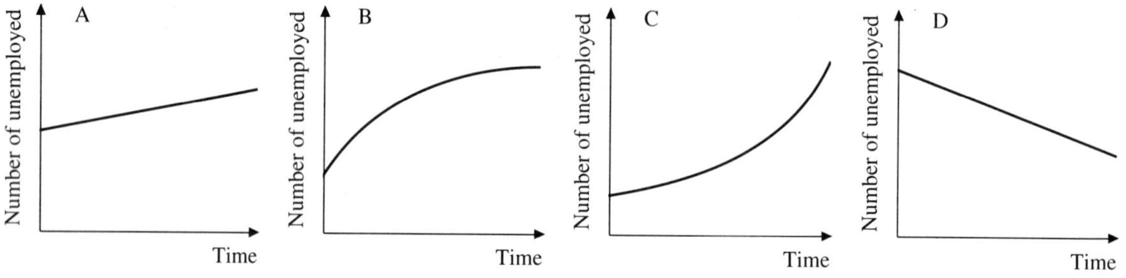

2. Which of the graphs A to D best fits the following statement: 'The price of oil was rising more rapidly in 1993 than at any time in the previous ten years'.

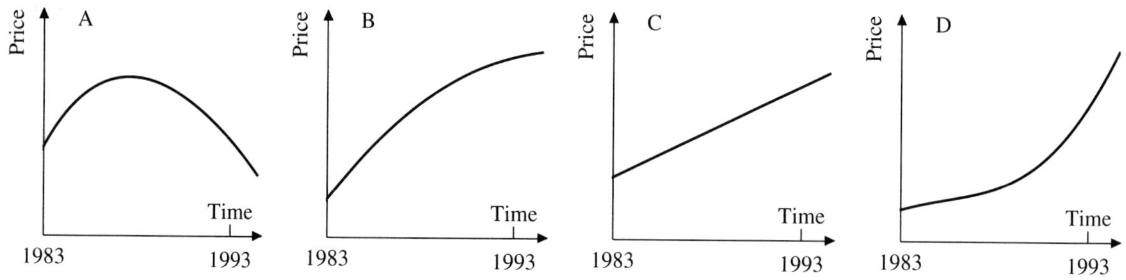

3. Which of the graphs A to D below best fits each of the following statements:

(a) The birthrate was falling but is now steady.

(b) Unemployment, which rose slowly until 1980, is now rising rapidly.

(c) Inflation, which has been rising steadily, is now beginning to fall.

(d) The price of gold has fallen steadily over the last year.

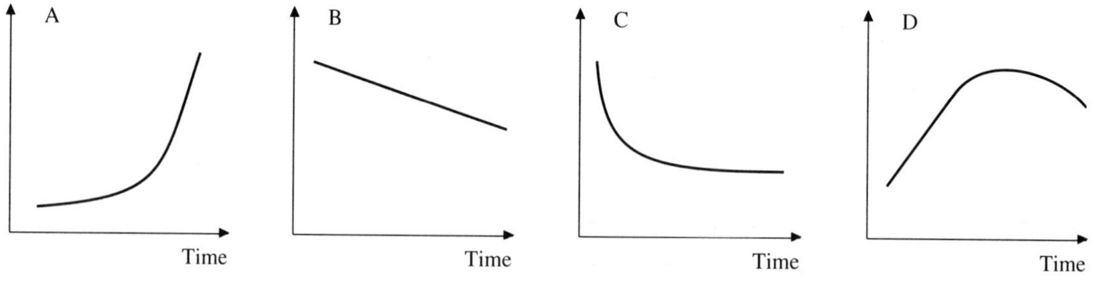

4. The graph shows the motion of three cars A, B and C along the same road.
Answer the following questions giving estimates where necessary.
(a) Which car is in front after
(i) 10 s, (ii) 20 s?
(b) When is B in the front?
(c) When are B and C going at the same speed?
(d) When are A and C going at the same speed?
(e) Which car is going fastest after 5 s?
(f) Which car starts slowly and then goes faster and faster?

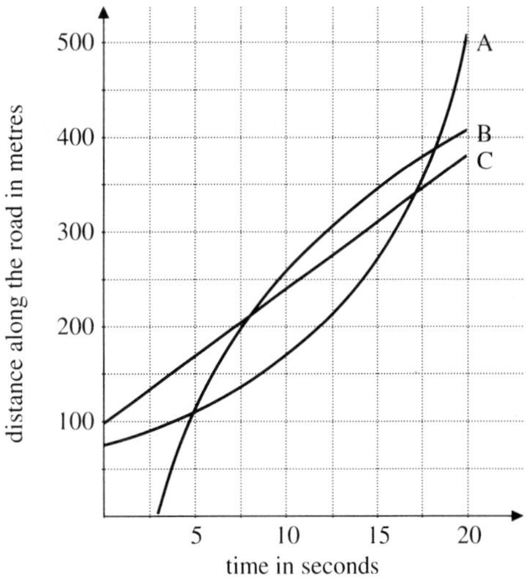

5. Three girls Hanna, Fateema and Carine took part in an egg and spoon race. Describe what happened, giving as many details as possible.

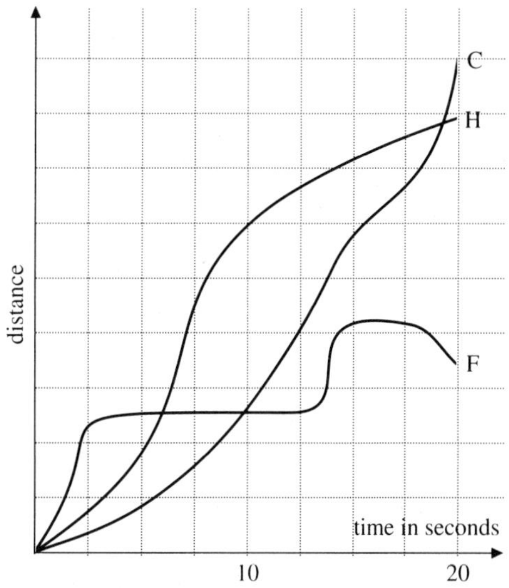

6. The graph shows the speed of the baton during a 4 × 100 m relay race.

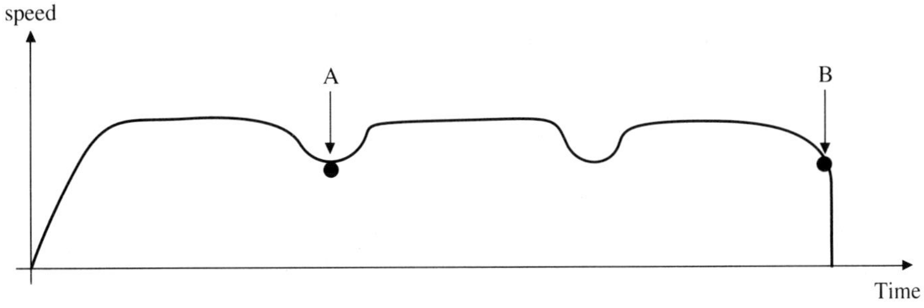

(a) Describe what is happening at point A.
(b) Describe what is happening at point B.

6.5 Flow diagrams

3/7b, 5/7a

A flow diagram is used to break down a calculation or operation into a series of simple steps connected by direction arrows. Flow diagrams are sometimes used as a first step in writing a computer program.

Exercise 11

In Questions **1** to **5**, put each of the numbers 1, 2, 3, 4, 5, 6, 7 in at the box marked N. Work out what number would be printed in each case. Record the results in a table:

Input	1	2	3	4	5	6	7
Output							

1.

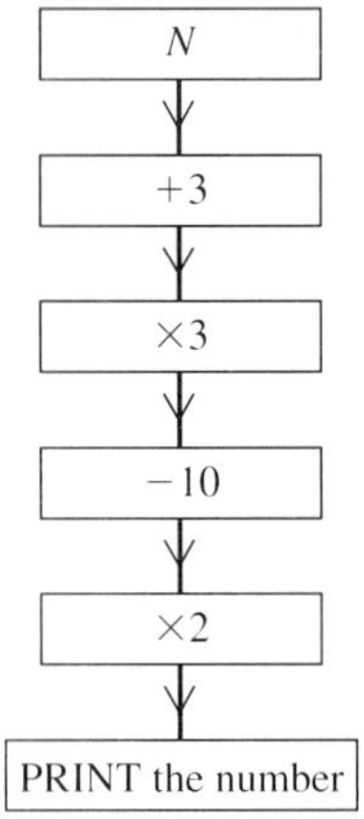

2.

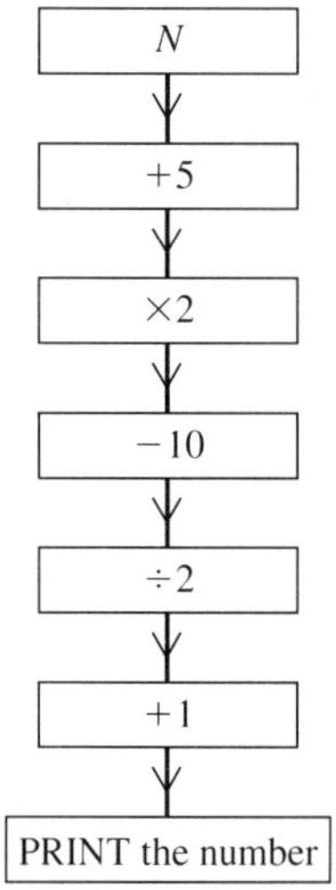

3.

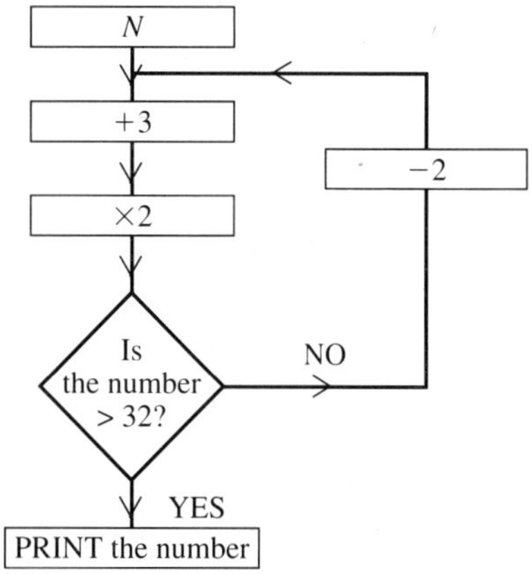

4.

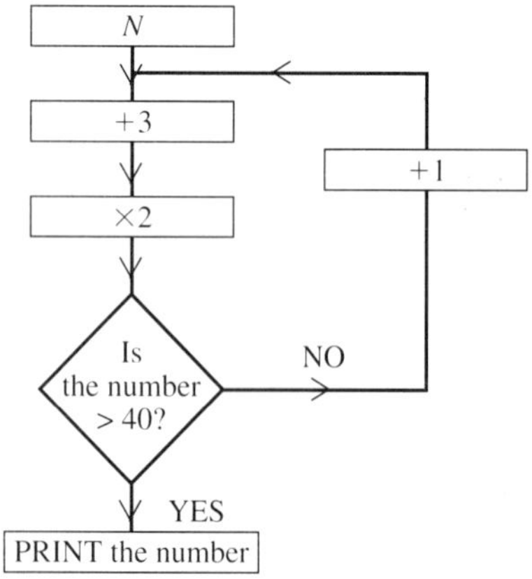

5.

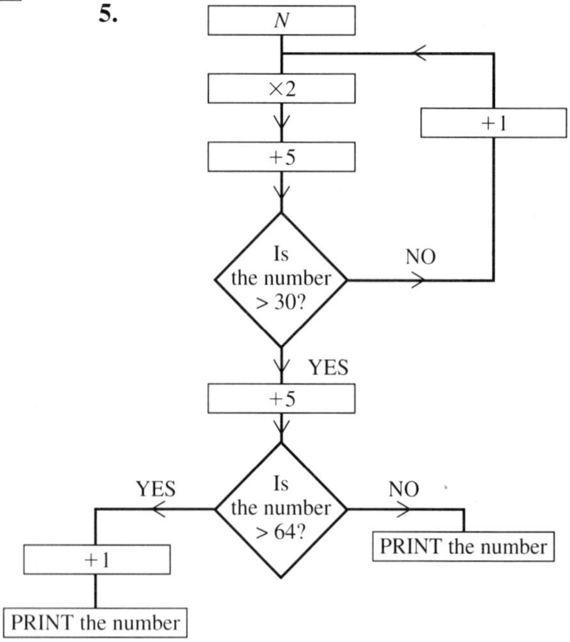

In Questions **6** and **7** use $N = 1, 2, 3, \ldots 9$.

6.

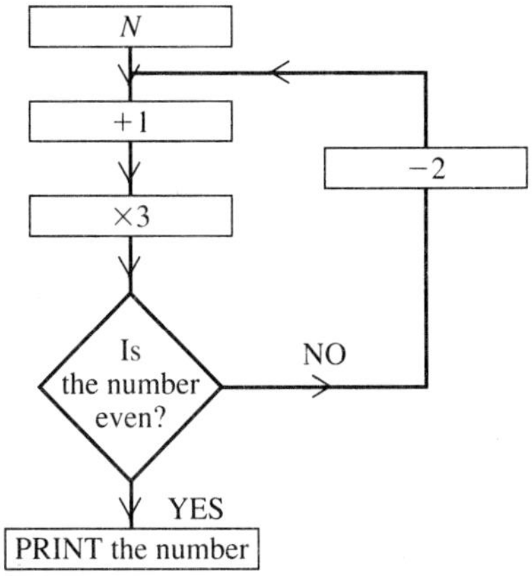

7.

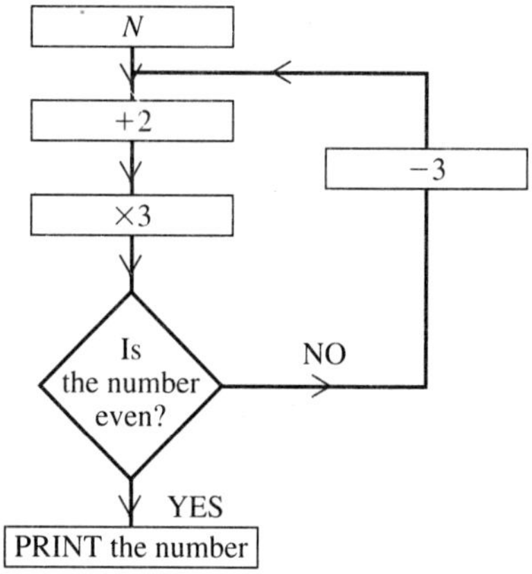

8. This flow diagram has three variables X, Y and Z.
(a) What two numbers will be printed?
(b) In Box 1 Z is changed from 20 to 600. What will be printed now?

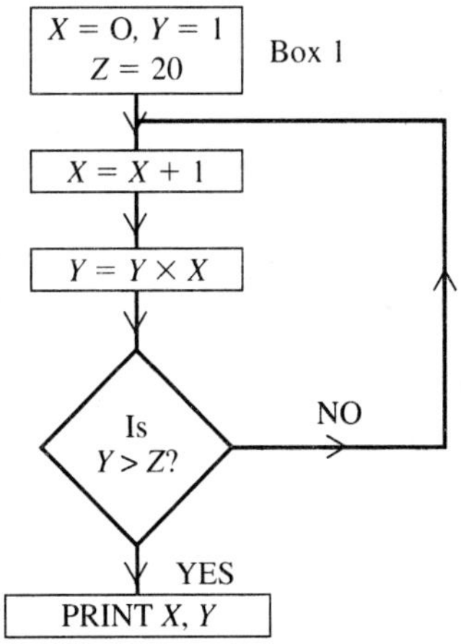

9. (a) Work through this flow diagram several times. Take any value of Z that you like (say 7, 11, 197, −17).
What do you notice?

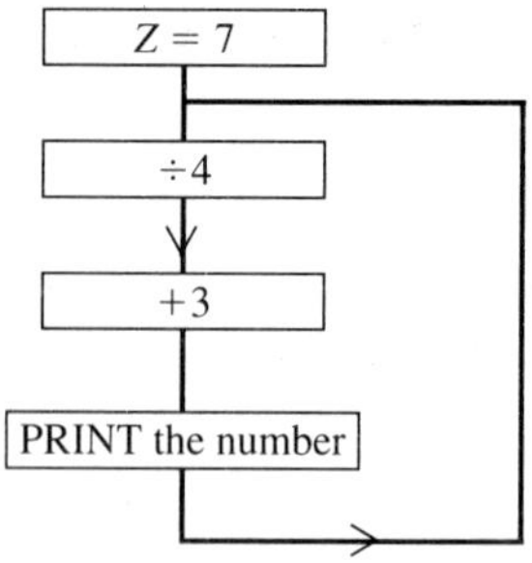

(b) This flow diagram can be checked by running the BASIC program below on a computer.

```
10    Z= 7
20    FOR N= 1 TO 25
30    Z=Z/4
40    Z=Z+3
50    PRINT Z
60    NEXT N
70    END
RUN
```

Line 10, gives Z a starting value. You can try '$Z = 11$', '$Z = 197$', '$Z = -11$' afterwards.
Line 20 with line 60 tells the computer to go around the loop 25 times.
Line 30 makes the new value of Z a quarter of the old value.
Line 40 make the new value of Z three more than the old value.
Run the program on a computer to see if you get the same result as before.

10. Here is another flow diagram with its program written in BASIC.

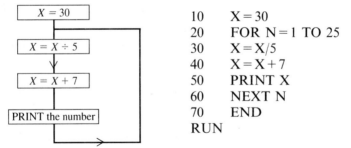

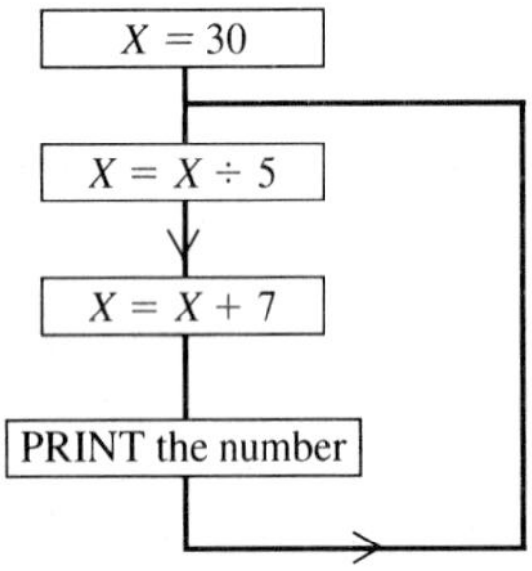


```
10    X=30
20    FOR N=1 TO 25
30    X=X/5
40    X=X+7
50    PRINT X
60    NEXT N
70    END
RUN
```

(a) Run the program with $X = 30$, $X = 8$, $X = 17{\cdot}3$ or any other value in line 10.
What do you notice about the output?
(b) Change line 30 to '30 $X = X/7$'.
What do you notice about the output?
(c) Make other changes to lines 30 and 40 and run the programs.

Find the operation

Exercise 12

In the flow charts, the boxes A, B, C and D each contain a single mathematical operation (like +5, ×4, −15,. ÷2).

Look at flow charts (i) and (ii) together and work out what is the same operation which will replace A. Complete the flow chart by replacing B, C and D.

Now copy and complete each flow chart on the right, using the same operations.

1. (i) 1 → [A] → 8 → [B] → 16 → [C] → 5 → [D] → 15

(ii) 3 → [A] → 10 → [B] → 20 → [C] → 9 → [D] → 27

(a) 4 → [A] → ? → [B] → ? → [C] → ? → [D] → ?

(b) 5 → [A] → ? → [B] → ? → [C] → ? → [D] → ?

(c) ? → [A] → ? → [B] → 28 → [C] → ? → [D] → ?

(d) ? → [A] → 16 → [B] → ? → [C] → ? → [D] → ?

(e) ? → [A] → ? → [B] → ? → [C] → 25 → [D] → ?

(f) ? → [A] → ? → [B] → ? → [C] → ? → [D] → 87

2. (i) 2 → [A] → 4 → [B] → 19 → [C] → 12 → [D] → 3

(ii) 4 → [A] → 8 → [B] → 23 → [C] → 16 → [D] → 4

(a) 6 → [A] → ? → [B] → ? → [C] → ? → [D] → ?

(b) 3 → [A] → ? → [B] → ? → [C] → ? → [D] → ?

(c) ? → [A] → 16 → [B] → ? → [C] → ? → [D] → ?

(d) ? → [A] → ? → [B] → 35 → [C] → ? → [D] → ?

(e) ? → [A] → ? → [B] → ? → [C] → ? → [D] → $2\frac{1}{2}$

(f) ? → [A] → ? → [B] → ? → [C] → ? → [D] → 8

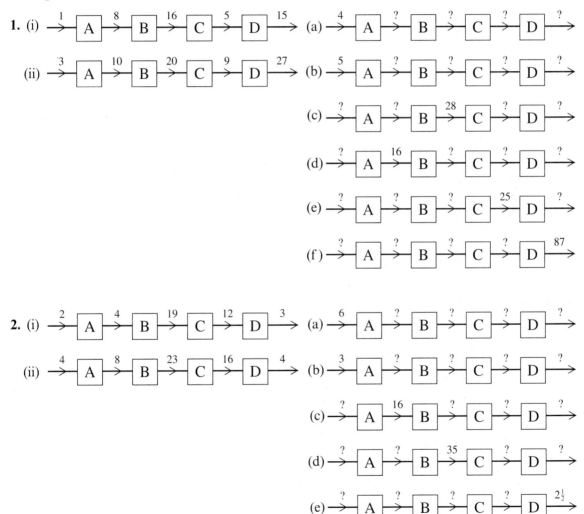

3. (i) $\xrightarrow{2}$ A $\xrightarrow{17}$ B $\xrightarrow{34}$ C $\xrightarrow{12}$ D $\xrightarrow{3}$

(ii) $\xrightarrow{4}$ A $\xrightarrow{19}$ B $\xrightarrow{38}$ C $\xrightarrow{16}$ D $\xrightarrow{4}$

(a) $\xrightarrow{7}$ A $\xrightarrow{?}$ B $\xrightarrow{?}$ C $\xrightarrow{?}$ D $\xrightarrow{?}$

(b) $\xrightarrow{10}$ A $\xrightarrow{?}$ B $\xrightarrow{?}$ C $\xrightarrow{?}$ D $\xrightarrow{?}$

(c) $\xrightarrow{?}$ A $\xrightarrow{?}$ B $\xrightarrow{62}$ C $\xrightarrow{?}$ D $\xrightarrow{?}$

(d) $\xrightarrow{?}$ A $\xrightarrow{15\frac{1}{2}}$ B $\xrightarrow{?}$ C $\xrightarrow{?}$ D $\xrightarrow{?}$

(e) $\xrightarrow{?}$ A $\xrightarrow{?}$ B $\xrightarrow{?}$ C $\xrightarrow{208}$ D $\xrightarrow{?}$

(f) $\xrightarrow{?}$ A $\xrightarrow{?}$ B $\xrightarrow{?}$ C $\xrightarrow{?}$ D $\xrightarrow{14}$

4. (i) $\xrightarrow{2}$ A $\xrightarrow{4}$ B $\xrightarrow{12}$ C $\xrightarrow{2}$ D $\xrightarrow{1}$

(ii) $\xrightarrow{3}$ A $\xrightarrow{9}$ B $\xrightarrow{27}$ C $\xrightarrow{17}$ D $\xrightarrow{8\frac{1}{2}}$

(a) $\xrightarrow{4}$ A $\xrightarrow{16}$ B $\xrightarrow{?}$ C $\xrightarrow{?}$ D $\xrightarrow{?}$

(b) $\xrightarrow{5}$ A $\xrightarrow{?}$ B $\xrightarrow{?}$ C $\xrightarrow{?}$ D $\xrightarrow{?}$

(c) $\xrightarrow{?}$ A $\xrightarrow{?}$ B $\xrightarrow{108}$ C $\xrightarrow{?}$ D $\xrightarrow{?}$

(d) $\xrightarrow{?}$ A $\xrightarrow{?}$ B $\xrightarrow{?}$ C $\xrightarrow{182}$ D $\xrightarrow{?}$

(e) $\xrightarrow{?}$ A $\xrightarrow{?}$ B $\xrightarrow{3}$ C $\xrightarrow{?}$ D $\xrightarrow{?}$

(f) $\xrightarrow{?}$ A $\xrightarrow{?}$ B $\xrightarrow{?}$ C $\xrightarrow{?}$ D $\xrightarrow{145}$

In Questions **5, 6, 7** find the operations A,B,C,D.

5. (i) $\xrightarrow{4}$ A $\xrightarrow{16}$ B $\xrightarrow{4}$ C $\xrightarrow{-6}$ D $\xrightarrow{12}$

(ii) $\xrightarrow{9}$ A $\xrightarrow{36}$ B $\xrightarrow{6}$ C $\xrightarrow{-4}$ D $\xrightarrow{8}$

6. (i) $\xrightarrow{5}$ A $\xrightarrow{\frac{1}{5}}$ B $\xrightarrow{1\cdot2}$ C $\xrightarrow{1\cdot44}$ D $\xrightarrow{0\cdot48}$

(ii) $\xrightarrow{\frac{1}{2}}$ A $\xrightarrow{2}$ B $\xrightarrow{3}$ C $\xrightarrow{9}$ D $\xrightarrow{3}$

7. (i)

$\xrightarrow{-1}$ A $\xrightarrow{2}$ B $\xrightarrow{8}$ C $\xrightarrow{-4}$ D $\xrightarrow{96}$

(ii)

$\xrightarrow{7}$ A $\xrightarrow{10}$ B $\xrightarrow{1000}$ C $\xrightarrow{-500}$ D $\xrightarrow{-400}$

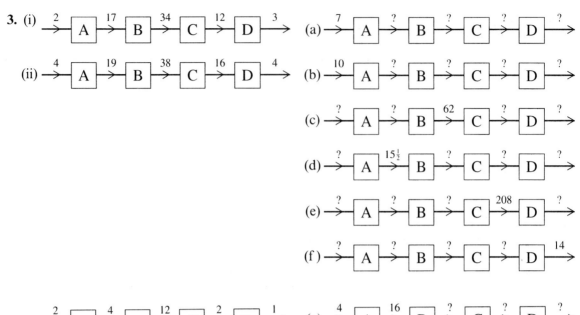

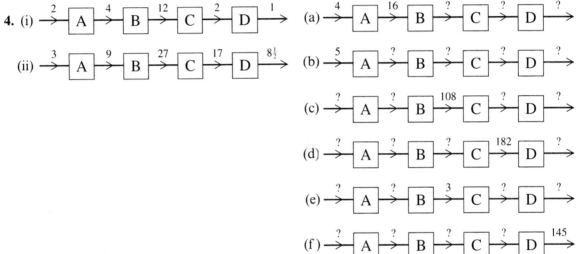

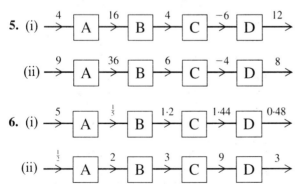

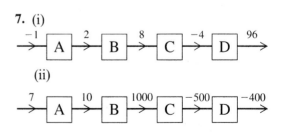

7 Number 2

7.1 Percentage change

2/6a

Price changes are sometimes more significant when expressed as a percentage of the original price. For example if the price of a car goes up from £7000 to £7070, this is only a 1% increase. If the price of a jacket went up from £100 to £170 this would be a 70% increase! In both cases the actual increase is the same: £70.

$$\text{Percentage increase} = \frac{\text{(actual increase)}}{\text{(original value)}} \times \frac{100}{1}$$

The price of a car is increased from £6400 to £6800.

$$\text{Percentage increase} = \frac{400}{6400} \times \frac{100}{1} = 6\tfrac{1}{4}\%$$

For a *decrease*:

$$\text{Percentage decrease} = \frac{\text{actual decrease}}{\text{original value}} \times \frac{100}{1}$$

Exercise 1

In Questions **1** to **10** calculate the percentage increase.

	Original price	Final price
1.	£50	£54
2.	£80	£88
3.	£180	£225
4.	£100	£102
5.	£75	£78
6.	£400	£410
7.	£5000	£6000
8.	£210	£315
9.	£600	£690
10.	\$4000	\$7200

In Questions **11** to **20** calculate the percentage decrease.

	Original price	Final price
11.	£800	£600
12.	£50	£40
13.	£120	£105
14.	£420	£280
15.	£6000	£1200
16.	\$880	\$836
17.	\$15 000	\$14 100
18.	\$7·50	\$6·00
19.	£8·20	£7·79
20.	£16 000	£15 600

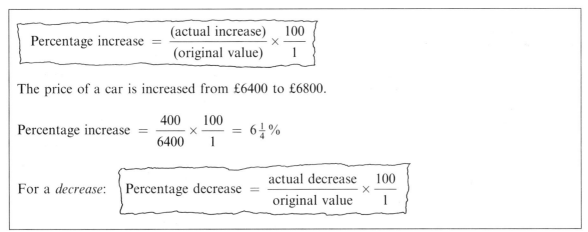

Exercise 2

Find the percentage profit/loss using either the formula:

$$\text{percentage profit} = \frac{(\text{actual profit})}{(\text{cost price})} \times \frac{100}{1}$$

or

$$\text{percentage loss} = \frac{(\text{actual loss})}{(\text{cost price})} \times \frac{100}{1}$$

Give the answers correct to one decimal place.

	Cost price	Selling price
1.	£11	£15
2.	£21	£25
3.	£36	£43
4.	£41	£50
5.	£411	£461
6.	£5·32	£5·82
7.	£6·14	£7·00
8.	£2·13	£2·50
9.	£6·11	£8·11
10.	£18·15	£20

	Cost price	Selling price
11.	£20	£18·47
12.	£17	£11
13.	£13	£9
14.	£211	£200
15.	£8·15	£7
16.	£2·62	£3
17.	£1·52	£1·81
18.	\$13·50	\$13·98
19.	\$3·05	\$4·00
20.	\$1705	\$1816

Exercise 3

1. The number of people employed by a firm increased from 250 to 280. Calculate the percentage increase in the workforce.

2. During the first four weeks of her life a baby's weight increases from 3000 g to 3870 g. Calculate the percentage increase in the baby's weight.

3. Before cooking, a joint of meat weighs 2·5 kg. After cooking the same joint of meat weighs only 2·1 kg. Calculate the percentage decrease in the weight of the joint.

4. When cold, an iron rod is 200 cm long. After being heated, the length increases to 200·5 cm. Calculate the percentage increase in the length of the rod.

5. A man buys a car for £4000 and sells it for £4600. Calculate the percentage profit.

6. A shopkeeper buys jumpers for £6·20 and sells them for £9·99. Calculate the percentage profit correct to one decimal place.

7. A grocer buys bananas at 20p per pound but after the fruit are spoiled he has to sell them at only 17p per pound. Calculate the percentage loss.

8. Before a service the petrol consumption of a car was 31 miles per gallon. After the service the consumption improved to 35·4 miles per gallon. Calculate the percentage improvement in the petrol consumption, correct to one decimal place.

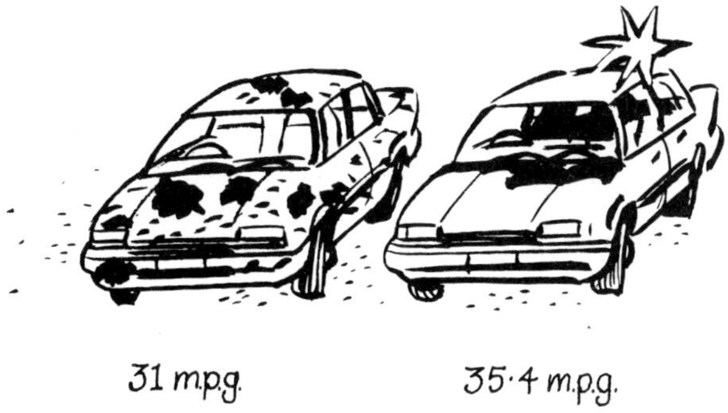

9. After an outbreak of smallpox, the population of a town went down from 22 315 to 21 987. Calculate the percentage reduction, correct to one decimal place.

10. In 1986 a tennis player earned £2 410 200. In 1987 the same player earned £2 985 010. Calculate the percentage increase in his income, correct to one decimal place.

Exercise 4

This exercise is more difficult.

1. A shopkeeper bought 40 articles for £10 and sold them at 32p each. Calculate
   (a) the cost price of each article.
   (b) the total selling price of the 40 articles.
   (c) the total profit.
   (d) the percentage profit.

2. A shopkeeper bought a crate of 40 tins of pears at 25p per tin.
   (a) Find the total cost of the crate of pears.
   (b) He sold 10 tins at 37p per tin, and the rest of the crate at 35p per tin.
      (i) How much profit did he make?
      (ii) Express this profit as a percentage of his total cost price.

3. ABCD is a square of side 100 cm. Side AB is increased by 20% and side AD is reduced by 25% to form rectangle APQR.

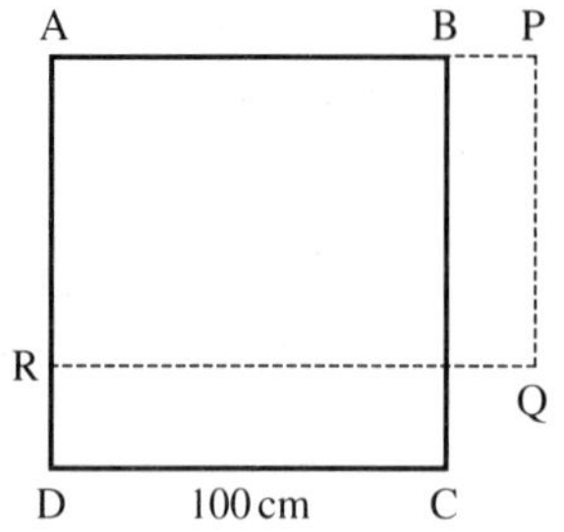

(a) Calculate (i) the length of AP
(ii) the length of AR
(iii) the area of square ABCD
(iv) the area of rectangle APQR.

(b) By what percentage has the area of the square been reduced?

4. When a house was built in 1994 the total cost was made up of the following:

wages	£30 000
materials	£16 000
overheads	£4 000

(a) Find the total cost of the house in 1994.

(b) In 1995 the cost of wages increased by 10%, the cost of materials increased by 5% and the overheads remained at their previous cost.
(i) Find the total cost of the house in 1995
(ii) Calculate the percentage increase from 1994 to 1995.

5. Four maths teachers calculate the area of the shape given and they all get different answers,
As usual Mr Gibson is wrong by 20% but surprisingly Mr Rayner is also wrong, but by only 5%.
Here are the four answers:
$237{\cdot}5\ m^2$, $250\ m^2$, $260\ m^2$, $300\ m^2$.
Which is the correct answer?

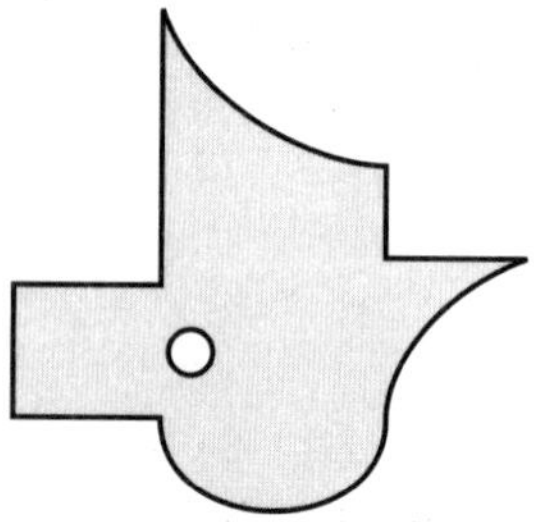

7.2 Fractions, ratio, decimals and percentage

2/6b

Percentages are simply a convenient way of expressing fractions or decimals. '50% of £60' is the same as '$\frac{1}{2}$ of £60'. You should be able to convert readily from one form to another.

(a) Change $\frac{7}{8}$ to a decimal.

Divide 8 into 7 $\quad 8\overline{)7 \cdot 000}$ = $0 \cdot 875$

(b) Change 0·35 to a fraction.

$0{\cdot}35 = \frac{35}{100} = \frac{7}{20}$

(c) Change $\frac{3}{8}$ to a percentage.

$\frac{3}{8} = \frac{3}{8} \times 100\% = 37\frac{1}{2}\%$

(d) Work out $\frac{1}{6} + 0{\cdot}72$

$\frac{1}{6} = 0{\cdot}1666\ldots$ [divide 6 into 1]

$\therefore \frac{1}{6} + 0{\cdot}72 = 0{\cdot}1666$
$\qquad\qquad\quad 0{\cdot}7200+$
$\qquad\qquad\quad 0{\cdot}8866$

Answer = 0·89 (2 d.p.)

Exercise 5

1. Two shops had sale offers on an article which previously cost £69. One shop had '$\frac{1}{3}$ off' and the other had '70% of old price'. Which shop had the lower price?

2. Shareholders in a company can opt for either '$\frac{1}{6}$ of £5000' or '15% of £5000'. Which is the greater amount?

3. A photo copier increases the sides of a square in the ratio 4 : 5. By what percentage are the sides increased?

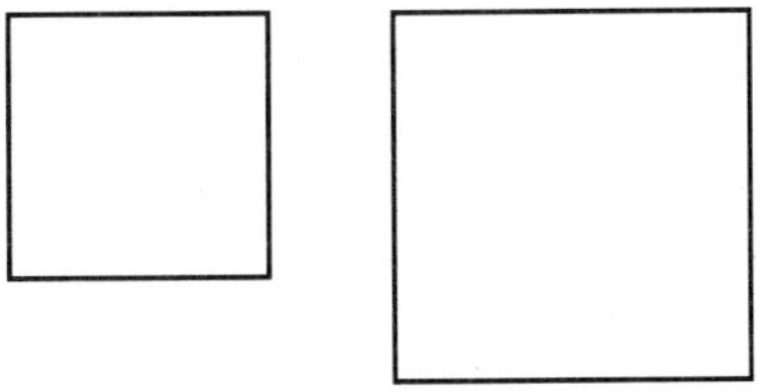

4. In an alloy the ratio of copper to iron to lead is 5 : 7 : 3. What percentage of the alloy is lead?

5. Change the fractions to decimals.

(a) $\frac{1}{4}$ (b) $\frac{2}{5}$ (c) $\frac{3}{8}$
(d) $\frac{5}{12}$ (e) $\frac{1}{6}$ (f) $\frac{2}{7}$

6. Change the decimals to fractions and simplify.

(a) 0·2 (b) 0·45 (c) 0·36
(d) 0·125 (e) 1·05 (f) 0·007

7. Change to percentages.

(a) $\frac{1}{4}$ (b) $\frac{1}{10}$ (c) 0·72

(d) 0·075 (e) 0·02 (f) $\frac{1}{3}$

8. Copy and complete the table:

	Fraction	Decimal	Percentage
(a)	$\frac{1}{4}$		
(b)		0·2	
(c)			80%
(d)	$\frac{1}{100}$		
(e)			30%
(f)	$\frac{1}{3}$		

9. Work out (a) $\frac{3}{4}$ of 65% of 0·3

(b) 11% of $\frac{3}{5}$ of £240

10. Arrange in order of size (smallest first)

(a) $\frac{1}{2}$; 45%; 0·6 (b) 0·38; $\frac{6}{16}$; 4% (c) 0·111; 11%; $\frac{1}{9}$

Evaluate, giving the answer to 2 decimal places:

11. $\frac{1}{4}+\frac{1}{3}$ **12.** $\frac{2}{3}+0{\cdot}75$ **13.** $\frac{8}{9}-0{\cdot}24$

14. $\frac{7}{8}+\frac{5}{9}+\frac{2}{11}$ **15.** $\frac{1}{3}\times 0{\cdot}2$ **16.** $\frac{5}{8}\times\frac{1}{4}$

17. $\frac{8}{11}\div 0{\cdot}2$ **18.** $(\frac{4}{7}-\frac{1}{3})\div 0{\cdot}4$

19. Pure gold is 24 carat gold. What percentage of pure gold is 15 carat gold?

7.3 Estimating

2/6c

In some circumstances it is unrealistic to work out the exact answer to a problem. It might be quite satisfactory to give an estimate for the answer. For example a builder does not know *exactly* how many bricks a new garage will require. He may estimate that he needs 2500 bricks and place an order for that number. In practice he may need only 2237.

Exercise 6

Estimate which answer is closest to the actual answer.

1. The height of a double-decker bus:

A	B	C
3 m	6 m	10 m

2. The height of the tallest player in the Olympic basketball competition:

A	B	C
1·8 m	3·0 m	2·2 m

3. The weight of a £1 coin:

A	B	C
1 g	10 g	100 g

4. The weight of a pint of milk in a cardboard carton:

A	B	C
500 g	1000 g	5000 g

5. The volume of your classroom:

A	B	C
700 cu.ft.	7000 cu.ft.	70 000 cu.ft.

6. The top speed of a Grand Prix racing car:

A	B	C
600 km/h	80 km/h	300 km/h

7. The number of times your heart beats in one day (24 h).

A	B	C
10 000	100 000	1 000 000

8. The thickness of one page in this book:

A	B	C
0·01 cm	0·001 cm	0·0001 cm

9. The number of cars in a traffic jam 10 km long on a 3-lane motorway:

A	B	C
4000	40 000	200 000

10. The time it takes to walk one mile:

A	B	C
10 minutes	20 minutes	60 minutes

11. The cost of a 5 minute telephone call to New York at 10.00 am on a weekday:

A	B	C
£2·80	£7·50	£15·00

12. The weight of an ordinary apple is:

A	B	C
100 g	250 g	400 g

13. The cheap rate telephone charge to Australia is 70p per minute. The number of words you will be able to say in a call costing £4 is:

A	B	C
120	500	1200

14. The speed at which the hair on your head grows in km/h is:

A	B	C
0·0001	0·000 01	0·000 001

15. Mr Gibson, the famous maths teacher, has won the pools. He decides to give a rather unusual prize for the person who comes top in his next maths test. The prize winner receives his or her own weight in coins and they can choose to have either 1p, 2p, 5p, 10p, 20p, 50p or £1 coins. All the coins must be the same.

Shabeza is the winner and she weighs 47 kg. *Estimate* the highest value of her prize.
To improve your estimate you can use the following equipment at home: kitchen scales, lots of coins, calculator.

16. The largest tree in the world has a diameter of 11 m.
Estimate the number of 'average' 15 year olds required to circle the tree so that they form an unbroken chain.

17. • When you multiply by a number greater than 1 you make it bigger.

so **5·3** × 1·03 > **5·3** and **6·75** × 0·89 < **6·75**

• When you divide by a number greater than 1 you make it smaller.

so **8·92** ÷ 1·13 < **8·92** and **11·2** ÷ 0·73 > **11·2**

State whether true or false:

(a) 3·72 × 1·3 > 3·72
(b) 253 × 0·91 < 253
(c) 0·92 × 1·04 > 0·92
(d) 8·5 ÷ 1·4 > 8·5
(e) 113 ÷ 0·73 < 113
(f) 17·4 ÷ 2·2 < 17·4
(g) 0·73 × 0·73 < 0·73
(h) 2511 ÷ 0·042 < 2511
(i) 614 × 0·993 < 614

Estimate the answers to the following questions:

(a) $9{\cdot}7 \times 3{\cdot}1 \approx 10 \times 3$. About 30.

(b) $81{\cdot}4 \times 98{\cdot}2 \approx 80 \times 100$. About 8000.

(c) $19{\cdot}2 \times 49{\cdot}1 \approx 20 \times 50$. About 1000.

(d) $102{\cdot}7 \div 19{\cdot}6 \approx 100 \div 20$. About 5.

Exercise 7

Write down each question and decide (by estimating) which answer is correct. Do not do the calculations exactly.

	Question	Answer A	Answer B	Answer C
1.	$7{\cdot}79 \div 1{\cdot}9$	8·2	4·1	1·9
2.	$27{\cdot}03 \div 5{\cdot}1$	5·3	0·5	8·7
3.	$59{\cdot}78 \div 9{\cdot}8$	12·2	2·8	6·1
4.	$58{\cdot}4 \times 102$	600·4	5956·8	2450·4
5.	$6{\cdot}8 \times 11{\cdot}4$	19·32	280·14	77·52
6.	$97 \times 1{\cdot}08$	104·76	55·66	1062·3
7.	$972 \times 20{\cdot}2$	2112·4	19 634·4	8862·4
8.	$7{\cdot}1 \times 103$	74·3	731·3	7210·3
9.	$18{\cdot}9 \times 21$	396·9	58·7	201·9
10.	$1{\cdot}078 \div 0{\cdot}98$	6·4	10·4	1·1
11.	$1250{\cdot}5 \div 6{\cdot}1$	21·4	205	66·2
12.	$20{\cdot}48 \div 3{\cdot}2$	6·4	12·2	2·8
13.	$25{\cdot}11 \div 3{\cdot}1$	8·1	15·1	19·3
14.	$216 \div 0{\cdot}9$	56·3	24·3	240
15.	$19{\cdot}2 + 0{\cdot}41$	23·3	8·41	19·61
16.	$207 + 18{\cdot}34$	25·34	225·34	1248
17.	$68{\cdot}2 - 1{\cdot}38$	97·82	48·82	66·82
18.	$7 - 0{\cdot}64$	6·36	1·48	0·48
19.	$974 \times 0{\cdot}11$	9·14	107·14	563·14
20.	$551{\cdot}1 \div 11$	6·92	50·1	5623
21.	$207{\cdot}1 + 11{\cdot}65$	310·75	23·75	218·75
22.	$664 \times 0{\cdot}51$	256·2	338·64	828·62
23.	$(5{\cdot}6 - 0{\cdot}21) \times 39$	389·21	210·21	20·51
24.	$\dfrac{17{\cdot}5 \times 42}{2{\cdot}5}$	294	504	86
25.	$(906 + 4{\cdot}1) \times 0{\cdot}31$	473·21	282·131	29·561
26.	$\dfrac{543 + 472}{18{\cdot}1 + 10{\cdot}9}$	65	35	85
27.	$\dfrac{112{\cdot}2 \times 75{\cdot}9}{6{\cdot}9 \times 5{\cdot}1}$	242	20·4	25·2

28. There are about 7000 cinemas in the U.K. and every day about 300 people visit each one. The population of the U.K. is about 60 million.

Here is a film magazine report.

WHICH
CINEMA
MAGAZINE

Over 3% of British people go to the cinema everyday

Is the magazine report fair?
Show the working you did to decide.

29. The petrol consumption of a car is 22 miles per gallon and petrol costs £2·45 per gallon.
Jasper estimates that the petrol costs of a round trip of about 1200 miles will be £130. Is this a reasonable estimate?

30. The 44 teachers in a rather difficult school decide to buy 190 canes at £2·42 each. They share the cost equally between them. The headmaster used a calculator to work out the cost per teacher and got an answer of £1·05 to the nearest penny.
Without using a calculator, work out an estimate for the answer to check whether or not he got it right. Show your working.

31. Each year in Britain about 150 million trees are cut down to make paper. One tree is enough to make about 650 kg of paper.

(a) Weigh several newspapers (large and small) and estimate the number of newspapers which can be made from one tree.
(b) Estimate the number of newspapers which could be made from all the trees cut down each year.
(c) Weigh some of the exercise books you use at school. Estimate the number of books your class will use in a whole year and hence estimate the number of trees required to supply the paper for your class for one year.

7.4 Measurement is approximate

2/6d, 2/7c

(a) If you measure the length of some cloth for a dress you might say the length is 145 cm to the nearest cm. The actual length could be anything from 144·5 cm to 145·49999... cm if we use the normal convention which is to round up a figure of 5 or more. Clearly 145·4999... is effectively 145·5 and we could use this figure.

(b) If you measure the length of a page in a book you might say the length is 437 mm to the nearest mm. In this case the actual length could be anywhere from 436·5 mm to 437·5 mm. We write 'length is between 436·5 mm and 437·5 mm'.

> In both cases (a) and (b) the measurement expressed to a given unit is in *possible error* of *half a unit.*

(c) (i) Similarly if you say you weigh 57 kg to the nearest kg you could actually weigh anything from 56·5 kg to 57·5 kg.
(ii) If your brother was weighed on more sensitive scales and the result was 57·2 kg, his actual weight could be from 57·15 kg to 57·25 kg.
(iii) The weight of a butterfly might be given as 0·032 g. The actual weight could be from 0·0315 g to 0·0325 g.

Exercise 8

1. In a DIY store the height of a door is given as 195 cm to the nearest cm. Write down the greatest possible height of the door.
2. A vet weighs a sick goat at 37 kg to the nearest kg. What is the least possible weight of the goat?
3. A cook's weighing scales weigh to the nearest 0·1 kg. What is the greatest possible weight of a chicken which she weighs at 3·2 kg?
4. A surveyor using a laser beam device can measure distances to the nearest 0·1 m. What is the least possible length of a warehouse which he measures at 95·6 m?

5. In the county sports Jill was timed at 28·6 s for the 200 m. What is the greatest time she could have taken?

6. The length of a telephone is measured as 193 mm, to the nearest mm. The length lies between:

A	B	C
192 and 194 mm	192·5 and 193·5 mm	188 and 198 mm

7. The weight of a labrador is 35 kg, to the nearest kg. The weight lies between:

A	B	C
30 and 40 kg	34 and 36 kg	34·5 and 35·5 kg

8. Liz and Julie each measure a different worm and they both say that their worm is 11 cm long to the nearest cm. Does this mean that both worms are the same length?

In Questions **9** to **23** you are given a measurement. Write down the upper and lower bounds of the number. For example if you are given a length as 13 cm you can write 'length is between 12·5 cm and 13·5 cm'.

9. mass = 17 kg
10. d = 256 km
11. length = 2·4 m
12. m = 0·34 grams
13. v = 2·04 m/s
14. x = 12·0 cm [N.B. not 12 cm!]
15. T = 81·4°C
16. M = 0·3 kg
17. d = 4·80 cm
18. y = 0·07 m
19. mass = 0·7 tonne
20. t = 615 seconds
21. d = 7·13 m
22. n = 52 million (nearest million)
23. x = 85·0 seconds

In Questions **24** to **31** you are given the answer to a calculation. Write 'Yes' if the answer is sensible and 'No' if the answer is not.

24. Total weight of apples off a large tree = 62 kg.

25. Cost of a school meal in U.S.A. = $35·80.

26. Time taken by an aircraft to fly non-stop from London to Hong Kong = 14·2 h.

27. Ratio of population of China to population of U.K. = 200 : 1.

28. Daily takings at a Tesco superstore = £42 400

29. Number of bricks needed to build an 'average' size house = 3·2 million.

30. Time required for your maths teacher to run 100 m = 11·2 seconds.

31. Weight of a 'typical' saloon car = 384 600 kg.

7.5 Mental arithmetic

2/7a

Ideally these questions should be read out by a teacher or friends and you should not be looking at them. Each question should be repeated once and then the answer, and only the answer, should be written down.
Each test, including the recording of results, should take about 30 minutes.
If you do not have anyone to read out the questions for you, try to do the test without writing down any detailed working.

Test 1

1. Find the cost in pounds of ten books at 35 pence each.
2. Add together £4·20 and 75 pence.
3. What number divided by six gives an answer of eight?
4. I spend £1·60 and pay with £2. My change consists of three coins. What are they?
5. Find the difference between $13\frac{1}{2}$ and 20.
6. Write one centimetre as a fraction of one metre.
7. How many ten pence coins are there in a pile worth £5.60?
8. Ten per cent of the pupils in a school play hockey, 15% play basketball and the rest play football. What percentage play football?
9. In a room of 20 people, three quarters were women. What was the number of women?
10. Four lemons costing eleven pence each are bought with a one pound coin. What is the change?
11. I arrive at the railway station at 5.20 p.m. and my train is due at 6.10 p.m. How long do I have to wait?
12. What number is ten times a big as 0·65?
13. A hockey pitch measures 25 metres by 40 metres. Find the distance around the pitch.
14. Write the number 768 correct to the nearest ten.
15. By how many does a half of 62 exceed 20?
16. How many 2p coins are worth the same as ten 5p coins?
17. What number must be added to $1\frac{1}{4}$ to make $2\frac{1}{2}$?
18. Three books cost six pounds. How much will five books cost?
19. A rubber costs 20 pence. How many can be bought for £2?
20. What number is a hundred times as big as 0·605?
21. How many millimetres are there in $5\frac{1}{2}$ cm?
22. Find the average of 12 and 20.
23. A car travelling at 80 kilometres per hour takes 30 minutes for a journey. How long will the car take at 40 kilometres per hour?
24. A certain number multiplied by itself gives 81 as the answer. What is half of that number?
25. The difference between two numbers is 15. One of the numbers is 90. What is the other?
26. How many half-litre glasses can be filled from a vessel containing ten litres?
27. How much will a dozen oranges cost at 20 pence each?
28. On a coach forty-one out of fifty people are men. What percentage is this?
29. A prize of £400 000 is shared equally between one hundred people. How much does each person receive?
30. If electric cable is 6 pence for 50 cm, how much will 4 metres cost?

Test 2

1. What are 48 twos?
2. How many fives are there in ninety-five?
3. What is 6.30 a.m. on the 24-hour clock?
4. Add together £2·25 and 50 pence.
5. I go shopping with £2·80 and buy a magazine for ninety pence. How much money have I left?
6. Two angles of a triangle are 65° and 20°. What is the third angle?
7. Write in figures the number 'five million, eighteen thousand and one.'
8. How many 20 pence biros can be bought for £3?
9. Work out 1% of £600.
10. A packet of 10 small cakes costs 35 pence. How much does each cake cost?
11. Add eight to 9 fives.
12. A packet of flour weighing 2400 grams is divided into three equal parts. How heavy is each part?

13. Add together 7, 23 and 44.
14. A car does 40 miles per gallon of petrol. How far does the car travel on seven gallons of petrol?
15. How many twenty pence coins are needed to make eight pounds?
16. A certain butterfly lives for just 96 hours. How many days is this?
17. What number is 25 more than 37?
18. Find the average of 2, 5 and 8.
19. Pears cost eleven pence each. How many can I buy for sixty pence?
20. How many minutes are there in eight hours?
21. What number is twice as big as seventy-nine?
22. How many minutes are there between 6.25 p.m. and 8.00 p.m.?
23. Write one-fifth as a decimal.
24. Which is the larger: 0·7, or 0·071?
25. If a woman earns £8·40 per hour, how much does she earn in ten hours?
26. A car costing £2500 is reduced by £45. What is the new price?
27. How many half kilogram packets of sugar can be filled from a large bowl containing 32 kilograms?
28. My daily paper costs 15 pence and I buy the paper six days a week. What is my weekly bill?
29. A car journey of 110 miles took two hours. What was the average speed of the car?
30. How many days will there be in February 2003?

Test 3

1. What number is fifteen more than fifty-five?
2. What is a tenth of 2400?
3. What is twenty times forty-five?
4. Write in figures the number ten thousand, seven hundred and five.
5. A play lasting $2\frac{1}{4}$ hours starts at half-past eight. When does it finish?
6. What number is fifty-five less than 300?
7. How many twelves are there in 240?
8. A book costs £1·95. How much change do I receive from a five pound note?
9. Find the cost of eight biros at 22 pence each.
10. What four coins make 61 pence?
11. Work out $\frac{1}{2}$ plus $\frac{1}{4}$ and give the answer as a decimal.
12. A box holds 16 cans. How many boxes are needed for 80 cans?
13. If the 25th of December is a Tuesday, what day of the week is the first of January?
14. By how much is two kilos more than 500 g?
15. Write down fifteen thousand and fifty pence in pounds and pence.
16. The sides of a square field measure 160 metres. Find the total distance around the field.
17. A three-piece suite costing £970 is reduced by £248. What is the new price?
18. A bingo prize of £150 000 is shared equally between six people. How much does each person receive?
19. Ice creams cost twenty-four pence each. How many can I buy with one pound?
20. A bag contains 22 five pence coins. How much is in the bag?
21. How many pounds are there in two stones?
22. A wine merchant puts 100 bottles in crates of 12. How many crates does he need?
23. Add together 73 and 18.
24. What is 5% of £120?
25. Peaches cost fourteen pence each. How much do I pay for seven peaches?
26. A toy costs 54 pence. Find the change from a five pound note.
27. A boy goes to and from school by bus and a ticket costs 33 pence each way. How much does he spend in a five-day week?
28. In your purse, you have two ten pound notes, three five pound notes and seven one pound coins. How much have you got altogether?
29. What are eighty twelves?
30. Sweets cost 72 pence a pound. How much do I pay if I buy four ounces of sweets?

Test 4

1. What is the change from a £10 note for goods costing £1·95?
2. Add 12 to 7 nines.
3. How many 20 pence coins are needed to make £5?
4. A pile of 100 sheets of paper is 10 cm thick. How thick is each sheet?
5. Lemons cost 7 pence each or 60 pence a dozen. How much is saved by buying a dozen instead of 12 separate lemons?
6. How many weeks are there in two years?

7. What is 1% of £40?
8. How much more than £92 is £180?
9. My watch reads five past 6. It is 15 minutes fast. What is the correct time?
10. If a pint of beer costs 82p, how much does a man pay for a round of 10 pints?
11. A cycle track is 800 metres long. How far do I go in kilometres if I complete 5 laps of the track?
12. A train travels at an average speed of 30 mph for $1\frac{1}{2}$ hours. How far does it travel?
13. I go shopping with £5 and buy 3 items at 25 pence each. How much money have I left?
14. From one thousand and seven take away nine.
15. If I can cycle a mile in 3 minutes, how many miles can I cycle in one hour?
16. How many millimetres are there in 20 cm?
17. A metal rod 90 cm long is cut into four equal parts. How long is one part?
18. Find the cost of fifteen items at 5 pence each.
19. A 2 pence coin is about 2 mm thick. How many coins are in a pile which is 2 cm high?
20. Add up the first four odd numbers.
21. Add up the first four even numbers.
22. My daily paper costs 18 pence. I pay for it with a £10 note. What change do I receive?
23. A film starts at 8.53 p.m. and finishes at 9.15 p.m. How long is the film?
24. We finish school at twenty to four. What is that on the 24-hour clock?
25. Add together £2·34 and £5·60.
26. What is 10% of £7?
27. How many 2 pence coins are needed to make £4?
28. 35% of a class prefer BBC1 and 30% prefer ITV. What percentage prefer the other two channels?
29. How many minutes is it between 6.20 p.m. and 8.00 p.m.?
30. What is the cost of 1000 books at £2·50 each?

The questions in the next three tests are a little harder.

Test 5

1. I bought an article costing 63p and paid with a one pound coin. My change consisted of four coins. What were they?
2. I bought two books costing £2·50 and £1·90. How much did I spend altogether?
3. What is the cost of six items at thirty-five pence each?
4. Tickets for a concert cost £6·50 each. What is the cost of four tickets?
5. It takes me 24 minutes to walk to school. I cycle three times as fast as I walk. How long do I take to cycle to school?
6. Work out as a single number, four squared plus three squared.
7. Write down an approximate value for forty-nine times eleven.
8. Write one metre as a fraction of one kilometre.
9. What number is exactly half-way between 2·5 and 2·8?
10. The First World War started in 1914. How long ago was that?
11. Lottery tickets cost £2·50 each. How much is raised from the sale of six thousand tickets?
12. Train fares are increased by ten per cent. If the old fare was £3·50, what is the new fare?
13. If a man earns £5·50 per hour, how much does he earn in five hours?
14. A beer crate holds twelve bottles. How many crates are needed for 90 bottles?
15. When playing darts you score double ten, double twenty and treble eight. What is your total score?
16. How many inches are there in three yards?
17. A petrol pump delivered $2\frac{1}{2}$ litres in 5 seconds. How many litres will it deliver in one minute?
18. A square has sides of length 5 cm. How long is a diagonal to the nearest centimetre?
19. How much more than 119 is 272?
20. What is the cube root of 64?
21. Find the average of 4, 8 and 9.
22. A rectangular lawn is 7 yards wide and 15 yards long. What area does it cover?
23. How many centimetres are there in 20 km?
24. A ship was due at noon on Tuesday, but arrived at 15 00 on Thursday. How many hours late was it?
25. A litre of wine fills 9 glasses. How many litre bottles are needed to fill 50 glasses?
26. Work out 15% of £40.
27. A cake weighs two pounds. How many ounces is that?

28. How many seconds are there in $2\frac{1}{2}$ minutes?
29. How many days are there altogether in 19 weeks?
30. If the eighth of May is a Monday, what day of the week is the seventeenth?

Test 6

1. What is the angle between the hands of a clock at two o'clock?
2. What is a half of a half of 0·2?
3. In a test Paul got 16 out of 20. What percentage is that?
4. Work out $2 \times 20 \times 200$.
5. Two friends share a bill for £33·80. How much does each person pay?
6. Work out $\frac{1}{2}$ plus $\frac{1}{5}$ and give the answer as a decimal.
7. How long will it take a car to travel 320 miles at an average speed of 60 m.p.h.?
8. What is $\frac{1}{8}$ as a percentage?
9. What is the height of a triangle with base 12 cm and area 36 cm^2?
10. Work out 0·1 cubed.
11. Between which two consecutive whole numbers does the square root of 58 lie?
12. What is eight per cent of £25?
13. A car has a 1795 c.c. engine. What is that approximately in litres?
14. The mean of four numbers is 12·3. What is their sum?
15. Find the cost of smoking 40 cigarettes a day for five days if a packet of 20 costs £1·25.
16. How many minutes are there in $2\frac{3}{4}$ hours?
17. A pie chart has a red sector representing 20% of the whole chart. What is the angle of the sector?
18. How many five pence coins are needed to make £12?
19. I buy three pounds of oranges for £1·02. How much do they cost per pound?
20. A rectangular pane of glass is 3 feet long and 2 feet wide. Glass costs £1·50 per square foot. How much will the pane cost?
21. A car journey of 150 miles took $2\frac{1}{2}$ hours. What was the average speed?
22. Add 218 to 84.
23. Pencils cost 5 pence each. How many can I buy with £2·50?
24. Write down the next prime number after 31.
25. A ruler costs 37 pence. What is the total cost of three rulers?
26. A salesman receives commission of $1\frac{1}{2}$% on sales. How much commission does he receive when he sells a computer for £1000?
27. How many edges does a cube have?
28. Between which two consecutive whole numbers does the square root of 80 lie?
29. A coat is marked at a sale price of £60 after a reduction of 25%. What was the original price?
30. Theatre tickets cost £3·45 each. How much will four tickets cost?

Test 7

1. Two angles of a triangle are 42° and 56°. What is the third angle?
2. Telephone charges are increased by 20%. What is the new charge for a call which previously cost 60p?
3. What number is exactly half way between 0·1 and 0·4?
4. A boat sails at a speed of 18 knots for five hours. How far does it go?
5. How many 23p stamps can be bought for £2?
6. The mean age of three girls is 12 years. If two of the girls are aged 9 and 16 years, how old is the third girl?
7. Multiply $3\frac{1}{4}$ by 100.
8. What is a quarter of a third?
9. A prize of five million pounds is shared between 200 people. How much does each person receive?
10. The attendance at an athletics meeting was forty-eight thousand, seven hundred and eleven. Write this number correct to two significant figures.
11. Work out 0·1 multiplied by 63.
12. Find the cost of 6 litres of wine at £1·45 per litre.
13. Three people agree to share a bill equally. The cost comes to £7·20. How much does each person pay?
14. A pump removes water at a rate of 6 gallons per minute. How many hours will it take to remove 1800 gallons?
15. Work out three-eighths of £100.
16. A metal rod of length 27·1 cm is cut exactly in half. How long is each piece?

17. A square has sides of length 7 cm. How long is a diagonal to the nearest centimetre?

18. The cost of five tins of salmon is £7·50. How much will six tins cost?

19. What number is a thousand times as big as 0·2?

20. Pencils cost five pence each. How much will two dozen pencils cost?

21. How many fours are there in a thousand?

22. Work out the area, in square metres, of a rectangular field of width twenty metres and length twenty-five metres.

23. A packet of peanuts costs 65 pence. I buy two packets and pay with a ten pound note. Find the change.

24. What is a half of a half of 0·1?

25. I bought three kilograms of flour and I use four hundred and fifty grams of it. How many grams of flour do I have left?

26. A bingo prize of two hundred thousand pounds is shared equally between five people. How much does each person receive?

27. What is the angle between the hands of a clock at 5 o'clock?

28. Five boys and three girls share £240. How much do the boys get altogether?

29. How many 17p stamps can I buy for £2?

30. A milk crate has space for 24 bottles. How many crates are needed for 200 bottles?

Mathematical magic

Here is a trick which you can perform to demonstrate that you can add even quicker than a calculator!

(a) Ask someone to give a five-digit number with the figures all jumbled up to make it more 'difficult'.

(b) Ask for two more five-digit numbers. You may now have:

47563 ...A
25608 ...B
87265 ...C

(c) Pretend to add two more five-digit numbers at random. In fact choose the fourth number so that when added to number B it makes 99999. Similarly the fifth number is chosen so that when added to number C it also makes 99999. We now have:

47563
25608
87265
74391
12734

(d) You now add them together 'in your head' and write down the answer. (Check this on a calculator.)

Answer = 247561

How does it work?

The first digit is always a '2'.
The next five digits are simply 2 less than number A.
i.e. 47563 − 2 = 47561.

Here is another example.

58627
43817
38065
56182
\+ 61934
258625

Can you work out why it works?

Now challenge your friends or relatives to an addition race: your brain versus their calculator.

7.6 Using a calculator

2/7b

Order of operations

Calculators cannot think for themselves. *You* have to decide in which order the buttons have to be pressed.

Always perform operations in the following order:
(a) Brackets
(b) Divide and multiply
(c) Add and subtract.

(a) $7 + 6 \div 3 = 7 + 2$
$= 9$

(b) $6 \times 4 - 8 \div 2 = 24 - 4$
$= 20$

(c) $5 + (28 + 5) \div 3 = 5 + 33 \div 3$
$= 5 + 11$
$= 16$

(d) $\dfrac{4{\cdot}2}{1{\cdot}2 - 0{\cdot}7} = \dfrac{4{\cdot}2}{0{\cdot}5}$
$= 8{\cdot}4$

Notice that the division line ——— acts like a pair of brackets so that we work out 1·2 − 0·7 first.

Exercise 9

Work out, without a calculator.

1. $11 + 8 \div 1$ **2.** $60 - 7 \times 8$ **3.** $15 - 2 \times 6$
4. $15 \div 5 - 3$ **5.** $30 + 15 \div 3$ **6.** $9 \times 5 + 15$
7. $40 - 3 \times 8$ **8.** $12 - 36 \div 6$ **9.** $3 + 20 \div 2$
10. $13 + 8 \div 8$ **11.** $2 \times 4 + 3 \times 5$ **12.** $6 \times 6 + 7 \times 5$
13. $1 \times 6 + 7 \times 2$ **14.** $2 \times 8 + 2 \times 10$ **15.** $3 \times 5 - 12 \div 2$
16. $3 \times 5 - 28 \div 4$ **17.** $7 \times 4 + 2 \times 2$ **18.** $30 \div 3 + 5 \times 4$
19. $20 \div 2 - 3 \times 2$ **20.** $8 \div 8 - 1 \times 1$ **21.** $\dfrac{27 + 3 \times 3}{(3 \times 2)}$
22. $\dfrac{6 + 8 \times 3}{(8 \times 2 - 10)}$ **23.** $\dfrac{13 - 12 \div 4}{4 + 3 \times 2}$ **24.** $\dfrac{11 + 6 \times 6}{5 - 8 \div 2}$
25. $\dfrac{12 + 3 \times 6}{4 + 3 \div 3}$ **26.** $\dfrac{24 - 18 \div 3}{1{\cdot}5 + 4{\cdot}5}$

27. $(42 - 5 \times 6) \times (8 - 4 \times 2) + (7 + 3 \times 3)$
28. $(10 - 24 \div 3) + (8 + 3 \times 4) \div (8 - 6 \times 1)$
29. $7 + 9 \times (8 - 6 \div 2)$
30. $[(7 - 2) \times 5] - (6 \times 3 - 2 \times 4)$
31. $[(60 - 7 \times 5) \div 5] + (12 + 7 \times 10)$
32. $(15 - 3 \times 4) \times 4 + [60 \div (24 \div 2)]$
33. $[(9 - 7) \times 12] - (7 \times 3 - 5 \times 4)$
34. $(50 - 8 \times 6) \times 2 + [40 \div (5 \times 2)]$
35. $[(12 - 8) \times 4] \div (11 - 3 \times 1)$
36. $(7 \times 2 - 6) + (7 + 16 \div 8) \times (10 - 4 \times 2)$

Exercise 10

This exercise is more difficult. Write down each question and find the missing signs. (+, −, ×, ÷). There are no brackets.

1. 7 5 4 = 27
2. 3 5 10 = 25
3. 4 2 3 = 5
4. 11 3 3 = 20
5. 31 10 2 = 11
6. 10 6 5 = 40
7. 4 8 7 = 25
8. 12 9 2 = 30
9. 18 4 4 = 2
10. 28 10 2 = 8
11. 21 3 5 = 2
12. 7 3 3 = 16
13. 10 2 3 = 8
14. 10 3 12 = 42
15. 18 3 7 = 13
16. 31 40 5 = 39
17. 15 16 4 = 11
18. 15 8 9 = 87
19. 37 35 5 = 44
20. 11 5 9 = 64
21. 8 3 2 4 = 10
22. 12 3 3 1 = 4
23. 11 4 1 6 = 9
24. 15 5 2 4 = 11
25. 7 2 3 3 = 5
26. 12 2 3 4 = 22
27. 8 9 6 11 = 6
28. 20 20 9 0 = 1
29. 20 30 10 8 = 25
30. 30 6 11 11 = 85

Calculator

(a) Work out $8{\cdot}43 + \dfrac{9{\cdot}72}{3{\cdot}3}$ correct to four significant figures.

Perform the division first and *don't forget* to press the [=] button.

[9·72] [÷] [3·3] [=] [+] [8·43] [=]

Answer = 11·38 (to 4 s.f.)

(b) Work out $(5{\cdot}2 - 4{\cdot}737)^2$.

[5·2] [−] [4·737] [=] [x^2]

Answer = 0·2144 (to 4 s.f.)

Exercise 11

Work out, correct to four significant figures.

1. $85{\cdot}3 \times 21{\cdot}7$
2. $18{\cdot}6 \div 2{\cdot}7$
3. $10{\cdot}074 \div 8{\cdot}3$
4. $0{\cdot}112 \times 3{\cdot}74$
5. $8 - 0{\cdot}11111$
6. $19 + 0{\cdot}3456$
7. $0{\cdot}841 \div 17$
8. $11{\cdot}02 \times 20{\cdot}1$
9. $18{\cdot}3 \div 0{\cdot}751$
10. $0{\cdot}982 \times 6{\cdot}74$
11. $\dfrac{8{\cdot}3 + 2{\cdot}94}{3{\cdot}4}$
12. $\dfrac{6{\cdot}1 - 4{\cdot}35}{0{\cdot}76}$
13. $\dfrac{19{\cdot}7 + 21{\cdot}4}{0{\cdot}985}$
14. $7{\cdot}3 + \left(\dfrac{8{\cdot}2}{9{\cdot}5}\right)$
15. $\left(\dfrac{6{\cdot}04}{18{\cdot}7}\right) - 0{\cdot}214$
16. $\dfrac{2{\cdot}4 \times 0{\cdot}871}{4{\cdot}18}$
17. $19{\cdot}3 + \left(\dfrac{2{\cdot}6}{1{\cdot}95}\right)$
18. $6{\cdot}41 + \dfrac{9{\cdot}58}{2{\cdot}6}$

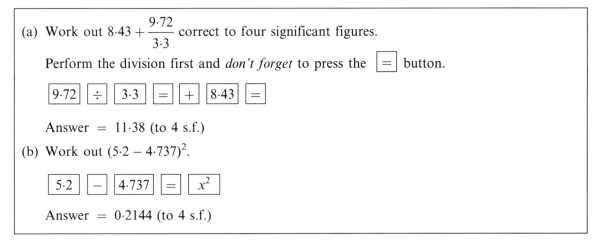

19. $\dfrac{19.3 \times 0.221}{0.689}$

20. $8.3 + \dfrac{0.64}{0.325}$

21. $2.4 + (9.7 \times 0.642)$

22. $11.2 + (9.75 \times 1.11)$

23. $0.325 + \dfrac{8.6}{11.2}$

24. $8.35^2 - 25$

25. $6.71^2 + 0.64$

26. $3.45^3 + 11.8$

27. $2.93^3 - 2.641$

28. $\dfrac{7.2^2 - 4.5}{8.64}$

29. $\dfrac{13.9 + 2.97^2}{4.31}$

30. $(3.3 - 2.84)^2$

Using the memory

(a) Work out $\dfrac{4.2 + 1.75}{3.63 - 2.14}$, correct to 4 s.f., using the memory buttons.

Find the bottom line first:

[3.63] [−] [2.14] [=] [Min] [C] [4.2] [+] [1.75] [=] [÷] [MR] [=]

The calculator reads 3.9932886

$\therefore$ Answer = 3.993 (to 4 s.f.)

(b) Work out $18.75 - 2.11^3$.

[2.11] [x^y] [3] [=] [Min] [18.75] [−] [MR] [=]

Answer = 9.356 (to 4 s.f.)

Exercise 12

Work out the following, correct to four significant figures. Use the memory buttons where necessary.

1. $\dfrac{7.3 + 2.14}{3.6 - 2.95}$

2. $\dfrac{2.3 + 0.924}{1.3 + 0.635}$

3. $\dfrac{5.89}{7 - 3.83}$

4. $\dfrac{102}{58.1 + 65.32}$

5. $\dfrac{18.8}{3.72 \times 1.86}$

6. $\dfrac{904}{65.3 \times 2.86}$

7. $12.2 - \left(\dfrac{2.6}{1.95}\right)$

8. $8.047 - \left(\dfrac{6.34}{10.2}\right)$

9. $14.2 - \left(\dfrac{1.7}{2.4}\right)$

10. $\dfrac{9.75 - 8.792}{4.31 - 3.014}$

11. $\dfrac{19.6 \times 3.01}{2.01 - 1.958}$

12. $3.7^2 - \left(\dfrac{8.59}{24}\right)$

13. $8.27 - 1.56^2$

14. $111.79 - 5.04^2$

15. $18.3 - 2.841^2$

16. $(2.93 + 71.5)^2$

17. $(8.3 - 6.34)^4$

18. $54.2 - 2.6^4$

19. $(8.7 - 5.95)^4$

20. $\sqrt{68.4} + 11.63$

21. $9.45 - \sqrt{8.248}$

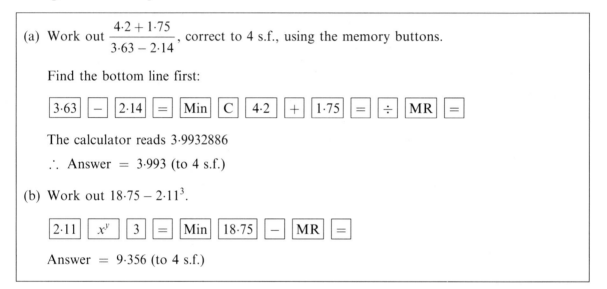

22. $3{\cdot}24^2 - \sqrt{1{\cdot}962}$

23. $\dfrac{3{\cdot}54 + 2{\cdot}4}{8{\cdot}47^2}$

24. $2065 - \sqrt{44\,000}$

25. $\sqrt{(5{\cdot}69 - 0{\cdot}0852)}$

26. $\sqrt{(0{\cdot}976 + 1{\cdot}03)}$

27. $\sqrt{\left(\dfrac{17{\cdot}4}{2{\cdot}16 - 1{\cdot}83}\right)}$

28. $\sqrt{\left(\dfrac{28{\cdot}9}{\sqrt{8{\cdot}47}}\right)}$

29. $257 - \dfrac{6{\cdot}32}{0{\cdot}059}$

30. $75\,000 - 5{\cdot}6^4$

31. $\dfrac{11{\cdot}29 \times 2{\cdot}09}{2{\cdot}7 + 0{\cdot}082}$

32. $85{\cdot}5 - \sqrt{105{\cdot}8}$

33. $\dfrac{4{\cdot}45^2}{8{\cdot}2^2 - 51{\cdot}09}$

34. $\left(\dfrac{8{\cdot}53 + 7{\cdot}07}{6{\cdot}04 - 4{\cdot}32}\right)^4$

35. $2{\cdot}75 + \dfrac{5}{8{\cdot}2} + \dfrac{11{\cdot}2}{4{\cdot}3}$

36. $8{\cdot}2 + \dfrac{6{\cdot}3}{0{\cdot}91} + \dfrac{2{\cdot}74}{8{\cdot}4}$

37. $\dfrac{18{\cdot}5}{1{\cdot}6} + \dfrac{7{\cdot}1}{0{\cdot}53} + \dfrac{11{\cdot}9}{25{\cdot}6}$

38. $\dfrac{83{\cdot}6}{105} + \dfrac{2{\cdot}95}{2{\cdot}7} + \dfrac{81}{97}$

39. $\left(\dfrac{98{\cdot}76}{103} + \dfrac{4{\cdot}07}{3{\cdot}6}\right)^2$

40. $\dfrac{(5{\cdot}843 - \sqrt{2{\cdot}07})^2}{88{\cdot}4}$

41. $\left(\dfrac{1}{7{\cdot}6} - \dfrac{1}{18{\cdot}5}\right)^3$

42. $\dfrac{\sqrt{(4{\cdot}79)} + 1{\cdot}6}{9{\cdot}63}$

43. $\dfrac{(0{\cdot}761)^2 - \sqrt{(4{\cdot}22)}}{1{\cdot}96}$

44. $\sqrt[3]{\left(\dfrac{1{\cdot}74 \times 0{\cdot}761}{0{\cdot}0896}\right)}$

45. $\left(\dfrac{8{\cdot}6 \times 1{\cdot}71}{0{\cdot}43}\right)^3$

46. $\dfrac{\sqrt[3]{(86{\cdot}6)}}{\sqrt[4]{(4{\cdot}71)}}$

47. $\dfrac{1}{8{\cdot}2^2} - \dfrac{3}{19^2}$

48. $\dfrac{100}{11^3} + \dfrac{100}{12^3}$

Exercise 13

If we work out $25 \times 503 \times 4 + 37$ on a calculator we should obtain the number 50337. If we turn the calculator upside down (and use a little imagination) we see the word 'LEEDS'.

Find the words given by the clues below.

1. $83 \times 85 + 50$ (Lots of this in the garden)
2. $211 \times 251 + 790$ (Tropical or Scilly)
3. $19 \times 20 \times 14 - 2{\cdot}66$ (Not an upstanding man)
4. $(84 + 17) \times 5$ (Dotty message)
5. $0{\cdot}01443 \times 7 \times 4$ (Three times as funny)
6. $79 \times 9 - 0{\cdot}9447$ (Greasy letters)
7. $50{\cdot}19 - (5 \times 0{\cdot}0039)$ (Not much space inside)
8. $2 \div 0{\cdot}5 - 3{\cdot}295$ (Rather lonely)
9. $0{\cdot}034 \times 11 - 0{\cdot}00292$; $9^4 - (8 \times 71)$ (two words) (Nice for breakfast)
10. $7420 \times 7422 + 118^2 - 30$ (Big Chief)

11. $(13 \times 3 \times 25 \times 8 \times 5) + 7$ (Dwelling for masons)
12. $71^2 - 11^2 - 5$ (Sad gasp)
13. $904^2 + 89621818$ (Prickly customer)
14. $(559 \times 6) + (21 \times 55)$ (What a surprise!)

15. $566 \times 711 - 23617$ (Bolt it down)

16. $\dfrac{9999 + 319}{8{\cdot}47 + 2{\cdot}53}$ (Sit up and plead)

17. $\dfrac{2601 \times 6}{4^2 + 1^2}$; $(401 - 78) \times 5^2$ (two words) (Not a great man)

18. $0{\cdot}4^2 - 0{\cdot}1^2$ (Little Sidney)

19. $\dfrac{(27 \times 2000 - 2)}{(0{\cdot}63 \div 0{\cdot}09)}$ (Not quite a mountain)

20. $(5^2 - 1^2)^4 - 14239$ (Just a name)

21. $48^4 + 102^2 - 4^2$ (Pursuits)

22. $615^2 + (7 \times 242)$ (Almost a goggle)

23. $14^4 - 627 + 29$ (Good book, by God!)

24. $6{\cdot}2 \times 0{\cdot}987 \times 1\,000\,000 - 860^2 + 118$ (Flying ace)

25. $(426 \times 474) + (318 \times 487) + 22018$ (Close to a bubble)

26. $\dfrac{36^3}{4} - 1530$ (Foreign-sounding girl's name)

27. $(594 \times 571) - (154 \times 132) - 38$ (Female Bobby)

28. $(7^2 \times 100) + (7 \times 2)$ (Lofty)

29. $240^2 + 134$; $241^2 - 7^3$ (two words) (Devil of a chime)

30. $1384{\cdot}5 \times 40 - 1{\cdot}991$ (Say this after sneezing)

31. $(2 \times 2 \times 2 \times 2 \times 3)^4 + 1929$ (Unhappy ending)

32. $141918 + 83^3$ (Hot stuff in France)

7.7 Problems 2

2/7b

Income tax

The tax which an employee pays on his income depends on
(a) how much he is paid (b) his allowances (c) the rate of taxation.

Tax is paid only on the 'taxable income'.
(i) Taxable income = Total income – allowances.

Allowances depend on whether a person is married or single and on various expenses involved in doing the job.
You can check your allowances by looking at the 'Tax Code Number' on your payslip.

(ii) Allowances = (Tax Code Number) × 10

A man earns £6500 per year. If his Tax Code Number is 238, calculate his taxable income.

Allowances = 238×10 = £2380. Taxable income = £6500 – £2380
= £4120.

Exercise 14

Calculate the taxable income from the details given.

	Earnings	Tax Code Number		Earnings	Tax Code Number
1.	£3500 per year	213	**2.**	£5000 per year	274
3.	£8000 per year	315	**4.**	£4200 per year	289
5.	£3650 per year	265	**6.**	£9800 per year	341
7.	£8655 per year	286	**8.**	£600 per month	412
9.	£450 per month	263	**10.**	£825 per month	311
11.	£710 per month	278	**12.**	£985 per month	415
13.	£160 per week	342	**14.**	£144 per week	214
15.	£180 per week	289			

A woman earns £95 per week and her Tax Code Number is 215. Find the total amount of tax paid in a year when the tax rate is 30%.

Amount earned in year = £95 × 52
= £4940

Allowances = 215 × 10 = £2150

∴ Taxable income = £4940 − £2150
= £2790

Tax paid = 30% of £2790
$= \frac{30}{100} \times \frac{2790}{1} =$ £837

Exercise 15

In all questions the tax rate is 30%.

1. A man earns £110 per week and his Tax Code Number is 304. Find the total amount of tax paid in a year.

2. A man earns £204 per week and his Tax Code Number is 361. Find the total amount of tax paid in a year.

3. Ann earns £165 per week. How much tax does she pay in a year if her Tax Code Number is 247?

4. John earns £148·50 per week. How much tax does he pay in a year if his Tax Code Number is 302?

5. Louise earns a salary of £620 per month. How much tax does she pay in a year if her Tax Code Number is 342?

6. David earns £950 per month and his Tax Code Number is 357. Find the total amount of tax paid in a year.

7. Mr Tebbit's salary is £9650 per year and his Tax Code Number is 465. Find the total amount of tax paid in a year.

Mixed questions

Exercise 16

1. Four dozen bags of grain weigh 2016 kg. How much does each bag weigh?

2. An office building has twelve floors and each floor has twenty windows.
A window cleaner charges 50p per window. How much will he charge to clean all the windows in the building?

3. Write the following to the degree of accuracy stated:

(a) 7·243 (to 1 d.p.)
(b) 11·275 (to 2 d.p.)
(c) 0·115 (to 1 d.p.)
(d) 0·0255 (to 3 d.p.)
(e) 28·21 (to 1 d.p.)
(f) 0·0072 (to 2 d.p.)

4. Work out, without using a calculator.

(a) $0·6 + 2·72$
(b) $3·21 - 1·6$
(c) $2·8 - 1·34$
(d) $8 - 3·6$
(e) $100 \times 0·062$
(f) $27·4 \div 10$

5. A rectangular wheat field is 200 m by 400 m. One hectare is 10 000 m^2 and each hectare produces 3 tonnes of wheat.

(a) What is the area of the field in hectares?
(b) How much wheat is produced in this field?

6. A powerful computer is hired out at a rate of 50p per minute. How much will it cost to hire the computer from 06 30 to 18 00?

7. An old sailor keeps all of his savings in gold. Altogether the gold weighs ten pounds. One day the price of gold goes up by \$40 an ounce to \$520 an ounce.

(a) By how much did his gold rise in value?
(b) How much was it worth after the rise?
(1 pound = 16 ounces).

8. This packet of sugar cubes costs 60p. How much would you have to pay for this packet?

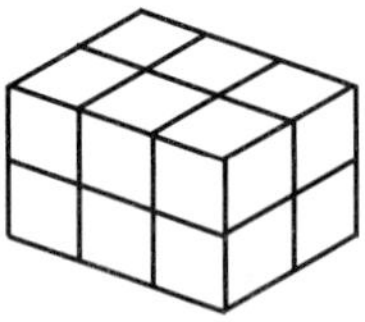

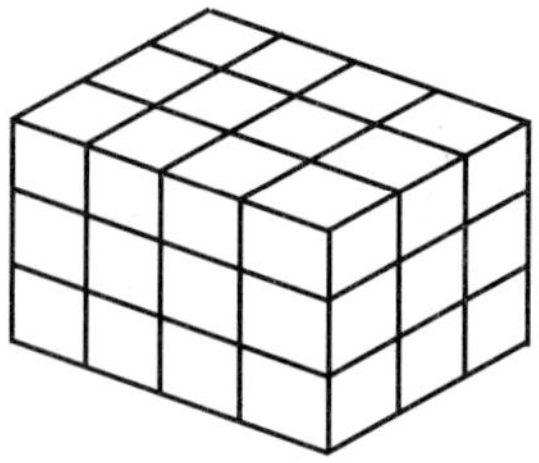

9. A wall measuring 3 m by 2 m is to be covered with square tiles of side 10 cm.
(a) How many tiles are needed?
(b) If the tiles cost £3·40 for ten, how much will it cost?

10. Draw the next member of the sequence.

(a) 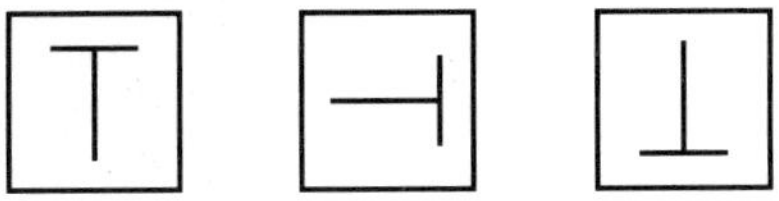

(b) 

(c) 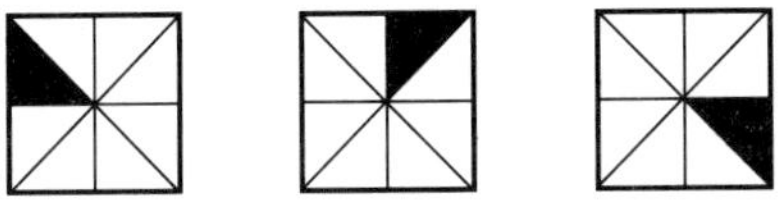

Exercise 17

1. The results of a test given to 50 children are shown below.

Mark	0	1	2	3	4	5
Number of pupils	1	4	10	12	15	8

(a) How many pupils scored less than 3 marks?
(b) Find the percentage of the pupils who scored
(i) 2 marks (ii) 5 marks
(iii) 3 marks or more (iv) No marks.

2. The thirteenth number in the sequence 1, 3, 9, 27, ... is 531 441. What is
(a) the twelfth number
(b) the fourteenth number?

3. 6 sacks of corn will feed 80 hens for 12 days.
Copy and complete the following:
(a) 18 sacks of corn will feed 80 hens for ... days.
(b) 6 sacks of corn will feed 40 hens for ... days.
(c) 60 sacks of corn will feed 40 hens for ... days.
(d) 30 sacks of corn will feed 80 hens for ... days.

4. Calculate the area of the shape below. Take $\pi = 3$.

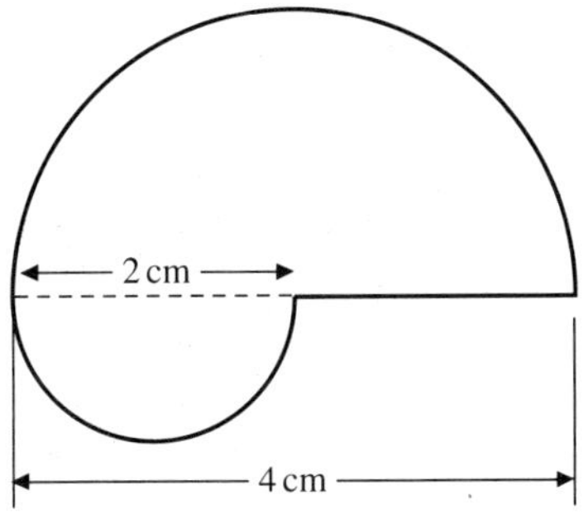

5. The mileometer of a car shows a reading of 14 941 miles. This number is called 'palindromic' because it reads the same backwards or forwards.
   (a) What will be the reading when the next palindromic number appears?
   (b) How far will the car have travelled by then?

6. Copy and complete the telephone bill shown.

DATE	METER READING	UNITS USED	PRICE PER UNIT	AMOUNT (£)
29/7/95	18714			
30/4/95	17956	______	3·80p	______
		Rental Charges		21·50
		Total Charges (excluding VAT)		______
		Value Added Tax at $17\frac{1}{2}\%$		______
		Total Charges (including VAT)		______

7. A salesman is paid a basic salary of £5400 per year, plus commission of 5% on all his sales. Calculate his total salary if his sales totalled £40 000.

8. Petrol costs 54·3 pence per litre. How any litres can be bought for £8? Give your answer to one decimal place.

Exercise 18

1. A slimmer's calorie guide shows how many calories are contained in various foods:

   Bread 1·2 calories per g
   Cheese 2·5 calories per g
   Meat 1·6 calories per g
   Butter 6 calories per g

   Calculate the number of calories in the following meals:
   (a) 50 g bread, 40 g cheese, 100 g meat, 15 g butter.
   (b) 150 g bread, 85 g cheese, 120 g meat, 20 g butter.

2. Write as a single number.
   (a) 8^2 (b) 1^4 (c) 10^2
   (d) 3×10^3 (e) 2^5 (f) 3^4

3. A cylinder has a volume of 200 cm^3 and a height of 10 cm. Calculate the area of its base.

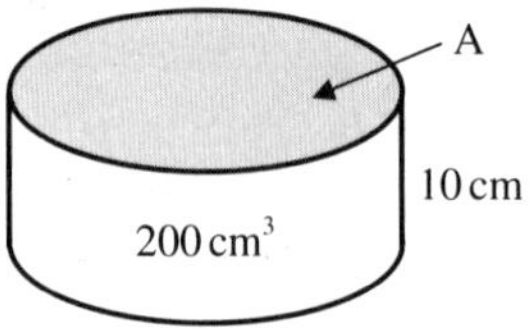

4. The diagram represents a railway siding. Each ● is a junction where a train can turn left or right. A turn to the left has a code 0 and a turn to the right has a code 1.

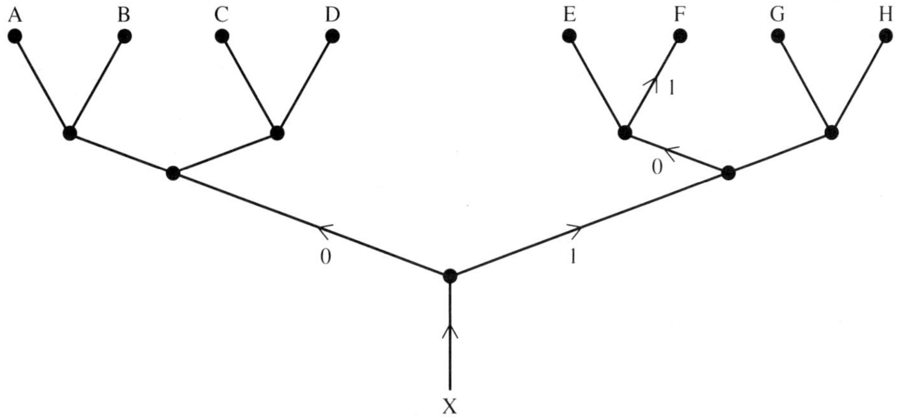

For example, a train starting at X would have code 101 in order to arrive at F.
Copy and complete the table below.

Point	A	B	C	D	E	F	G	H
Code						101		

5. A group of four adults are planning a holiday in France. The ferry costs, for the return journey, are:

Adult	£25
Car	£62

Travel around France is estimated at 2000 km and petrol costs 5 francs per litre. The car travels 10 km on one litre of petrol.
(a) Calculate the total cost of the return journey on the ferry.
(b) Calculate the number of litres of petrol to be used.
(c) Calculate the total cost, in francs, of the petrol.
(d) Calculate the cost of the petrol in pounds, if £1 is equivalent to 10 francs.

6. A journey by boat takes 2 hours 47 minutes. How long will it take at half the speed?

7. Copy the following tables and write down the next *two* lines

(a)
$$2^2 = 1^2 + 3$$
$$3^2 = 2^2 + 5$$
$$4^2 = 3^2 + 7$$
$$5^2 = 4^2 + 9$$

(b)
$$3^2 = 4 + 1^2 + 2^2$$
$$5^2 = 12 + 2^2 + 3^2$$
$$7^2 = 24 + 3^2 + 4^2$$
$$9^2 = 40 + 4^2 + 5^2$$

8. The area of a county is 6000 km^2. What volume of rain falls on the county during a day when there is 2 cm of rain? Give the answer in m^3.

9. Ten posts are equally spaced in a straight line. It is 450 m from the first to the tenth post. What is the distance between successive posts?

10. Find the smallest whole number that is exactly divisible by all the numbers 1 to 10 inclusive.

Exercise 19

1. Seven fig rolls together weigh 560 g. A calorie guide shows that 10 g of fig roll contains 52 calories.
(a) How much does one fig roll weigh?
(b) How many calories are there in 1 g of fig roll?
(c) How many calories are there in one fig roll?

2. Two numbers x and t are such that t is greater than 6 and x is less than 4. Arrange the numbers 5, t and x in order of size, starting with the smallest.

3. To the nearest whole number 5·84, 16·23 and 7·781 are 6, 16 and 8 respectively.
(a) Use these approximate values to obtain an approximate result for $\dfrac{5{\cdot}84 \times 16{\cdot}23}{7{\cdot}781}$
(b) Use the same approach to obtain approximate results for
(i) $\dfrac{15{\cdot}72 \times 9{\cdot}78}{20{\cdot}24}$ (ii) $\dfrac{23{\cdot}85 \times 9{\cdot}892}{4{\cdot}867}$

4. King Richard is given three coins which look identical, but in fact one of them is an overweight fake.
Describe how he could discover the fake using an ordinary balance and only *one* weighing operation.

5. A light aircraft flies 375 km on 150 litres of fuel. How much fuel is needed for a journey of 500 km?

6. A pile of 400 sheets of paper is 2·5 cm thick. What is the thickness in cm of one sheet of paper?

7. A map uses a scale of 1 to 100 000.
(a) Calculate the actual length, in km, of a canal which is 5·4 cm long on the map.
(b) A path is 600 m long. Calculate, in cm, the length this would be on the map.

8. Given the circumference C of a circle it is possible to estimate the area A by the following method:

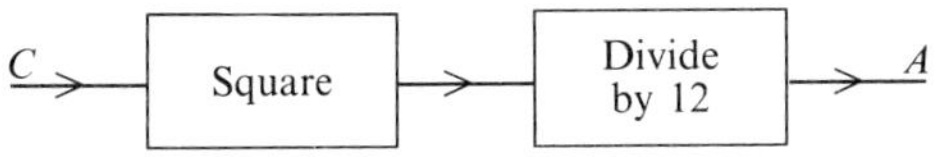

(a) Find A when $C = 6$ cm.
(b) Find A when $C = 18$ cm.
(c) Write down the formula involving A and C.

9. I think of a number. If I subtract 4 and then divide the result by 4 the answer is 3. What number was I thinking of?

10. Try to draw four straight lines which pass through all of the 9 points below, without taking your pen from the paper and without going over any line twice.

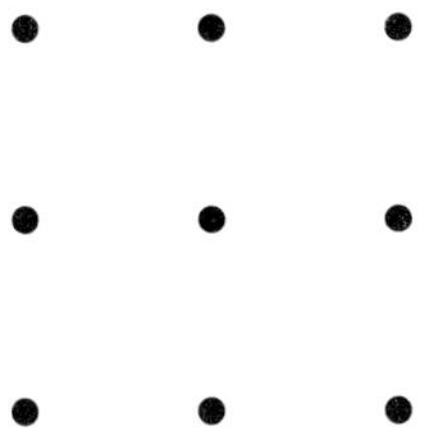

(Hint: The lines may go outside the pattern of dots).

8 Probability

8.1 One event

5/5d

The probability of an event is a measure of how likely it is to occur. This probability can be any number between 0 and 1 (inclusive).

- Events which are very likely to occur have a probability of nearly 1.
  For example, the probability of failing to select the ace of diamonds at random from an ordinary pack of cards is equal to $\frac{51}{52}$.
- Events which are very unlikely to occur have a probability of nearly 0.
  e.g. the probability of your maths teacher becoming prime minister one day is 0·000 001 (approximately).
- Events which are certain to occur have a probability of 1.
- Events which can not occur have a probability of 0.
  For example,
  the probability that tomorrow is Tuesday if today is Monday is 1;
  the probability that one day a man will run a mile in under ten seconds is 0.

There are four different ways of estimating probabilities.

Method A Use symmetry

- The probability of rolling a 3 on a fair dice is $\frac{1}{6}$.
  This is because all the scores 1, 2, 3, 4, 5, 6 are equally likely.
- Similarly the probability of getting a head when tossing a fair coin is $\frac{1}{2}$.

Method B Conduct an experiment or survey to collect data

- Suppose I wanted to estimate the probability of a drawing pin landing point upwards when dropped onto a hard surface. I could not use symmetry for obvious reasons but I could conduct an experiment to see what happened in say 500 trials.

- I might want to know the probability that the next car going past the school gates is driven by a woman.
  I could conduct a survey in which the drivers of cars are recorded over a period of time.

Method C Look at past data

- If I wanted to estimate the probability of my plane crashing as it lands at Heathrow airport I could look at accident records at Heathrow over the last five years or so.

Method D Make a subjective estimate

We have to use this method when the event is not repeatable. It is not really a 'method' in the same sense as are methods A, B, C.

- We might want to estimate the probability of England beating France in a soccer match next week. We could look at past results but these could be of little value for all sorts of reasons. We might consult 'experts' but even they are notoriously inaccurate in their predictions.

Exercise 1

In Questions **1** to **12** state which method A, B, C or D you would use to estimate the probability of event given.

1. The probability that a person chosen at random from a class will be left handed.

2. The probability that there will be snow in the ski resort to which a school party is going in February next year.

3. The probability of drawing an 'ace' from a pack of playing cards.

4. The probability that you hole a six foot put when playing golf.

5. The probability that the world record for running 1500 m will be under 3 min 20 seconds by the year 2020.

6. The probability that a person who smokes will suffer from lung cancer later in life.

7. The probability of rolling a 3 using a dice which is suspected of being biased.

8. The probability that a person selected at random would vote 'Labour' in a general election tomorrow.

9. The probability that a train will arrive within ten minutes of its scheduled arrival time.

10. The probability of winning first prize in a raffle if you have 5 tickets and 1000 are sold.

11. The probability that the current Wimbledon Ladies Champion will successfully defend her title next year.

12. The probability that the next pupil expelled from a certain school will be a girl.

Working out probabilities

The probability of an event occuring can be calculated using symmetry. We argue, for example, that when we toss a coin we have an equal chance of getting a 'head' or a 'tail'. So the probability of spinning a 'head' is a half.
We write 'p (spinning a head) = $\frac{1}{2}$'.

A single card is drawn from a pack of 52 playing cards. Find the probability of the following results:
(a) the card is a Queen,
(b) the card is a Club,
(c) the card is the Jack of Hearts.

There are 52 equally likely outcomes of the 'trial' (drawing a card).
(a) p (Queen) $= \frac{4}{52} = \frac{1}{13}$
(b) p (Club) $= \frac{13}{52} = \frac{1}{4}$
(c) p (Jack of Hearts) $= \frac{1}{52}$.

Exercise 2

1. If one card is picked at random from a pack of 52 playing cards, what is the probability that it is:
(a) a King,
(b) the Ace of Clubs,
(c) a Heart?

2. Nine counters numbered 1, 2, 3, 4, 5, 6, 7, 8, 9 are placed in a bag. One is taken out at random. What is the probability that it is:
(a) a '5', (b) divisible by 3,
(c) less than 5, (d) divisible by 4?

3. A bag contains 5 green balls, 2 red balls and 4 yellow balls. One ball is taken out at random. What is the probability that it is:
(a) green,
(b) red,
(c) yellow?

4. A cash bag contains two 20p coins, four 10p coins, five 5p coins, three 2p coins and three 1p coins. Find the probability that one coin selected at random is:
(a) a 10p coin,
(b) a 2p coin,
(c) a silver coin.

5. A bag contains 8 orange balls, 5 green balls and 4 silver balls. Find the probability that a ball picked out at random is:
(a) silver,
(b) orange,
(c) green.

6. One card is selected at random from those below.

Find the probability of selecting:
(a) a Heart,
(b) an Ace,
(c) the 10 of Clubs,
(d) a Spade,
(e) a Heart or a Diamond.

7. A pack of playing cards is well shuffled and a card is drawn. Find the probability that the card is:
(a) a Jack.
(b) a Queen or a Jack,
(c) the ten of Hearts,
(d) a Club higher than the 9 (count the Ace as high).

8. The numbers of matches in ten boxes is as follows:
48, 46, 45, 49, 44, 46, 47, 48, 45, 46.
One box is selected at random. Find the probability of the box containing:
(a) 49 matches,
(b) 46 matches,
(c) more than 47 matches.

9. One ball is selected at random from those below.

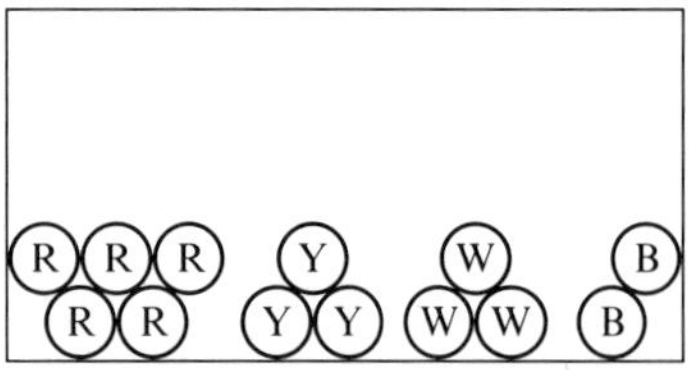

R = red
Y = yellow
W = white
B = black

Find the probability of selecting:
(a) a white ball,
(b) a yellow or a black ball,
(c) a ball which is not red.

10. (a) A bag contains 5 red balls, 6 green balls and 2 black balls. Find the probability of selecting:
(i) a red ball (ii) a green ball.
(b) One black ball is removed from the bag. Find the new probability of selecting:
(i) a red ball (ii) a black ball.

11. A small pack of 20 cards consists of the Ace, King, Queen, Jack and ten of all four suits. Find the probability of selecting from this pack:
(a) an Ace,
(b) the Queen of Spades,
(c) a red card,
(d) any King or Queen.

12. A bag contains 12 white balls, 12 green balls and 12 purple balls. After 3 white balls, 4 green balls and 9 purple balls have been removed, what is the probability that the next ball to be selected will be white?

13. A large firm employs 3750 people. One person is chosen at random. What is the probability that that person's birthday is on a Monday in the year 2000?

14. The numbering on a set of 28 dominoes is as follows:

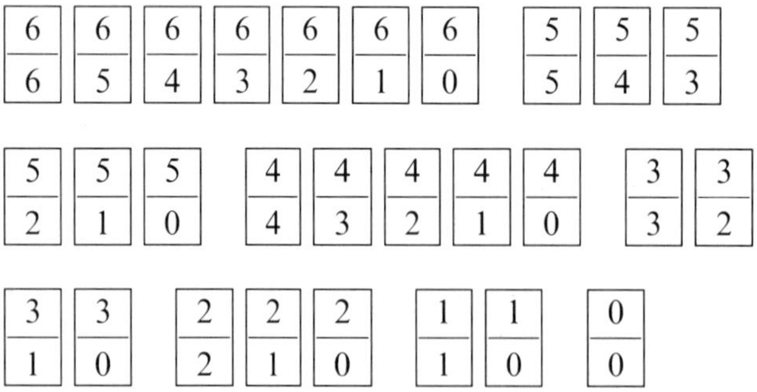

(a) What is the probability of drawing a domino from a full set with
  (i) at least one six on it?
  (ii) at least one four on it?
  (iii) at least one two on it?
(b) What is the probability of drawing a 'double' from a full set?
(c) If I draw a double five which I do not return to the set, what is the probability of drawing another domino with a five on it?

A fair dice is rolled 240 times. How many times would you expect to roll a number greater than 4?

We can roll a 5 or a 6 out of the six equally likely outcomes.
$\therefore\ p(\text{number greater than 4}) = \frac{2}{6} = \frac{1}{3}$.

Expected number of successes = (probability of a success) × (number of trials)

Expected number of scores greater than 4 $= \frac{1}{3} \times 240$
$= 80$

Exercise 3

1. A fair dice is rolled 300 times. How many times would you expect to roll:
(a) an even number
(b) a 'six'?

2. The spinner shown has four equal sectors. How many 3's would you expect in 100 spins?

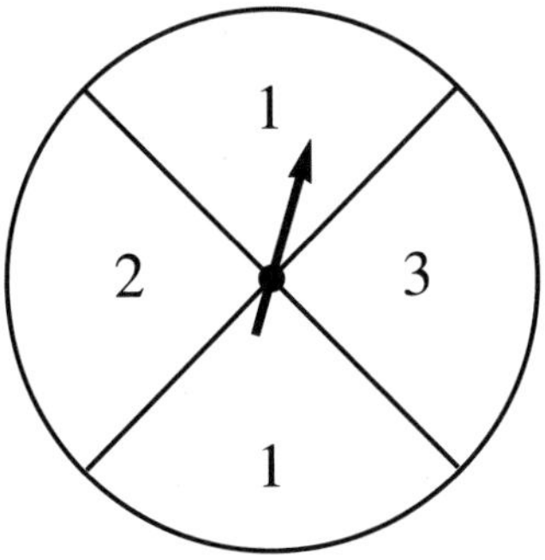

3. About one in eight of the population is left-handed. How many left-handed people would you expect to find in a firm employing 400 people?

4. A bag contains a large number of marbles of which one in five is red. If I randomly select one marble on 200 occasions how many times would I expect to select a red marble?

5. The spinner shown is used for a simple game. A player pays 10p and then spins the pointer, winning the amount indicated.

(a) What is the probability of winning nothing?

(b) If the game is played by 200 people how many times would you expect the 50p to be won?

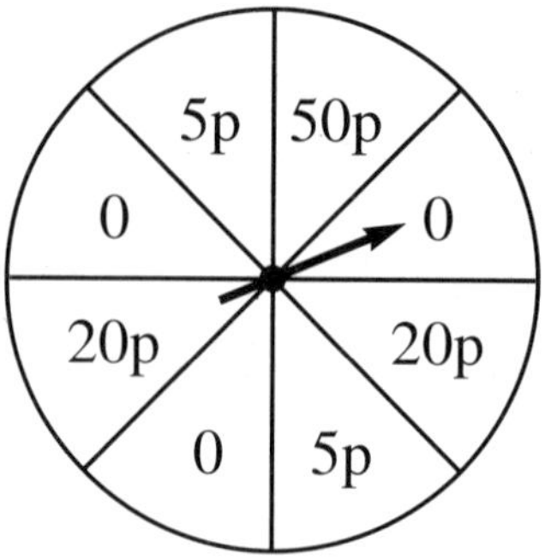

6. The numbered cards are shuffled and put into a pile.

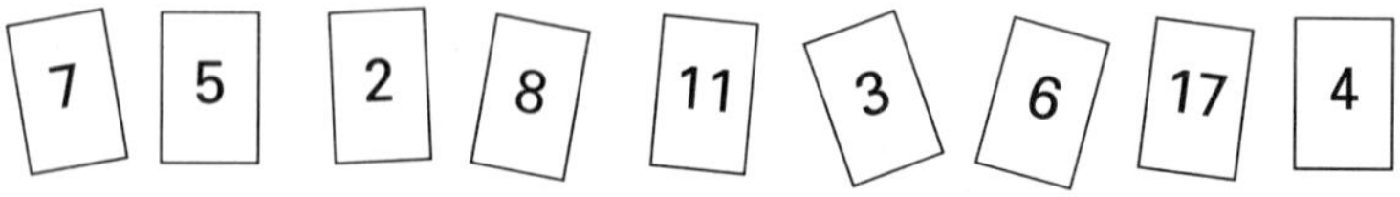

One card is selected at random and not replaced. A second card is then selected.

(a) If the first card was the '11' find the probability of selecting an even number with the second draw.

(b) If the first card was an odd number, find the probability of selecting another odd number.

7. A pack of playing cards is split so that all the picture cards (Kings, Queens, Jacks) are in Pile A and all the other cards are in Pile B.

Find the probability of selecting:

(a) the Queen of clubs from pile A.

(b) the seven of spades from pile B.

(c) any heart from pile B.

8.2 Two events

5/6c, 5/6d

Listing possible outcomes

When a 10p coin and a 50p coin are tossed together we have two events occurring:

- tossing the 10p coin
- tossing the 50p coin.

The result of tossing the 10p coin does not affect the result of the 50p coin.
We say the two events are *independent*.
We can list all the possible outcomes as shown:

(10p first)	head,	head
	head,	tail
	tail,	head
	tail,	tail.

A red dice and a black dice are thrown together. Show all the possible outcomes.

We could list them in pairs with the red dice first:

(1,1), (1,2), (1,2), ... (1,6)
(2,1), (2,2), ...
and so on.

In this example it is easier to see all the possible outcomes when they are shown on a grid.

The X shows 6 on the red dice and 2 on the black.

The ○ shows 3 on the red dice and 5 on the black.

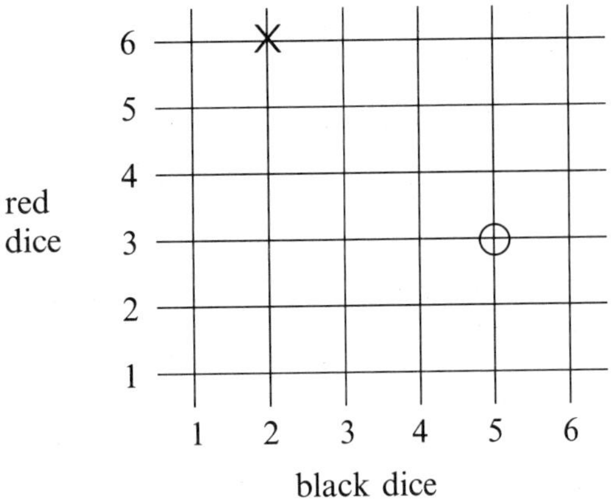

Exercise 4

1. Three coins (10p, 20p, 50p) are tossed together. List all the possible ways in which they could land.

2. List all the possible outcomes when four coins are tossed together. How many are there altogether?
3. A black dice and a white dice are thrown together
   (a) Draw a grid to show all the possible outcomes.
   (b) How many ways can you get a total of nine on the two dice?
4. A red spinner and a white spinner are spun together.

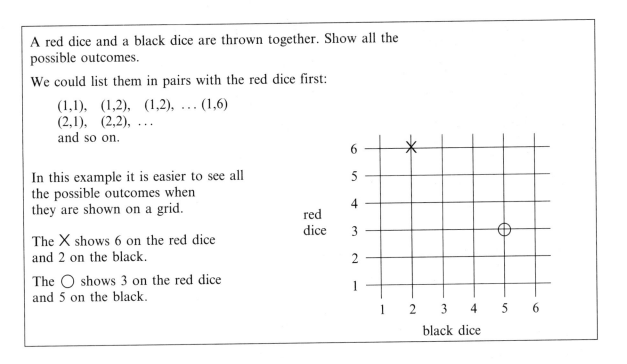

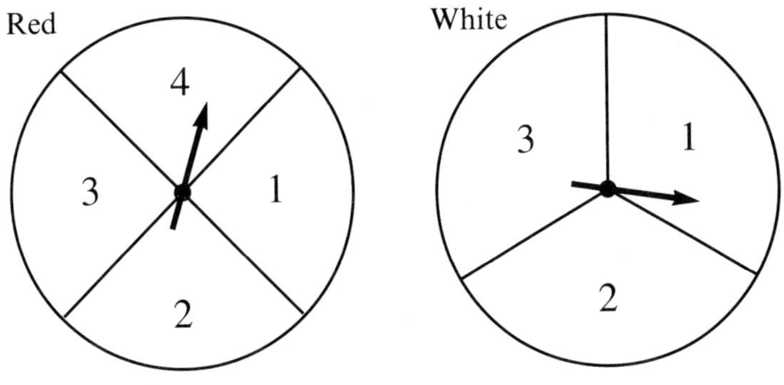

   (a) List all the possible outcomes.
   (b) In how many ways can you get a total of 4?

5. Four friends, Wayne, Xavier, Yves and Zara, each write their name on a card and the four cards are placed in a hat. Two cards are chosen to decide who does the maths homework that night.
List all the possible combinations.

6. The spinner is spun and the dice is thrown at the same time.

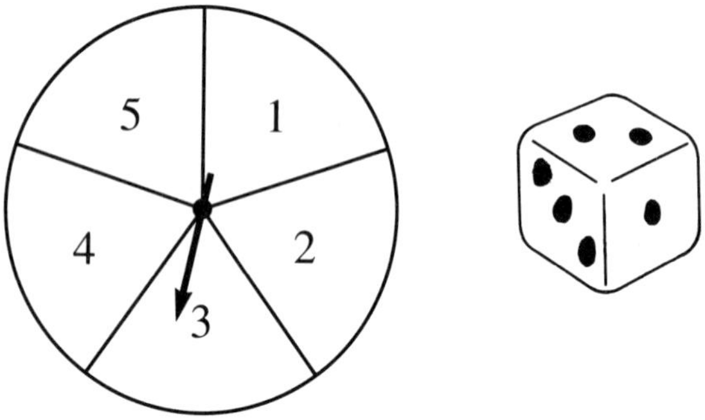

(a) Draw a grid to show all the possible outcomes.
(b) A 'win' occurs when the number on the spinner is greater than or equal to the number on the dice. In how many ways can a 'win' occur?

7. The menu in a restaurant has two choices of starter, three choices of main course and two choices of dessert.
List all the different combinations I could choose from this menu.

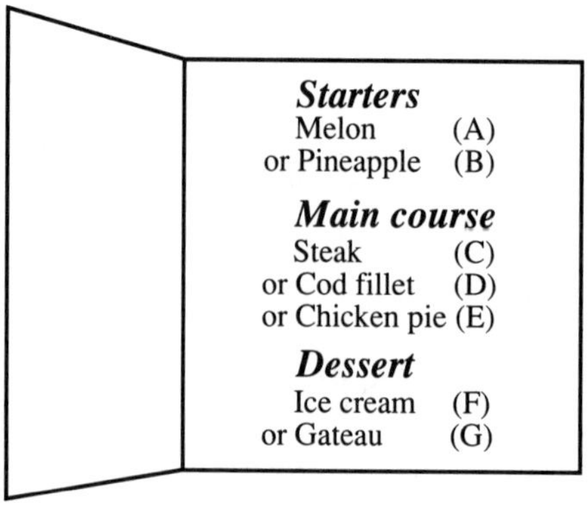

8. A motorway service station offers a meal consisting of four courses: soup, salad, meat, dessert.

There are:	two kinds of soup	A and B
	three kinds of salad	C, D and E
	four kinds of meat	F, G, H and I
	two kinds of dessert	J and K.

How many different choices of meal are there altogether?

9. By a strange coincidence the Branson family, the Green family and the Webb family all have the same first names for the five members of their families: James, Don, Samantha, Laura and Kate. One year Father Christmas decides to give each person a monogrammed handkerchief with two initials.

(a) How many different handkerchiefs does he need for these three families?

(b) How many different monograms are there if *any* first name and *any* surname is possible [e.g. 'Zak Quilfeldt']?

10. Keith, Len, Mike and Neil enter a cycling race.

(a) List all the possible orders in which they could finish. State the number of different finishing orders.

(b) In how many of the above does Mike finish in front of Len?

11. In Gibson Academy there are six forms (A, B, C, D, E, F) in Year 10 and the Mathematics Department has been asked to work out a schedule so that, over 5 weeks, each team can play each of the others in a soccer competition.
The games are all played at lunch time on Wednesdays and three games have to be played at the same time.
For example in Week 1 we could have

Form A *v* Form B
Form C *v* Form D
Form E *v* Form F

Work out a schedule for the remaining four weeks so that each team plays each of the others. Check carefully that each team plays every other team just once.

12. In Mongolia there are not many cars and the licence plates have one letter (A, B, C, . . . , Z) and 3 digits (1, 2, . . . , 9)

For example **M 357**

Apparently the Mongolians consider it unlucky to have a 'zero' in the number and they must have all three digits. So the number must be from 111 to 999.
How many different licence plates can be made?

13. In neighbouring Siberia there are more cars and the licence plates have 2 letters and 4 digits.

For example **ME 7238**

How many different licence plates can be made?

8.3 Exclusive events

5/6d, 5/7c

Events are *mutually exclusive* if they cannot occur at the same time.

Examples
- Selecting an ace } from a
  Selecting a ten } pack of cards

- Tossing a 'head'
  Tossing a 'tail'

- Getting a total of 5 on two dice
  Getting a total of 7 on two dice

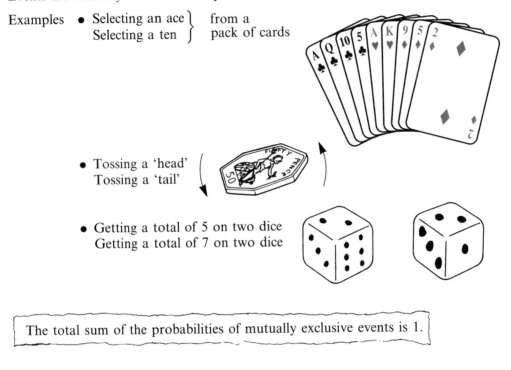

> The total sum of the probabilities of mutually exclusive events is 1.

> The probability of something happening is 1 minus the probability of it not happening.

Every day Anna has the choice of going to work by bus, by train or by taxi.
The probability of choosing to go by bus is 0·5 and the probability of choosing to go by train is 0·3.
Find:
(a) the probability of choosing not to go by train
(b) the probability of choosing to go by taxi

The three events 'going by bus', 'going by train' and 'going by taxi' are mutually exclusive.

(a) $p(\text{not going by train}) = 1 - p(\text{going by train})$
$= 1 - 0{\cdot}3$
$= 0{\cdot}7$

(b) The sum of the probabilities is 1.
$\therefore\ p(\text{going by taxi}) = 1 - (0{\cdot}5 + 0{\cdot}3)$
$= 0{\cdot}2$

Exercise 5

1. A bag contains a large number of balls including some red balls. The probability of selecting a red ball is $\frac{1}{5}$. What is the probability of selecting a ball which is not red?

2. A card is selected from a pack of 52. Find the probability of selecting
   (a) a 'King'
   (b) a card which is not a 'King'
   (c) any picture card (King, Queen or Jack)
   (d) a card which is not a picture card.

3. On a roulette wheel the probability of getting '21' is $\frac{1}{36}$. What is the probability of not getting '21'?

4. A motorist does a survey at some traffic lights on his way to work every day. He finds that the probability that the lights are 'red' when he arrives is $0{\cdot}24$. What is the probability that the lights are not 'red'?

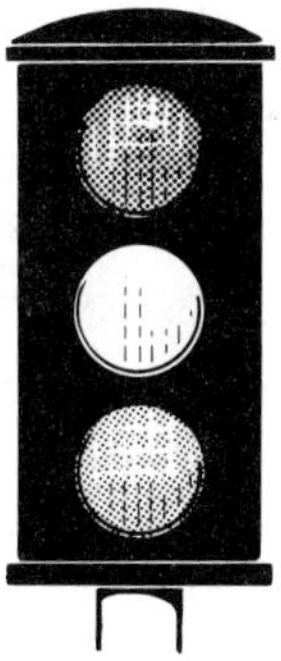

5. Government birth statistics show that the probability of a woman giving birth to a boy is $0{\cdot}506$. What is the probability of having a girl?

6. The spinner has 8 equal sectors. Find the probability of
   (a) spinning a 5
   (b) not spinning a 5
   (c) spinning a 2
   (d) not spinning a 2
   (e) spinning a 7
   (f) not spinning a 7.

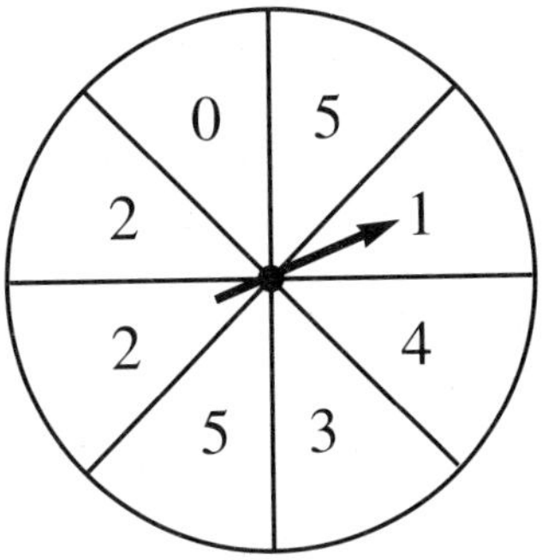

7. The King of clubs is removed from a normal pack of cards. One card is selected from the remaining cards. Find the probability of
   (a) selecting a King
   (b) not selecting a King
   (c) selecting a club

8. A bag contains a large number of balls coloured red, white, black or green. The probabilities of selecting each colour are as follows:

colour	red	white	black	green
probability	0·3	0·1		0·3

Find the probability of selecting a ball
(a) which is black
(b) which is not white.

9. In a survey the number of people in cars is recorded. When a car passes the school gates the probability of having 1, 2, 3, ... occupants is as follows.

number of people	1	2	3	4	more than 4
probability	0·42	0·23		0·09	0·02

(a) Find the probability that the next car past the school gates contains (i) three people (ii) less than 4 people.
(b) One day 2500 cars passed the gates. How many of the cars would you expect to have 2 people inside?

10. Percy is a gardener whose eyesight is not what is was. One day he accidently mixes lettuce and carrot seeds so that $\frac{5}{12}$ of the mixture is lettuce seeds. He plants 600 seeds from the mixture.
(a) What is the probability that the first seed he plants is not a lettuce?
(b) If all the seeds germinate, how many carrots would he expect to grow?

The 'OR' rule:

For exclusive events A and B

$$p(\text{A or B}) = p(\text{A}) + p(\text{B})$$

One ball is selected at random from a bag containing 5 red balls, 2 yellow balls and 4 white balls. Find the probability of selecting a red ball or a white ball.

The two events are exclusive.

$$\begin{aligned} p(\text{red ball } \textit{or} \text{ white ball}) &= p(\text{red}) + p(\text{white}) \\ &= \tfrac{5}{11} + \tfrac{4}{11} \\ &= \tfrac{9}{11}. \end{aligned}$$

Many questions involving exclusive events can be done without using the addition rule.

A card is selected at random from a pack of 52 playing cards. What is the probability of selecting any King or Queen?

(a) This question can be done by counting the number of ways in which we can get a King or a Queen. That is 8 ways.

$$p\text{(selecting a King or a Queen)} = \tfrac{8}{52} = \tfrac{2}{13}.$$

(b) Since 'selecting a King' and 'selecting a Queen' are exclusive events we could use the addition law.

$$p\text{(selecting a King)} = \tfrac{4}{52}$$

$$p\text{(selecting a Queen)} = \tfrac{4}{52}$$

$$\therefore\ p\text{(selecting a King or a Queen)} = \tfrac{4}{52} + \tfrac{4}{52} = \tfrac{8}{52} \text{ as before.}$$

You can decide for yourself which method is easier in any given question.

Important!
If the events are not exclusive we cannot use the addition rule.

Here is a spinner with numbers and colours.

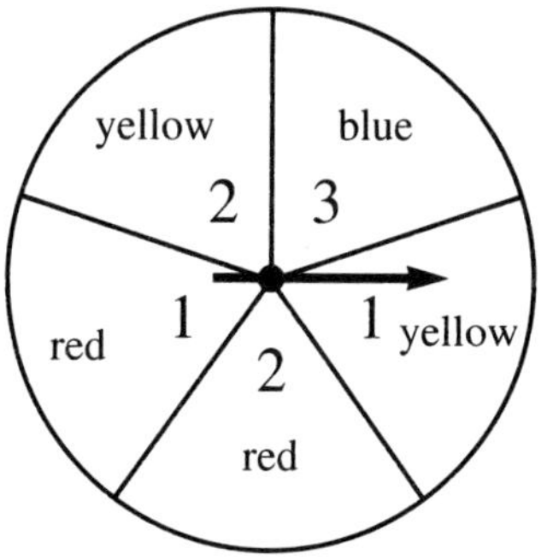

The events 'spinning a red' and 'spinning a 1' are *not* exclusive because we can get a red and a 1 at the same time.

Exercise 6

1. A bag contains 10 red balls, 5 blue balls and 7 green balls. Find the probability of selecting at random:
(a) a red ball, (b) a green ball,
(c) a blue *or* a red ball, (d) a red *or* a green ball.

2. A roulette wheel has the numbers 1 to 36. What is the probability of spinning either a 10 or a 20?

3. A fair dice is rolled. What is the probability of rolling either a 1 or a 6?

4. From a pack of cards I have already selected the King, Queen, Jack and ten of diamonds.
What is the probability that on my next draw I will select either the ace or the nine of diamonds?

5. The grid shows the 36 equally likely outcomes when two dice are rolled.
(a) How many outcomes give a total of 9?
(b) Find the probability of getting a total of
(i) 9
(ii) 7
(iii) 4

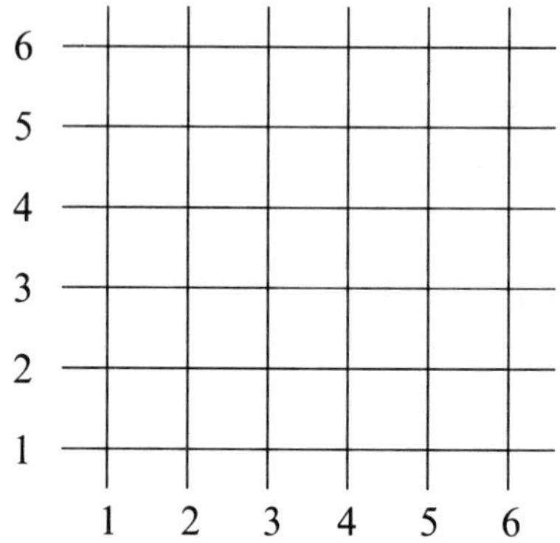

6. Two dice are thrown together. Find the probability of getting
(a) a total of 10 or 11
(b) a total less than 6
(c) the same number on both dice or a total of 5.

7. Three coins are tossed at the same time. List all the possible outcomes. Find the probability of getting
(a) three heads
(b) three heads or three tails
(c) two heads and one tail (in any order).

8. (a) How many possible outcomes are there when four coins are tossed together?
(b) What is the probability of tossing either four heads or four tails?

9. Two dice are thrown together and the 'score' is the *difference* between the two numbers showing. So if I throw a '4' and a '6' the score is 2.
Copy and complete the table showing the scores for two dice.
Find the probability of obtaining a score of
(a) 2 (b) 0
(c) 5 (d) 6

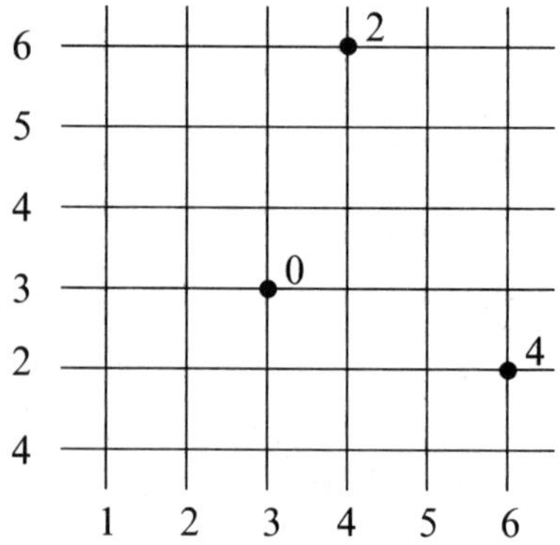

10. Two special dice are made.

Dice A has two 1's
two 3's
two 5's

Dice B has two 2's
two 4's
two 6's.

(a) Draw a grid to show all the possible outcomes when the two dice are thrown together.
(b) Find the probability of getting a total of
(i) 11 (ii) 7 (iii) 8
(iv) either 3 or 11 (v) either 3 or 9 or 11.

11. The spinner shown has four equal sectors.
(a) Which of the following pairs of events are exclusive?
(i) 'spinning 1', 'spinning green'.
(ii) 'spinning 3', 'spinning 2'.
(iii) 'spinning blue', 'spinning 1'.
(b) What is the probability of spinning either a 1 or a green?

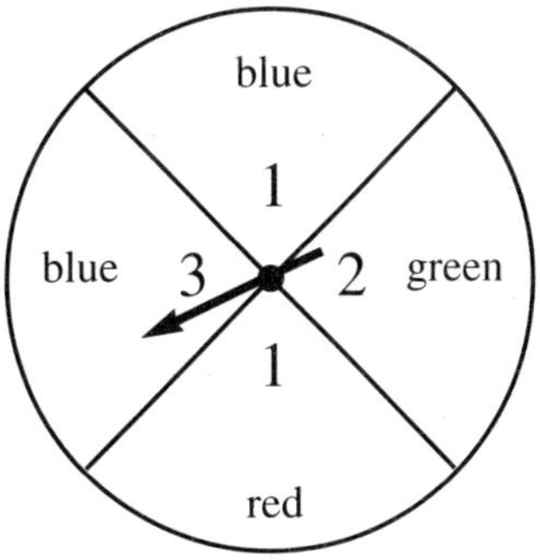

12. Here is a spinner with unequal sectors. When the pointer is spun, the probability of getting each colour and number is given in the tables.

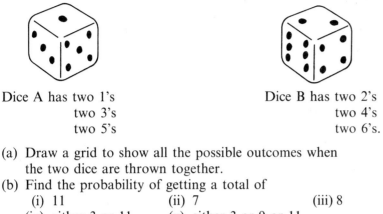

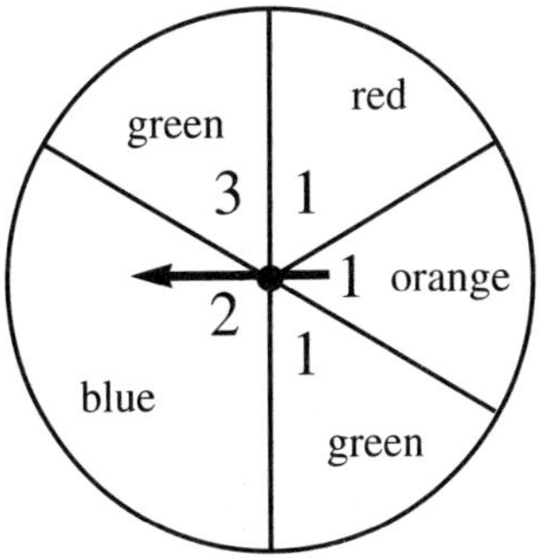

colour	probability
red	0·1
blue	0·3
orange	0·2
green	0·4

number	probability
1	0·5
2	0·3
3	0·2

(a) What is the probability of spinning either 1 or 2?
(b) What is the probability of spinning either blue or green?
(c) Why is the probability of spinning either 1 or green *not* $0{\cdot}5 + 0{\cdot}4$?

13. Shirin and Dipika are playing a game in which three coins are tossed. Shirin wins if there are no heads or one head. Dipika wins if there are either two or three heads. Is the game fair to both players?

14. Pupils X, Y and Z play a game in which four coins are tossed.

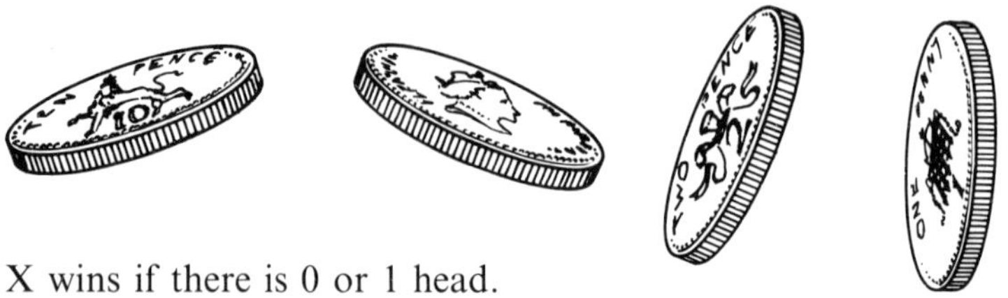

X wins if there is 0 or 1 head.
Y wins if there are 2 heads.
Z wins if there are 3 or 4 heads.

Is the game fair to all three players?

15. Four cards numbered 2, 4, 5 and 7 are mixed up and placed face down.

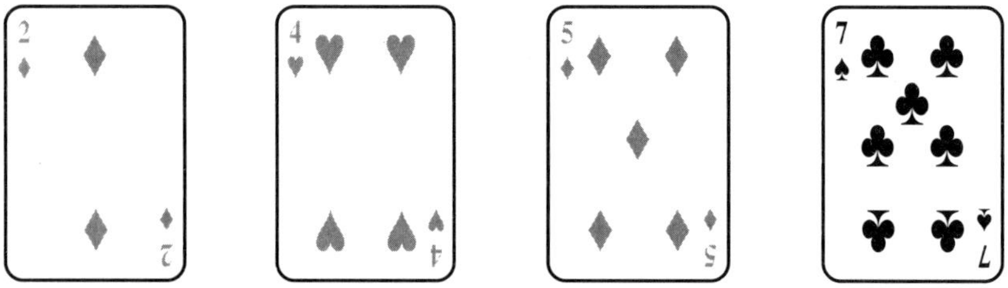

In a game you pay 10p to select two cards. You win 25p if the total of the two cards is nine.
How much would you expect to win or lose if you played the game 12 times?

8.4 Relative frequency

5/7b

To work out the probability of a drawing pin landing point up we can conduct an experiment in which a drawing pin is dropped many times. If the pin lands 'point up' on x occasions out of a total number of N trials, the *relative frequency* of landing 'point up' is $\frac{x}{N}$.

When an experiment is repeated many times we can use the relative frequency as an estimate of the probability of the event occuring.

Here are the results of an experiment in which a dice, suspected of being biased, was rolled 300 times. After each set of 25 rolls the number of sixes obtained was noted and the results were as follows:

5 4 6 6 6 5 3 7 6 5 6 5

After 25 rolls the relative frequency of sixes $= \frac{5}{25} = 0{\cdot}2$

After 50 rolls the relative frequency of sixes $= \frac{5+4}{50} = 0{\cdot}18$

After 75 rolls the relative frequency of sixes $= \frac{5+4+6}{75} = 0{\cdot}173$

and so on.

The results are plotted on the graph below.

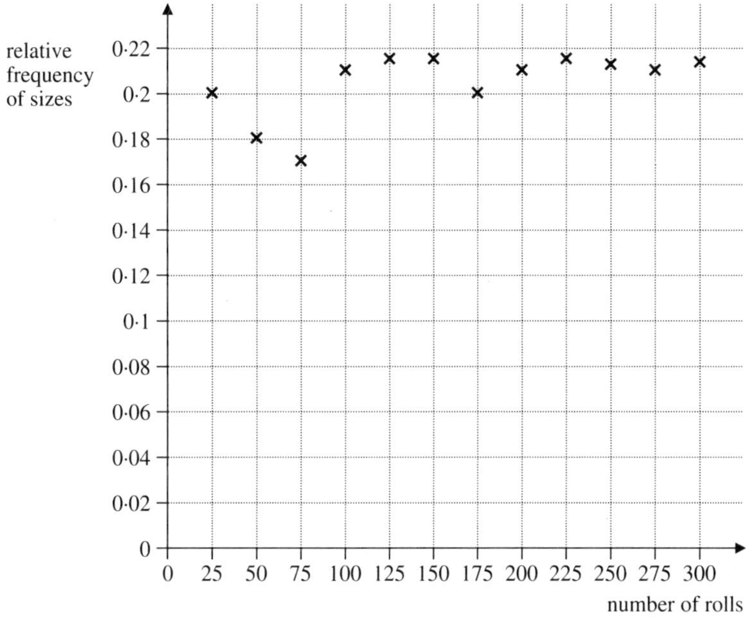

As we include more and more results, the average number of sixes per roll settles down at slightly over 0·21.

For this dice we say the *relative frequency* of sixes was just over 0·21.

If the dice was fair we would expect to get a 6 on $\frac{1}{6}$ of the throws. So the relative frequency would be $0{\cdot}1\dot{6}$. The dice in the experiment does appear to be biased so that sixes occur more frequently than we would expect for a fair dice.

Exercise 7

1. Conduct an experiment where you cannot predict the result.
You could roll a dice with a piece of 'blu-tack' stuck to it.
Or make a spinner where the axis is not quite in the centre.
Or drop a drawing pin.
Conduct the experiment many times and work out the relative frequency of a 'success' after every 10 or 20 trials.
Plot a relative frequency graph like the one above to see if the results 'settle down' to a consistent value.

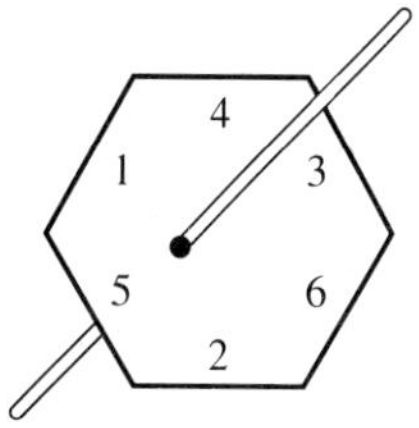

2. The spinner has an equal chance of giving any digit from 0 to 9.
Four friends did an experiment when they spun the pointer a different number of times and recorded the number of zeroes they got.
Here are their results.

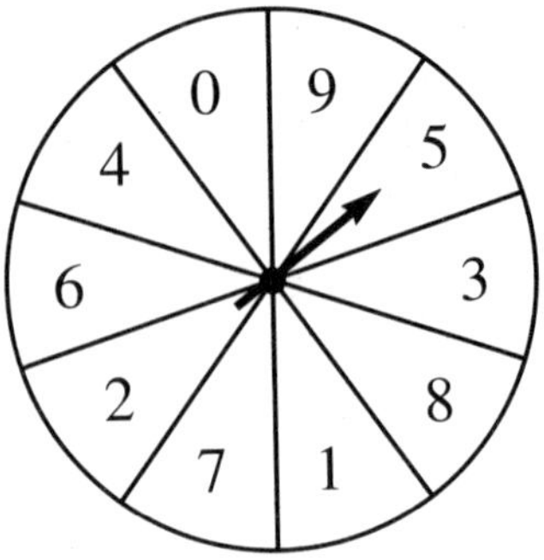

	Number of spins	Number of zeroes	Relative frequency
Steve	10	2	0·2
Nick	150	14	0·093
Mike	200	41	0·205
Jason	1000	104	0·104

One of the four recorded his results incorrectly. Say who you think this was and explain why.

3. The RAN # button on a calculator generates random numbers between ·000 and ·999. It can be used to simulate tossing three coins.
We could say any *odd* digit is a *tail* and any *even* digit is a *head.*
So the number ·568 represents THH
and ·605 represents HHT

Use the RAN # button to simulate the tossing of three coins.
'Toss' the three coins 32 times and work out the relative frequencies of (a) three heads and (b) two heads and a tail.
Compare your results with the values that you would expect to get theoretically.

4. When a coin is tossed, a head means 'turn left' and a tail means 'turn right'
I tossed a coin four times and got head, head, tail, head so that I ended at point B.

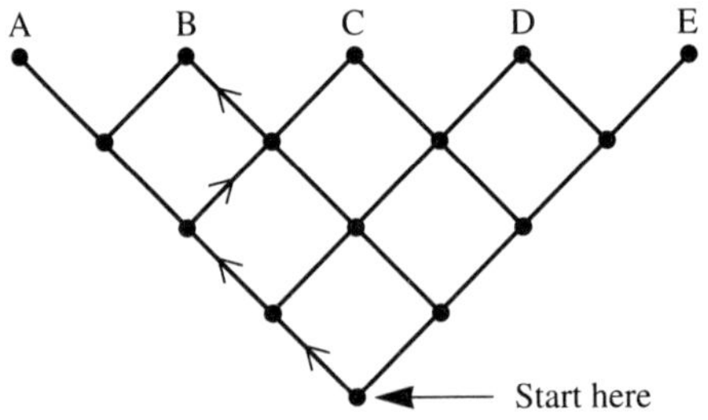

A 'trial' consists of tossing a coin four times and recording the destination. Perform 64 trials and record the results on a relative frequency graph.
Work out the theoretical probability of arriving at point A and compare it with your experimental result.
Repeat for the points B, C, D, E.

[You could use the RAN # button for three of the coins to speed up the experiment].

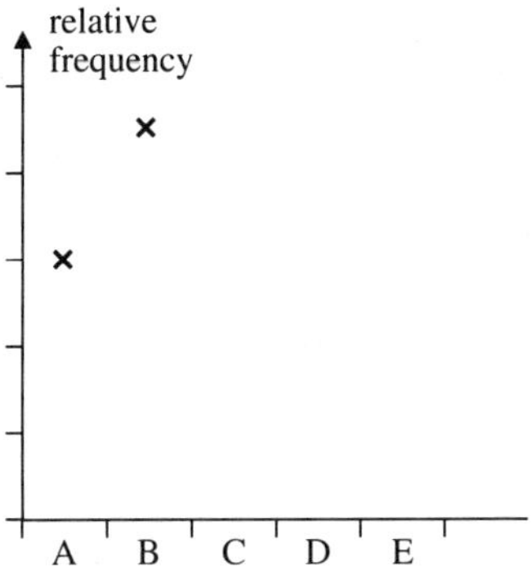

5. A calculator can be used to simulate throwing imaginary dice with 10 faces numbered 0, 1, 2, 3, 4, 5, 6, 7, 8, 9.
The RAN # button gives a random 3 digit number between 0·000 and 0·999. We can use the first 2 digits after the point to represent the numbers on two ten-sided dice.
So 0·763 means 7 on one dice and 6 on the second.
and 0·031 means 0 on one dice and 3 on the second.
We add the numbers on the two 'dice' to give the total.
So for 0·763 the total is 13 and for 0·031 the total is 3.
Press the RAN # button lots of times and record the totals in a tally chart.

Total	0	1	2	...	18
Tally		||	||||	...	

This grid can be used to predict the result. There are 100 equally likely outcomes like 3,7 or 4,1. The ten results shown each give a total of 9 which is the most likely score. So in 100 throws you could expect to get a total of 9 on ten occasions.
Plot your results on a frequency graph.
Compare your results with the values you would expect.

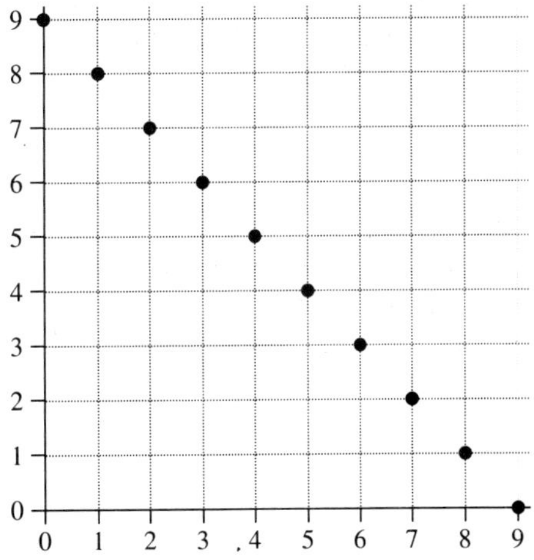

8.5 Independent events

5/8c

Two events are *independent* if the occurrence of one event is unaffected by the occurrence of the other.
e.g. Obtaining a 'head' on one coin, and a tail on another coin when the coins are tossed at the same time.

> The 'AND' rule:
>
> $p(\text{A } \textit{and} \text{ B}) = p(\text{A}) \,.\, p(\text{B})$
>
> where $p(\text{A})$ = probability of A occuring etc.

This is the multiplication law. It only works for independent events.

When two coins are tossed we have seen previously by listing the outcomes [HH, HT, TH, TT] that the probability of tossing two heads is $\frac{1}{4}$.
By the multiplication rule for independent events:

$$p(\text{two heads}) = p(\text{head on first coin}) \times p(\text{head on second coin})$$
$$\therefore\ p(\text{two heads}) = \tfrac{1}{2} \times \tfrac{1}{2}$$
$$= \tfrac{1}{4} \text{ as before.}$$

A fair coin is tossed and a fair dice is rolled. Find the probability of obtaining a 'head' and a 'six'.

The two events are independent.

$$p(\text{head } \textit{and} \text{ six}) = p(\text{head}) \times p(\text{six})$$
$$= \tfrac{1}{2} \times \tfrac{1}{6}$$
$$= \tfrac{1}{12}.$$

When the two spinners are spun, what is the probability of getting a B on the first and a 3 on the second?

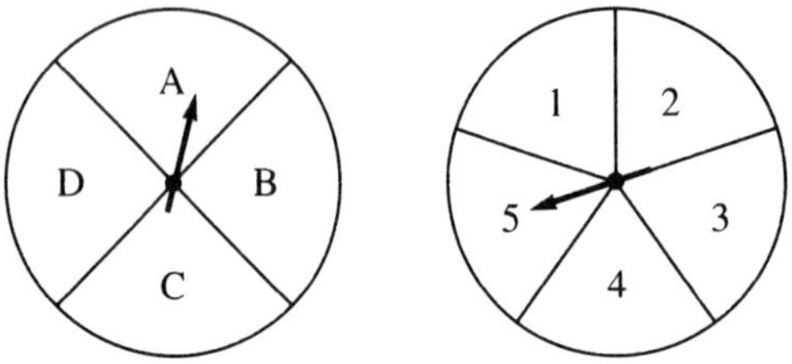

The events 'B on the first spinner' and '3 on the second spinner' are independent.

$$\therefore\ p(\text{spinning B and 3}) = p(\text{B}) \times p(3)$$
$$= \tfrac{1}{4} \times \tfrac{1}{5}$$
$$= \tfrac{1}{20}.$$

Exercise 8

1. A card is drawn from a pack of playing cards and a dice is thrown. Events A and B are as follows:
   A: 'a Jack is drawn from the pack'
   B: 'a three is thrown on the dice'.
   (a) Write down the values of $p(\text{A})$, $p(\text{B})$.
   (b) Write down the value of $p(\text{A and B})$.

2. A coin is tossed and a dice is thrown. Write down the probability of obtaining
   (a) a 'head' on the coin,
   (b) an odd number on the dice,
   (c) a 'head' on the coin and an odd number on the dice.

3. Box A contains 3 red balls and 3 white balls. Box B contains 1 red and 4 white balls.

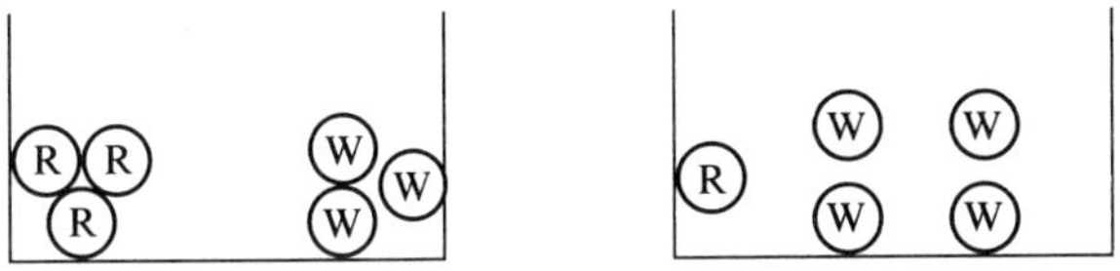

A B

   One ball is randomly selected from box A and from box B. What is the probability that both balls selected are red?

4. In an experiment, a card is drawn from a pack of playing cards and a dice is thrown.
   Find the possibility of obtaining:
   (a) A card which is an ace and a six on the dice,
   (b) the king of clubs and an even number on the dice,
   (c) a heart and a 'one' on the dice.

5. A card is taken at random from a pack of playing cards and replaced. After shuffling, a second card is selected.
   Find the probability of obtaining:
   (a) two cards which are clubs,
   (b) two Kings,
   (c) two picture cards.

6. A ball is selected at random from a bag containing 3 red balls, 4 black balls and 5 green balls. The first ball is replaced and a second is selected. Find the probability of obtaining:
   (a) two red balls,
   (b) two green balls.

7. The letters of the word 'INDEPENDENT' are written on individual cards and the cards are put into a box. A card is selected and then replaced and then a second card is selected.
   Find the probability of obtaining:
   (a) the letter 'P' twice,
   (b) the letter 'E' twice.

8. A fruit machine has three reels and pays out a Jackpot of £100 when three apples are obtained.

Each reel has 15 pictures. The first reel has 3 apples, the second has 4 apples and the third has 2 apples.
Find the probability of winning the Jackpot.

9. Three coins are tossed and two dice are thrown at the same time. Find the probability of obtaining:
(a) three heads and a total of 12 on the dice,
(b) three tails and a total of 9 on the dice.

10. A coin is biased so that it shows 'Heads' with a probability of $\frac{2}{3}$. The same coin is tossed three times. Find the probability of obtaining:
(a) two tails on the first two tosses,
(b) a head, a tail and a head (in that order).

11. A fair dice and a biased dice are thrown together. The probabilities of throwing the numbers 1 to 6 are shown for the biased dice.

Fair

Biased

$p(6) = \frac{1}{4}$; $p(1) = \frac{1}{12}$

$p(2) = p(3) = p(4) = p(5) = \frac{1}{6}$

Find the probability of obtaining a total of 12 on the two dice.

12. Philip and his sister toss a coin to decide who does the washing up. If it's heads Philip does it. If it's tails his sister does it. What is the probability that Philip does the washing up every day for a week (7 days)?

13. Here is the answer sheet for five questions in a multiple choice test.
What is the probability of getting all five correct by guessing?

Answer sheet

1.	(A)	(B)	(C)	
2.	(A)	(B)		
3.	(A)	(B)	(C)	
4.	(A)	(B)	(C)	(D)
5.	(A)	(B)		

Tree diagrams

A bag contains 5 red balls and 3 green balls.
A ball is drawn at random and then replaced.
Another ball is drawn.

What is the probability that both balls are green?

The branch marked * involves the selection of a green ball twice.
The probability of this event is obtained by simply multiplying the fractions on the two branches.

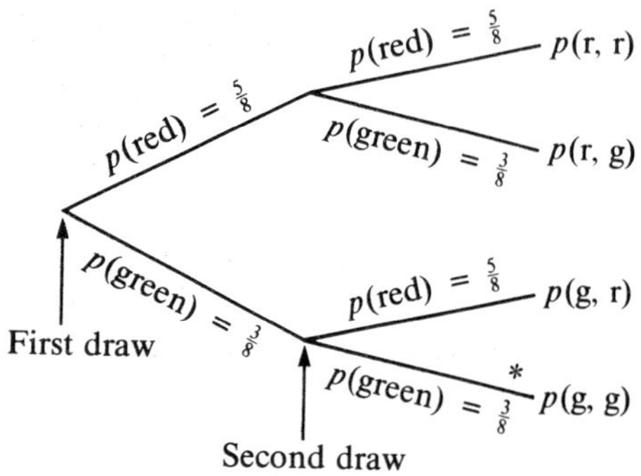

$\therefore \quad p(\text{two green balls}) = \frac{3}{8} \times \frac{3}{8} = \frac{9}{64}$

A bag contains 5 red balls and 3 green balls.
A ball is selected at random and *not* replaced.
A second ball is then selected.
Find the probability of selecting
(a) two green balls
(b) one red ball and one green ball.

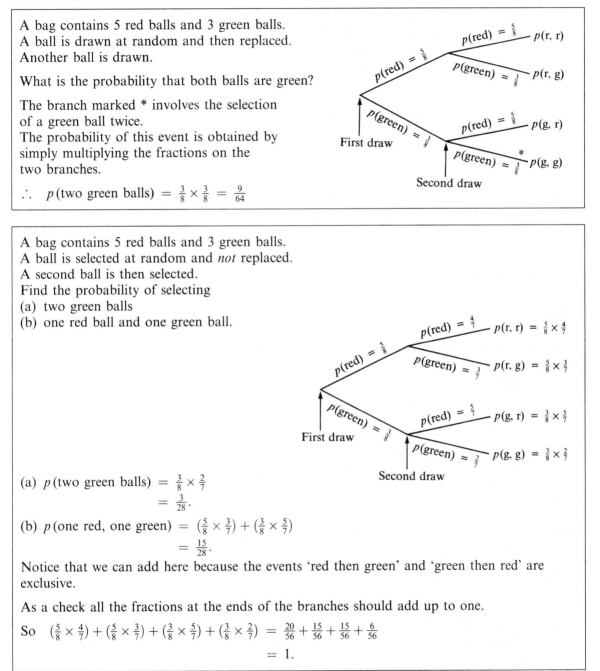

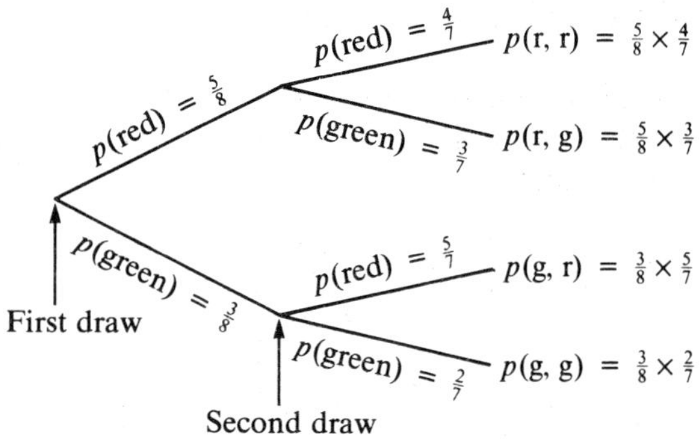

(a) $p(\text{two green balls}) = \frac{3}{8} \times \frac{2}{7}$
$= \frac{3}{28}.$

(b) $p(\text{one red, one green}) = (\frac{5}{8} \times \frac{3}{7}) + (\frac{3}{8} \times \frac{5}{7})$
$= \frac{15}{28}.$

Notice that we can add here because the events 'red then green' and 'green then red' are exclusive.

As a check all the fractions at the ends of the branches should add up to one.

So $(\frac{5}{8} \times \frac{4}{7}) + (\frac{5}{8} \times \frac{3}{7}) + (\frac{3}{8} \times \frac{5}{7}) + (\frac{3}{8} \times \frac{2}{7}) = \frac{20}{56} + \frac{15}{56} + \frac{15}{56} + \frac{6}{56}$
$= 1.$

Exercise 9

1. A bag contains 10 discs; 7 are black and 3 white. A disc is selected, and then replaced. A second disc is selected. Copy and complete the tree diagram showing all the probabilities and outcomes.

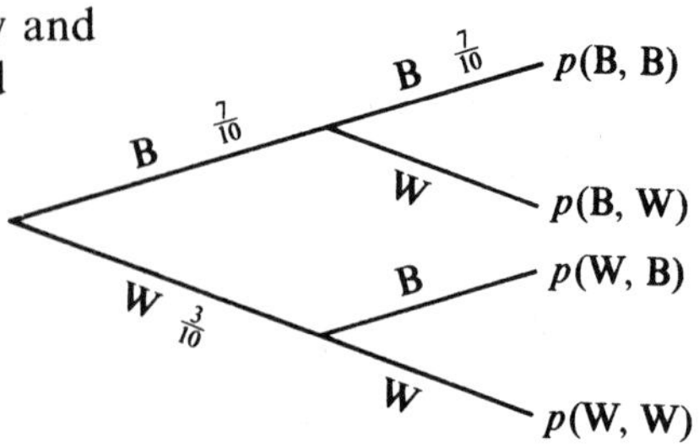

Find the probability of the following:
(a) both discs are black,
(b) both discs are white.

2. A bag contains 5 red balls and 3 green balls.
A ball is drawn and then replaced before a ball is drawn again. Draw a tree diagram to show all the possible outcomes. Find the probability that
(a) two green balls are drawn,
(b) the first ball is red and the second is green.

3. A bag contains 7 green discs and 3 blue discs. A disc is drawn and *not* replaced.
A second disc is drawn. Copy and complete the tree diagram.

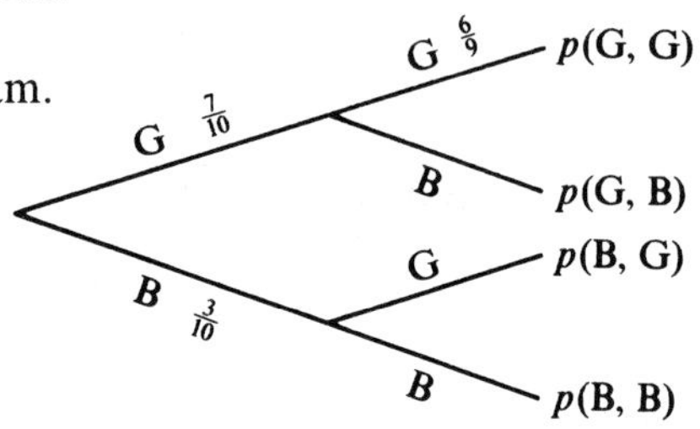

Find the probability that
(a) both discs are green
(b) both discs are blue.

4. A bag contains 5 red balls, 3 blue balls and 2 yellow balls. A ball is drawn and not replaced. A second ball is drawn.

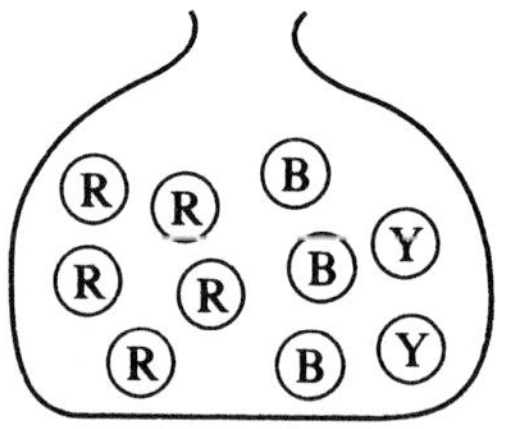

Find the probability of drawing:
(a) two red balls,
(b) one blue ball and one yellow ball,
(c) two yellow balls.

5. A bag contains 4 red balls, 2 green balls and 3 blue balls. A ball is drawn and not replaced. A second ball is drawn.

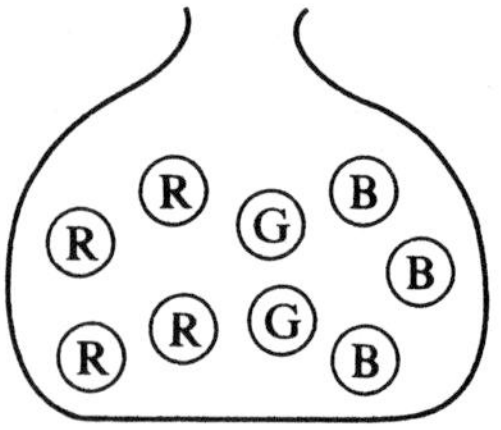

Find the probability of drawing:
(a) two blue balls,
(b) two red balls,
(c) one red ball and one blue ball (in any order),
(d) one green ball and one red ball (in any order).

6. A six-sided dice is thrown three times. Complete the tree diagram, showing at each branch the two events: 'three' and 'not three' (written $\bar{3}$).

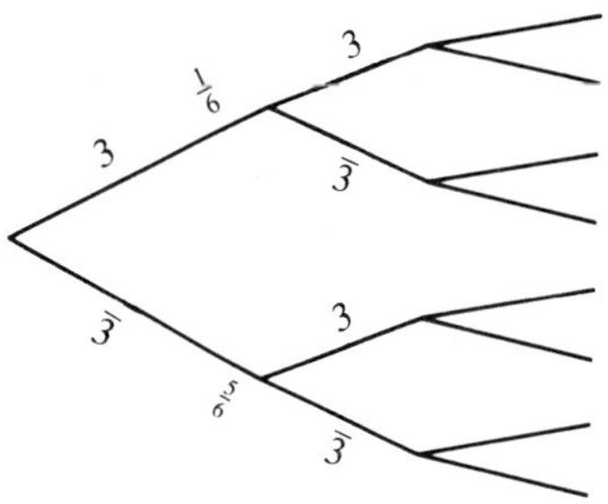

What is the probability of throwing a total of
(a) three threes,
(b) no threes,
(c) one three,
(d) at least one three (use part (b))?

7. A card is drawn at random from a pack of 52 playing cards. The card is replaced and a second card is drawn. This card is replaced and a third card is drawn. What is the probability of drawing:
(a) three hearts?
(b) at least two hearts?
(c) exactly one heart?

8. A bag contains 6 red marbles and 4 blue marbles. A marble is drawn at random and not replaced. Two further draws are made, again without replacement. Find the probability of drawing:
(a) three red marbles,
(b) three blue marbles,
(c) no red marbles,
(d) at least one red marble.

9. When a cutting is taken from a geranium the probability that it grows is $\frac{3}{4}$. Three cuttings are taken. What is the probability that
(a) all three grow,
(b) none of them grow?

10. A dice has its six faces marked 0, 1, 1, 1, 6, 6. Two of these dice are thrown together and the total score is recorded. Draw a tree diagram.

(a) How many different totals are possible?
(b) What is the probability of obtaining a total of 7?

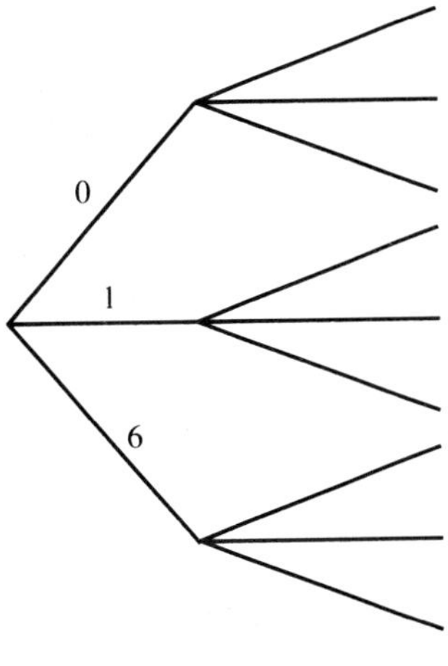

11. A coin is biased so that the probability of a 'head' is $\frac{3}{4}$. Find the probability that, when tossed three times, it shows:
(a) three tails,
(b) two heads and one tail,
(c) one head and two tails,
(d) no tails.
Write down the sum of the probabilities in (a), (b), (c) and (d).

12. A teacher decides to award exam grades A, B or C by a new fairer method. Out of 20 children, three are to receive A's, five B's and the rest C's. She writes the letters A, B and C on 20 pieces of paper and invites the pupils to draw their exam result, going through the class in alphabetical order. Find the probability that:
(a) the first three pupils all get grade 'A'.
(b) the first three pupils all get grade 'B'.
(c) the first four pupils all get grade 'B'.
(Do not cancel down the fractions.)

13. The probability that George, an amateur golfer, actually hits the ball is (regrettably for all concerned) only $\frac{1}{10}$.

If four separate attempts are made, find the probability that George will hit the ball:
(a) four times
(b) not at all
(c) at least once (hint: use part (b)).

9 Shape and space 3

9.1 Similar shapes

4/8a

If one shape is an enlargement of another, the two shapes are mathematically *similar*.

The two triangles A and B are similar if they have the same angles.

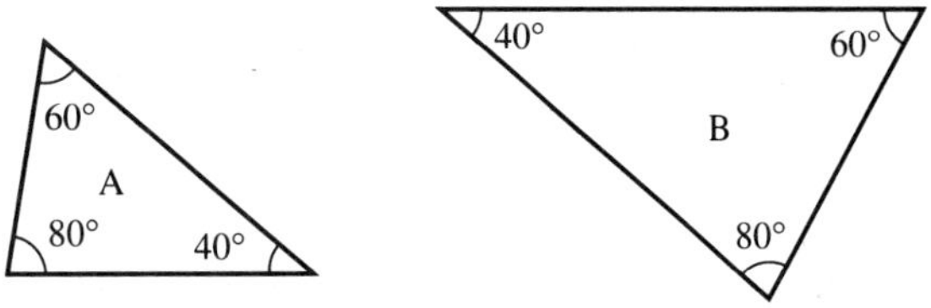

For other shapes to be similar, not only must corresponding angles be equal, but also corresponding edges must be in the same proportion.

The two quadrilaterals C and D are similar. All the edges of shape D are twice as long as the edges of shape C.

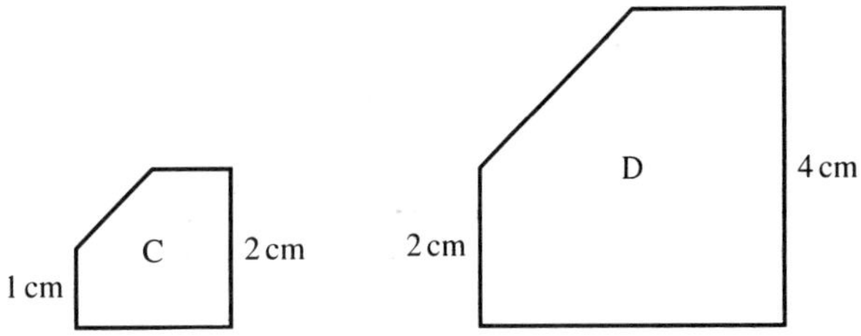

The two rectangles E and F are not similar even though they have the same angles.

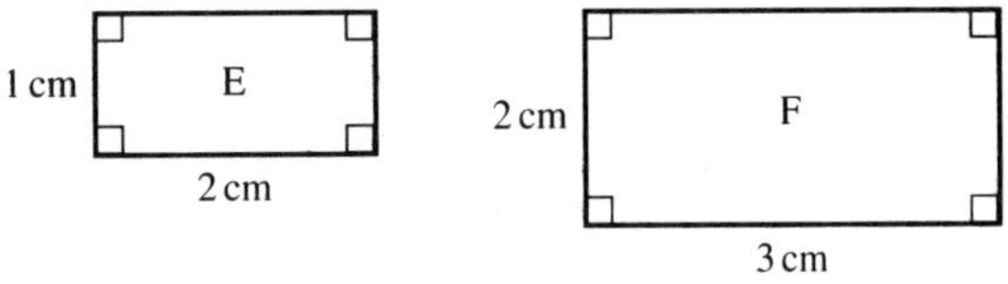

(a) Show that triangles PQR and PST are similar.
(b) Given the lengths shown, work out QS.

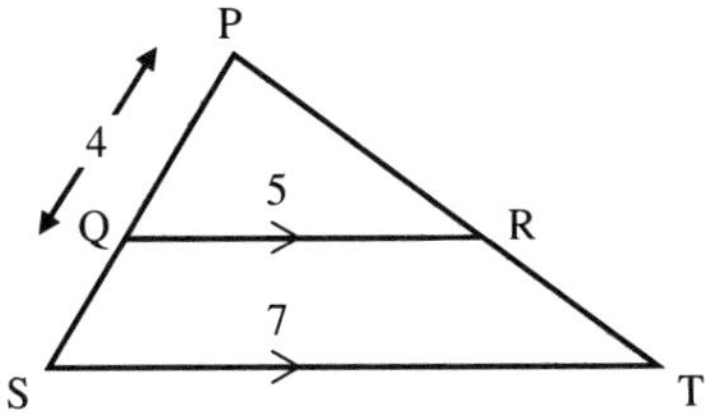

(a) In the triangles PQR and PST:
Angle P is common
$P\hat{Q}R = P\hat{S}T$ (corresponding angles)
$\therefore$ Triangles PQR and PST are similar.

(b) $\frac{ST}{QR} = \frac{PS}{PQ}$ so $\frac{7}{5} = \frac{PS}{4}$

$\therefore \quad PS = \frac{28}{5} = 5\frac{3}{5}$

$\therefore \quad QS = 5\frac{3}{5} - 4 = 1\frac{3}{5}$

Exercise 1

1. Which of the shapes B, C, D is/are similar to shape A?

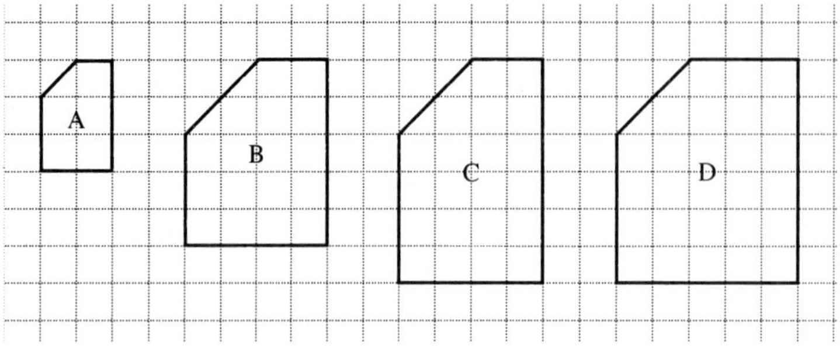

In Questions **2** to **8**, find the sides marked with letters; all lengths are given in cm.

2.

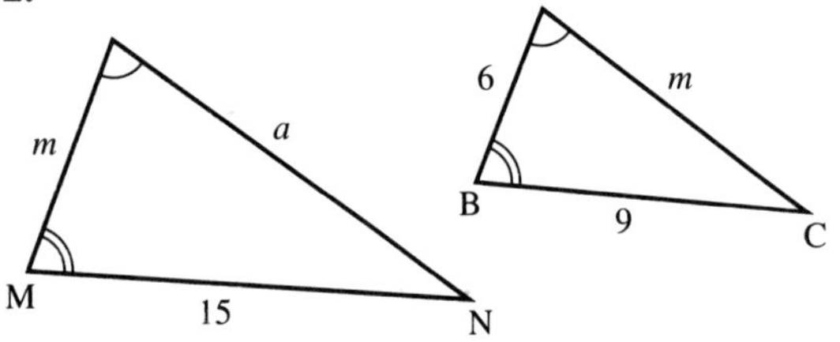

3.

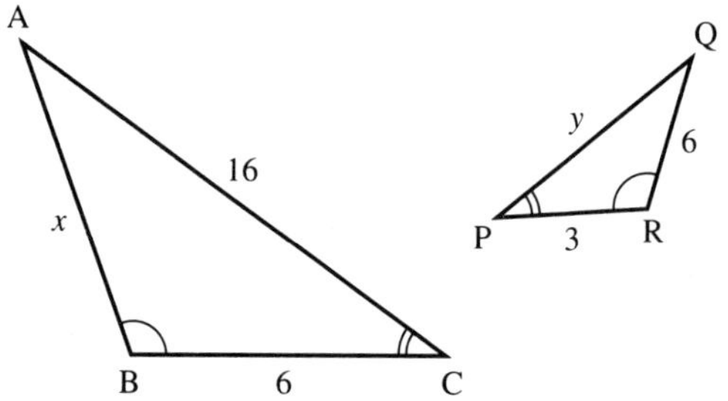

4.

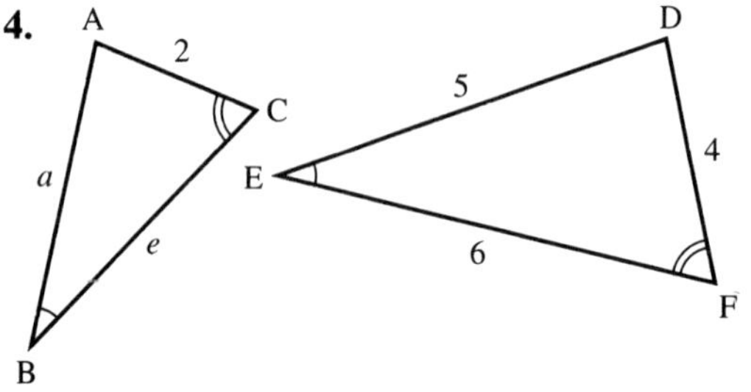

5.

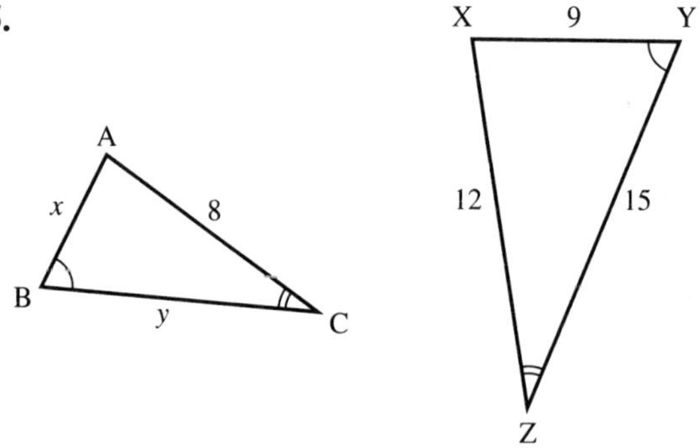

6.

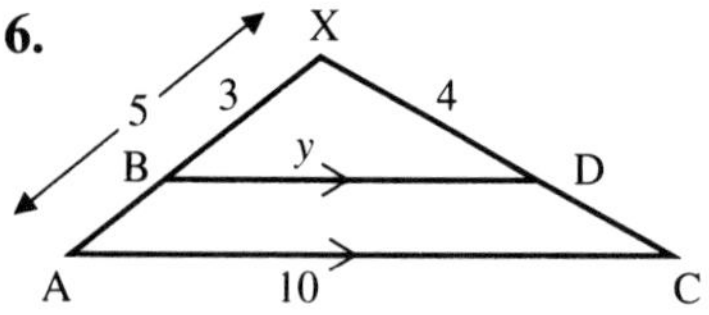

7.

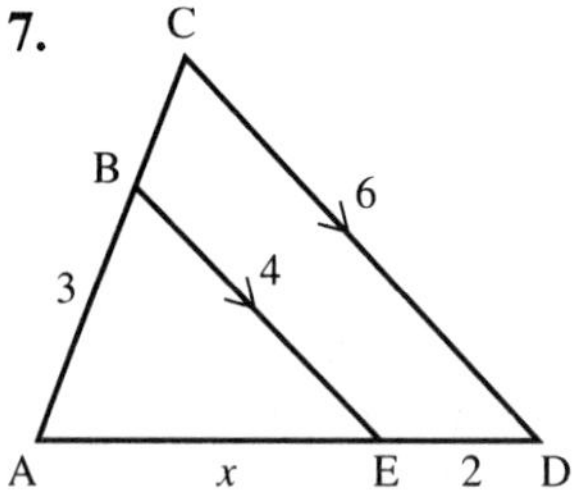

8.

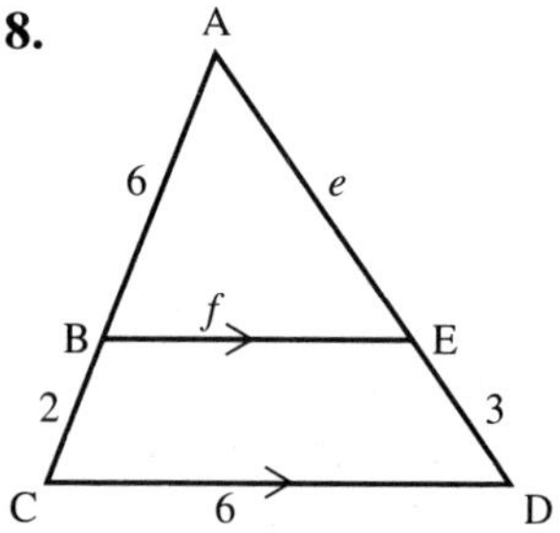

9. Picture B is an enlargement of picture A. Calculate the length x.

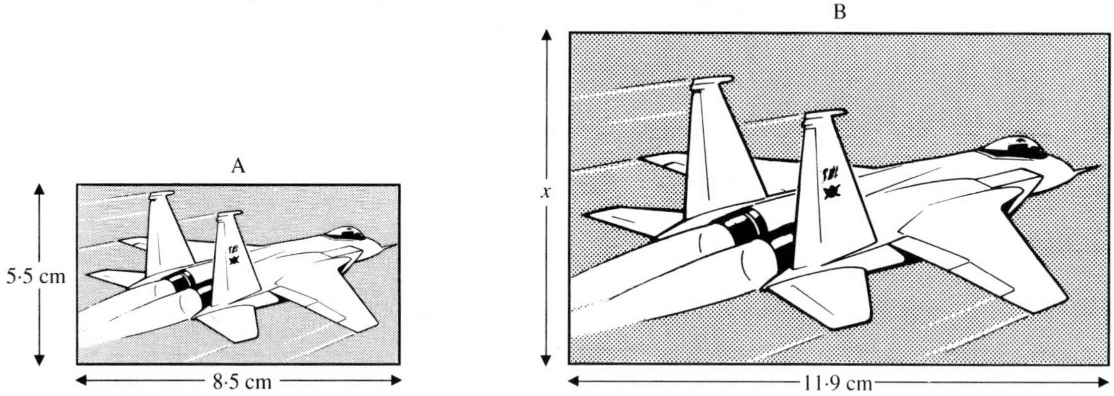

10. The drawing shows a rectangular picture 16 cm × 8 cm surrounded by a border of width 4 cm. Are the two rectangles similar?

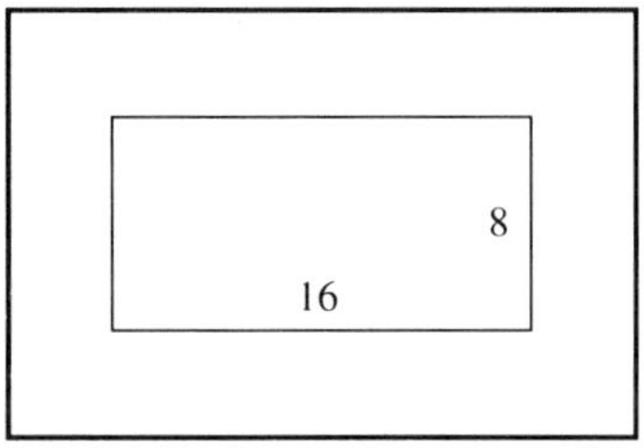

11. The diagonals of a trapezium ABCD intersect at O. AB is parallel to DC, AB = 3 cm and DC = 6 cm. Show that triangles ABO and CDO are similar. If CO = 4 cm and OB = 3 cm, find AO and DO.

12. A tree of height 4 m casts a shadow of length 6·5 m. Find the height of a house casting a shadow 26 m long.

13. Triangles ABC and EBD are similar but DE is *not* parallel to AC. Work out the length x.

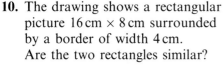

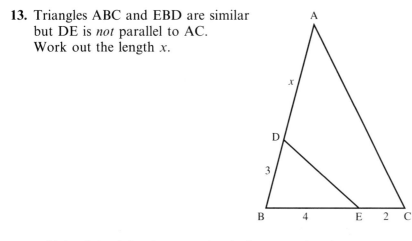

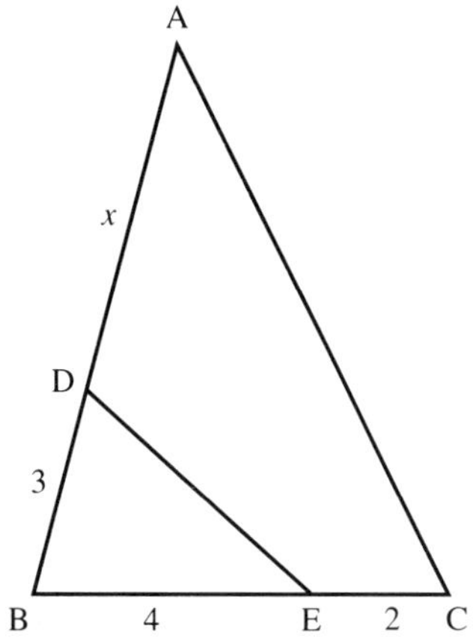

14. Which of the following *must* be similar to each other.

(a) Two equilateral triangles.
(b) Two rectangles.
(c) Two isosceles triangles.
(d) Two squares.
(e) Two regular pentagons.
(f) Two kites.
(g) Two rhombuses.
(h) Two circles.

15. A small cone is cut from a larger cone. Find the radius of the smaller cone.

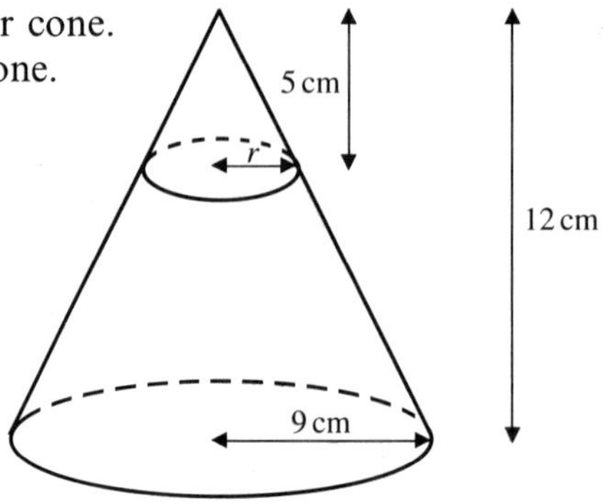

16. The diagram shows the side view of a swimming pool being filled with water. Calculate the length x.

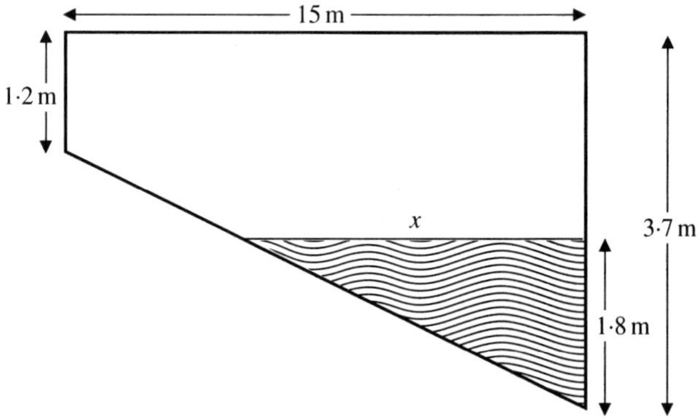

9.2 Trigonometry

4/8b

Trigonometry is used to calculate sides and angles in triangles. The triangle must have a right angle.

The side opposite the right angle is called the *hypotenuse* (H). It is the longest side.

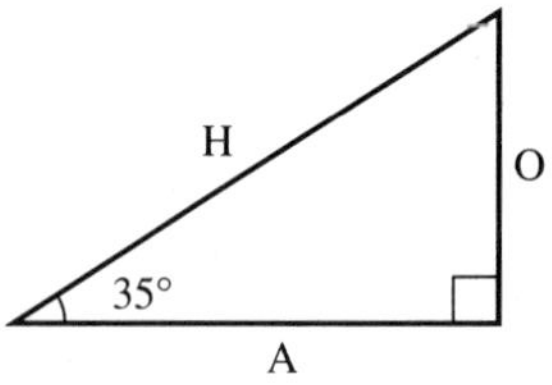

The side opposite the marked angle m is called the opposite (O).

The other side is called the adjacent (A).

Consider two triangles, one of which is an enlargement of the other.
It is clear that, for the angle 30°, the

$$\text{ratio} = \frac{\text{opposite}}{\text{hypotenuse}} = \frac{6}{12} = \frac{2}{4} = \frac{1}{2}$$

This is the same for both triangles.

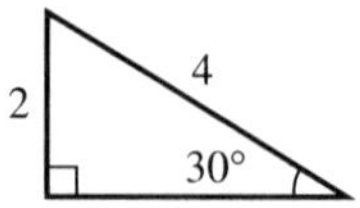

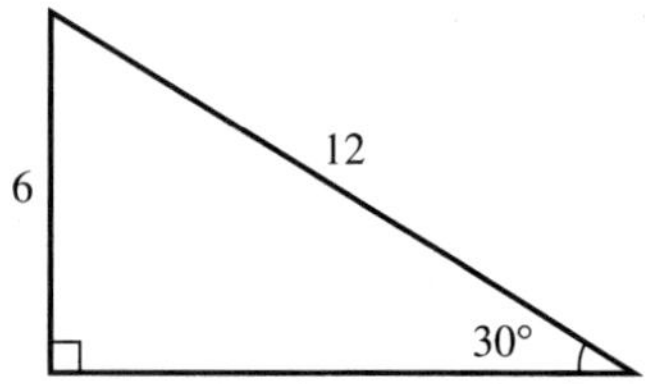

Sine, cosine, tangent

Three important ratios are defined for angle x.

$$\sin x = \frac{\text{O}}{\text{H}} \qquad \cos x = \frac{\text{A}}{\text{H}} \qquad \tan x = \frac{\text{O}}{\text{A}}$$

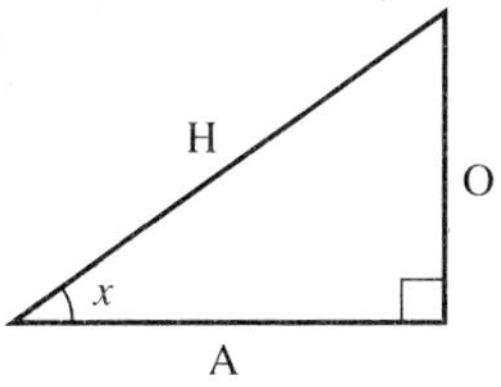

It is important to get the letters in the correct positions.

Some people find a simple sentence helpful where the first letters of each word describe sine, cosine or tangent, Hypotenuse, Opposite or Adjacent. An example is:

Silly Old Harry Caught A Herring Trawling Off Afghanistan

e.g. S O H $\quad \sin = \frac{\text{O}}{\text{H}}$

Finding the length of a side

Find the length of l.

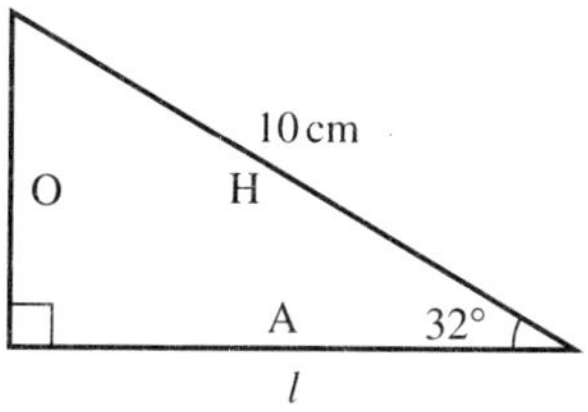

$$\cos 32° = \frac{\text{A}}{\text{H}} = \frac{l}{10}$$

$$\therefore\ l = 10 \times \cos 32°$$

$$l = 8{\cdot}48 \text{ cm (to 3 s.f.)}$$

Exercise 2

Find the lengths marked with letters. All lengths are in cm. Give answers correct to 3 s.f.

1.
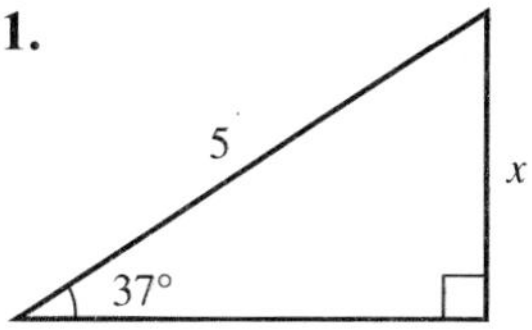

2.
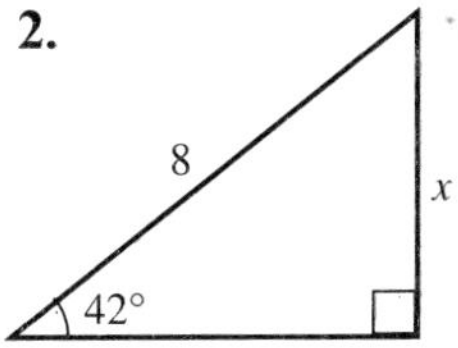

3.
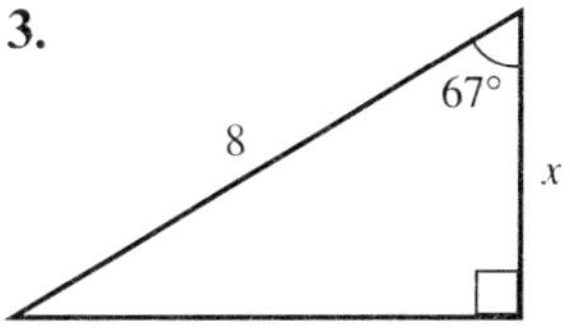

4.
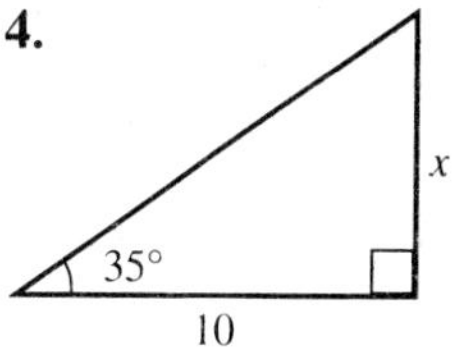

5.
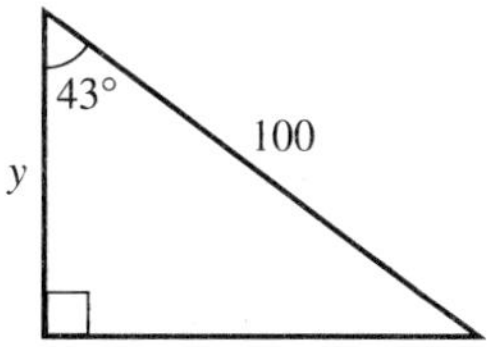

6.
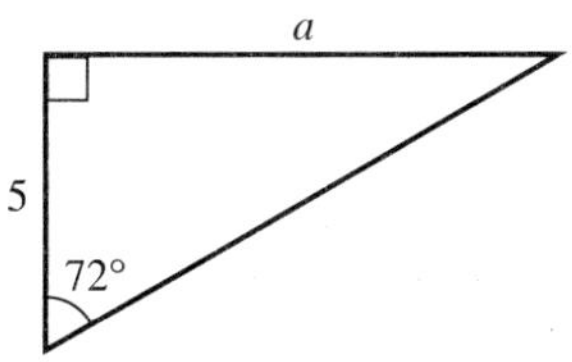

7.
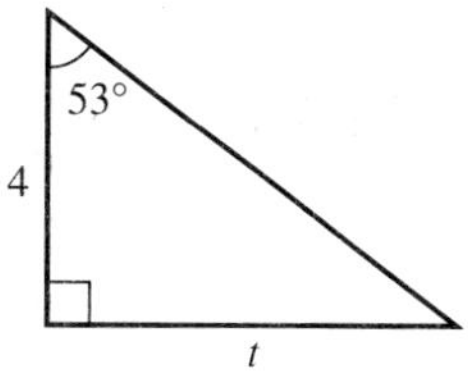

8.
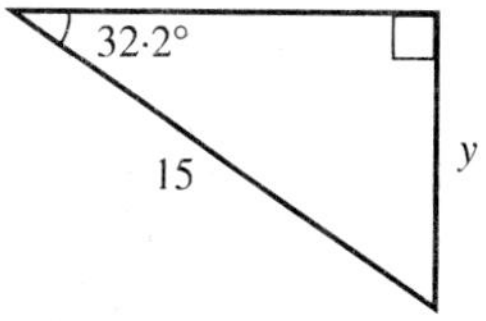

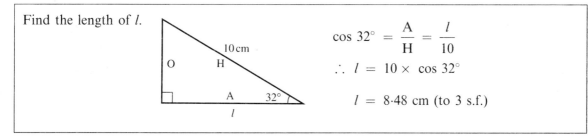

9.

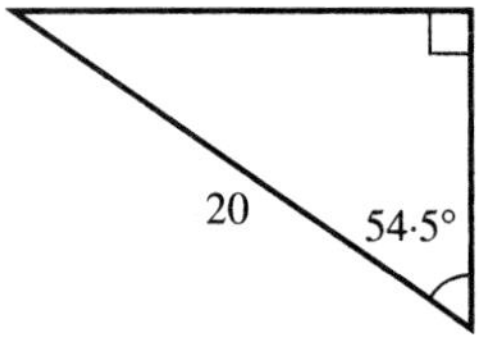

10.

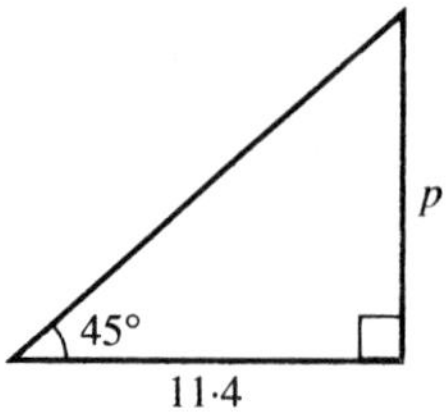

11.

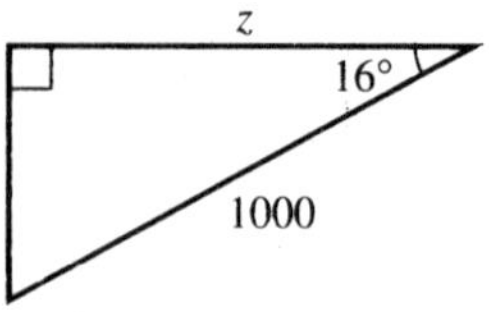

12.

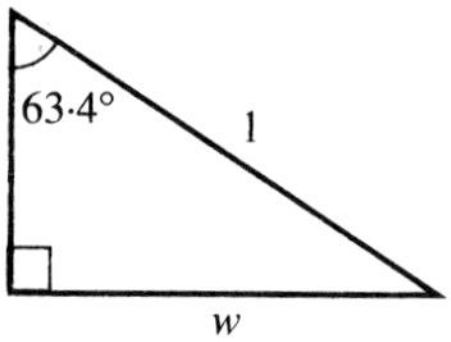

13.

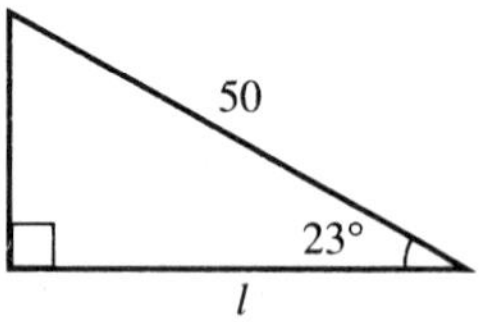

14.

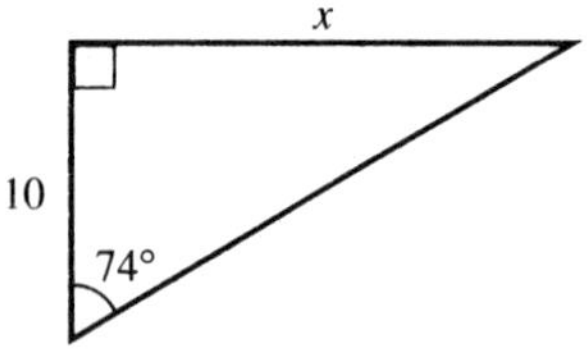

15.

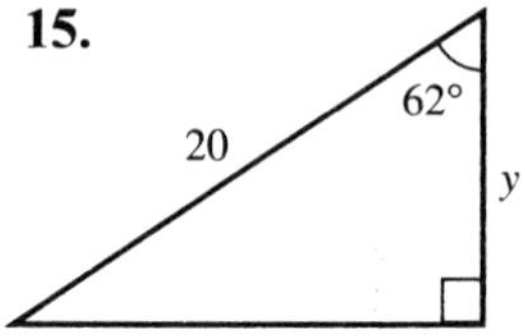

16.

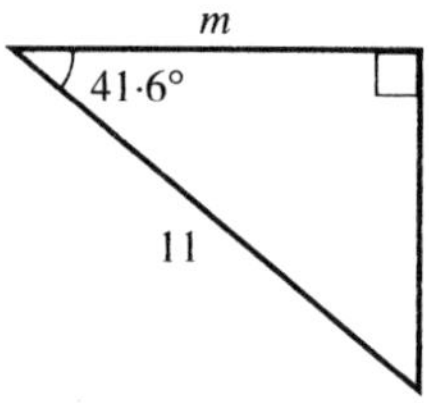

17.

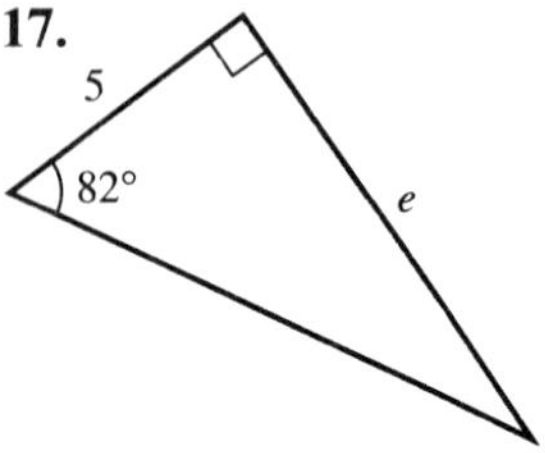

18.

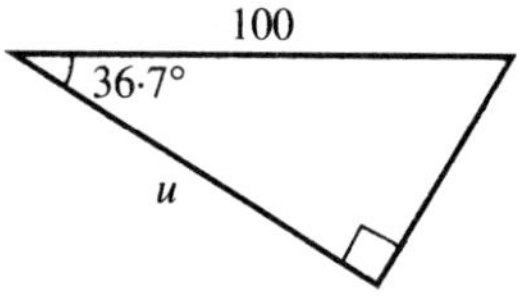

19.

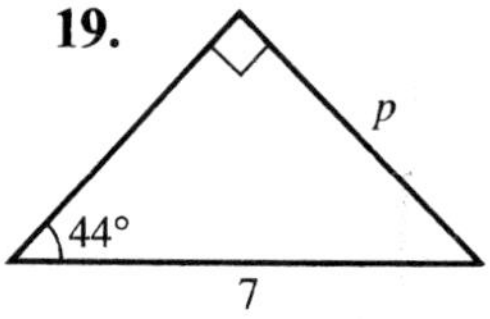

20.

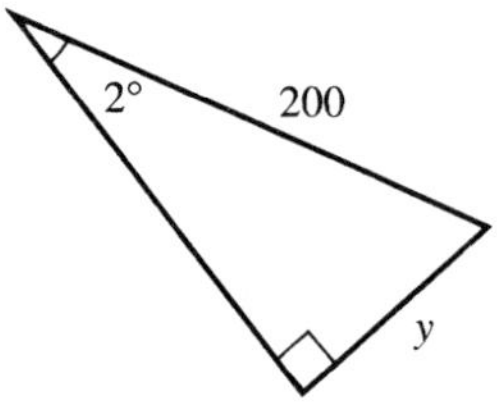

Find the length of x.

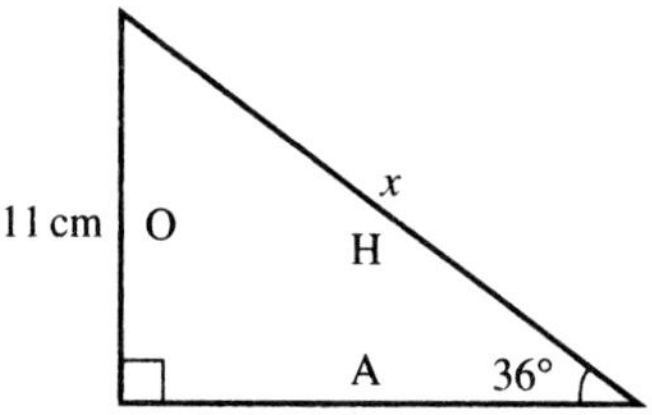

$$\sin 36° = \frac{O}{H} = \frac{11}{x}$$

$$\therefore\ x \sin 36° = 11 \quad \text{[Multiply by } x\text{]}$$

$$x = \frac{11}{\sin 36°} = 18{\cdot}7 \text{ cm (to 3 s.f.)}$$

Exercise 3

This exercise is more difficult. Find the lengths marked with letters.

1.

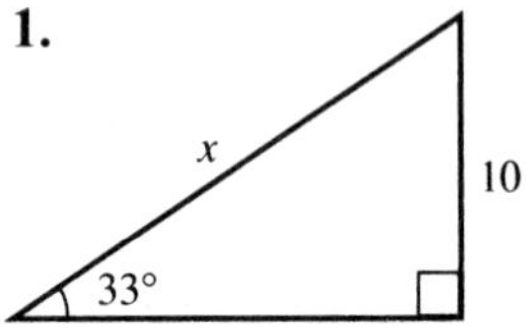

2.

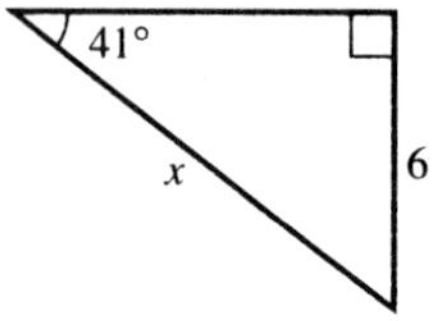

3.

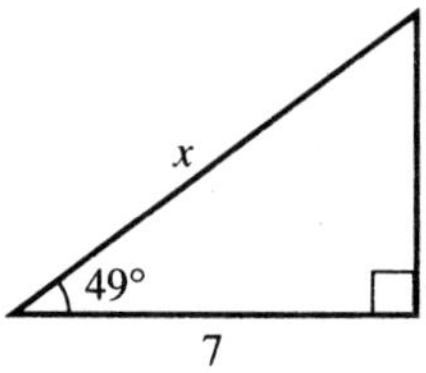

4.

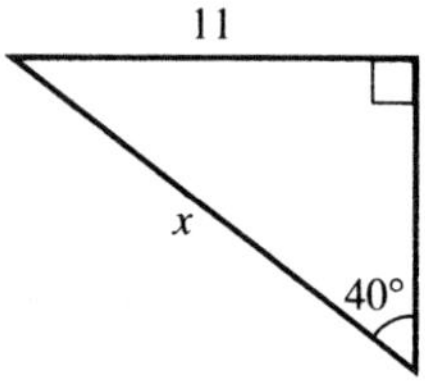

5.

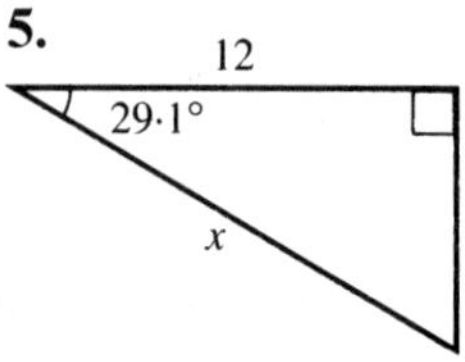

6.

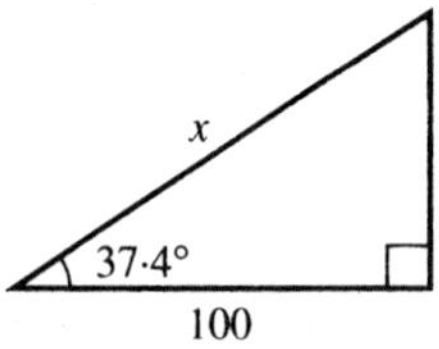

7.

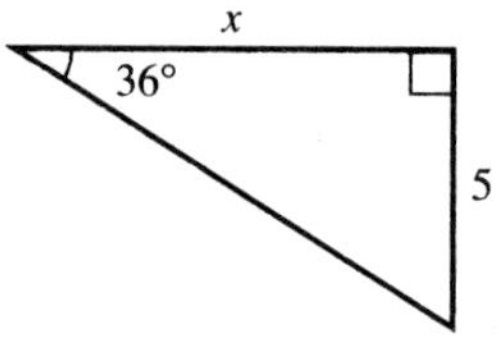

8.

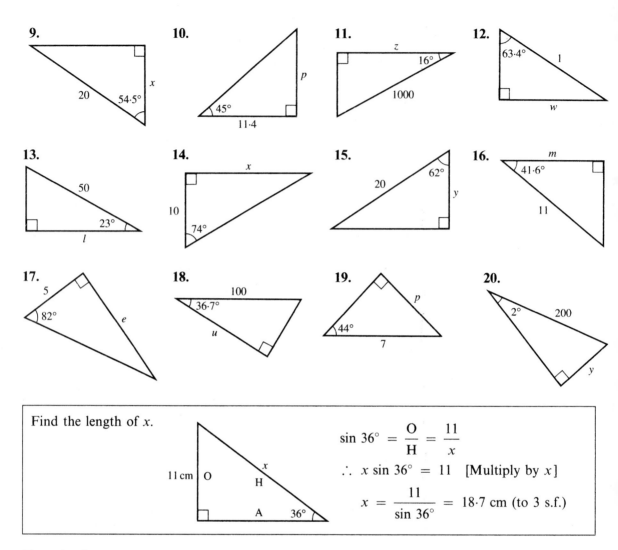

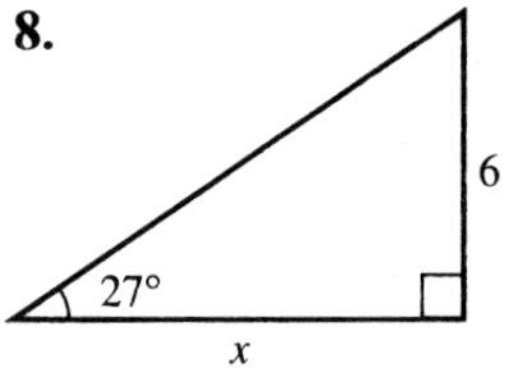

9.

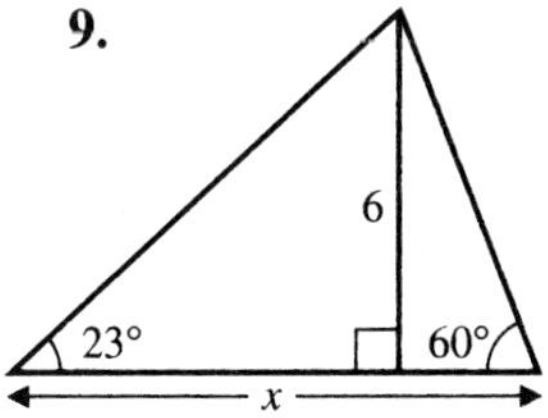

10.

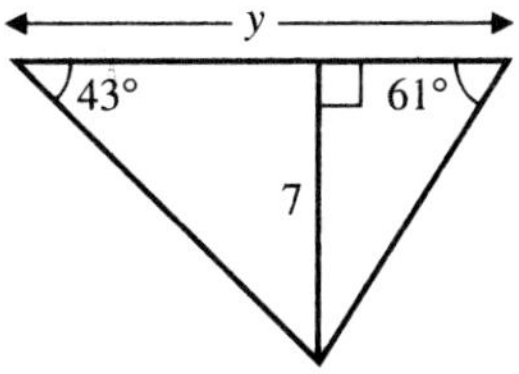

11.

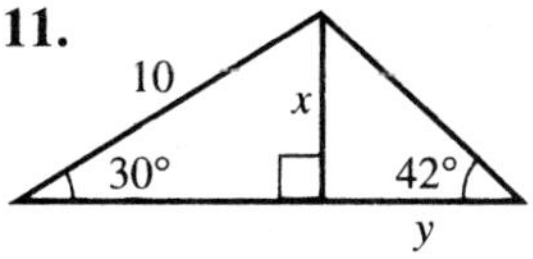

12.

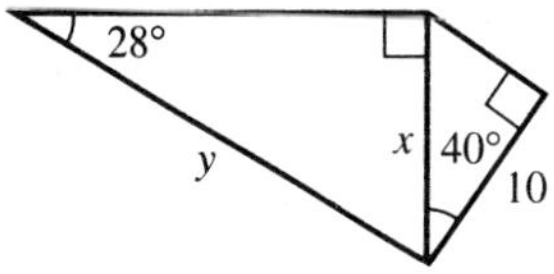

13.

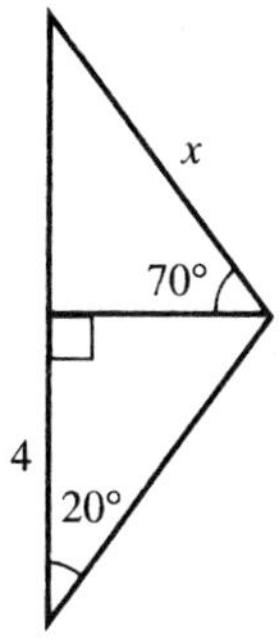

14.

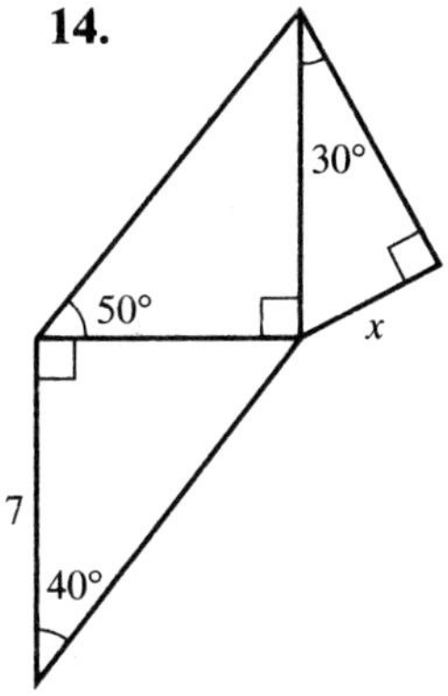

15.

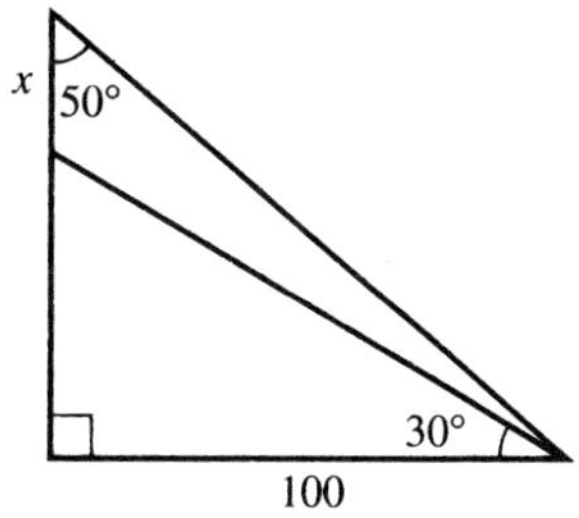

16.

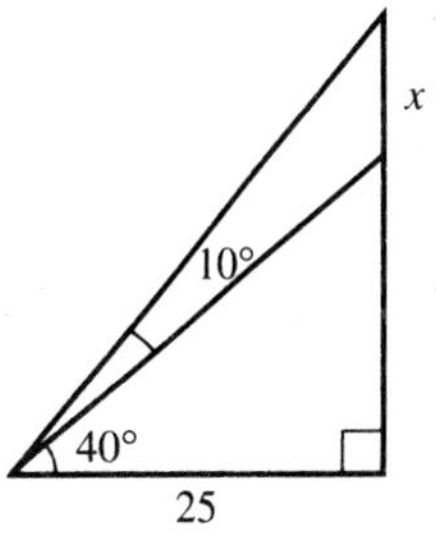

Finding angles

Find the angle x.

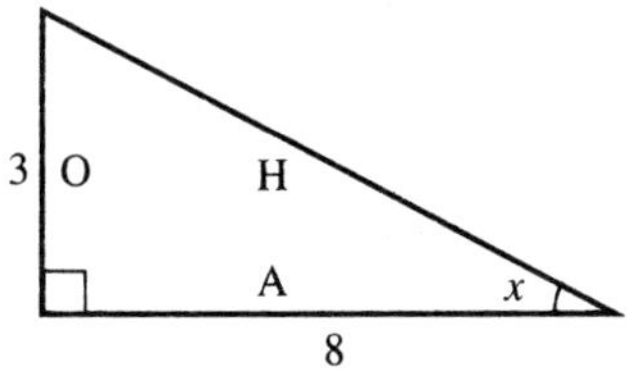

$$\tan x = \frac{O}{A} = \frac{3}{8}$$

$$\tan x = 0{\cdot}375$$
$$x = 20{\cdot}6°\text{(to 1 d.p.)}$$

On a calculator:

[3] [÷] [8] [=] [INV] [tan]

Exercise 4

Find the angles marked with letters. All the lengths are in cm.

1.

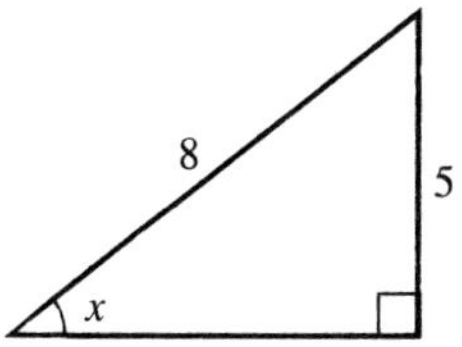

2.

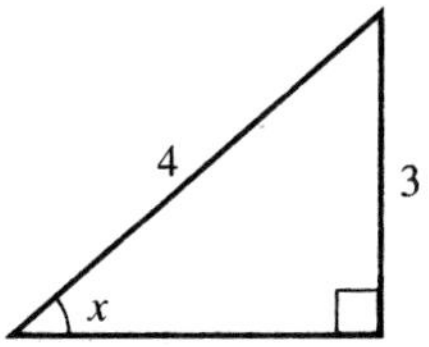

3.

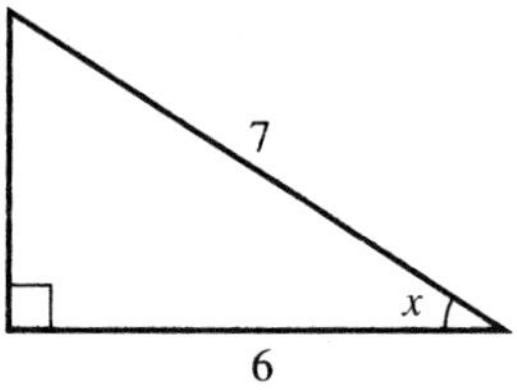

4.

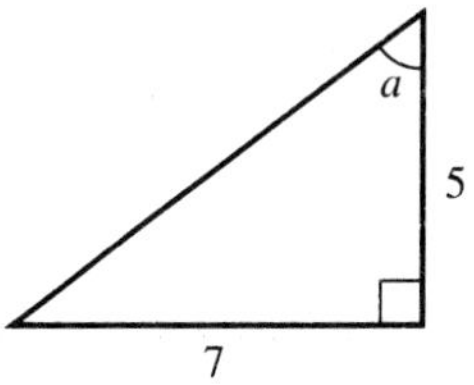

5.

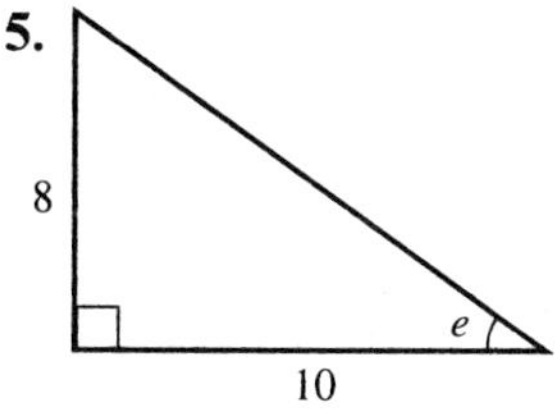

6.

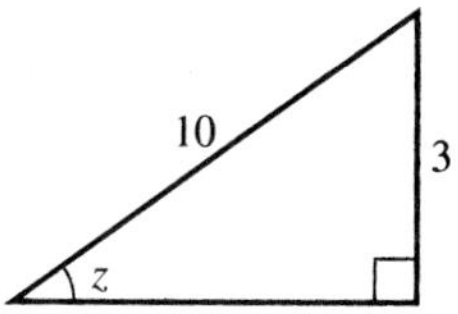

7.

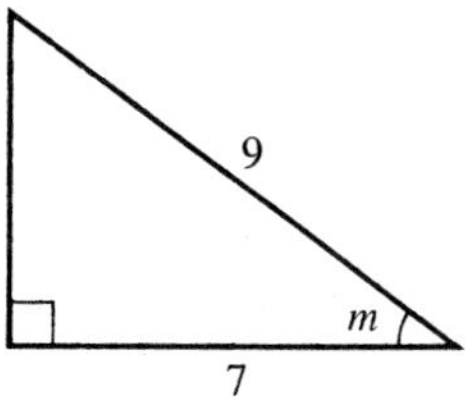

8.

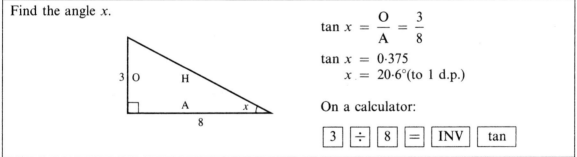

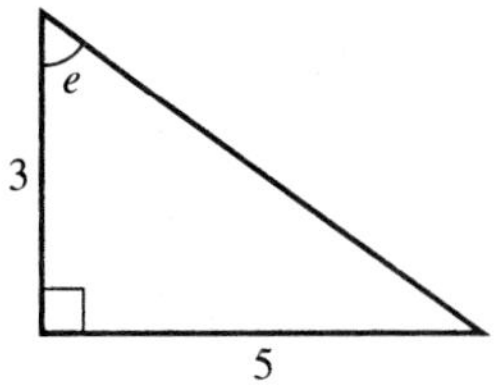

9.

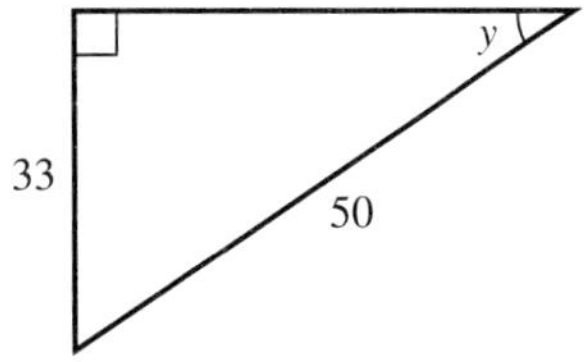

10.

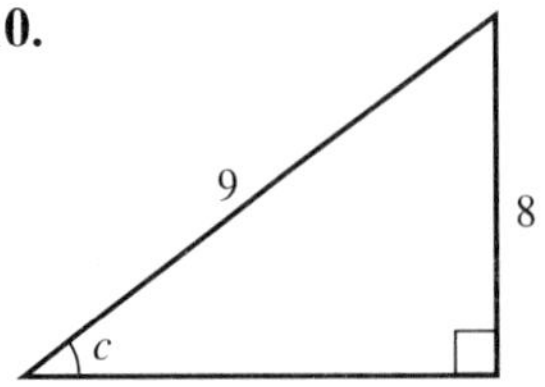

11.

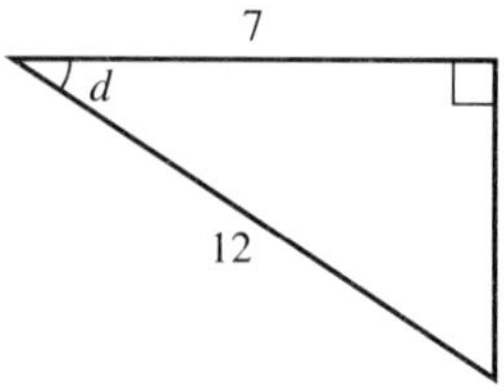

12.

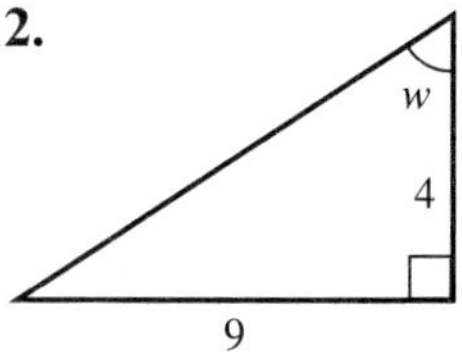

13.

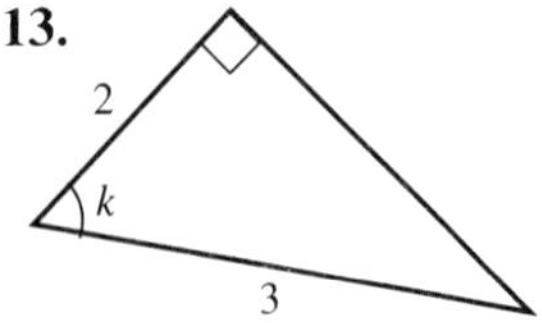

14.

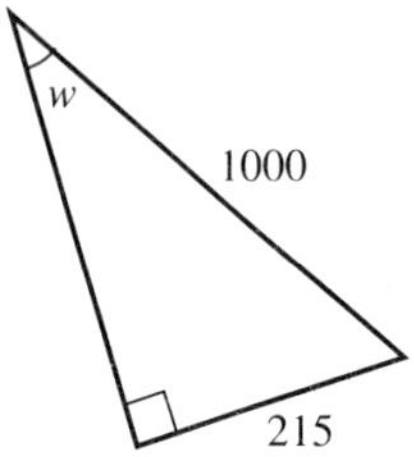

15.

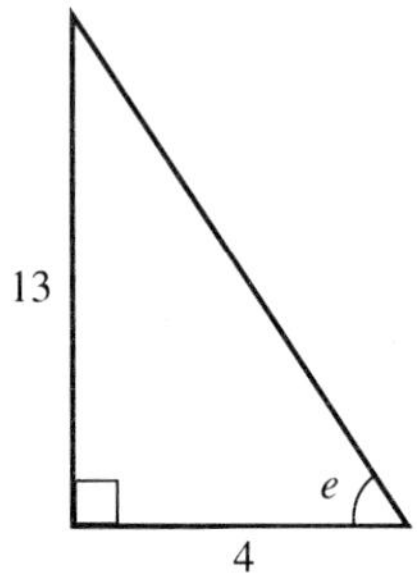

16.

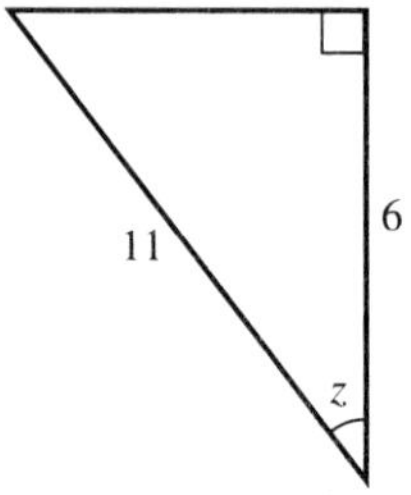

17.

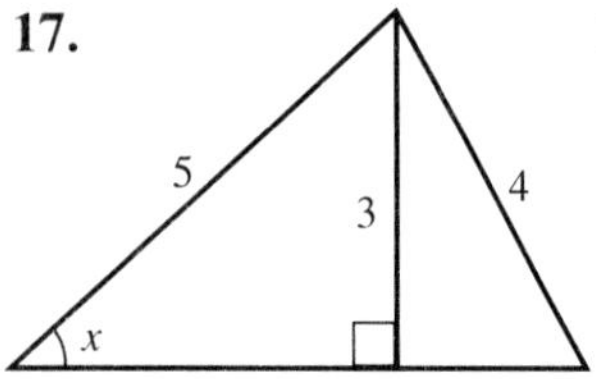

18.

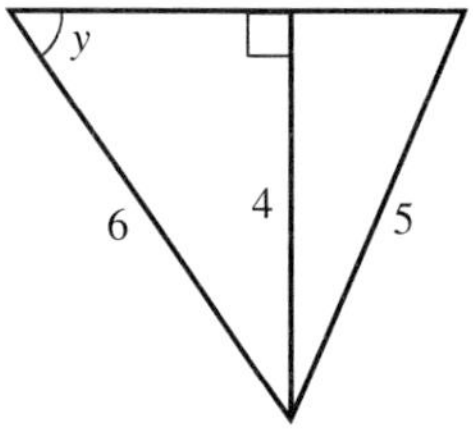

19.

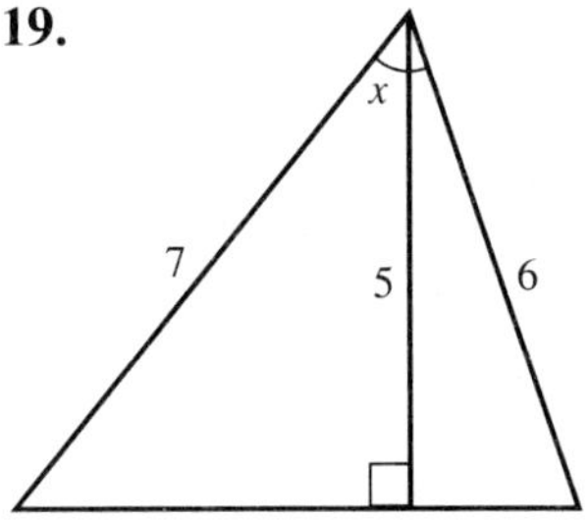

20.

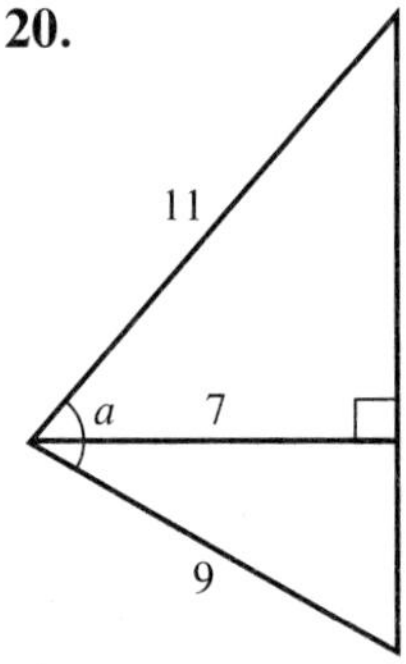

Angles of elevation and depression

(a)

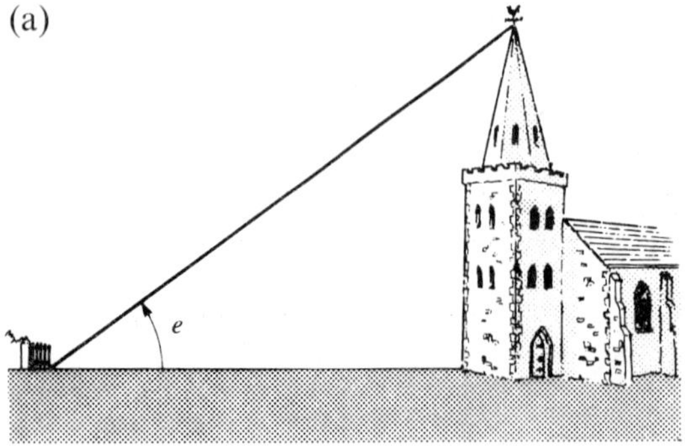

e is the angle of elevation of the Steeple from the Gate.

(b)

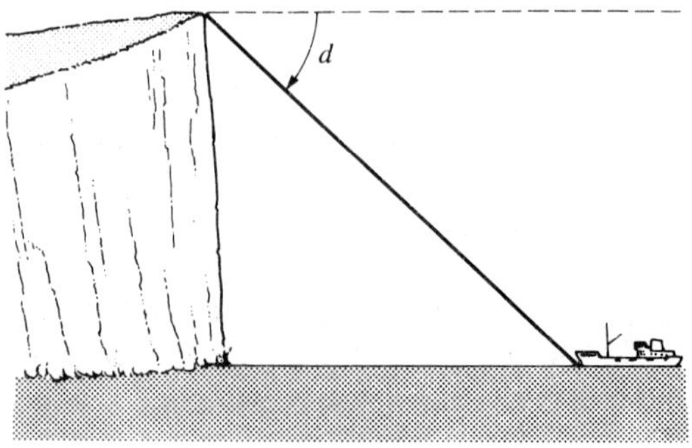

d is the angle of depression of the Boat from the Cliff top.

Exercise 5

Begin each question by drawing a large clear diagram.

1. A ladder of length 4 m rests against a vertical wall so that the base of the ladder is 1·5 m from the wall.
   Calculate the angle between the ladder and the ground.

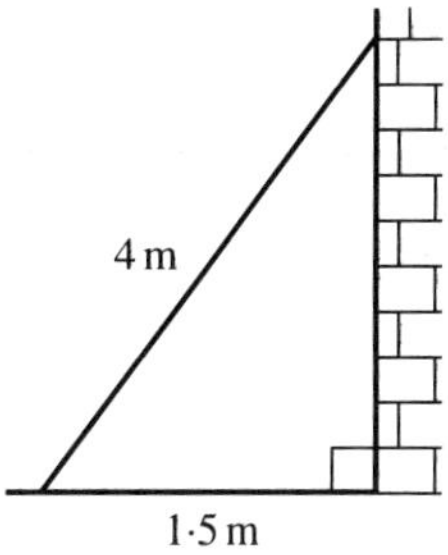

2. A ladder of length 4 m rests against a vertical wall so that the angle between the ladder and the ground is 66°. How far up the wall does the ladder reach?

3. From a distance of 20 m the angle of elevation to the top of a tower is 35°.

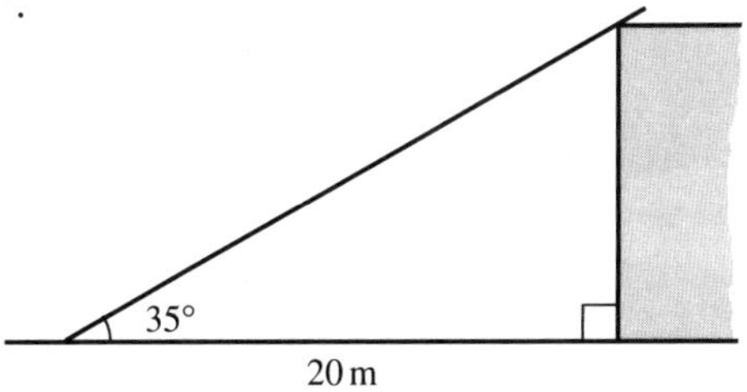

   How high is the tower?

4. A point G is 40 m away from a building, which is 15 m high. What is the angle of elevation to the top of the building from G?

5. A boy is flying a kite from a string of length 60 m.
   If the string is taut and makes an angle of 71° with the horizontal, what is the height of the kite?
   Ignore the height of the boy.

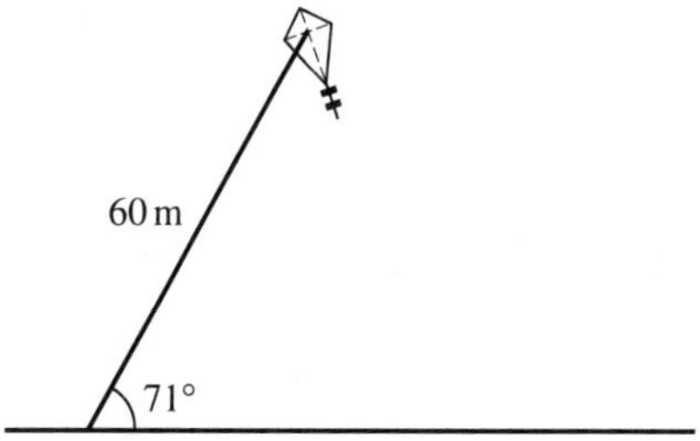

6. A straight tunnel is 80 m long and slopes downwards at an angle of 11° to the horizontal. Find the vertical drop in travelling from the top to the bottom of the tunnel.

7. The frame of a bicycle is shown in the diagram.
   Find the length of the cross bar.

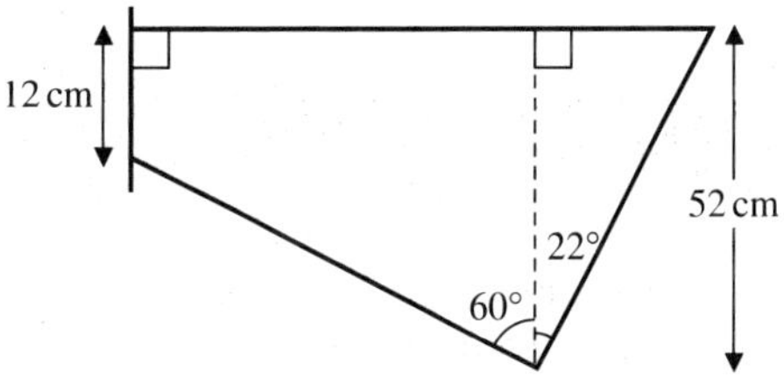

8. Calculate the length x.

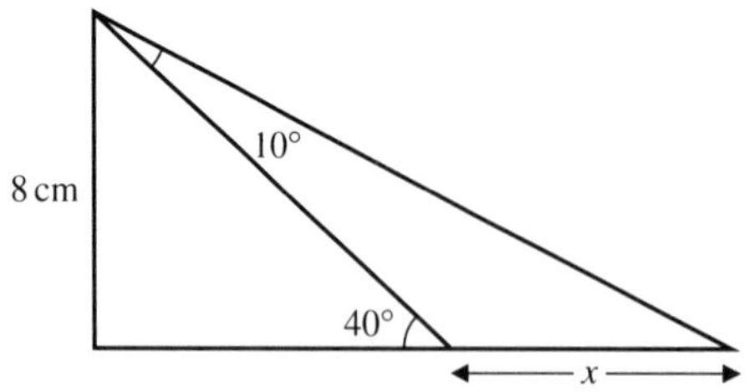

9. AB is a chord of a circle of radius 5 cm and centre O.

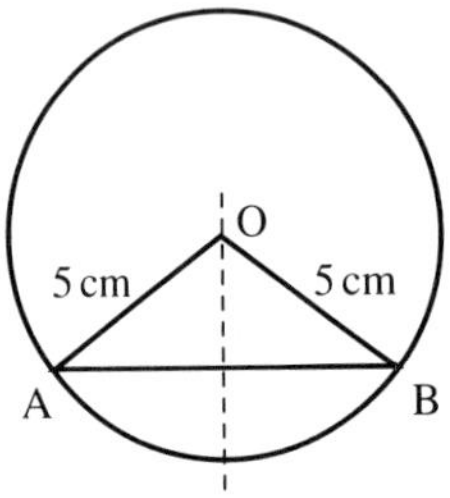

The perpendicular bisector of AB passes through O and also bisects the angle AOB. If $A\hat{O}B = 100°$ calculate the length of the chord AB.

10. A ship is due South of a lighthouse. It sails on a bearing of 055° for a distance of 80 km until it is due East of the lighthouse.

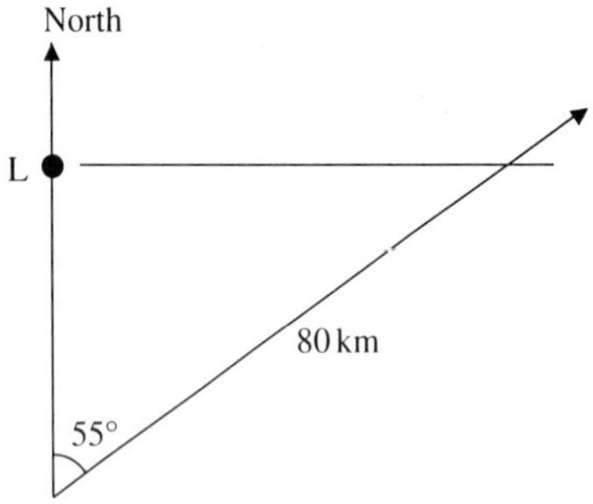

How far is it now from the lighthouse?

11. A ship is due South of a lighthouse. It sails on a bearing of 071° for a distance of 200 km until it is due East of the lighthouse. How far is it now from the lighthouse?

12. A ship is due North of a lighthouse. It sails on a bearing of 200° at a speed of 15 km/h for five hours until it is due West of the lighthouse. How far is it now from the lighthouse?

13. From the top of a tower of height 75 m, a guard sees two prisoners, both due West of him.

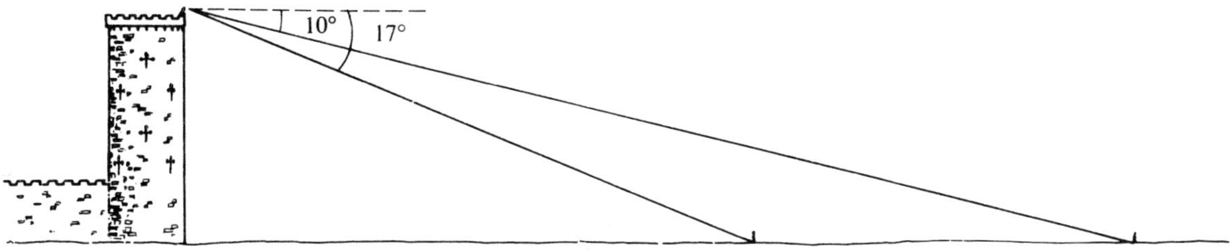

If the angles of depression of the two prisoners are 10° and 17°, calculate the distance between them.

14. From a horizontal distance of 40 m, the angle of elevation to the top of a building is 35·4°. From a point further away from the building the angle of elevation is 20·2°. What is the distance between the two points?

15. An isosceles triangle has sides of length 8 cm, 8 cm and 5 cm. Find the angle between the two equal sides.

16. The angles of an isosceles triangle are 66°, 66° and 48°. If the shortest side of the triangle is 8·4 cm, find the length of one of the two equal sides.

17. A regular pentagon is inscribed in a circle of radius 7 cm.

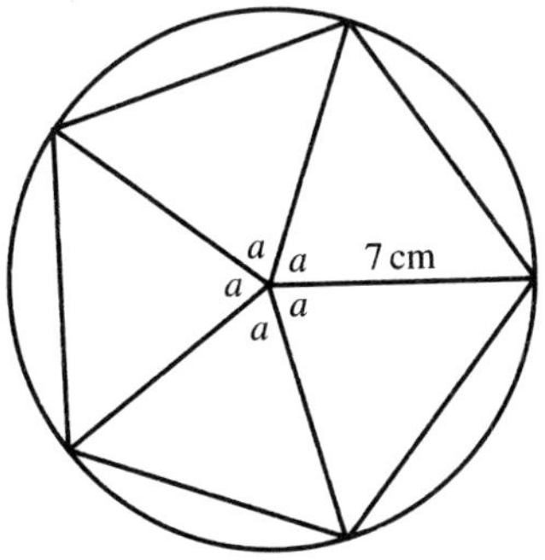

Find the angle a and then the length of a side of the pentagon.

18. Find the acute angle between the diagonals of a rectangle whose sides are 5 cm and 7 cm.

9.3 Dimensions of formulas

4/8c

Here are some formulas for finding volumes, areas and lengths.

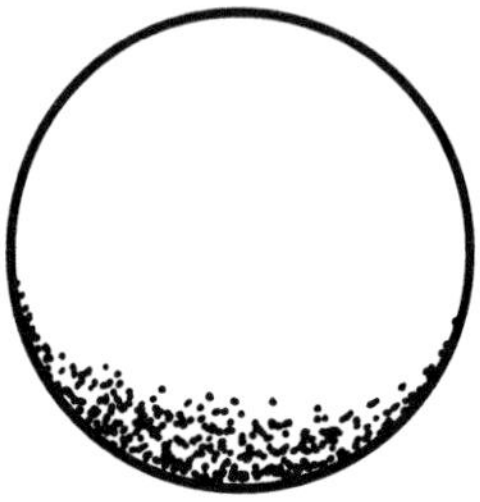

sphere: volume $= \frac{4}{3}\pi \boldsymbol{r}^3$

surface area $= 4\pi \boldsymbol{r}^2$

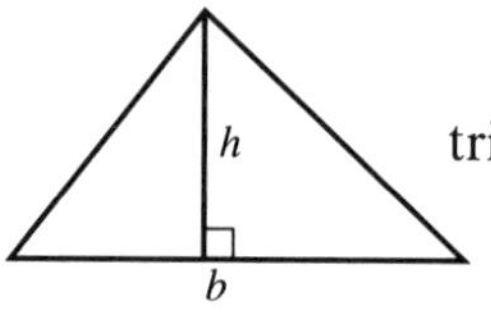

triangle: area $= \frac{1}{2}\boldsymbol{bh}$

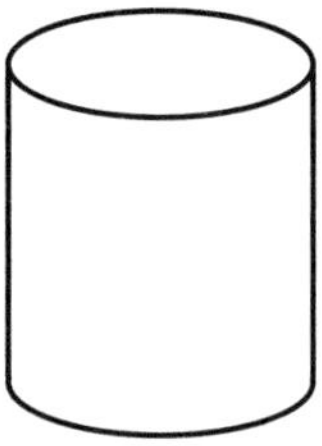

cylinder: volume $= \pi \boldsymbol{r}^2 \boldsymbol{h}$

curved surface area $= 2\pi \boldsymbol{rh}$

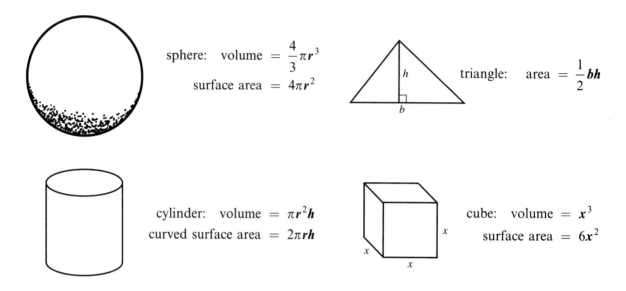

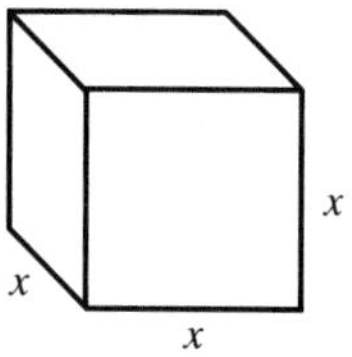

cube: volume $= \boldsymbol{x}^3$

surface area $= 6\boldsymbol{x}^2$

All the symbols in bold type are lengths. They have the *dimension* of length and are measured in cm, metres, km, etc. The other symbols are numbers (including π) and have no dimensions.

(a) It is not hard to see that all the formulas for volume have *three* lengths multiplied together. They have three dimensions.
(b) All the formulas for area have *two* lengths multiplied together. They have two dimensions.
(c) Any formula for the length of an object will involve just *one* length (or one dimension).

It is quite possible that a formula can have more than one term. The formula $A = \pi r^2 + 3rd$ has two terms and each term has two dimensions.
It is not possible to have a mixture of terms some with, say, two dimensions and some with three dimensions.
So the formula $A = \pi r^2 + 3r^2 d$ could not possibly represent volume.

The formula $z = \frac{2\pi r^2 h}{L}$ has three dimensions on the top line and one dimension on the bottom. The dimensions can be 'cancelled' so the expression for z has only two dimensions and can only represent an area.
We can use these facts to check that any formula we may be using has the correct number of dimensions.

Here are four formulas where the letters c, d, r represent lengths:

(a) $t = 3c^2$ (b) $k = \frac{\pi}{3}r^3 + 4r^2d$

(c) $m = \pi(c + d)$ (d) $f = 4c + 3cd$

State whether the formula gives:
(i) a length (ii) an area
(iii) a volume (iv) an impossible expression.

(a) $t = 3c^2 = 3c \times c$
This has *two* dimensions so t is an *area*.

(b) $k = \frac{\pi}{3}r^3 + 4r^2d.$

Both $\frac{\pi}{3}r^3$ and $4r^2d$ have *three* dimensions so k is a *volume*.

(c) $m = \pi(c + d) = \pi c + \pi d$
πc is a length and πd is a length.
So m is a length plus a length.
$\therefore$ m is a length.

(d) $f = 4c + 3cd$
$4c$ is a length.
$3cd$ is a length multiplied by a length and is an area.
So f is a length plus an area which is an *impossible* expression.

Exercise 6

The symbols a, b, d, h, l, r represent lengths.

1. State the number of dimensions for each of the following:

(a) πl^2 (b) $3\pi lr$ (c) $\frac{\pi}{2}b^2h$

(d) $\pi(a + b)$ (e) $\frac{ab + h^2}{6}$ (f) $abd \sin 30°$

2. Give the number of dimensions that a formula for each of the following should have.
(a) Total area of windows in a room.
(b) Volume of sand in a lorry.
(c) Area of a sports field.
(d) The diagonal of a rectangle.
(e) The capacity of an oil can.
(f) The perimeter of a trapezium.
(g) The number of people in a cinema.
(h) The surface area of the roof of a house.

3. From this list of expressions, choose the *two* that represent volume, the four that represent area and the *one* that represents a length. The other expression is impossible.

(a) $\pi rh + \pi r^2$ (b) $5a + 6c$

(c) $3{\cdot}5\,abd$ (d) $4hl + \pi rh$

(e) $3r^2hl$ (f) $2\pi r(r + h)$

(g) $2(rb^2 + h^3)$ (h) $\frac{\pi}{2}(l + d)^2$

4. In Sam's notes, the formula for the volume of a container was written with Tippex over the index for r. The formula was

$V = \frac{\pi}{3}r^{\bigcirc}h$. What was the missing index?

5. Work out the missing index numbers in these formulas:

(a) Area $= 3(a^{\bigcirc} + bd)$ (b) Volume $= \frac{\pi L^{\bigcirc}}{3}$

(c) Length $= \frac{\pi r^{\bigcirc}}{3}$ (d) Area $= 3(a^{\bigcirc} + b^{\bigcirc}d)$

(e) Volume $= 2\pi(r^{\bigcirc} + b^{\bigcirc})$ (f) Area $= \frac{3\pi}{4}(a + b)^{\bigcirc}$

6. A physicist worked out a formula for the surface area of a complicated object and got

$$S = 3\pi(a + b)^2 \sin 20^\circ + \frac{\pi}{2}a$$

Explain why the formula could not be correct.

10 Algebra 3

10.1 Brackets and factors

3/8a

Two brackets

Suppose we need to work out $(x + 3)(x + 2)$. We can use the area of a rectangle to help.

Total area $= (x+3)(x+2)$
$= x^2 + 2x + 3x + 6$
$= x^2 + 5x + 6$

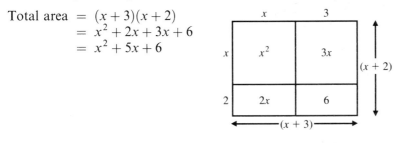

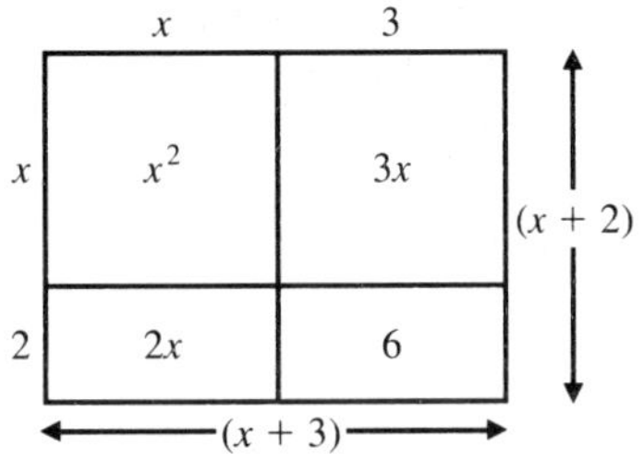

After a little practice, it is possible to do without the diagram.

(a) $(3x-2)(2x-1) = 3x(2x-1) - 2(2x-1)$
$= 6x^2 - 3x - 4x + 2$
$= 6x^2 - 7x + 2$

(b) $3(x+1)(x-2) = 3[x(x-2) + 1(x-2)]$
$= 3[x^2 - 2x + x - 2]$
$= 3x^2 - 3x - 6$

Exercise 1

Remove the brackets and simplify.

1. $(x+1)(x+3)$
2. $(x+3)(x+2)$
3. $(y+4)(y+5)$
4. $(x-3)(x+4)$
5. $(x+5)(x-2)$
6. $(x-3)(x-2)$
7. $(a-7)(a+5)$
8. $(z+9)(z-2)$
9. $(x-3)(x+3)$
10. $(k-11)(k+11)$
11. $(2x+1)(x-3)$
12. $(3x+4)(x-2)$
13. $(2y-3)(y+1)$
14. $(7y-1)(7y+1)$
15. $(3x-2)(3x+2)$
16. $(5-x)(4+x)$
17. $2(x-1)(x+2)$
18. $3(x-1)(2x+3)$
19. $4(2y-1)(3y+2)$
20. $2(3x+1)(x-2)$

Be careful with an expression like $(x-3)^2$. It is not x^2-9, or even x^2+9.

$$\begin{aligned}(x-3)^2 &= (x-3)(x-3)\\ &= x(x-3)-3(x-3)\\ &= x^2-6x+9\end{aligned}$$

Exercise 2

Remove the brackets and simplify:

1. $(x+4)^2$
2. $(x+2)^2$
3. $(x-2)^2$
4. $(2x+1)^2$
5. $(y-5)^2$
6. $(3y+1)^2$
7. $3(x+2)^2$
8. $(3-x)^2$
9. $(3x+2)^2$
10. $2(x+1)^2$
11. $(x+1)^2+(x+2)^2$
12. $(x-2)^2+(x+3)^2$
13. $(x+2)^2+(2x+1)^2$
14. $(y-3)^2+(y-4)^2$
15. $(x+2)^2-(x-3)^2$
16. $(x-3)^2-(x+1)^2$

Solve the equation.

$$\begin{aligned}(x+3)^2 &= (x+2)^2+3^2\\ (x+3)(x+3) &= (x+2)(x+2)+9\\ x^2+6x+9 &= x^2+4x+4+9\\ 6x+9 &= 4x+13\\ 2x &= 4\\ x &= 2\end{aligned}$$

Exercise 3

Solve the following equations:

1. $x^2+4 = (x+1)(x+3)$
2. $x^2+3x = (x+3)(x+1)$
3. $(x+3)(x-1) = x^2+5$
4. $(x+1)(x+4) = (x-7)(x+6)$
5. $(x-2)(x+3) = (x-7)(x+7)$
6. $(x-5)(x+4) = (x+7)(x-6)$
7. $2x^2+3x = (2x-1)(x+1)$
8. $(2x-1)(x-3) = (2x-3)(x-1)$
9. $x^2+(x+1)^2 = (2x-1)(x+4)$
10. $x(2x+6) = 2(x^2-5)$

In Questions **11** and **12**, form an equation in x by means of Pythagoras' Theorem, and hence find the length of each side of the triangle.
(All the lengths are in cm.)

11.

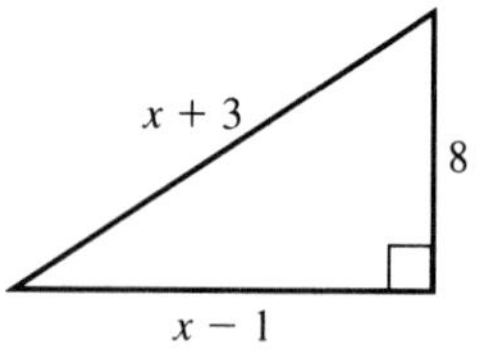

12.

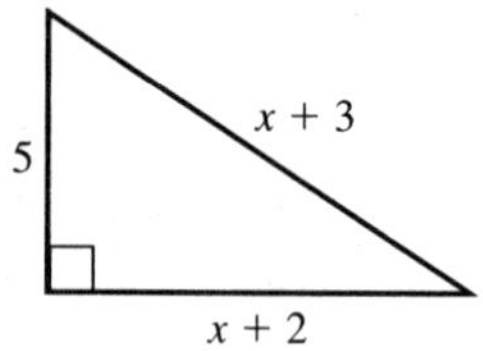

13. The area of the rectangle shown exceeds the area of the square by $2\,\text{cm}^2$. Find x.

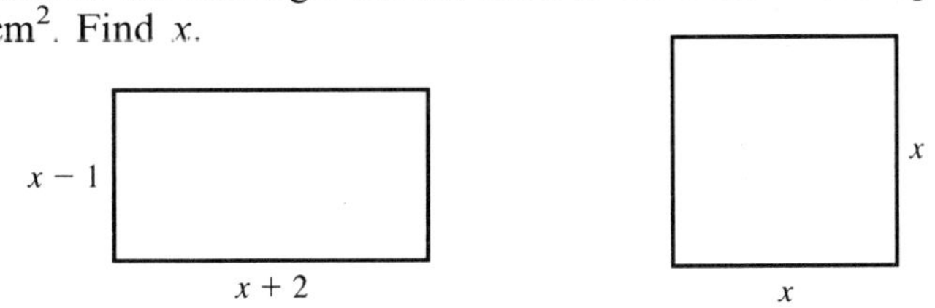

14. The area of the square exceeds the area of the rectangle by $13\,\text{m}^2$. Find y.

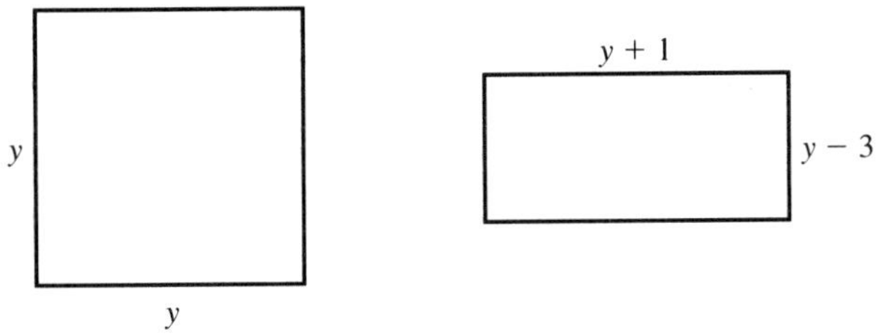

Factors

> Factorise the following (a) $12a - 15b$
> (b) $3x^2 - 2x$
> (c) $2xy + 6y^2$
>
> (a) $12a - 15b = 3(4a - 5b)$
> (b) $3x^2 - 2x = x(3x - 2)$
> (c) $2xy + 6y^2 = 2y(x + 3y)$

Exercise 4

In Questions **1** to **10** copy and complete the statement.

1. $6x + 4y = 2(3x + \quad)$
2. $9x + 12y = 3(\quad + 4y)$
3. $10a + 4b = 2(5a + \quad)$
4. $4x + 12y = 4(\quad + \quad)$
5. $10a + 15b = 5(\quad + \quad)$
6. $18x - 24y = 6(3x - \quad)$
7. $8u - 28v = \quad (\quad - 7v)$
8. $15s + 25t = \quad (3s + \quad)$
9. $24m + 40n = \quad (3m + \quad)$
10. $27c - 72d = \quad (\quad - 8d)$

In Questions **11** to **30** factorise the expression.

11. $20a + 8b$
12. $30x - 24y$
13. $27c - 33d$
14. $35u + 49v$
15. $12s - 32t$
16. $40x - 16t$
17. $24x + 84y$
18. $12x + 8y + 16z$
19. $12a - 6b + 9c$
20. $10x - 20y + 25z$
21. $20a - 12b - 28c$
22. $48m + 8n - 24x$
23. $42x + 49y - 21z$
24. $6x^2 + 15y^2$
25. $20x^2 - 15y^2$
26. $7a^2 + 28b^2$
27. $27a + 63b - 36c$
28. $12x^2 + 24xy + 18y^2$
29. $64p - 72q - 40r$
30. $36x - 60y + 96z$

10.2 Changing the subject of a formula

3/8a

Make x the subject in the formulae below.

(a) $ax - p = t$
$ax = t + p$
$x = \dfrac{t+p}{a}$

(b) $y(x+y) = v^2$
$yx + y^2 = v^2$
$yx = v^2 - y^2$
$x = \dfrac{v^2 - y^2}{y}$

Exercise 5

Make x the subject

1. $x + b = e$
2. $x - t = m$
3. $x - f = a + b$
4. $x + h = A + B$
5. $x + t = y + t$
6. $a + x = b$
7. $k + x = m$
8. $v + x = w + y$
9. $ax = b$
10. $hx = m$
11. $mx = a + b$
12. $kx = c - d$
13. $vx = e + n$
14. $3x = y + z$
15. $xp = r$
16. $xm = h - m$
17. $ax + t = a$
18. $mx - e = k$
19. $ux - h = m$
20. $ex + q = t$
21. $kx - u^2 = v^2$
22. $gx + t^2 = s^2$
23. $xa + k = m^2$
24. $xm - v = m$
25. $a + bx = c$
26. $t + sx = y$
27. $y + cx = z$
28. $a + hx = 2a$
29. $mx - b = b$
30. $kx + ab = cd$
31. $a(x - b) = c$
32. $c(x - d) = e$
33. $m(x + m) = n^2$
34. $k(x - a) = t$
35. $h(x - h) = k$
36. $m(x + b) = n$
37. $a(x - a) = a^2$
38. $c(a + x) = d$
39. $m(b + x) = e$

Formulae involving fractions

Make x the subject in the formulae below.

(a) $\dfrac{x}{a} = p$
$x = ap$

(b) $\dfrac{m}{x} = t$
$m = xt$
$\dfrac{m}{t} = x$

Exercise 6

Make x the subject.

1. $\dfrac{x}{t} = m$
2. $\dfrac{x}{e} = n$
3. $\dfrac{x}{p} = a$
4. $am = \dfrac{x}{t}$
5. $bc = \dfrac{x}{a}$
6. $e = \dfrac{x}{y^2}$

7. $\frac{x}{a} = (b+c)$
8. $\frac{x}{t} = (c-d)$
9. $\frac{x}{m} = s+t$
10. $\frac{x}{k} = h+i$
11. $\frac{x}{b} = \frac{a}{c}$
12. $\frac{x}{m} = \frac{z}{y}$
13. $\frac{x}{h} = \frac{c}{d}$
14. $\frac{m}{n} = \frac{x}{e}$
15. $\frac{b}{e} = \frac{x}{h}$
16. $\frac{x}{(a+b)} = c$
17. $\frac{x}{(h+k)} = m$
18. $\frac{x}{u} = \frac{m}{y}$
19. $\frac{x}{(h-k)} = t$
20. $\frac{x}{(a+b)} = (z+t)$
21. $t = \frac{e}{x}$
22. $a = \frac{e}{x}$
23. $m = \frac{h}{x}$
24. $\frac{a}{b} = \frac{c}{x}$
25. $\frac{u}{x} = \frac{c}{d}$
26. $\frac{m}{x} = t^2$
27. $\frac{h}{x} = \sin 20°$
28. $\frac{e}{x} = \cos 40°$
29. $\frac{m}{x} = \tan 46°$
30. $\frac{a^2}{b^2} = \frac{c^2}{x}$

Formulae with x^2 and negative x terms

Make x the subject of the formulae.

(a)
$$ax^2 = e$$
$$x^2 = \frac{e}{a}$$
$$x = \pm\sqrt{\left(\frac{e}{a}\right)}$$

(b)
$$h - bx = m$$
$$h = m + bx \quad \text{[Make the } x \text{ term positive].}$$
$$h - m = bx$$
$$\frac{h-m}{b} = x$$

Exercise 7

Make x the subject.

1. $cx^2 = h$
2. $bx^2 = f$
3. $x^2t = m$
4. $x^2y = (a+b)$
5. $mx^2 = (t+a)$
6. $x^2 - a = b$
7. $x^2 + c = t$
8. $x^2 + y = z$
9. $x^2 - a^2 = b^2$
10. $x^2 + t^2 = m^2$
11. $x^2 + n^2 = a^2$
12. $ax^2 = c$
13. $hx^2 = n$
14. $cx^2 = z+k$
15. $ax^2 + b = c$
16. $dx^2 - e = h$
17. $gx^2 - n = m$
18. $x^2m + y = z$
19. $a + mx^2 = f$
20. $a^2 + x^2 = b^2$
21. $a - x = y$
22. $h - x = m$
23. $z - x = q$
24. $v = b - x$
25. $m = k - x$
26. $h - cx = d$
27. $y - mx = c$
28. $k - ex = h$
29. $a^2 - bx = d$
30. $m^2 - tx = n^2$
31. $v^2 - ax = w$
32. $y - x = y^2$
33. $k - t^2x = m$
34. $e = b - cx$
35. $z = h - gx$
36. $a + b = c - dx$
37. $y^2 = v^2 - kx$
38. $h = d - fx$
39. $a(b-x) = c$
40. $h(m-x) = n$

Exercise 8

Make the letter in brackets the subject.

1. $ax - d = h$ $[x]$
2. $zy + k = m$ $[y]$
3. $d(y + e) = f$ $[y]$
4. $m(a + k) = d$ $[k]$
5. $a + bm = c$ $[m]$
6. $ae^2 = b$ $[e]$
7. $yt^2 = z$ $[t]$
8. $x^2 - c = e$ $[x]$
9. $my - n = b$ $[y]$
10. $a(z + a) = b$ $[z]$
11. $\frac{a}{x} = d$ $[x]$
12. $\frac{k}{m} = t$ $[k]$
13. $\frac{u}{m} = n$ $[u]$
14. $\frac{y}{x} = d$ $[x]$
15. $\frac{a}{m} = t$ $[m]$
16. $\frac{d}{g} = n$ $[g]$
17. $\frac{t}{k} = (a + b)$ $[t]$
18. $y = \frac{v}{e}$ $[e]$
19. $c = \frac{m}{y}$ $[y]$
20. $\frac{a^2}{m} = b$ $[a]$
21. $g(m + a) = b$ $[m]$
22. $h(h + g) = x^2$ $[g]$
23. $y - t = z$ $[t]$
24. $me^2 = c$ $[e]$
25. $a(y + x) = t$ $[x]$
26. $uv - t^2 = y^2$ $[v]$
27. $k^2 + t = c$ $[k]$
28. $k - w = m$ $[w]$
29. $b - an = c$ $[n]$
30. $m(a + y) = c$ $[y]$
31. $pq - x = ab$ $[x]$
32. $a^2 - bk = t$ $[k]$
33. $v^2z = w$ $[z]$
34. $c = t - u$ $[u]$
35. $xc + t = 2t$ $[c]$
36. $m(n + w) = k$ $[w]$
37. $v - mx = t$ $[m]$
38. $c = a(y + b)$ $[y]$
39. $m(a - c) = e$ $[c]$
40. $ba^2 = c$ $[a]$
41. $\frac{a}{p} = q$ $[p]$
42. $\frac{a}{n^2} = e$ $[n]$
43. $\frac{h}{f^2} = m$ $[f]$
44. $\frac{v}{x^2} = n$ $[x]$
45. $v - ac = t^3$ $[c]$
46. $a(a^2 + y) = b^3$ $[y]$
47. $ah^2 - d = b$ $[h]$
48. $h(h + k) = bc$ $[k]$
49. $u^2 - n^2 = v^2$ $[n]$
50. $m(b - z) = b^3$ $[z]$

Exercise 9

Make x the subject.

1. $a + x = p$
2. $y + x = m$
3. $z = k + x$
4. $u^2 = t^2 + x$
5. $a = bc + mx$
6. $z = k + ax$
7. $u^2 = e^2 + kx$
8. $m(a + x) = b$
9. $h = k(a + x)$
10. $y = p(p + x)$
11. $\frac{x}{k} = y$
12. $\frac{x}{m} = n$
13. $q = \frac{x}{q}$
14. $mn = \frac{x}{n}$
15. $\frac{m}{x} = a$
16. $e = \frac{n}{x}$
17. $w = \frac{u}{x}$
18. $\sin 32° = \frac{e}{x}$
19. $\frac{1}{2}zx = y$
20. $\frac{1}{3}kx = p$
21. $x^2 - n = m$
22. $v + x^2 = a - b$
23. $bx^2 - n = n^2$
24. $a(x - b) = d + e$
25. $k(x^2 - k) = mp$
26. $y - x = m$
27. $e(x - d) = u$
28. $a(y + x) = z$
29. $y(ex - f) = w$
30. $t(m + ax) = m$
31. $\frac{x}{(c + d)} = y$
32. $\frac{(a - b)}{x} = p$

10.3 Direct and inverse proportion

3/8a

Direct proportion

(a) When you buy petrol, the more you buy the more money you have to pay. So if 2·2 litres costs 121p, then 4·4 litres will cost 242p.
We say the cost of petrol is *directly proportional* to the quantity bought.
To show that quantities are proportional, we use the symbol '$\propto$'.
So in our example if the cost of petrol is c pence and the number of litres of petrol is l, we write

$$c \propto l$$

The '$\propto$' sign can always be replaced by '$= k$' where k is a constant.

So $c = kl$

From above, if $c = 121$ when $l = 2{\cdot}2$

so $121 = k \times 2{\cdot}2$

$$k = \frac{121}{2{\cdot}2} = 55$$

We can then write $c = 55l$, and this allows us to find the value of c for any value of l, and *vice versa*.

(b) If a quantity z is proportional to a quantity x, we have

$z \propto x$ or $z = kx$

Two other expressions are sometimes used when quantities are directly proportional. We could say

'z varies as x'

or 'z varies directly as x'.

The graph connecting z and x is a straight line which passes through the origin.

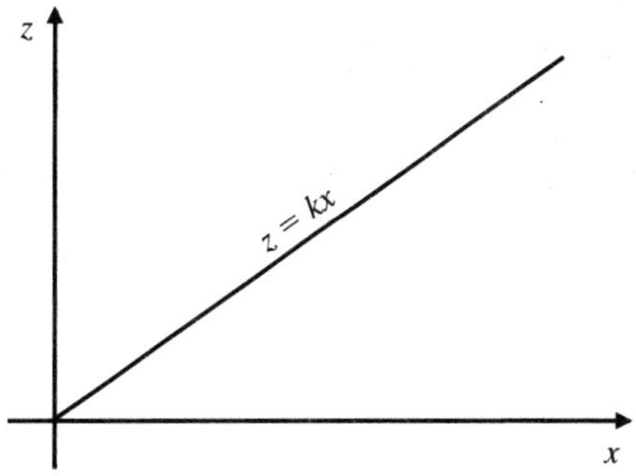

y varies as z, and $y = 2$ when $z = 5$; find

(a) the value of y when $z = 6$
(b) the value of z when $y = 5$

Because $y \propto z$, then $y = kz$ where k is a constant.

$$y = 2 \text{ when } z = 5$$
$$\therefore \quad 2 = k \times 5$$
$$k = \tfrac{2}{5}$$
$$\text{So} \quad y = \tfrac{2}{5}z$$

(a) When $z = 6$, $y = \frac{2}{5} \times 6 = 2\frac{2}{5}$.

(b) When $y = 5$, $5 = \frac{2}{5}z$; $z = \frac{25}{2} = 12\frac{1}{2}$.

The value V of a diamond is proportional to the square of its weight W. If a diamond weighing 10 grams is worth £200, find

(a) the value of a diamond weighing 30 grams
(b) the weight of a diamond worth £5000.

$$V \propto W^2$$

or $V = kW^2$ where k is a constant.

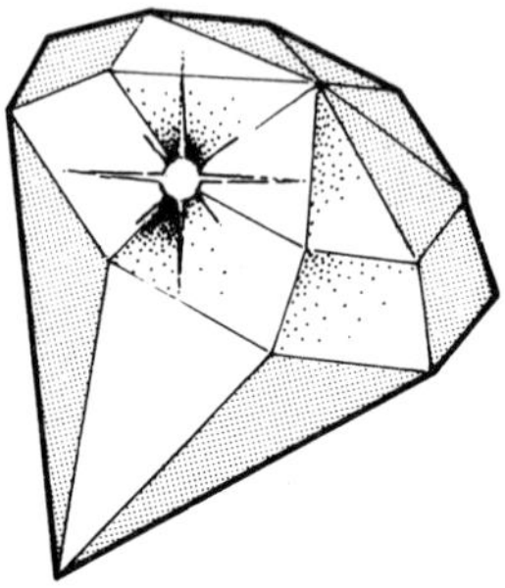

$V = 200$ when $W = 10$

$\therefore \quad 200 = k \times 10^2$

$k = 2$

So $\quad V = 2W^2$

(a) When $W = 30$,

$V = 2 \times 30^2 = 2 \times 900$

$V = £1800$

So a diamond of weight 30 grams is worth £1800.

(b) When $V = 5000$,

$5000 = 2 \times W^2$

$$W^2 = \frac{5000}{2} = 2500$$

$W = \sqrt{2500} = 50$

So a diamond of value £5000 weighs 50 grams.

Exercise 10

1. Rewrite the statement connecting each pair of variables using a constant k instead of '$\propto$'.
   (a) $S \propto e$ (b) $v \propto t$ (c) $x \propto z^2$
   (d) $y \propto \sqrt{x}$ (e) $T \propto \sqrt{L}$

2. y is proportional to t. If $y = 6$ when $t = 4$, calculate
   (a) the value of y, when $t = 6$
   (b) the value of t, when $y = 4$.

3. z is proportional to m. If $z = 20$ when $m = 4$, calculate
   (a) the value of z, when $m = 7$
   (b) the value of m, when $z = 55$.

4. A is proportional to r^2. If $A = 12$, when $r = 2$, calculate
   (a) the value of A, when $r = 5$
   (b) the value of r, when $A = 48$.

5. Given that $z \propto x$, copy and complete the table.

x	1	3		$5\frac{1}{2}$
z	4		16	

6. Given that $V \propto r^3$, copy and complete the table.

r	1	2		$1\frac{1}{2}$
V	4		256	

7. The pressure of the water P at any point below the surface of the sea is proportional to the depth of the point below the surface d. If the pressure is 200 newtons/cm^2 at a depth of 3 m, calculate the pressure at a depth of 5 m.

8. The distance d through which a stone falls from rest is proportional to the square of the time taken t. If the stone falls 45 m in 3 seconds, how far will it fall in 6 seconds?
How long will it take to fall 20 m?

9. The energy E stored in an elastic band is proportional to the square of the extension x. When the elastic is extended by 3 cm, the energy stored is 243 joules. What is the energy stored when the extension is 5 cm?
What is the extension when the stored energy is 36 joules?

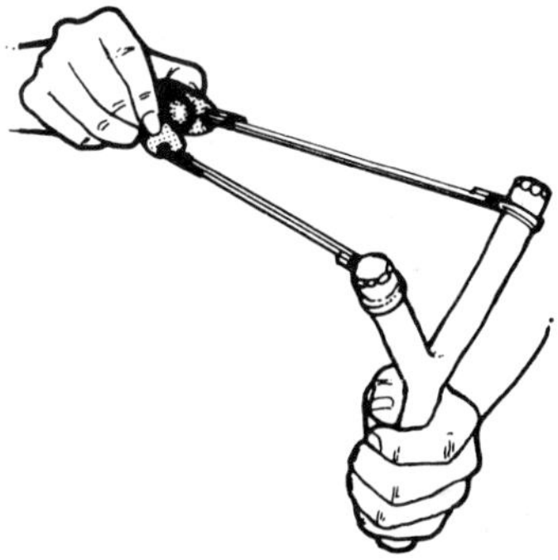

10. The resistance to motion of a car is proportional to the square of the speed of the car. If the resistance is 4000 newtons at a speed of 20 m/s, what is the resistance at a speed of 30 m/s? At what speed is the resistance 6250 newtons?

11. In an experiment, measurements of w and p were taken.

w	2	5	7
p	1·6	25	68·6

Which of these laws fits the results?

$p \propto w, \qquad p \propto w^2, \qquad p \propto w^3.$

12. A road research organisation recently claimed that the damage to road surfaces was proportional to the fourth power of the axle load. The axle load of a 44-ton HGV is about 15 times that of a car. Calculate the ratio of the damage to road surfaces made by a 44-ton HGV and a car.

Inverse proportion

If you travel a distance of 200 m at 10 m/s, the time taken is 20 s.
If you travel the same distance at 20 m/s, the time taken is 10 s.
As you *double* the speed, you *halve* the time taken.
For a fixed journey, the time taken is *inversely proportional* to the speed at which you travel.
If t is inversely proportional to s, we write

$$s \propto \frac{1}{t}$$

or $s = k \times \frac{1}{t}$

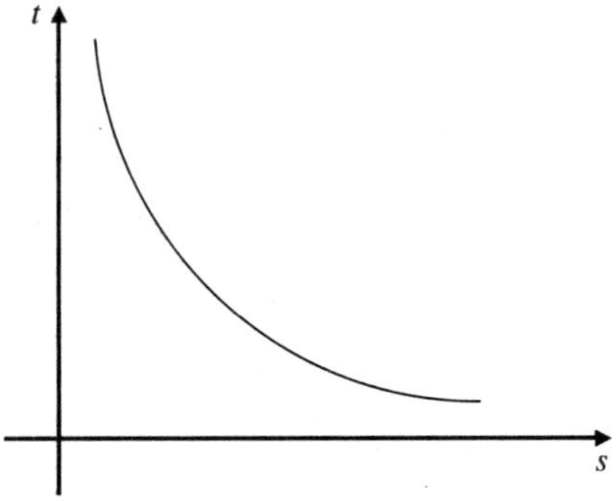

Notice that the product $s \times t$ is constant.
The graph connecting s and t is a curve.

The shape of the curve is the same as $y = \frac{1}{x}$.

Note: Sometimes we write 'x varies inversely as y'.
It means the same as 'x is inversely proportional to y'.

---

z is inversely proportional to t^2 and $z = 4$ when $t = 1$.

Calculate z when $t = 2$

We have $z \propto \frac{1}{t^2}$ or $z = k \times \frac{1}{t^2}$ (k is a constant)

$z = 4$ when $t = 1$,

$\therefore \quad 4 = k\left(\frac{1}{1^2}\right)$

so $k = 4$

$\therefore \quad z = 4 \times \frac{1}{t^2}$

When $t = 2$, $z = 4 \times \frac{1}{2^2} = 1$.

Exercise 11

1. Rewrite the statements connecting the variables using a constant of variation, k.

(a) $x \propto \frac{1}{y}$ (b) $s \propto \frac{1}{t^2}$ (c) $t \propto \frac{1}{\sqrt{q}}$

(d) m varies inversely as w

(e) z is inversely proportional to t^2.

2. b is inversely proportional to e. If $b = 6$ when $e = 2$, calculate
(a) the value of b when $e = 12$
(b) the value of e when $b = 3$.

3. x is inversely proportional to y^2. If $x = 4$ when $y = 3$, calculate
(a) the value of x when $y = 1$
(b) the value of y when $x = 2\frac{1}{4}$.

4. p is inversely proportional to $\sqrt{y}$. If $p = 1{\cdot}2$ when $y = 100$, calculate
(a) the value of p when $y = 4$
(b) the value of y when $p = 3$.

5. Given that $z \propto \frac{1}{y}$, copy and complete the table:

y	2	4		$\frac{1}{4}$
z	8		16	

6. Given that $v \propto \frac{1}{t^2}$, copy and complete the table:

t	2	5		10
v	25		$\frac{1}{4}$	

7. The volume V of a given mass of gas varies inversely as the pressure P. When $V = 2\ \text{m}^3$, $P = 500\ \text{N/m}^2$. Find the volume when the pressure is $400\ \text{N/m}^2$. Find the pressure when the volume is $5\ \text{m}^3$.

8. The number of hours N required to dig a certain hole is inversely proportional to the number of men available x.

When 6 men are digging, the hole takes 4 hours. Find the time taken when 8 men are available. If it takes $\frac{1}{2}$ hour to dig the hole, how many men are there?

9. The force of attraction F between two magnets varies inversely as the square of the distance d between them. When the magnets are 2 cm apart, the force of attraction is 18 newtons. How far apart are they if the attractive force is 2 newtons?

10. The life expectancy L of a rat varies inversely as the square of the density d of poison distributed around his home.

When the density of poison is 1 g/m^2 the life expectancy is 50 days. How long will he survive if the density of poison is

(a) 5 g/m^2? (b) $\frac{1}{2}$ g/m^2?

11. When cooking snacks in a microwave oven, a French chef assumes that the cooking time is inversely proportional to the power used. The five levels on his microwave have the powers shown in the table.

Level	Power used
Full	600 W
Roast	400 W
Simmer	200 W
Defrost	100 W
Warm	50 W

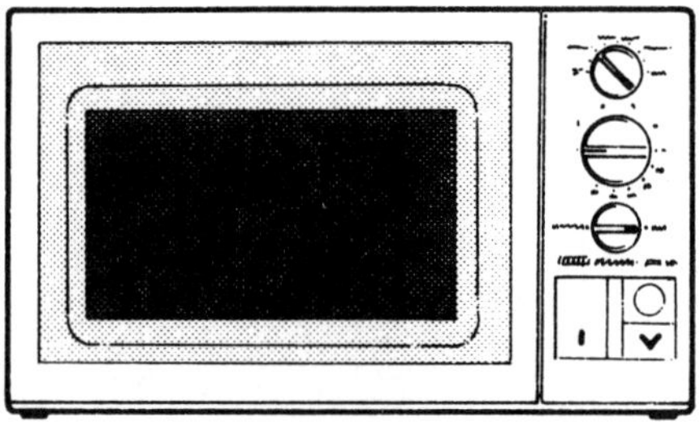

(a) Escargots de Bourgogne take 5 minutes on 'Simmer'. How long will they take on 'Warm'?
(b) Escargots à la Provençale are normally cooked on 'Roast' for 3 minutes. How long will they take on 'Full'?

10.4 Inequalities and regions

3/7b, 3/8b

Symbols:

Here is the meaning of inequality symbols used.

$x < 4$ means 'x is *less than* 4'
$y > 7$ means 'y is *greater than* 7'
$z \leqslant 10$ means 'z is *less than or equal to* 10'
$t \geqslant -3$ means 't is *greater than or equal to* -3'

With two symbols in one statement look at each part separately. For example, if n is an *integer* and $3 < n \leqslant 7$, n has to be greater than 3 but at the same time it has to be less than or equal to 7.

So n could be 4, 5, 6 or 7 only.

Solving inequalities

We follow the same procedure used for solving equations except that when we multiply or divide by a *negative* number the inequality is *reversed.*

e.g. $4 > -2$ but multiplying by -2, $-8 < 4$

It is best to avoid dividing by a negative number as in the following example.

Solve the inequalities

(a) $2x - 1 > 5$

$2x > 5 + 1$

$x > \frac{6}{2}$

$x > 3$

(b) $5 - 3x \leqslant 1$

$5 \leqslant 1 + 3x$

$5 - 1 \leqslant 3x$

$\frac{4}{3} \leqslant x$

Exercise 12

Solve the following inequalities:

1. $x - 3 > 10$
2. $x + 1 < 0$
3. $5 > x - 7$
4. $2x + 1 \leqslant 6$
5. $3x - 4 > 5$
6. $10 \leqslant 2x - 6$
7. $5x < x + 1$
8. $2x \geqslant x - 3$
9. $4 + x < -4$
10. $3x + 1 < 2x + 5$
11. $2(x + 1) > x - 7$
12. $7 < 15 - x$
13. $9 > 12 - x$
14. $4 - 2x \leqslant 2$
15. $3(x - 1) < 2(1 - x)$
16. $7 - 3x < 0$
17. $\frac{x}{3} < -1$
18. $\frac{2x}{5} > 3$
19. $2x > 0$
20. $\frac{x}{4} < 0$

(Hint: in Questions **21** to **25**, solve the two inequalities separately.)

21. $10 \leqslant 2x \leqslant x + 9$
22. $x < 3x + 2 < 2x + 6$
23. $10 \leqslant 2x - 1 \leqslant x + 5$
24. $3 < 3x - 1 < 2x + 7$
25. $x - 10 < 2(x - 1) < x$

Squares and square roots in inequalities need care.

The equation $x^2 = 4$ becomes $x = \pm 2$, which is correct.
We would say $x = \pm 2$, which is correct.

For the inequality $x^2 < 4$, we might wrongly write $x < \pm 2$.
Consider $x = -3$, say.
-3 is less than -2 and is also less than $+2$.
But $(-3)^2$ is not less than 4 and so
$x = -3$ does not satisfy the inequality $x^2 < 4$.

The correct solution for $x^2 < 4$
is $-2 < x < 2$

Solve the inequality $2x^2 - 1 > 17$

$$2x^2 - 1 > 17$$
$$2x^2 > 18$$
$$x^2 > 9$$
$$x > 3 \text{ or } x < -3$$

[Avoid the temptation to write $x > \pm 3$]!

Exercise 13

Solve the inequalities.

1. $x^2 < 25$
2. $x^2 \leqslant 16$
3. $x^2 > 1$
4. $2x^2 \geqslant 72$
5. $3x^2 + 5 > 5$
6. $5x^2 - 2 < 18$

For Questions **7** to **13**, list the solutions which satisfy the given condition.

7. $3a + 1 < 20$; a is a positive integer.

8. $b - 1 \geqslant 6$; b is a prime number less than 20.

9. $1 < z < 50$; z is a square number.

10. $2x > -10$; x is a negative integer.

11. $x + 1 < 2x < x + 13$; x is an integer.

12. $0 \leqslant 2z - 3 \leqslant z + 8$; z is a prime number.

13. $\frac{a}{2} + 10 > a$; a is a positive even number.

14. Given that $4x > 1$ and $\frac{x}{3} \leqslant 1\frac{1}{3}$, list the possible integer values of x.

15. State the smallest integer n for which $4n > 19$.

16. Given that $-4 \leqslant a \leqslant 3$ and $-5 \leqslant b \leqslant 4$, find
(a) the largest possible value of a^2
(b) the smallest possible value of ab
(c) the largest possible value of ab
(d) the value of b if $b^2 = 25$

17. For any shape of triangle ABC, complete the statement AB + BC □ AC, by writing $<, >$ or $=$ inside the box.

18. Find a simple fraction r such at $\frac{1}{3} < r < \frac{2}{3}$.

19. Find the largest prime number p such that $p^2 < 400$.

20. Find the integer n such that $n < \sqrt{300} < n + 1$.

21. If $f(x) = 2x - 1$ and $g(x) = 10 - x$ for what values of x is $f(x) > g(x)$?

22. If $2^r > 100$, what is the smallest integer value of r?

23. Given $\left(\frac{1}{3}\right)^x < \frac{1}{200}$, what is the smallest integer value of x?

24. Find the smallest integer value of x which satisfies $x^x > 10\,000$.

25. What integer values of x satisfy
$100 < 5^x < 10\,000$?

Shading regions

It is useful to represent inequalities on a graph, particularly where two variables (x and y) are involved.

Draw a sketch graph and shade the area which represents the set of points that satisfy each of these inequalities.

(a) $x > 2$ (b) $1 \leqslant y \leqslant 5$ (c) $x + y \leqslant 8$

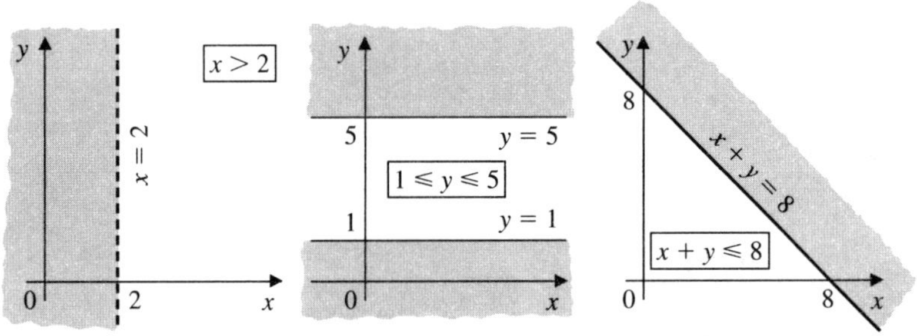

In each graph, the unwanted region is shaded. This is done to make it clearer when several regions are shown on the same diagram.

In (a), the line $x = 2$ is shown as a broken line to indicate that the points on the line are not included.

In (b) and (c) points on the line *are* included 'in the region' and the lines are drawn unbroken.

To decide which side to shade when the line is sloping, we take a *trial point*. This can be any point which is not actually on the line.

In (c) above, the trial point could be (1, 1).

Is (1, 1) in the region $x + y \leqslant 8$?
It satisfies $x + y < 8$ because $1 + 1 = 2$, which is less than 8.
So below the line is $x + y < 8$. We have shaded the unwanted region.

Exercise 14

In Questions **1** to **6**, describe the region left unshaded.

1.

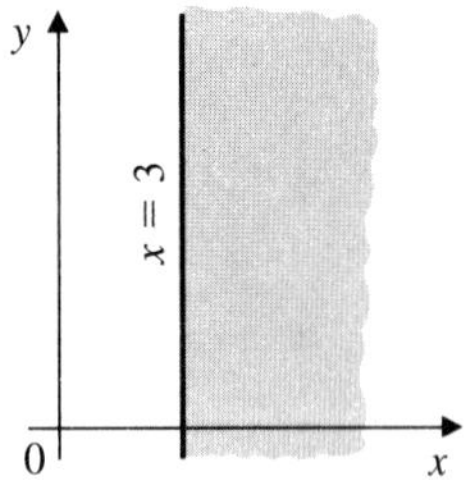

2.

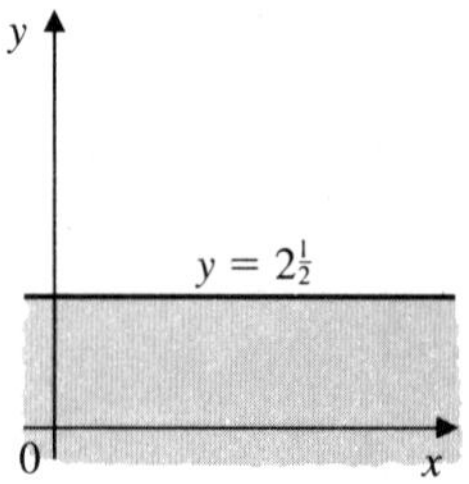

3.

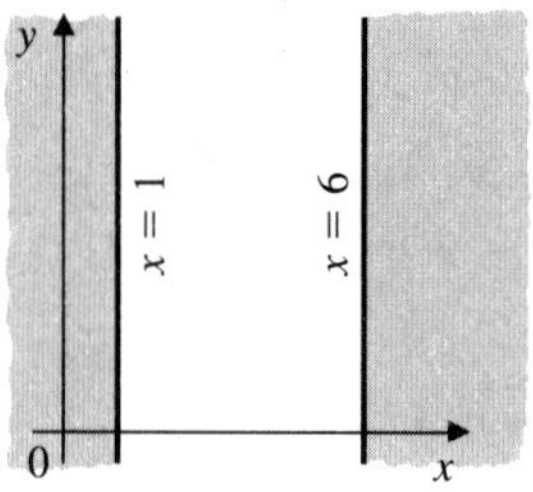

4.

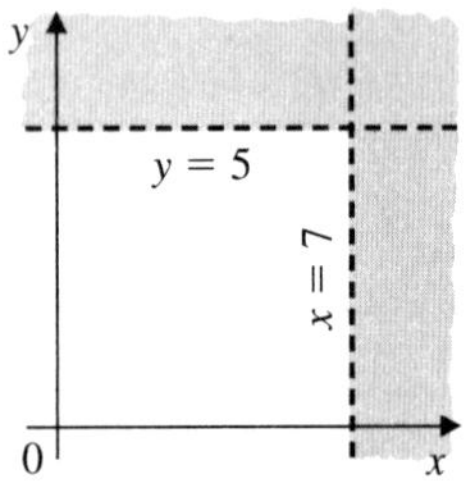

5.

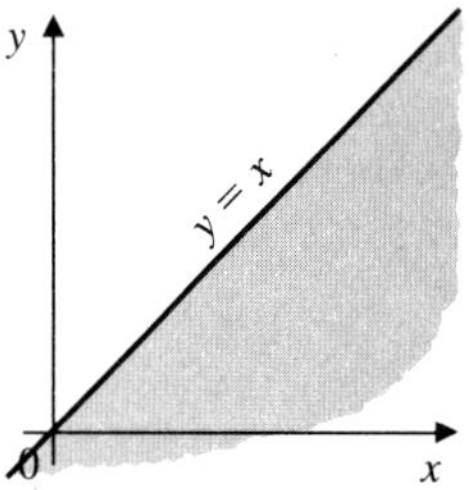

6.

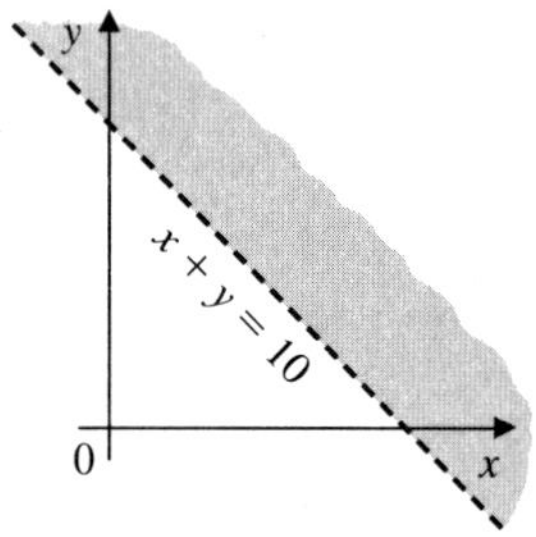

7. The point (1, 1), marked *, lies in the unshaded region. Use this as a trial point to describe the unshaded region.

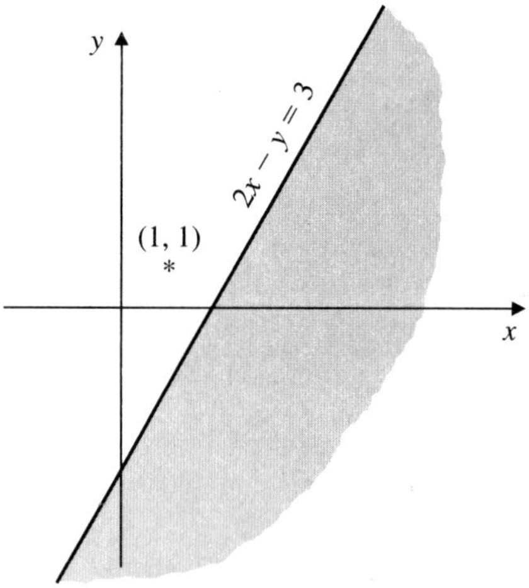

8. The point (3, 1), marked *, lies in the unshaded triangle. Use this as a trial point to write down the three inequalities which describe the unshaded region.

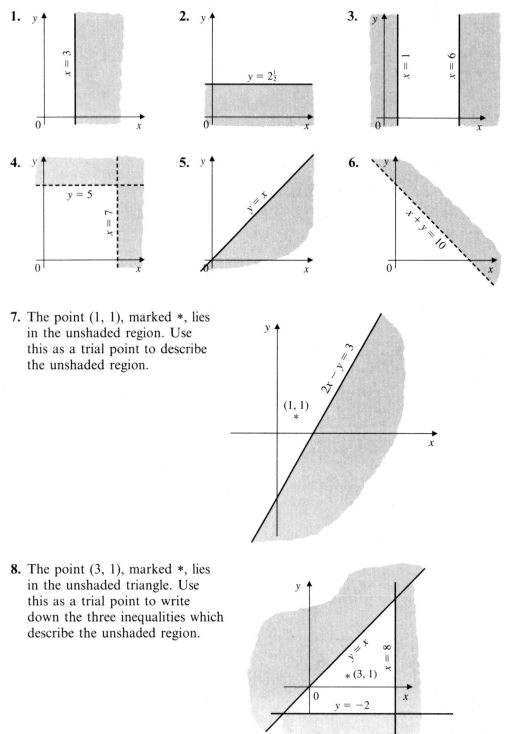

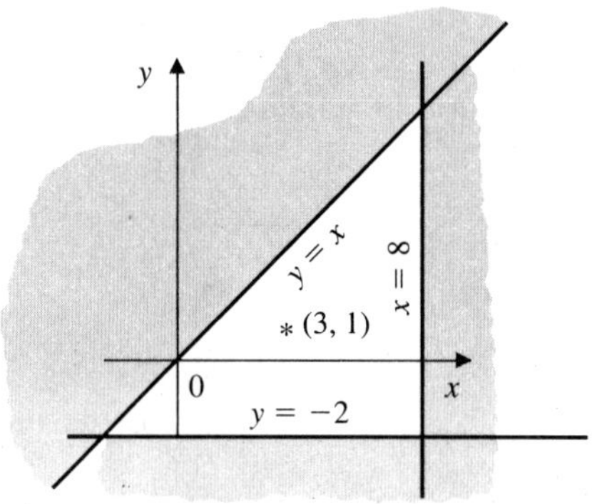

9. A trial point (1, 1) lies inside the unshaded triangles. Write down the three inequalities which describe each unshaded region.

(a)

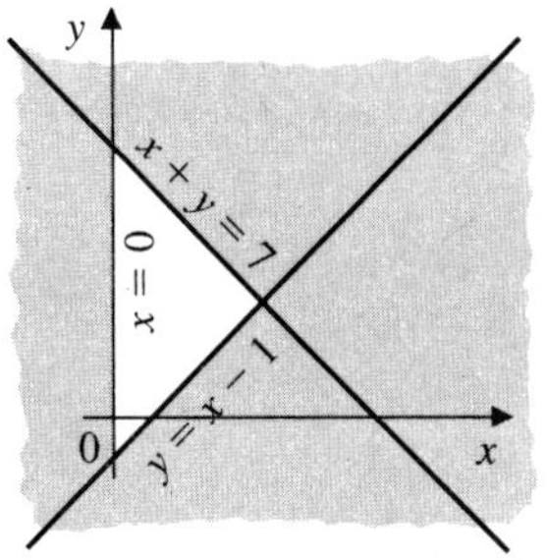

(b)

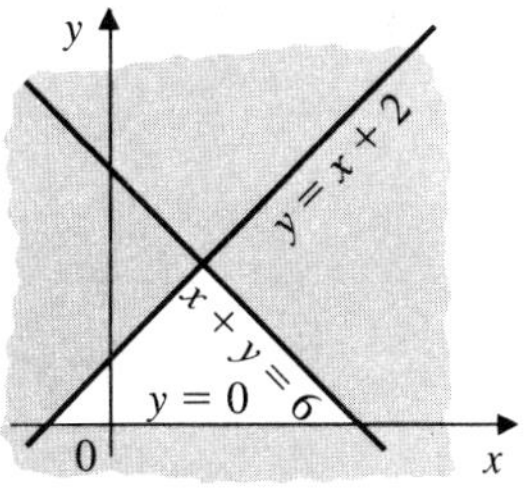

For Questions **10** to **27**, draw a sketch graph similar to those above and indicate the set of points which satisfy the inequalities by shading the unwanted region.

10. $2 < x < 7$

11. $0 < y < 3\frac{1}{2}$

12. $-2 < x < 2$

13. $x < 6$ and $y < 4$

14. $0 < x < 5$ and $y < 3$

15. $1 < x < 6$ and $2 < y < 8$

16. $-3 < x < 0$ and $-4 < y < 2$

17. $y < x$

18. $x + y < 5$

19. $y > x + 2$ and $y < 7$

20. $x > 0$ and $y > 0$ and $x + y < 7$

21. $x > 0$ and $x + y < 10$ and $y > x$

22. $8 > y > 0$ and $x + y > 3$

23. $x + 2y < 10$ and $x > 0$ and $y > 0$

24. $3x + 2y < 18$ and $x > 0$ and $y > 0$

25. $x > 0$, $y > x - 2$, $x + y < 10$

26. $3x + 5y < 30$ and $y > \dfrac{x}{2}$

27. $y > \dfrac{x}{2}$, $y < 2x$ and $x + y < 8$

28. The two lines $y = x + 1$ and $x + y = 5$ divide the graph into four regions A, B, C, D.

Write down the two inequalities which describe each of the regions A, B, C, D.

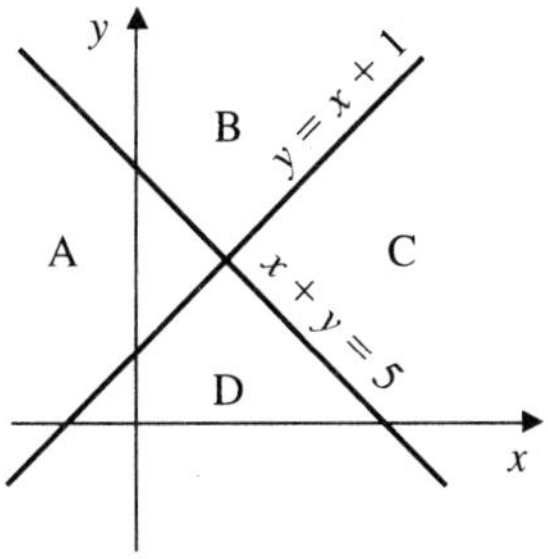

29. Using the same axes, draw the graphs of $xy = 10$ and $x + y = 9$ for values of x from 1 to 10.
Hence find all pairs of positive integers whose product is greater than 10 and whose sum is less than 9.

10.5 Sketching graphs

3/8a, 3/8c

Gradient

The gradient of a straight line is a measure of how steep it is.

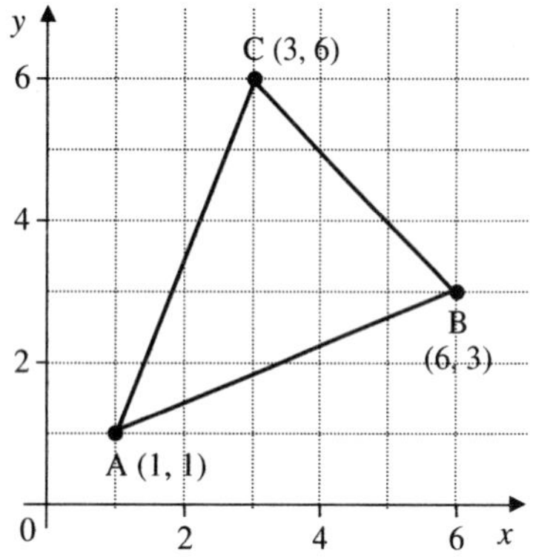

Gradient of line AB $= \frac{3-1}{6-1} = \frac{2}{5}$.

Gradient of line AC $= \frac{6-1}{3-1} = \frac{5}{2}$.

Gradient of line BC $= \frac{6-3}{3-6} = -1$.

A line which slopes upwards to the right has a *positive* gradient.

A line which slopes upwards to the left has a *negative* gradient.

$$\text{Gradient} = \frac{\text{difference in } y\text{-coordinates}}{\text{difference in } x\text{-coordinates}}$$

Exercise 15

1. Find the gradients of AB, BC, AC.

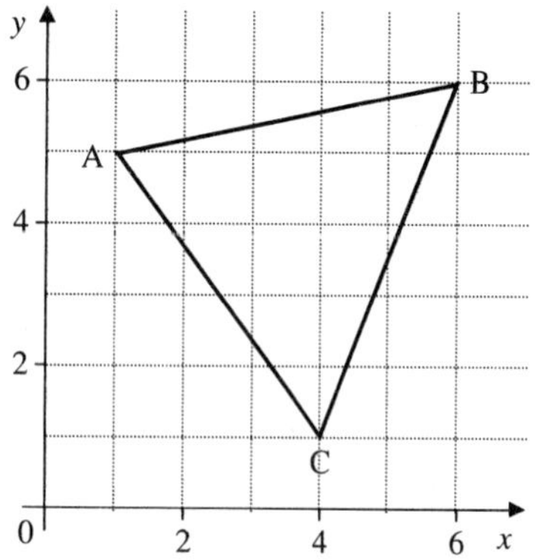

2. Find the gradients of PQ, PR, QR.

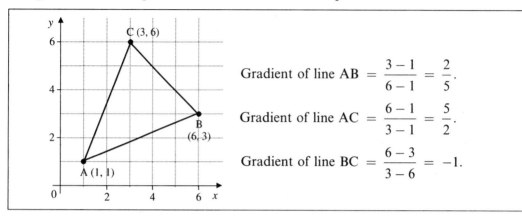

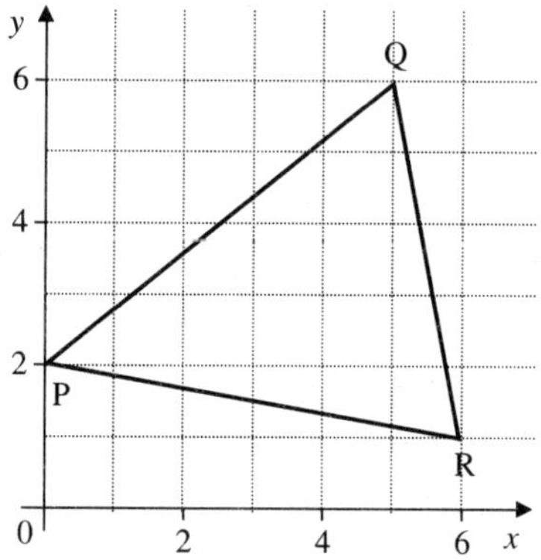

3. Find the gradients of the lines joining the following pairs of points:

(a) $(5, 2) \rightarrow (7, 8)$ (b) $(-1, 3) \rightarrow (1, 6)$

(c) $(\frac{1}{2}, 1) \rightarrow (\frac{3}{4}, 2)$ (d) $(3{\cdot}1, 2) \rightarrow (3{\cdot}2, 2{\cdot}5)$

4. Find the value of a if the line joining the points $(3a, 4)$ and $(a, -3)$ has a gradient of 1.

5. (a) Write down the gradient of the line joining the points $(2m, n)$ and $(3, -4)$,
(b) Find the value of n if the line is parallel to the x-axis,
(c) Find the value of m if the line is parallel to the y-axis.

The form $y = mx + c$

Here are two straight lines.

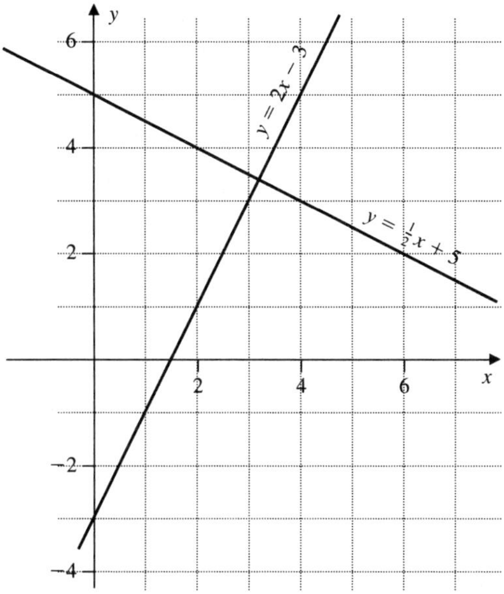

For $y = 2x - 3$, the gradient is 2 and the y-intercept is -3.

For $y = -\frac{1}{2}x + 5$, the gradient is $-\frac{1}{2}$ and the y-intercept is 5.

These two lines illustrate a general rule.
When the equation of a straight line is written in the form $y = mx + c$, the gradient of the line is m and the intercept on the y-axis is c.

Draw the line $y = 2x + 3$ on a sketch graph.

The word 'sketch' implies that we do not plot a series of points but simply show the position and slope of the line.

The line $y = 2x + 3$ has a gradient of 2 and cuts the y-axis at $(0, 3)$.

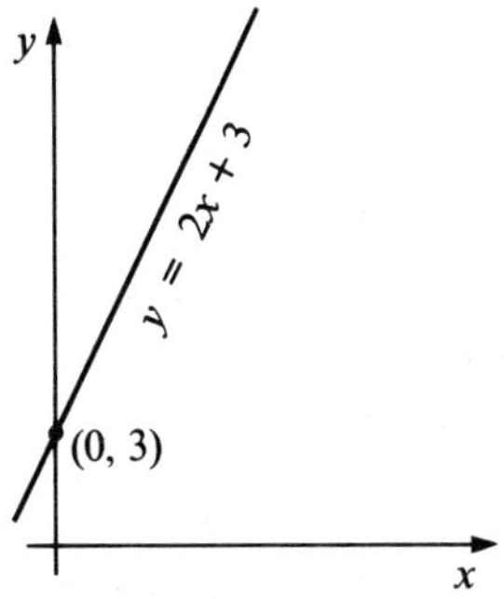

Draw the line $x + 2y - 6 = 0$ on a sketch graph.

(a) Rearrange the equation to make y the subject.

$$x + 2y - 6 = 0$$
$$2y = -x + 6$$
$$y = -\tfrac{1}{2}x + 3.$$

(b) The line has a gradient of $-\tfrac{1}{2}$ and cuts the y-axis at (0, 3).

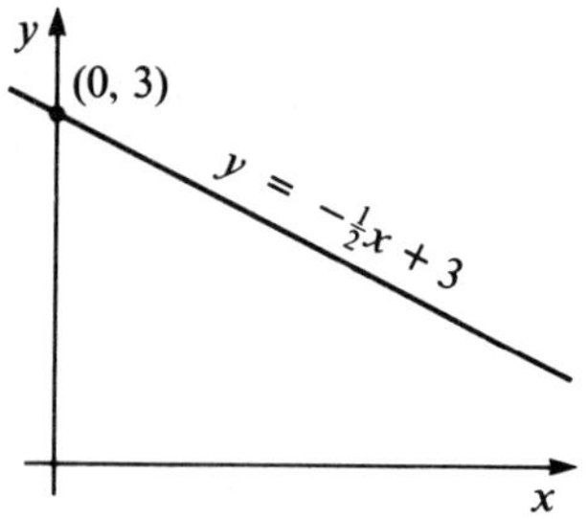

Exercise 16

In Questions **1** to **20**, find the gradient of the line and the intercept on the y-axis. Hence draw a small sketch graph of each line.

1. $y = x + 3$ **2.** $y = x - 2$ **3.** $y = 2x + 1$
4. $y = 2x - 5$ **5.** $y = 3x + 4$ **6.** $y = \tfrac{1}{2}x + 6$
7. $y = 3x - 2$ **8.** $y = 2x$ **9.** $y = \tfrac{1}{4}x - 4$
10. $y = -x + 3$ **11.** $y = 6 - 2x$ **12.** $y = 2 - x$
13. $y + 2x = 3$ **14.** $3x + y + 4 = 0$ **15.** $2y - x = 6$
16. $3y + x - 9 = 0$ **17.** $4x - y = 5$ **18.** $3x - 2y = 8$
19. $10x - y = 0$ **20.** $y - 4 = 0$

21. Find the equations of the lines A and B.

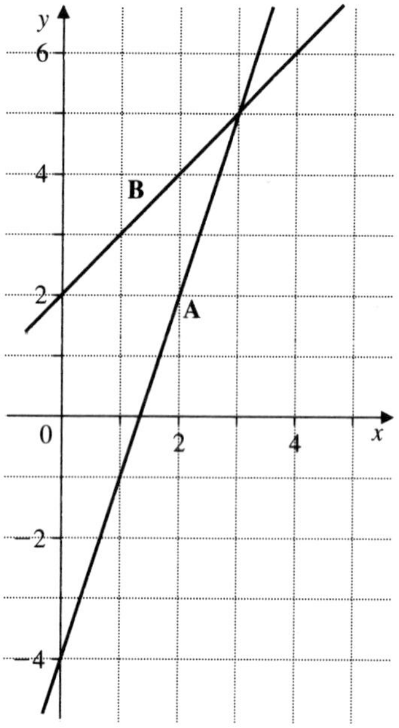

22. Find the equations of the lines C and D.

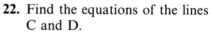

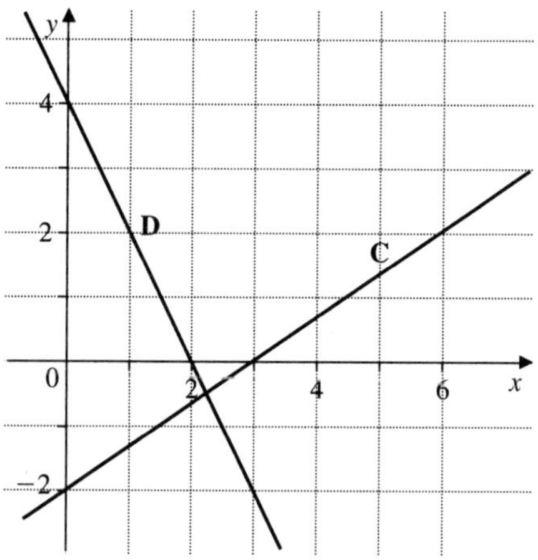

11 Number 3

11.1 Index notation

2/7b, 3/7a, 2/8a

Indices are used as a mathematical shorthand.

(a) $2 \times 2 \times 2 \times 2 = 2^4$

(b) $5 \times 5 \times 5 = 5^3$

(c) $7 \times 7 \times 2 \times 2 \times 2 = 7^2 \times 2^3$

(d) $3 \times 3 \times 3 \times 3 \times 10 \times 10 = 3^4 \times 10^2$

(e) Express 6930 as a product of primes.

$2\overline{)69^1 3^1 0}$	(divide by 2)
$3\overline{)34^1 6^1 5}$	(divide by 3)
$3\overline{)11^2 5^1 5}$	(divide by 2)
$5\overline{)\ 3\ 8^3 5}$	(divide by 5)
$7\overline{)\ \ 77}$	(divide by 7)
11	(stop because 11 is prime)

$\therefore\ 6930 = 2 \times 3 \times 3 \times 5 \times 7 \times 11$

Exercise 1

Write in a form using indices.

1. $3 \times 3 \times 3 \times 3$

2. 5×5

3. $6 \times 6 \times 6$

4. $10 \times 10 \times 10 \times 10 \times 10$

5. $1 \times 1 \times 1 \times 1 \times 1 \times 1 \times 1$

6. $8 \times 8 \times 8 \times 8$

7. $7 \times 7 \times 7 \times 7 \times 7 \times 7$

8. $2 \times 2 \times 2 \times 5 \times 5$

9. $3 \times 3 \times 7 \times 7 \times 7 \times 7$

10. $3 \times 3 \times 10 \times 10 \times 10$

11. $5 \times 5 \times 5 \times 5 \times 11 \times 11$

12. $2 \times 3 \times 2 \times 3 \times 3$

13. $5 \times 3 \times 3 \times 5 \times 5$

14. $2 \times 2 \times 3 \times 3 \times 3 \times 11 \times 11$

15. Express each of the following numbers as a product of primes.
(a) 600 (b) 693 (c) 2464
(d) 3510 (e) 4000 (f) 22 540

16. (a) Write the number 576 as a product of its prime factors.
(b) Without a calculator, work out the square root of 576.
(c) Given that $99\,225 = 3 \times 3 \times 3 \times 3 \times 5 \times 5 \times 7 \times 7$ work out the square root of 99 225 (without a calculator of course!).

17. (a) Express 1008 and 840 as products of their prime factors.
(b) Find the H.C.F. (highest common factor) of 1008 and 840.
(c) Find the smallest number which can be multiplied by 1008 to give a square number.

18. If you take a piece of paper, fold it and then cut along the fold, you will have 2 pieces.

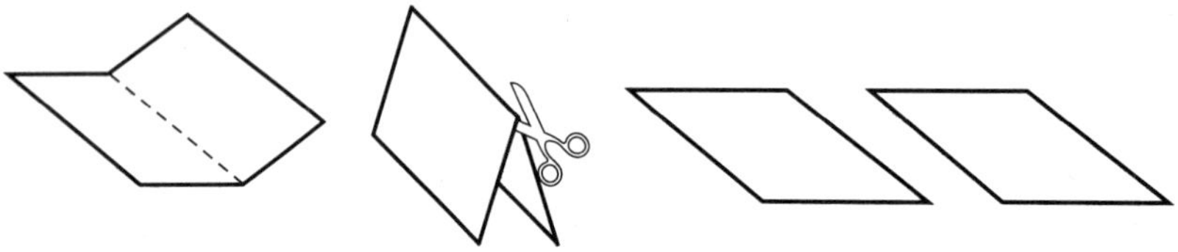

If you take the two pieces, fold them and then cut along the fold you will have 4 pieces.
After another 'fold and cut', you will have 8 pieces.
(a) After 20 'fold and cuts' *estimate* how many sheets you will have.

A	B	C	D	E
100	1000	10 000	100 000	1 000 000

(b) Now work it out as follows:
After 1 'fold and cut' you have $2\ (= 2^1)$ pieces.
After 2 'fold and cuts' you have $4\ (= 2^2)$ pieces.
After 3 'fold and cuts' you have $8\ (= 2^3)$ pieces.
So after 20 'fold and cuts' you have ______ pieces.

19. In a laboratory, we start with 2 cells in a dish. The number of cells in the dish doubles every 30 minutes.
(a) How many cells are in the dish after four hours?
(b) After what time are there 2^{13} cells in the dish?
(c) After $10\frac{1}{2}$ hours there are 2^{22} cells in the dish and an experimental fluid is added which eliminates half of the cells.
How many cells are left?

20. Solve the equations for x.
(a) $2^x = 8$ (b) $3^x = 81$ (c) $5^{2x} = 125$

21. Find two solutions to the equation $x^2 = 2^x$.

Negative indices

$$2^{-3} = \frac{1}{2^3} = \frac{1}{8} \qquad 3^{-2} = \frac{1}{3^2} = \frac{1}{9}$$

In general, $x^{-5} = \frac{1}{x^5}$

Exercise 2

In Questions **1** to **12**, work out the value of the number given.

1. 2^{-2} **2.** 4^{-2} **3.** 10^{-2} **4.** 1^{-4}
5. 3^{-3} **6.** 4^{-3} **7.** 10^{-3} **8.** 5^{-2}
9. 7^{-2} **10.** 5^{-3} **11.** 9^{-2} **12.** 1^{-7}

In Questions **13** to **30** answer 'true' or 'false'.

13. $2^3 = 8$ **14.** $3^2 = 6$ **15.** $5^3 = 125$ **16.** $2^{-1} = \frac{1}{2}$
17. $10^{-2} = \frac{1}{20}$ **18.** $3^{-3} = \frac{1}{9}$ **19.** $2^2 > 2^3$ **20.** $2^3 < 3^2$
21. $2^{-2} > 2^{-3}$ **22.** $3^{-2} < 3^3$ **23.** $1^9 = 9$ **24.** $(-3)^2 = -9$
25. $5^{-2} = \frac{1}{10}$ **26.** $10^{-3} = \frac{1}{1000}$ **27.** $10^{-2} > 10^{-3}$ **28.** $5^{-1} = 0{\cdot}2$
29. $10^{-1} = 0{\cdot}1$ **30.** $2^{-2} = 0{\cdot}25$

Multiplying and dividing

$3^2 \times 3^4 = (3 \times 3) \times (3 \times 3 \times 3 \times 3) = 3^6$

$2^3 \times 2^2 = (2 \times 2 \times 2) \times (2 \times 2) = 2^5$

$7^3 \times 7^5 = 7^8$ [add the indices].

$$2^4 \div 2^2 = \frac{2 \times 2 \times 2 \times 2}{2 \times 2} = 2^2$$

$$\left.\begin{array}{l} 5^6 \div 5^2 = 5^4 \\ 7^8 \div 7^3 = 7^5 \end{array}\right\} \text{[subtract the indices].}$$

Exercise 3

Write in a more simple form.

1. $5^2 \times 5^4$ **2.** $6^3 \times 6^2$ **3.** $10^4 \times 10^5$ **4.** $7^5 \times 7^3$
5. $3^6 \times 3^4$ **6.** $8^3 \times 8^3$ **7.** $2^3 \times 2^{10}$ **8.** $3^6 \times 3^{-2}$
9. $5^4 \times 5^{-1}$ **10.** $7^7 \times 7^{-3}$ **11.** $5^{-3} \times 5^5$ **12.** $3^{-2} \times 3^{-2}$
13. $6^{-3} \times 6^8$ **14.** $5^{-2} \times 5^{-8}$ **15.** $7^{-3} \times 7^9$ **16.** $7^4 \div 7^2$
17. $6^7 \div 6^2$ **18.** $8^5 \div 8^4$ **19.** $5^{10} \div 5^2$ **20.** $10^7 \div 10^5$
21. $9^6 \div 9^8$ **22.** $3^8 \div 3^{10}$ **23.** $2^6 \div 2^2$ **24.** $3^3 \div 3^5$
25. $7^2 \div 7^8$ **26.** $3^{-2} \div 3^2$ **27.** $5^{-3} \div 5^2$ **28.** $8^{-1} \div 8^4$
29. $5^{-4} \div 5^1$ **30.** $6^2 \div 6^{-2}$

11.2 Standard form

2/8a

When dealing with either very large or very small numbers, it is not convenient to write them out in full in the normal way. It is better to use standard form. Most calculators represent large and small numbers in this way.

This calculator shows $2{\cdot}3 \times 10^8$.

The number $a \times 10^n$ is in standard form when $1 \leq a < 10$ and n is a positive or negative integer.

Write the following numbers in standard form:

(a) $2000 = 2 \times 1000 = 2 \times 10^3$

(b) $150 = 1{\cdot}5 \times 100 = 1{\cdot}5 \times 10^2$

(c) $0{\cdot}0004 = 4 \times \dfrac{1}{10\,000} = 4 \times 10^{-4}$

Exercise 4

Write the following numbers in standard form:

1. 4000	**2.** 500	**3.** 70 000
4. 60	**5.** 2400	**6.** 380
7. 46 000	**8.** 46	**9.** 900 000
10. 2560	**11.** 0·007	**12.** 0·0004
13. 0·0035	**14.** 0·421	**15.** 0·000 055
16. 0·01	**17.** 564 000	**18.** 19 million

19. The population of China is estimated at 1 100 000 000. Write this in standard form.

20. A hydrogen atom weighs 0·000 000 000 000 000 000 000 001 67 grams. Write this weight in standard form.

21. The area of the surface of the Earth is about 510 000 000 km^2. Express this in standard form.

22. A certain virus is 0·000 000 000 25 cm in diameter. Write this in standard form.

23. Avogadro's number is 602 300 000 000 000 000 000 000. Express this in standard form.

24. The speed of light is 300 000 km/s. Express this speed in cm/s in standard form.

25. A very rich oil sheikh leaves his fortune of £$3{\cdot}6 \times 10^8$ to be divided between his 100 children.

How much does each child receive? Give the answer in standard form.

Work out $1500 \times 8\,000\,000$

$$1500 \times 8\,000\,000 = (1{\cdot}5 \times 10^3) \times (8 \times 10^6)$$
$$= 12 \times 10^9$$
$$= 1{\cdot}2 \times 10^{10}$$

Notice that we multiply the numbers and the powers of 10 separately.

Many calculators have an [EXP] button which is used for standard form.

(a) To enter $1{\cdot}6 \times 10^7$ into the calculator:

press [1·6] [EXP] [7]

(b) To enter $3{\cdot}8 \times 10^{-3}$

press [3·8] [EXP] [3] [+/−]

(c) To calculate $(4{\cdot}9 \times 10^{11}) \div (3{\cdot}5 \times 10^{-4})$:

[4·9] [EXP] [11] [÷] [3·5] [EXP] [4] [+/−] [=]

The answer is $1{\cdot}4 \times 10^{15}$.

Exercise 5

In Questions **1** to **22**, give the answer in standard form.

1. 5000×3000
2. $60\,000 \times 5000$
3. $0{\cdot}000\,07 \times 400$
4. $0{\cdot}0007 \times 0{\cdot}000\,01$
5. $8000 \div 0{\cdot}004$
6. $(0{\cdot}002)^2$
7. $150 \times 0{\cdot}0006$
8. $0{\cdot}000\,033 \div 500$
9. $0{\cdot}007 \div 20\,000$
10. $(0{\cdot}0001)^4$
11. $(2000)^3$
12. $0{\cdot}005\,92 \div 8000$
13. $(1{\cdot}4 \times 10^7) \times (3{\cdot}5 \times 10^4)$
14. $(8{\cdot}8 \times 10^{10}) \div (2 \times 10^{-2})$
15. $(1{\cdot}2 \times 10^{11}) \div (8 \times 10^7)$
16. $(4 \times 10^5) \times (5 \times 10^{11})$

17. $(2{\cdot}1 \times 10^{-3}) \times (8 \times 10^{15})$

18. $(8{\cdot}5 \times 10^{14}) \div 2000$

19. $(3{\cdot}3 \times 10^{12}) \times (3 \times 10^{-5})$

20. $(2{\cdot}5 \times 10^{-8})^2$

21. $(1{\cdot}2 \times 10^{5})^2 \div (5 \times 10^{-3})$

22. $(6{\cdot}2 \times 10^{-4}) \times (1{\cdot}1 \times 10^{-3})$

23. If $a = 512 \times 10^2$
$b = 0{\cdot}478 \times 10^6$
$c = 0{\cdot}0049 \times 10^7$
arrange a, b and c in order of size (smallest first).

24. If the number $2{\cdot}74 \times 10^{15}$ is written out in full, how many zeros follow the 4?

25. If the number $7{\cdot}31 \times 10^{-17}$ is written out in full, how many zeros would there be between the decimal point and the first significant figure?

26. If $x = 2 \times 10^5$ and $y = 3 \times 10^{-3}$, find the values of

(i) xy (ii) $\dfrac{x}{y}$

27. Oil flows through a pipe at a rate of $40\,\text{m}^3/\text{s}$. How long will it take to fill a tank of volume $1{\cdot}2 \times 10^5\,\text{m}^3$?

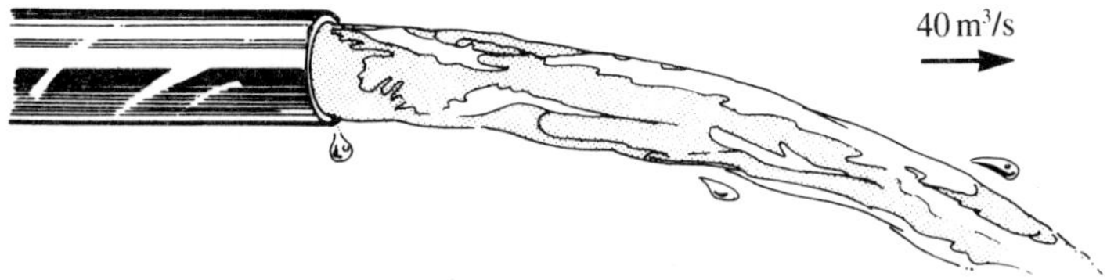

28. Given that $L = 2\sqrt{\dfrac{a}{k}}$, find the value of L in standard form when $a = 4{\cdot}5 \times 10^{12}$ and $k = 5 \times 10^7$.

29. A light year is the distance travelled by a beam of light in a year. Light travels at a speed of approximately 3×10^5 km/s.
(a) Work out the length of a light year in km.
(b) Light takes about 8 minutes to reach the Earth from the Sun. How far is the Earth from the Sun in km?

30. Percy, a rather mean gardener, is trying to estimate the number of seeds in a 50 gram packet. He counts 30 seeds from the packet and finds their weight is 6×10^{-2} grams.

Use his sample to estimate the total number of seeds in the packet.

11.3 Fractions

2/8b

Common fractions are added or subtracted from one another directly only when they have a common denominator.

(a) $\frac{3}{4}+\frac{2}{5} = \frac{15}{20}+\frac{8}{20} = \frac{23}{20} = 1\frac{3}{20}$

(b) $2\frac{3}{8}-1\frac{5}{12} = \frac{19}{8}-\frac{17}{12} = \frac{57}{24}-\frac{34}{24} = \frac{23}{24}$

(c) $\frac{2}{5}\times\frac{6}{7} = \frac{12}{35}$

(d) $2\frac{2}{5}\div 6 = \frac{12}{5}\div\frac{6}{1} = \frac{12}{5}\times\frac{1}{6} = \frac{2}{5}$

Exercise 6

Work out and simplify where possible.

1. $\frac{1}{3}+\frac{1}{2}$	**2.** $\frac{1}{3}\times\frac{1}{2}$	**3.** $\frac{1}{3}\div\frac{1}{2}$	**4.** $\frac{3}{4}-\frac{1}{3}$
5. $\frac{3}{4}\times\frac{1}{3}$	**6.** $\frac{3}{4}\div\frac{1}{3}$	**7.** $\frac{2}{5}+\frac{1}{2}$	**8.** $\frac{2}{5}\times\frac{1}{2}$
9. $\frac{2}{5}\div\frac{1}{2}$	**10.** $\frac{3}{7}+\frac{1}{2}$	**11.** $\frac{3}{7}\times\frac{1}{2}$	**12.** $\frac{3}{7}\div\frac{1}{2}$
13. $\frac{5}{8}-\frac{1}{4}$	**14.** $\frac{5}{8}\times\frac{1}{4}$	**15.** $\frac{5}{8}\div\frac{1}{4}$	**16.** $\frac{1}{6}+\frac{4}{5}$
17. $\frac{1}{6}\times\frac{4}{5}$	**18.** $\frac{1}{6}\div\frac{4}{5}$	**19.** $\frac{3}{7}+\frac{1}{3}$	**20.** $\frac{3}{7}\times\frac{1}{3}$
21. $\frac{3}{7}\div\frac{1}{3}$	**22.** $\frac{4}{5}-\frac{1}{4}$	**23.** $\frac{4}{5}\times\frac{1}{4}$	**24.** $\frac{4}{5}\div\frac{1}{4}$
25. $\frac{2}{3}-\frac{1}{8}$	**26.** $\frac{2}{3}\times\frac{1}{8}$	**27.** $\frac{2}{3}\div\frac{1}{8}$	**28.** $\frac{5}{9}+\frac{1}{4}$
29. $\frac{5}{9}\times\frac{1}{4}$	**30.** $\frac{5}{9}\div\frac{1}{4}$	**31.** $2\frac{1}{2}-\frac{1}{4}$	**32.** $2\frac{1}{2}\times\frac{1}{4}$
33. $2\frac{1}{2}\div\frac{1}{4}$	**34.** $3\frac{3}{4}-\frac{2}{3}$	**35.** $3\frac{3}{4}\times\frac{2}{3}$	**36.** $3\frac{3}{4}\div\frac{2}{3}$
37. $\dfrac{\frac{1}{2}+\frac{1}{5}}{\frac{1}{2}-\frac{1}{5}}$	**38.** $\dfrac{\frac{3}{4}-\frac{1}{3}}{\frac{3}{4}+\frac{1}{3}}$	**39.** $\dfrac{2\frac{1}{4}\times\frac{4}{5}}{\frac{3}{5}-\frac{1}{2}}$	**40.** $\dfrac{3\frac{1}{2}\times 2\frac{2}{3}}{\frac{1}{2}+1\frac{1}{18}}$

Exercise 7

1. Arrange the fractions in order of size:

(a) $\frac{7}{12}, \frac{1}{2}, \frac{2}{3}$ (b) $\frac{3}{4}, \frac{2}{3}, \frac{5}{6}$

(c) $\frac{1}{3}, \frac{17}{24}, \frac{5}{8}, \frac{3}{4}$ (d) $\frac{5}{6}, \frac{8}{9}, \frac{11}{12}$

2. Find the fraction which is mid-way between the two fractions given:

(a) $\frac{2}{5}, \frac{3}{5}$ (b) $\frac{5}{8}, \frac{7}{8}$

(c) $\frac{2}{3}, \frac{3}{4}$ (d) $\frac{1}{3}, \frac{4}{9}$

(e) $\frac{4}{15}, \frac{1}{3}$ (f) $\frac{3}{8}, \frac{11}{24}$

3. In the equation on the right, all the asterisks stand for the same number. What is the number?

$$\left[\frac{*}{*}-\frac{*}{6}=\frac{*}{30}\right]$$

4. Work out one half of one third of 65% of £360.

5. Find the value of n if
$(1\frac{1}{3})^n - (1\frac{1}{3}) = \frac{28}{27}$

6. A rubber ball is dropped from a height of 300 cm. After each bounce, the ball rises to $\frac{4}{5}$ of its previous height.
How high, to the nearest cm, will it rise after the fourth bounce?

7. Steve Braindead spends his income as follows:
(a) $\frac{2}{5}$ of his income goes in tax,
(b) $\frac{2}{3}$ of what is left goes on food, rent and transport,
(c) he spends the rest on cigarettes, beer and betting.
What fraction of his income is spent on cigarettes, beer and betting?

8. A formula used by opticians is

$$\frac{1}{f} = \frac{1}{u} + \frac{1}{v}$$

Given that $u = 3$ and $v = 2\frac{1}{2}$, find the exact value of f.

9. A set of drills starts at $\frac{1}{8}$ inch and goes up to $\frac{5}{8}$ inch in steps of $\frac{1}{16}$ inch.
(a) How many drills are there in the full set?
(b) Which size is half way between $\frac{1}{4}$ inch and $\frac{3}{8}$ inch?

10. A fraction is equivalent to $\frac{2}{3}$ and its denominator (bottom number) is 8 more than its numerator (top number). What is the fraction?

11. When it hatches from its egg, the shell of a certain crab is 1 cm across. When fully grown the shell is approximately 10 cm across. Each new shell is one-third bigger than the previous one. How many shells does a fully grown crab have during its life?

12. Figures 1 and 2 show an equilateral triangle divided into thirds and quarters. They are combined in Figure 3. Calculate the fraction of Figure 3 that is shaded.

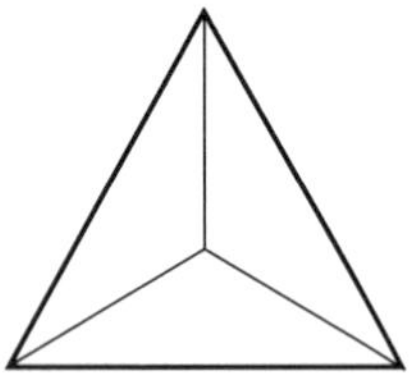
Fig. 1

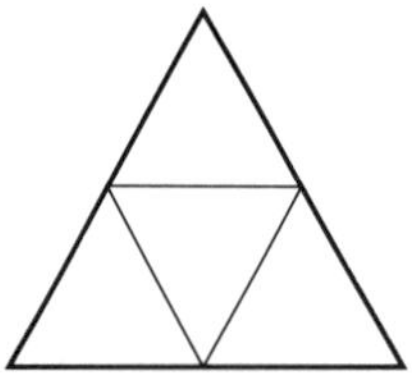
Fig. 2

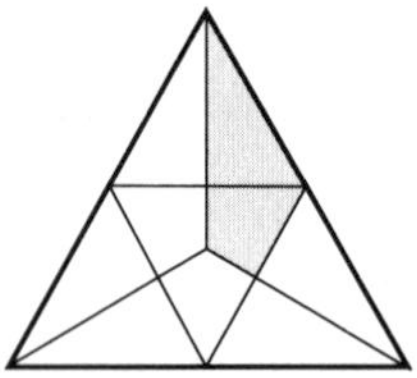
Fig. 2

13. Glass a contains 10 ml of water and glass B contains 100 ml of wine.

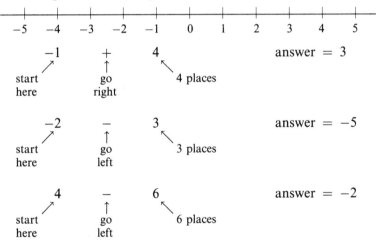

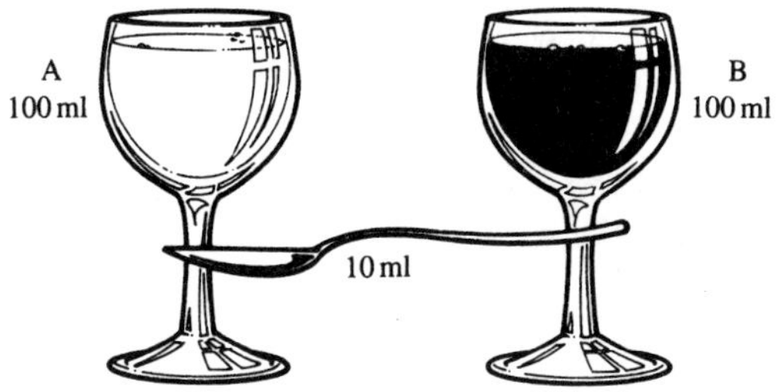

A 10 ml spoonful of wine is taken from glass B and mixed thoroughly with the water in glass A. A 10 ml spoonful of the mixture from A is returned by B. Is there now more wine in the water or more water in the wine?

11.4 Negative numbers

2/8b

For adding and subtracting use the number line.

−5 −4 −3 −2 −1 0 1 2 3 4 5

$-1 \quad + \quad 4$ answer = 3

start here ↗ ; ↑ go right ; ↖ 4 places

$-2 \quad - \quad 3$ answer = −5

start here ↗ ; ↑ go left ; ↖ 3 places

$4 \quad - \quad 6$ answer = −2

start here ↗ ; ↑ go left ; ↖ 6 places

When you have two (+) or (−) signs together use this rule:

$++ = +$ $\qquad +- = -$

$-- = +$ $\qquad -+ = -$

(a) $3-(-6) = 3+6 = 9$

(b) $-4+(-5) = -4-5 = -9$

(c) $-5-(+7) = -5-7 = -12$

Exercise 8

Work out

1. $-6+2$	**2.** $-7-5$	**3.** $-3-8$	**4.** $-5+2$
5. $-6+1$	**6.** $8-4$	**7.** $4-9$	**8.** $11-19$
9. $4+15$	**10.** $-7-10$	**11.** $16-20$	**12.** $-7+2$
13. $-6-5$	**14.** $10-4$	**15.** $-4+0$	**16.** $-6+12$
17. $-7+7$	**18.** $2-20$	**19.** $8-11$	**20.** $-6-5$
21. $-3+(-5)$	**22.** $-5-(+2)$	**23.** $4-(+3)$	**24.** $-3-(-4)$
25. $6-(-3)$	**26.** $16+(-5)$	**27.** $-4+(-4)$	**28.** $20-(-22)$
29. $-6-(-10)$	**30.** $95+(-80)$	**31.** $-3-(+4)$	**32.** $-5-(+4)$
33. $6+(-7)$	**34.** $-4+(-3)$	**35.** $-7-(-7)$	**36.** $3-(-8)$
37. $-8+(-6)$	**38.** $7-(+7)$	**39.** $12-(-5)$	**40.** $9-(+6)$

When two directed numbers with the same sign are multiplied together, the answer is positive.
(a) $+7 \times (+3) = +21$
(b) $-6 \times (-4) = +24$

When two directed numbers with different signs are multiplied together, the answer is negative.
(a) $-8 \times (+4) = -32$
(b) $+7 \times (-5) = -35$
(c) $-3 \times (+2) \times (+5) = -6 \times (+5) = -30$

When dividing directed numbers, the rules are the same as in multiplication.
(a) $-70 \div (-2) = +35$
(b) $+12 \div (-3) = -4$
(c) $-20 \div (+4) = -5$

Exercise 9

1. $-3 \times (+2)$	**2.** $-4 \times (+1)$	**3.** $+5 \times (-3)$	**4.** $-3 \times (-3)$
5. $-4 \times (2)$	**6.** $-5 \times (3)$	**7.** $6 \times (-4)$	**8.** $3 \times (2)$
9. $-3 \times (-4)$	**10.** $6 \times (-3)$	**11.** $-7 \times (3)$	**12.** $-5 \times (-5)$
13. $6 \times (-10)$	**14.** $-3 \times (-7)$	**15.** $8 \times (6)$	**16.** $-8 \times (2)$
17. $-7 \times (6)$	**18.** $-5 \times (-4)$	**19.** $-6 \times (7)$	**20.** $11 \times (-6)$
21. $8 \div (-2)$	**22.** $-9 \div (3)$	**23.** $-6 \div (-2)$	**24.** $10 \div (-2)$
25. $-12 \div (-3)$	**26.** $-16 \div (4)$	**27.** $4 \div (-1)$	**28.** $8 \div (-8)$
29. $16 \div (-8)$	**30.** $-20 \div (-5)$	**31.** $-16 \div (1)$	**32.** $18 \div (-9)$
33. $36 \div (-9)$	**34.** $-45 \div (-9)$	**35.** $-70 \div (7)$	**36.** $-11 \div (-1)$
37. $-16 \div (-1)$	**38.** $1 \div (-\frac{1}{2})$	**39.** $-2 \div (\frac{1}{2})$	**40.** $50 \div (-10)$
41. $-8 \times (-8)$	**42.** $-9 \times (3)$	**43.** $10 \times (-60)$	**44.** $-8 \times (-5)$
45. $-12 \div (-6)$	**46.** $-18 \times (-2)$	**47.** $-8 \div (4)$	**48.** $-80 \div (10)$
49. $-16 \times (-10)$	**50.** $32 \div (-16)$		

Questions on negative numbers are more difficult when the different sorts are mixed together. The remaining questions are given in the form of six short tests.

Test 1

1. $-8-8$	**2.** $-8\times(-8)$	**3.** -5×3	**4.** $-5+3$
5. $8-(-7)$	**6.** $20-2$	**7.** $-18\div(-6)$	**8.** $4+(-10)$
9. $-2+13$	**10.** $+8\times(-6)$	**11.** $-9+(+2)$	**12.** $-2-(-11)$
13. $-6\times(-1)$	**14.** $2-20$	**15.** $-14-(-4)$	**16.** $-40\div(-5)$
17. $5-11$	**18.** -3×10	**19.** $9+(-5)$	**20.** $7\div(-7)$

Test 2

1. $-2\times(+8)$	**2.** $-2+8$	**3.** $-7-6$	**4.** $-7\times(-6)$
5. $+36\div(-9)$	**6.** $-8-(-4)$	**7.** $-14+2$	**8.** $5\times(-4)$
9. $11+(-5)$	**10.** $11-11$	**11.** $-9\times(-4)$	**12.** $-6+(-4)$
13. $3-10$	**14.** $-20\div(-2)$	**15.** $16+(-10)$	**16.** $-4-(+14)$
17. $-45\div 5$	**18.** $18-3$	**19.** $-1\times(-1)$	**20.** $-3-(-3)$

Test 3

1. $-10\times(-10)$	**2.** $-10-10$	**3.** $-8\times(+1)$	**4.** $-8+1$
5. $5+(-9)$	**6.** $15-5$	**7.** $-72\div(-8)$	**8.** $-12-(-2)$
9. $-1+8$	**10.** $-5\times(-7)$	**11.** $-10+(-10)$	**12.** $-6\times(+4)$
13. $6-16$	**14.** $-42\div(+6)$	**15.** $-13+(-6)$	**16.** $-8-(-7)$
17. $5\times(-1)$	**18.** $2-15$	**19.** $21+(-21)$	**20.** $-16\div(-2)$

11.5 Substituting into formulas

2/8b

When a calculation is repeated many times it is often helpful to use a formula. When a building society offers a mortgage it may use a formula like '$2\frac{1}{2}$ times the main salary plus the second salary'. Publishers use a formula to work out the selling price of a book based on the production costs and the expected sales of the book.

(a) A formula connecting velocities with acceleration and time is $v = u + at$.
Find the value of v when $u = 3$, $a = 4$, $t = 6$.

$$v = u + at$$
$$v = 3 + (4\times 6)$$
$$v = 27$$

(b) A formula for the tension in a spring is $T = \frac{kx}{a}$.
Find the value of T when $k = 13$, $x = 5$, $a = 2$.

$$T = \frac{kx}{a}$$
$$T = \frac{13\times 5}{2}$$
$$T = 32\tfrac{1}{2}$$

Exercise 10

1. A formula involving force, mass and acceleration is $F = ma$. Find the value of F when $m = 12$ and $a = 3$.

2. The height of a growing tree is given by the formula $h = 2t + 15$. Find the value of h when $t = 7$.

3. The time required to cook a joint of meat is given by the formula $T = (\text{mass of joint}) \times 3 + \frac{1}{2}$. Find the value of T when $(\text{mass of joint}) = 2\frac{1}{2}$.

4. An important formula in Physics states that $I = mu - mv$. Find the value of I when $m = 6$, $u = 8$, $v = 5$.

5. The distance travelled by an accelerating car is given by the formula $s = \left(\frac{u+v}{2}\right)t$. Find the value of s when $u = 17$, $v = 25$ and $t = 4$.

6. Einstein's famous formula states that $E = mc^2$. Find the value of E when $m = 0{\cdot}0001$ and $c = 3 \times 10^8$.

7. The height of a stone thrown upwards is given by $h = ut - 5t^2$. Find the value of h when $u = 70$ and $t = 3$.

8. The speed of an accelerating particle is given by the formula $v^2 = u^2 + 2as$. Find the value of v when $u = 11$, $a = 5$ and $s = 6$.

9. The time period T of a simple pendulum is given by the formula $T = 2\pi\sqrt{\left(\frac{\ell}{g}\right)}$, where ℓ is the length of the pendulum and g is the gravitational acceleration. Find T when $\ell = 0{\cdot}65$, $g = 9{\cdot}81$ and $\pi = 3{\cdot}142$.

10. The sum S of the squares of the integers from 1 to n is given by $S = \frac{1}{6}n(n+1)(2n+1)$. Find S when $n = 12$.

If $x = 3$, $y = -4$, work out the following.

(a) $2x + y$
$= 6 + -4$
$= 6 - 4$
$= 2$

(b) $xy - y$
$= -12 - -4$
$= -12 + 4$
$= -8$

Do some of the working in your head.

Exercise 11

If $a = -4$, $b = 5$, $c = -2$, work out

1. $2a + 3$	**2.** $3b - 7$	**3.** $4a - 1$	**4.** $2b + c$
5. $5c - 2a$	**6.** $6a - 3$	**7.** $2c + b$	**8.** $3a - 2b$
9. $6c - 2b$	**10.** $3c + 4a$	**11.** $3c - 4$	**12.** $2a - 3c$
13. $7b + 3a$	**14.** $8a + 6c$	**15.** $2b - 4a$	**16.** $4b + 5$
17. $3a + 8$	**18.** $2c - a$	**19.** $5a - 2c$	**20.** $3b + 7$

If $n = 3$, $x = -1$, $y = 6$, work out

21. $2x - 3$	**22.** $3y + 4n$	**23.** $5n + 2x$	**24.** $4y - x$
25. $7y - 2$	**26.** $3x + 2n$	**27.** $10x + 5$	**28.** $6x - y$
29. $4x - 5y$	**30.** $2y - 10$	**31.** $8n - 2y$	**32.** $7n + 3y$
33. $6y + 4$	**34.** $4n + 5x$	**35.** $2n + 3x$	**36.** $5y - 20$
37. $9y - n$	**38.** $8x + 2n$	**39.** $5x + 6$	**40.** $3n - 2x$

$a^2 = a \times a$

$a^3 = a \times a \times a$

$2a^2 = 2(a^2)$

$(2a)^2 = 2a \times 2a$

$a(b - c)$: Work out the term in brackets first

$\dfrac{a+b}{c}$: The division line works like a bracket, so work out $a + b$ first.

If $y = -3$, $x = 2$, work out (a) y^2, (b) $3x^2$

(a) $y^2 = -3 \times -3 = 9$ (b) $3x^2 = 3 \times 4 = 12$

Exercise 12

If $m = 2$, $t = -2$, $x = -3$, $y = 4$, work out

1. m^2	**2.** t^2	**3.** x^2	**4.** y^2
5. m^3	**6.** t^3	**7.** x^3	**8.** y^3
9. $2m^2$	**10.** $(2m)^2$	**11.** $2t^2$	**12.** $(2t)^2$
13. $2x^2$	**14.** $(2x)^2$	**15.** $3y^2$	**16.** $4m^2$
17. $5t^2$	**18.** $6x^2$	**19.** $(3y)^2$	**20.** $3m^3$
21. $x^2 + 4$	**22.** $y^2 - 6$	**23.** $t^2 - 3$	**24.** $m^3 + 10$
25. $x^2 + t^2$	**26.** $2x^2 + 1$	**27.** $m^2 + xt$	**28.** my^2
29. $(mt)^2$	**30.** $(xy)^2$	**31.** $(xt)^2$	**32.** yx^2
33. $m - t$	**34.** $t - x$	**35.** $y - m$	**36.** $m - y^2$
37. $t + x$	**38.** $2m + 3x$	**39.** $3t - y$	**40.** $xt + y$
41. $3(m + t)$	**42.** $4(x + y)$	**43.** $5(m + 2y)$	**44.** $2(y - m)$
45. $m(t + x)$	**46.** $y(m + x)$	**47.** $x(y - m)$	**48.** $t(2m + y)$
49. $m^2(y - x)$	**50.** $t^2(x^2 + m)$		

Exercise 13

If $w = -2$, $x = 3$, $y = 0$, $z = -\frac{1}{2}$, work out

1. $\frac{w}{z} + x$ **2.** $\frac{w+x}{z}$ **3.** $y\left(\frac{x+z}{w}\right)$ **4.** $x^2(z + wy)$

5. $x\sqrt{(x + wz)}$ **6.** $w^2\sqrt{(z^2 + y^2)}$ **7.** $2(w^2 + x^2 + y^2)$ **8.** $2x(w - z)$

9. $\frac{z}{w} + x$ **10.** $\frac{z+w}{x}$ **11.** $\frac{x+w}{z^2}$ **12.** $\frac{y^2 - w^2}{xz}$

13. $z^2 + 4z + 5$ **14.** $\frac{1}{w} + \frac{1}{z} + \frac{1}{x}$ **15.** $\frac{4}{z} + \frac{10}{w}$ **16.** $\frac{yz - xw}{xz - w}$

17. Find $K = \sqrt{\left(\frac{a^2 + b^2 + c^2 - 2c}{a^2 + b^2 + 4c}\right)}$ if $a = 3$, $b = -2$, $c = -1$.

18. Find $W = \frac{kmn(k + m + n)}{(k + m)(k + n)}$ if $k = \frac{1}{2}$, $m = -\frac{1}{3}$, $n = \frac{1}{4}$.

11.6 Problems 3

2/7b, 2/8c

Exercise 14

1. A maths teacher bought 40 calculators at £8.20 each and a number of other calculators costing £2.95 each. In all she spent £387. How many of the cheaper calculators did she buy?

2. The total mass of a jar one quarter full of jam is 250 g. The total mass of the same jar three quarters full of jam is 350 g.

What is the mass of the empty jar?

3. I have lots of 1p, 2p, 3p and 4p stamps. How many different combinations of stamps can I make which total 5p?

4. 8% of 2500 + 37% of P = 348. Find the value of P.

5. Express 419 965 in terms of its prime factors.

6. A map is 278 mm wide and 445 mm long. When reduced on a photocopier, the copy is 360 mm long. What is the width of the copy, to the nearest millimetre?

7. How many prime numbers are there between 120 and 130?

8. You are given that $41 \times 271 = 11\,111$. Work out the following *in your head*.
(a) 246×271
(b) $22\,222 \div 271$

9. Booklets have a mass of 19 g each, and they are posted in an envelope of mass 38 g. Postage charges are shown in the table below

Mass (in grams) not more than	60	100	150	200	250	300	350	600
Postage (in pence)	24	30	37	44	51	59	67	110

(a) A package consists of 15 booklets in an envelope. What is the total mass of the package?
(b) The mass of a second package is 475 g. How many booklets does it contain?
(c) What is the postage charge on a package of mass 320 g?
(d) The postage on a third package was £1.10. What is the largest number of booklets it could contain?

10. A rabbit runs at $7\,\text{m}\,\text{s}^{-1}$ and a hedgehog at $\frac{1}{2}\,\text{m}\,\text{s}^{-1}$. They are 90 m apart and start to run towards each other.
How far does the hedgehog run before they meet?

Exercise 15

1. A wicked witch stole a new born baby from its parents.
On the baby's first birthday the witch sent the grief-stricken parents 1 penny.
On the second birthday she sent 2 pence.
On the third birthday she sent 4 pence and so on, doubling the amount each time.
How much did the witch send the parents on the twenty-first birthday?

2. The diagrams show magic squares in which the sum of the numbers in any row, column or diagonal is the same. Find the value of x in each square.

(a)

	x	6
3		7
		2

(b)

4		5	16
x		10	
	7	11	2
1			13

3. Find a pair of positive integers a and b for which $18a + 65b = 1865$.

4. Work out $100 - 99 + 98 - 97 + 96 - \ldots + 4 - 3 + 2 - 1$.

5. The smallest three-digit product of a one-digit prime and a two-digit prime is

(A)	(B)	(C)	(D)	(E)
102	103	104	105	106

6. Apart from 1, 3 and 5 all odd numbers less than 100 can be written in the form $p + 2^n$ where p is a prime number and n is greater than or equal to 2.

e.g. $43 = 11 + 2^5$
$27 = 23 + 2^2$

For the odd numbers 7, 9, 11, ... 39 write as many as you can in the form $p + 2^n$.

7. Evaluate

(a) $\frac{1}{3} \times \frac{2}{4} \times \frac{3}{5} \times \ldots \times \frac{9}{11} \times \frac{10}{12}$.

(b) $[(-2)^{-2}]^{-2}$

8. What is the smallest number greater than 1000 that is exactly divisible by 13 and 17?

9. Find the smallest value of n for which

$1^2 + 2^2 + 3^2 + 4^2 + 5^2 + \ldots + n^2 > 800$

10. The reciprocal of 2 is $\frac{1}{2}$. The reciprocal of 7 is $\frac{1}{7}$. The reciprocal of x is $\frac{1}{x}$.
Find the square root of the reciprocal of the square root of the reciprocal of ten thousand.

11. S_1 is the sum of all the even numbers from 2 to 1000 inclusive.
S_2 is the sum of all the odd numbers from 1 to 999 inclusive.
Work out $S_1 - S_2$.

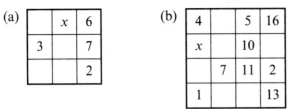

12 Handling data 2

12.1 Averages

5/7a

If you have a set of data, say exam marks or heights, and are told to find the 'average', just what are you trying to find? The answer is: a single number which can be used to represent the entire set of data. This could be done in three different ways.

(a) The median

The data is arranged in order from the smallest to the largest; the middle number is then selected. This is really the central number of the range and is called the median.
If there are two 'middle' numbers, the median is in the middle of these two numbers.

Median

(b) The mean

All the data is added up and the total divided by the number of items. This is called the mean and is equivalent to sharing out all the data evenly.

(c) The mode

The number of items which occurs most frequently in a frequency table is selected. This is the most popular value and is called the mode (from the french 'a la mode' meaning 'fashionable')

Each 'average' has its purpose and sometimes one is preferable to the others.

The median is fairly easy to find and has an advantage in being hardly affected by untypical values such as very large or very small values that occur at the ends of the distribution.
Consider these exam marks:

20, 21, 21, 22, 23, 23, 25, 27, 27, 27, 29, 98, 98
↑

The median (25) gives a truer picture of the centre of the distribution than the mean (35·5).
The mean takes account of all of the data and is the 'average' which most people readily think of. It does, of course, take a little longer to calculate than either the mode or the median.
The mode of this data is 27. It is easy to calculate and it eliminates some of the effects of extreme values. However it does have disadvantages, particularly in data which has two 'most popular' values, and it is not widely used.

Range

In addition to knowing the centre of a distribution, it is useful to know the range or spread of the data.

range = (largest value) – (smallest value)

For the examination marks, range = 98 – 20 = 78.

Find the median, the mean, the mode and the range of this set of 10 numbers: 5, 4, 10, 3, 3, 4, 7, 4, 6, 5.

(a) Arrange the numbers in order of size to find the median.
3, 3, 4, 4, 4, 5, 5, 6, 7, 10
↑
the median is the 'average' of 4 and 5.
∴ median = 4·5

(b) $\text{Mean} = \dfrac{(5+4+10+3+3+4+7+4+6+5)}{10} = \dfrac{51}{10} = 5{\cdot}1$

(c) mode = 4 because there are more 4's then any other number.

(d) range = 10 – 3 = 7

Exercise 1

1. Find the mean, median and mode of the following sets of numbers:
   (a) 3, 12, 4, 6, 8, 5, 4
   (b) 7, 21, 2, 17, 3, 13, 7, 4, 9, 7, 9
   (c) 12, 1, 10, 1, 9, 3, 4, 9, 7, 9
   (d) 8, 0, 3, 3, 1, 7, 4, 1, 4, 4.
2. The temperature in °C on 17 days was:
   1, 0, 2, 2, 0, 4, 1, 3, 2, 1, 2, 3, 4, 5, 4, 5, 5.
   What was the modal temperature?
3. A dice was thrown 14 times as follows:

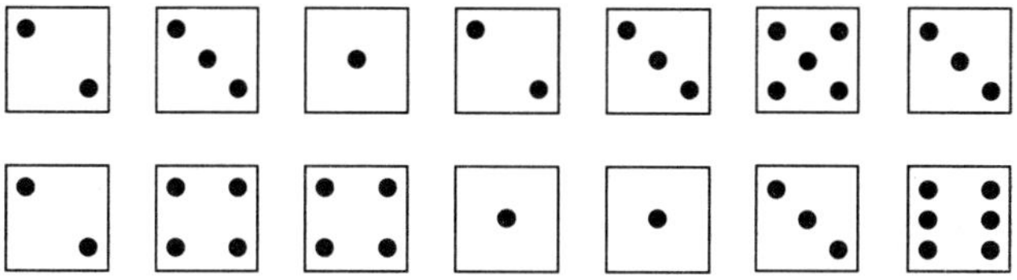

   (a) What was the modal score?
   (b) What was the median score?
4. Write down five numbers so that:
   the mean is 6
   the median is 5
   the mode is 4.
5. Louise claims that she is better at maths than her brother Peter. Louise's last five marks were 63, 72, 58, 84 and 75 and Peter's last four marks were 69, 73, 81 and 70. Find the mean mark for Louise and for Peter. Is Louise better than Peter?
6. The bar chart shows the marks scored in a test. What was the modal mark?

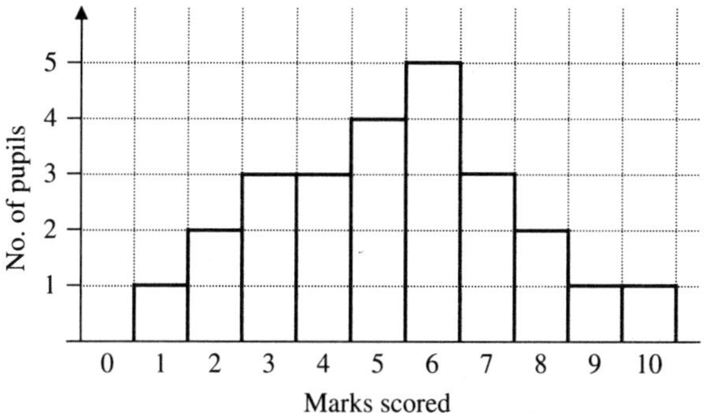

7. Six boys have heights of 1·53 m, 1·49 m, 1·60 m, 1·65 m, 1·90 m and 1·43 m.
   (a) Find the mean height of the six boys.
   (b) Find the mean height of the remaining five boys when the shortest boy leaves.

8. Seven ladies have weights of 44 kg, 51 kg, 57 kg, 63 kg, 48 kg, 49 kg and 45 kg.
(a) Find the mean weight of the seven ladies.
(b) Find the mean weight of the remaining five ladies after the lightest and the heaviest ladies leave.

9. In a maths test the marks for the boys were 9, 7, 8, 7, 5 and the marks for the girls were 6, 3, 9, 8, 2, 2.
(a) Find the mean mark for the boys.
(b) Find the mean mark for the girls.
(c) Find the mean mark for the whole class.

10. The following are the salaries of 5 employees in a small business:
Mr A: £22,500 Mr B: £17,900 Mr C: £21,400
Mr D: £22,500 Mr E: £155,300.
(a) Find the mean, median and mode of their salaries.
(b) Which does *not* give a fair 'average'? Explain why in one sentence.

11. A farmer has 32 cattle to sell. The weights of the cattle in kg are:

81	81	82	82	83	84	84	85
85	86	86	87	87	88	89	91
91	92	93	94	96	150	152	153
154	320	370	375	376	380	381	390

[Total weight = 5028 kg].

On the telephone to a potential buyer, the farmer describes the cattle and says the 'average' weight is 'over 157 kg'.
(a) Find the mean weight and the median weight.
(b) Which 'average' has the farmer used to describe his animals?
Does this average describe the cattle fairly?

12. A gardening magazine sells seedlings of a plant through the post and claims that the average height of the plants after one year's growth will be 85 cm. A sample of 24 of the plants were measured after one year with the following results (in cm)

6	7	7	9	34	56	85	89
89	90	90	91	91	92	93	93
93	94	95	95	96	97	97	99

[The sum of the heights is 1788 cm].

(a) Find the mean and the median height of the sample.
(b) Is the magazine's claim about average height justified?

Calculating the mean from a frequency table

The frequency table shows the weights of the eggs bought in a supermarket.

weight	58 g	59 g	60 g	61 g	62 g	63 g
frequency	3	7	11	9	8	2

(a) mean weight of eggs

$$= \frac{(58 \times 3) + (59 \times 7) + (60 \times 11) + (61 \times 9) + (62 \times 8) + (63 \times 2)}{(3 + 7 + 11 + 9 + 8 + 2)}$$

$$= \frac{2418}{40} = 60{\cdot}45 \text{ g}$$

(b) There are 40 eggs so the median weight is the number between the 20th and 21st numbers. By inspection, both the 20th and 21st numbers are 60 g.

$\therefore$ Median weight $=$ 60 g

(c) The modal weight $=$ 60 g.

Exercise 2

1. The frequency table shows the weights of the 40 apples sold in a shop.

weight	70 g	80 g	90 g	100 g	110 g	120 g
frequency	2	7	9	11	8	3

Calculate the mean weight of the apples.

2. The frequency table shows the price of a packet of butter in 30 different shops.

price	49p	50p	51p	52p	53p	54p
frequency	2	3	5	10	6	4

Calculate the mean price of a packet of butter.

3. A box contains 50 nails of different lengths as shown in the frequency table.

length of nail	2 cm	3 cm	4 cm	5 cm	6 cm	7 cm
frequency	4	7	9	12	10	8

Calculate the mean length of the nails.

4. The following tables give the distribution of marks obtained by different classes in various tests. For each table, find the mean, median and mode.

(a)

mark	0	1	2	3	4	5	6
frequency	3	5	8	9	5	7	3

(b)

mark	15	16	17	18	19	20
frequency	1	3	7	1	5	3

5. A teacher conducted a mental arithmetic test for 26 pupils and the marks out of 10 were as follows.

mark	3	4	5	6	7	8	9	10
frequency	6	3	1	2	0	5	5	4

(a) Find the mean, median and mode.
(b) The teacher congratulated the class saying that "over three quarters were above 'average' ". Which 'average' justifies this statement?

6. The number of goals scored in a series of football matches was as follows:

number of goals	1	2	3
number of matches	8	8	x

(a) If the mean number of goals is 2·04, find x.
(b) If the modal number of goals is 3, find the smallest possible value of x.
(c) If the median number of goals is 2, find the largest possible value of x.

7. In a survey of the number of occupants in a number of cars, the following data resulted.

number of occupants	1	2	3	4
number of cars	7	11	7	x

(a) If the mean number of occupants is $2\frac{1}{3}$, find x.
(b) If the mode is 2, find the largest possible value of x.
(c) If the median is 2, find the largest possible value of x.

Data in groups

The results of 51 students in a test are given in the frequency table.
Find the (a) mean, (b) median, (c) mode.

mark	30–39	40–49	50–59	60–69
frequency	7	14	21	9

In order to find the mean we approximate by saying each interval is represented by its mid-point. For the 30–39 interval we say there are 7 marks of 34·5 [ie $(30 + 39) \div 2 = 34{\cdot}5$].

(a) mean $= \dfrac{(34{\cdot}5 \times 7) + (44{\cdot}5 \times 14) + (54{\cdot}5 \times 21) + (64{\cdot}5 \times 9)}{(7 + 14 + 21 + 9)}$

$= 50{\cdot}7745098$

$= 51 \quad (2 \text{ s.f.})$

Don't forget this is only an *estimate* because we do not have the raw data and we have made an assumption with the mid-point of each interval.

(b) The median is the 26th mark which is in the interval 50–59. We cannot find the exact median. [Later we will get an estimate by drawing a cumulative frequency curve].

(c) The *modal group* is 50–59. You cannot find an exact mode.

Exercise 3

1. The results of 24 students in a test are given below.

mark	40–54	55–69	70–84	85–99
frequency	5	8	7	4

Find the mid-point of each group of marks and calculate an estimate of the mean mark.

2. The number of letters delivered to the 26 houses in a street was as follows.

number of letters delivered	number of houses (i.e. frequency)
0–2	10
3–4	8
5–7	5
8–12	3

Calculate an estimate of the mean number of letters delivered per house.

3. The heights of the 60 athletes in the 1992 British Olympic team were as follows.

height (cm)	frequency
$150 \leqslant h < 160$	4
$160 \leqslant h < 170$	10
$170 \leqslant h < 180$	14
$180 \leqslant h < 185$	18
$185 \leqslant h < 190$	8
$190 \leqslant h < 200$	6

Calculate the mean height of the 60 athletes.

12.2 Frequency polygons

5/7a

We have seen earlier on page 92 how a frequency distribution can be shown in the form of a bar chart.

The number of peas in 40 pea pods is shown below. Note: Frequency goes on the vertical axis.

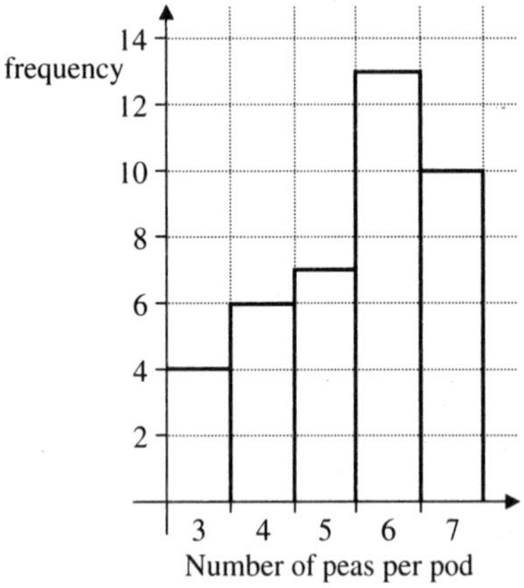

A *frequency polygon* is formed by joining the mid-points of the tops of the bars in a bar chart by straight lines.

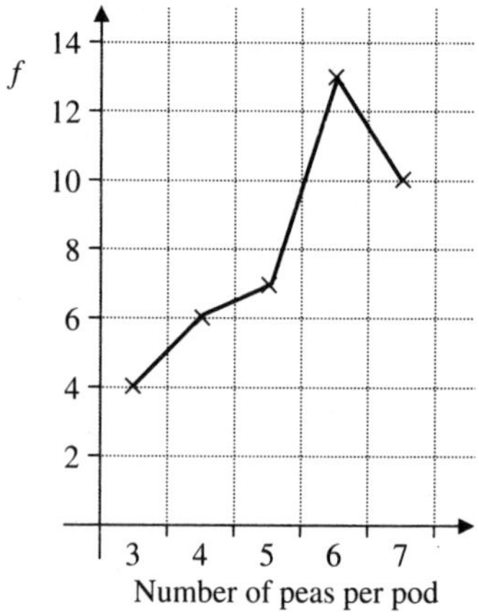

Discrete and continuous data

The data that we record can be either *discrete* or *continuous*.
Discrete data can take only certain values:

- the number of peas in a pod
- the number of children in a class
- shoe sizes.

Continuous data comes from measuring and can take any value:

- height of a child
- weight of an apple
- time taken to boil a kettle.

Class boundaries

The lengths of 40 pea pods were measured and rounded to the nearest mm. So a pea pod which is actually 59·2 mm long is rounded off to 59 mm.

52	80	65	82	77	60	72	83	63
78	84	75	53	73	70	86	55	88
85	59	76	86	73	89	91	76	92
66	93	84	62	79	90	73	68	71

This data can be put into a grouped frequency table.

Length (mm)	Tally	Frequency
$50 \leqslant l < 60$	||||	4
$60 \leqslant l < 70$	~~||||~~ |	6
$70 \leqslant l < 80$	~~||||~~ ~~||||~~ ||	12
$80 \leqslant l < 90$	~~||||~~ ~~||||~~	10
$90 \leqslant l < 100$	||||	4

For the class $50 \leqslant l < 60$, the class boundaries are 50 and 60. The bar will go from 50 to 60 mm.

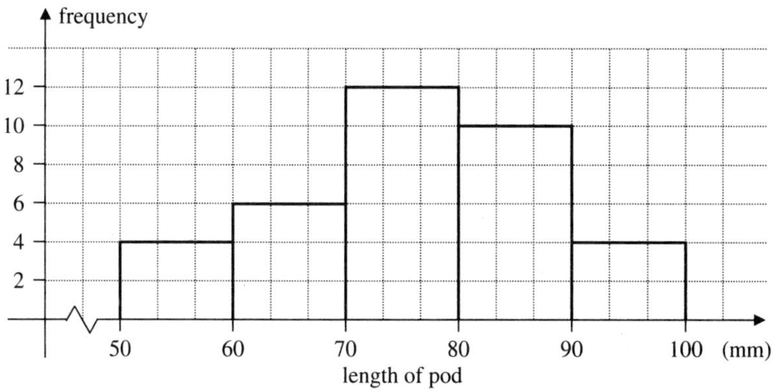

The frequency polygon for this data can be drawn in the same way as with discrete data. Note that you can draw the frequency polygon *without* drawing a bar chart first. You must calculate the mid-points of each group.

For the $50 \leqslant l < 60$ group:

$$\text{mid-point} = \frac{50 + 60}{2} = 55$$

Frequency polygon

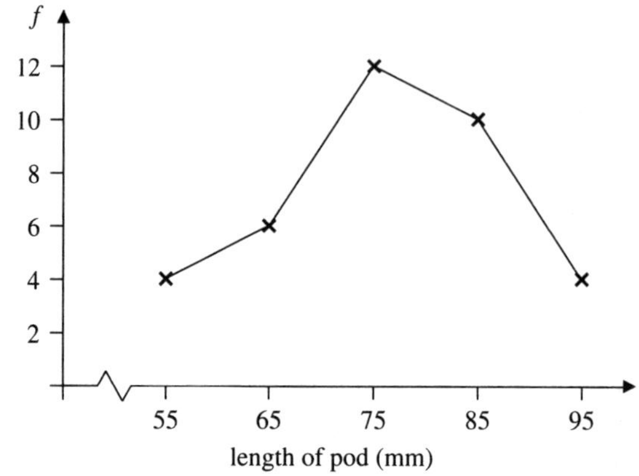

Mid-points

The mid-points of other groups can be calculated as follows:

(a)

mark	mid-point
0–9	4·5 $\left(\frac{0+9}{2}\right)$
10–19	14·5 $\left(\frac{10+19}{2}\right)$

(b)

height	mid-point
$150 \leqslant h < 155$	152·5 $\left(\frac{150+155}{2}\right)$
$155 \leqslant h < 160$	157·5 $\left(\frac{155+160}{2}\right)$

Exercise 4

1. In a survey the number of people in 100 cars passing a set of traffic lights was counted. Here are the results:

number of people in car	0	1	2	3	4	5	6
frequency	0	10	35	25	20	10	0

(a) Draw a bar chart to illustrate this data.
(b) On the same graph draw the frequency polygon.

Here we have started the bar chart.
For frequency, use a scale of 1 cm for 5 units.

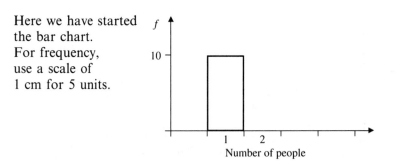

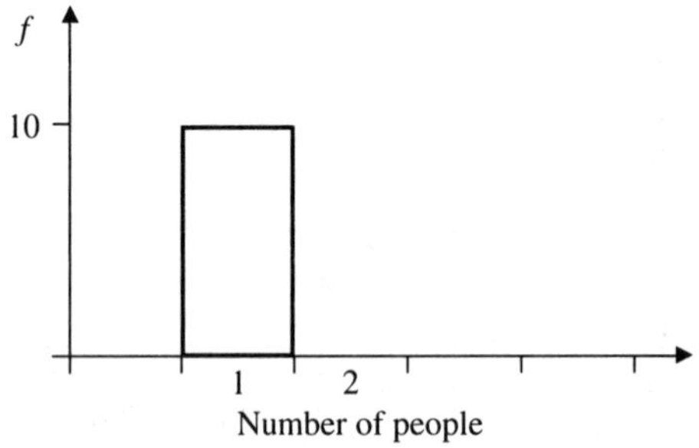

2. The frequency polygon shows the marks obtained by pupils in a maths test.
(a) How many pupils got 7 marks?
(b) How many pupils were there altogether?

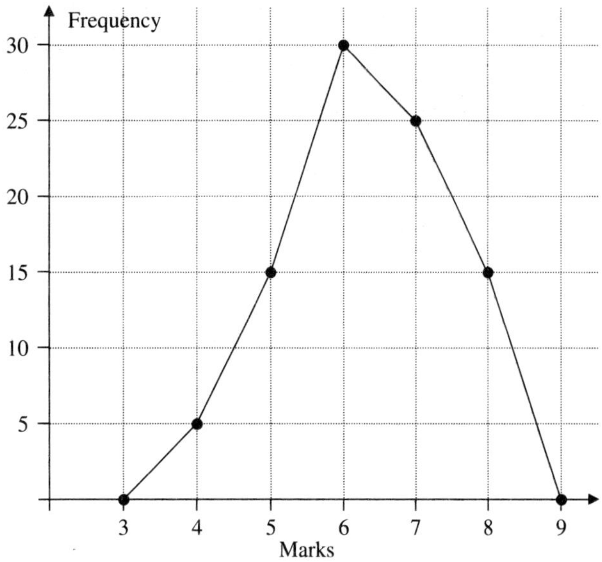

3. The members of several professional basketball teams were measured for their heights. The results were:

height	frequency
$180 \leqslant h < 185$	5
$185 \leqslant h < 190$	8
$190 \leqslant h < 195$	15
$195 \leqslant h < 200$	11
$200 \leqslant h < 205$	6
$205 \leqslant h < 210$	2

Draw a bar chart and a frequency polygon to illustrate this data.

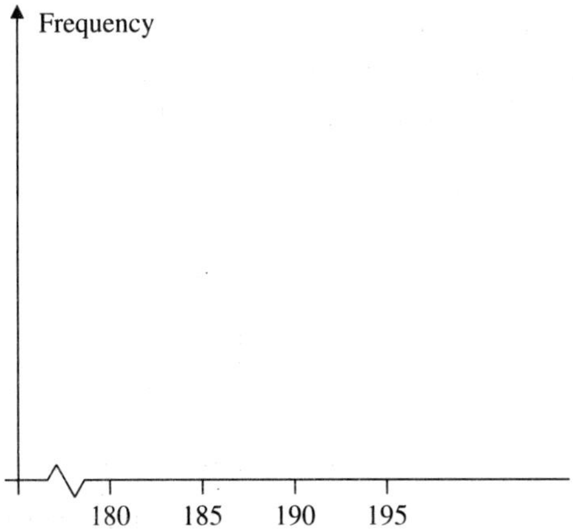

4. Two frequency polygons are shown giving the distribution of the weights of players in two different sports A and B.

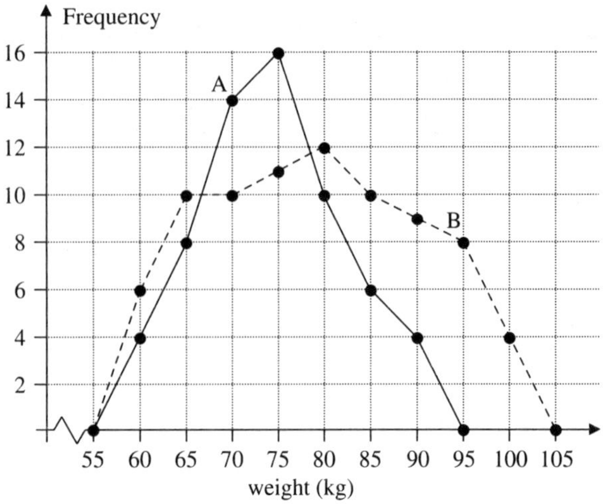

(a) How many people played sport A?
(b) Comment on two differences between the two frequency polygons.
(c) Either for A or for B suggest a sport where you would expect the frequency polygon of weights to have this shape. Explain in one sentence why you have chosen that sport.

5. A scientist at an agricultural college is studying the effect of a new fertilizer for raspberries. She measures the heights of the plants and also the total weight of fruit collected. She does this for two sets of plants: one with the new fertilizer and one without it. Here are the frequency polygons:

[- - - with fertilizer
—— without fertilizer]

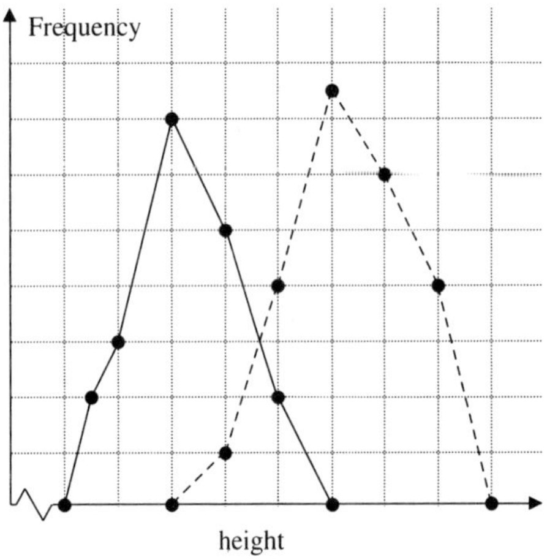

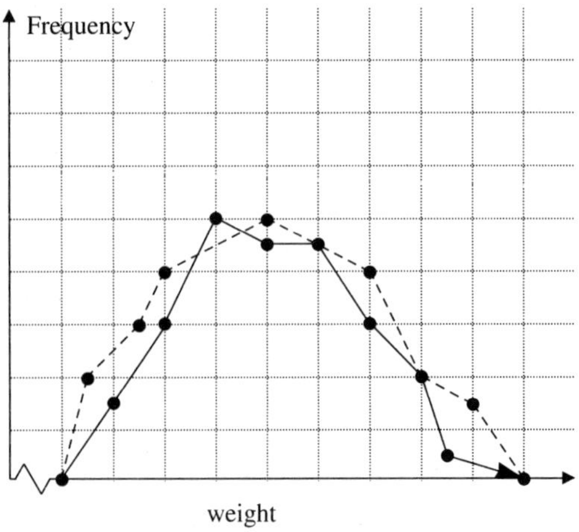

(a) What effect did the fertilizer have on the heights of the plants?
(b) What effect was there on the weights of fruit collected?

12.3 Cumulative frequency

5/8b

Data given in a frequency table can be used to calculate cumulative frequencies. These new values, when plotted and joined, form a cumulative frequency curve, sometimes called an S-shaped curve or ogive.

It is a simple matter to find the median from the halfway point of a cumulative frequency curve.
Other points of location can also be found from this curve. The cumulative frequency axis can be diviided into 100 parts.

- The upper quartile is at the 75% point
- The lower quartile is at the 25% point

The quartiles are particularly useful in finding the central 50% of the range of the distribution; this is known as the interquartile range.

Interquartile range = upper quartile − lower quartile

The interquartile range is an important measure of spread in that it shows how widely the data is spread.
Half the distribution is in the interquartile range. If the interquartile range is small, then the middle half of the distribution is bunched together.

In a survey, 200 people were asked to state their weekly earnings. The results were plotted on the cumulative frequency curve.

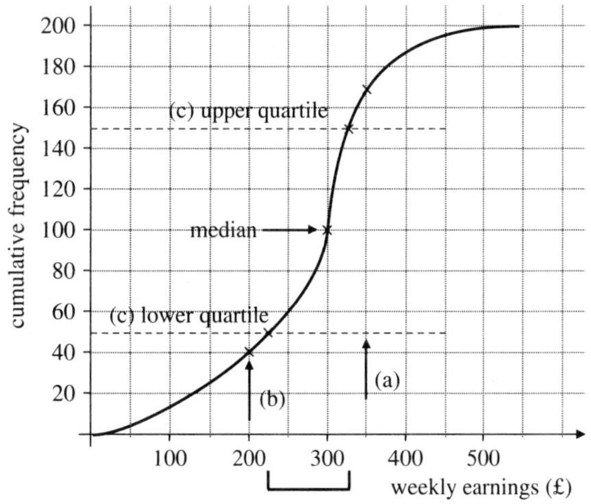

(a) How many people earned up to £350 a week?

From the curve about 170 people earned up to £350 a week.

(b) How many people earned more than £200 a week?

About 40 people earned up to £200 per week. There are 200 people in the survey. So 160 people earned more than £200 a week.

(c) Find the interquartile range.

Lower quartile (50 People) = £225
Upper quartile (150 People) = £325
∴ Interquartile range = 325 − 225
= £100.

A pet shop owner likes to weigh all his mice every week as a check on their state of health. The weights of the 80 mice are shown below.

weight (g)	frequency	cumulative frequency	weight represented by cumulative frequency
0–10	3	3	$\leqslant$ 10 g
10–20	5	8	$\leqslant$ 20 g
20–30	5	13	$\leqslant$ 30 g
30–40	9	22	$\leqslant$ 40 g
40–50	11	33	$\leqslant$ 50 g
50–60	15	48	$\leqslant$ 60 g
60–70	14	62	$\leqslant$ 70 g
70–80	8	70	$\leqslant$ 80 g
80–90	6	76	$\leqslant$ 90 g
90–100	4	80	$\leqslant$ 100 g

The table also shows the cumulative frequency. Plot a cumulative frequency curve and hence estimate
(a) the median
(b) the interquartile range.

Note: The points on the graph are plotted at the *upper limit* of each group of weights.

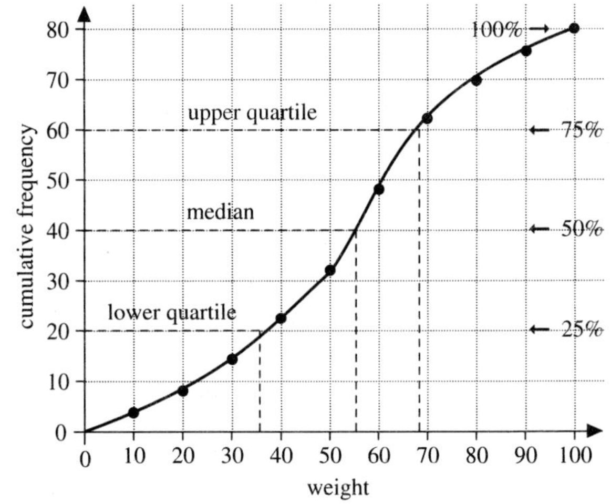

From the cumulative frequency curve,

median = 55 g
lower quartile = 37·5 g
upper quartile = 68 g
interquartile range = (68 − 37·5) g
= 30·5 g

Exercise 5

1. The graph shows the cumulative frequency curve for the marks of 60 students in an examination. From the graph, estimate
(a) the median mark
(b) the mark at the lower quartile and at the upper quartile
(c) the interquartile range
(d) the pass mark if two-thirds of the students passed

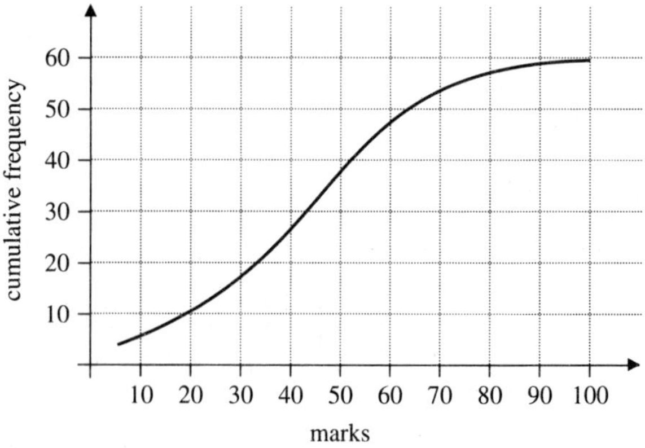

2. The lifetime of 500 electric light bulbs was measured in a laboratory. The results are shown in the cumulative frequency diagram.
   (a) How many bulbs had a lifetime of 1500 hours or less?
   (b) How many bulbs had a lifetime of between 2000 and 3000 hours?
   (c) After how many hours were 70% of the bulbs dead?
   (d) What was the shortest lifetime of a bulb?

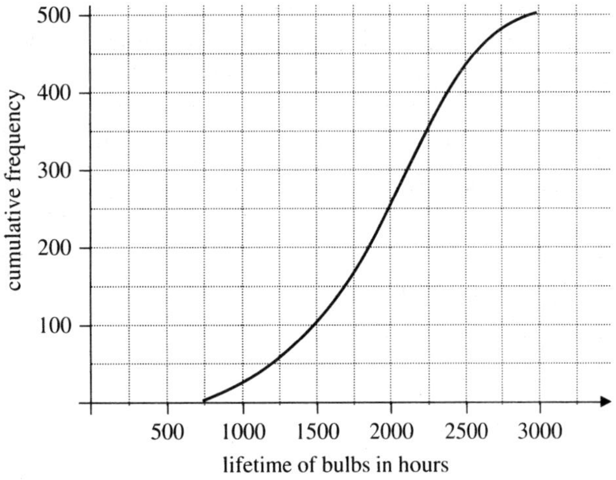

3. The graph shows the cumulative frequency curve for the marks of 140 students in an examination. From the graph estimate
   (a) the median mark
   (b) the mark at the lower quartile and at the upper quartile
   (c) the interquartile range
   (d) the pass mark if two-thirds of the students passed
   (e) the number of students achieving more than 30 marks.

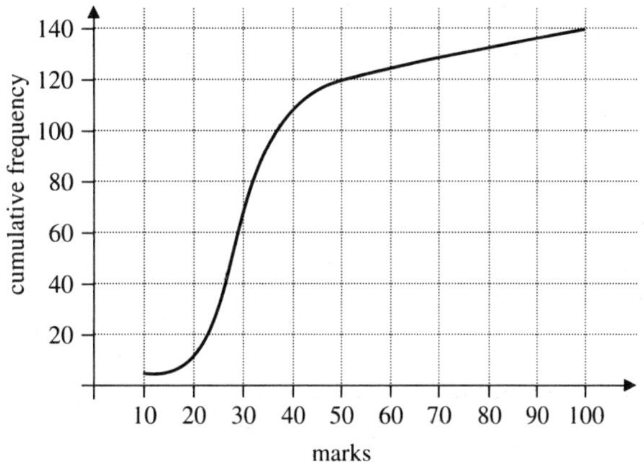

4. A photographer measures all the snakes required for a scene in a film involving a snake pit.
   (a) Draw a cumulative frequency curve for the results below.

length (cm)	frequency	cumulative frequency	upper limit
0–10	0	0	$\leqslant 10$
10–20	2	2	$\leqslant 20$
20–30	4	6	$\leqslant 30$
30–40	10	16	$\leqslant 40$
40–50	17		⋮
50–60	11		⋮
60–70	3		⋮
70–80	3		⋮

Use a scale of 2 cm for 10 units across the page for the lengths and 2 cm for 10 units up the page for the cumulative frequency. Remember to plot points at the *upper* end of the classes (10, 20, 30 etc).
   (b) Find (i) the median (ii) the interquartile range.

5. As part of a medical inspection, a nurse measures the heights of 48 pupils in a school.
(a) Draw a cumulative frequency curve for the results below.

height (cm)	frequency	cumulative frequency
$140 \leqslant h < 145$	2	2 [$\leqslant$145 cm]
$145 \leqslant h < 150$	4	6 [$\leqslant$150 cm]
$150 \leqslant h < 155$	8	14 [$\leqslant$155 cm]
$155 \leqslant h < 160$	9	
$160 \leqslant h < 165$	12	
$165 \leqslant h < 170$	7	
$170 \leqslant h < 175$	4	
$175 \leqslant h < 180$	2	

Use a scale of 2 cm for 5 units across the page and 2 cm for 10 units up the page.

(b) Find (i) the median
(ii) the interquartile range.

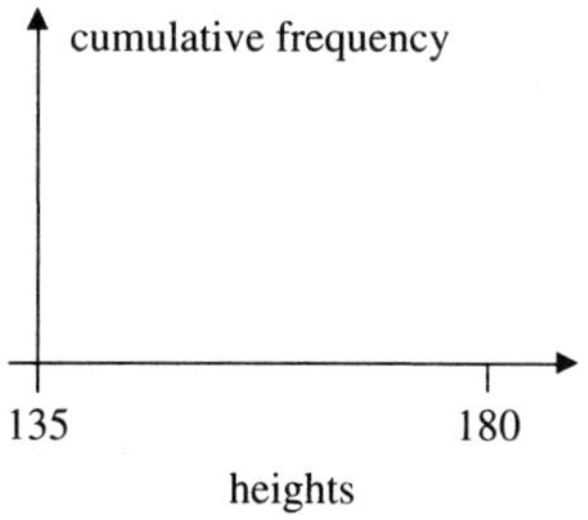

6. In an international competition 60 children from Britain and France did the same science test.

Marks	Britain frequency	France frequency
1–5	1	2
6–10	2	5
11–15	4	11
16–20	8	16
21–25	16	10
26–30	19	8
31–35	10	8

Note: The upper class boundaries for the marks are 5·5, 10·5, 15·5 etc.
The cumulative frequency graph should be plotted for values $\leqslant 5{\cdot}5$, $\leqslant 10{\cdot}5$, $\leqslant 15{\cdot}5$ and so on.
(a) Using the same axes, draw the cumulative frequency curves for the British and French results.
Use a scale of 2 cm for 5 marks across the page and 2 cm for 10 people up the page.
(b) Find the median mark for each country.
(c) Find the interquartile range for the British results.
(d) Describe in one sentence the main difference between the two sets of results.

7. The age distribution of the populations of two countries, A and B, is shown below

Age	Number of people in A (millions)	Number of people in B (millions)
Under 10	15	2
10–19	11	3
20–39	18	5
40–59	7	13
60–79	3	14
80–99	1	7

(a) Copy and complete the cumulative frequency tables below

Age	Country A	Country B
Under 10	15	
Under 20	26	
Under 40		
Under 60		
Under 80		
Under 100		

(b) Using the same axes draw cumulative frequency curves for countries A and B.
Use a scale of 2 cm to 20 years across the page
and 2 cm to 10 million up the page.
(c) State the population of country B.
(d) State the median age for the two countries.
(e) Describe the main difference in the age distribution of the two countries.

13 Using and applying mathematics

13.1 Coursework tasks

There are a large number of possible starting points for investigations here so it may be possible to allow students to choose investigations which appeal to them. On other occasions the same investigation may be set to a whole class.

Here are a few guidelines for pupils:
(a) If the set problem is too complicated try an easier case;
(b) Draw your own diagrams;
(c) Make tables of your results and be systematic;
(d) Look for patterns;
(e) Is there a rule or formula to describe the results?
(f) Can you *predict* further results?
(f) Can you *explain* any rules which you may find?
(h) Where possible extend the task further by asking questions like 'what happens if ...'

1 Opposite corners

Here the numbers are arranged in 9 columns.

1	2	3	4	5	6	7	8	9
10	11	12	13	14	15	16	17	18
19	20	21	22	23	24	25	26	27
28	29	30	31	32	33	34	35	36
37	38	39	40	41	42	43	44	45
46	47	48	49	50	51	52	53	54
55	56	57	58	59	60	61	62	63
64	65	66	67	68	69	70	71	72
73	74	75	76	77	78	79	80	81
82	83	84	85	86	87	88	89	90

In the 2×2 square ...

6	7
15	16

$6 \times 16 = 96$
$7 \times 15 = 105$

... the difference between them is 9.

22	23	24
31	32	33
40	41	42

In the 3×3 square ...

$22 \times 42 = 924$
$24 \times 40 = 960$

... the difference between them is 36.

Investigate to see if you can find any rules or patterns connecting the size of square chosen and the difference.
If you find a rule, use it to *predict* the difference for larger squares.
Test your rule by looking at squares like 8 × 8 or 9 × 9.
Can you *generalise* the rule?

[What is the difference for a square of size $n \times n$?]

Can you *prove* the rule?

Hint:
In a 3 × 3 square . . .

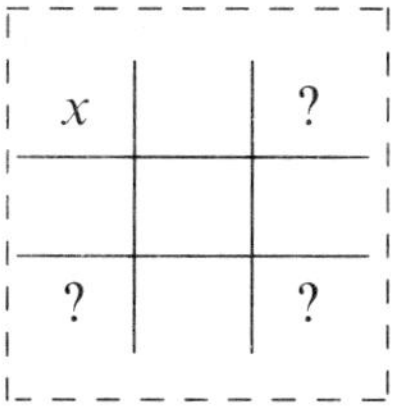

What happens if the numbers are arranged in six columns or seven columns?

1	2	3	4	5	6
7	8	9	10	11	12
13	14	15	16	17	18
19					

1	2	3	4	5	6	7
8	9	10	11	12	13	14
15	16	17	18	19	20	21
22						

2 Hiring a car

You are going to hire a car for one week (7 days).
Which of the firms below should you choose?

Gibson car hire	Snowdon rent-a-car	Hav-a-car
£170 per week unlimited mileage	£10 per day 6·5 p per mile	£60 per week 500 miles without charge 22p per mile over 500 miles.

Work out as detailed an answer as possible.

3 Half-time score

The final score in a football match was 3–2. How many different scores were possible at half-time?

Investigate for other final scores where the difference between the teams is always one goal. [1–0, 5–4, etc.]. Is there a pattern or rule which would tell you the number of possible half-time scores in a game which finished 58–57?

Suppose the game ends in a draw. Find a rule which would tell you the number of possible half-time scores if the final score was 63–63.

Investigate for other final scores [3–0, 5–1, 4–2, etc.].
Find a rule which gives the number of different half-time scores for *any* final score (say $a - b$).

4 An expanding diagram

Look at the series of diagrams below.

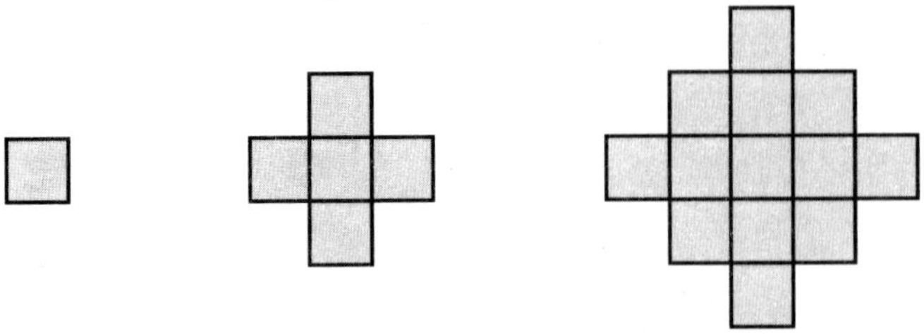

1 2 3

Continue the series by drawing the fourth, fifth and sixth diagrams in the sequence. Each new diagram is obtained by drawing squares all around the outside of the previous diagram. For each diagram count the number of squares it contains.
Using the results of the first six diagrams, can you predict the number of squares in the seventh diagram? See if you were right by drawing the diagram.
Can you predict the number of squares in the eighth diagram? Again draw the diagram to see if you were right.
Can you predict the number of squares in
(a) the 12th diagram, (b) the 20th diagram?
Try to find a rule which will enable you to predict the number of squares for any member of the sequence of diagrams.

5 Maximum box

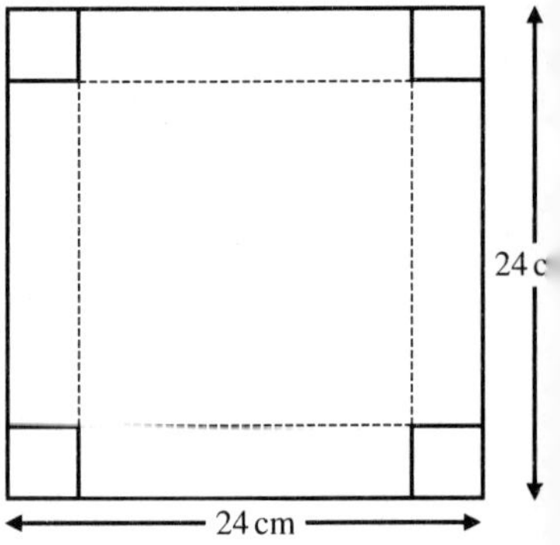

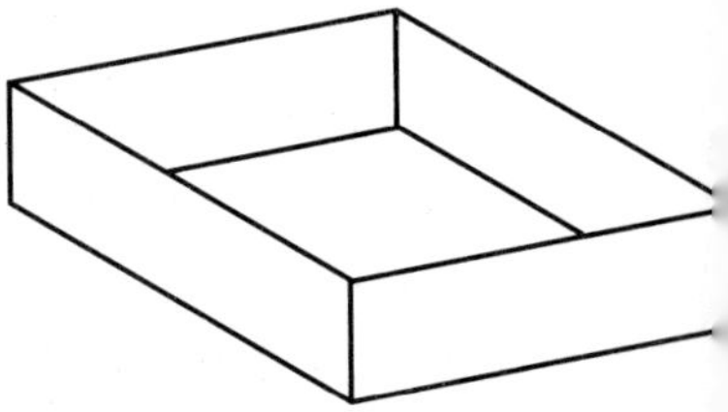

(a) You have a square sheet of card 24 cm by 24 cm.
You can make a box (without a lid) by cutting squares from the corners and folding up the sides.
What size corners should you cut out so that the volume of the box is as large as possible?
Try different sizes for the corners and record the results in a table.

Length of the side of the corner square (cm)	Dimensions of the open box (cm)	Volume of the box (cm^3)
1	$22 \times 22 \times 1$	484
2		
–		
–		

Now consider boxes made from different sized cards:
15 cm × 15 cm and 20 cm by 20 cm.
What size corners should you cut out this time so that the volume of the box is as large as possible?
Is there a connection between the size of the corners cut out and the size of the square card?

(b) Investigate the situation when the card is not square.
Take rectangular cards where the length is twice the width (20×10, 12×6, 18×9 etc.)
Again, for the maximum volume is there a connection between the size of the corners cut out and the size of the original card?

6 Timetabling

(a) Every year a new timetable has to be written for the school. We will look at the problem of writing the timetable for one department (mathematics). The department allocates the teaching periods as follows:

U6	2 sets (at the same times); 8 periods in 4 doubles.
L6	2 sets (at the same times); 8 periods in 4 doubles.
Year 5	6 sets (at the same times); 5 single periods.
Year 4	6 sets (at the same times); 5 single periods.
Year 3	6 sets (at the same times); 5 single periods.
Year 2	6 sets (at the same times); 5 single periods.
Year 1	5 mixed ability forms; 5 single periods not necessarily at the same times.

Here are the teachers and the maximum number of maths periods which they can teach.

A	33	F	15	(Must be Years 5, 4, 3)
B	33	G	10	(Must be Years 2, 1)
C	33	H	10	(Must be Years 2, 1)
D	20	I	5	(Must be Year 3)
E	20			

Furthermore, to ensure some continuity of teaching, teachers B and C must teach the U6 and teachers A, B, C, D, E, F must teach year 5.

Here is a timetable form which has been started

M	5					U6 B, C	U6 B, C			
Tu		5		U6 B, C	U6 B, C					
W						5				
Th							5		U6 B, C	U6 B, C
F	U6 B, C	U6 B, C			5					

Your task is to write a complete timetable for the mathematics department subject to the restrictions already stated.

(b) If that was too easy, here are some changes.

U6 and L6 have 4 sets each (still 8 periods)
Two new teachers:
J 20 periods maximum
K 15 periods maximum but cannot teach on Mondays.

Because of games lessons: A cannot teach Wednesday afternoon
B cannot teach Tuesday afternoon
C cannot teach Friday afternoon

Also: A, B, C and E must teach U6
A, B, C, D, E, F must teach year 5

For the pupils, games afternoons are as follows:
Monday year 2; Tuesday year 3; Wednesday year 5 L6, U6;
Thursday year 4; Friday year 1.

7 Diagonals

In a 4×7 rectangle, the diagonal passes through 10 squares.

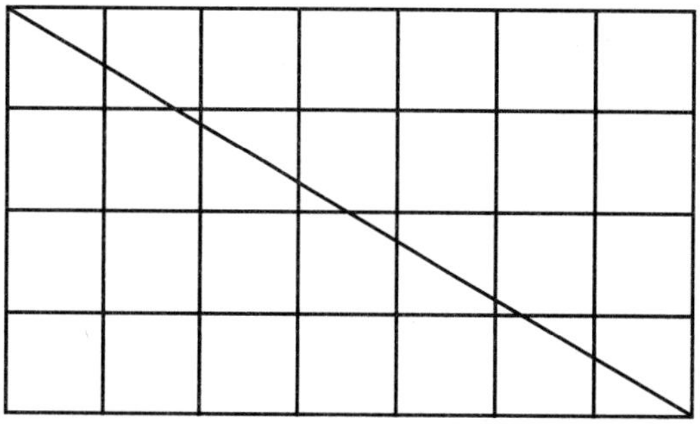

Draw rectangles of your own choice and count the number of squares through which the diagonal passes.
A rectangle is 640×250. How many squares will the diagonal pass through?

8 Painting cubes

The large cube on the right consists of 27 unit cubes.

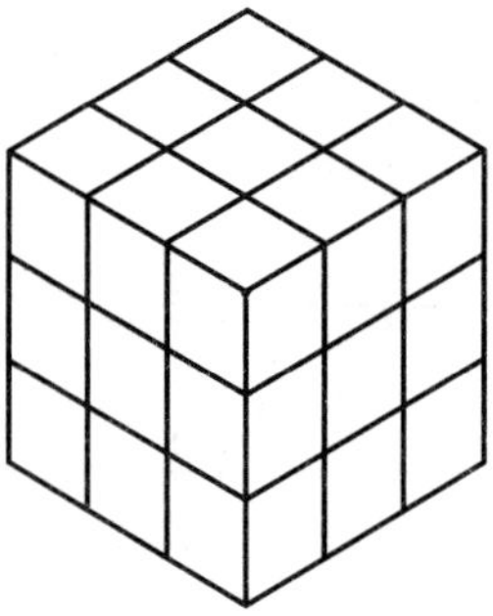

All six faces of the large cube are painted green.

- How many unit cubes have 3 green faces?
- How many unit cubes have 2 green faces?
- How many unit cubes have 1 green face?
- How many unit cubes have 0 green faces?

Answer the four questions for the cube which is $n \times n \times n$.

13.2 Puzzles and games

1 Crossnumbers

Draw a copy of the crossnumber pattern below and work out the answers using the clues. You can check your working by doing *all* the across and *all* the down clues.

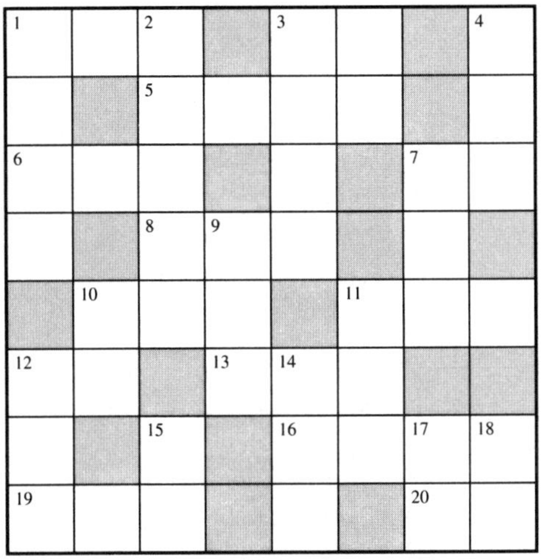

Part A

Across

1. $327 + 198$
2. $245 \div 7$
5. $3146 - 729$
6. $248 - 76$
7. 2^6
8. $850 \div 5$
10. $10^2 + 1^2$
11. $3843 \div 7$
12. $1000 - 913$
13. $37 \times 5 \times 3$
16. $152\,300 \div 50$
19. 3^6
20. $100 - \left(\frac{17 \times 10}{5}\right)$

Down

1. $3280 + 1938$
2. $65\,720 - 13\,510$
3. $3{\cdot}1 \times 1000$
4. $1284 \div 6$
7. $811 - 127$
9. 65×11
10. $(12^2 - 8) \div 8$
11. $(7^2 + 1^2) \times 11$
12. $7 + 29 + 234 + 607$
14. $800 - 265$
15. $1 + 2 + 3 + 4 + 5 + 6 + 7 + 8 + 13$
17. $(69 \times 6) \div 9$
18. $3^2 + 4^2 + 5^2 + 2^4$

Part B Draw decimal points on the lines between squares where necessary.

Across

1. $4{\cdot}2 + 1{\cdot}64$
3. $7 \times 0{\cdot}5$
5. $20{\cdot}562 \div 6$
6. $(2^3 \times 5) \times 10 - 1$
7. $0{\cdot}034 \times 1000$
8. $61 \times 0{\cdot}3$
10. $8 - 0{\cdot}36$
11. 19×50
12. $95{\cdot}7 \div 11$
13. $8{\cdot}1 \times 0{\cdot}7$
16. $(11 \times 5) \div 8$
19. $(44 - 2{\cdot}8) \div 5$
20. Number of inches in a yard

Down

1. $62{\cdot}6 - 4{\cdot}24$
2. $48{\cdot}73 - 4{\cdot}814$
3. $25 + 7{\cdot}2 + 0{\cdot}63$
4. $2548 \div 7$
7. $0{\cdot}315 \times 100$
9. $169 \times 0{\cdot}05$
10. $770 \div 100$
11. $14{\cdot}2 + 0{\cdot}7 - 5{\cdot}12$
12. $11{\cdot}4 - 2{\cdot}64 - 0{\cdot}18$
14. $0{\cdot}0667 \times 10^3$
15. $0{\cdot}6 + 0{\cdot}7 + 0{\cdot}8 + 7{\cdot}3$
17. 0·73 m written in cm
18. $0{\cdot}028 \times 200$

Part C

Across

1. Eleven squared take away six
3. Next in the sequence 21, 24, 28, 33
5. Number of minutes in a day
6. $2 \times 13 \times 5 \times 5$
7. Next in the sequence 92, 83, 74
8. 5% of 11 400
10. $98 + 11^2$
11. $(120 - 9) \times 6$
12. $1\frac{2}{5}$ as a decimal
13. $2387 \div 7$
16. $9{\cdot}05 \times 1000$
19. 8 m − 95 cm (in cm)
20. 3^4

Down

1. Write 18·6 m in cm
2. Fifty-one thousand and fifty-one
3. Write 3·47 km in m
4. $1\frac{1}{4}$ as a decimal
7. 7 m − 54 cm (in cm)
9. $0{\cdot}0793 \times 1000$
10. 2% of 1200
11. $\frac{1}{5}$ of 3050
12. $127 \div 100$
14. Number of minutes between 12 00 and 20 10
15. 4% of 1125
17. $7^2 + 3^2$
18. Last two digits of (67×3)

Part D

Across

1. $1\frac{3}{4}$ as a decimal
3. Two dozen
5. Forty less than ten thousand
6. Emergency
7. 5% of 740
8. Nine pounds and five pence
10. 1·6 m written in cm
11. $5649 \div 7$
12. One-third of 108
13. $6 - 0{\cdot}28$
16. A quarter to midnight on the 24 h clock
20. $3300 \div 150$

Down

1. Twelve pounds 95 pence
2. Four less than sixty thousand
3. 245×11
4. James Bond
7. Number of minutes between 09 10 and 15 30
9. $\frac{1}{20}$ as a decimal
10. Ounces in a pound
11. 8·227 to two decimal places
12. 4 m − 95 cm (in cm)
14. Three to the power 6
15. 20·64 to the nearest whole number
17. $(6\frac{1}{2})^2$ to the nearest whole number
18. Number of minutes between 14 22 and 15 14

2 Crossnumbers without clues

Here we have five cross number puzzles with a difference. There are no clues, only answers, and it is your task to find where the answers go.

(a) Copy out the crossnumber pattern.

(b) Fit all the given numbers into the correct spaces.
Tick off the numbers from the lists as you write them in the square.

1.

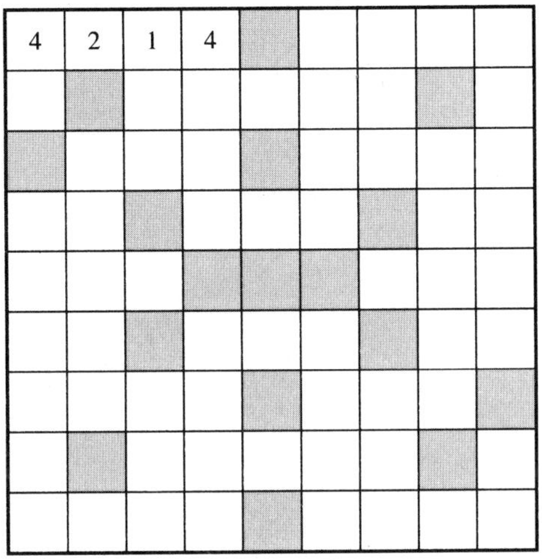

2 digits	*3 digits*	*4 digits*	*5 digits*	*6 digits*
26	215	5841	21862	134953
41	427	9217	83642	727542
19	106	9131	21362	
71	872	1624	57320	
63	725	1506		
76	385	4214		
	156	5216		
	263	4734		
	234	2007		
	180	2637		

2.

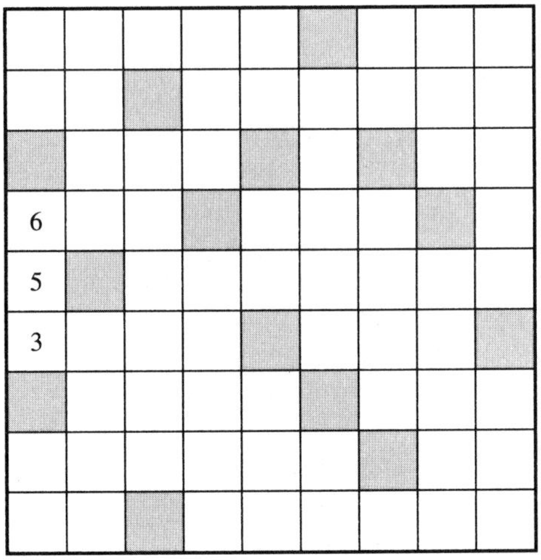

2 digits	*3 digits*	*4 digits*	*5 digits*	*6 digits*
99	571	9603	24715	387566
25	918	8072	72180	338472
52	131	4210	54073	414725
26	328	3824	71436	198264
42	906	8916	82125	
57	249			
30	653			*7 digits*
53	609			8592070
14	111			
61	127			
	276			

The next three are more difficult but they are possible! Don't give up.

3.

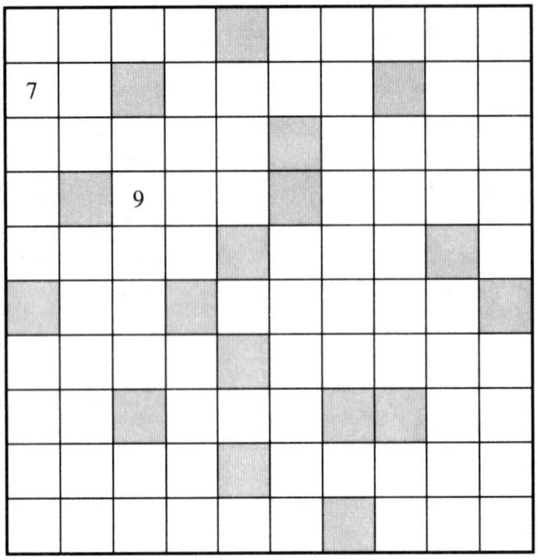

2 digits	*3 digits*	*4 digits*	*5 digits*	*6 digits*
26	306	3654	38975	582778
28	457	3735	49561	585778
32	504	3751	56073	728468
47	827	3755	56315	
49	917	3819	56435	*7 digits*
52	951	6426	57435	8677056
70		7214	58535	
74		7315	58835	
		7618	66430	
		7643	77435	
		9847	77543	

4.

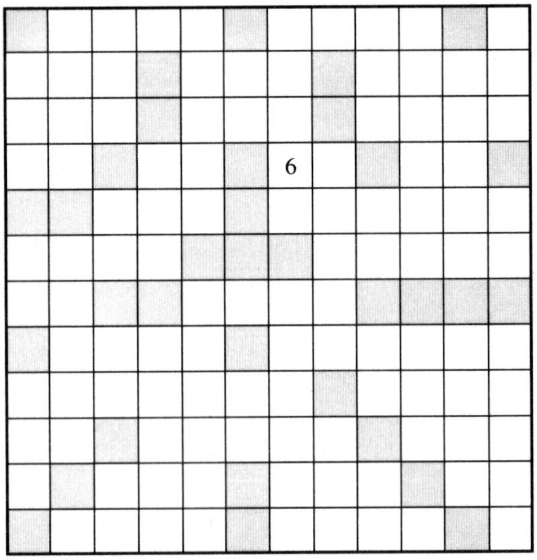

2 digits	*3 digits*	*4 digits*	*5 digits*	*6 digits*
11	121	2104	14700	216841
17	147	2356	24567	588369
18	170	2456	25921	846789
19	174	3714	26759	861277
23	204	4711	30388	876452
31	247	5548	50968	
37	287	5678	51789	
58	324	6231	78967	
61	431	6789	98438	
62	450	7630		*7 digits*
62	612	9012		6645678
70	678	9921		
74	772			
81	774			
85	789			
94	870			
99				

5.

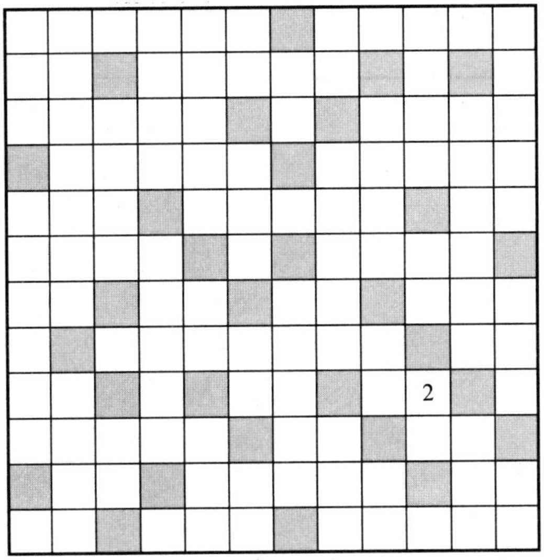

2 digits		*3 digits*	*4 digits*	*5 digits*	*6 digits*
12	47	129	2096	12641	324029
14	48	143	3966	23449	559641
16	54	298	5019	33111	956782
18	56	325	5665	33210	
20	63	331	6462	34509	
21	67	341	7809	40551	
23	81	443	8019	41503	
26	90	831	8652	44333	*7 digits*
27	91	923		69786	1788932
32	93			88058	5749306
38	98			88961	
39	99			90963	
46				94461	
				99654	

3 *Number messages*

(a) Start at the box containing the letter 'Q'.
(b) Work out the answer to the question in the box.
(c) Look for the answer in the corner of another box.
(d) Write down the letter in the box and then work out the answer to the problem in the box.
(e) Look for the answer as before and continue until you arrive back at box 'Q'.
(f) Read the message.

1.

27 **Q** $99 - 27$	99 **S** $2212 \div 7$	125 **W** $211 - 99$	444 **N** 110×9
766 **I** $(18 - 13)^2$	112 **O** $(21 - 18)^3$	615 **N** 18×20	25 **S** $108 + 209$
317 **T** $625 \div 5$	990 **E** $840 \div 3$	72 **O** $123 + 321$	118 **U** $3^2 \times 11$
166 **L** $19 + 99$	360 **E** $1000 - 234$	316 **O** $5 + 55 + 555$	280 **P** $200 - 34$

2.

0·42 **Q** 8·1 + 5	3·3 **R** 6·1 ÷ 5	4·1 **B** 19 − 13·7	10·5 **R** 14·5 − 3
5·3 **I** 3·24 ÷ 9	11·5 **S** 0·84 ÷ 4	1·22 **E** 11 − 8·95	0·01 **H** 4·2 × 0·1
2·05 **R** 0·313 × 100	31·3 **U** 8·8 + 9·9	13·1 **S** 8 − 3·7	0·21 **A** 0·33 × 10
4·3 **P** 2·4 + 7	0·36 **S** 10 − 9·99	18·7 **B** 8·2 × 0·5	9·4 **U** 2·1 × 5

3.

6 **Q** 10 + 3 × 2	13 **S** 22 + 20 ÷ 10	33 **R** 19 − 12 ÷ 6	71 **N** 7 × 4 − 15 ÷ 5
7 **E** 8 + 9 ÷ 3	53 **O** 39 − 17 × 2	25 **D** (25 + 23) ÷ 8	19 **E** 13 − 3 × 2
55 **H** 2 × 3 + 4 × 2	5 **U** 8 × 7 + 3 × 5	16 **T** 12 − 4 × 2	17 **T** (4 + 7) × 5
4 **H** 6 × 3 + 1	24 **R** 3 × 14 + 11	14 **I** 3 × 5 − 1 × 2	11 **A** 5 × 7 − 2

4.

50 **Q** 2·5 × 4 + 3	8·1 **O** 5 × 9 − 2 × 9	2·13 **N** 7 − 0·04 × 10	2 **N** 0·5 × 2 + 17
7·2 **L** 0·3 × 100 − 7	3·5 **O** 8 × 5 + 6 × 7	84 **G** 11 × 9 − 7 × 7	52·2 **G** 10 × (3·4 + 5)
6 **A** 1·7 + 3 ÷ 10	23 **A** 13 ÷ 100 + 2	13 **C** 8 − 0·2 × 10	7·24 **B** 8 + 1 ÷ 10
82 **U** 6·2 ÷ 5 + 6	27 **I** 8 − 0·4 × 2	6·6 **E** 3·2 + 7 × 7	18 **Y** 12·5 − 3 × 3

5.

−13 **Q** $-6+2$	−7 **C** $(-3)^2+4^2$	12 **Y** $12 \div (-2)$	0 **A** $12 \times (-10)$	−14 **A** $-8+17$
−120 **R** $16 \div (-16)$	−8 **H** $-3-15$	−18 **E** $(-2)^2$	8 **E** $(-8) \div (-8)$	4 **R** $-3+7-9$
−6 **T** $-8-9$	13 **E** $-2+1-1$	−4 **M** $(-3) \times (-4)$	25 **L** $-7+20$	1 **R** $-3-2-8$
9 **C** $(-8) \div 1$	−5 **S** $0 \times (-17)$	−2 **V** $6-(-2)$	−1 **E** $-2+6-11$	−17 **E** -2×7

6.

3·62 **Q** $12-8{\cdot}99$	8 **O** $45 \div 9 - 5$	25 **U** $90 \times 2 - 5$	300 **S** $-8-6$	1·3 **L** $6+9 \div 3$
−9 **A** $2{\cdot}6 \times 0{\cdot}5$	6 **Y** $0{\cdot}7 \div 100$	0·27 **R** $(-1)^2+(-2)^2$	21 **N** $200-41$	159 **G** $25{\cdot}34 \div 7$
0 **R** $1{\cdot}4+19$	1·24 **A** $9 \times 5 - 3 \times 7$	3·01 **M** $18 - 3 \times 4$	5 **O** $6 \times (11-7{\cdot}5)$	175 **L** $6{\cdot}2 \div 5$
9 **C** $(-2)^2+21$	−14 **W** $2{\cdot}7 \times 0{\cdot}1$	20·4 **I** $0{\cdot}3 \times 1000$	24 **T** $-7+15$	0·007 **C** $-36 \div 4$

4. Calculator words

On a calculator the number 4915 looks like the word 'SIGH' when the calculator is held upside down.

Find the words given by the clues below.

1. $221 \times 7 \times 5$ (Sounds like 'cell')
2. $5 \times 601 \times 5 \times 3$ (Wet blow)
3. $88^2 - 6$ (Ringer)
4. $0{\cdot}9 \times 5900 - 1$ (Leaves)
5. $62^2 - (4 \times 7 \times 5)$ (Nothing to it)
6. $0{\cdot}88^2 - \frac{1}{1000}$ (O Hell)
7. $(5 \times 7 \times 10^3) + (3 \times 113)$ (Gaggle)
8. 44^4 + Half of 67 682 (Readable)
9. $5 \times 3 \times 37 \times 1000 - 1420$ (Stick in mind)
10. $3200 - 1320 \div 11$ (Woodwind)

11. $48^4 + 8929$ (Deceitful dame)
12. $31^2 \times 32^2 - 276^2 + 30$ (Not a twig)
13. $(130 \times 135) + (23 \times 3 \times 11 \times 23)$ (Wobbly)
14. $164 \times 166^2 + 734$ (Almost big)
15. $8794^2 + 25 \times 342{\cdot}28 + 120 \times 25$ (Thin skin)
16. $0{\cdot}08 - (3^2 \div 10^4)$ (Ice house)
17. $235^2 - (4 \times 36{\cdot}5)$ (Shiny surface)
18. $(80^2 + 60^2) \times 3 + 81^2 + 12^2 + 3013$ (Ship gunge)
19. $3 \times 17 \times (329^2 + 2 \times 173)$ (Unlimbed)
20. $230 \times 230\frac{1}{2} + 30$ (Fit feet)
21. $33 \times 34 \times 35 + 15 \times 3$ (Beleaguer)
22. $0{\cdot}32^2 + \frac{1}{1000}$ (Did he or didn't he?)
23. $(23 \times 24 \times 25 \times 26) + (3 \times 11 \times 10^3) - 20$ (Help)
24. $(16^2 + 16)^2 - (13^2 - 2)$ (Slander)
25. $(3 \times 661)^2 - (3^6 + 22)$ (Pester)
26. $(22^2 + 29{\cdot}4) \times 10$; $(3{\cdot}03^2 - 0{\cdot}02^2) \times 100^2$ (Four words) (Goliath)
27. $1{\cdot}25 \times 0{\cdot}2^6 + 0{\cdot}2^2$ (Tissue time)
28. $(710 + (1823 \times 4)) \times 4$ (Liquor)
29. $(3^3)^2 + 2^2$ (Wriggler)
30. $14 + (5 \times (83^2 + 110))$ (Bigger than a duck)
31. $2 \times 3 \times 53 \times 10^4 + 9$ (Opposite to hello, almost!)
32. $(177 \times 179 \times 182) + (85 \times 86) - 82$ (Good salesman)

5 The milk crate problem

You have 18 bottles to put into the crate below which has space for 24 bottles.

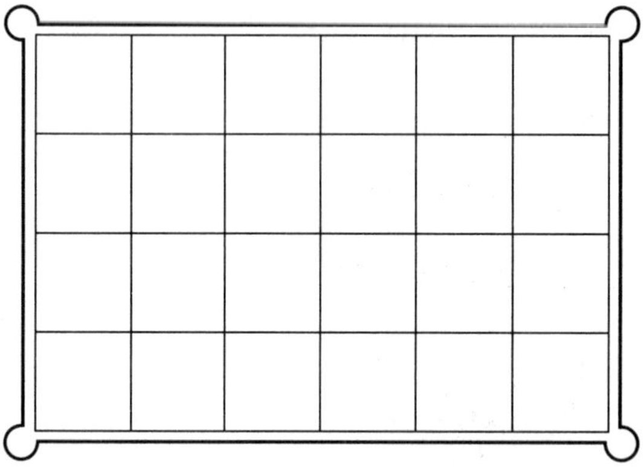

The only condition is that you have to put an *even* number of bottles into every row and every column. Good luck.

6 Estimating game

This is a game for two players. On squared paper draw an answer grid with the numbers shown.

Answer grid

891	7047	546	2262	8526	429
2548	231	1479	357	850	7938
663	1078	2058	1014	1666	3822
1300	1950	819	187	1050	3393
4350	286	3159	442	2106	550
1701	4050	1377	4900	1827	957

The players now take turns to choose two numbers from the question grid below and multiply them on a calculator.

Question grid

11	26	81
17	39	87
21	50	98

The number obtained is crossed out on the answer grid using the players' own colour.
The game continues until all the numbers in the answer grid have been crossed out. The object is to get four answers in a line (horizontally, vertically or diagonally). The winner is the player with most lines of four.
A line of *five* counts as *two* lines of four.
A line of *six* counts as *three* lines of four.

7 Creating numbers

Using only the numbers 1, 2, 3 and 4 once each and the operations $+, -, \times, \div, !$ create every number from 1 to 100.
You can use the numbers as powers and you must use all of the numbers 1, 2, 3 and 4.
[4! is pronounced 'four factorial' and means $4 \times 3 \times 2 \times 1$ (i.e. 24)
similarly $3! = 3 \times 2 \times 1 = 6$
$5! = 5 \times 4 \times 3 \times 2 \times 1 = 120$]

Examples: $1 = (4-3) \div (2-1)$
$20 = 4^2 + 3 + 1$
$68 = 34 \times 2 \times 1$
$100 = (4! + 1)(3! - 2!)$

8 Pentominoes

A pentomino is a set of five squares joined along their edges. You probably know of the game of dominoes. A domino is just two squares joined together; there is only one possible shape because the two shapes here count as the same.

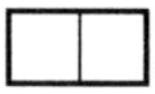
counts the same as

1. See how many different pentominoes you can design on squared paper. Here are a few.

(a) 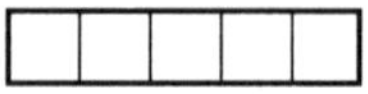 (b) 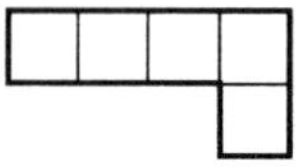 (c) 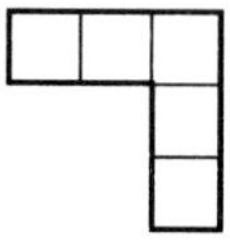

You may find that some of your designs are really the same, for example

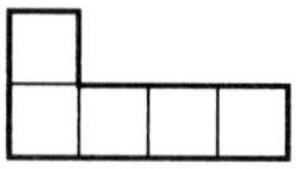
and
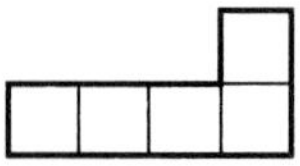

You can use a piece of tracing paper to check if some of your designs are really the same or different.

After about fifteen minutes, compare your designs with those of other people in your class. There are in fact twelve different pentomino shapes. Make a neat copy of these.

2. Fit these five pentominoes together to form a square.

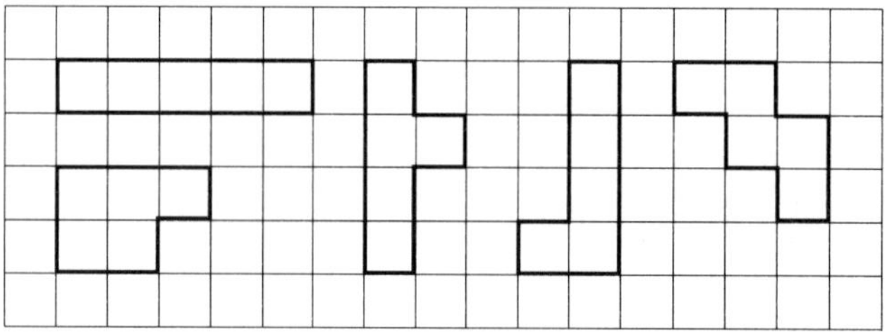

3. On squared paper, draw a square having eight units on each side. Somewhere inside the square draw a small square having two units on each side and shade it.

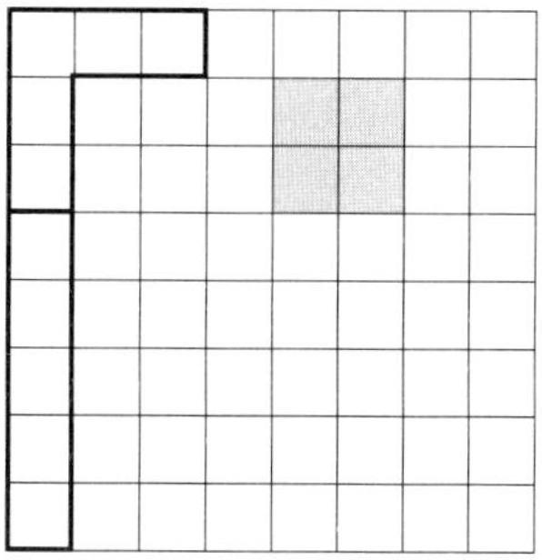

Now fill up the rest of the square with as many different pentominoes as you can. There should be no 'holes' left by the time you have finished.

A start has been made in the diagram above.

4. Take some more squared paper and draw a rectangle measuring 10 by 6. Fill up the rectangle with as many different pentominoes as you can. This problem is more difficult than the 8 by 8 square.

9 'I can read your mind'

Here is a trick where you can demonstrate your ability to read a friend's mind.

	Example
Start by writing any number between 1 and 50 on a card but do not let your friend see it.	I will choose 31
Now ask your friend to do the following:	
1. Write any number between 50 and 100.	74 (say)
2. Add ______ to your number. [The number is 99 minus the number on *your* card] i.e. 99 − 31 = 68	Add 68 74 + 68 = 142
3. Cross out the left-hand digit.	~~1~~42
4. Add this digit to the number remaining.	42 + 1 = 43
5. Subtract this number from the number you chose at the start. (i.e. In Line 1 above)	74 − 43 = 31

Now, with a flourish, show your friend your card with the correct number written on it.

10 The chess board problem

On the 4×4 square below we have placed four objects subject to the restriction that nowhere are there two objects on the same row, column or diagonal.

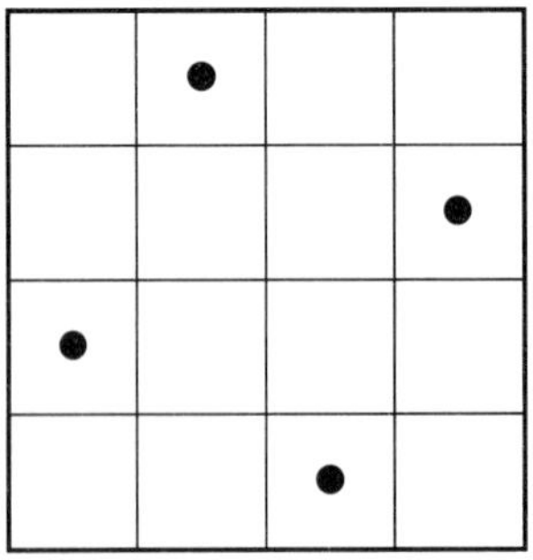

Subject to the same restrictions:
(i) find a solution for a 5×5 square, using five objects,
(ii) find a solution for a 6×6 square, using six objects,
(iii) find a solution for a 7×7 square, using seven objects,
(iv) find a solution for a 8×8 square, using eight objects.

It is called the chess board problem because the objects could be 'Queens' which can move any number of squares in any direction.

11 Miscellaneous puzzles

1. This shape can be divided into equal pieces in several ways. Each piece must be exactly the same size and shape.

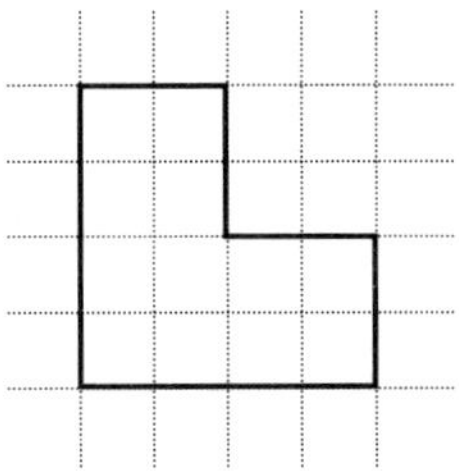

We can easily divide the shape into two equal pieces.
Draw the shape three times and show how it can be divided into
(a) 3 pieces
(b) 6 pieces
(c) (harder) 4 pieces.

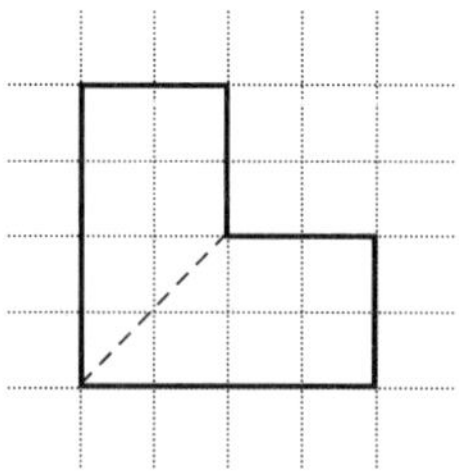

Draw this shape three times and show how it can be divided into
(a) 3 pieces
(b) 6 pieces
(c) (harder) 8 pieces.

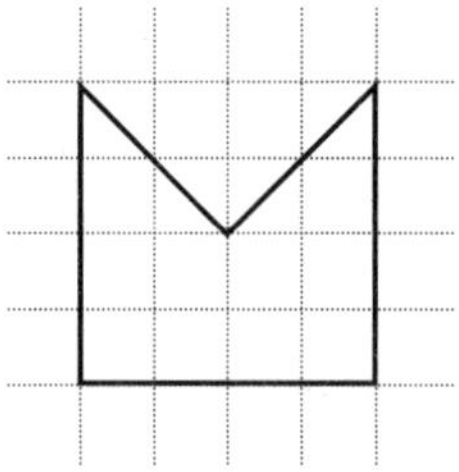

2. King John is given nine coins which look identical but in fact one of the coins is an underweight fake.
Describe how you can use a balance to find the fake in just two weighings.

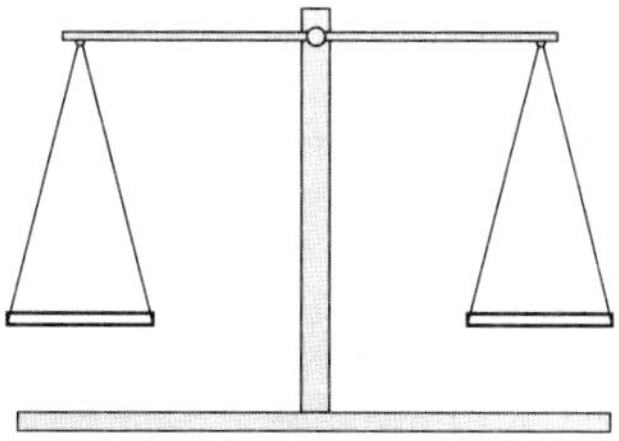

3. Here we have used 12 matches to enclose an area of 9 squares. Draw four diagrams to show how 12 matches can be used to enclose areas of 8, 7, 6 and 5 squares.

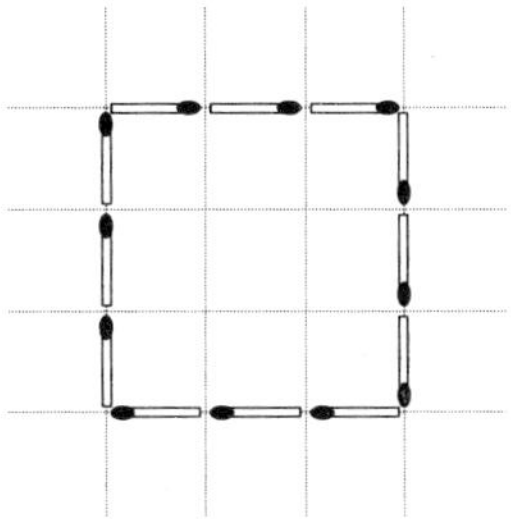

4. There is a fire in the kitchens of Gibson College and the principal, Mr Gibson, is stranded on the roof of the burning building.

Firemen are on the roof of the library and they have two ladders each 20 feet long. The shortest distance from the library to the kitchen roof is 22 feet. How can the firemen rescue Mr Gibson?

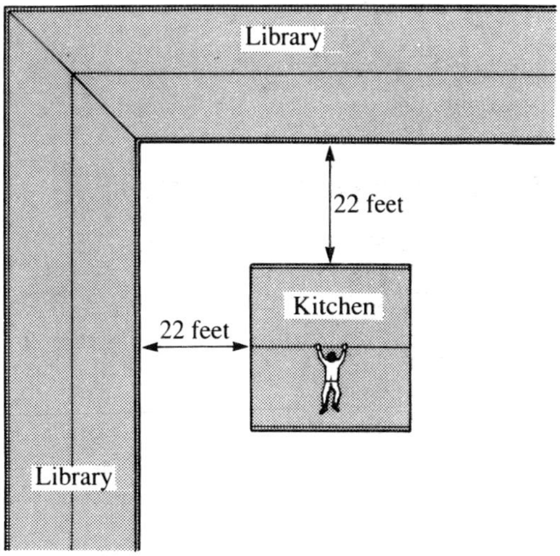

5. Two coins have a total value of 60p. One of them is *not* a 50p coin. What are the two coins?

6. In a 24 hour day, from midnight to midnight, how many times are the hands of a clock at right angles to each other?

14 Revision

14.1 Revision exercises

Exercise 1

1. Copy the following bill and complete it by filling in the four blank spaces.

8 rolls of wallpaper at £3·20 each	= £ ...
3 tins of paint at £ ... each	= £ 20·10
... brushes at £2·40 each	= £ 9·60
Total	= £ ...

2. Write down each sequence and find the next two numbers.
   (a) 2, 9, 16, 23,
   (b) 20, 18, 16, 14,
   (c) −5, −2, 1, 4,
   (d) 128, 64, 32, 16,
   (e) 8, 11, 15, 20,

3. A man buys 500 pencils at 2·4 pence each. What change does he receive from £20?

4. Every day at school Stephen buys a roll for 14p, crisps for 11p and a drink for 21p. How much does he spend in pounds in the whole school year of 200 days?

5. An athlete runs 25 laps of a track in 30 minutes 10 seconds.
   (a) How many seconds does he take to run 25 laps?
   (b) How long does he take to run one lap, if he runs the 25 laps at a constant speed?

6. A pile of 250 tiles is 2 m thick. What is the thickness of one tile in cm?

7. Work out
   (a) 20% of £65
   (b) 37% of £400
   (c) 8·5% of £2000.

8. In a test, the marks of nine pupils were 7, 5, 2, 7, 4, 9, 7, 6, 6. Find
   (a) the mean mark
   (b) the median mark
   (c) the modal mark.

9. Work out
   (a) $-6-5$ (b) $-7+30$
   (c) $-13+3$ (d) -4×5
   (e) -3×-2 (f) $-4+-10$

10. Given $a=3$, $b=-2$ and $c=5$, work out
   (a) $b+c$ (b) $a-b$
   (c) ab (d) $a+bc$

11. Solve the equations
   (a) $x-6=3$ (b) $x+9=20$
   (c) $x-5=-2$ (d) $3x+1=22$

12. Which of the nets below can be used to make a cube?

(a)
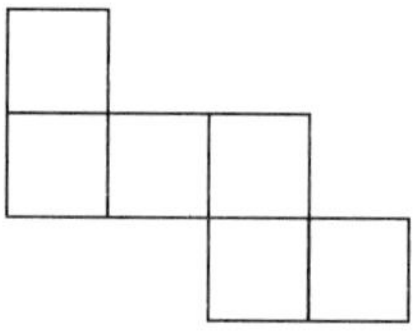

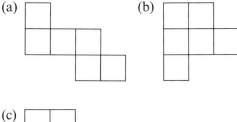

(b)
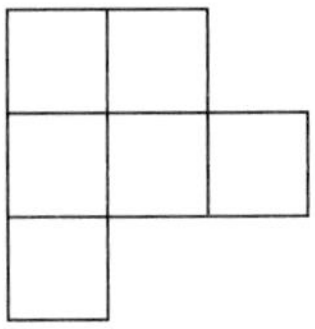

(c)
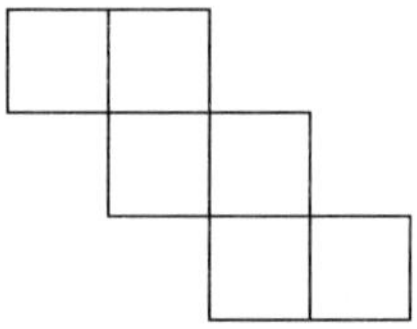

13.

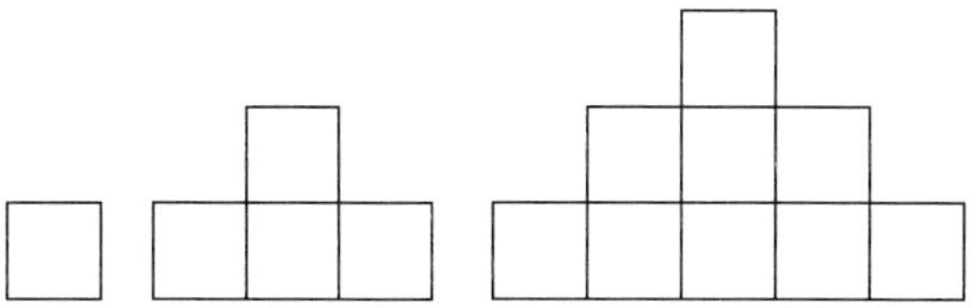

(a) Draw the next diagram in this sequence.
(b) Write down the number of squares in each diagram.
(c) Describe in words the sequence you obtain in part (b).
(d) How many squares will there be in the diagram which has 13 squares on the base?

14. *Estimate* the area of this shape correct to 1 s.f. (take $\pi = 3$)

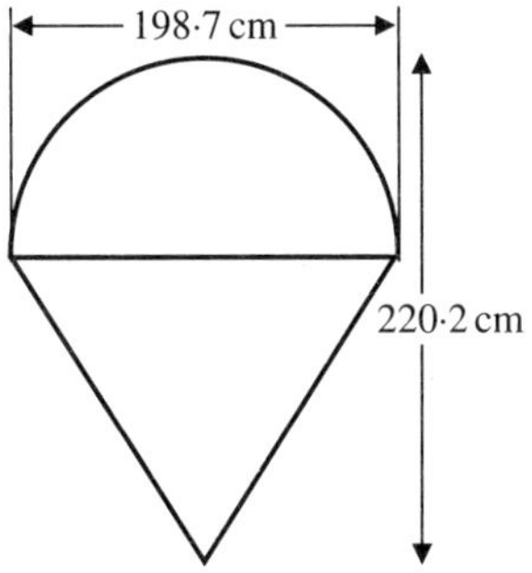

Exercise 2

1. Solve the equations
(a) $3x - 1 = 20$ (b) $4x + 3 = 4$
(c) $5x - 7 = -3$

2. Copy the diagrams and then calculate x, correct to 3 s.f.

(a)
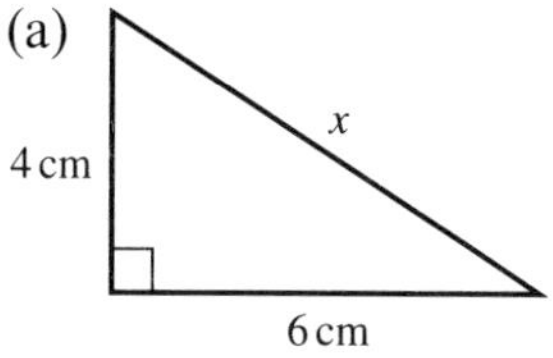

(b)
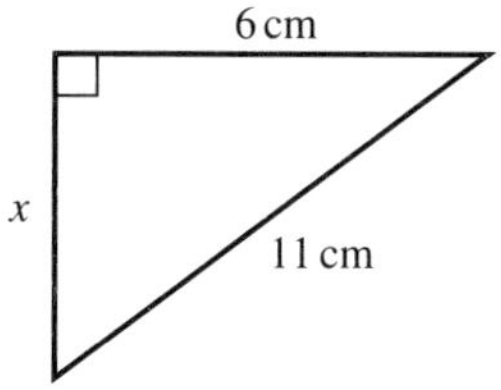

(c)
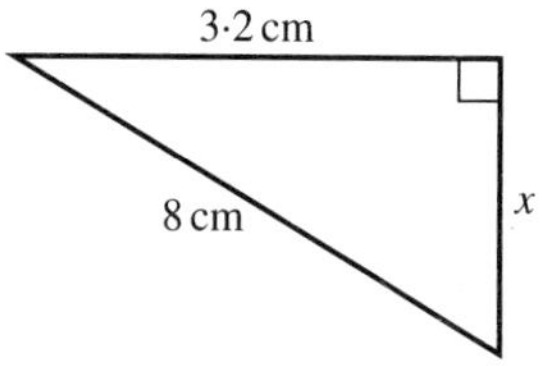

3. A bag contains 3 red balls and 5 white balls. Find the probability of selecting:
(a) a red ball,
(b) a white ball.

4. A box contains 2 yellow discs, 4 blue discs and 5 green discs. Find the probability of selecting:
(a) a yellow disc,
(b) a green disc,
(c) a blue or a green disc.

5. A school decides to have a disco from 8 p.m. to midnight. The price of the tickets will be 20p. The costs are as follows:

Disco and D.J., £25
Hire of hall, £5 an hour
200 cans of soft drinks at 15p each
200 packets of crisps at 10p each
Printing of tickets, £5

(i) What is the total cost of putting on the disco?
(ii) How many tickets must be sold to cover the cost?
(iii) If 400 tickets are sold, all the drinks are sold at 20p each and all the packets of crisps at 12p each, calculate the profit or loss the school finally makes.

6. Work out on a calculator, correct to 4 s.f.
(a) $3{\cdot}61 - (1{\cdot}6 \times 0{\cdot}951)$
(b) $\dfrac{(4{\cdot}65 + 1{\cdot}09)}{(3{\cdot}6 - 1{\cdot}714)}$

7. Find the area, correct to 3 s.f.

(a)
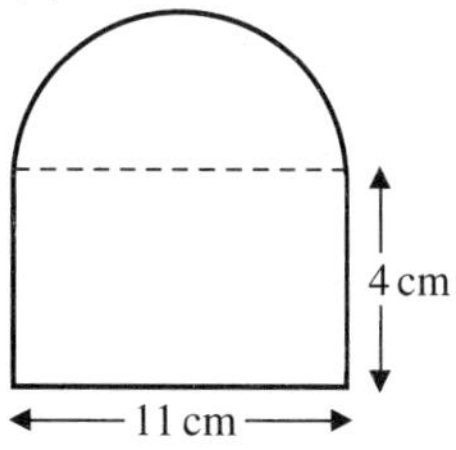

(b)
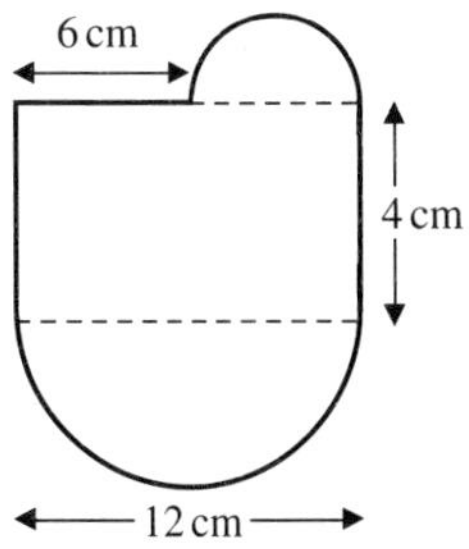

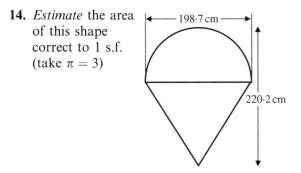

8. Look at the diagram below

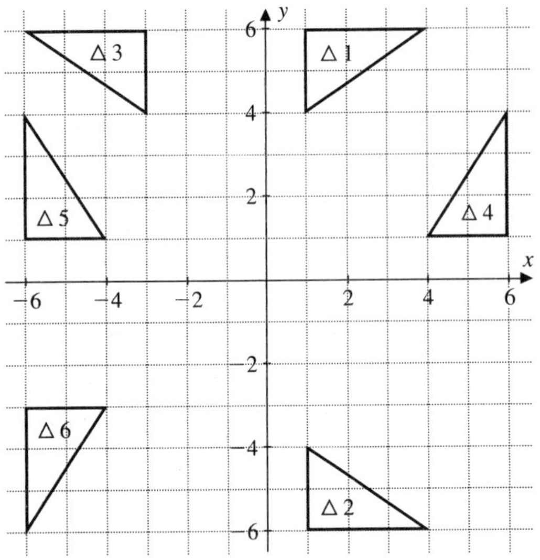

Describe fully the following transformations.

(a) △1 → △2 (b) △1 → △3
(c) △1 → △4 (d) △5 → △1
(e) △5 → △6 (f) △4 → △6

9. Plot and label the following triangles.
△1: (−3, −6), (−3, −2), (−5, −2)
△2: (−5, −1), (−5, −7), (−8, −1)
△3: (−2, −1), (2, −1), (2, 1)
△4: (6, 3), (2, 3), (2, 5)
△5: (8, 4), (8, 8), (6, 8)
△6: (−3, 1), (−3, 3), (−4, 3)

Describe fully the following transformations.

(a) △1 → △2 (b) △1 → △3
(c) △1 → △4 (d) △1 → △5
(e) △1 → △6 (f) △3 → △5
(g) △6 → △2

10. A train travels between Watford and Coventry, a distance of 108 km, in 45 minutes, at a steady speed. It passes through Rugby 40 minutes after leaving Watford. How far, in km, is it from Rugby to Coventry?

Exercise 3

1. The tables show the rail fares for adults and part of a British Rail timetable for trains between Cambridge and Bury St. Edmunds.

Fares for *one* adult

Cambridge				
£1·00	Dullingham			
£1·20	40p	Newmarket		
£1·30	£1·00	60p	Kennett	
£2·00	£1·30	£1·20	80p	Bury St. Edmunds

Train times

Cambridge	11 20
Dullingham	11 37
Newmarket	11 43
Kennett	11 52
Bury St. Edmunds	12 06

(a) How much would it cost for four adults to travel from Dullingham to Bury St. Edmunds?
(b) How long does this journey take?

2. The sketch of a clock tower is shown.

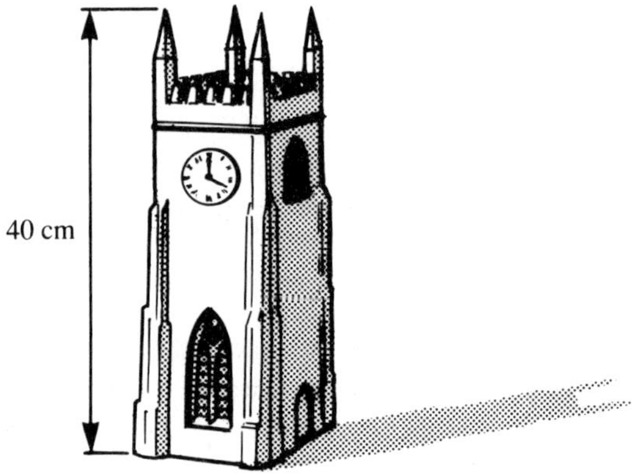

A model of the tower is made using a scale of 1 to 20.
(a) The minute hand on the tower clock is 40 cm long. What is the length of the minute hand on the model?
(b) The height of the model is 40 cm. What is the height h, in metres, of the clock tower?

3. Look at the number pattern below.

$(2 \times 1) - 1 = 2 - 1$
$(3 \times 3) - 2 = 8 - 1$
$(4 \times 5) - 3 = 18 - 1$
$(5 \times 7) - 4 = 32 - 1$
$(6 \times a) - 5 = b - 1$

(i) What number does the letter a stand for?
(ii) What number does the letter b stand for?
(iii) Write down the next line in the pattern.

4. (a) Plot and label
$\triangle 1$: $(-3, 4)$, $(-3, 8)$, $(-1, 8)$
$\triangle 5$: $(-8, -2)$, $(-8, -6)$, $(-6, -2)$

(b) Draw the triangles $\triangle 2$, $\triangle 3$, $\triangle 4$, $\triangle 6$ and $\triangle 7$ as follows:

(i) $\triangle 1 \to \triangle 2$: translation $\begin{pmatrix} 9 \\ -4 \end{pmatrix}$.

(ii) $\triangle 2 \to \triangle 3$: translation $\begin{pmatrix} -4 \\ -8 \end{pmatrix}$.

(iii) $\triangle 3 \to \triangle 4$: reflection in the line $y = x$.

(iv) $\triangle 5 \to \triangle 6$: rotation 90° anticlockwise, centre $(-4, -1)$.

(v) $\triangle 6 \to \triangle 7$: rotation 180°, centre $(0, -1)$.

(c) Write down the coordinates of the 'pointed ends' of triangles $\triangle 2$, $\triangle 3$, $\triangle 4$, $\triangle 6$, and $\triangle 7$.

5. The faces of a round and square clock are exactly the same area. If the round clock has a radius of 10 cm, how wide is the square clock?

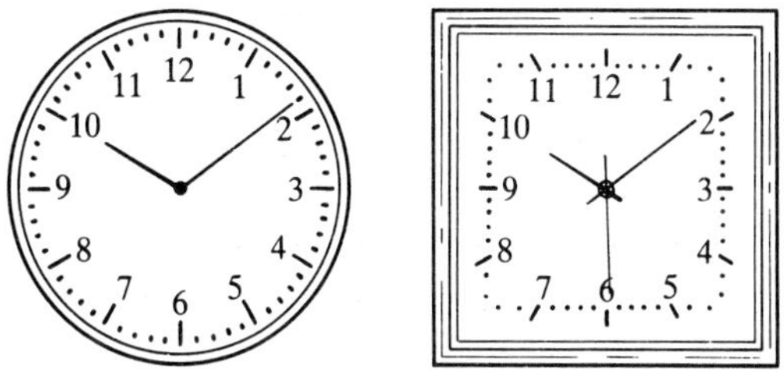

6. Here are three diagrams with lines and dots

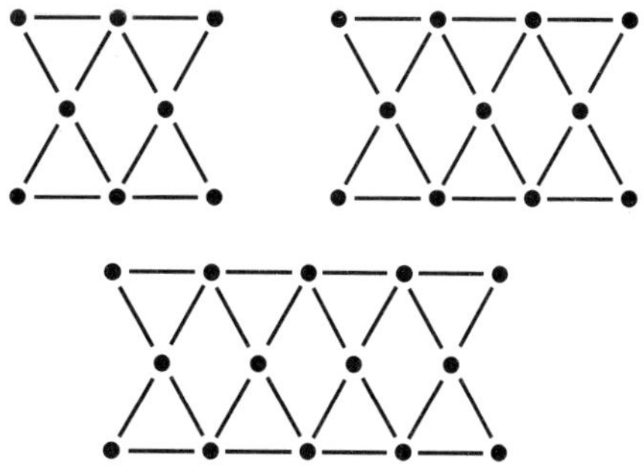

(a) Find a formula connecting the number of lines l and the number of dots d.
(b) How many dots are there in a diagram with 294 lines?

7. A factory cafeteria contains a vending machine which sells drinks. On a typical day:

the machine starts half full,
no drinks are sold before 9 a.m. and after 5 p.m.,
drinks are sold at a slow rate throughout the day, except during the morning and lunch breaks (10.30–11 a.m. and 1–2 p.m.) when there is a greater demand.
the machine is filled up just before the lunch break. (It takes about 10 minutes to fill.)

Sketch a graph showing how the number of drinks in the machine may vary from 8 a.m. to 6 p.m.

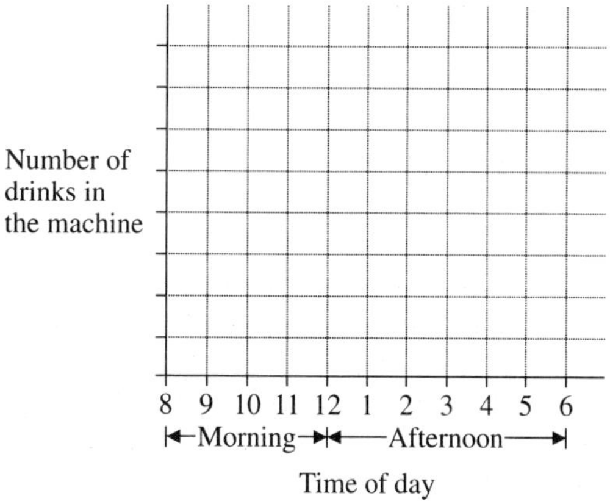

8. A metal ingot is in the form of a solid cylinder of length 7 cm and radius 3 cm.
(a) Calculate the volume, in cm^3, of the ingot.
The ingot is to be melted down and used to make cylindrical coins of thickness 3 mm and radius 12 mm.
(b) Calculate the volume, in mm^3, of each coin.
(c) Calculate the number of coins which can be made from the ingot, assuming that there is no wastage of metal.

Exercise 4

1. In December 1984, a factory employed 220 men, each man being paid £130 per week.
(a) Calculate the total weekly wage bill for the factory.
(b) In January 1985, the work force of 220 was reduced by 10 per cent. Find the number of men employed at the factory after the reduction.
(c) Also in January 1985, the weekly wage of £130 was increased by 10 per cent. Find the new weekly wage.
(d) Calculate the total weekly wage bill for the factory in January 1985.
(e) Calculate the difference between the total weekly wage bills in December 1984 and January 1985.

2. A motorist travelled 800 miles during May, when the cost of petrol was 50 pence per litre. In June the cost of petrol increased by 10% and he reduced his mileage for the month by 5%.
(a) What was the cost, in pence per litre, of petrol in June?
(b) How many miles did he travel in June?

3. $1+3 = 2^2$. $1+3+5 = 3^2$.
(a) $1+3+5+7 = x^2$. Calculate x.
(b) $1+3+5+\ldots+n = 100$. Calculate n.

4. The distance-time graphs for several objects are shown. Decide which line represents each of the following:
- hovercraft from Dover
- car ferry from Dover
- cross-channel swimmer
- marker buoy outside harbour
- train from Dover
- car ferry from Calais

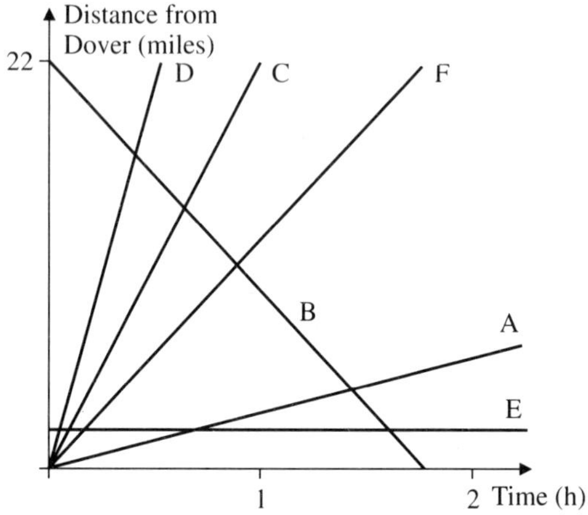

5. (a) The mean mass of 10 boys in a class is 56 kg.
(i) Calculate the total mass of these 10 boys.
(ii) Another boy, whose mass is 67 kg, joins the group. Calculate the mean mass of the 11 boys.
(b) A group of 10 boys whose mean mass is 56 kg joins a group of 20 girls whose mean mass is 47 kg. Calculate the mean mass of the 30 children.

6. Two girls walk at the same speed from A to B. Aruni takes the large semicircle and Deepa takes the three small semicircles. Who arrives at B first?

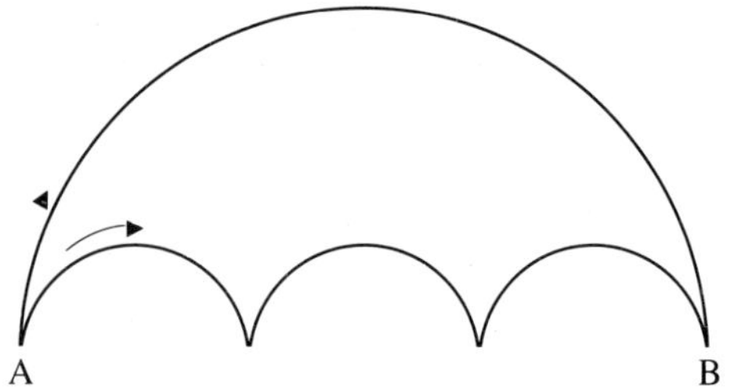

7. This electricity bill is not complete.

NEA

Northern Electricity Authority
P.O. Box 6984
Manchester M49 2QQ

Tel: 061 555 2718

Customer:
G.J. Spinner
21 Silk Street
Macclesfield SK27 3BJ

Ref: 0248-6879-5

METER READING on 07-11-84	26819 units	
METER READING on 04-02-85	☐ units	
ELECTRICITY USED	1455 units	
1455 units at 5·44 pence per unit		£ ☐
Quarterly charge		£ 6·27
TOTAL (now due)		£ ☐

(i) Write down the correct amount to be placed in each box.
(ii) In 1984, in what month was the meter read?

8. The diagram shows a lawn in the shape of a rectangle from which two semicircles have been removed. The diameter of each semicircle is 7 metres.

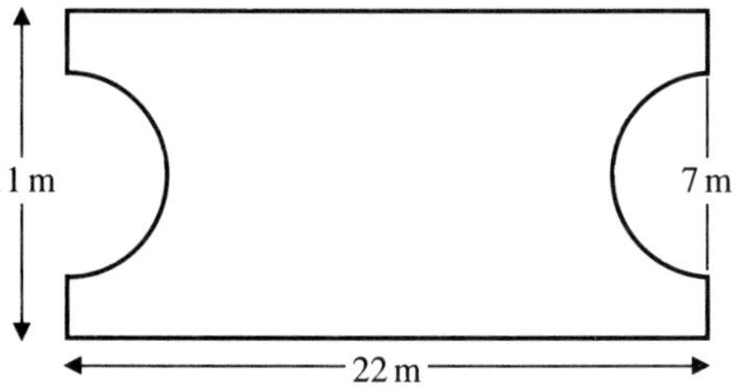

Taking π as $\frac{22}{7}$, calculate, in metres, the perimeter of the lawn.

9. A swimming pool is of width 10 m and length 25 m. The depth of water in the pool increases uniformly from the shallow end, where the depth is 1·5 m to the deep end, where the depth is 2·5 m.
(a) Calculate the volume of water in the pool.
(b) This water is emptied into a cylindrical tank of radius 3·5 m. Calculate the depth of water in the tank.

10. The following are the first six numbers, written in order of size, of a pattern.
4, 13, 28, 49, 76, 109.
(a) Which of these numbers are:
(i) odd numbers,
(ii) square numbers,
(iii) prime numbers?
(b) The difference between the first and second numbers, that is 13–4, is 9; between the second and the third it is 15, between the third and the fourth it is 21. Work out the difference between
(i) the fourth and the fifth,
(ii) the fifth and the sixth.
(c) By considering your answers in (b), find the seventh and eighth numbers of the pattern.
Explain how you reached this decision.
(d) Use the method you have described to write down the next two terms in the following pattern.
1, 4, 12, 25, 43, 66, —, —.

Exercise 5

1. $a = \frac{1}{2}$, $b = \frac{1}{4}$. Which one of the following has the greatest value?
(i) ab (ii) $a + b$ (iii) $\frac{a}{b}$
(iv) $\frac{b}{a}$ (v) $(ab)^2$

2. Solve the simultaneous equations
(a) $7c + 3d = 29$
$5c - 4d = 33$
(b) $2x - 3y = 7$
$2y - 3x = -8$

3. Calculate the side or angle marked with a letter.

(a)
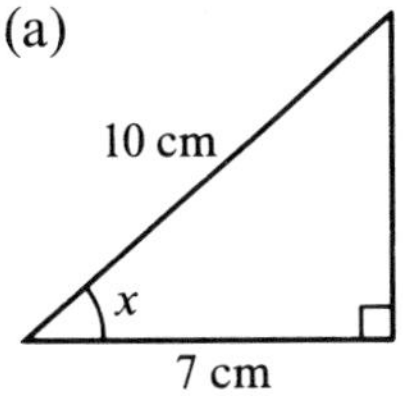

(b)
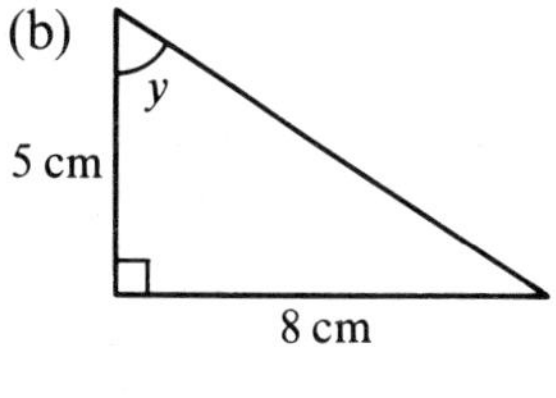

(c)
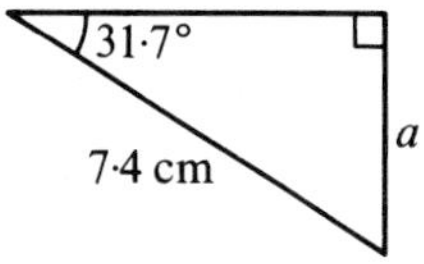

(d)
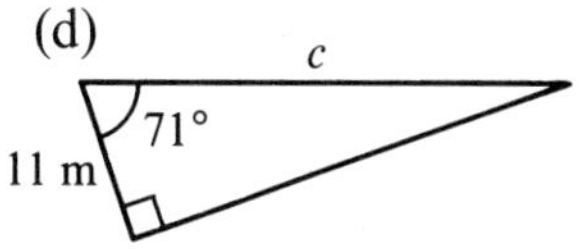

4. (a) Calculate the speed (in metres per second) of a slug which moves a distance of 30 cm in 1 minute.
(b) Calculate the time taken for a bullet to travel 8 km at a speed of 5000 m/s.
(c) Calculate the distance flown, in a time of four hours, by a pigeon which flies at a speed of 12 m/s.

5. Given $a = 3$, $b = 4$ and $c = -2$, evaluate
(a) $2a^2 - b$ (b) $a(b - c)$
(c) $2b^2 - c^2$

6. When two dice are thrown simultaneously, what is the probability of obtaining the same number on both dice?

7. In Figure 1 a circle of radius 4 cm is inscribed in a square. In Figure 2 a square is inscribed in a circle of radius 4 cm. Calculate the shaded area in each diagram.

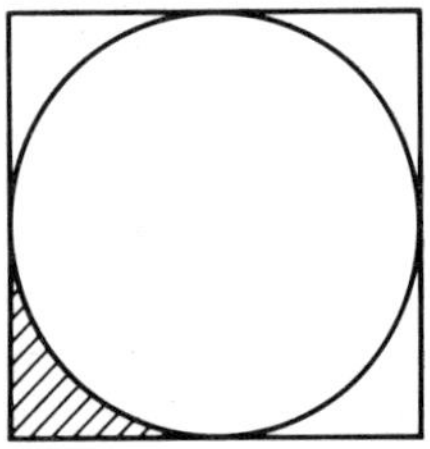
Fig. 1

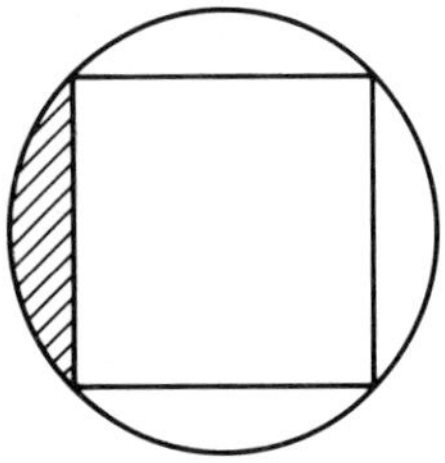
Fig. 2

8. (a) A lies on a bearing of 040° from B. Calculate the bearing of B from A.
(b) The bearing of X from Y is 115°. Calculate the bearing of Y from X.

9. In the diagram, the equations of the lines are $y = 3x$, $y = 6$, $y = 10 - x$ and $y = \frac{1}{2}x - 3$.

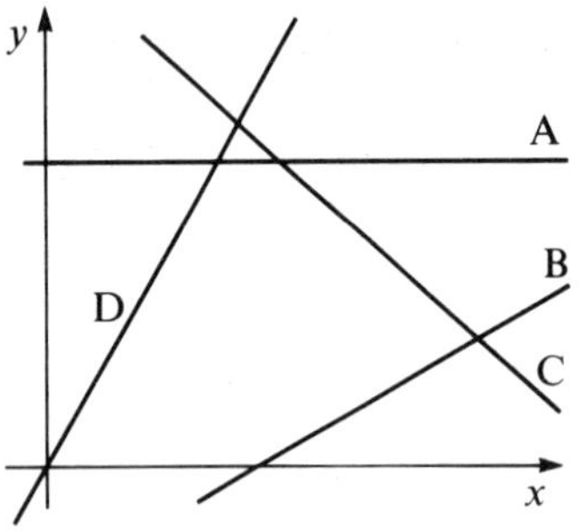

Find the equation corresponding to each line.

10. Given that $s - 3t = rt$, express
(a) s in terms of r and t
(b) r in terms of s and t

11. The mean height of 10 boys is 1·60 m and the mean height of 15 girls is 1·52 m. Find the mean height of the 25 boys and girls.

12. Find x.

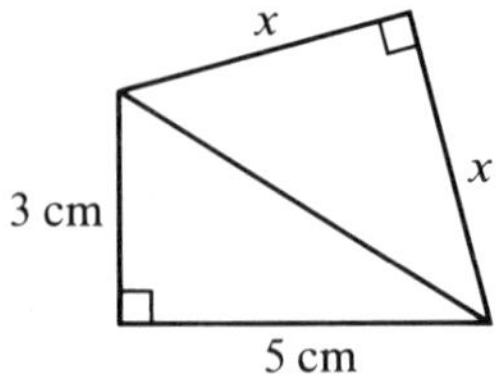

13. A cylinder of radius 8 cm has a volume of 2 litres. Calculate the height of the cylinder.

14. The shaded region A is formed by the lines $y = 2$, $y = 3x$ and $x + y = 6$. Write down the three inequalities which define A.

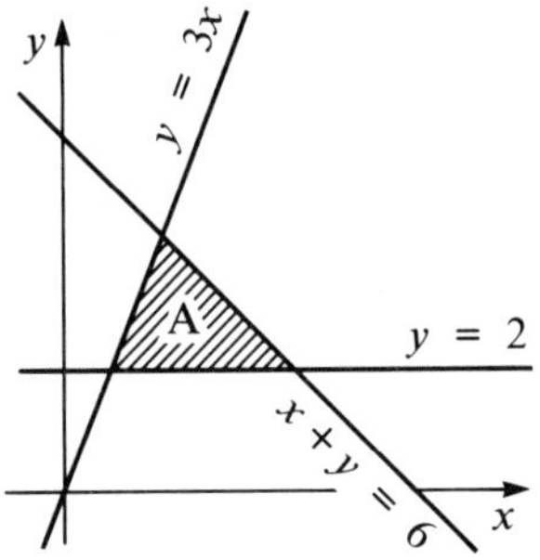

Exercise 6

1. The pump shows the price of petrol in a garage.

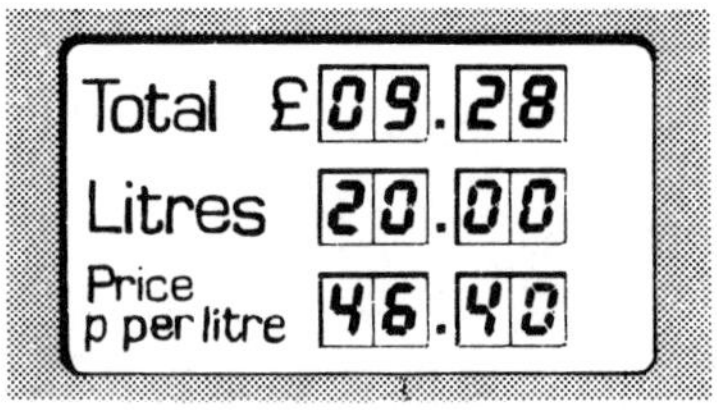

One day I buy £20 worth of petrol: How many litres do I buy?

2. Given that $x = 4$, $y = 3$, $z = -2$, evaluate
(a) $2x(y + z)$ (b) $(xy)^2 - z^2$
(c) $x^2 + y^2 + z^2$ (d) $(x + y)(x - z)$

3. Twenty-seven small wooden cubes fit exactly inside a cubical box without a lid. How many of the cubes are touching the sides or the bottom of the box?

4. The square has sides of length 3 cm and the arcs have centres at the corners. Find the shaded area.

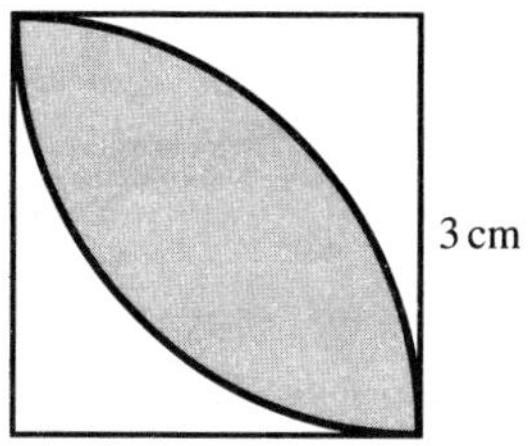

5. A coin is tossed four times. What is the probability of obtaining at least three 'heads'?

6. Each diagram in the sequence below consists of a number of dots.

Diagram number	1	2	3
	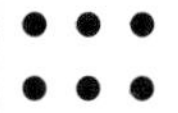	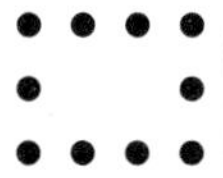	

(a) Draw diagram number 4, diagram number 5 and diagram number 6.
(b) Copy and complete the table below:

Diagram number	Number of dots
1	6
2	10
3	
4	
5	
6	

(c) Without drawing the diagrams, state the number of dots in
  (i) diagram number 10
  (ii) diagram number 15
(d) If we write x for the diagram number and n for the number of dots, write down a formula involving x and n.

7. (a) On a map, the distance between two points is 16 cm. Calculate the scale of the map if the actual distance between the points is 8 km.
(b) On another map, two points appear 1·5 cm apart and are in fact 60 km apart. Calculate the scale of the map.

8. In a mixed school there are twice as many boys as girls and ten times as many girls as teachers. Using the letters b, g, t to represent the number of boys, girls and teachers, find an expression for the total number of boys, girls and teachers. Give your answer in terms of b only.

9. Calculate the length of AB.

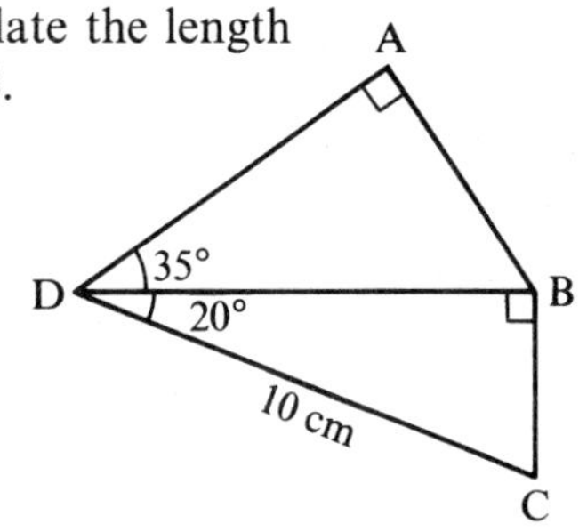

10.

Marks	3	4	5	6	7	8
Number of pupils	2	3	6	4	3	2

The table shows the number of pupils in a class who scored marks 3 to 8 in a test. Find
(a) the mean mark,
(b) the modal mark,
(c) the median mark.

11. In the diagram, triangles ABC and EBD are similar but DE is *not* parallel to AC. Given that AD = 5 cm, DB = 3 cm and BE = 4 cm, calculate the length of BC.

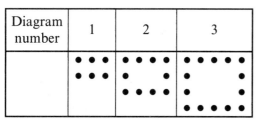

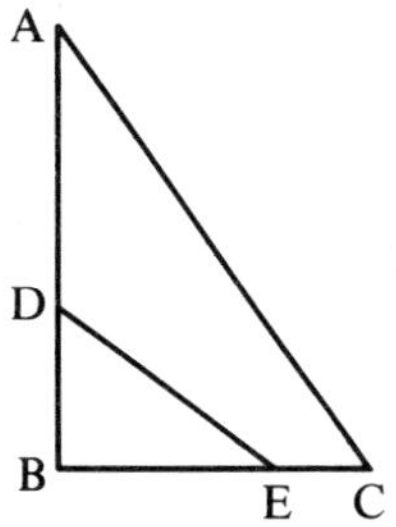

12. (a) Given that $x - z = 5y$, express z in terms of x and y.
(b) Given that $mk + 3m = 11$, express k in terms of m.
(c) For the formula $T = C\sqrt{z}$, express z in terms of T and C.

Exercise 7

1. The mass of the planet Jupiter is about 350 times the mass of the Earth. The mass of the earth is approximately $6{\cdot}03 \times 10^{21}$ tonnes. Give an estimate correct to 2 significant figures for the mass of Jupiter.

2. This graph shows a car journey from Gateshead to Middlesbrough and back again.

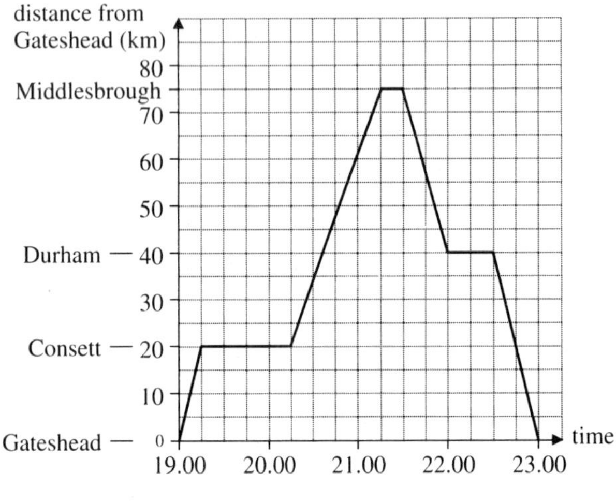

(a) Where is the car
  (i) at 19·15 h
  (ii) at 22·15 h
  (iii) at 22·45 h?
(b) How far is it
  (i) from Consett to Middlesbrough
  (ii) from Durham to Gateshead?
(c) At what speed does the car travel
  (i) from Gateshead to Consett
  (ii) from Consett to Middlesbrough
  (iii) from Middlesbrough to Durham
  (iv) from Durham to Gateshead?
(d) For how long is the car stationary during the journey?

3. Work out the difference between one ton and one tonne.

1 tonne	=	1000 kg
1 ton	=	2240 lb
1 lb	=	454 g

Give your answer to the nearest kg.

4. A motorist travelled 200 miles in five hours. Her average speed for the first 100 miles was 50 m.p.h. What was her average speed for the second 100 miles?

5. Evaluate the following and give the answers to 3 significant figures:

(a) $\sqrt[3]{(9{\cdot}61 \times 0{\cdot}0041)}$

(b) $\left(\frac{1}{9{\cdot}5} - \frac{1}{11{\cdot}2}\right)^3$

(c) $\frac{15{\cdot}6 \times 0{\cdot}714}{0{\cdot}0143 \times 12}$ (d) $\sqrt[4]{\left(\frac{1}{5 \times 10^3}\right)}$

6. Throughout his life Mr Cram's heart has beat at an average rate of 72 beats per minute. Mr Cram is sixty years old. How many times has his heart beat during his life? Give the answer in standard form correct to two significant figures.

7. Two dice are thrown. What is the probability that the *product* of the numbers on top is
(a) 12, (b) 4, (c) 11?

8. The shaded region **B** is formed by the lines $x = 0$, $y = x - 2$ and $x + y = 7$.

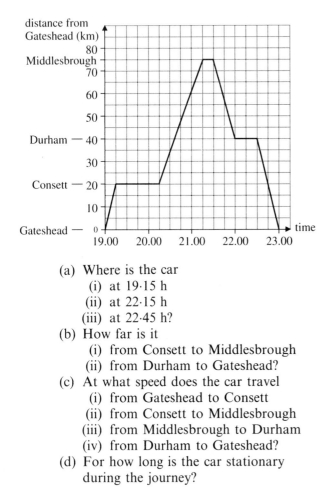

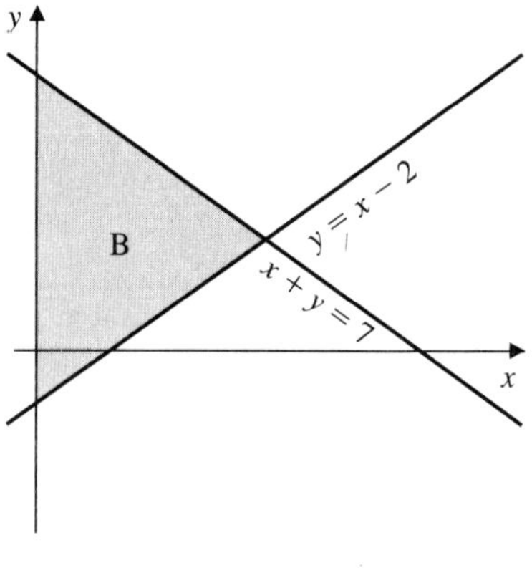

Write down the three inequalities which define **B**.

9. Estimate the answer correct to one significant figure. Do not use a calculator.

(a) $(612 \times 52) \div 49{\cdot}2$
(b) $(11{\cdot}7 + 997{\cdot}1) \times 9{\cdot}2$
(c) $\sqrt{\left(\frac{91{\cdot}3}{10{\cdot}1}\right)}$ (d) $\pi\sqrt{(5{\cdot}2^2 + 18{\cdot}2^2)}$

10. In the quadrilateral PQRS, PQ = QS = QR, PS is parallel to QR and $Q\hat{R}S = 70°$.
Calculate
(a) $R\hat{Q}S$
(b) $P\hat{Q}S$.

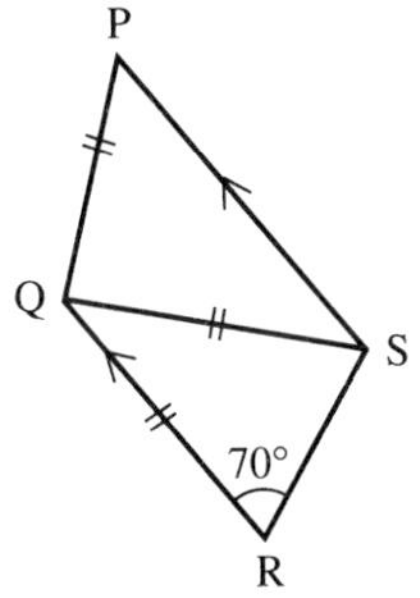

11. A bag contains x green discs and 5 blue discs. A disc is selected. Find, in terms of x, the probability of selecting a green disc.

12. In the diagram, the equations of the lines are $2y = x - 8$, $2y + x = 8$, $4y = 3x - 16$ and $4y + 3x = 16$.

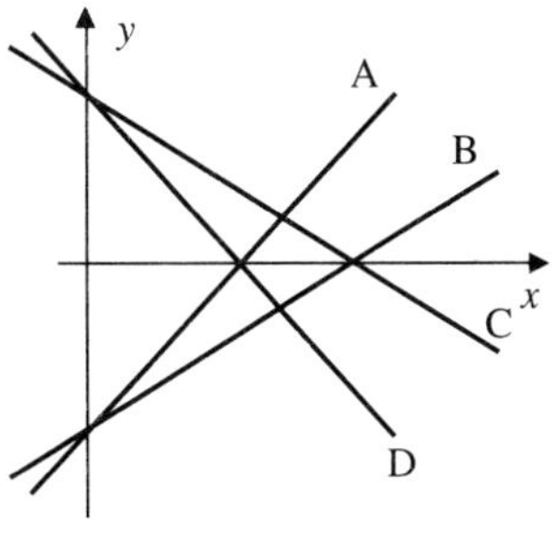

Find the equation corresponding to each line.

Exercise 8

1. Sainsburys sell their 'own-label' raspberry jam in two sizes.

Which jar represents the better value for money? You are given that 1 kg = 2·20 lb.

2. A photo 21 cm by 12 cm is enlarged as shown.

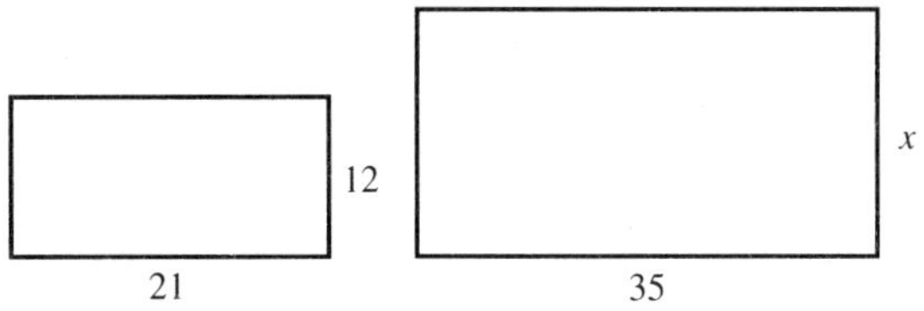

(a) What is the scale factor of the enlargement?
(b) Work out the length x.

3. Nadia said: 'I thought of a number, multiplied it by 6, then added 15. My answer was less than 200'.

(a) Write down Nadia's statement in symbols, using x as the starting number.
(b) Nadia actually thought of a prime number. What was the largest prime number she could have thought of?

4. In the diagram the area of the smaller square is $10\,\text{cm}^2$. Find the area of the larger square.

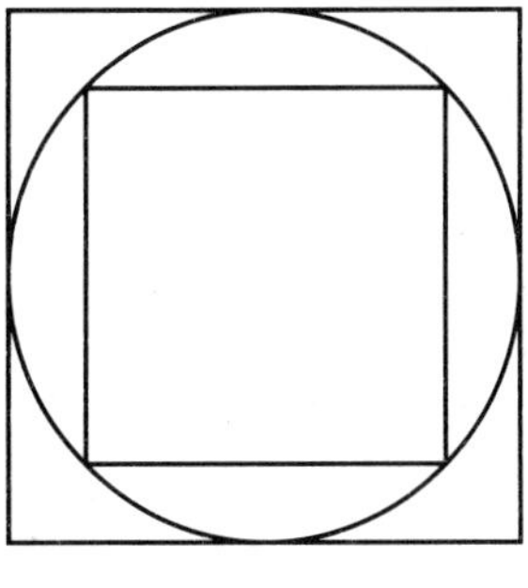

5. Write down the coordinates of the points A, B, C, D.

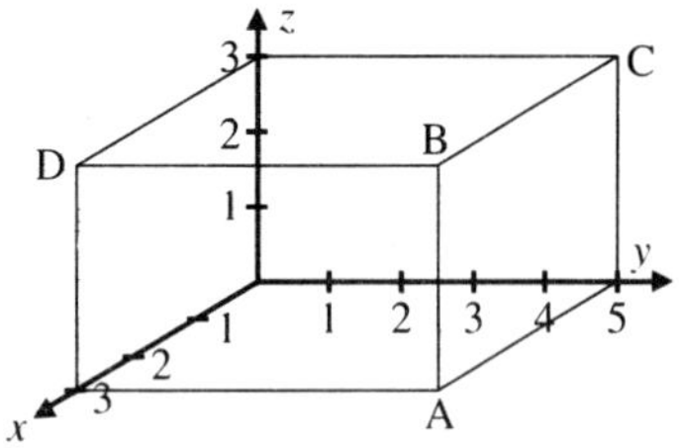

6. Point B is on a bearing 120° from point A. The distance from A to B is 110 km.

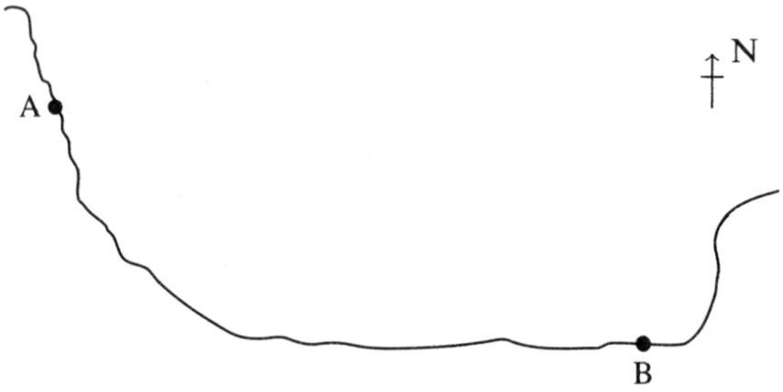

(a) Draw a diagram showing the positions of A and B. Use a scale of 1 cm to 10 km.
(b) Ship S is on a bearing 072° from A. Ship S is on a bearing 325° from B. Show S on your diagram and state the distance from S to B.

7. A regular octagon of side length 20 cm is to be cut out of a square card.

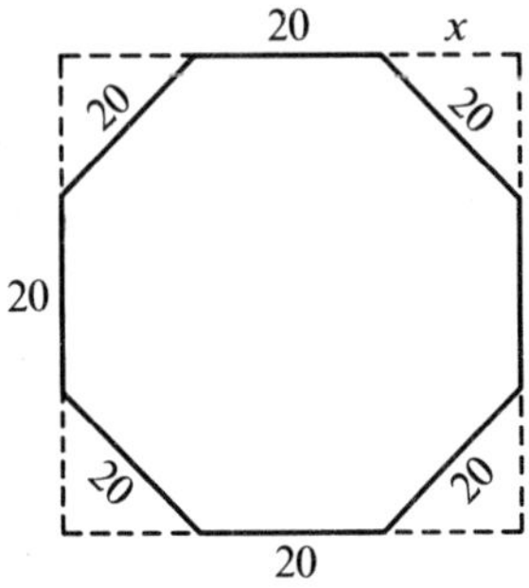

(a) Find the length x and hence find the size of the smallest square card from which this octagon can be cut.
(b) Calculate the area of the octagon, correct to 3 s.f.

8. Evaluate the following using a calculator: (answers to 4 sig. fig.)

(a) $\dfrac{0{\cdot}74}{0{\cdot}81 \times 1{\cdot}631}$ (b) $\sqrt{\left(\dfrac{9{\cdot}61}{8{\cdot}34 - 7{\cdot}41}\right)}$

(c) $\left(\dfrac{0{\cdot}741}{0{\cdot}8364}\right)^4$ (d) $\dfrac{8{\cdot}4 - 7{\cdot}642}{3{\cdot}333 - 1{\cdot}735}$

9. The mean of four numbers is 21.
(a) Calculate the sum of the four numbers.
Six other numbers have a mean of 18.
(b) Calculate the mean of the ten numbers.

10. Given BD = 1 m, calculate the length AC.

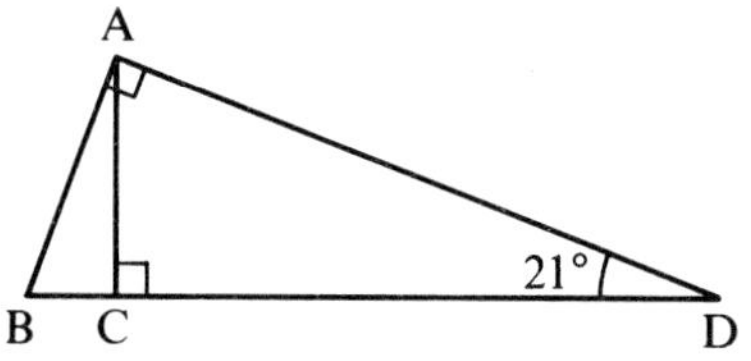

11. Use the method of trial and improvement to find a solution of the equation $x^5 = x^3 + 1$, giving your answer correct to 2 decimal places.

12. Given that $y = \dfrac{k}{k + w}$
(a) Find the value of y when $k = \frac{1}{2}$ and $w = \frac{1}{3}$
(b) Express w in terms of y and k.

14.2 Multiple choice tests

Test 1

1. How many mm are there in 1 m 1 cm?

A 1001
B 1110
C 1010
D 1100

2. The circumference of a circle is 16π cm. The radius, in cm, of the circle is:

A 2
B 4
C $\frac{4}{\pi}$
D 8

3. In the triangle below the value of $\cos x$ is:

A 0·8
B 1·333
C 0·75
D 0·6

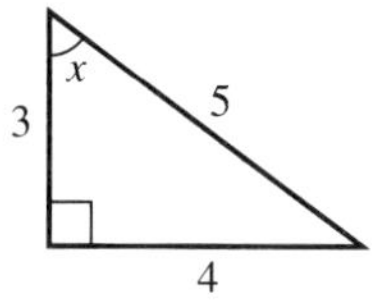

4. The line $y = 2x - 1$ cuts the x-axis at P. The coordinates of P are:

A $(0, -1)$
B $(\frac{1}{2}, 0)$
C $(-\frac{1}{2}, 0)$
D $(-1, 0)$

5. The mean weight of a group of 11 men is 70 kg. What is the mean weight of the remaining group when a man of weight 90 kg leaves?

A 80 kg
B 72 kg
C 68 kg
D 62 kg

6. A, B, C and D are points on the sides of a rectangle. Find the area in cm^2 of quadrilateral ABCD.

A $27\frac{1}{2}$
B 28
C $28\frac{1}{2}$
D cannot be found

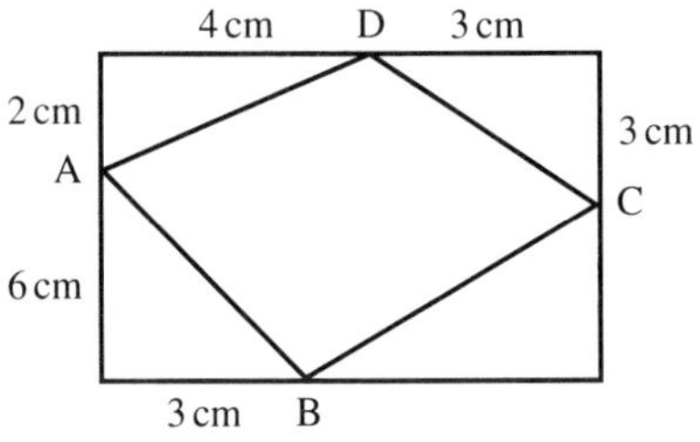

7. The formula $b + \frac{x}{a} = c$ is rearranged to make x the subject. What is x?

A $a(c - b)$
B $ac - b$
C $\frac{c - b}{a}$
D $ac + ab$

8. In standard form the value of $2000 \times 80\,000$ is:

A 16×10^6
B $1{\cdot}6 \times 10^9$
C $1{\cdot}6 \times 10^7$
D $1{\cdot}6 \times 10^8$

9. The sum of the lengths of the edges of a cube is 36 cm. The volume, in cm^3, of the cube is:

A 36
B 27
C 64
D 48

10. In the triangle the size of angle x is:

A 35°
B 70°
C 110°
D 40°

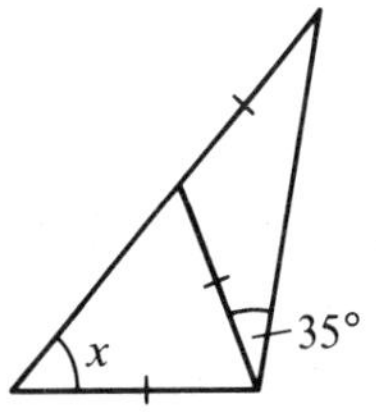

11. A man paid tax on £9000 at 30%. He paid the tax in 12 equal payments. Each payment was:

A £2·25
B £22·50
C £225
D £250

12. The approximate value of $\frac{3{\cdot}96 \times (0{\cdot}5)^2}{97{\cdot}1}$ is:

A 0·01
B 0·02
C 0·04
D 0·1

13. Given that $\frac{3}{n} = 5$, then $n =$

A 2
B -2
C $1\frac{2}{3}$
D 0·6

14. Cube A has side 2 cm. Cube B has side 4 cm. $\left(\frac{\text{Volume of B}}{\text{Volume of A}}\right) =$

A 2
B 4
C 8
D 16

15. How many tiles of side 50 cm will be needed to cover the floor shown?

A 16
B 32
C 64
D 84

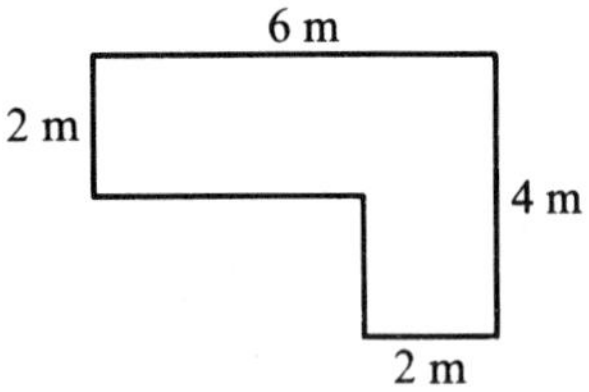

16. The equation $ax^2 + x - 6 = 0$ has a solution $x = -2$. What is a?

A 1
B -2
C $\sqrt{2}$
D 2

17. Which of the following is/are correct?
1. $\sqrt{0{\cdot}16} = 0{\cdot}4$
2. $0{\cdot}2 \div 0{\cdot}1 = 0{\cdot}2$
3. $\frac{4}{7} > \frac{3}{5}$

A **1** only
B **2** only
C **3** only
D **1** and **2**

18. How many prime numbers are there between 30 and 40?

A 0
B 1
C 2
D 3

19. A man is paid £180 per week after a pay rise of 20%. What was he paid before?

A £144
B £150
C £160
D £164

20. A car travels for 20 minutes at 45 m.p.h. and then for 40 minutes at 60 m.p.h. The average speed for the whole journey is:

A $52\frac{1}{2}$ m.p.h.
B 50 m.p.h
C 54 m.p.h.
D 55 m.p.h.

21. The point $(3, -1)$ is reflected in the line $y = 2$. The new coordinates are:

A $(3, 5)$
B $(1, -1)$
C $(3, 4)$
D $(0, -1)$

22. Given the equation $5^x = 120$, the best approximate solution is $x =$

A 2
B 3
C 4
D 25

23. The rectangle ABCD is cut out of paper and the edges AB and DC are joined to make a cylinder. The radius of the cylinder in cm is:

A 6
B 7
C $\frac{6}{\pi}$
D $\frac{12}{\pi}$

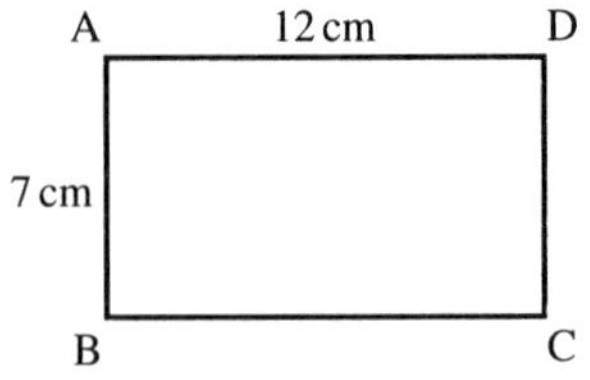

24. The shaded area in cm^2 is:

A $16 - 2\pi$
B $16 - 4\pi$
C $\frac{4}{\pi}$
D $64 - 8\pi$

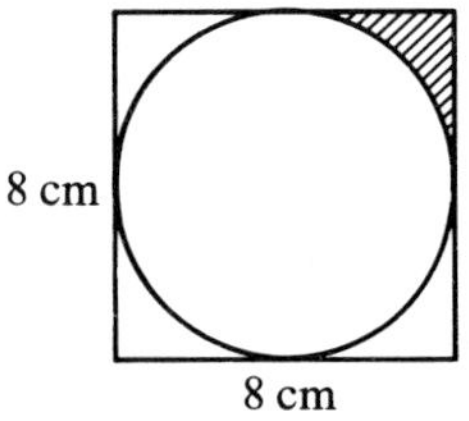

25. What is the sine of 45°?

A 1
B $\frac{1}{2}$
C $\frac{1}{\sqrt{2}}$
D $\sqrt{2}$

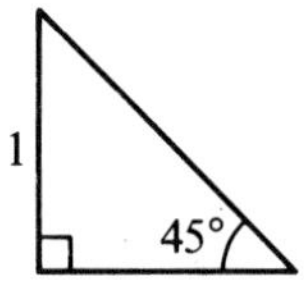

Test 2

1. What is the value of the expression $(x - 2)(x + 4)$ when $x = -1$?

A 9
B -9
C 5
D -5

2. The perimeter of a square is 36 cm. What is its area?

A 36 cm^2
B 324 cm^2
C 81 cm^2
D 9 cm^2

3. The gradient of the line $2x + y = 3$ is:

A 3
B -2
C $\frac{1}{2}$
D $-\frac{1}{2}$

4. The shape consists of four semi-circles placed round a square of side 2 m. The area of the shape in m^2 is:

A $2\pi + 4$
B $2\pi + 2$
C $4\pi + 4$
D $\pi + 4$

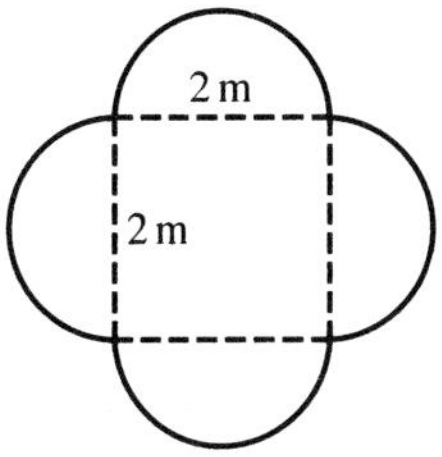

5. A firm employs 1200 people, of whom 240 are men. The percentage of employees who are men is:

A 40%
B 10%
C 15%
D 20%

6. A car is travelling at a constant speed of 30 m.p.h. How far will the car travel in 10 minutes?

A $\frac{1}{3}$ mile
B 3 miles
C 5 miles
D 6 miles

7. What are the coordinates of the point $(1, -1)$ after reflection in the line $y = x$?

A $(-1, 1)$
B $(1, 1)$
C $(-1, -1)$
D $(1, -1)$

8. $\frac{1}{3} + \frac{2}{5} =$

A $\frac{2}{8}$
B $\frac{3}{8}$
C $\frac{3}{15}$
D $\frac{11}{15}$

9. In the triangle the size of the largest angle is:

A 30°
B 90°
C 120°
D 80°

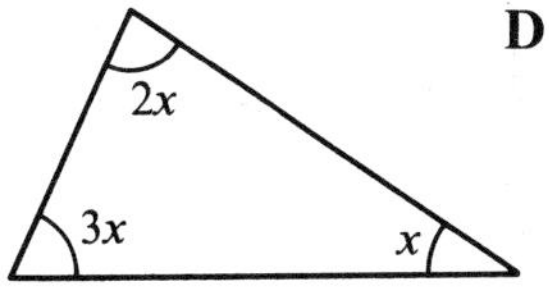

10. 800 decreased by 5% is:

A 795
B 640
C 760
D 400

11. Which of the statements is (are) true?
1. $\tan 60° = 2$
2. $\sin 60° = \cos 30°$
3. $\sin 30° > \cos 30°$

A **1** only
B **2** only
C **3** only
D **2** and **3**

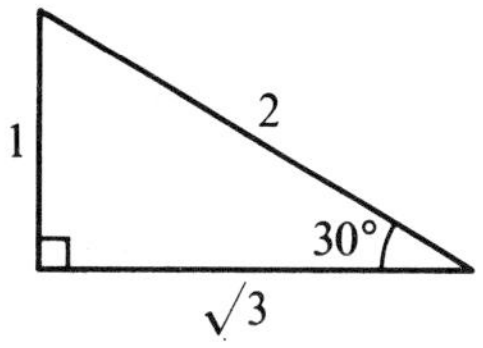

12. Given $a = \frac{3}{5}$, $b = \frac{1}{3}$, $c = \frac{1}{2}$ then:

A $a < b < c$
B $a < c < b$
C $a > b > c$
D $a > c > b$

13. The *larger* angle between South-West and East is:

A 225°
B 240°
C 135°
D 315°

14. In a triangle PQR, $P\hat{Q}R = 50°$ and point X lies on PQ such that QX = XR. Calculate $Q\hat{X}R$.

A 100°
B 50°
C 80°
D 65°

15. What is the value of $1 - 0{\cdot}05$ as a fraction?

A $\frac{1}{20}$
B $\frac{9}{10}$
C $\frac{19}{20}$
D $\frac{5}{100}$

16. Find the length x.

A 5
B 6
C 8
D $\sqrt{50}$

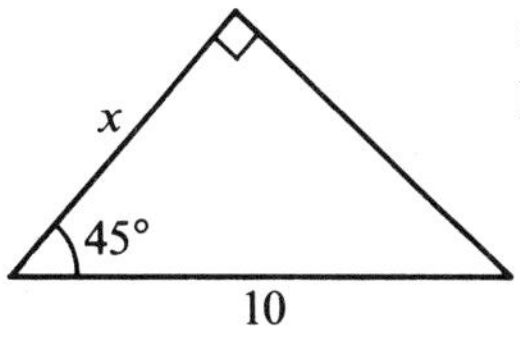

17. Given that $m = 2$ and $n = -3$, what is mn^2?

A -18
B 18
C -36
D 36

18. The graph of $y = (x-3)(x-2)$ cuts the y-axis at P. The coordinates of P are:
A (0, 6) **B** (6, 0) **C** (2, 0) **D** (3, 0)

19. £240 is shared in the ratio 2 : 3 : 7. The largest share is:
A £130 **B** £140 **C** £150 **D** £160

20. Adjacent angles in a parallelogram are $x°$ and $3x°$. The smallest angles in the parallelogram are each:
A 30° **B** 45° **C** 60° **D** 120°

21. When the sides of a square are increased by 10% the area is increased by:
A 10% **B** 20% **C** 21% **D** 15%

22. The volume, in cm^3, of the cylinder is:
A 9π **B** 12π **C** 600π **D** 900π

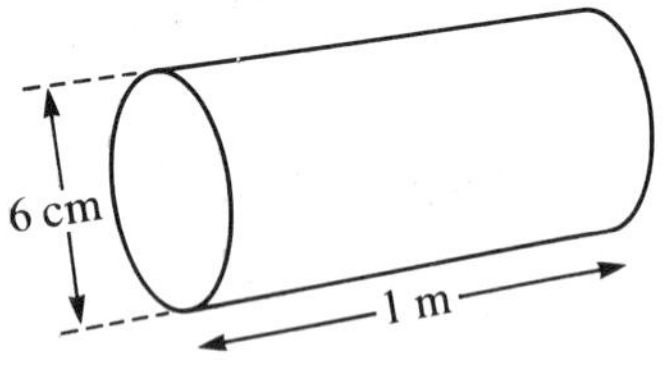

23. A car travels for 10 minutes at 30 m.p.h. and then for 20 minutes at 45 m.p.h. The average speed for the whole journey is:
A 40 m.p.h. **B** $37\frac{1}{2}$ m.p.h. **C** 20 m.p.h. **D** 35 m.p.h.

24. Four people each toss a coin. What is the probability that the fourth person will toss a 'tail'?
A $\frac{1}{2}$ **B** $\frac{1}{4}$ **C** $\frac{1}{8}$ **D** $\frac{1}{16}$

25. A rectangle 8 cm by 6 cm is inscribed inside a circle. What is the area, in cm^2, of the circle?
A 10π **B** 25π **C** 49π **D** 100π

Test 3

1. The price of a T.V. changed from £240 to £300. What is the percentage increase?
A 15% **B** 20% **C** 60% **D** 25%

2. Find the length x.
A 6 **B** 5 **C** $\sqrt{44}$ **D** $\sqrt{18}$

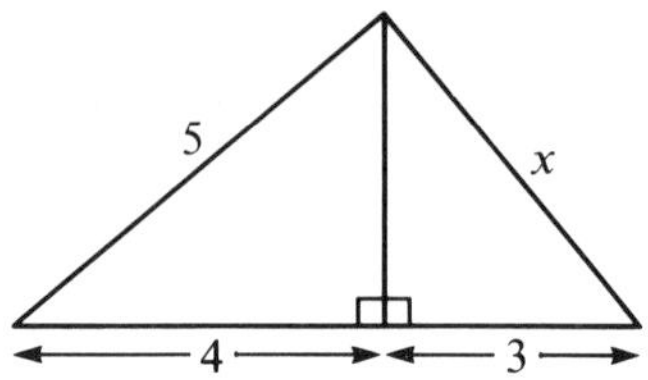

3. The bearing of A from B is 120°. What is the bearing of B from A ?
A 060° **B** 120° **C** 240° **D** 300°

4. Numbers m, x and y satisfy the equation $y = mx^2$. When $m = \frac{1}{2}$ and $x = 4$ the value of y is:
A 4 **B** 8 **C** 1 **D** 2

5. A school has 400 pupils, of whom 250 are boys. The ratio of boys to girls is:
A 5 : 3 **B** 3 : 2 **C** 3 : 5 **D** 8 : 5

6. A train is travelling at a speed of 30 km per hour. How long will it take to travel 500 m?
A 2 minutes **B** $\frac{3}{50}$ hour **C** 1 minute **D** $\frac{1}{2}$ hour

7. The approximate value of $\dfrac{9{\cdot}65 \times 0{\cdot}203}{0{\cdot}0198}$ is:
A 99 **B** 9·9 **C** 0·99 **D** 180

8. Which point does *not* lie on the curve $y = \dfrac{12}{x}$?
A (6, 2) **B** $(\frac{1}{2}, 24)$ **C** (−3, −4) **D** (3, −4)

9. $t = \frac{c^3}{y}$, $y =$

A $\frac{t}{c^3}$
B $c^3 t$
C $c^3 - t$
D $\frac{c^3}{t}$

10. The largest number of 1 cm cubes which will fit inside a cubical box of side 1 m is:

A 10^3
B 10^6
C 10^8
D 10^{12}

11. I start with x, then square it, multiply by 2 and finally subtract 3. The final result is:

A $(2x)^2 - 3$
B $(2x - 3)^2$
C $2x^2 - 3$
D $2(x - 3)^2$

12. Which of the following has the largest value?

A $\sqrt{100}$
B $\sqrt{\frac{1}{0{\cdot}1}}$
C $\sqrt{1000}$
D $\frac{1}{0{\cdot}01}$

13. Two dice numbered 1 to 6 are thrown together and their scores are added. The probability that the sum will be 12 is:

A $\frac{1}{6}$
B $\frac{1}{12}$
C $\frac{1}{18}$
D $\frac{1}{36}$

14. The length, in cm, of the minor arc is:

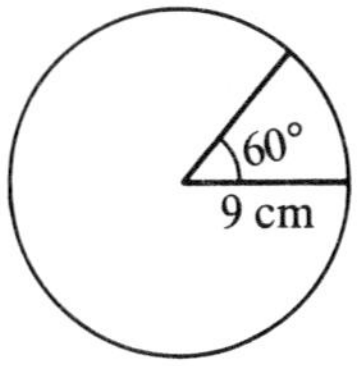

A 2π
B 3π
C 6π
D $13\frac{1}{2}\pi$

15. Metal of weight 84 kg is made into 40 000 pins. What is the weight, in kg, of one pin?

A 0·0021
B 0·0036
C 0·021
D 0·21

16. What is the value of x which satisfies both equations?
$3x + y = 1$
$x - 2y = 5$

A -1
B 1
C -2
D 2

17. What is the new fare when the old fare of £250 is increased by 8%?

A £258
B £260
C £270
D £281·25

18. What is the area of this triangle?

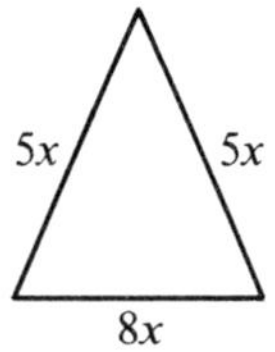

A $12x^2$
B $15x^2$
C $16x^2$
D $30x^2$

19. What values of x satisfy the inequality $2 - 3x > 1$?

A $x < -\frac{1}{3}$
B $x > -\frac{1}{3}$
C $x > \frac{1}{3}$
D $x < \frac{1}{3}$

20. A right-angled triangle has sides in the ratio 5 : 12 : 13. The tangent of the smallest angle is:

A $\frac{12}{5}$
B $\frac{12}{13}$
C $\frac{5}{13}$
D $\frac{5}{12}$

21. To one significant figure, $\sqrt{0{\cdot}1}$ is:

A 0·01
B 0·1
C 0·3
D 0·5

22. The number of letters in the word SNAIL that have line symmetry is:

A 0
B 1
C 2
D 3

23. The probability of an event occurring is 0·35. The probability of the event *not* occurring is:

A $\frac{1}{0{\cdot}35}$
B 0·65
C 0·35
D 0

24. What fraction of the area of the rectangle is the area of the triangle?

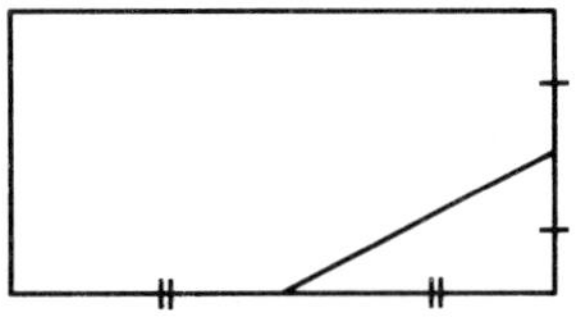

A $\frac{1}{4}$
B $\frac{1}{8}$
C $\frac{1}{16}$
D $\frac{1}{32}$

25. On a map a distance of 36 km is represented by a line of 1·8 cm. What is the scale of the map?

A 1 : 2000
B 1 : 20 000
C 1 : 200 000
D 1 : 2000 000

Test 4

1. What is the value of x satisfying the simultaneous equations
$3x + 2y = 13$
$x - 2y = -1$?

A 7
B 3
C $3\frac{1}{2}$
D 2

2. A straight line is 4·5 cm long. $\frac{2}{5}$ of the line is:

A 0·4 cm
B 1·8 cm
C 2 cm
D 0·18 cm

3. The mean of four numbers is 12. The mean of three of the numbers is 13. What is the fourth number?

A 9
B 12·5
C 7
D 1

4. How many cubes of edge 3 cm are needed to fill a box with internal dimensions 12 cm by 6 cm by 6 cm?

A 8
B 18
C 16
D 24

5. The value of 4865·355 correct to 2 significant figures is:

A 4865·36
B 4865·35
C 4900
D 49

6. What values of y satisfy the inequality $4y - 1 < 0$?

A $y < 4$
B $y < -\frac{1}{4}$
C $y > \frac{1}{4}$
D $y < \frac{1}{4}$

For Questions **7** to **9** use the diagram below.

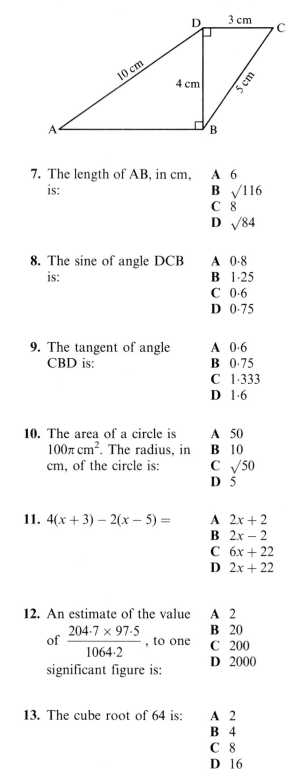

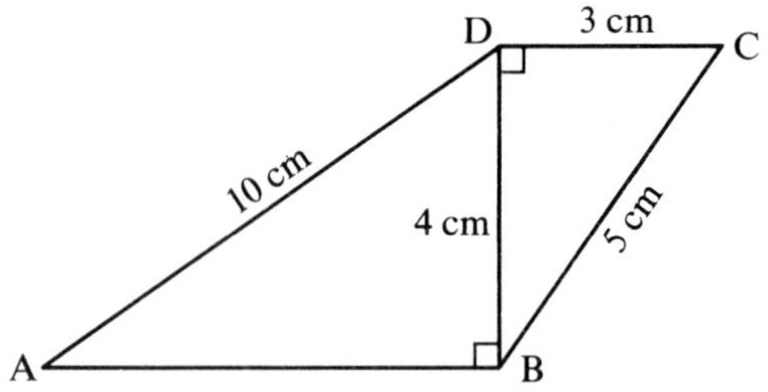

7. The length of AB, in cm, is:

A 6
B $\sqrt{116}$
C 8
D $\sqrt{84}$

8. The sine of angle DCB is:

A 0·8
B 1·25
C 0·6
D 0·75

9. The tangent of angle CBD is:

A 0·6
B 0·75
C 1·333
D 1·6

10. The area of a circle is 100π cm^2. The radius, in cm, of the circle is:

A 50
B 10
C $\sqrt{50}$
D 5

11. $4(x + 3) - 2(x - 5) =$

A $2x + 2$
B $2x - 2$
C $6x + 22$
D $2x + 22$

12. An estimate of the value of $\dfrac{204{\cdot}7 \times 97{\cdot}5}{1064{\cdot}2}$, to one significant figure is:

A 2
B 20
C 200
D 2000

13. The cube root of 64 is:

A 2
B 4
C 8
D 16

14. Here are four statements about the diagonals of a rectangle. The statement which is not *always* true is
A They are equal in length
B They divide the rectangle into four triangles of equal area
C They cross at right angles
D They bisect each other

15. Given $16^x = 4^4$, what is x?
A -2
B $-\frac{1}{2}$
C $\frac{1}{2}$
D 2

16. What is the area, in m^2, of a square with each side 0·02 m long?
A 0·0004
B 0·004
C 0·04
D 0·4

17. I start with x, then square it, multiply by 3 and finally subtract 4. The final result is:
A $(3x)^2 - 4$
B $(3x - 4)^2$
C $3x^2 - 4$
D $3(x - 4)^2$

18. How many prime numbers are there between 50 and 60?
A 1
B 2
C 3
D 4

19. What are the coordinates of the point (2, −2) after reflection in the line $y = -x$?
A (−2, 2)
B (2, −2)
C (−2, −2)
D (2, 2)

20. The area of a circle is 36π cm^2. The circumference, in cm, is:
A 6π
B 18π
C $12\sqrt{\pi}$
D 12π

21. The gradient of the line $2x - 3y = 4$ is:
A $\frac{2}{3}$
B $1\frac{1}{2}$
C $-\frac{4}{3}$
D $-\frac{3}{4}$

22. When all three sides of a triangle are trebled in length, the area is increased by a factor of:
A 3
B 6
C 9
D 27

23. $a = \sqrt{\left(\frac{m}{x}\right)}$

$x =$
A a^2m
B $a^2 - m$
C $\frac{m}{a^2}$
D $\frac{a^2}{m}$

24. A coin is tossed three times. The probability of getting three 'heads' is:
A $\frac{1}{3}$
B $\frac{1}{6}$
C $\frac{1}{8}$
D $\frac{1}{16}$

25. A triangle has sides of length 5 cm, 5 cm and 6 cm. What is the area, in cm^2?
A 12
B 15
C 18
D 20

ANSWERS

Shape and space 1

page 1 ***Exercise 1***

1. 7·3 cm **2.** 7·9 cm **3.** 8·0 cm **4.** 10·3 cm **5.** 6·4 cm
6. 6·8 cm **7.** 9·0 cm **8.** 9·6 cm **9.** 7·6 cm **10.** 8·7 cm
11. 8·2 cm **12.** 5·3 cm **13.** $60\frac{1}{2}°$ **14.** $85\frac{1}{2}°$ **15.** 72°
16. 121° **17.** 10 000 m^2 **18.** 10 300 or 10 400 m^2

page 5 ***Exercise 3***

1. 70° **2.** 100° **3.** 70° **4.** 100°
5. 44° **6.** 80° **7.** 40° **8.** 48°
9. 40° **10.** 35° **11.** $a = 40°$, $b = 140°$ **12.** $x = 108°$, $y = 72°$

page 6 ***Exercise 4***

1. 50° **2.** 70° **3.** 29° **4.** 30°
5. 70° **6.** 42° **7.** 40° **8.** $a = 55°$, $b = 70°$
9. 60° **10.** $x = 122°$, $y = 116°$ **11.** 135° **12.** 30°
13. 154° **14.** 75° **15.** $x = 30°$ **16.** 28°

page 7 ***Exercise 5***

1. 72° **2.** 98° **3.** 80°
4. 74° **5.** 86° **6.** 88°
7. $x = 95°$, $y = 50°$ **8.** $a = 87°$, $b = 74°$ **9.** $a = 65°$, $c = 103°$
10. $a = 68°$, $b = 42°$ **11.** $y = 65°$, $z = 50°$ **12.** $a = 55°$, $b = 75°$, $c = 50°$

page 8 ***Exercise 6***

1. 108° **2.** 50° **3.** 76° **4.** 270°
5. $a = 119°$, $b = 25°$ **6.** $c = 70°$, $d = 60°$ **7.** $a = 45°$ **12.** $a = 45°$, $b = 67\frac{1}{2}°$

page 9 ***Exercise 7***

1. 42° **2.** 68° **3.** 100°
4. 73° **5.** 120° **6.** 52°
7. 100° **8.** $a = 70°$, $b = 60°$ **9.** $x = 58°$, $y = 109°$
10. 66° **11.** 65° **12.** $e = 70°$, $f = 30°$
13. $x = 72°$, $y = 36°$ **14.** $a = 68°$, $b = 72°$, $c = 68°$ **15.** 4°
16. $28\frac{1}{2}°$ **17.** 20° **18.** $x = 62°$, $y = 28°$

19. 34° **20.** 58° **21.** $x = 60°$, $y = 48°$
22. $a = 65°$, $b = 40°$ **23.** $x = 49°$, $y = 61°$ **24.** $a = 60°$, $b = 40°$
25. 136° **26.** 80° **27.** $x = 65°$, $y = 35°$, $z = 55°$
28. 26°

page 11 ***Exercise 8***

1. (a) 1 (b) 1 **2.** (a) 1 (b) 1 **3.** (a) 4 (b) 4
4. (a) 2 (b) 2 **5.** (a) 0 (b) 6 **6.** (a) 0 (b) 2
7. (a) 0 (b) 2 **8.** (a) 4 (b) 4 **9.** (a) 0 (b) 4
10. (a) 4 (b) 4 **11.** (a) 6 (b) 6 **12.** (a) infinite (b) infinite

page 13 ***Exercise 10***

1. 3 **2.** (a) 1 (b) 1 (c) 1 **3.** 9 **5.** 4

page 14 ***Exercise 11***

1. a, b, c, e, f, g, h are traversable
2. (a) ADCFG (= 15 miles)
(b) ABFCDEG (= 29 miles)
(c) AEDCBFG (= 30 miles)
3. (a) ABCI (= 12 miles)
(b) AEGHFDBCI (= 24 miles)
4. (a) ABCDBEDFEFA (= 43 units)
(b) ACEFBDABA (= 44 units)
(c) AEBABCDEFDFA (= 51 units)
(d) (traversable) ABEGFCDBCA (= 46 units)

page 17 ***Exercise 12***

1. 34·6 cm **2.** 25·1 cm **3.** 37·7 cm **4.** 15·7 cm **5.** 28·3 cm
6. 53·4 m **7.** 44·6 m **8.** 72·3 m **9.** 13 mm **10.** 8·48 m
11. 212 **12.** 400 m **13.** 22·6 cm **14.** (a) 823 m (b) 655
15. 643 cm **16.** 23 or 24 **17.** 45 000

page 20 ***Exercise 13***

1. 95·0 cm^2 **2.** 78·5 cm^2 **3.** 28·3 m^2 **4.** 38·5 m^2
5. 113 cm^2 **6.** 201 cm^2 **7.** 19·6 m^2 **8.** 380 cm^2
9. 29·5 cm^2 **10.** 125 m^2 **11.** 21·5 cm^2 **12.** 4580 g
13. 30; (a) 1508 cm^2 (b) 508 cm^2 **14.** (a) 40·8 m^2 (b) 6 **15.** 118 m^2

page 22 ***Exercise 14***

1. 23·1 cm **2.** 38·6 cm **3.** 20·6 m **4.** 8·23 cm **5.** 28·6 cm **6.** 39·4 m
7. 17·9 cm **8.** 28·1 m **9.** 24·8 cm **10.** 46·3 m **11.** 28·8 cm

page 23 ***Exercise 15***

1. 35·9 cm^2 **2.** 84·1 cm^2 **3.** 37·7 cm^2 **4.** 74·6 cm^2 **5.** 13·7 cm^2 **6.** 25·1 cm^2
7. (a) 12·5 cm^2 (b) 50 cm^2 (c) 78·5 cm^2 (d) 28·5 cm^2

page 24 ***Exercise 16***

1. 2·39 cm **2.** 4·46 cm **3.** 1·11 m **4.** 4·15 cm **5.** 3·48 cm **6.** 3·95 m
7. 2·55 m **8.** 4·37 cm **9.** 4·62 cm **10.** 5·75 cm **11.** 15·9 cm **12.** 5·09 cm
13. 9·2 m **14.** 58·6 cm **15.** 5·39 cm **16.** 17·8 cm **17.** 195 km **18.** 3·95 cm
19. 215 m^2 **20.** 3·88 m **21.** 575 m^2 **22.** 5·41 cm **23.** 4·5 m

page 26 ***Exercise 17***

1. 24 cm^2 **2.** 14 cm^2 **3.** 36 cm^2 **4.** 77 cm^2 **5.** 54 cm^2 **6.** 25 cm^2
7. 36 cm^2 **8.** 48 cm^2 **9.** 51 cm^2 **10.** 36 cm^2 **11.** 24 cm^2 **12.** 24 cm^2
13. 57 cm^2 **14.** 48 cm^2 **15.** 36 cm^2 **16.** 41 cm^2

page 27 ***Exercise 18***

1. (a) 14·6 m (b) 6 (c) £19·20 (d) 11·22 m^2
2. A (a) 13·2 m (b) 6 (c) £19·20 (d) 9·32 m^2
B (a) 19·4 m (b) 9 (c) £28·80 (d) 13 m^2

page 28 ***Exercise 19***

Questions **1** to **7** answers in square units.

1. (b) 10, 6, 3 (c) 36 (d) 17
2. (b) 5, 14, 6 (c) 42 (d) 17
3. $13\frac{1}{2}$ **4.** $14\frac{1}{2}$ **5.** 24 **6.** 22 **7.** 21
8. (a) 248 cm^2 (b) 120

page 29 ***Exercise 20***

1. 42 cm^2 **2.** 22 cm^2 **3.** 103 cm^2 **4.** 60·5 cm^2
5. 143 cm^2 **6.** 9 cm^2 **7.** 47 cm^2 **8.** 81·75 cm^2
9. (a) 4000 000 m^2; 400 hectares (b) 314 hectares; 785 acres **10.** £252

page 31 ***Exercise 22***

1. 150 cm^3 **2.** 60 m^3 **3.** 480 cm^3 **4.** 300 cm^3 **5.** 56 m^3
6. 280 cm^3 **7.** 145 cm^3 **8.** 448 cm^3 **9.** 108 cm^3

page 32 ***Exercise 23***

1. 62·8 cm^3 **2.** 113 cm^3 **3.** 198 cm^3 **4.** 763 cm^3
5. 157 cm^3 **6.** 385 cm^3 **7.** 770 m^3 **8.** 176 m^3
9. 228 m^3 **10.** 486 cm^3 **11.** 113 litres **12.** 141 cm^3, 25·1 cm

page 33 ***Exercise 24***

1. 2400 cm^3 **2.** (a) 200 m^2 (b) 2400 m^3 **3.** 770 cm^3
4. (a) 2·25 cm^2 (b) 0·451 cm^3 (c) 4510 cm^3 **5.** 125
6. (a) 76 cm^2 (b) 30 400 cm^3 (c) 237 kg (d) 33 **7.** 8 cm^3
8. (a) 7 (b) 35, 6 (c) 1200 cm^3, 14 000 cm^3 (d) 48 p, £5·60, £50·40 (e) 140
9. No **10.** 1570 cm^3, 12·6 kg **11.** 53 times
12. 191 cm **13.** 98 min **14.** 144

page 37 ***Exercise 25***

1. 12 cm^3 **2.** 12 cm^3 **3.** 10 cm^3 **4.** 19 cm^3 **5.** 18 cm^3

Algebra 1

page 39 ***Exercise 1***

1. (a) 7, 11, 18, 29, 47, 76, 123 (b) 12, 19, 31, 50
2. (a) $6 \times 7 = 6 + 6^2$ $7 \times 8 = 7 + 7^2$ (b) $10 \times 11 = 10 + 10^2$ $30 \times 31 = 30 + 30^2$
3. (a) $\frac{1}{3}, \frac{2}{6}, \frac{3}{9}, \frac{4}{12}, \frac{5}{15}, \frac{6}{18}, \frac{7}{21}, \frac{8}{24}$ (b) $\frac{2}{5}, \frac{4}{10}, \frac{6}{15}, \frac{8}{20}, \frac{10}{25}, \frac{12}{30}, \frac{14}{35}$
(c) $\frac{1}{4}, \frac{2}{8}, \frac{3}{12}, \frac{4}{16}, \frac{5}{20}, \frac{6}{24}$ (d) $\frac{3}{7}, \frac{6}{14}, \frac{9}{21}, \frac{12}{28}$
4. 63, 3968, 15745023 **5.** 3, 5, 5
6. (a) 48 (b) 40 (c) $12\frac{1}{2}$ (d) 121 (e) 162 (f) 0·56 (g) 720 (h) 21
7. (a) Yes (b) (i) 5 (ii) 10 (iii) 1331 **8.** (b) $(1 + 2 + 3 + \ldots + 10)^2 = 55^2 = 3025$
10. $5 + 9 \times 1234 = 11111$
$6 + 9 \times 12345 = 111111$
$7 + 9 \times 123456 = 1111111$

page 42 ***Exercise 2***

1. (a) 16 (b) 15 (c) 26 (d) 25
2. (a) 113 (b) (i) 90 (ii) 105 (iii) 199 (iv) 437
3. (a) (i) 24 (ii) 36 (iii) 75
(b) (i) 23 (ii) 35 (iii) 59
(c) (i) 28 (ii) 39 (iii) 50 (iv) 88
(d) (i) 40 (ii) 21 (iii) 31 (iv) 50
4. (b) 2, 5, 8, 11, 14 **5.** (a) $\times 5$, $+2$ (b) $\times 3$, $+3$
6. (a) 48 (b) 80 (c) 52 (d) 84 (e) 120 (f) 156 Multiply ‘A’ number by 8.
7. (a) 29 (b) 41 (c) 281 (d) 59 (e) 79 (f) 399
8. (a) 44 (b) 41 (c) 599; Multiply by 6, subtract 1.

page 45 ***Exercise 3***

1. 60 **2.** (a) 45 **3.** 48 **4.** (a) 14 (b) 35
5. (a) 54 (b) 21 (c) 36 **6.** (a) 42, 59 (b) 51, 67 (c) 37, 50
7. (a) 57, 21, 6 **8.** (a) 91, 133 (b) 101, 145
9. (a) 112 (b) 217 (c) 87 **10.** 2559

page 50 ***Exercise 5***

1. 4 kg **2.** 3 kg **3.** 3 kg **4.** 2 kg **5.** 4 kg **6.** 3 kg

page 51 ***Exercise 6***

1. 12 **2.** 9 **3.** 18 **4.** 4 **5.** 17 **6.** -5 **7.** 6
8. -7 **9.** 4 **10.** 8 **11.** 17 **12.** -5 **13.** 5 **14.** 6
15. 2 **16.** $\frac{4}{5}$ **17.** $2\frac{1}{3}$ **18.** $7\frac{1}{2}$ **19.** $1\frac{5}{6}$ **20.** 0 **21.** $\frac{5}{9}$
22. 1 **23.** $\frac{1}{5}$ **24.** $\frac{2}{7}$ **25.** $\frac{3}{4}$ **26.** $\frac{2}{3}$ **27.** $1\frac{1}{4}$ **28.** $1\frac{1}{5}$
29. $1\frac{5}{9}$ **30.** $\frac{1}{3}$ **31.** $\frac{1}{2}$ **32.** $\frac{1}{10}$ **33.** $-\frac{3}{8}$ **34.** $\frac{9}{50}$ **35.** $\frac{1}{2}$
36. $\frac{3}{5}$ **37.** $-\frac{4}{9}$ **38.** 0 **39.** $4\frac{5}{8}$ **40.** $-1\frac{3}{7}$ **41.** $2\frac{1}{3}$ **42.** $\frac{3}{4}$
43. 1 **44.** $3\frac{3}{5}$ **45.** $\frac{1}{3}$ **46.** $2\frac{1}{14}$ **47.** -1 **48.** $-\frac{5}{6}$ **49.** $8\frac{1}{4}$
50. -55

page 51 ***Exercise 7***

1. $2\frac{3}{4}$ **2.** $1\frac{2}{3}$ **3.** 2 **4.** $\frac{1}{5}$ **5.** $\frac{1}{2}$ **6.** 2 **7.** $5\frac{1}{3}$
8. $1\frac{1}{5}$ **9.** 0 **10.** $\frac{2}{9}$ **11.** $1\frac{1}{2}$ **12.** $\frac{1}{6}$ **13.** $1\frac{1}{3}$ **14.** $\frac{6}{7}$
15. $\frac{4}{7}$ **16.** 7 **17.** $\frac{5}{8}$ **18.** 5 **19.** $\frac{2}{5}$ **20.** $\frac{1}{3}$ **21.** 4
22. -1 **23.** 1 **24.** $\frac{6}{7}$ **25.** $1\frac{1}{4}$ **26.** 1 **27.** $\frac{7}{9}$ **28.** $-1\frac{1}{2}$
29. $\frac{2}{9}$ **30.** $-1\frac{1}{2}$

page 52 ***Exercise 8***

1. 3 **2.** 5 **3.** $10\frac{1}{2}$ **4.** -8 **5.** $\frac{1}{3}$ **6.** $-4\frac{1}{2}$ **7.** $3\frac{1}{3}$
8. $3\frac{1}{2}$ **9.** $3\frac{2}{3}$ **10.** -2 **11.** $-5\frac{1}{2}$ **12.** $4\frac{1}{5}$ **13.** $\frac{3}{7}$ **14.** $\frac{7}{11}$
15. $4\frac{4}{5}$ **16.** 5 **17.** 9 **18.** $-2\frac{1}{3}$ **19.** $\frac{2}{5}$ **20.** $\frac{3}{5}$ **21.** -1
22. 13 **23.** 9 **24.** $4\frac{1}{2}$ **25.** $3\frac{1}{3}$

page 52 ***Exercise 9***

1. $\frac{3}{5}$ **2.** $\frac{4}{7}$ **3.** $\frac{11}{12}$ **4.** $\frac{6}{11}$ **5.** $\frac{2}{3}$ **6.** $\frac{5}{9}$ **7.** $\frac{7}{9}$
8. $1\frac{1}{3}$ **9.** $\frac{1}{2}$ **10.** $\frac{2}{3}$ **11.** 3 **12.** $1\frac{1}{2}$ **13.** 24 **14.** 15
15. -10 **16.** 21 **17.** 21 **18.** $2\frac{2}{3}$ **19.** $4\frac{3}{8}$ **20.** $1\frac{1}{2}$ **21.** $3\frac{3}{4}$
22. $1\frac{1}{3}$ **23.** $3\frac{3}{5}$ **24.** 2 **25.** $\frac{5}{8}$ **26.** $\frac{7}{19}$ **27.** $-\frac{3}{5}$ **28.** -24
29. -70 **30.** $8\frac{1}{4}$ **31.** 220 **32.** -500 **33.** $-\frac{98}{99}$ **34.** 6 **35.** 30
36. $1\frac{1}{2}$ **37.** 84 **38.** 6 **39.** $\frac{5}{7}$ **40.** $\frac{3}{5}$

page 53 ***Exercise 10***

1. 2 **2.** 3 **3.** 2 **4.** 2 **5.** 2 **6.** 3 **7.** 6 **8.** 1

page 54 ***Exercise 11***

1. 3 **2.** $\frac{3}{4}$ **3.** $4\frac{1}{2}$ **4.** $-\frac{3}{10}$ **5.** $-\frac{1}{2}$ **6.** $17\frac{2}{3}$
7. $\frac{1}{6}$ **8.** 5 **9.** 12 **10.** $3\frac{1}{3}$ **11.** $4\frac{2}{3}$ **12.** -9

page 55 ***Exercise 12***

1. $\frac{3}{4}$ **2.** $\frac{1}{4}$ **3.** $1\frac{3}{8}$ **4.** $1\frac{1}{4}$ **5.** 7
6. (a) $3\frac{3}{5}$ (b) $\frac{3}{4}$ **7.** (a) 41 (b) 31 **8.** 29
9. (a) 53 (b) 65 **10.** 55, 56, 57 **11.** 41, 42, 43, 44
12. (a) (i) $x-3$ (ii) $2(x-3)$ (b) $x = 12\frac{1}{2}$ **13.** $x = 8$, perimeter = 60 cm
14. 11 **15.** £6 **16.** $x = 3$ **17.** $x = 47$ **18.** 27 cm

page 59 ***Exercise 14***

14. (a) 10·7 cm^2 (b) $5\cdot3 \times 1\cdot7$ (c) 12·25 cm^2 (d) $3\cdot5 \times 3\cdot5$
15. (c) $x = 7$ (d) 2058 cm^3 **16.** (d) 3·5 s (e) 3 s (f) 20 m

Number 1

page 62 ***Exercise 1***

1. 805 **2.** 459 **3.** 650 **4.** 1333 **5.** 2745
6. 1248 **7.** 4522 **8.** 30 368 **9.** 28 224 **10.** 8568
11. 46 800 **12.** 66 281 **13.** 57 602 **14.** 89 516 **15.** 97 525

page 63 ***Exercise 2***

1. 32 **2.** 25 **3.** 18 **4.** 13 **5.** 35
6. 22 r 2 **7.** 23 r 24 **8.** 18 r 10 **9.** 27 r 18 **10.** 13 r 31
11. 35 r 6 **12.** 23 r 24 **13.** 64 r 37 **14.** 151 r 17 **15.** 2961 r 15

page 63 ***Exercise 3***

1. £47·04 **2.** 46 **3.** 7592 **4.** 21, 17 p change
5. 8 **6.** £80·64 **7.** £14 million **8.** £85 **9.** £21 600

page 64 ***Exercise 4***

1.

5	×	12	→	60
×		÷		
20	+	24	→	44
↓		↓		
100	×	$\frac{1}{2}$	→	50

2.

7	×	6	→	42
÷		÷		
14	−	3	→	11
↓		↓		
$\frac{1}{2}$	×	2	→	1

3.

19	×	2	→	38
−		÷		
12	×	4	→	48
↓		↓		
7	−	$\frac{1}{2}$	→	$6\frac{1}{2}$

4.

17	×	10	→	170
−		÷		
9	÷	100	→	0·09
↓		↓		
8	−	0·1	→	7·9

5.

0·3	×	20	→	6
+		−		
11	÷	11	→	1
↓		↓		
11·3	−	9	→	2·3

6.

$\frac{1}{2}$	×	50	→	25
−		÷		
0·1	+	$\frac{1}{2}$	→	0·6
↓		↓		
0·4	×	100	→	40

7.

7	×	0·1	→	0·7
÷		×		
4	÷	0·2	→	20
↓		↓		
1·75	+	0·02	→	1·77

8.

1·4	+	8	→	9·4
−		×		
0·1	×	0·1	→	0·01
↓		↓		
1·3	+	0·8	→	2·1

9.

100	×	0·3	→	30
−		×		
2·5	÷	10	→	0·25
↓		↓		
97·5	+	3	→	100·5

10.

3	÷	2	→	1·5
÷		÷		
8	÷	16	→	$\frac{1}{2}$
↓		↓		
$\frac{3}{8}$	+	$\frac{1}{8}$	→	$\frac{1}{2}$

11.

$\frac{1}{4}$	−	$\frac{1}{16}$	→	$\frac{3}{16}$
×		×		
$\frac{1}{2}$	÷	4	→	$\frac{1}{8}$
↓		↓		
$\frac{1}{8}$	+	$\frac{1}{4}$	→	$\frac{3}{8}$

12.

0·5	−	0·01	→	0·49
+		×		
3·5	×	10	→	35
↓		↓		
4	÷	0·1	→	40

13.

5·2	−	1·8	→	3·4
−		÷		
4·56	×	5	→	22·8
↓		↓		
0·64	+	0·36	→	1

14.

0·7	×	30	→	21
×		−		
16	−	−19	→	35
↓		↓		
11·2	−	49	→	−37·8

15.

−12	×	−6	→	72
÷		+		
4	+	7	→	1
↓		↓		
−3	+	1	→	−2

page 65 ***Exercise 5***

1. £12 **2.** £8 **3.** £10 **4.** £3 **5.** £2·40 **6.** £24 **7.** £45
8. £72 **9.** £244 **10.** £9·60 **11.** \$42 **12.** \$88 **13.** 8 kg **14.** 12 kg
15. 272 g **16.** 45 m **17.** 40 km **18.** \$710 **19.** 4·94 kg **20.** 60 g **21.** £204

page 66 ***Exercise 6***

1. £0·28 **2.** £1·16 **3.** £1·22 **4.** £2·90 **5.** £3·57 **6.** £0·45 **7.** £0·93
8. £37·03 **9.** £16·97 **10.** £0·38 **11.** £0·79 **12.** £1·60 **13.** £13·40 **14.** £50
15. £2·94 **16.** £11·06 **17.** £1·23 **18.** £4·40 **19.** £11·25 **20.** £22·71 **21.** £9·19

page 67 ***Exercise 7***

1. £63 **2.** £736 **3.** £77·55 **4.** £104 **5.** £1960 **6.** £792 **7.** £132
8. £45·75 **9.** £110·30 **10.** £42 **11.** £12·03 **12.** £9·49 **13.** £7·35 **14.** £7·01
15. £12·34 **16.** £16·92 **17.** £31·87 **18.** £9·02 **19.** £8·88 **20.** £14·14

page 67 ***Exercise 8***

1. £35·20 **2.** £5724 **3.** £171·50 **4.** £88·35 **5.** 2·828 kg **6.** £58·50
7. 24 **8.** 59 400 **9.** £9·52 **10.** 3·348 kg **11.** 13·054 kg **12.** £2762·50

page 68 ***Exercise 9***

1. £17·51 **2.** £40·66 **3.** £77·96 **4.** £185·34
5. (a) £28 (b) £21 **6.** (a) £480 (b) (i) £16·20 (ii) £1053

page 69 ***Exercise 10***

1. (a) £168 (b) £8736 **2.** (a) £176 (b) £8096 **3.** (a) £184 (b) £8464
4. (a) (i) £4 (ii) £5·75 (iii) £482·31 (iv) £24·12 (b) (i) £9·60 (ii) £13·80 (iii) £57·88

page 70 ***Exercise 11***

1. 200 m **2.** 500 m **3.** (b) 200 m (c) 1 km (d) 0·6 km **4.** 63 m
5. 24 km **6.** 120 m **7.** (a) 2·8 km (b) 3·25 km (c) 2·7 km

page 71 ***Exercise 12***

1. 150 cm **2.** 125 cm **3.** 28 cm **4.** 5·9 cm
5. (a) 60 cm (b) 84 cm (c) 56 cm (d) 140 cm (e) 100 cm **6.** 2·5 cm

page 72 ***Exercise 13***

1. £10, £20 **2.** £45, £15 **3.** 330 g, 550 g **4.** \$480, \$600 **5.** 36, 90
6. £10, £20, £30 **7.** £70 **8.** £50 **9.** 3250

page 73 ***Exercise 14***

1. 8	**2.** 5	**3.** 9	**4.** 30 g zinc, 40 g tin
5. 24	**6.** 2·4 kg	**7.** 6	**8.** 18 cm
9. 22·5 cm	**10.** 7·2 cm	**11.** 300 g	**12.** 5 : 3
13. £200	**14.** 42 p	**15.** £175 000	**16.** $\frac{1}{4}$ m^3

page 75 ***Exercise 15***

1. 2·35	**2.** 0·814	**3.** 26·2	**4.** 35·6	**5.** 113	**6.** 211
7. 0·825	**8.** 0·0312	**9.** 5·9	**10.** 1·2	**11.** 0·55	**12.** 0·72
13. 0·14	**14.** 1·8	**15.** 25	**16.** 31	**17.** 486·7	**18.** 500·4
19. 2·889	**20.** 3·113	**21.** 0·07154	**22.** 3·041	**23.** 2464	**24.** 488 900
25. 0·513	**26.** 5·8	**27.** 66	**28.** 587·6	**29.** 0·6	**30.** 0·07
31. 5·84	**32.** 88	**33.** 2500	**34.** 52700	**35.** 0·006	**36.** 7000

page 75 ***Exercise 16***

1. 5·38	**2.** 11·05	**3.** 0·41	**4.** 0·37	**5.** 8·02	**6.** 87·04	**7.** 9·01
8. 0·07	**9.** 8·4	**10.** 0·7	**11.** 0·4	**12.** 0·1	**13.** 6·1	**14.** 19·5
15. 8·1	**16.** 7·1	**17.** 8·16	**18.** 3·0	**19.** 0·545	**20.** 0·0056	**21.** 0·71
22. 6·83	**23.** 0·8	**24.** 19·65	**25.** 0·0714	**26.** 60·1	**27.** −7·3	**28.** −5·42

29. (a) 5·9 cm by 3·3 cm; 5·1 cm by 2·9 cm (b) 19·5 cm^2, 14·8 cm^2

page 76 ***Exercise 17***

1. 0·57	**2.** 3·45	**3.** 431	**4.** 19·3	**5.** 0·22	**6.** 3942·7
7. 53	**8.** 18·4	**9.** 0·059	**10.** 1·1	**11.** 6140	**12.** 127·89
13. 20·3	**14.** 47·6	**15.** 599·1	**16.** 0·16		

page 76 ***Exercise 18***

1. 0·85 m	**2.** 2400 m	**3.** 63 cm	**4.** 0·25 m	**5.** 0·7 cm
6. 20 mm	**7.** 1200 m	**8.** 700 cm	**9.** 580 m	**10.** 0·815 m
11. 0·65 km	**12.** 2·5 cm	**13.** 5000 g	**14.** 4200 g	**15.** 6400 g
16. 3000 g	**17.** 800 g	**18.** 0·4 kg	**19.** 2000 kg	**20.** 0·25 kg
21. 500 kg	**22.** 620 kg	**23.** 0·007 t	**24.** 1·5 kg	**25.** 0·8 l
26. 2000 ml	**27.** 1 l	**28.** 4500 ml	**29.** 6000 ml	**30.** 3000 cm^3
31. 2000 l	**32.** 5500 l	**33.** 900 cm^3	**34.** 0·6 l	**35.** 15 000 l
36. 0·24 l	**37.** 0·28 m	**38.** 550 cm	**39.** 0·305 kg	**40.** 46 m
41. 0·016 l	**42.** 0·208 m	**43.** 2·8 cm	**44.** 0·27 m	**45.** 0·788 km
46. 14 000 kg	**47.** 1300 g	**48.** 0·09 m^3	**49.** 2900 kg	**50.** 0·019 l

51. (For discussion)

page 77 ***Exercise 19***

1. 24	**2.** 48	**3.** 30	**4.** 4480	**5.** 48	**6.** 17 600
7. 36	**8.** 70	**9.** 4	**10.** 880	**11.** 3	**12.** 2
13. 3520	**14.** 80	**15.** 140	**16.** 12	**17.** 48	**18.** 22 400
19. 5280	**20.** 2	**21.** 30	**22.** 62	**23.** 76	**24.** 101
25. 18	**26.** 8	**27.** 58	**28.** 92	**29.** 4	**30.** 152

page 78 ***Exercise 20***

1. 25·4 **2.** 45·5 **3.** 45·4 **4.** 56·8 **5.** 3·22 **6.** 0·908
7. 16·1 **8.** 10·16 **9.** 2·27 **10.** 0·284 **11.** 6·21 **12.** 22
13. 6·6 **14.** 62·1 **15.** 88 **16.** 4·4 **17.** 1·242 **18.** 1·1
19. 44 **20.** 12·42 **21.** 30·48 **22.** 2·84 **23.** 0·66 **24.** 7·62
25. 3105 **26.** (a) $\frac{1}{2}$ (b) 10 mins **27.** (a) 48·3 km/h (b) 49·7 mph
28. (a) Britain (b) 28 p or 29 p **29.** 26·7 yards **30.** $\frac{1}{8}$ inch **31.** 28 g

page 79 ***Exercise 21***

(For discussion)
1. (a) Nelson's column 184 feet (b) Empire State Building 1472 feet
(c) Mount Everest 29 000 feet
2. (a) No (b) No **3.** (a) No (b) No
4. (a) No (b) Probably **5.** (a) Yes (b) about 54 times

page 80 ***Exercise 22***

1. 4 p **2.** 11 p **3.** 9 p **4.** 10 p **5.** 4 p **6.** 18 p **7.** 6 p
8. 13 p **9.** £1·75 **10.** 36 p **11.** 2·5 p **12.** £7·25 **13.** 15 p **14.** 5 p
15. 16 p **16.** £0·89 **17.** 14 p **18.** 2 p **19.** £3·60 **20.** 15 p

page 81 ***Exercise 23***

1. 4·3 **2.** 0·7 **3.** 9·4 **4.** 1·2 **5.** 16 **6.** 23.4
7. 17·4 **8.** 128 **9.** 11 **10.** 0·24 **11.** 1·92 **12.** 5·2
13. 53 **14.** 1·76 **15.** 3·13 **16.** 105 **17.** 50 **18.** 1·9

page 82 ***Exercise 24***

1. (a) 45 (b) 30 (c) 30 (d) 20 **2.** 2 h 10 min **3.** 2005
4. 'The London Blackout Murders' **5.** 15 min **6.** 225 min (= $3\frac{3}{4}$ h)
7. 11 h 5 min **8.** 21 10 **9.** 5 **10.** 1 h 45 min
11. 18 00 **12.** 15 min **13.** 15 h 10 min

page 83 ***Exercise 25***

1. 582 **2.** £5·12 **3.** 130 years **4.** £28·50 **5.** 1455
6. 15 h 5 min **7.** £10·35 **8.** £21·10 **9.** 3854 **10.** £704

page 84 ***Exercise 26***

1. £0·78, £1·80, 7, £14·63 **2.** 6 p
3. (a) double 18 (b) £11 111 **4.** 140
5. (a) 50, 20, 5, 2 (b) 50, 20, 10, 5, 1 (c) £1, 50, 5, 1, 1 or 50, 50, 50, 5, 2
6. *m*, 9, *z* **7.** 24 **8.** Both same (!) **9.** 1·50 m

page 85 ***Exercise 27***

1. 9 **2.** (a) 5 m (b) 50 m (c) 6 km **3.** 51·4°
4. (a) 40 acres (b) 15 acres (c) 10%; 30%; 37·5%, 22·5% **5.** 78
6. £184·50 **7.** £839·50 **8.** £5·85
9. (a) $99 + \frac{9}{9}$ (b) $6 + \frac{6}{6}$ (c) $55 + 5$ (d) $55 + 5 + \frac{5}{5}$ (e) $\frac{7+7}{7+7}$ (f) $\frac{88}{8}$
10. From left to right (a) 7, 3 (b) 4, 3 (c) 7, 8, 6 (d) 3, 7, 0 (e) 3, 6 (f) 6, 8, 0

page 86 ***Exercise 28***

1. £3·26 **2.** £1·70 **3.** (a) 108 m^2 (b) 3
5. 100 m **6.** (a) £800 (b) 8% **7.** 10 h 30 min
8. (a) 0·54 (b) 40 (c) 0·004 (d) 2·2 (e) £9 (f) £40 **9.** 260 million
10. (a) 4, 3 (b) 7, 6 (c) 8, 4 (d) 24, 2

page 88 ***Exercise 29***

1. (a) 69 (b) 65 **2.** 120 **3.** 360 000 kg
4. 0·012, 0·021, 0·03, 0·12, 0·21 **5.** 16 **7.** 64 mph
8. (a) Yes (b) No (c) Yes (d) Yes (e) Yes (f) Yes (g) Yes (h) No

Handling data 1

page 89 ***Exercise 1***

1. (a) £425 (b) £150 (c) £250 (d) £75
2. (a) £1333·33 (b) £1500 (c) £666·67 (d) £1000 (e) £1200
3. (a) £21 600 000 (b) £8 000 000 (c) £1 000 000
4. (a) 8 min, 34 min, 10 min (b) 18°

page 90 ***Exercise 2***

1. (a) (i) 45° (ii) 200° (iii) 110° (iv) 5° **2.** (a) $\frac{3}{10}$, $\frac{4}{10}$, $\frac{1}{5}$, $\frac{1}{10}$ **3.** $x = 60°$, $y = 210°$
4. Barley 60°, Oats 90°, Rye 165°, Wheat 45° **5.** (a) 180° (b) 36° (c) 90° (d) 54°

page 92 ***Exercise 3***

1. (a) 5 (b) 19 (c) 23 (d) 55 (e) $\frac{6}{23}$
3. (a) £3000 approx.
(b) Profits increase in months before Christmas. Very few sales after Christmas.

page 94 ***Exercise 4***

1. (a) 5 (b) 24 (c) 35 (d) Expect this shape.
2. (a) D (b) A (c) A (d) C (e) C (f) B
3. Field A (assuming the fertilizer increases the weight).
4. No significant change.

page 97 ***Exercise 5***

1. (a) (i) \$2·50 (ii) \$2 (iii) \$3 (b) (i) £0·80 (ii) £2·80 (iii) £2
2. (a) (i) 2·5 kg (ii) 3·6 kg (iii) 0.9 kg (b) (i) 4·4 lb (ii) 6·6 lb (iii) 3·3 lb (c) 2·2 lb (d) 3·2 kg
3. (a) DM 0·6 less (b) 25%
4. (a) 10°C (b) 68°F (c) −18°C

page 105 ***Exercise 7***

2. (b) about 44
3. (b) about 6·7 km
4. (b) Bogota, high in the Andes (c) about 73°
5. For discussion

page 108 ***Exercise 8***

1. (b) 31·0% (c) 34·5%
2. (b) 57·7% (c) 86·8% (d) many more over 16's preferred BBC2
3. (a) 47·6% (b) 155 (c) 9·68% (d) not surprisng
4. (a) 5°C (b) −10°C (c) 0°C (d) second feels colder (e) (i) Bitterly cold (ii) No: too cold
5. (a) 68·9% (b) 61·0% (c) fertilizer does produce a (slight) improvement
(d) Mark II fertilizer is not efficient.

Shape and space 2

page 112 ***Exercise 2***

2. (a) (7, −7), (−5, 5), (5, 7)
3. (d) (7, 5), (−5, 7), (5, −7)
4. (g) (−3, 6), (−6, 6), (−6, 4)
5. (g) (3, 1), (7, 1), (7, 3)
6. (a) $y = 0$ (x-axis) (b) $x = 1$ (c) $y = 1$ (d) $y = -x$

page 114 ***Exercise 3***

7. Shape 1: C, 90° CW; Shape 2: B, 180°
Shape 3: A, 90° ACW; Shape 4: B, 90° CW; Shape 5: F, 180°

page 115 ***Exercise 4***

2. (e) (3, −4), (2, −7), (−1, −4)
3. (e) (−6, 2), (−6, 6), (−4, 4)

page 116 **Exercise 5**

4. (a) (0, 0) (b) (1, 2) (c) (0, 0) (d) (−1, 1)
5. (b) (i) (2, 3) (ii) (0, 0) (iii) (2, 0) (iv) (−1, 1)
6. (b) (i) (0, 0) (ii) (−5, 0) (iii) (−7, 4) (iv) (−1, −5)

page 118 **Exercise 6**

1. (a) Yes (b) No (c) Yes (d) Yes
2. 78 mm
3. $y = 24$ mm, $z = 67{\cdot}5$ mm
7. OA′ = 2 × OA, OB′ = 2 × OB
9. (b) Scale factor = $1\frac{1}{2}$

page 122 **Exercise 7**

7. (e) (3, 0), (−5, −1), (3, −1) **8.** (e) (3, 3), (−6, −1), (3, −3) **9.** (e) (3, −1), (2, −1), (5, −7)

page 125 **Exercise 9**

1. (a) No (b) No (c) No (d) No (e) No
(f) Yes (g) No (h) Yes (i) No (j) No
(k) No (l) No (m) Yes (n) No

2. (a) $\begin{pmatrix}4\\6\end{pmatrix}$ (b) $\begin{pmatrix}6\\4\end{pmatrix}$ (c) $\begin{pmatrix}0\\3\end{pmatrix}$ (d) $\begin{pmatrix}6\\0\end{pmatrix}$ (e) $\begin{pmatrix}5\\-2\end{pmatrix}$

(f) $\begin{pmatrix}-2\\-3\end{pmatrix}$ (g) $\begin{pmatrix}-2\\5\end{pmatrix}$ (h) $\begin{pmatrix}2\\-2\end{pmatrix}$ (i) $\begin{pmatrix}-4\\-3\end{pmatrix}$ (j) $\begin{pmatrix}2\\-6\end{pmatrix}$

(k) $\begin{pmatrix}1\\-8\end{pmatrix}$ (l) $\begin{pmatrix}-6\\-1\end{pmatrix}$ (m) $\begin{pmatrix}0\\-4\end{pmatrix}$ (n) $\begin{pmatrix}6\\1\end{pmatrix}$

page 129 **Exercise 11**

1. (a) 115° (b) 90° (c) 80°
3. C(−3, −3), D(−4, 2)
4. (a) 34° (b) 56°
5. (a) 35° (b) 35°
6. (a) 72° (b) 108° (c) 80°
7. (a) 40° (b) 30° (c) 110°
8. (a) 116° (b) 32° (c) 58°
9. (a) 55° (b) 55°
10. (a) 26° (b) 26° (c) 77°
11. (a) 52° (b) 64° (c) 116°
12. 110°
13. (a) 54° (b) 72° (c) 36°
14. (a) 60° (b) 15° (c) 75°

page 131 **Exercise 12**

1. A 035°, B 070°, C 155°, D 220°, E 290°, L 340°
2. A 040°, B 065°, C 130°, D 160°, E 230°, F 330°

page 132 **Exercise 13**

1. (a) $147\frac{1}{2}$° (b) 122° (c) 090°
2. (a) 286° (b) 225° (c) 153°
3. (a) 061° (b) $327\frac{1}{2}$°
4. (a) 302° (b) 344° (c) 045°

page 134 ***Exercise 16***

1. 11·5 km **2.** 14·1 km **3.** 12·5 km, 032° **4.** 6·9 km
5. 8·5 km, 074° **6.** 8·4 km, 029° **7.** (b) 5·2 h **8.** No

page 136 ***Exercise 17***

1. A (2, 4, 0) B (0, 4, 3) C (2, 4, 3) D (2, 0, 3)
2. (a) B (3, 0, 0) C (3, 4, 0) Q (3, 0, 2) R (3, 4, 2)
(b) (i) (0, 2, 0) (ii) (0, 4, 1) (iii) ($1\frac{1}{2}$, 4, 0)
(c) (i) ($1\frac{1}{2}$, 2, 0) (ii) ($1\frac{1}{2}$, 2, 2) (iii) ($1\frac{1}{2}$, 4, 1) (d) ($1\frac{1}{2}$, 2, 1)
3. (a) C (2, 2, 0) R (2, 2, 3) B (2, −2, 0) P (0, −2, 3) Q (2, −2, 3)
(b) (i) (2, −2, $1\frac{1}{2}$) (ii) (1, −2, 3)
4. (i) 5 (ii) 5·83 (iii) 6·40 **5.** (i) (2, $3\frac{1}{2}$, 5) (ii) (2, 7, $2\frac{1}{2}$) (iii) (2, $3\frac{1}{2}$, 0)
6. (20, 45, 5) **7.** (a) 4 (b) 5 (c) $5\sqrt{2}$ **8.** Square-based pyramid
9. (a) 10 (b) 45° **10.** 29·9 m

page 139 ***Exercise 18***

8. 10 cm, 40 cm **9.** (a) anticlockwise (b) 15 (c) 200 rpm **11.** a plane

page 142 ***Exercise 19***

1. 10 cm **2.** 4·12 cm **3.** 10.6 cm **4.** 5·66 cm **5.** 4·24 cm **6.** 990
7. 4·58 cm **8.** 5·20 cm **9.** 9·85 cm **10.** 7·07 cm **11.** 3·46 m **12.** 40·3 km
13. 9·49 cm **14.** 32·6 cm **15.** 5·39 units **16.** Yes **17.** 6·63 cm **18.** 5·57
19. 8·72 **20.** 5·66 **21.** 6·63 cm **22.** 2·24 **23.** (a) (i) 13 (ii) 25 (iii) 9
24. (a) 5 cm (b) 7·81 cm **25.** (a) 8·06 cm (b) 9 cm **26.** Philip

page 145 ***Exercise 20***

1. 113 litres **2.** 17·3 litres **3.** (a) $\frac{1}{3}$ (b) $\frac{4}{9}$ (c) 25 cm^2 **4.** 2500
5. 1100 m **6.** (a) 24 cm^2 (b) 35 cm^2 **7.** 740 cm^3 **8.** 2·4 cm
9. (a) 2·5 cm (b) 3·25 cm **10.** 40 **11.** 100 **12.** 900
13. (a) 384 cm^2 (b) 80 cm **14.** (a) 6 (b) 12 (c) 8 (d) 1

Algebra 2

page 149 ***Exercise 1***

1. $w = b + 4$ **2.** $w = 2b + 6$ **3.** $w = 2b - 12$ **4.** $m = 2t + 1$ **5.** $m = 3t + 2$
6. $s = t + 2$ **7.** (a) $p = 5n - 2$ (b) $k = 7n + 3$ (c) $w = 2n + 11$
8. (a) $y = 3n + 1$ (b) $h = 4n - 3$ (c) $k = 3n + 5$ **9.** $m = 8c + 4$
10. (a) $t = 2n + 4$ (b) $e = 3n + 11$ (c) $e = \dfrac{3t + 10}{2}$

page 152 ***Exercise 2***

1. 6 × 12 **2.** 15 × 5 **3.** (a) 26 × 13 (b) 16 × 8 (c) 32 × 16 (d) 9 × 4·5 (e) 6·5 × 3·25
4. (a) 6 × 5 (b) 12 × 11 (c) 20 × 19 (d) 6·5 × 5·5 (e) 8·7 × 7·7 **5.** Not given

page 154 ***Exercise 3***

1. (a) 9·51/9·52 (b) 7·57/7·58 **2.** (a) 5·14/5·15 (b) 3·82/3·83 (c) 6·69/6·70 (d) 3·37/3·38 (e) 5·82/5·83 or 0·17/0·18 (f) 3·15/3·16 (g) 3·59/3·60 **3.** 8·07/8·08
4. 9·55/9·56 **5.** (a) $x + 10$ (c) $32 \times 42 \times 6$ **6.** $x = 3{\cdot}8$ **7.** $x = 1{\cdot}62$

page 156 ***Exercise 4***

1. (a) (3, 7) (b) (1, 3) (c) (11, −1) **2.** (2, 4) **3.** (2, 3) **4.** (3, 1) **5.** (1, 5)
6. (5, 3) **7.** (a) (4, 0) (b) (1, 6) (c) (−2, −3) (d) (8, −1) (e) (−0·6, 1·2)

page 158 ***Exercise 5***

1. $x = 2, y = 1$ **2.** $x = 4, y = 2$ **3.** $x = 3, y = 1$ **4.** $x = -2, y = 1$
5. $x = 3, y = 2$ **6.** $x = 5, y = -2$ **7.** $x = 2, y = 1$ **8.** $x = 5, y = 3$
9. $x = 3, y = -1$ **10.** $a = 2, b = -3$ **11.** $a = 5, b = \frac{1}{4}$ **12.** $a = 1, b = 3$
13. $m = \frac{1}{2}, n = 4$ **14.** $w = 2, x = 3$ **15.** $x = 6, y = 3$ **16.** $x = \frac{1}{2}, z = -3$
17. $m = 1\frac{15}{17}, n = \frac{11}{17}$ **18.** $c = 1\frac{16}{23}, d = -2\frac{12}{23}$

page 159 ***Exercise 6***

1. $x = 2, y = 4$ **2.** $x = 1, y = 4$ **3.** $x = 2, y = 5$ **4.** $x = 3, y = 7$
5. $x = 5, y = 2$ **6.** $a = 3, b = 1$ **7.** $x = 1, y = 3$ **8.** $x = 1, y = 3$
9. $x = -2, y = 3$ **10.** $x = 4, y = 1$ **11.** $x = 1, y = 5$ **12.** $x = 0, y = 2$
13. $x = \frac{5}{7}, y = 4\frac{3}{7}$ **14.** $x = 1, y = 2$ **15.** $x = 2, y = 3$ **16.** $x = 4, y = -1$
17. $x = 3, y = 1$ **18.** $x = 1, y = 2$ **19.** $x = 2, y = 1$ **20.** $x = -2, y = 1$

page 159 ***Exercise 7***

1. $5\frac{1}{2}, 9\frac{1}{2}$ **2.** 6, 3 or $2\frac{2}{5}, 5\frac{2}{5}$ **3.** 4, 10
4. 10·5, 7·5 **5.** $a = 2, c = 7$ **6.** $m = 4, c = -3$
7. $a = 30, b = 5$ **8.** TV £200, video £450 **9.** w 2 oz, b $3\frac{1}{2}$ oz
10. 2 p × 15, 5 p × 25 **11.** 10 p × 14, 50 p × 7 **12.** 12 m, 24 m
13. (4, −3), (−2, 3) **14.** man £50, woman £70 **15.** current 4 m/s, kipper 10 m/s

page 162 ***Exercise 8***

1. (a) 40 km (b) 60 km (c) York, Scarborough (d) 15 min (e) (i) 1100 (ii) 1345 (f) (i) 40 km/h (ii) 60 km/h (iii) 100 km/h
2. (a) 25 km (b) 15 km (c) 0945 (d) 1 h (e) (i) 26·7 km/h (ii) 5 km/h (iii) 30 km/h (iv) 40 km/h
3. (a) (i) 1400 (ii) 1345 (b) (i) 1545 (ii) towards Aston (c) (i) 15 mph (ii) 40 mph (iii) 40 mph (iv) 20 mph (d) $1607\frac{1}{2}$
4. (a) 45 min (b) 0915 (c) 60 km/h (d) 100 km/h (e) 57·1 km/h
5. (a) 0915 (b) 64 km/h (c) 37·6 km/h (d) 47 km (e) 80 km/h
6. (b) 1105 **7.** (a) 1242 **8.** (b) 1235

page 165 ***Exercise 9***

1. (a) 740 p (b) £280 (c) £14 000 (d) £11 000
4. (a) 6 gallons (b) 40 mpg; 30 mpg (c) $33\frac{1}{3}$ mpg; $5\frac{1}{2}$ gallons
5. 180 miles
6. 2·5 h

page 168 ***Exercise 10***

1. B
2. D
3. (a) C (b) A (c) D (d) B
4. (a) (i) B (ii) A (b) 8 s to 18 s (c) about 15 s (d) about 9 s (e) B (f) A
6. (a) runners slow down for takeover (b) baton dropped at third takeover

page 170 ***Exercise 11***

1. 4, 10, 16, 22, 28, 34, 40
2. 2, 3, 4, 5, 6, 7, 8
3. 38, 46, 54, 62, 34, 38, 42
4. 56, 64, 72, 80, 88, 44, 48
5. 54, 62, 71, 38, 42, 46, 50
6. 6, 24, 12, 42, 18, 60, 24, 78, 30
7. 24, 12, 42, 18, 60, 24, 78, 30, 96
8. (a) 4, 24 (b) 6, 720

page 173 ***Exercise 12***

1. (a) 11, 22, 11, 33 (b) 12, 24, 13, 39 (c) 7, 14, 28, 17, 51
(d) 9, 16, 32, 21, 63 (d) 11, 18, 36, 25, 75 (f) 13, 20, 40, 29, 87
2. (a) 6, 12, 27, 20, 5 (b) 3, 6, 21, 14, $3\frac{1}{2}$ (c) 8, 16, 31, 24, 6
(d) 10, 20, 35, 28, 7 (e) 1, 2, 17, 10, $2\frac{1}{2}$ (f) 12, 24, 39, 32, 8
3. (a) 7, 22, 44, 22, $5\frac{1}{2}$ (b) 10, 25, 50, 28, 7 (c) 16, 31, 62, 40, 10
(d) $\frac{1}{2}$, $15\frac{1}{2}$, 31, 9, $2\frac{1}{4}$ (e) 100, 115, 230, 208, 52 (f) 24, 39, 78, 56, 14
4. (a) 4, 16, 48, 38, 19 (b) 5, 25, 75, 65, $32\frac{1}{2}$ (c) 6, 36, 108, 98, 49
(d) 8, 64, 192, 182, 91 (e) 1, 1, 3, −7, $-3\frac{1}{2}$ (f) 10, 100, 300, 290, 145
5. × 4, square root, −10, × −2
6. reciprocal, +1, square, ÷3
7. +3, cube, ÷−2, +100

Number 2

page 175 ***Exercise 1***

1. 8% **2.** 10% **3.** 25% **4.** 2% **5.** 4%
6. $2\frac{1}{2}$% **7.** 20% **8.** 50% **9.** 15% **10.** 80%
11. 25% **12.** 20% **13.** $12\frac{1}{2}$% **14.** $33\frac{1}{3}$% **15.** 80%
16. 5% **17.** 6% **18.** 20% **19.** 5% **20.** $2\frac{1}{2}$%

page 176 ***Exercise 2***

1. 36·4% **2.** 19·0% **3.** 19·4% **4.** 22·0% **5.** 12·2%
6. 9·4% **7.** 14·0% **8.** 17·4% **9.** 32·7% **10.** 10·2%
11. 7·7% **12.** 35·3% **13.** 30·8% **14.** 5·2% **15.** 14·1%
16. 14·5% **17.** 19·1% **18.** 3·6% **19.** 31·1% **20.** 6·5%

page 176 ***Exercise 3***

1. 12% **2.** 29% **3.** 16% **4.** 0·25% **5.** 15%
6. 61·1% **7.** 15% **8.** 14·2% **9.** 1·5% **10.** 23·8%

page 177 ***Exercise 4***

1. (a) 25 p (b) £12·80 (c) £2·80 (d) 28% **2.** (a) £10 (b) (i) £4·20 (ii) 42%
3. (a) (i) 120 cm (ii) 75 cm (iii) 10 000 cm^2 (iv) 9000 cm^2 (b) 10%
4. (a) £50 000 (b) (i) £53 800 (ii) 7·6% **5.** 250 m^2

page 179 ***Exercise 5***

1. '$\frac{1}{3}$ off' **2.** $\frac{1}{6}$ of £5000 **3.** 25% **4.** 20%
5. (a) 0·25 (b) 0·4 (c) 0·375 (d) $0{\cdot}41\dot{6}$ (e) $0{\cdot}1\dot{6}$ (f) $0{\cdot}\dot{2}8571\dot{4}$
6. (a) $\frac{1}{5}$ (b) $\frac{9}{20}$ (c) $\frac{9}{25}$ (d) $\frac{1}{8}$ (e) $1\frac{1}{20}$ (f) $\frac{7}{1000}$
7. (a) 25% (b) 10% (c) 72% (d) 7·5% (e) 2% (f) $33\frac{1}{3}$%
8. (a) $\frac{1}{4}$, 0·25, 25% (b) $\frac{1}{5}$, 0·2, 20% (c) $\frac{4}{5}$, 0.8, 80% (d) $\frac{1}{100}$, 0·01, 1%
(e) $\frac{3}{10}$, 0·3, 30% (f) $\frac{1}{3}$, $0{\cdot}\dot{3}$, $33\frac{1}{3}$% **9.** (a) 0·14625 (b) £15·84
10. (a) 45%; $\frac{1}{2}$; 0·6 (b) 4%; $\frac{6}{16}$; 0·38 (c) 11%; 0·111; $\frac{1}{9}$ **11.** 0·58
12. 1·42 **13.** 0·65 **14.** 1·61 **15.** 0·07
16. 0·16 **17.** 3·64 **18.** 0·60 **19.** 62·5%

page 181 ***Exercise 6***

1. B **2.** C **3.** B **4.** A **5.** B **6.** C **7.** B
8. B **9.** A **10.** B **11.** A **12.** A **13.** C (or B) **14.** C
15. £5200 [assuming one pound coin weighs 9 g] **16.** about 20
17. (a) True (b) True (c) True (d) False (e) False (f) True (g) True
(h) False (i) True

page 183 ***Exercise 7***

1. B **2.** A **3.** C **4.** B **5.** C **6.** A **7.** B
8. B **9.** A **10.** C **11.** B **12.** A **13.** A **14.** C
15. C **16.** B **17.** C **18.** A **19.** B **20.** B **21.** C
22. B **23.** B **24.** A **25.** B **26.** B **27.** A **28.** Yes
29. Yes **30.** He got it wrong. Correct answer is £10·45 each
31. (a) (Say) 200 g per paper : 3250 papers per tree (b) about 5×10^{11} (c) For discussion

page 185 ***Exercise 8***

1. 195·5 cm **2.** 36·5 kg **3.** 3·25 kg **4.** 95·55
5. 28·65 s **6.** B **7.** C **8.** Not necessarily
9. 16·5, 17·5 **10.** 255·5, 256·5 **11.** 2·35, 2·45 **12.** 0·335, 0·345

13. 2·035, 2·045 **14.** 11.95, 12·05 **15.** 81·35, 81·45 **16.** 0·25, 0·35
17. 4·795, 4·805 **18.** 0·065, 0·075 **19.** 0·65, 0·75 **20.** 614·5, 615·5
21. 7·125, 7.135 **22.** 51·5 million, 52·5 million **23.** 84·95, 85·05
24. to **31.** For discussion

page 187 ***Test 1***

1. £3·50	**2.** £4·95	**3.** 48	**4.** 10 p, 10 p, 20 p	**5.** $6\frac{1}{2}$	**6.** $\frac{1}{100}$
7. 56	**8.** 75%	**9.** 15	**10.** 56 p	**11.** 50 min	**12.** 6·5
13. 130 m	**14.** 770	**15.** 11	**16.** 25	**17.** $1\frac{1}{4}$	**18.** £10
19. 10	**20.** 60·5	**21.** 55	**22.** 16	**23.** 1 h	**24.** $4\frac{1}{2}$
25. 75 or 105	**26.** 20	**27.** £2·40	**28.** 82%	**29.** £4000	**30.** 48 p

page 187 ***Test 2***

1. 96	**2.** 19	**3.** 06 30	**4.** £2·75	**5.** £1·90	**6.** 95°
7. 5 018 001	**8.** 15	**9.** £6	**10.** 3·5 p	**11.** 53	**12.** 800 g
13. 74	**14.** 280 miles	**15.** 40	**16.** 4	**17.** 62	**18.** 5
19. 5	**20.** 480	**21.** 158	**22.** 95	**23.** 0·2	**24.** 0·7
25. £84	**26.** £2455	**27.** 64	**28.** 90 p	**29.** 55 mph	**30.** 28

page 188 ***Test 3***

1. 70	**2.** 240	**3.** 900	**4.** 10 705	**5.** 10 45	**6.** 245
7. 20	**8.** £3·05	**9.** £1·76	**10.** 20, 20, 20, 1 or 50, 5, 5, 1		
11. 0·75	**12.** 5	**13.** Tuesday	**14.** 1·5 kg	**15.** £150·50	**16.** 640 m
17. £722	**18.** £25 000	**19.** 4	**20.** £1·10	**21.** 28	**22.** 9
23. 91	**24.** £6	**25.** 98 p	**26.** £4·46	**27.** £3·30	**28.** £42
29. 960	**30.** 18 p				

page 188 ***Test 4***

1. £8·05	**2.** 75	**3.** 25	**4.** 0·1 cm	**5.** 24 p	**6.** 104
7. 40 p	**8.** £88	**9.** 5 : 50	**10.** £8·20	**11.** 4 km	**12.** 45 miles
13. £4·25	**14.** 998	**15.** 20	**16.** 200	**17.** 22·5 cm	**18.** 75 p
19. 10	**20.** 16	**21.** 20	**22.** £9·82	**23.** 22 min	**24.** 1540
25. £7·94	**26.** 70 p	**27.** 200	**28.** 35%	**29.** 100	**30.** £2500

page 189 ***Test 5***

1. 20, 10, 5, 2	**2.** £4·40	**3.** £2·10	**4.** £26	**5.** 8 min
6. 25	**7.** 500 ($\pm$ 50)	**8.** $\frac{1}{1000}$	**9.** 2·65	**10.** —
11. £15 000	**12.** £3·85	**13.** £27·50	**14.** 8	**15.** 84
16. 108	**17.** 30 litres	**18.** 7 cm	**19.** 153	**20.** 4
21. 7	**22.** 105 sq yd	**23.** 2 000 000	**24.** 51	**25.** 6
26. £6	**27.** 32	**28.** 150	**29.** 133	**30.** Wednesday

page 190 ***Test 6***

1. 60°	**2.** 0·05	**3.** 80%	**4.** 8000	**5.** £16·90
6. 0·7	**7.** 5 h 20 min	**8.** $12\frac{1}{2}$%	**9.** 6 cm	**10.** 0·001
11. 7, 8	**12.** £2	**13.** 1·8	**14.** 49·2	**15.** £12·50
16. 165	**17.** 72°	**18.** 240	**19.** 34 p	**20.** £9
21. 60 mph	**22.** 302	**23.** 50	**24.** 37	**25.** £1·11
26. £15	**27.** 12	**28.** 8, 9	**29.** £80	**30.** £13·80

page 190 ***Test 7***

1. 82°	**2.** 72 p	**3.** 0·25	**4.** 90 nautical miles
5. 8	**6.** 11	**7.** 325	**8.** $\frac{1}{12}$
9. £25 000	**10.** 49 000	**11.** 6·3	**12.** £8·70
13. £2·40	**14.** 5	**15.** £37·50	**16.** 13·55 cm
17. 10 cm	**18.** £9	**19.** 200	**20.** £1·20
21. 250	**22.** 500 m^2	**23.** £8·70	**24.** 0·025
25. 2550 g	**26.** £40 000	**27.** 150°	**28.** £150
29. 11	**30.** 9		

page 192 ***Exercise 9***

1. 19	**2.** 4	**3.** 3	**4.** 0	**5.** 35	**6.** 60
7. 16	**8.** 6	**9.** 13	**10.** 14	**11.** 23	**12.** 71
13. 20	**14.** 36	**15.** 9	**16.** 8	**17.** 32	**18.** 30
19. 4	**20.** 0	**21.** 6	**22.** 5	**23.** 1	**24.** 47
25. 6	**26.** 3	**27.** 16	**28.** 12	**29.** 52	**30.** 15
31. 87	**32.** 17	**33.** 23	**34.** 8	**35.** 2	**36.** 26

page 193 ***Exercise 10***

1. $7 + 5 \times 4$	**2.** $3 \times 5 + 10$	**3.** $4 \div 2 + 3$	**4.** $11 + 3 \times 3$
5. $31 - 10 \times 2$	**6.** $10 + 6 \times 5$	**7.** $4 \times 8 - 7$	**8.** $12 + 9 \times 2$
9. $18 - 4 \times 4$	**10.** $28 - 10 \times 2$	**11.** $21 \div 3 - 5$	**12.** $7 + 3 \times 3$
13. $10 \div 2 + 3$	**14.** $10 \times 3 + 12$	**15.** $18 \div 3 + 7$	**16.** $31 + 40 \div 5$
17. $15 - 16 \div 4$	**18.** $15 + 8 \times 9$	**19.** $37 + 35 \div 5$	**20.** $11 \times 5 + 9$
21. $8 + 3 \times 2 - 4$	**22.** $12 - 3 \times 3 + 1$	**23.** $11 + 4 - 1 \times 6$	**24.** $15 \div 5 + 2 \times 4$
25. $7 \times 2 - 3 \times 3$	**26.** $12 - 2 + 3 \times 4$	**27.** $8 \times 9 - 6 \times 11$	**28.** $20 \div 20 + 9 \times 0$
29. $20 - 30 \div 10 + 8$	**30.** $30 + 6 \times 11 - 11$		

page 193 ***Exercise 11***

1. 1851	**2.** 6·889	**3.** 1·214	**4.** 0·4189	**5.** 7·889	**6.** 19·35
7. 0·049 47	**8.** 221·5	**9.** 24·37	**10.** 6·619	**11.** 3·306	**12.** 2·303
13. 41·73	**14.** 8·163	**15.** 0·1090	**16.** 0·5001	**17.** 20·63	**18.** 10·09
19. 6·191	**20.** 10.27	**21.** 8·627	**22.** 22·02	**23.** 1·093	**24.** 44·72
25. 45·66	**26.** 52·86	**27.** 22·51	**28.** 5·479	**29.** 5·272	**30.** 0·2116

page 194 ***Exercise 12***

1. 14·52	**2.** 1·666	**3.** 1·858	**4.** 0·8264	**5.** 2·717	**6.** 4·840
7. 10·87	**8.** 7·425	**9.** 13·49	**10.** 0·7392	**11.** 1135	**12.** 13·33
13. 5·836	**14.** 86·39	**15.** 10·23	**16.** 5540	**17.** 14·76	**18.** 8·502
19. 57·19	**20.** 19·90	**21.** 6·578	**22.** 9·097	**23.** 0·082 80	**24.** 1855
25. 2·367	**26.** 1·416	**27.** 7·261	**28.** 3·151	**29.** 149·9	**30.** 74 020
31. 8·482	**32.** 75·21	**33.** 1·226	**34.** 6767	**35.** 5·964	**36.** 15·45
37. 25·42	**38.** 2·724	**39.** 4·366	**40.** 0·2194	**41.** 0·000 465 9	**42.** 0·3934
43. −0·7526	**44.** 2·454	**45.** 40 000	**46.** 3·003	**47.** 0·006 562	**48.** 0·1330

page 195 ***Exercise 13***

1. SOIL	**2.** ISLES	**3.** HE LIES	**4.** SOS
5. HO HO HO	**6.** ESSO OIL	**7.** SOLID	**8.** SOLO
9. BOILED EGGS	**10.** HE IS BOSS	**11.** LODGE	**12.** SIGH
13. HEDGEHOG	**14.** GOSH	**15.** GOBBLE	**16.** BEG
17. BIG SLOB	**18.** SID	**19.** HILL	**20.** LESLIE
21. HOBBIES	**22.** GIGGLE	**23.** BIBLE	**24.** BIGGLES
25. BOBBLE	**26.** HEIDI	**27.** BOBBIE	**28.** HIGH
29. HELLS BELLS	**30.** GOD BLESS	**31.** SHE DIES	**32.** SOLEIL

page 197 ***Exercise 14***

1. £1370	**2.** £2260	**3.** £4850	**4.** £1310	**5.** £1000
6. £6390	**7.** £5795	**8.** £3080	**9.** £2770	**10.** £6790
11. £5740	**12.** £7670	**13.** £4900	**14.** £5348	**15.** £6470

page 197 ***Exercise 15***

1. £804	**2.** £2099·40	**3.** £1833	**4.** £1410·60	**5.** £1206
6. £2349	**7.** £1500			

page 198 ***Exercise 16***

1. 42 kg **2.** £120 **3.** (a) 7·2 (b) 11·28 (c) 0·1 (d) 0·026 (e) 28·2 (f) 0·01
4. (a) 3·32 (b) 1·61 (c) 1·46 (d) 4·4 (e) 6·2 (f) 2·74
5. (a) 8 hectares (b) 24 tonnes **6.** £345 **7.** (a) \$6400 (b) \$83 200
8. £1·80 **9.** (a) 600 (b) £204 **10.** —

page 199 ***Exercise 17***

1. (a) 15 (b) (i) 20% (ii) 16% (iii) 70% (iv) 2% **2.** (a) 177 147 (b) 1 594 323
3. (a) 36 (b) 24 (c) 240 (d) 240 **4.** $7\frac{1}{2}$ cm^2
5. (a) 15051 (b) 110 miles **6.** Total charges = £59·11 **7.** £7400 **8.** 14·7

page 200 ***Exercise 18***

1. (a) 410 (b) 704·5
2. (a) 64 (b) 1 (c) 100 (d) 3000 (e) 32 (f) 81
3. 20 cm^2
4. 000, 001, 010, 011, 100, 101, 110, 111
5. (a) £162 (b) 200 (c) F 1000 (d) £100
6. 5 h 34 min
7. (a) $6^2 = 5^2 + 11$, $7^2 = 6^2 + 13$ (b) $11^2 = 60 + 5^2 + 6^2$, $13^2 = 84 + 6^2 + 7^2$
8. 120 000 000 m^3
9. 50 m
10. 2520

page 202 ***Exercise 19***

1. (a) 80 g (b) 5.2 (c) 416
2. *x*, 5, *t*
3. (a) 12 (b) (i) 8 (ii) 48
5. 200 litres
6. 0·006 25 cm
7. (a) 5·4 km (b) 0·6 cm
8. (a) 3 cm^2 (b) 27 cm^2 (c) $A = \frac{C^2}{12}$
9. 16

Probability

page 205 ***Exercise 1***

1. B **2.** C **3.** A **4.** B or C **5.** C or D **6.** C
7. B **8.** B **9.** C **10.** A **11.** D **12.** C or D

page 206 ***Exercise 2***

1. (a) $\frac{1}{13}$ (b) $\frac{1}{52}$ (c) $\frac{1}{4}$
2. (a) $\frac{1}{9}$ (b) $\frac{1}{3}$ (c) $\frac{4}{9}$ (d) $\frac{2}{9}$
3. (a) $\frac{5}{11}$ (b) $\frac{2}{11}$ (c) $\frac{4}{11}$
4. (a) $\frac{4}{17}$ (b) $\frac{3}{17}$ (c) $\frac{11}{17}$
5. (a) $\frac{4}{17}$ (b) $\frac{8}{17}$ (c) $\frac{5}{17}$
6. (a) $\frac{2}{9}$ (b) $\frac{2}{9}$ (c) $\frac{1}{9}$ (d) 0 (e) $\frac{5}{9}$
7. (a) $\frac{1}{13}$ (b) $\frac{2}{13}$ (c) $\frac{1}{52}$ (d) $\frac{5}{52}$
8. (a) $\frac{1}{10}$ (b) $\frac{3}{10}$ (c) $\frac{3}{10}$
9. (a) $\frac{3}{13}$ (b) $\frac{5}{13}$ (c) $\frac{8}{13}$
10. (a) (i) $\frac{5}{13}$ (ii) $\frac{6}{13}$ (b) (i) $\frac{5}{12}$ (ii) $\frac{1}{12}$
11. (a) $\frac{1}{5}$ (b) $\frac{1}{20}$ (c) $\frac{1}{2}$ (d) $\frac{2}{5}$
12. $\frac{9}{20}$
13. $\frac{1}{7}$
14. (a) (i) $\frac{1}{4}$ (ii) $\frac{1}{4}$ (iii) $\frac{1}{4}$ (b) $\frac{1}{4}$ (c) $\frac{6}{27} = \frac{2}{9}$

page 209 ***Exercise 3***

1. (a) 150 (b) 50 **2.** 25 **3.** 50 **4.** 40
5. (a) $\frac{3}{8}$ (b) 25 **6.** (a) $\frac{1}{2}$ (b) $\frac{1}{2}$ **7.** (a) $\frac{1}{12}$ (b) $\frac{1}{40}$ (c) $\frac{1}{4}$

page 211 ***Exercise 4***

1. 8 ways
2. 16 ways
3. 4
4. (a) 12 ways (b) 3
5. WX, WY, WZ, XY, XZ, YZ
6. (a) 30 outcomes (b) 15
7. 12 combinations
8. 48
9. (a) 15 (b) $26 \times 26 = 676$
10. (a) 24 orders (b) 12
12. 18 954
13. 4 435 236

page 215 ***Exercise 5***

1. $\frac{4}{5}$
2. (a) $\frac{1}{13}$ (b) $\frac{12}{13}$ (c) $\frac{3}{13}$ (d) $\frac{10}{13}$
3. $\frac{35}{36}$
4. 0·76
5. 0·494
6. (a) $\frac{1}{4}$ (b) $\frac{3}{4}$ (c) $\frac{1}{4}$ (d) $\frac{3}{4}$ (e) 0 (f) 1
7. (a) $\frac{3}{51} = \frac{1}{17}$ (b) $\frac{16}{17}$ (c) $\frac{12}{51} = \frac{4}{17}$
8. (a) 0·3 (b) 0·9
9. (a) (i) 0·24 (ii) 0·89 (b) 575
10. (a) $\frac{7}{12}$ (b) 350

page 217 ***Exercise 6***

1. (a) $\frac{5}{11}$ (b) $\frac{7}{22}$ (c) $\frac{15}{22}$ (d) $\frac{17}{22}$
2. $\frac{1}{18}$
3. $\frac{1}{3}$
4. $\frac{1}{24}$
5. (a) 4 (b) (i) $\frac{1}{9}$ (ii) $\frac{1}{6}$ (iii) $\frac{1}{12}$
6. (a) $\frac{5}{36}$ (b) $\frac{5}{18}$ (c) $\frac{5}{18}$
7. (a) $\frac{1}{8}$ (b) $\frac{1}{4}$ (c) $\frac{3}{8}$
8. (a) 16 (b) $\frac{1}{8}$
9. (a) $\frac{2}{9}$ (b) $\frac{1}{6}$ (c) $\frac{1}{18}$ (d) 0
10. (b) (i) $\frac{1}{9}$ (ii) $\frac{1}{3}$ (iii) 0 (iv) $\frac{2}{9}$ (v) $\frac{4}{9}$
11. (a) (i) exclusive (ii) exclusive (iii) not exclusive (b) $\frac{3}{4}$
12. (a) 0·8 (b) 0·7 (c) not exclusive
13. Yes
14. No. Y has the best chance
15. lose 45 p

page 221 ***Exercise 7***

2. Mike. With a large number of spins he should get zero with a probability of about $\frac{1}{10}$.

page 225 ***Exercise 8***

1. (a) $\frac{1}{13}$, $\frac{1}{6}$ (b) $\frac{1}{78}$
2. (a) $\frac{1}{2}$ (b) $\frac{1}{2}$ (c) $\frac{1}{4}$
3. $\frac{1}{10}$
4. (a) $\frac{1}{78}$ (b) $\frac{1}{104}$ (c) $\frac{1}{24}$
5. (a) $\frac{1}{16}$ (b) $\frac{1}{169}$ (c) $\frac{9}{169}$
6. (a) $\frac{1}{16}$ (b) $\frac{25}{144}$
7. (a) $\frac{1}{121}$ (b) $\frac{9}{121}$
8. $\frac{8}{1125}$
9. (a) $\frac{1}{288}$ (b) $\frac{1}{72}$
10. (a) $\frac{1}{9}$ (b) $\frac{4}{27}$
11. $\frac{1}{24}$
12. $\frac{1}{128}$
13. $\frac{1}{144}$

page 228 ***Exercise 9***

1. (a) $\frac{49}{100}$ (b) $\frac{9}{100}$
2. (a) $\frac{9}{64}$ (b) $\frac{15}{64}$
3. (a) $\frac{7}{15}$ (b) $\frac{1}{15}$
4. (a) $\frac{2}{9}$ (b) $\frac{2}{15}$ (c) $\frac{1}{45}$
5. (a) $\frac{1}{12}$ (b) $\frac{1}{6}$ (c) $\frac{1}{3}$ (d) $\frac{2}{9}$
6. (a) $\frac{1}{216}$ (b) $\frac{125}{216}$ (c) $\frac{25}{72}$ (d) $\frac{91}{216}$
7. (a) $\frac{1}{64}$ (b) $\frac{5}{32}$ (c) $\frac{27}{64}$
8. (a) $\frac{1}{6}$ (b) $\frac{1}{30}$ (c) $\frac{1}{30}$ (d) $\frac{29}{30}$
9. (a) $\frac{27}{64}$ (b) $\frac{1}{64}$
10. $\frac{1}{3}$
11. (a) $\frac{1}{64}$ (b) $\frac{27}{64}$ (c) $\frac{9}{64}$ (d) $\frac{27}{64}$; Sum = 1
12. $\frac{3}{20} \times \frac{2}{19} \times \frac{1}{18} \left(= \frac{1}{1140}\right)$ (b) $\frac{1}{4} \times \frac{4}{19} \times \frac{1}{6} \left(= \frac{1}{114}\right)$ (c) $\frac{5}{20} \times \frac{4}{19} \times \frac{3}{18} \times \frac{2}{17}$
13. (a) $\frac{1}{10\,000}$ (b) $\frac{6561}{10\,000}$ (c) $\frac{3439}{10\,000}$

Shape and space 3

page 232 ***Exercise 1***

1. C only **2.** $m = 10$, $a = 16\frac{2}{3}$ **3.** $x = 12$, $y = 8$ **4.** $a = 2\frac{1}{2}$, $e = 3$
5. $x = 6$, $y = 10$ **6.** $y = 6$ **7.** $x = 4$, $w = 1\frac{1}{2}$ **8.** $e = 9$, $f = 4\frac{1}{2}$
9. 7.7 cm **10.** No **11.** AO = 2 cm, DO = 6 cm **12.** 16 m
13. 5 **14.** (a) Yes (b) No (c) No (d) Yes (e) Yes (f) No (g) No (h) Yes
15. 3·75 cm **16.** 10·8 m

page 235 ***Exercise 2***

1. 3·01 cm **2.** 5.35 cm **3.** 3·13 cm **4.** 7·00 cm **5.** 73·1 cm
6. 15·4 cm **7.** 5·31 cm **8.** 7·99 cm **9.** 11·6 cm **10.** 11·4 cm
11. 961 cm **12.** 0·894 cm **13.** 46·0 cm **14.** 34·9 cm **15.** 9·39 cm
16. 8·23 cm **17.** 35·6 cm **18.** 80·2 cm **19.** 4·86 cm **20.** 6·98 cm

page 236 ***Exercise 3***

1. 18·4 **2.** 9.15 **3.** 10·7 **4.** 17·1
5. 13.7 **6.** 126 **7.** 6·88 **8.** 11·8
9. 17·6 **10.** 11·4 **11.** 5, 5·55 **12.** 13·1, 27·8
13. 4·26 **14.** 3·50 **15.** 26·2 **16.** 8·82

page 237 ***Exercise 4***

1. 38·7° **2.** 48·6° **3.** 31·0° **4.** 54.5° **5.** 38·7°
6. 17·5° **7.** 38·9° **8.** 59·0° **9.** 41·3° **10.** 62·7°
11. 54·3° **12.** 66·0° **13.** 48·2° **14.** 12.4° **15.** 72·9°
16. 56·9° **17.** 36·9° **18.** 41·8° **19.** 78·0° **20.** 89·4°

page 239 ***Exercise 5***

1. 68·0° **2.** 3·65 m **3.** 14·0 m **4.** 20·6° **5.** 56·7 m
6. 15.3 m **7.** 90·3 cm **8.** 4·32 cm **9.** 7·66 cm **10.** 65·5 km
11. 189 km **12.** 25·7 km **13.** 180 m **14.** 37·3 m **15.** 36.4°
16. 10·3 cm **17.** $a = 72°$, 8·23 cm **18.** 71·1°

page 243 ***Exercise 6***

1. (a) 2 (b) 2 (c) 3 (d) 1 (e) 2 (f) 3
2. (a) 2 (b) 3 (c) 2 (d) 1 (e) 3 (f) 1 (g) 0 (h) 2
3. (a) A (b) L (c) V (d) A (e) Impossible (f) A (g) V (h) A
4. 2 **5.** (a) 2 (b) 3 (c) 1 (d) 2, 1 (e) 3, 3 (f) 2

Algebra 3

page 245 **Exercise 1**

1. $x^2 + 4x + 3$ **2.** $x^2 + 5x + 6$ **3.** $y^2 + 9y + 20$ **4.** $x^2 + x - 12$
5. $x^2 + 3x - 10$ **6.** $x^2 - 5x + 6$ **7.** $a^2 - 2a - 35$ **8.** $z^2 + 7z - 18$
9. $x^2 - 9$ **10.** $k^2 - 121$ **11.** $2x^2 - 5x - 3$ **12.** $3x^2 - 2x - 8$
13. $2y^2 - y - 3$ **14.** $49y^2 - 1$ **15.** $9x^2 - 4$ **16.** $20 + x - x^2$
17. $2x^2 + 2x - 4$ **18.** $6x^2 + 3x - 9$ **19.** $24y^2 + 4y - 8$ **20.** $6x^2 - 10x - 4$

page 246 **Exercise 2**

1. $x^2 + 8x + 16$ **2.** $x^2 + 4x + 4$ **3.** $x^2 - 4x + 4$ **4.** $4x^2 + 4x + 1$
5. $y^2 - 10y + 25$ **6.** $9y^2 + 6y + 1$ **7.** $3x^2 + 12x + 12$ **8.** $9 - 6x + x^2$
9. $9x^2 + 12x + 4$ **10.** $2x^2 + 4x + 2$ **11.** $2x^2 + 6x + 5$ **12.** $2x^2 + 2x + 13$
13. $5x^2 + 8x + 5$ **14.** $2y^2 - 14y + 25$ **15.** $10x - 5$ **16.** $-8x + 8$

page 246 **Exercise 3**

1. $\frac{1}{4}$ **2.** -3 **3.** 4 **4.** $-7\frac{2}{3}$ **5.** -43
6. 11 **7.** $-\frac{1}{2}$ **8.** 0 **9.** 1 **10.** $-1\frac{2}{3}$
11. 10, 8, 6 **12.** 13, 12, 5 **13.** 4 cm **14.** 5 m

page 247 **Exercise 4**

1. $2(3x + 2y)$ **2.** $3(3x + 4y)$ **3.** $2(5a + 2b)$ **4.** $4(x + 3y)$
5. $5(2a + 3b)$ **6.** $6(3x - 4y)$ **7.** $4(2u - 7v)$ **8.** $5(3s + 5t)$
9. $8(3m + 5n)$ **10.** $9(3c - 8d)$ **11.** $4(5a + 2b)$ **12.** $6(5x - 4y)$
13. $3(9c - 11d)$ **14.** $7(5u + 7v)$ **15.** $4(3s - 8t)$ **16.** $8(5x - 2t)$
17. $12(2x + 7y)$ **18.** $4(3x + 2y + 4z)$ **19.** $3(4a - 2b + 3c)$ **20.** $5(2x - 4y + 5z)$
21. $4(5a - 3b - 7c)$ **22.** $8(6m + n - 3x)$ **23.** $7(6x + 7y - 3z)$ **24.** $3(2x^2 + 5y^2)$
25. $5(4x^2 - 3y^2)$ **26.** $7(a^2 + 4b^2)$ **27.** $9(3a + 7b - 4c)$ **28.** $6(2x^2 + 4xy + 3y^2)$
29. $8(8p - 9q - 5r)$ **30.** $12(3x - 5y + 8z)$

page 248 **Exercise 5**

1. $e - b$ **2.** $m + t$ **3.** $a + b + f$ **4.** $A + B - h$ **5.** y
6. $b - a$ **7.** $m - k$ **8.** $w + y - v$ **9.** $\frac{b}{a}$ **10.** $\frac{m}{h}$
11. $\frac{a+b}{m}$ **12.** $\frac{c-d}{k}$ **13.** $\frac{e+n}{v}$ **14.** $\frac{y+z}{3}$ **15.** $\frac{r}{p}$
16. $\frac{h-m}{m}$ **17.** $\frac{a-t}{a}$ **18.** $\frac{k+e}{m}$ **19.** $\frac{m+h}{u}$ **20.** $\frac{t-q}{e}$

21. $\frac{v^2+u^2}{k}$ 22. $\frac{s^2-t^2}{g}$ 23. $\frac{m^2-k}{a}$ 24. $\frac{m+v}{m}$ 25. $\frac{c-a}{b}$

26. $\frac{y-t}{s}$ 27. $\frac{z-y}{c}$ 28. $\frac{a}{h}$ 29. $\frac{2b}{m}$ 30. $\frac{cd-ab}{k}$

31. $\frac{c+ab}{a}$ 32. $\frac{e+cd}{c}$ 33. $\frac{n^2-m^2}{m}$ 34. $\frac{t+ka}{k}$ 35. $\frac{k+h^2}{h}$

36. $\frac{n-mb}{m}$ 37. $2a$ 38. $\frac{d-ac}{c}$ 39. $\frac{e-mb}{m}$

page 248 **Exercise 6**

1. mt 2. en 3. ap 4. amt 5. abc
6. ey^2 7. $a(b+c)$ 8. $t(c-d)$ 9. $m(s+t)$ 10. $k(h+i)$

11. $\frac{ab}{c}$ 12. $\frac{mz}{y}$ 13. $\frac{ch}{d}$ 14. $\frac{em}{k}$ 15. $\frac{hb}{e}$

16. $c(a+b)$ 17. $m(h+k)$ 18. $\frac{mu}{y}$ 19. $t(h-k)$ 20. $(z+t)(a+b)$

21. $\frac{e}{7}$ 22. $\frac{e}{a}$ 23. $\frac{h}{m}$ 24. $\frac{bc}{a}$ 25. $\frac{ud}{c}$

26. $\frac{m}{t^2}$ 27. $\frac{h}{\sin 20°}$ 28. $\frac{e}{\cos 40°}$ 29. $\frac{m}{\tan 46°}$ 30. $\frac{b^2c^2}{a^2}$

page 249 **Exercise 7**

1. $\pm\sqrt{\frac{h}{c}}$ 2. $\pm\sqrt{\frac{f}{b}}$ 3. $\pm\sqrt{\frac{m}{t}}$ 4. $\pm\sqrt{\frac{a+b}{y}}$ 5. $\pm\sqrt{\frac{t+a}{m}}$

6. $\pm\sqrt{(a+b)}$ 7. $\pm\sqrt{(t-c)}$ 8. $\pm\sqrt{(z-y)}$ 9. $\pm\sqrt{(a^2+b^2)}$ 10. $\pm\sqrt{(m^2-t^2)}$

11. $\pm\sqrt{(a^2-n^2)}$ 12. $\pm\sqrt{\frac{c}{a}}$ 13. $\pm\sqrt{\frac{n}{h}}$ 14. $\pm\sqrt{\frac{z+k}{c}}$ 15. $\pm\sqrt{\frac{c-b}{a}}$

16. $\pm\sqrt{\frac{h+e}{d}}$ 17. $\pm\sqrt{\frac{m+n}{g}}$ 18. $\pm\sqrt{\frac{z-y}{m}}$ 19. $\pm\sqrt{\frac{f-a}{m}}$ 20. $\pm\sqrt{(b^2-a^2)}$

21. $a-y$ 22. $h-m$ 23. $z-q$ 24. $b-v$ 25. $k-m$

26. $\frac{h-d}{c}$ 27. $\frac{y-c}{m}$ 28. $\frac{k-h}{e}$ 29. $\frac{a^2-d}{b}$ 30. $\frac{m^2-n^2}{t}$

31. $\dfrac{v^2 - w}{a}$ **32.** $y - y^2$ **33.** $\dfrac{k - m}{t^2}$ **34.** $\dfrac{b - e}{c}$ **35.** $\dfrac{h - z}{g}$

36. $\dfrac{c - a - b}{d}$ **37.** $\dfrac{v^2 - y^2}{k}$ **38.** $\dfrac{d - h}{f}$ **39.** $\dfrac{ab - c}{a}$ **40.** $\dfrac{hm - n}{h}$

page 250 ***Exercise 8***

1. $\dfrac{h + d}{a}$ **2.** $\dfrac{m - k}{z}$ **3.** $\dfrac{f - ed}{d}$ **4.** $\dfrac{d - ma}{m}$ **5.** $\dfrac{c - a}{b}$

6. $\pm\sqrt{\left(\dfrac{b}{a}\right)}$ **7.** $\pm\sqrt{\left(\dfrac{z}{y}\right)}$ **8.** $\pm\sqrt{(e + c)}$ **9.** $\dfrac{b + n}{m}$ **10.** $\dfrac{b - a^2}{a}$

11. $\dfrac{a}{d}$ **12.** mt **13.** mn **14.** $\dfrac{y}{d}$ **15.** $\dfrac{a}{t}$

16. $\dfrac{d}{n}$ **17.** $k(a + b)$ **18.** $\dfrac{v}{y}$ **19.** $\dfrac{m}{c}$ **20.** $\pm\sqrt{mb}$

21. $\dfrac{b - ag}{g}$ **22.** $\dfrac{x^2 - h^2}{h}$ **23.** $y - z$ **24.** $\pm\sqrt{\left(\dfrac{c}{m}\right)}$ **25.** $\dfrac{t - ay}{a}$

26. $\dfrac{y^2 + t^2}{u}$ **27.** $\pm\sqrt{(c - t)}$ **28.** $k - m$ **29.** $\dfrac{b - c}{a}$ **30.** $\dfrac{c - am}{m}$

31. $pq - ab$ **32.** $\dfrac{a^2 - t}{b}$ **33.** $\dfrac{w}{v^2}$ **34.** $t - c$ **35.** $\dfrac{t}{x}$

36. $\dfrac{k - mn}{m}$ **37.** $\dfrac{v - t}{x}$ **38.** $\dfrac{c - ab}{a}$ **39.** $\dfrac{ma - e}{m}$ **40.** $\pm\sqrt{\dfrac{c}{b}}$

41. $\dfrac{a}{q}$ **42.** $\pm\sqrt{\left(\dfrac{a}{e}\right)}$ **43.** $\pm\sqrt{\left(\dfrac{h}{m}\right)}$ **44.** $\pm\sqrt{\left(\dfrac{v}{n}\right)}$ **45.** $\dfrac{v - t^3}{a}$

46. $\dfrac{b^3 - a^3}{a}$ **47.** $\pm\sqrt{\left(\dfrac{b + d}{a}\right)}$ **48.** $\dfrac{bc - h^2}{h}$ **49.** $\pm\sqrt{(u^2 - v^2)}$ **50.** $\dfrac{mb - b^3}{m}$

page 250 ***Exercise 9***

1. $p - a$ **2.** $m - y$ **3.** $z - k$ **4.** $u^2 - t^2$

5. $\dfrac{a - bc}{m}$ **6.** $\dfrac{z - k}{a}$ **7.** $\dfrac{u^2 - e^2}{k}$ **8.** $\dfrac{b - ma}{m}$

9. $\dfrac{h - ka}{k}$ **10.** $\dfrac{y - p^2}{p}$ **11.** ky **12.** mn

13. q^2 **14.** mn^2 **15.** $\frac{m}{a}$ **16.** $\frac{n}{e}$

17. $\frac{u}{w}$ **18.** $\frac{e}{\sin 32°}$ **19.** $\frac{2y}{z}$ **20.** $\frac{3p}{k}$

21. $\pm\sqrt{(m+n)}$ **22.** $\pm\sqrt{(a-b-v)}$ **23.** $\pm\sqrt{\left(\frac{n^2+n}{b}\right)}$ **24.** $\frac{d+e+ab}{a}$

25. $\pm\sqrt{\left(\frac{mp+k^2}{k}\right)}$ **26.** $y-m$ **27.** $\frac{u+ed}{e}$ **28.** $\frac{z-ay}{a}$

29. $\frac{w+yf}{ye}$ **30.** $\frac{m-tm}{at}$ **31.** $y(c+d)$ **32.** $\frac{a-b}{p}$

page 252 ***Exercise 10***

1. (a) $S=ke$ (b) $v=kt$ (c) $x=kz^2$ (d) $y=k\sqrt{x}$ (e) $T=k\sqrt{L}$ **2.** (a) 9 (b) $2\frac{2}{3}$
3. (a) 35 (b) 11 **4.** (a) 75 (b) 4

5.

x	1	3	4	$5\frac{1}{2}$
z	4	12	16	22

6.

r	1	2	4	$1\frac{1}{2}$
V	4	32	256	$13\frac{1}{2}$

7. 333 N/cm^2 **8.** 180 m; 2 s **9.** 675 J; $\sqrt{\frac{4}{3}}$ cm
10. 9000 N; 25 m/s **11.** $p \propto w^3$ **12.** $15^4:1$ (50625 : 1)

page 254 ***Exercise 11***

1. (a) $x=\frac{k}{y}$ (b) $s=\frac{k}{t^2}$ (c) $t=\frac{k}{\sqrt{q}}$ (d) $m=\frac{k}{w}$ (e) $z=\frac{k}{t^2}$

2. (a) 1 (b) 4 **3.** (a) 36 (b) ± 4 **4.** (a) 6 (b) 16

5.

y	2	4	1	$\frac{1}{4}$
z	8	4	16	64

6.

t	2	5	20	10
v	25	4	$\frac{1}{4}$	1

7. 2·5 m^3; 200 N/m^2 **8.** 3 h; 48 men **9.** 6 cm
10. 2 days; 200 days **11.** (a) 20 min (b) 2 min

page 257 ***Exercise 12***

1. $x>13$ **2.** $x<-1$ **3.** $x<12$ **4.** $x \leqslant 2\frac{1}{2}$ **5.** $x>3$
6. $x \geqslant 8$ **7.** $x<\frac{1}{4}$ **8.** $x \geqslant -3$ **9.** $x<-8$ **10.** $x<4$
11. $x>-9$ **12.** $x<8$ **13.** $x>3$ **14.** $x \geqslant 1$ **15.** $x<1$
16. $x>2\frac{1}{3}$ **17.** $x<-3$ **18.** $x>7\frac{1}{2}$ **19.** $x>0$ **20.** $x<0$
21. $5 \leqslant x \leqslant 9$ **22.** $-1<x<4$ **23.** $\frac{11}{2} \leqslant x \leqslant 6$ **24.** $\frac{4}{3}<x<8$ **25.** $-8<x<2$

page 258 ***Exercise 13***

1. $-5 < x < 5$ **2.** $-4 \leqslant x \leqslant 4$ **3.** $x > 1$, $x < -1$
4. $x \geqslant 6$, $x \leqslant -6$ **5.** all values except zero **6.** $-2 < x < 2$
7. 1, 2, 3, 4, 5, 6 **8.** 7, 11, 13, 17, 19 **9.** 4, 9, 16, 25, 36, 49
10. $-4, -3, -2, -1$ **11.** 2, 3, 4, ... 12 **12.** 2, 3, 5, 7, 11
13. 2, 4, 6, ... 18 **14.** 1, 2, 3, 4 **15.** 5
16. 16, -16, 20, -5 **17.** $>$ **18.** $\frac{1}{2}$ (or others)
19. 19 **20.** 17 **21.** $x > 3\frac{2}{3}$ **22.** 7 **23.** 5 **24.** 6 **25.** 3, 4, 5

page 260 ***Exercise 14***

1. $x \leqslant 3$ **2.** $y \geqslant 2\frac{1}{2}$ **3.** $1 \leqslant x \leqslant 6$ **4.** $x < 7$, $y < 5$
5. $y \geqslant x$ **6.** $x + y < 10$ **7.** $2x - y \leqslant 3$ **8.** $y \leqslant x$, $x \leqslant 8$, $y \geqslant -2$
9. (a) $x + y \leqslant 7$, $x \geqslant 0$, $y \geqslant x - 1$ (b) $x + y \leqslant 6$, $y \geqslant 0$, $y \leqslant x + 2$
28. A: $x + y < 5$, $y > x + 1$ B: $x + y > 5$, $y > x + 1$
C: $x + y > 5$, $y < x + 1$ D: $x + y < 5$, $y < x + 1$
29. (2, 6), (3, 5), (3, 4), (4, 4), (4, 3), (5, 3), (6, 2)

page 262 ***Exercise 15***

1. $\frac{1}{5}, \frac{5}{2}, -\frac{4}{3}$ **2.** $\frac{4}{5}, -\frac{1}{6}, -5$ **3.** (a) 3 (b) $\frac{3}{2}$ (c) 4 (d) 5
4. $a = 3\frac{1}{2}$ **5.** (a) $\dfrac{n+4}{2m-3}$ (b) $n = -4$ (c) $m = 1\frac{1}{2}$

page 264 ***Exercise 16***

21. A: $y = 3x - 4$; B: $y = x + 2$ **22.** C: $y = \frac{2}{3}x - 2$; D: $y = -2x + 4$

Number 3

page 265 ***Exercise 1***

1. 3^4 **2.** 5^2 **3.** 6^3 **4.** 10^5 **5.** 1^7
6. 8^4 **7.** 7^6 **8.** $2^3 \times 5^2$ **9.** $3^2 \times 7^4$ **10.** $3^2 \times 10^3$
11. $5^4 \times 11^2$ **12.** $2^2 \times 3^3$ **13.** $3^2 \times 5^3$ **14.** $2^2 \times 3^3 \times 11^2$
15. (a) $2^3 \times 3 \times 5^2$ (b) $3^2 \times 7 \times 11$ (c) $2^5 \times 7 \times 11$
(d) $2 \times 3^3 \times 5 \times 13$ (e) $2^5 \times 5^3$ (f) $2^2 \times 5 \times 7^2 \times 23$
16. (a) $2^6 \times 3^2$ (b) $2^3 \times 3 (= 24)$ (c) 315
17. (a) $1008 = 2^4 \times 3^2 \times 7$, $840 = 2^3 \times 3 \times 5 \times 7$ (b) H.C.F. $= 8 \times 3 \times 7 = 168$ (c) 7
18. (a) E (b) 1 048 576 ($= 2^{20}$) **19.** (a) 512 (b) 6 h (c) 2^{21}
20. (a) 3 (b) 4 (c) $1\frac{1}{2}$ **21.** $x = 2$ or 4

page 267 ***Exercise 2***

1. $\frac{1}{4}$ **2.** $\frac{1}{16}$ **3.** $\frac{1}{100}$ **4.** 1 **5.** $\frac{1}{27}$ **6.** $\frac{1}{64}$
7. $\frac{1}{1000}$ **8.** $\frac{1}{25}$ **9.** $\frac{1}{49}$ **10.** $\frac{1}{125}$ **11.** $\frac{1}{81}$ **12.** 1
13. T **14.** F **15.** T **16.** T **17.** F **18.** F
19. F **20.** T **21.** T **22.** T **23.** F **24.** F
25. F **26.** T **27.** T **28.** T **29.** T **30.** T

page 267 **Exercise 3**

1. 5^6	**2.** 6^5	**3.** 10^9	**4.** 7^8	**5.** 3^{10}	**6.** 8^6
7. 2^{13}	**8.** 3^4	**9.** 5^3	**10.** 7^4	**11.** 5^2	**12.** 3^{-4}
13. 6^5	**14.** 5^{-10}	**15.** 7^6	**16.** 7^2	**17.** 6^5	**18.** 8^1
19. 5^8	**20.** 10^2	**21.** 9^{-2}	**22.** 3^{-2}	**23.** 2^4	**24.** 3^{-2}
25. 7^{-6}	**26.** 3^{-4}	**27.** 5^{-5}	**28.** 8^{-5}	**29.** 5^{-5}	**30.** 6^4

page 268 **Exercise 4**

1. 4×10^3	**2.** 5×10^2	**3.** 7×10^4	**4.** 6×10	**5.** $2{\cdot}4 \times 10^3$
6. $3{\cdot}8 \times 10^2$	**7.** $4{\cdot}6 \times 10^4$	**8.** $4{\cdot}6 \times 10$	**9.** 9×10^5	**10.** $2{\cdot}56 \times 10^3$
11. 7×10^{-3}	**12.** 4×10^{-4}	**13.** $3{\cdot}5 \times 10^{-3}$	**14.** $4{\cdot}21 \times 10^{-1}$	**15.** $5{\cdot}5 \times 10^{-5}$
16. 1×10^{-2}	**17.** $5{\cdot}64 \times 10^5$	**18.** $1{\cdot}9 \times 10^7$	**19.** $1{\cdot}1 \times 10^9$	**20.** $1{\cdot}67 \times 10^{-24}$
21. $5{\cdot}1 \times 10^8$	**22.** $2{\cdot}5 \times 10^{-10}$	**23.** $6{\cdot}023 \times 10^{23}$	**24.** 3×10^{10}	**25.** £$3{\cdot}6 \times 10^6$

page 269 **Exercise 5**

1. $1{\cdot}5 \times 10^7$	**2.** 3×10^8	**3.** $2{\cdot}8 \times 10^{-2}$	**4.** 7×10^{-9}
5. 2×10^6	**6.** 4×10^{-6}	**7.** 9×10^{-2}	**8.** $6{\cdot}6 \times 10^{-8}$
9. $3{\cdot}5 \times 10^{-7}$	**10.** 10^{-16}	**11.** 8×10^9	**12.** $7{\cdot}4 \times 10^{-7}$
13. $4{\cdot}9 \times 10^{11}$	**14.** $4{\cdot}4 \times 10^{12}$	**15.** $1{\cdot}5 \times 10^3$	**16.** 2×10^{17}
17. $1{\cdot}68 \times 10^{13}$	**18.** $4{\cdot}25 \times 10^{11}$	**19.** $9{\cdot}9 \times 10^7$	**20.** $6{\cdot}25 \times 10^{-16}$
21. $2{\cdot}88 \times 10^{12}$	**22.** $6{\cdot}82 \times 10^{-7}$	**23.** c, a, b	**24.** 13
25. 16	**26.** (i) 6×10^2 (ii) $6{\cdot}67 \times 10^7$		**27.** 50 min
28. 6×10^2	**29.** (a) $9{\cdot}46 \times 10^{12}$ km (b) 144 million km		**30.** 25 000

page 271 **Exercise 6**

1. $\frac{5}{6}$	**2.** $\frac{1}{6}$	**3.** $\frac{2}{3}$	**4.** $\frac{5}{12}$	**5.** $\frac{1}{4}$	**6.** $2\frac{1}{4}$	**7.** $\frac{9}{10}$	**8.** $\frac{1}{5}$
9. $\frac{4}{5}$	**10.** $\frac{13}{14}$	**11.** $\frac{3}{14}$	**12.** $\frac{6}{7}$	**13.** $\frac{3}{8}$	**14.** $\frac{5}{32}$	**15.** $2\frac{1}{2}$	**16.** $\frac{29}{30}$
17. $\frac{2}{15}$	**18.** $\frac{5}{24}$	**19.** $\frac{16}{21}$	**20.** $\frac{1}{7}$	**21.** $1\frac{2}{7}$	**22.** $\frac{11}{20}$	**23.** $\frac{1}{5}$	**24.** $3\frac{1}{5}$
25. $\frac{13}{24}$	**26.** $\frac{1}{12}$	**27.** $5\frac{1}{3}$	**28.** $\frac{29}{36}$	**29.** $\frac{5}{36}$	**30.** $2\frac{2}{9}$	**31.** $2\frac{1}{4}$	**32.** $\frac{5}{8}$
33. 10	**34.** $3\frac{1}{12}$	**35.** $2\frac{1}{2}$	**36.** $5\frac{5}{8}$	**37.** $2\frac{1}{3}$	**38.** $\frac{5}{13}$	**39.** 18	**40.** 6

page 271 **Exercise 7**

1. (a) $\frac{1}{2}, \frac{7}{12}, \frac{2}{3}$ (b) $\frac{2}{3}, \frac{3}{4}, \frac{5}{6}$ (c) $\frac{1}{3}, \frac{5}{8}, \frac{17}{24}, \frac{3}{4}$ (d) $\frac{5}{6}, \frac{8}{9}, \frac{11}{12}$

2. (a) $\frac{1}{2}$ (b) $\frac{3}{4}$ (c) $\frac{17}{24}$ (d) $\frac{7}{18}$ (e) $\frac{3}{10}$ (f) $\frac{5}{12}$

3. 5	**4.** £39	**5.** 3	**6.** 123 cm	**7.** $\frac{1}{5}$	**8.** $1\frac{4}{11}$
9. (a) 9 (b) $\frac{5}{16}$		**10.** $\frac{16}{24}$	**11.** 9	**12.** $\frac{5}{24}$	**13.** same

page 274 ***Exercise 8***

1. −4	**2.** −12	**3.** −11	**4.** −3	**5.** −5	**6.** 4	**7.** −5	**8.** −8
9. 19	**10.** −17	**11.** −4	**12.** −5	**13.** −11	**14.** 6	**15.** −4	**16.** 6
17. 0	**18.** −18	**19.** −3	**20.** −11	**21.** −8	**22.** −7	**23.** 1	**24.** 1
25. 9	**26.** 11	**27.** −8	**28.** 42	**29.** 4	**30.** 15	**31.** −7	**32.** −9
33. −1	**34.** −7	**35.** 0	**36.** 11	**37.** −14	**38.** 0	**39.** 17	**40.** 3

page 274 ***Exercise 9***

1. −6	**2.** −4	**3.** −15	**4.** 9	**5.** −8	**6.** −15	**7.** −24	**8.** 6
9. 12	**10.** −18	**11.** −21	**12.** 25	**13.** −60	**14.** 21	**15.** 48	**16.** −16
17. −42	**18.** 20	**19.** −42	**20.** −66	**21.** −4	**22.** −3	**23.** 3	**24.** −5
25. 4	**26.** −4	**27.** −4	**28.** −1	**29.** −2	**30.** 4	**31.** −16	**32.** −2
33. −4	**34.** 5	**35.** −10	**36.** 11	**37.** 16	**38.** −2	**39.** −4	**40.** −5
41. 64	**42.** −27	**43.** −600	**44.** 40	**45.** 2	**46.** 36	**47.** −2	**48.** −8
49. 160	**50.** −2						

page 275 ***Test 1***

1. −16	**2.** 64	**3.** −15	**4.** −2	**5.** 15	**6.** 18	**7.** 3	**8.** −6
9. 11	**10.** −48	**11.** −7	**12.** 9	**13.** 6	**14.** −18	**15.** −10	**16.** 8
17. −6	**18.** −30	**19.** 4	**20.** −1				

page 275 ***Test 2***

1. −16	**2.** 6	**3.** −13	**4.** 42	**5.** −4	**6.** −4	**7.** −12	**8.** −20
9. 6	**10.** 0	**11.** 36	**12.** −10	**13.** −7	**14.** 10	**15.** 6	**16.** −18
17. −9	**18.** 15	**19.** 1	**20.** 0				

page 275 ***Test 3***

1. 100	**2.** −20	**3.** −8	**4.** −7	**5.** −4	**6.** 10	**7.** 9	**8.** −10
9. 7	**10.** 35	**11.** −20	**12.** −24	**13.** −10	**14.** −7	**15.** −19	**16.** −1
17. −5	**18.** −13	**19.** 0	**20.** 8				

page 276 ***Exercise 10***

1. 36	**2.** 29	**3.** 8	**4.** 18	**5.** 84
6. 9×10^{12}	**7.** 165	**8.** $\sqrt{181}$	**9.** 1·62	**10.** 650

page 277 ***Exercise 11***

1. −5	**2.** 8	**3.** −17	**4.** 8	**5.** −2	**6.** −27	**7.** 1	**8.** −22
9. −22	**10.** −22	**11.** −10	**12.** −2	**13.** 23	**14.** −44	**15.** 26	**16.** 25
17. −4	**18.** 0	**19.** −16	**20.** 22	**21.** −5	**22.** 30	**23.** 13	**24.** 25
25. 40	**26.** 3	**27.** −5	**28.** −12	**29.** −34	**30.** 2	**31.** 12	**32.** 39
33. 40	**34.** 7	**35.** 3	**36.** 10	**37.** 51	**38.** −2	**39.** 1	**40.** 11

page 277 ***Exercise 12***

1. 4 **2.** 4 **3.** 9 **4.** 16 **5.** 8 **6.** −8 **7.** −27 **8.** 64
9. 8 **10.** 16 **11.** 8 **12.** 16 **13.** 18 **14.** 36 **15.** 48 **16.** 16
17. 20 **18.** 54 **19.** 144 **20.** 24 **21.** 13 **22.** 10 **23.** 1 **24.** 18
25. 13 **26.** 19 **27.** 10 **28.** 32 **29.** 16 **30.** 144 **31.** 36 **32.** 36
33. 4 **34.** 1 **35.** 2 **36.** −14 **37.** −5 **38.** −5 **39.** −10 **40.** 10
41. 0 **42.** 4 **43.** 50 **44.** 4 **45.** −10 **46.** −4 **47.** −6 **48.** −16
49. 28 **50.** 44

page 278 ***Exercise 13***

1. 7 **2.** −2 **3.** 0 **4.** $-4\frac{1}{2}$ **5.** 6 **6.** 2
7. 26 **8.** −9 **9.** $3\frac{1}{4}$ **10.** $-\frac{5}{6}$ **11.** 4 **12.** $2\frac{2}{3}$
13. $3\frac{1}{4}$ **14.** $-2\frac{1}{6}$ **15.** −13 **16.** 12 **17.** $1\frac{1}{3}$ **18.** $-\frac{5}{36}$

page 278 ***Exercise 14***

1. 20 **2.** 200 g **3.** 6 **4.** 400
5. $5 \times 7 \times 13 \times 71$ **6.** 225 mm **7.** 1 **8.** (a) 66666 (b) 82
9. (a) 323 g (b) 23 (c) 67 p (d) 29 **10.** 6 m

page 279 ***Exercise 15***

1. £10 485·76 **2.** (a) 1 (b) 15 **3.** $a = 100$, $b = 1$ **4.** 50 **5.** E
7. (a) $\frac{1}{66}$ (b) 16 **8.** 1105 **9.** 13 **10.** 10 **11.** 500

Handling data 2

page 283 ***Exercise 1***

1. (a) mean = 6, median = 5, mode = 4 (b) mean = 9, median = 7, mode = 7
(c) mean = 6·5, median = 8, mode = 9 (d) mean = 3·5, median = 3·5, mode = 4
2. 2°C **3.** (a) 3 (b) 3 **5.** 70·4, 73·25, No **6.** 6
7. (a) 1·6 m (b) 1·634 m **8.** (a) 51 kg (b) 50 kg **9.** (a) 7·2 (b) 5 (c) 6
10. (a) mean = £47 920, median = £22 500, mode = £22 500
(b) The mean is skewed by one large number.
11. (a) mean = 157·1 kg, median = 91 kg
(b) mean. No: over three quarters of the cattle are below the mean weight.
12. (a) mean = 74·5 cm, median = 91 cm, (b) Yes

page 285 ***Exercise 2***

1. 96·25 g **2.** 51·9 p **3.** 4·82 cm
4. (a) mean = 3·025, median = 3, mode = 3, (b) mean = 17·75, median = 17, mode = 17
5. (a) mean = 6·62, median = 8, mode = 3, (b) the mode
6. (a) 9 (b) 9 (c) 15 **7.** (a) 5 (b) 10 (c) 10

page 287 ***Exercise 3***

1. 68·25 **2.** 3·8 **3.** 177·9 cm

page 290 ***Exercise 4***

2. (a) 25 (b) 90
4. (a) 62 (b) Sport B has more heavy people. Sport A has a much smaller range of weights compared to sport B.
5. (a) Plants with fertilizer are significantly taller (b) No significant effect

page 294 ***Exercise 5***

1. (a) 46 (b) 28; 62 (c) 34 (d) 35 [all approximate]
2. (a) 100 (b) 250 (c) 2250 h (d) 750 h
3. (a) 28 (b) 25; 37 (c) 12 (d) about 27 (e) 60 [all approx]
4. (b) (i) 45 (ii) 17
5. (b) (i) about 160·5 cm (ii) about 13 cm
6. (b) France 18·5; Britain 24·5 (c) 8·5
(d) Results for Britain bunched together more closely with a higher median
7. (c) 44 million (d) A: 21; B: 59 (e) A has much younger population

Revision

page 316 ***Exercise 1***

1. £25·60, £6·70, 4, £55·30
2. (a) 30, 37 (b) 12, 10 (c) 7, 10 (d) 8, 4 (e) 26, 33
3. £8
4. £92
5. (a) 1810 s (b) 72·4 s
6. 0·8 cm
7. (a) £13 (b) £148 (c) £170
8. (a) 5·89 (b) 6 (c) 7
9. (a) −11 (b) 23 (c) −10 (d) −20 (e) 6 (f) −14
10. (a) 3 (b) 5 (c) −6 (d) −7
11. (a) 9 (b) 11 (c) 3 (d) 7
12. (a) Yes (b) No (c) Yes
13. (c) Sequence of square numbers (d) 49
14. 30 000 cm^2

page 317 ***Exercise 2***

1. (a) 7 (b) $\frac{1}{4}$ (c) $\frac{4}{5}$
2. (a) 7·21 cm (b) 9·22 cm (c) 7·33 cm
3. (a) $\frac{3}{8}$ (b) $\frac{5}{8}$
4. (a) $\frac{2}{11}$ (b) $\frac{5}{11}$ (c) $\frac{9}{11}$
5. (i) £100 (ii) 500 (iii) £44 profit
6. (a) 2·088 (b) 3·043
7. (a) 91·5 cm^2 (b) 119 cm^2
8. (a) reflection in the x-axis (b) reflection in $x = -1$ (c) reflection in $y = x$
(d) rotation, centre (0, 0), 90° clockwise (e) reflection in $y = -1$
(f) rotation, centre (0, −1), 180°
9. (a) enlargement; scale factor $1\frac{1}{2}$, (1, −4) (b) rotation 90° clockwise, (0, −4)
(c) reflection in $y = -x$ (d) translation $\begin{pmatrix} 11 \\ 10 \end{pmatrix}$ (e) enlargement; scale factor $\frac{1}{2}$, (−3, 8)
(f) rotation 90° anticlockwise, $(\frac{1}{2}, 6\frac{1}{2})$ (g) enlargement; scale factor 3, (−2, 5)
10. 12 km

page 318 **Exercise 3**

1. (a) £5·20 (b) 29 min **2.** (a) 2 cm (b) 8 m **3.** (i) 9 (ii) 50 (iii) $(7 \times 11) - 6 = 72 - 1$
4. (c) $\triangle 2\,(6, 0); \triangle 3\,(2, -8); \triangle 4\,(-8, 2); \triangle 6\,(1, -5); \triangle 7\,(-1, 3)$
5. 17·7 cm **6.** (a) $l = 2d - 4$ (b) 149 **8.** (a) 198 cm^3 (b) 1357 mm^3 (c) 145

page 320 **Exercise 4**

1. (a) £28 600 (b) 198 (c) £143 (d) £28 314 (e) £286 **2.** (a) 55 p (b) 760
3. (a) 4 (b) 19 **4.** A swimmer, B car ferry from Calais, C hovercraft, D train from Dover, E marker buoy, F car ferry from Dover
5. (a) 560 kg, 57 kg (b) 50 kg **6.** Both arrive at the same time
7. 28 274, £79·15, £85·42, November **8.** 74 m **9.** (a) 500 m^3 (b) 13 m
10. (a) (i) 13, 49, 109 (ii) 4, 49 (iii) 13, 109 (b) (i) 27 (ii) 33 (c) 148, 193 (d) 94, 127

page 321 **Exercise 5**

1. $\dfrac{a}{b}$ **2.** (a) $c = 5, d = -2$ (b) $x = 2, y = -1$
3. (a) 45·6° (b) 58·0° (c) 3·89 cm (d) 33·8 m **4.** (a) 0·005 m/s (b) 1·6 s (c) 173 km
5. (a) 14 (b) 18 (c) 28 **6.** $\frac{1}{6}$ **7.** 3·43 cm^2, 4·57 cm^2 **8.** (a) 220° (b) 295°
9. A : $y = 6$; B : $y = \frac{1}{2}x - 3$; C : $y = 10 - x$; D : $y = 3x$
10. (a) $s = t(r + 3)$ (b) $r = \dfrac{s - 3t}{t}$ **11.** 1·552 m **12.** 4·12 cm **13.** 9·95 cm
14. $y \geqslant 2,\ x + y \leqslant 6;\ y \leqslant 3x$

page 322 **Exercise 6**

1. 43·1 litres **2.** (a) 8 (b) 140 (c) 29 (d) 42 (e) 6 (f) −6
3. 25 **4.** 5·14 cm^2 **5.** $\frac{5}{16}$
6. (b) $3 \rightarrow 14,\ 4 \rightarrow 18,\ 5 \rightarrow 22,\ 6 \rightarrow 26$ (c) (i) 42 (ii) 62 (d) $n = 4x + 2$
7. (a) 1 : 50 000 (b) 1 : 4 000 000 **8.** $\frac{31}{20}b$ **9.** 5·39 cm **10.** (a) 5·45 (b) 5 (c) 5
11. 6 cm **12.** (a) $z = x - 5y$ (b) $k = \dfrac{11 - 3m}{m}$ (c) $z = \dfrac{T^2}{C^2}$

page 324 **Exercise 7**

1. $2{\cdot}1 \times 10^{24}$ tonnes
2. (a) (i) Consett (ii) Durham (iii) Consett (b) (i) 55 km (ii) 40 km
(c) (i) 80 km/h (ii) 55 km/h (iii) 70 km/h (iv) 80 km/h (d) $1\frac{3}{4}$ hours
3. 17 kg **4.** $33\frac{1}{3}$ mph **5.** (a) 0·340 (b) $4{\cdot}08 \times 10^{-6}$ (c) 64·9 (d) 0·119
6. $2{\cdot}3 \times 10^{9}$ **7.** (a) $\frac{1}{9}$ (b) $\frac{1}{12}$ (c) 0 **8.** $x \geqslant 0,\ y \geqslant x - 2,\ x + y \leqslant 7$
9. (a) 600 (b) 9000 or 10 000 (c) 3 (d) 60 **10.** 40° (b) 100°
11. $\dfrac{x}{x + 5}$ **12.** A : $4y = 3x - 16$; B : $2y = x - 8$; C : $2y + x = 8$; D : $4y + 3x = 16$

page 325 ***Exercise 8***

1. 95 p for 1 lb **2.** (a) $1\frac{2}{3}$ (b) 20 cm **3.** (a) $6x + 15 < 200$ (b) 29 **4.** 20 cm^2
5. A (3, 5, 0), B (3, 5, 3), C (0, 5, 3), D (3, 0, 3) **6.** (b) 85·5 km ($\pm$ 1·5 km)
7. (a) $x = 14{\cdot}1$ cm, size of card = 48·3 cm (b) 1930 cm^2
8. (a) 0·5601 (b) 3·215 (c) 0·6161 (d) 0·4743 **9.** (a) 84 (b) 19·2 **10.** 0·335 m
11. 1·24 **12.** (a) $\frac{3}{5}$ (b) $w = \dfrac{k(1-y)}{y}$

page 327 ***Test 1***

1. C	**2.** D	**3.** D	**4.** B	**5.** C
6. C	**7.** A	**8.** D	**9.** B	**10.** B
11. C	**12.** A	**13.** D	**14.** C	**15.** C
16. D	**17.** A	**18.** C	**19.** B	**20.** D
21. A	**22.** B	**23.** C	**24.** B	**25.** C

page 328 ***Test 2***

1. B	**2.** C	**3.** B	**4.** A	**5.** D
6. C	**7.** A	**8.** D	**9.** B	**10.** C
11. B	**12.** D	**13.** A	**14.** C	**15.** C
16. D	**17.** B	**18.** A	**19.** B	**20.** B
21. C	**22.** D	**23.** A	**24.** A	**25.** B

page 330 ***Test 3***

1. D	**2.** D	**3.** D	**4.** B	**5.** A
6. C	**7.** A	**8.** D	**9.** D	**10.** B
11. C	**12.** D	**13.** D	**14.** B	**15.** A
16. B	**17.** C	**18.** A	**19.** D	**20.** D
21. C	**22.** C	**23.** B	**24.** B	**25.** D

page 332 ***Test 4***

1. B	**2.** B	**3.** A	**4.** C	**5.** C
6. D	**7.** D	**8.** A	**9.** B	**10.** B
11. D	**12.** B	**13.** B	**14.** C	**15.** D
16. A	**17.** C	**18.** B	**19.** B	**20.** D
21. A	**22.** C	**23.** C	**24.** C	**25.** A

INDEX